ARTHURIAN STUDIES L.

ARTHURIANISM IN EARLY PLANTAGENET ENGLAND

ARTHURIAN STUDIES

ISSN 0261-9814

General Editor: Norris J. Lacy

Previously published volumes in the series
are listed at the back of this book

ARTHURIANISM IN EARLY PLANTAGENET ENGLAND

From Henry II to Edward I

Christopher Michael Berard

THE BOYDELL PRESS

First published 2019
The Boydell Press, Woodbridge
Paperback edition 2021

ISBN 978 1 78327 374 4 hardback
ISBN 978 1 78327 606 6 paperback

The Boydell Press is an imprint of Boydell & Brewer Ltd
PO Box 9, Woodbridge, Suffolk, IP12 3DF, UK
and of Boydell & Brewer Inc.
668 Mount Hope Avenue, Rochester, NY 14620–2731, USA
website: www.boydellandbrewer.com

The publisher has no responsibility for the continued existence
or accuracy of URLs for external or third-party internet
websites referred to in this book, and does not guarantee that
any content on such websites is, or will remain,
accurate or appropriate

A CIP catalogue record for this book is available
from the British Library

This publication is printed on acid-free paper

Printed and bound in Great Britain by
TJ International Ltd, Padstow, Cornwall

Contents

Contents

Abbreviations

HRB   *Historia regum Britannie*
MGH   *Monumenta Germaniae Historica*
PL   J.-P. Migne, ed. *Patrologiae Cursus Completus... Series Latina.* 221
         vols. Paris, 1844–64
RS   Rolls Series

Genealogical Table of the Sovereigns of England from William I to Edward II

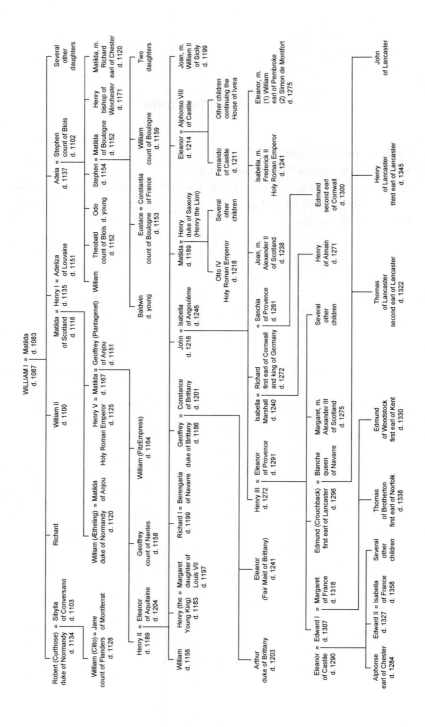

Introduction

Arthur the Briton emerged in the twelfth century as one of the great kings of European literature. But, unlike his counterparts Alexander the Great and Charlemagne, his basis in fact is tenuous. The historical foundation for the character, if any, is a sixth-century warrior of the same name who is said to have resisted the Anglo-Saxon invasion of post-Roman Britain. The earliest surviving accounts of this 'historical' Arthur and his military successes were composed over two centuries after this figure's putative lifetime, and it is possible that Arthur was purely a figure of folklore that over time was historicized.[1] By virtue of being quasi-historical and also from an obscure moment in British history, Arthur has always been a malleable character.

Although Arthurian literature is traditionally set in post-Roman Britain (400–600), medieval authors gave Arthur contemporary dress and fashioned his world after the political realities of their own. Anachronism is by no means unique to the Matter of Britain, but it is a hallmark of it. Not uncommonly, the characterization of Arthur in chronicles and romance was modeled after high and late medieval princes and potentates. Even more interestingly, there are numerous historical accounts of high and late medieval kings and noblemen fashioning themselves after the figure of Arthur and engaging in chivalric and dramatic enactments of episodes from Arthurian literature. Princes and lords, who saw themselves as imitating paladins from the distant past, were actually modeling themselves after idealized representations of their own more recent forebears. Arthurianism (Arthurian imitation and role-playing) is thus an example of life imitating art imitating life.

Pertinent for the classification of this phenomenon within larger categories of human behavior is the term 'ostension' as applied in Folklore Studies: the conscious adoption of a narrative as a model (or

---

[1] These early sources include the *Historia Brittonum* (c. 830) and the *Annales Cambriae* (tenth century). On the historicization of Arthur, see Oliver J. Padel, 'The Nature of Arthur', *Cambrian Medieval Celtic Studies* 27 (1994): 1–31.

script) for human action.[2] Recognizable, contemporary examples of ostension include copycat crimes – imitations either of documented crimes or of fictitious but practicable narratives of crime.[3] Carl Lindahl defines ostension as 'the folklorist's term for legendary role-playing that breaks the boundaries of play to transform itself into something far more earnest'.[4] Imitation exists on a spectrum. It may be as self-contained as a one-time instance of fancy dress or as far-reaching as a sustained persona that influences one's construction of identity, course of action, and life goals. It is worth pointing out that the imitator requires a model that is either drawn from real life or could have been – a model that has verisimilitude. With respect to Arthurianism, what medieval kings and nobles seem to have understood to be reenactment of the past, we understand to be enactment, an actualization of narrative content that we know to be largely fictitious. Even this statement is problematic because much of what Arthurian imitators set out to do had been done – just not by Arthur.

Rather than perform a strictly New-Historicist reading of Arthurian literature with the aim of isolating the influence of historical actors on literature, I have sought to identify the influence of literature on living people. In 2006, Michel Pastoureau lamented the 'rareté des études consacrées à la réception de cette légende [arthurienne] et à ses prolongements sur l'ensemble de la société', and he called for 'une approche interdisciplinaire' to this matter that would take into account chivalric rituals (including tournaments and feasts), anthroponymy, iconography, and heraldry.[5] To date Pastoureau's appeal has gone unanswered. This book responds to the call. Historical cases of the imitation and evocation of Arthur in their immediate political and broader cultural contexts are its subject. Modes of Arthurianism under consideration include: hosting and participation in Arthurian sport and spectacle, including, but not limited to, 'round table' ludic events; patronage of literature (in its broadest sense), heraldry, monuments,

---

[2] Linda Dégh and Andrew Vázsonyi, 'Does the Word "Dog" Bite? Ostensive Action: A Means of Legend-Telling', *Journal of Folklore Research* 20, n. 1 (1983): 7–9. Also see Bill Ellis, 'Death by Folklore: Ostension, Contemporary Legend, and Murder', *Western Folklore* 48, n. 3 (1989): 202.

[3] Dégh and Vázsonyi, 'Ostensive Action', 13–14.

[4] Carl Lindahl, 'Three Ways of Coming Back: Folkloric Perspectives on Arthur's Return', in *King Arthur's Modern Return*, ed. Debra N. Mancoff (New York: Garland Publishing, 1998), 20.

[5] Michel Pastoureau, 'Jouer aux chevaliers de la Table Ronde à la fin du Moyen Age', *Le goût du lecture* à la fin du *moyen âge*, ed. Danielle Bohler (Paris: Léopard d'Or, 2006), 66.

regalia, and coinage that elicit comparison between contemporaneous figures and Arthur and his knights; and lastly, the creation of rituals that were either directly modeled after or demonstrably evocative of Arthur and his fellowship of the Round Table. Medieval chronicles (monastic and secular, Latin and vernacular), chivalric biographies, and occasional poetry from the British Isles and Continental Europe constitute the raw materials of this study and my objective has been to determine, when possible, the varied motivations behind and consequences of Arthurianism.

Also fundamental to my work is reconstructing the ways in which the pseudo-historical Arthur existed in historical memory in the time and places under consideration. The history of Arthurian self-fashioning provided here is concomitantly a reception study on medieval understandings of Arthur.

This approach to the study of historical cases of Arthurianism is, by virtue of the topic and source materials, multidisciplinary; however, the questions asked are those of a political historian, namely: when, where, and how did the practice of Arthurianism have political significance beyond its immediate entertainment value? What did the orchestrator of each Arthurian imitation hope to achieve? Who were the intended audience? How effective was Arthurianism as a means of symbolic communication? I have adapted for these purposes the methodological suggestions offered by Kelly DeVries with respect to the use of medieval chronicles in recreating medieval military history. For each suggestion or explicit statement of Arthurianism, I have considered the 'presence or non-presence of the chronicler' at the event in question and how the chronicler's nationality, vocation, education, agenda, and intended audience may have affected his description of events.[6] Whenever possible I have crosschecked chronicle entries against documentary sources, alternative accounts, and surviving records of material history. In addition to DeVries' methodological recommendations, I have been attentive to the generic conventions at play in each text.

The method by which I have reconstructed the ways in which Arthur existed in historical memory also breaks new ground. Rather than follow in the footsteps of existing scholarship, which often restricts itself to assessing Arthur's portrayal in those texts in which the figure plays an essential role (especially in Arthurian chronicles and romances), I have called attention to his numerous, yet lesser known, cameo appearances

[6] Kelly DeVries, 'The Use of Chronicles in Recreating Medieval Military History', *Journal of Medieval Military History* 2 (2004): 15.

in law books, political treatises, religious writing, and conduct literature. This approach has been suggested by other scholars but not fully implemented. Christopher Dean, for example, in his *Arthur of England: English Attitudes to King Arthur and the Knights of the Round Table in the Middle Ages and the Renaissance*, recognized the importance of collecting and analyzing mentions of Arthur outside of Arthurian literature proper in order to analyze medieval understandings of the figure. He provided a useful catalogue of 'Arthurian References in Non-Arthurian Literature' – typically short asides and allusions that offer clues as to the perception of the court of King Arthur. Dean's catalogue, however, only contains mentions of Arthur in English-language texts from 1250–1650.[7] It does not take into account the considerable mass of Latin and Anglo-Norman writings about Arthur produced in England during his somewhat arbitrarily defined 400-year range of study, and it does not offer context for the entries that are included. When considering appearances of Arthur in 'non-Arthurian' literature, it is important to be mindful of the overall textual agenda of each work. We must conduct a part-to-whole analysis: how does the appearance of Arthur fit the greater purpose of the work that contains it? We must also attempt to determine which predetermined aspects of the character, if any, informed the deployment and representation of Arthur. Understanding the trends in and variety of such utilizations of Arthur grants us fresh insight into not only medieval perceptions and applications of this particular figure but also medieval engagement with the existing narratives of the past.

In addition to analyzing Arthur in 'non-Arthurian' literature, David A. Summers has invited us to analyze non-literary references to Arthur. He has called for an 'aggregate history of Arthur as a cultural icon' that takes into account not only the romance and chronicle traditions but also 'those encoded scraps of evidence which help the attentive reader reconstruct a more complete sense of "what was in the air" with regard to the popular sentiment concerning Arthur: local pageants, anecdotal asides, and other varied bits and pieces of Arthurian imagery and references that crop up in public life and discourse'.[8] And yet Summers freely acknowledges that his monograph is not such a work, and he expresses doubt whether writing a comprehensive history of this sort is even possible.[9] The issue

---

[7] Christopher Dean, *Arthur of England: English Attitudes to King Arthur and the Knights of the Round Table in the Middle Ages and the Renaissance* (Toronto: University of Toronto Press, 1987), 128–62.

[8] See David A. Summers, *Spenser's Arthur: The British Arthurian Tradition and* The Faerie Queene (Lanham, MD: University Press of America, 1997), 23–4.

[9] Summers, *Spenser's Arthur*, 24.

of feasibility can be addressed by limiting the geographical and temporal parameters of the history to be written.

The lands most typically associated with King Arthur – the duchy of Brittany, the earldom of Cornwall, the kingdom of England, the petty kingdoms of Wales, and the kingdom of France – have constituted the primary geographical focus of my research. My coverage begins with the earliest known political usage of the figure of King Arthur, which comes in the form of the 'Breton Hope' (*exspectare Arthurum*) – the supposedly indigenous Brittonic belief that Arthur did not die and was fated to return to rid Britain of its 'foreign' oppressors and to restore it to its former greatness.[10] This is a singularly appropriate starting point for analysis because the myth of Arthur's return provides a rationale for the practice of Arthurianism. As Lindahl has noted, besides returning Arthur to life in the flesh,

> [a] second way of bringing Arthur back is the 'return-through-re-enactment,' in which hero worshippers restore the vanished hero by playing his part. This is a doubly vicarious victory: Arthur lives on in a second form at the same time that his emulators live through Arthur. The return-through-re-enactment affirms that the hero, wherever he may be, has not died yet, because we can restore him through imitation.[11]

The spirit of Arthur, regardless of whether it is understood literally or figuratively, inhabits the imitator and directs his actions. Arthur is real within the mind of the imitator, and the imitator's actions externalize and materialize that reality. The earliest undisputed written attestation of the Breton Hope appears in the first version of the *Gesta regum Anglorum* of William of Malmesbury, which was completed in 1125. A decade later, Geoffrey of Monmouth completed his enormously influential *Historia regum Britannie* (c.1136–8), which furnished for the first time the complete biography of King Arthur from his peculiar conception at Tintagel to his mysterious disappearance at the close of the Battle of Camlann.

While it is true that this book explores the historical phenomenon of Arthurianism generally speaking and my historical coverage extends back to the 1120s, I have fixed my gaze on the well-known Arthurian self-fashioning of the Plantagenet dynasty of England beginning with the founder of this royal dynasty, Count Henry of Anjou (1133–89). When

---

[10] *Exspectare Arthurum* has been a phrase for the myth of Arthur's return since at least the time of Charles du Fresne, sieur Du Cange (1610–88). See 'Arturum Exspectare', in Du Cange, et al., *Glossarium mediae et infimae latinitatis*, rev. edn. (Niort, France: L. Favre, 1883–7), I, col. 414b.

[11] Lindahl, 'Three Ways of Coming Back', 19.

Henry of Anjou won the throne of England by force in 1153 and became Henry II of England the following year, he was in search of a precursor from the supposed past to legitimize his exercise of power. Geoffrey of Monmouth's newly minted version of British history was in many ways a serviceable model. Chronology confirms that Henry II was the first incoming king of England who had the opportunity to present himself as the embodiment of the Galfridian depiction of 'King' Arthur.[12] Whether Henry II actually did so is a subject of scholarly debate. The nature and extent of Henry's use of Arthurian legend is thus the natural starting point for my study.

Scholars are divided over whether Arthur was more commonly perceived in Plantagenet England as a spiritual progenitor to Henry or as a specter representing Henry's marginalized Celtic opponents. Whether the figure of Arthur was an asset or a liability to the Plantagenets is also debated. Responses to these questions have been impressionistic because to date no one has completed an aggregate history of Arthur as a cultural icon.[13] Through systematic study of the references to Arthur beyond Arthurian literature proper, I have reconstructed ways in which Arthur was remembered and deployed. My book proceeds diachronically, and the reigns of the first five Plantagenet kings provide its chapter divisions. This chronological structure facilitates the assessment of continuity and change in the understandings of Arthur.

My first chapter emphasizes the duality of Arthur in historical memory during the reign of Henry II. Arthur, as introduced in Geoffrey's *Historia*, is a hero of monarchical imperialism but also a Brittonic champion of resistance against foreign occupation. Twelfth-century political leaders in the 'Celtic Fringe' lands of Wales and Brittany rallied behind the latter aspect of Arthur's legacy in their opposition to 'French' (i.e. Plantagenet) territorial expansion. I contend that Henry II's propagandists responded to the Brittonic proprietary claim to Arthur in two ways. First, they portrayed Arthur as a king of *England* whose manner of kingship and territorial possessions matched those of Henry

---

[12] See Alexander Ostmann, 'Die Bedeutung der Arthurtradition für die englische Gesellschaft des 12. und 13. Jahrhunderts' (Ph.D. diss., Freie Universität Berlin, 1975), 175.

[13] It is often said that England's medieval kings exploited Arthur as a 'vehicle to enhance their prestige and as a symbol of centralized power and authority'. See Geraldine Barnes, 'Arthurian Chivalry in Old Norse', *Arthurian Literature* VII (1987): 55; Robert Allen Rouse and Cory James Rushton, 'Arthurian Geography', in *The Cambridge Companion to the Arthurian Legend*, ed. Elizabeth Archibald and Ad Putter (Cambridge, UK: Cambridge University Press, 2009), 219. Pastoureau has questioned this assumption. See his 'Jouer aux chevaliers', 65 n. 2.

II. Second, they promoted the myth that the Brittonic Celts mistakenly believed Arthur to be their special savior, who would return from the dead to aid them in their time of need. So construed, the 'Breton Hope', far from constituting a threat to the English, provided an opportunity for Henry's writers to repurpose anti-Jewish polemic against the Brittonic Celts. I situate this misrepresentation within the larger colonial discourse in which the French-speaking colonizers of Britain emerge as culturally advanced and righteous Christians while the native Celtic peoples are presented as treacherous barbarians and 'bad' Christians.

The anglicization of Arthur and the othering of the Brittonic Celts continue to be central themes in my second chapter, which treats the use of Arthur during the reign of Richard I. Although a renowned warrior-king in his own right, Richard the Lionheart does not stand out in the annals of history as an imitator of King Arthur. Rather, he seems to have been interested in carving out his own legacy as a great knight and crusader. Richard eschewed Arthurian self-fashioning in deference to his nephew, Arthur of Brittany (1187–1203), the posthumous son of Richard's younger brother Geoffrey, duke of Brittany (1158–86). In 1190, Richard declared that, in the event he should die without offspring, Arthur of Brittany would be his successor to the throne of England. The king also arranged for Arthur to marry the daughter of King Tancred of Sicily (r. 1189–94). In 1191, Richard reportedly gave Tancred King Arthur's legendary sword, Caliburn. Richard, as I argue, intended for Tancred to use Caliburn to knight Arthur of Brittany, thereby affirming the idea that this Arthur of the Plantagenet dynasty was the long-awaited second coming of Arthur. In this chapter, I also analyze the earliest accounts of the alleged discovery of King Arthur's tomb at Glastonbury Abbey (1191) and contend that the monks of Glastonbury produced the bones of Arthur in the hope that their monastery would obtain royal patronage from the newly named heir-apparent, Arthur of Brittany. My research also supports J. S. P. Tatlock's suggestion that Laȝamon wrote his *Brut*, the earliest English-language narrative of Arthur, with Arthur of Brittany in mind.

Near the close of my second chapter and throughout my third chapter, I call attention to changing views on Arthur in England. In some quarters, Arthur was disowned as the 'Celtic Other'. This move is most notable in William of Newburgh's *Historia rerum Anglicarum* (c.1196–8). It was, I argue, a consequence of the succession dispute between the English-born Prince John and his Breton-born nephew, Arthur of Brittany. While Arthur was alive, John had no hope of outdoing his nephew as an imitator of the legendary king. Even after Arthur's sudden disappearance in 1203, King John still could not readily cultivate an Arthurian image. Nor could he make effective use of the figure of Arthur without attracting unwanted attention to Prince Arthur's disappearance. Consequently, John distanced himself from all things Arthurian. As he did so, the barons of England took over the reins of the Arthurian narrative. In the concluding section of my third chapter, I discuss how the barons of London, around the time of the sealing of Magna Carta (1215), fabricated laws validating local self-government that were allegedly instituted by Arthur. These laws show how Arthur came to be remembered as a king who upheld aristocratic privileges and ruled with the advice and consent of his barons, a mode of governance consistent with the burgeoning English parliamentary system.

In my fourth chapter, I trace the continued transition of Arthur from champion of the monarchy to hero of the high nobility. Henry III preferred the saint-king model of Edward the Confessor (r. 1042–66), but Arthur remained popular with the great lords of the realm, including members of the royal family. I discuss how Henry III's younger brother, Richard, earl of Cornwall (1209–72), cultivated an Arthurian likeness. Richard was the undisputed heir to the throne of England until the birth of Henry III's son, Lord Edward, in 1239. Richard refurbished Tintagel Castle, the supposed birthplace of Arthur, in the first half of the 1230s when it was still uncertain whether Henry III would have offspring. In this chapter, I also investigate how the advent of round table games at beginning of the thirteenth century promoted an *esprit de corps* among the nobility that often stood against the wishes of Henry III. Additionally, I explore the evocation of Arthur by the princely House of Gwynedd in North Wales. Llywelyn ap Iorwerth (r. 1195–1240) and his grandson Llywelyn ap Gruffudd (r. 1246–82) took advantage of Henry III's difficulties with his barons in order to increase their hegemony in Wales. These princes made reference to Arthur and other legendary British kings as their predecessors.

The use of Arthur by Edward I of England (r. 1272–1307) is the subject of my fifth and final chapter. I show how Edward reasserted control over the Arthurian narrative by representing himself as a champion of parliamentary government, by assuming a chivalric kingly persona, and by participating in and presiding over round tables. That Edward cultivated an Arthurian image to obtain loyalty from his subjects and to galvanize support for his wars is well known, but I explore the mechanics and symbolism of each of his Arthurian gestures. I also call attention to instances in which Edward's Arthurian persona proved to be a liability. In the Anglo-Norman verse *Chronicle of Pierre de Langtoft* (c.1307), for example, Edward is negatively compared to the figure of King Arthur.

The end of the reign of Edward I is a fitting terminus for the present study, not because Arthurian self-fashioning came to an end, but because

Edward brought about the subjugation of Wales to the kingdom of England. By his conquest of Wales, Edward, for a time, put to rest the ideological conflict between Arthur the Brittonic freedom fighter and Arthur the champion of English institutional authority.

Although medieval Arthurianism is a popular digression in scholarship on medieval court culture, tournaments, political ritual, kingship, and chivalry, there has not been a systematic collection of chronicle accounts of the practice of Arthurianism nor any exhaustive contextual or comparative study devoted exclusively to this topic.[14] Much of the discussion of pre-Tudor Arthurian play and display derives from Roger Sherman Loomis' 'Chivalric and Dramatic Imitations of Arthurian Romance' (1939)[15] and Ruth Huff Cline's 'The Influence of Romances on Tournaments of the Middle Ages' (1945).[16] These pioneering works are descriptive in nature and aim to promote further interest in Arthurian pageantry. They stress that round table festivals were cosmopolitan affairs that took place both in England and on the Continent. Yet neither Loomis nor Cline suggest that these grand events had practical or symbolic value beyond that of any other great tournament, feast, or masque.

The scholarly work nearest in purpose and design to my own is Alexander Ostmann's unpublished dissertation: 'Die Bedeutung der Arthurtradition für die englische Gesellschaft des 12. und 13. Jahrhunderts' (1975). Ostmann's study is partly thematic, partly diachronic. He includes sections on Arthur in oral tradition and Arthur in hagiography, and he

---

[14] Article-length discussions of the socio-political symbolism of King Arthur include Martin Aurell, 'Henry II and Arthurian Legend', trans. Nicholas Vincent, in *Henry II: New Interpretations*, ed. Christopher Harper-Bill and Nicholas Vincent, (Woodbridge, UK: Boydell, 2007), 362–94; Jean Flori, *Aliénor d'Aquitaine: La reine insoumise*, trans. Olive Classe as *Eleanor of Aquitaine: Queen and Rebel* (Edinburgh: Edinburgh University Press, 2007), 294–313; Peter Johanek, 'König Arthur und die Plantagenets: Über den Zusammenhang von Historiographie und höfischer Epik in mittelalterlicher Propaganda', *Frühmittelalterliche Studien* 21 (1987): 346–89; Karl Heinz Göller, 'The Figure of King Arthur as a Mirror of Political and Religious Views', in *Functions of Literature: Essays Presented to Erwin Wolff on his Sixtieth Birthday*, ed. Ulrich Brioch, Theo Stemmler, and Gerd Stratmann (Tübingen: M. Niemeyer, 1984), 55–79; Wilhelm Störmer, 'König Artus als aristokratisches Leitbild während des späteren Mittelalters, gezeigt an Beispielen der Ministerialität und des Patriziats', *Zeitschrift für bayerische Landesgeschichte* 35 (1972): 946–71.

[15] Roger Sherman Loomis, 'Chivalric and Dramatic Imitations of Arthurian Romance', in *Medieval Studies in Memory of A. Kingsley Porter*, vol. 1, ed. Wilhelm R.W. Koehler (Cambridge, MA: Harvard University Press, 1939), 79–97. See Roger Sherman Loomis, 'Arthurian Influence on Sport and Spectacle', in *Arthurian Literature in the Middle Ages: A Collaborative History*, ed. Roger Sherman Loomis (Oxford: Clarendon Press, 1959), 553–9.

[16] Ruth Huff Cline, 'The Influence of Romances on Tournaments of the Middle Ages', *Speculum* 20, n. 2 (1945): 204–11.

considers the figure's relationship with the Church and with different strata of English society. In the sixth section of his dissertation he examines the significance of the Arthurian tradition for the native princes of Wales, and in the thirteenth section of his work he surveys how the post-Conquest kings of England from William I to Edward I were understood as successors to King Arthur. Ostmann notes some lesser-known chronicle sources that compare English kings to the figure of Arthur. Ostmann's work provides historical context for his discussion of the different social functions of Arthur, and he rightly recognizes Arthur of Brittany as a significant personage in the English Arthurian tradition. His study, although ambitious and far-reaching, is diffuse and his discussion of Plantagenet Arthurian self-fashioning can be described as an overview that points out (but does not critically engage with) many of the key primary sources.

In addition to addressing a lacuna in Arthurian scholarship, my book makes inroads into an interdisciplinary gray zone which literary scholars and historians have been somewhat hesitant to probe too deeply. Such a foray requires a demonstration of how 'literary' texts can be judiciously put to use as primary sources for historical analysis. For instance, being mindful of intertextuality and literary *topoi* enables one to catch false dedications to historical kings such as Henry II and Edward I in the narrative framework of prose Arthurian romances. In turn, these false dedications can and have been misconstrued as positive proof of kingly interest in Arthurian literature.

Careful attention to the details of history combined with knowledge of the evolution of the Arthurian tradition has also enabled me to narrow the dating of anonymous and little-studied works, including a commentary on Geoffrey of Monmouth's *Prophetia Merlini*, contained in London, British Library, MS Cotton Claudius B vii, 224r–233v. My research into the history of Arthurianism also adds new weight and meaning to Tatlock's linkage of Laȝamon's Arthur with Arthur of Brittany and to his suggested dating of Laȝamon's *Brut* to 1189–99. Thus my work contributes to both historical and literary studies.

Further collapsing the disciplinary divisions between literature and history, and also theology, is the tendency of medieval chroniclers to write their histories in typological terms. The understanding of events as part of an ever-unfolding, recurrent pattern underpins Plantagenet Arthurianism. Caroline D. Eckhardt has rightly called attention to this approach to medieval Christian historical writing and has termed it 'history as typology' and explains that this understanding assumes the recurrence of human experiences and situations: events at one time virtually call forth or compel corresponding events at later times, in order to fulfill a necessary overarching pattern. The direction of historical sequence is not simply linear but touches back upon itself, echoes itself, conducts as it were a conversation with itself, an interaction in which people and episodes take part of their meaning from their earlier or later manifestations.[17]

Typology is a mode of Christian biblical exegesis concerned with identifying and explaining how historical figures and events described in the Hebrew scriptures parallel and anticipate those of the New Testament. All are, according to Christian thought, part of the same unfolding narrative of sacred history. Supporters of the Plantagenet dynasty, *mutatis mutandis*, coopted this hermeneutic. Geoffrey of Monmouth's *Historia regum Britanniae*, which contains within it the *Prophetia Merlini*, was made an analogue to the Hebrew Bible, and the contemporary deeds of the post-Conquest kings of England were presented as a New Testament of sorts, fulfilling the hopes, promises, and prophecies of this remote past. Indeed, the *Brut* chronicle tradition, which gradually took shape between the reigns of Henry II and Edward I, joins as seamlessly as possible the ancient British past and the insular present; this, of course, calls to mind the Christian Bible, a marriage of Hebrew scriptures and the New Testament. Just as Jesus is the 'New Adam', Henry II, Arthur of Brittany, and Edward I were each, in turn, presented as the 'New Arthur'. Chroniclers, especially the continuator of Pierre de Langtoft's *Chronicle*, aligned as much as possible the histories of the kings of the ancient British past with those of their post-Conquest counterparts.

Adding a further knot to this pattern is the interweaving of sacred and secular typologies in medieval historiography. Arthur of Brittany, for example, came to be portrayed not only as the 'New Arthur', but also as a 'New David' and as a Jesus figure; John, the jealous king and persecutor of Arthur of Brittany, is described alternately as a 'New Saul' and a 'New Herod'. The concept of 'history as typology' is itself the most significant recurrent thematic thread in this book. Being attentive to it enhances one's understanding of medieval historiography, royal political ideology, and, of course, Arthurianism.

---

[17] See Caroline D. Eckhardt, 'Prophecy and Nostalgia: Arthurian Symbolism at the Close of the English Middle Ages', in *The Arthurian Tradition: Essays in Convergence*, ed. Mary Flowers Braswell and John Bugge (Tuscaloosa: University of Alabama Press, 1988), 118.

1
Arthurianism during the reign of Henry II, 1154–1189

The political orientation of the figure of King Arthur

Between 1185 and 1216, Laʒamon, a priest of the Worcestershire village now known as Areley Kings, wrote a history of 'England' in early Middle English. In his preface, he announces 'þet he wolde of Engle þa æðelæn tellen' (that he would relate the noble origins of the English).[1] This description is misleading because Laʒamon's text centers on the vicissitudes of the British ancestors of the Welsh and their eventual loss of the core of Britain to the Anglo-Saxons. Laʒamon's main source was Wace's *Roman de Brut* (1155), itself an Anglo-Norman verse translation of Geoffrey of Monmouth's *Historia regum Britannie* (c. 1136–8). Although Laʒamon amplified his source material, his adaptation largely upholds the symmetry of the Galfridian chronicle tradition. Arthur thus features prominently in Laʒamon's *Brut*. The text is distinctive not only for furnishing the earliest known appearance of Arthur in an English-language text but also for the extent of its anglicization of the king. Under Laʒamon's quill, Arthur became an epic hero after the fashion of his mortal enemies, the Anglo-Saxons. Laʒamon dressed Arthur in Anglo-Saxon battle dress. Arthur wore a corselet of woven steel and steel hose fashioned by an elven smith named Wygar, an analogue to Weland, the elven weapon smith who appears in *Beowulf* and the Old

---

[1] *Laʒamon's Brut, or Hystoria Brutonum*, ed. and trans. W. R. J. Barron and S. C. Weinberg (Harlow, UK: Longman Group, 1995), 2–3, line 7. For comparison with the Otho manuscript, see Laʒamon, *Brut, Edited from British Museum MS. Cotton Caligula A.ix and British Museum MS. Cotton Otho C.xiii*, ed. G. L. Brook and R. F. Leslie, 2 vols. (London: Oxford University Press, 1963–78), 3, line 7. Laʒamon describes the relics of saints Columkille, Brendan, and Bride in his *Brut*. Their remains were discovered in 1185 and furnish a *terminus a quo* for the text. The lack of differentiation between Henry II and III in the *Brut*'s prologue indicates that Henry III had not yet assumed the throne. The year of Henry III's elevation, 1216, thus furnishes a *terminus ad quem*. See Françoise H. M. Le Saux, *Laʒamon's Brut: The Poem and its Sources* (Cambridge, UK: D. S. Brewer, 1989), 6–10. For a later thirteenth-century dating of Laʒamon's *Brut* that assumes archaism, see W. R. J. Barron, 'The Idiom and the Audience of Laʒamon's *Brut*', in *Laʒamon: Contexts, Language, and Interpretation*, ed. Rosamund Allen, Lucy Perry, and Jane Roberts (London: King's College London Centre for Late Antique and Medieval Studies, 2002), 157–60.

English Boethius.[2] And although Laȝamon was expressly aware of the distinction between Britain and England, he 'slipped' into anachronism and spoke of Arthur as ruling over England on at least two occasions.[3] Most remarkably, Laȝamon made Arthur a messianic hero not simply for the descendants of the Britons but for the English as well.[4]

Laȝamon lived only about an hour's ride from the Welsh March[5] and conceivably had some knowledge of Welsh prophetic tradition, but he need not have drawn upon Welsh sources for his account of the myth of King Arthur's survival. Indeed, he likely did not turn to Welsh tradition in this instance. By the time he was writing, the idea that the Britons (the Bretons, the Cornish, and the Welsh) were awaiting Arthur's return had long been a cliché in Insular and Continental writing. Laȝamon perpetuated this stereotype of the Britons. He emphatically stated that it was the Britons who believed in Arthur's return. And yet, a mere two sentences later, he affirmed the truth of an otherwise unattested prophecy of Merlin which held that another Arthur would come. This Arthur would be a hero for all the people inhabiting England, including the descendants of Arthur's sworn enemies, the Anglo-Saxons.[6]

This chapter will explore the development of the myth of Arthur's survival and the assimilation of Arthur into English culture. With respect to the anglicization of Arthur, it will concentrate on when and how Arthur became an advantageous model for English royal self-fashioning and the post-Conquest kings of England began to imitate him.[7] As will be illustrated, our responses to these questions hinge on our sense of the

---

[2] *Laȝamon's Brut*, 542–3, lines 10542–6; Laȝamon, *Brut* (Otho), II, 551, lines 10542–8.

[3] See *Laȝamon's Brut*, 526–7, lines 10197–9 and 632–3, line 12305. The earlier 'slippage' occurs in the Otho manuscript, see Laȝamon, *Brut*, II, 531, line 10197, but not the latter (645, line 12305).

[4] *Laȝamon's Brut*, 732–3, lines 14288–97. The Otho text removes the indefinite article and changes 'English' to 'British' undoing the anglicization of the Breton Hope. See Laȝamon, *Brut*, II, 751, line 14297. This observation has been made by Karl Heinz Göller, 'The Legend of King Arthur's Survival and Its Political Impact', in *The Legacy of History: English and American Studies and the Significance of the Past*, vol. 1: *Literature*, ed. Teresa Bela and Justyna Leśniewska (Kraków: Jagiellonian University, 2003), 85.

[5] Laȝamon appears to have had some knowledge of Welsh prophetic tradition. See Simon Meecham-Jones, '"Þe Tide of Þisse Londe": Finding and Losing Wales in Laȝamon's *Brut*', in *Reading Laȝamon's* Brut: *Approaches and Explorations*, ed. Rosamund Allen, Jane Roberts, and Carole Weinberg (Amsterdam: Rodopi, 2013), 72.

[6] Göller calls this process the 'Englishing of Arthur'. See his 'Legend of King Arthur's Survival', p. 84.

[7] See J. S. P. Tatlock, *The Legendary History of the Kings of Britain: Geoffrey of Monmouth's Historia regum Britanniae and Its Early Vernacular Versions* (Berkeley: University of California Press, 1950), 485; W. R. J. Barron, '*Bruttene Deorling*: An Arthur for Every Age', in *The Fortunes of King Arthur*, ed. Norris J. Lacy (Cambridge, UK: D. S. Brewer, 2005), 56.

flexibility of Arthur as a cultural icon in the twelfth century and on the expansiveness of our understanding of imitation.

Arthur obtained qualities that made him especially suitable for use by the kings of England in the *Historia regum Britannie* of the Oxford-based *magister* Geoffrey of Monmouth (d.1155).[8] Geoffrey transformed Arthur, who had previously been depicted as a Brittonic *dux bellorum* and as a fantastical demigod, into a champion of institutional authority and imperialism.[9] Geoffrey's *Historia* had three known dedicatees, all Anglo-Normans, and the poet tailored his account of British history for these Anglo-Norman patrons. They included Robert, earl of Gloucester (d.1147), Henry I's illegitimate son who supported the succession of his half-sister, Empress Matilda (1102–67), to the throne of England; Waleran de Meulan, earl of Worcester (d.1166), who was a supporter of Stephen of Blois' claim to England; and Stephen of Blois himself, the nephew of Henry I (who reigned as king of England from 1135 to 1154). Geoffrey lifted details from the deeds and ceremonial practices of the first three post-Conquest kings of England for his portrait of Arthur. In his description, the king's coronation feast at Caerleon and his council with his magnates in particular resembled elements of Anglo-Norman custom.[10] Arthur's campaigns seem to have been modeled in part after those of William the Conqueror (r. 1066–87).[11] Geoffrey evidently hoped his Anglo-Norman readers would catch such parallels and receive them as flattery. Arthur had been fashioned after the Anglo-Norman kings of England, and this enabled the reigning kings of England to identify with the figure of Arthur and fashion themselves after Arthur.

---

[8] All citations and translations of this source, unless otherwise noted, are from *The History of the Kings of England: An Edition and Translation of De gestis Britonum*, ed. Michael D. Reeve, trans. Neil Wright (Woodbridge, UK: Boydell, 2007). I am following this edition's practice of citing section and line numbers. On the life of Geoffrey of Monmouth, see Julia Crick, *The Historia regum Britannie of Geoffrey of Monmouth IV: Dissemination and Reception in the Later Middle Ages* (Cambridge, UK: D. S. Brewer 1991), 4–5. Hereafter this source will be cited as *HRB Dissemination and Reception*. See also Geoffrey of Monmouth, *Vita Merlini*, ed. and trans. Basil Clarke (Cardiff: University of Wales Press, 1973), 26–35, and Julia Crick, *The Historia regum Britannie of Geoffrey of Monmouth III: A Summary Catalogue of the Manuscripts* (Cambridge, UK: D. S. Brewer, 1989). Hereafter this source will be cited as *HRB Summary Catalogue*.

[9] I am employing Tatlock's definition of imperialism: 'the extension of a king's rule beyond the realm he began with, perhaps to provide apanages for *his* younger sons as well as revenue and feudal prestige for himself' (*Legendary History*, 305).

[10] Antonia Gransden, *Historical Writing in England*, 2 vols. (Ithaca, NY: Cornell University Press, 1974–82), I, 206; Tatlock, *Legendary History*, 293–4 and 301–2.

[11] See Tatlock, *Legendary History*, 308–9.

The interweaving of the Arthurian 'past' with the Anglo-Norman present is evident when we compare Geoffrey's presentation of Arthur's royal household with accounts of William the Conqueror's son and eventual successor Henry I 'Beauclerc' (r. 1100–35). Geoffrey, it should be noted, was at work on his *Prophetia Merlini* and *Historia regum Britannie* immediately after Henry I's death, and in these works he made favorable allusions to the late king. The 'leo iusticiae' (lion of justice) mentioned in the *Prophetia Merlini* was quickly identified by Geoffrey's readers, including Orderic Vitalis (c.1136), as Henry I.[12] Fifty years later, Walter Map in his *De Nugis Curialium* fondly commemorated Henry I for being very generous toward his barons and royal household.[13] Walter added that Henry's itinerant court was sumptuous and a hub of commerce that attracted countymen and visiting foreigners alike, 'eratque scola uirtutum et sapiencie curia regis illius ante meridiem, post, comitatis et reuerende leticie' (and this king's court was in the forenoon a school of virtues and of wisdom, and in the afternoon one of hilarity and decent mirth).[14] Geoffrey had introduced Arthur in much the same way, stating that he was exceptionally generous, a great patron of knights, and a king whose court was an internationally renowned center of cultural refinement.[15]

Geoffrey set forth Arthur as an exemplum for Anglo-Norman magnates vying with one another to be recognized as Henry I's rightful successor. Walter Map was using Henry I for the same purpose, but his patron was Henry I's grandson, Henry II of England (r. 1154–89). If Walter provided a largely faithful – albeit idealized – portrait of the king, then it would appear that Geoffrey modeled Arthur's court after the court of Henry I. Once again we see the reciprocal influence and circularity of life and art: Geoffrey invited Henry I's heirs to imitate a literary representation of Arthur that had been modeled in part after Henry I.

But William I and Henry I were not the only models on which Geoffrey based his Arthur. The Arthur of the *Historia* is very much an amalgamation of the great kings of Western culture but whose aspirations and accomplishments are attuned to the political circumstances and

---

[12] Orderic Vitalis, *The Ecclesiastical History of Orderic Vitalis* 12.47, ed. and trans. Marjorie Chibnall, vol. 6 (Oxford: Clarendon Press, 1978), 386–9.
[13] Walter Map, *De Nugis Curialium* 5.5, ed and trans. M. R. James, rev. C. N. L. Brooke and R. A. B Mynors (Oxford: Clarendon Press, 1983), 438–9.
[14] Walter Map, *De Nugis Curialium* 5.5, pp. 438–9. Also see 5.6, pp. 470–1.
[15] Geoffrey of Monmouth, *Historia regum Britannie* 154.225–32, pp. 204–5.

aspirations of Geoffrey's Anglo-Norman dedicatees.[16] Arthur's first royal act in the *Historia* was to reconquer land lost to the heathen Saxons, and, according to Geoffrey, he was entitled by lawful inheritance to be monarch of all Britain.[17] Arthur's central base of power, Loegria, was situated in the same place and had the same dimensions as Anglo-Norman England, but he held suzerainty over Scotland, Cornwall, Demetia (Dyfed / South Wales), and Venedotia (Gwynedd / North Wales). The petty or sub-kings of these lands swore homage to Arthur at his coronation feast.[18] The Anglo-Norman kings of England likewise sought to extend their rule from England into these territories.[19] After Arthur had conquered the British Isles, he is said to have aimed to put under his sway the whole of Europe.[20] William the Conqueror again comes to mind as an analogue because he sought to expand his lordship from Normandy into Maine and Brittany.[21] Geoffrey would have us believe that Arthur was on the brink of realizing his objectives when news of his nephew Mordred's treachery compelled him to make his fateful return to Britain. Geoffrey had crafted Arthur in such a way that the figure could function as a legitimizing precedent for Anglo-Norman imperialism.

The Arthur of the *Historia* also furnished the Anglo-Normans with a founding father to rival Charlemagne, whom the Capetian kings of France vaunted as their most illustrious predecessor. Arthur was an insular monarch whose *imperium* extended onto the Continent.[22] But it

[16] There are parallels between Geoffrey's life of Arthur and the legends of King David, Alexander the Great, Æthelstan (r. 925–40), Charlemagne, and Cnut (r. 1017–35). See Susan M. Shwartz, 'The Founding and Self-Betrayal of Britain: An Augustian Approach to Geoffrey of Monmouth's *Historia Regum Britanniae*', *Medievalia et Humanistica*, New Series 10 (1981): 41–6; M. Victoria Guerin, 'The King's Sin: The Origins of the David–Arthur Parallel', in *The Passing of Arthur: New Essays in Arthurian Tradition*, ed. Christopher Baswell and William Sharpe (New York and London: Garland, 1988), 15–30; Tatlock, *Legendary History*, 310–11, 320; W. G. Collingwood 'Arthur and Athelstan', *Saga-Book of the Viking Society for Northern Research* 10 (1928–9): 132–44; and Gordon Hall Gerould, 'King Arthur and Politics', *Speculum* 2, no. 1 (1927): 33–51. For analysis of how Geoffrey's Arthur reflects Anglo-Norman political interests, see Maureen Fries, 'The Arthurian Moment: History and Geoffrey of Monmouth's *Historia regum Britannie*', *Arthuriana* 8, n. 4 (1998): 90; James Noble, 'Patronage, Politics, and the Figure of Arthur in Geoffrey of Monmouth, Wace, and Layamon', *The Arthurian Yearbook* 2 (1992): 161–2.

[17] Geoffrey of Monmouth, *Historia regum Britannie* 143.14–18, pp. 192–3.

[18] Geoffrey of Monmouth, *Historia regum Britannie* 157.359–63, pp. 212–13. See Michael A. Faletra, *Wales and the Medieval Colonial Imagination: The Matters of Britain in the Twelfth Century* (New York: Palgrave Macmillan, 2014), 31, 42–4.

[19] Tatlock, *Legendary History*, 308; Faletra, *Wales and Medieval Colonial Imagination*, 3–4.

[20] Geoffrey of Monmouth, *Historia regum Britannie* 154.234–6, pp. 204–5.

[21] Tatlock, *Legendary History*, p. 308.

[22] Faletra, *Wales and Medieval Colonial Imagination*, 43.

must be emphasized that the association of the British kings, specifically Arthur, with the post-Conquest kings of England remained implicit in Geoffrey's *Historia*. Further cultivation of the association was needed to establish an explicit, and fully exploitable, connection.

There was, however, a complication to the retroactive adoption of Arthur as a precursor to the post-Conquest kings, one that arguably had the potential to undermine the representation of any contemporary English monarch as another Arthur. This obstacle was the proprietary claim to Arthur held by his cultural descendants, the Brittonic Celts. Just as the Arthur of Geoffrey's *Historia* could be interpreted as a spiritual predecessor to the kings of England, so too could he be interpreted as a champion of Welsh and Breton resistance against foreign occupation. R. R. Davies refers to this as the 'British problem' and the 'Welsh challenge'.[23] The British problem's chief cultural manifestation in the twelfth century, so it would seem, was the 'Breton Hope', the idea that Arthur the sixth-century British *dux bellorum* was a 'sleeping hero' destined to rise again and deliver *his* people in *their* hour of greatest need. Just how significant an obstacle the 'British problem' was to the adoption of Arthur by the post-Conquest kings of England is the central concern of this chapter.

One finds a maximalist view of the potency of the British problem, especially the Breton Hope element, in the scholarship of John Gillingham. He is a leading voice of dissent against the once prevailing assumption that Henry II consistently fashioned himself as Arthur's heir. In 'The Context and Purposes of Geoffrey of Monmouth's *History of the Kings of Britain*', Gillingham maintains that until the Breton Hope was debunked through the discovery of Arthur's remains at Glastonbury (c. 1191), Arthur remained the exclusive cultural property of the Brittonic Celts.[24] Subsequently, Gillingham nuanced his position slightly by remarking that during the reign of Henry II, 'the figure of King Arthur was not regarded as a cultural asset specific to the Angevin dynasty'.[25] This rephrasing allows for the possibility of Arthurian self-fashioning by Henry II, but Gillingham still holds that at the beginning of Henry II's reign Arthur 'in Anglo-Norman circles ... conjured up the image of a powerful enemy' and that even at the turn of the thirteenth century, 'Arthur was still too

[23] R. R. Davies, *The First English Empire: Power and Identities in the British Isles, 1093–1343* (Oxford: Oxford University Press, 2000), 48–9.

[24] John Gillingham, 'The Context and Purposes of Geoffrey of Monmouth's *History of the Kings of Britain*', *Anglo-Norman Studies* XIII (1991): 102–3.

[25] See John Gillingham, 'The Cultivation of History, Legend, and Courtesy at the Court of Henry II', in *Writers of the Reign of Henry II: Twelve Essays*, ed. Ruth Kennedy and Simon Meecham-Jones (New York: Palgrave Macmillan, 2006), 28.

closely associated with the Welsh and Bretons to be readily exploited as a specifically Plantagenet hero'.[26] Thus Gillingham suggests that Arthur had become emblematic of colonial anxiety in Anglo-Norman society.[27] His claim relies heavily on a choice passage contained in an anonymous twelfth-century Anglo-Norman *Description of England* in which Arthur appears as a figure standing against the French-speaking colonizers of the British Isles.[28] Gillingham's assessment of Arthur's place in twelfth-century historical memory has not been corroborated by a systematic analysis of all available primary source material on the subject of Arthur in twelfth-century historical memory.

Gillingham's reading of the relationship between the twelfth-century kings of England and the figure of Arthur has been influential. Martin Aurell, for example, assents that '[i]n the reign of Henry II, political "Arthurianism" remained far more Welsh or Breton than Angevin or English' and that in comparison to the reign of Edward I of England (r. 1272–1307), the 'few indications' that we have of Henry II's seeking 'to appropriate the *matière de Bretagne* seem entirely innocent' and do not amount to 'a deliberate deployment of ideology'.[29] Ralph V. Turner presents these ideas with even more forceful language, declaring that the 'contention that Henry viewed Arthur as a predecessor offering him an imperial mythology cannot be substantiated'.[30]

Gillingham, Aurell, and Turner have effectively demonstrated that King Arthur was not an uncomplicated 'hero' for the post-Conquest kings of England. That being said, they counter a flawed generalization with an equally flawed generalization. Their conclusion that just *one* definition of the figure of King Arthur as a hero of Brittonic resistance held sway is problematic. With reference to a variety of twelfth-century texts, especially commentaries on the prophecies of Merlin, I shall show that there was an ongoing dialectic in the twelfth century regarding Arthur's place in historical memory. To some, Arthur was a hero of Brittonic resistance and to others he was a champion of the prevailing institutional

---

[26] Gillingham, 'Cultivation of History', 36–7.

[27] For evidence of 'colonial anxiety' in the late twelfth century, see Gerald of Wales, *Itinerarium Kambriae* 1.2, ed. James F. Dimock, in *Giraldi Cambrensis opera*, vol. 6, ed. James F. Dimock, RS 21/6 (London: Longmans, Green, Reader, and Dyer, 1868), 34–5.

[28] The Anglo-Norman expansion into Wales and Ireland has been called 'feudal colonialism'. See Robert Bartlett, *Gerald of Wales, 1146–1223* (Oxford: Clarendon Press, 1982), 2.

[29] Aurell, 'Henry II and Arthurian Legend', 388, 393.

[30] Ralph V. Turner, 'England in 1215: An Authoritarian Angevin Dynasty Facing Multiple Threats', in *Magna Carta and the England of King John*, ed. Janet S. Loengard (Woodbridge, UK: Boydell, 2010), 22.

authority in England. Whether he belonged to the Brittonic Celts by virtue of blood and language or to the post-Conquest kings of England by virtue of royal office and geographical domain had not been resolved. Both interpretations of Arthur are attested in twelfth-century writings. Whereas Gillingham and Aurell privilege his ethnic dimension, I seek to emphasize the duality of the figure of Arthur in the twelfth century. This duality, a hallmark of the Arthur of the twelfth century, has not been sufficiently recognized in existing scholarship.[31]

We need only take into account the *Prophetia Merlini* commentary tradition to illustrate this point. Around 1136, Orderic Vitalis had asserted in his *Historia Ecclesiastica* that the *Prophetia Merlini* told of recent political events and that Merlin's prophecies, if read correctly, may well hold the key to deciphering the future. Learned clerics at the time went about producing Latin commentaries on Geoffrey's cryptic text.[32] Some of the Latin commentaries, especially John of Cornwall's (c.1153), were – it is true – anti-Norman.[33] However, not all of the twelfth-century readings of the *Prophetia Merlini* were hostile to the post-Conquest kings of England. Orderic Vitalis, as we have seen, believed that Henry I of England was the Lion of Justice described in the *Prophetia Merlini*.

Another aspect of the analysis of Gillingham and Aurell that, in my opinion, skews their conclusions is their method of assessing the nature and extent of Henry II's 'political Arthurianism'. They search for evidence that Henry II performed as King Arthur in a manner comparable to his successors, and come away largely empty-handed.[34] Rather than compare Henry's known or putative use of the figure of Arthur against that of his successors, it is, I believe, more fruitful to situate the discourse on Arthur in its own historical moment – in relation to the intellectual and cultural developments of the twelfth century.

As has been widely discussed, the eleventh and twelfth centuries saw an increase in literacy and a growing perception that facts were 'embodied in text' and that the truths of the past could be arrived at through exegesis (textuality) rather than through complete dependence

---

[31] An exception is Jean Blacker, *The Faces of Time: Portrayal of the Past in Old French and Latin Historical Narrative of the Anglo-Norman Regnum* (Austin: University of Texas Press, 1994), p. 164.

[32] See Orderic Vitalis, *The Ecclesiastical History of Orderic Vitalis* 12.47, ed. and trans. Marjorie Chibnall (Oxford: Clarendon Press, 1978), VI, 380–9.

[33] See Michael J. Curley, 'A New Edition of John of Cornwall's *Prophetia Merlini*', *Speculum* 57, n. 2 (1982): 217–49.

[34] See Gillingham, 'Context and Purposes', 103.

on collective memory (orality).[35] Angevin 'political Arthurianism', the use of the figure of Arthur to advance a political and/or social agenda, seems to have been textual in its character during Henry II's reign. This, at least, is what we can gather from the surviving primary sources. The principal political objective was to establish that a post-Conquest king of England could and should be understood as Arthur's legitimate successor. How then did twelfth-century writers make the case that the post-Conquest kings of England had a stronger claim to the mantle of Arthur than his cultural descendants, the Brittonic Celts? To answer this question we must delve further into twelfth-century intellectual history.

At the beginning of the twelfth century, Western Christendom was expanding its horizons both intellectually and geographically. Spurred on by the military success of the First Crusade (1096–9), Christian thinkers of the West were seeking to define their civilization's place in Salvation History. It was already a universal Christian belief that Christians were the *verus Israel*, but the crusading movement of the late eleventh and early twelfth centuries reinforced this idea. According to the *Historia Iherosolimitana* of Robert the Monk, the crusader Bohemond of Taranto (c.1058–1111) told his troops that the same God who had led the sons of Israel out of Egypt and towards the Promised Land was now leading the soldiers of Christ (*milites Christi*) and tireless pilgrims to the Holy Sepulchre.[36] After defeating the Turks at Dorylaeum, Bohemond's victorious army burst into the same song that the Israelites sang during their exodus from Egypt.[37] Ralph of Caen writes in his *Gesta Tancredi* that the Lord heard the prayers of the crusaders in Jerusalem just as he had heard those of the Israelites at the Red Sea (Psalm 136:13–14).[38]

The taking of Jerusalem in 1099 gave substance to the interpretation of Christians as the *verus Israel* and new *Populus Dei*.[39] Christian writers still,

---

[35] See Brian Stock, *The Implications of Literacy: Written Language and Models of Interpretation in the Eleventh and Twelfth Centuries* (Princeton: Princeton University Press, 1983), 62; M. T. Clanchy, *From Memory to Written Record: England 1066–1307*, 3rd edn. (Oxford: Wiley-Blackwell, 2013), passim.

[36] See Robert of Reims, *Historia Iherosolimitana* 2.16, trans. Carol Sweetenham as *Robert the Monk's History of the First Crusade* (Aldershot: Ashgate, 2005), 98.

[37] Robert of Reims, *Historia Iherosolimitana* 3.14, pp. 111–12.

[38] Ralph of Caen, *Gesta Tancredi* 125, trans. Bernard S. Bachrach and David S. Bachrach as *The Gesta Tancredi of Ralph of Caen: A History of the Normans on the First Crusade* (Aldershot: Ashgate, 2005), 141.

[39] See Kenneth Stow, 'Conversion, Apostasy, and Apprehensiveness: Emicho of Floheim and the Fear of the Jews in the Twelfth Century', *Speculum* 76, n. 4 (2001): 912–13; David Berger, 'Mission to the Jews and Jewish-Christian Contacts in the Polemical Literature of the High Middle Ages', *American Historical Review* 91, n. 3 (1986): 577–8; David Berger, 'The Attitude of St. Bernard of Clairvaux toward the Jews', *Proceedings of the American Academy for Jewish Research* 40 (1972): 98.

however, found it necessary to rationalize how they could take the place of the Jews as God's Chosen People. Anti-Jewish polemics were a key genre for this activity, and biblical exegesis was the principal analytical tool employed.[40] The frame of many of these tracts is a disputation between a Jew and a Christian over the correct interpretation of Scripture, and the most common Christian charge against Jewish readings is that they are too literal and simplistic. Christian polemicists employed invective and negative stereotyping to lend weight to their arguments: if Jews are blind or have veiled sight and if Jews are foolish, carnal, hard-hearted, and possess at best a 'bovine intellect', how then can anyone take seriously their interpretations of Scripture?[41]

Negative ethnic profiling was employed along similar lines by the Anglo-Normans against the Welsh and the Irish and by Germans against the Scandinavians, Slavs, and Magyars. The Anglo-Normans aimed to acquire Welsh and Irish lands, and the Germans had the same ambition for Scandinavian, Baltic, and Slavic territories. Both would-be colonizers maligned their opponents as primitives: economically and politically backward, brutal, faithless, lawless, licentious, lacking in reason, and bestial in physiognomy and dress.[42] Many of the Germans' opponents were pagan, which enabled their northward and eastward campaigns to be presented as a crusade. The same did not apply in the Insular context. The Welsh and the Irish were already Christians. But, as Robert Bartlett has noted, '[w]hile the Celts could not be called pagans, they were criticized as being the next worse thing – very bad Christians, semi-pagans. It is clear that some kind of religious deficiency was a crucial part of the concept "barbarian"'.[43] But what relevance does this have to the Arthurian discourse?

The Brittonic Celts were not simply portrayed as barbaric, 'bad Christians'; they were portrayed as 'Jew-like'. Analogies were drawn between the Jewish wait for the Davidic messiah and the British wait for the Arthurian messiah. There are definite parallels between Jewish–Christian and Brittonic–'French' (Anglo-Norman / Angevin) conflicts in the twelfth century. The Anglo-Normans in 1066 came into possession

---

[40] See Anna Sapir Abulafia, 'Jewish–Christian Disputations and the Twelfth-century Renaissance', *Journal of Medieval History* 15, n. 2 (1989): 105–25. Also see Lawrence Warner, 'Geoffrey of Monmouth and the De-Judaized Crusade', *Parergon* 21, n. 1 (2004): 19–37 and Shwartz, 'Founding and Self-betrayal', 33–53.

[41] See Peter the Venerable (d. 1156), *Adversus Iudeorum inveteratam duritiem* 3.47, trans. Irven M. Resnick as *Against the Inveterate Obduracy of the Jews* (Washington: Catholic University of America Press, 2013), 103; Berger, 'Attitude of St. Bernard', 102–3.

[42] See Faletra, *Wales and Medieval Colonial Imagination*, 7, 34–5.

[43] Bartlett, *Gerald of Wales*, 169.

of what in biblical times had belonged to the Brittonic Celts; Western Christendom in 1099 came into possession of what in biblical times had belonged to the Jews. The Brittonic Celts were a dispossessed and proximate Other to the Anglo-Normans, and, of course, Jews were a dispossessed and proximate Other to Christians all across Medieval Europe. The *Historia regum Britannie*, which features both historical and prophetic modes of discourse, is a text that contains material of ideological value to the Anglo-Normans / Plantagenets as well as to Brittonic Celts; the Hebrew Bible, which features both historical and prophetic modes of discourse, is, of course, a text of great ideological significance to Jews and Christians alike. The *Historia regum Britannie* has messianic elements which, depending on the interpretation of them, are either consistent with or antagonistic to the Anglo-Norman / Plantagenet interests; the Hebrew Bible has messianic elements which, depending on the interpretation of them, are either consistent with or antagonistic to Christians. Fifth and finally, the crux of the Galfridian debate centers on literal versus figurative modes of textual interpretation and whether the messianic hope will be of primary benefit to the Brittonic Celts; the crux of the biblical debate centers on literal versus figurative modes of textual interpretation and whether the messianic hope will be of primary benefit to the Jews. Just as Geoffrey looked back to King David when constructing the character of King Arthur, so too did he at times fashion the Britons after the ancient Hebrews, specifically as they were depicted in the Book of Exodus. Geoffrey also used events in biblical history as synchronisms for events in his legendary history of the Britons.[44] Moreover, two of Geoffrey's leading sources, Gildas' *De excidio et conquestu Britanniae* (c. 547) and the *Historia Brittonum* (829–30), likened the Britons and their plight to the ancient Israelites and their hardships.[45]

The writers of Henry II's court observed many, if not all, of these parallels and employed anti-Jewish polemical tactics against the Brittonic Celts, sometimes even so much as explicitly comparing the Breton Hope to Jewish political messianism. This was also done in an effort to make Galfridian history politically useful to the kings of England, namely to add further legitimation to Henry's imperialist agenda (dominion over the entirety of the British Isles and lordship over substantial portions of

---

[44] See Shwartz, 'Founding and Self-betrayal', 36–40; David C. Fowler, 'Some Biblical Influences on Geoffrey of Monmouth's Historiography', *Traditio* 14 (1958): 379.

[45] See, for example, Gildas, *De excidio Britonum / The Ruin of the Britain and other Documents*, ed. and trans. Michael Winterbottom (London and Chichester: Phillimore, 1978), at 1.7 and 1.13 (pp. 15 and 88). Also see Shwartz, 'Founding and Self-betrayal', 37–8.

present-day France). I shall begin by reviewing what we know of the Breton Hope's genesis. My exploration will illustrate that the idea of Arthur as an avenging British cultural hero may not have been a longstanding, deeply entrenched, and wholly Brittonic construct. Next, I shall consider contemporary responses to the Welsh Challenge and the Breton Hope, many of which emanated from the court of Henry II of England. I shall demonstrate that the expropriation of Arthur, his alienation from the Brittonic Celts, and his adoption by the English crown, was an ongoing process which was underway at Henry's court long before the unearthing of Arthur's remains at Glastonbury. The Breton Hope was not a problem or threat to Henry II; rather, Henry's court poets recognized the idea to be a useful racial myth, which enabled Christian anti-Jewish rhetoric to be repurposed to undermine Arthur's Brittonic ties and to justify Angevin expansion into the Celtic Fringe.

Exspectare Arthurum: native belief or colonial construct?

The strain of political messianism known as the Breton Hope has long been understood to be 'an idea as deeply rooted in Celtic culture as the Davidic Hope is in Jewish culture' and one that 'offered a totally unacceptable challenge to the sovereignty of the English reigning monarch'.[46] But Oliver Padel and Virginie Greene have cogently challenged this understanding. As they and others have noted, not a single pre-twelfth-century Breton, Cornish, or Welsh formulation of Arthur as a returning avenger survives.[47] Admittedly, a great deal of British writing was surely lost during the Germanic invasions of post-Roman Britain. We gather from allusions in early Welsh poetry, especially the Welsh Triads (Trioedd Ynys Prydein), What Man is the Gatekeeper? (Pa gur yw y porthor?), The Spoils of Awnwfn

---

[46] Constance Bullock-Davies, '"Exspectare Arturum": Arthur and the Messianic Hope', Bulletin of the Board of Celtic Studies 29, n. 3 (1981): 439. Also see E. K. Chambers, Arthur of Britain, rev. edn. (Cambridge, UK: Speculum Historiale, 1964), 18 and 108–25; Roger Sherman Loomis, 'The Legend of Arthur's Survival', in Arthurian Literature in the Middle Ages: A Collaborative History, ed. Roger Sherman Loomis (Oxford: Clarendon Press, 1959), 64–71; Henry H. Peyton III, 'The Myth of King Arthur's Immortality', Interpretations 5, n. 1 (1973): 55–71; Jean-Christophe Cassard, 'Arthur est vivant! Jalons pour une enquête sur le messianisme royal au moyen âge', Cahiers de civilization médiévale 32, n. 126 (1989): 135–46.

[47] See Padel, 'Nature of Arthur', 9–10; Virginie Greene, 'Qui croit au retour d'Arthur', Cahiers de civilization médiévale 45, n. 180 (2002): 332–3, and Bullock-Davies, 'Exspectare Arturum', 437; Bedwyr L. Jones, 'Williams (Ifor) (Ed.), Bromwich (Rachel) (Trans.), "Armes Prydein" (Book Review)', Medium Aevum 43 (1974): 183; Brynley F. Roberts, 'Geoffrey of Monmouth and Welsh Historical Tradition', Nottingham Mediaeval Studies 20 (1976): 35, 40 n. 37; Victoria Flood, 'Arthur's Return from Avalon: Geoffrey of Monmouth and the Development of Legend', Arthuriana 25, n. 2 (2015): 84–5.

(*Preiddeu Annwn*), and *Culhwch ac Olwen*, that there once was a healthy oral tradition involving monster-slaying, epic battles, and journeys to the Underworld. Expectation of Arthur's return might also have passed by word of mouth. Truly, it must be acknowledged that the absence of evidence is not evidence of absence. And yet, it is curious that the myth of Arthur's return does not appear in the *Historia Brittonum* or in the *Mirabilia* attached to it. For, just as the absence of mention of Arthur in Gildas' *De excidio et conquestu Brittanniae* calls into question Arthur's historicity, so too the absence of mention of *exspectare Arthurum* in the *Historia Brittonum* casts a shadow of doubt on the prevalence of this idea in the ninth century. In the vernacular prophecies of medieval Wales and in the onomastic tradition of its princes, Owain, Cadwallader, and Cynan were the names of power and of great expectation, and they typically filled the role of *y mab darogan*, the son of prophecy. Arthur did not have comparable standing.[48]

A slight indication that the Welsh regarded Arthur as a returning hero appears in the 'Stanzas of the Graves' (*Englynion y Beddau*), a Middle Welsh stanzaic poem that lists the burial sites of Welsh heroes of yore. The poem's date of composition is uncertain, but it is contained in the Black Book of Carmarthen, which was compiled around 1250. The forty-fourth stanza famously states: 'Anoeth bid bet y arthur' (*anoeth* of the world, a grave for Arthur).[49] *Anoeth* 'literally signifies something difficult, or even impossible, to obtain or achieve',[50] and Patrick Sims-Williams notes that this word is 'archaic and rare, occurring in prose only in *Culhwch* [*ac Olwen*], where it refers to the difficult or impossible tasks which Arthur's warriors undertake', adding that 'the word may allude to the story of Culhwch itself'.[51] If this is so, then the stanza might have been written after 1100, which is the conventional scholarly dating of *Culhwch ac Olwen*.

[48] See Juliet Wood, 'Where Does Britain End? The Reception of Geoffrey of Monmouth in Scotland and Wales', in *The Scots and Medieval Arthurian Legend*, ed. Rhiannon Purdie and Nicola Royan (Cambridge, UK: D. S. Brewer, 2005), 10, 15; Flood, 'Arthur's Return from Avalon', 84; Tatlock, *Legendary History*, 188, 217; Margaret Enid Griffiths, *Early Vaticination in Welsh*, ed. T. Gwynn Jones (Cardiff: University of Wales Press, 1937), 100, 145–55; Daniel Helbert, '"an Arður sculde ȝete cum": The Prophetic Hope in Twelfth-Century Britain', *Arthuriana* 26, n. 1 (2016): 96.

[49] For this translation, see John T. Koch, 'The Celtic Lands', in *Medieval Arthurian Literature: A Guide to Recent Research*, ed. Norris J. Lacy (New York: Garland, 1996), 266.

[50] A. O. H. Jarman, 'The Arthurian Allusions in the Black Book of Carmarthen', in *The Legend of Arthur in the Middle Ages Presented to A. H. Diverres*, ed. P. B. Grout, R. A. Lodge, C. E. Pickford, and E. K. C. Varty (Cambridge, UK: D. S. Brewer, 1983), 111.

[51] Patrick Sims-Williams, 'The Early Welsh Arthur Poems', in *The Arthur of the Welsh: The Arthurian Legend in Medieval Welsh Literature*, ed. Rachel Bromwich, A. O. H. Jarman, and Brynley F. Roberts (Cardiff: University of Wales Press, 1991), 49.

Even if we assume that stanza 44 is an early (pre-twelfth-century) attestation of Brittonic belief in Arthur's survival, we still lack concrete evidence that the Brittonic peoples regarded Arthur as a political messiah. The statement that Arthur's grave is impossible to find might imply that he does not have a grave because he is still alive. Nevertheless, Arthur could just as easily have been a giant, a demigod, or a great military hero who escaped the way of all flesh by entering a liminal space for eternity.[52]

Suggestion has been made that the myth of Arthur's survival stems from Brittany,[53] but this is not a testable hypothesis. As Victoria Flood acknowledges, '[w]e do not possess a body of recorded medieval political prophecy in Brittany comparative to that of Wales, and certainly no early written prophecies concerning Arthur's return'.[54] The idea depends heavily on a contestable interpretation of a short passage in the second book of Herman of Tournai's *Miracula sancte Marie Laudunensis*.[55] Book Two, which was redacted between 1136 and 1142, is a narrative of a relic tour that nine canons of Laon made through England between 24 March and 6 September 1113. Herman included in this narrative a vignette about a Cornishman with a withered hand who was seeking healing from the relics but also proclaiming that King Arthur was still alive. His claim sparked a quarrel over the question of Arthur's fate that almost resulted in violence and endangered the canons. Herman described the incident as follows:

> Quidam etiam vir ibidem manum aridam habens, coram feretro pro sanitate recipienda vigilabat. Sed sicut Britones solent iurgari cum Francis pro rege Arturo, idem vir cepit rixari cum uno ex famulis nostris, nomine Haganello, qui erat ex familia domni Widonis Laudunensis archidiaconi, dicens adhuc Arturum vivere. Unde non parvo tumultu exorto, cum armis ecclesiam irruunt plurimi, et nisi prefatus Algardus clericus obstitisset, pene usque ad sanguinis effusionem ventum fuisset. Quam rixam coram feretro suo factam credimus Domine nostre displicuisse, nam idem vir manum aridam habens, qui pro Arturo tumultum fecerat, sanitatem non recepit.[56]
>
> (Another fellow, who had a withered hand, was keeping watch in front of the reliquary in order to receive healing. But just as the Britons are accustomed to quarrel with the French on account of

---

52 Regarding the dating of stanza 44 and the meaning of *anoeth*, see Sims-William, 'Early Welsh Arthur Poems', 49 and Helbert, 'an Arður sculde ȝete cum', 89–90. On pre-Galfridian representations of Arthur, see Padel, 'Nature of Arthur', 14.

53 Flood, 'Arthur's Return from Avalon', 85.

54 Flood, 'Arthur's Return from Avalon', 91.

55 Hériman de Tournai, *Miracula sancte Marie Laudunensis*, ed. and trans. Alain Saint-Denis as *Les Miracles de sainte Marie de Laon* (Paris: CNRS Editions, 2008).

56 Hériman de Tournai, *Miracula sancte Marie Laudunensis* 2.16, p. 186.

King Arthur, this man began to quarrel violently with one of our servants, by the name of Haganellus, who was from the family of Lord Guido, archdeacon at Laon, saying that Arthur still lives. On account of this, not a small fracas arose with many rushing into the church with arms, and had not the aforesaid cleric Algardus stood in the way, it would have almost escalated to the spilling of blood. We believe this quarrel made in front of her bier displeased Our Lady, for the same man with the withered hand who had caused a fracas on account of Arthur did not receive healing.)

Two critical questions arise from this excerpt. First, should we interpret 'Britones' as the Brittonic Celts broadly speaking or as the inhabitants of Brittany?[57] The probable answer based on context (i.e. quarreling with the French) is the latter. Herman appears here to be offering an authorial aside explaining that just as the Bretons during his day were accustomed to quarrel with the French about Arthur, the canons of Laon found themselves in a heated debate with this man in Cornwall in 1113.

The second question concerns the reliability of the *Miracula* as a reflection of contemporary life and practice in England (including Cornwall) and France in 1113.[58] Herman had a source narrative dating from 1113. And yet, as Edmond Faral has demonstrated, Herman allowed his own more present knowledge to inform (or, from our perspective, contaminate) his source material.[59] Evidently, there had been a debate (either genuine or manufactured) between the Bretons and French over Arthur by 1142 when Herman completed the second book of his *Miracula*. If this were not the case, Herman's aside would not have made much sense to his immediate audience. The existence of a debate over the fate of Arthur in France around 1142 is not a groundbreaking discovery because Geoffrey's *Historia regum Britannie*, which contains veiled reference to the Breton Hope, was already in circulation in France by 1138 and the figure of Arthur was known in France even prior to the composition of Geoffrey's *Historia*.[60] The reference assumes much greater significance if

[57] This question is raised repeatedly by James Wade, *Fairies in Medieval Romance* (New York: Palgrave Macmillan, 2011), 43–4 and nn. 10 and 13.

[58] For doubt as to the account's veracity, see Edmond Faral, *La légende Arthurienne, études et documents*, 3 vols. Bibliothèque de l'École des Hautes-Études, fasc. 255–7 (Paris: Champion, 1929), I, 232–3. For acceptance of the account as genuine, see J. S. P. Tatlock, 'The English Journey of the Laon Canons', *Speculum* 8, n. 4 (1933): 464–5.

[59] Faral, *Légende Arthurienne*, I, 232–3.

[60] In his study of 300 cartularies that range from the ninth to the fourteenth centuries and span all the regions of France, Pierre Gallais has found that the name 'Arthur' (or a variant of it) began to be more frequently attested from about 1065. See his 'Bleheri, la cour de Poitiers et la diffusion des récits arthuriens sur le continent', *Journal of the International Arthurian Society* 2 (2014): 97–100.

it does show the Breton Hope to have been a living force among the Cornish in 1113.

Elsewhere, I have argued that the episode is not a dependable indicator of local Cornish belief in Arthur's survival at that time and is more likely a late accretion written in the context of the early dissemination of Geoffrey's *Historia regum Britannie* (c. 1138). Rather than being a value-neutral detail (reliable by virtue of being non-essential to the narrative), the Breton Hope reference serves as a preaching exemplum that participates in the overall didactic function of the work. It appears to have been modeled after the account of how Jesus healed a man with a withered hand (*homo habens manum aridam*) in the synagogue on the Sabbath (Matthew 12:9–14, Mark 3:1–6, and Luke 6:6–11). The passage juxtaposes Jesus, true and universal Messiah, and Arthur, a false and local messiah. Jesus healed the man with a withered hand who came to him; Arthur did not (and could not) provide healing to one of his 'believers'.[61] In short, there is no concrete evidence that the myth of Arthur's return existed prior to the twelfth century.

The earliest written expression of *exspectare Arthurum* appears in the *Gesta regum Anglorum* (completed in 1125) of the English and Norman Benedictine monk William of Malmesbury (d. c. 1142). William, after mentioning how the grave of Walwen (Gawain) was discovered in Ros in Wales during the reign of William II of England (r. 1087–1100), added: 'Sed Arturis sepulchrum nusquam uisitur, unde antiquitas neniarum adhuc eum uenturum fabulatur' (But the grave of Arthur is nowhere to be seen, whence comes the antiquity of idle talk that he will still return).[62] William introduced Arthur's second coming as age-old lore. Perhaps it was, but, as E. K. Chambers has noted, to us, '[t]he existence of these fables is the singular new fact in the development of the tradition'.[63] The only evidence we have for supposing that *exspectare Arturum* was a long-established part of Brittonic oral tradition are statements to that effect by non-Brittonic writers beginning with William of Malmesbury.

We have reason to question whether *exspectare Arturum* was a longheld Brittonic belief. Arthur might have assumed the revenant savior characteristics of Cynan, Cadwallon, Cadwallader, and Owain as tales of Arthur circulated among non-Brittonic audiences on the Continent. The

[61] Christopher Michael Berard, 'King Arthur and the Canons of Laon', *Arthuriana* 26, n. 3 (2016): 91–119.

[62] William of Malmesbury, *Gesta regum Anglorum* 3.287, ed. and trans. Roger Aubrey Baskerville Mynors, Rodney Malcolm Thomson, and Michael Winterbottom, 2 vols. (Oxford: Clarendon Press, 1998), I, 520–1. I have modified Mynors' translation slightly to be as literal as possible.

[63] Chambers, *Arthur of Britain*, 18, 108. Also see Tatlock, *Legendary History*, 229.

idea of Arthur as a messianic figure might also have been related to early twelfth-century Christian millenarian thinking, which was heightened by the First Crusade. The returning hero traditions surrounding Cynan, Cadwallader, and Owain could have been passed on to Arthur, but, given the late date of the earliest written attestation of Arthur's return (the first quarter of the twelfth century), it is possible that the understanding of Arthur as returning hero originated around the time of the First Crusade, that it came directly from Last Emperor prophecies, and even that it was not Brittonic in origin.

A strong case can be made that the inspiration behind *exspectare Arthurum* was the 'Last Emperor Prophecy' as formulated in the *Apocalypse* or *Revelations* (c. 685–92) attributed (erroneously) to Methodius of Olympus, a Christian bishop and writer who was martyred c.311.[64] As summarized by Michael Twomey, '[t]he original Syriac version of Pseudo-Methodius narrates world history from Creation through the succession of empires (Alexander to Rome), then foretells the rise of Islam, the eventual triumph of the last Roman emperor, the coming of the Antichrist, and the end of the world'.[65] Pseudo-Methodius predicted that when the Sons of Ishmael (the forces of Islam) will have brought great tribulation upon Christians all across the Mediterranean world and when they will have boasted that Christians will have no hope of deliverance, they will experience a sudden downturn and 'exiliet super eos rex Gregorum, sive Romanorum, in furore magno et expergiscitur tamquam homo a somno vini, quem exaestimabant homines tamquam mortuum esse et in nihilo utilem' (the king of the Greeks, that is, of the Romans, will spring upon them in great anger and he will be aroused like a man from a drunken sleep, whom men reckoned to be dead and good for nothing).[66] The prophecy goes on to state that this king will defeat the sons of Ishmael in battle and impose a yoke on them. The downtrodden and dispossessed Christians will return to their native lands, rebuild their cities, and be at peace. Although not the messiah, the Last Emperor assumes the role of heroic avenger of the

---

[64] Pseudo-Methodius, *Apocalypse; An Alexandrian World Chronicle*, ed. and trans. Benjamin Garstad (Cambridge, MA: Harvard University Press, 2012), 1–139.

[65] Michael W. Twomey, 'The *Revelations* of Pseudo-Methodius and Scriptural Study at Salisbury in the Eleventh Century', in *Sources of Wisdom: Old English and Early Medieval Latin Studies in honour of Thomas D. Hill*, ed. Frederick M. Biggs, Thomas D. Hill, Charles D. Wright, and Thomas Hall (Toronto: University of Toronto Press, 2007), 371.

[66] Pseudo-Methodius, *Apocalypse* 13.11, pp. 126–9. On the waking of the Last Roman Emperor, see Paul J. Alexander, 'The Medieval Legend of the Last Roman Emperor and its Messianic Origin', *Journal of the Warburg and Courtauld Institutes* 41 (1978): 4. This element is absent from the second recension.

downtrodden and restorer of peace and prosperity.[67] The Last Emperor is fated to precede the Parousia (Christ's triumphant Second Coming) just as John the Baptist heralded Christ's earthly ministry. The sudden heroic rise of a sleeping military hero in the time of his people's great need has much in common with the Breton Hope.[68]

Elements from the Last Emperor Prophecy as found in Pseudo-Methodius' *Apocalypse* or an analogue may have been incorporated into the legend of Arthur prior to the twelfth century, but to date no one has advanced a compelling argument to this effect.[69] The *Apocalypse* of Pseudo-Methodius was originally composed in Syriac at a time of great Muslim expansion (late seventh century), a crowning achievement of which was the construction of the Dome of the Rock on the Temple Mount by the caliph 'Abd al-Malik in 691. The *Apocalypse* was translated into a variety of languages, including Latin. The earliest surviving manuscript of the Latin text dates from before 727 and 'linguistic details of the translation indicate that it was made into the Vulgar Latin of Merovingian Gaul'.[70] There are two Latin recensions of the *Apocalypse*: R1 and R2. Both cover the critical section on the Last Emperor. No fewer than twenty-two manuscripts of the *Apocalypse* in Latin predate the twelfth century,[71] and it has been established that the text was read and used in Anglo-Saxon England. The two earliest surviving manuscripts of English provenance (pre-1100) were

---

[67] Bernard McGinn characterizes the Last Emperor as 'a coming quasi-Messiah, or stand-in for the Returning Christ'. See his 'Apocalypticism and Violence: Aspects of Their Relationship in Antiquity and the Middle Ages', in *Scripture and Pluralism: Reading the Bible in the Religiously Plural Worlds of the Middle Ages and Renaissance*, ed. Thomas J. Heffernan and Thomas E. Burman (Leiden: Brill, 2005), 220.

[68] This clear parallel has also been noted by Valerie M. Lagorio, 'The Apocalyptic Mode in the Vulgate Cycle of Arthurian Romances', *Philological Quarterly* 57 (1978): 12.

[69] Judith Weiss writes: '[w]e know versions of the Tiburtine Sibylline prophecies circulated in Wales: these must have fused with, perhaps influenced, the prophecies of returns of popular heroes, such as Cynan and Cadwaladr', and Weiss sees this fusion as an antecedent to the 'later belief among the Brittonic peoples that Arthur would return'. See her 'Emperors and Antichrists: Reflections of Empire in Insular Narrative, 1130–1250', in *The Matter of Identity in Medieval Romance*, ed. Phillipa Hardman (Cambridge: D. S. Brewer, 2002), 93. The Welsh Tiburtine Sibylline prophecy cited by Weiss derives from a mid eleventh-century Latin translation. See Griffiths, *Early Vaticination in Welsh*, 41, and Bernard McGinn, *Visions of the End: Apocalyptic Traditions in the Middle Ages*, rev. edn. (New York: Columbia University Press, 1998), 43–50, 294–7. This Latin translation may reflect the influence of the *Apocalypse* of Pseudo-Methodius. See Christopher Bonura, 'When did the Legend of the Last Emperor Originate? A New Look at the Textual Relationship between *The Apocalypse of Pseudo-Methodius* and the *Tiburtine Sibyl*', *Viator* 47, n. 3 (2016): 47–100.

[70] Pseudo-Methodius, *Apocalypse*, ix.

[71] See Michael W. Twomey, 'Pseudo-Methodius Revelations', in *Sources of Anglo-Saxon Culture: The Apocrypha*, ed. Frederick M. Biggs (Kalamazoo, MI: Medieval Institute Publications, 2007), 19.

composed at the Salisbury Cathedral scriptorium, which was established no earlier than 1075; and the Old English text, 'Concerning the Coming of Antichrist', preserved in a twelfth-century manuscript, indicates that the lengthier R1 was in Anglo-Saxon England.[72] Fusion of the Last Emperor Prophecy and the legend of King Arthur need not have occurred in Britain; it could, in fact, have happened on the Continent.

Around the time of the First Crusade, the characteristics of the Last Emperor intermingled with those of Charlemagne.[73] Arthur, whose stories are thought to have accompanied the crusaders into Italy and the Holy Land, also might have come by 'messianic' attributes at this time. The monk of Corvey and pilgrim to Jerusalem, Ekkehard of Aura (d. 1126), reported that in 1095–6, when Urban II was urging Christians to take up the Cross (1095), Satan, the old enemy, stirred up 'pseudo-prophets' and saw to it that false brothers and dishonest women feigned devotion and joined the crusaders, and Ekkehard further remarked:

> Sicque per aliorum hypocrisin atque mendacia per aliorum vero nefarias pollutiones Christi greges adeo turpabantur, ut juxta boni pastoris vaticinium etiam electi in errorem ducerentur.[74] Inde fabulosum illud confictum est de Karolo Magno, quasi de mortuis in id ipsum resuscitato et alio nescio quo nihilominus redivivo, fribolum quoque illud de ansere quasi dominam suam deducente, multaque id genus.[75]

> (And thus through the hypocrisy and lies of others, indeed through the abominable pollutions of others, the flocks of Christ were sullied to the point that, according to the prophecy of the Good Shepherd, even the chosen ones were led into error. Thence, for this purpose, that fabulous story was concocted about Charlemagne having been resuscitated and some other person, I do not remember who, likewise having come back to life (*redivivus*), and also that frivolous story about a gander leading its lady, and many other tales of this sort.)

---

72 See Stephen Pelle, 'The *Revelations* of Pseudo-Methodius and "Concerning the Coming of Antichrist" in British Library MS Cotton Vespasian D. xiv', *Notes and Queries* 56, n. 3 (2009): 327–8.

73 This fusion occurs in an anonymous eleventh-century text by 'Pseudo-Alcuin'. See Matthew Gabriele, *An Empire of Memory: The Legend of Charlemagne, the Franks, and Jerusalem before the First Crusade* (Oxford: Oxford University Press, 2011), 124–5.

74 See Matthew 24:24. All citations and translations of the Latin Vulgate are from *The Vulgate Bible: Douay-Rheims Translation*, ed. Swift Edgar (vols. 1–3) and Angela M. Kinney (vols. 3–6), 6 vols. (Cambridge, MA: Harvard University Press, 2010–13). The passage above from *Matthew* appears in volume 6 (The New Testament), 140–1.

75 Ekkehard of Aura, *Ekkehardi Chronicon Universale ad a. 1106*, ed. Georg Heinrich Pertz, in *MGH Scriptores* 6, ed. Georg Heinrich Pertz (Hanover: Hahn, 1843), 214–15.

This passage is tantalizing, elusive, and significant for our purposes. After mentioning the idea of *Carolus Magnus redivivus*, Ekkehard makes reference to a second returning hero, whom he does not name. The chronicler might very well have been thinking of Arthur in this instance. *Alio nescio quo* is, of course, a common Latin construction; yet I would call the reader's attention to a well-known, albeit subsequent, instance in which it was used in connection with Arthur. Aelred of Rievaulx in his *Liber de speculo caritatis* (c. 1142–3) famously writes: 'Nam et in fabulis, quae uulgo de nescio quo finguntur Arthuro, memini me nonnunquam usque ad effusionem lacrimarum fuisse permotum.' (For when fables that are being made up in common speech about some Arthur – I don't know exactly whom – I remember being moved sometimes even to the point of weeping.) [76] After speaking of the unnamed second returning hero, Ekkehard speaks of a 'frivolous story about a gander leading its lady'. Here Ekkehard appears to have been making a flippant reference to the *Chevalier au Cygne* (Swan Knight), who, in the Old French Crusade cycle of *chanson de geste*, emerges as the ancestor of Godfrey of Bouillon. If my suggestions are correct, then Ekkehard was speaking about Charlemagne, King Arthur, and an ancestor of Godfrey of Bouillon in that order. Arthur, Charlemagne, and Godfrey would later (c. 1310) be celebrated as the Three Christian Worthies of the Nine Worthies of chivalry. If my admittedly speculative reading of this passage is correct, then in Ekkehard's universal chronicle to 1106 we have found what is quite possibly the earliest attestation of *Arthurus redivivus*, one that slightly predates William of Malmesbury's *Gesta regum Anglorum* and is decidedly non-Brittonic in provenance.

Ekkehard presents *Carolus Magnus redivivus* as a ridiculous falsehood. This description calls to mind how William of Malmesbury goes on to jeer at the idea of Arthur's return. Although Ekkehard dismissed the notion of Charlemagne's second coming as an untruth inspired by the devil, the first Christian ruler of Jerusalem, Godfrey of Bouillon, seems to have had use for it. He claimed descent from Charlemagne and Caesar Augustus, and he was an adoptive son of Byzantine Emperor Alexius. Moreover, apocalyptic visions of Godfrey as the new Moses, as *dux et praeceptor* of the Christian people, and as sitting on the throne of the kingdom of

---

[76] See Aelred of Rievaulx, *Liber de speculo caritatis* 2.17.51, in *Aelredi Rievallensis Opera omnia*, vol. 1 (*Opera ascetica*), ed. Anselm Hoste and Charles H. Talbot (Turnhout: Brepols, 1971), 90. For the English translation provided, see Aelred of Rievaulx, *Speculum caritatis*, trans. Elizabeth Connor as *The Mirror of Charity* (Kalamazoo, MI: Cistercian Publications, 1990), 199. Also see Berard, 'King Arthur and the Canons of Laon', 116, n. 60.

Jerusalem, were reported. The supporters of Godfrey were hinting that he was *Carolus Magnus redivivus*.[77]

Clearly, there was a place in popular Christian belief in the late eleventh and twelfth centuries for a quasi-messianic hero, and the *Carolus Magnus redivivus* construct illustrates that *exspectare Arthurum* fit comfortably with non-Celtic-specific developments in twelfth-century European popular thought. The contents of surviving codices further indicate that manuscript compilers associated the *Historia regum Britannie* with prophetic and apocalyptic writing, and this is logical given that Geoffrey included his *Prophetia Merlini* (c. 1135) in his *Historia regum Britannie*. Last Emperor prophecies and the *Historia regum Britannie* circulated together with some frequency. Full copies of the *Apocalypse* of Pseudo-Methodius appear together with the *Historia regum Britannie* in six manuscripts. Three further codices containing the *Historia* also contain epitomes of the *Apocalypse*. 'Adso's Letter', which involves a *rex Francorum* as the Last Emperor figure, appears with Geoffrey's *Historia* in two manuscripts.[78] And the Latin version of the prophecy of the Tiburtine Sibyl appears together with the *Historia* in eleven manuscripts.[79] Unless a pre-twelfth-century source comes to light which speaks of Arthur as a hero destined to return, we should not close our minds to possibilities that challenge the assumption that *exspectare Arthurum* was deeply embedded in Brittonic oral tradition.

In the 1130s, the understanding of Arthur as a returning savior was not even monolithic. Before examining the next set of references to the Breton Hope, some historical context is required. After William of Malmesbury completed his *Gesta*, Henry I of England died (1 December 1135), and England fell into a protracted civil war, 'the Anarchy', which lasted until 1154. England's difficulty was Wales' opportunity. By 1136, the Welsh took advantage of the discord in England to win back many of

---

77 See Jay Rubenstein, 'Godfrey of Bouillon versus Raymond of Saint-Gilles: How Carolingian Kingship Trumped Millenarianism at the End of the First Crusade', in *The Legend of Charlemagne in the Middle Ages: Power, Faith and Crusade*, ed. Matthew Gabriele and Jace Stuckey (New York: Palgrave Macmillan, 2008), 64–5, 69–70.

78 Adso (d. 992), abbot of the monastery Montier-en-Der, wrote a letter, *De ortu et tempore Antichristi* (c. 950), for Gerberga, wife of the Carolingian King Louis IV of West Francia (r. 936–54), that contains an idea quite close to *Carolus Magnus redivivus*. See McGinn, *Visions of the End*, 82–7. *De ortu et tempore Antichristi* was circulating in England by the 990s: the homiletic writings of Ælfric of Eynsham (c. 950–c.1010) and Wulfstan (d. 1023) reflect its influence. See Stephen Anthony Pelle, 'Continuity and Renewal in English Homiletic Eschatology, *ca.* 1150–1200' (Ph.D. diss., University of Toronto, 2012), 13–14. It is also worthy of note that 'Pseudo-Alcuin' identifies the Last Roman Emperor as a Carolingian in his eleventh-century revision of Adso's *De ortu et tempore Antichristi*.

79 See Crick, *HRB Dissemination and Reception*, 31, 58–9, 66–7.

their ancestral lands.[80] It is at this time that we find suggestion of Arthur being conscripted for the Welsh cause and Geoffrey of Monmouth's first mention of Arthur's fate.

Geoffrey's handling of Arthur's fate is ambiguous. In keeping with the Welsh prophetic tradition, Geoffrey casts post-Arthurian British heroes Cadwallader and Conan as returning heroes but does not say the same of Arthur.[81] In his *Prophetia Merlini*, which as noted above became part of the *Historia regum Britannie*, Geoffrey has Merlin prophesy to the tyrant Vortigern the advent of Arthur, *not* his second coming.[82] Merlin tells Vortigern that this Boar of Cornwall (*Aper Cornubiae*) will have an uncertain end (*exitus dubius*), but that his great deeds will be celebrated throughout the world and will be the sustenance of storytellers forever more.[83] From the perspective of the characters within the narrative (Merlin and Vortigern), this is a prophecy of things to come. For the outside audience, these utterances foreshadow events that occur later in Geoffrey's *Historia*.[84]

Complicating this matter are two subsequent boar-related prophecies in the *Prophetia Merlini* that are expected to occur after the diegesis of the *Historia* concludes. Merlin foretells that the cubs of the Lion (*catuli Leonis*), the offspring of Henry I, the Lion of Justice, will be transformed into fish, a reference to the White Ship disaster (25 November 1120), a shipwreck in the Channel that resulted in the drowning of Henry's only legitimate son and chosen heir, William.[85] After describing violence in Venedotia (Gwynedd) and the House of Corineus (Cornwall), Merlin prophesies:

> Nocturnis lacrimis madebit insula, unde omnes ad omnia prouocabuntur. Nitentur posteri transuolare superna, sed fauor nouorum sublimabitur. Nocebit possidenti ex impiis pietas donec sese genitore induerit. Apri igitur dentibus accinctus, cacumina montium et umbram galeati transcendet. Indignabitur Albania et conuocatis collateralibus sanguinem effundere uacabit. Dabitur maxillis eius

---

[80] See R. R. Davies, *The Age of Conquest: Wales, 1063–1415* (Oxford: Oxford University Press, 1987), 45–55; Faletra, *Wales and Medieval Colonial Imagination*, 4, 20.

[81] Geoffrey of Monmouth, *Historia regum Britannie* 115.110–14, pp. 148–9.

[82] See Lesley A. Coote, *Prophecy and Public Affairs in Later Medieval England* (York: York Medieval Press, 2000), 50–1.

[83] Geoffrey of Monmouth, *Historia regum Britannie* 112.39–43, pp. 144–5. The First Variant Version matches the Vulgate Version for this prophecy. See *The Historia regum Britannie of Geoffrey of Monmouth II, The First Variant Version: A Critical Edition*, ed. Neil Wright (Cambridge, UK: D. S. Brewer, 1988), 102. Hereafter this source will be cited as *HRB First Variant Version*.

[84] See Faletra, *Wales and Medieval Colonial Imagination*, 51.

[85] Geoffrey of Monmouth, *Historia regum Britannie* 113.84–6, pp. 146–7.

frenum, quod in Armorico sinu fabricabitur. Deaurabit illud aquila rupti foederis et tercia nidificatione gaudebit.[86]

(The island will be soaked in nightly tears, and so all men will be provoked to all things. Their progeny will try to fly beyond the heavens, but the favour of new men will be raised up. The possessor will be harmed by the goodness of the wicked until he dresses himself as his father. Girt thus with the teeth of the boar, he will rise above the mountain peaks and the shadow of the helmeted man. Scotland will be angered and, summoning its neighbours, will spend its time in bloodshed. Upon its jaws will be placed a bridle, made in the bay of Brittany. The eagle of the broken treaty will gild the bridle and rejoice in a third nesting.)

I will refer to this section of the *Prophetia Merlini* as the prophecy of the Boar-Toothed King. The sadness and mayhem that are to ensue on the island allude to the Anarchy. According to an incomplete commentary on the *Prophetia Merlini* thought to date from c. 1155–9, *posteri* signifies the descendants of Henry I of England, namely Empress Matilda and her son by Count Geoffrey of Anjou, Henry Plantagenet; *favor novorum* refers to the influence of young men who installed Stephen of Blois as king of England and brought about the unjust expulsion of Matilda and Henry Plantagenet; and *Donec sese genitore induerit* is a reference to Stephen's eventual adoption of Henry Plantagenet as his heir and royal successor (by the Treaty of Winchester, 1153).[87] The commentator glosses *Apri igitur dentibus accinctus* as 'ad modum Arthuri, ferocis hominis' (just like Arthur, the ferocious man).[88] Geoffrey of Monmouth could not have foreseen the Treaty of Winchester when he was writing the *Prophetia Merlini* in the mid 1130s, but he seems to have envisioned a post-Conquest king of England, possibly even Stephen, behaving like the Boar of Cornwall. Hence, the commentator hints that Stephen might have been the Boar-Toothed King. Further on in the *Prophetia Merlini*, immediately after prophesying Normandy's loss of the British Isles, the return of Cadwallader and Conan as allies, and their restoration of Britain to its former name and glory, Merlin declares:

Ex Conano procedet aper bellicosus, qui infra Gallicana nemora acumen dentium suorum exercebit. Truncabit namque quaeque maiora robora, minoribus uero tutelam praestabit. Tremebunt illum

---

[86] Geoffrey of Monmouth, *Historia regum Britannie* 113–14.86–94, pp. 148–9.
[87] This Merlin commentary is preserved in Bibliothèque nationale de France, Fonds Latin 6233, fols. 42r–49v and in Fonds Latin 4126, fols. 172r–173v. The text has been edited by Jacob Hammer, 'A Commentary on the *Prophetia Merlini* (Geoffrey of Monmouth's *Historia regum Britanniae*, Book VII)', *Speculum* 10, n. 1 (1935): 17.
[88] Hammer, 'Commentary on the *Prophetia Merlini*', 17.

Arabes et Affricani; nam impetum cursus sui in ulteriorem Hispaniam protendit.[89]

(From Conanus will come forth a warlike boar, who will sharpen his tusks on the forests of France. He will break all the tallest trees, but give protection to the smaller. The Arabs and Africans will tremble before him; for his charge will carry him all the way to further Spain.)

This prophecy clearly anticipates the arrival of a conquering hero cut from the same cloth as Arthur, but the Bellicose Boar need not be the original Boar of Cornwall returned.

Subsequent to the *Prophetia Merlini* in the *Historia regum Britannie* proper, Geoffrey opts to leave Arthur's fate uncertain. At the conclusion of his account of Arthur's reign, he writes that Arthur was mortally wounded and conceded the crown to his kinsman Constantine, but that it remained possible that the king's wounds would heal.[90] Geoffrey does not specify the location of Avalon. Near the close of the *Historia*, Geoffrey makes one final inscrutable reference to Arthur. He states that an angelic voice instructed Cadwallader not to continue with his plans to retake Britain from the English. Geoffrey then explains: 'Nolebat enim Deus Britones in insulam Britanniae diutius regnare antequam tempus illud uenisset quod Merlinus Arturo prophetauerat' (God did not want the Britons to rule over the island of Britain any longer, until the time came which Merlin had foretold to Arthur).[91] This is a perplexing passage because Merlin's previous appearance in the *Historia* occurs immediately prior to the begetting of Arthur. Unless 'Arturo' was mistakenly written in place of the more logical 'Vortegirno', as Lewis Thorpe has suggested, we must assume that Merlin meets a fully grown Arthur and divines for him the fate of the Britons.[92] Geoffrey does not narrate this encounter, and it is unclear whether the exchange occurs while Arthur is reigning as king of Britain or convalescing on the isle of Avalon. Although we are given to understand that Arthur knows when Britain will

---

[89] Geoffrey of Monmouth, *Historia regum Britannie* 115.114–18, pp. 148–9.

[90] As Neil Wright observes, the copy of Geoffrey's *Historia* preserved in Bern, Burgerbibliothek, MS. 568, fols. 18r–79v (twelfth century, after 1175), 'has no time for the Breton hope that Arthur would return, but records unequivocally that the national hero was dead'. See *The Historia regum Britannie of Geoffrey of Monmouth, I: Bern, Burgerbibliothek, MS. 568*, ed. Neil Wright (Cambridge, UK: D. S. Brewer, 1985), lix, 132. *HRB First Variant Version* does not deviate from the vulgate version on this point (174).

[91] Geoffrey of Monmouth, *Historia regum Britannie* 205.564–6, pp. 278–9. *HRB First Variant Version* replicates this prophecy of Merlin to Arthur (190).

[92] Lewis Thorpe, 'Merlin's Sardonic Laughter', in *Studies in Medieval Literature and Languages in Memory of Frederick Whitehead*, ed. W. Rothwell, W. R. J. Barron, David Blamires, and Lewis Thorpe (Manchester, UK: Manchester University Press, 1973), 323 n. 3.

be restored to the Brittonic Celts, we are left wondering whether Arthur is destined to play a role in the British restoration.

Why is Geoffrey unwilling to take a firm stance concerning Arthur's end? We know that Geoffrey knew William of Malmesbury's *Gesta regum Anglorum* because he mentions it at the conclusion of his *Historia*.[93] Geoffrey almost certainly had read William's claim that there was an ancient tradition that Arthur would someday return. Yet he chooses not to repeat this idea. Why is this the case? Tatlock suggests that Geoffrey is being deliberately obscure as to Arthur's fate because he wished to offend neither the Brittonic Celts nor the Normans.[94] However, Geoffrey does not shy away from reporting the Cadwallader / Conan prophecy, which was equally ominous to the Anglo-Norman occupiers of Britain. The idea of a returning Brittonic hero thus was not in and of itself repugnant to his political or religious sensibilities. Whatever his motives, Geoffrey's reluctance to offer closure regarding Arthur's fate instantly captured the imagination of his audience, and eventually led to a dispute regarding the location of Arthur's resting place.

As Geoffrey was putting the finishing touches on his *Historia*, the troubadour Marcabru (c.1130–49) also touched upon Arthur's end. After the sudden death of William VIII of Poitou (X of Aquitaine) in April 1137, Marcabru found himself in a precarious situation. He sent greetings near and far in search of other benefactors. Reflecting upon his circumstance, Marcabru pessimistically states '... puois lo Peitavis m'es faillitz, / serai mai cum Artus perdutz, (since the Poitevin has failed me, I will ever more be lost like Arthur).[95] What then is Marcabru telling us about Arthur? Arthur apparently has gone to a far-off place and will not return. Arthur might not be dead, but there is no hint that he is coming back. It is unclear whether William of Malmesbury's or Geoffrey's writings influenced Marcabru. In the 1120s and 1130s the question of Arthur's fate was a source of fascination for courtly society and the educated clergy.

For the next mention of Arthur's fate we must turn to the earliest known witness to the dissemination of Geoffrey's *Historia*, the 'Epistola ad Warinum' of the Anglo-Norman chronicler Henry of Huntington (c. 1088–1157). By January 1139, Robert of Torigni, the monk, chronicler, and future abbot of Mont-Saint-Michel (r. 1154–86), already had a copy of Geoffrey's *Historia* at his monastery, Le Bec in Normandy. We know this because in that month

---

[93] See Geoffrey of Monmouth, *Historia regum Britannie* 208.601–7, pp. 280–1.

[94] Tatlock, *Legendary History*, 204–5.

[95] Marcabru, 'Al prim comenz de l'invernailh' 10.59–60, in *Marcabru: A Critical Edition*, ed. and trans. Simon Gaunt, Ruth Harvey, and Linda Paterson (Cambridge, UK: D. S. Brewer, 2000), 84–5.

Robert reportedly showed his copy to Henry of Huntingdon. Henry was an archdeacon of the diocese of Lincoln and was with Robert at the monastery of Le Bec while en route to Rome.[96] Henry went on to compose a loose summary of Geoffrey's text in the form of an epistle addressed to a certain 'Warinus Brito', who, according to the text, had chided him for not covering the deeds of the Britons from the time of Brutus to that of Julius Caesar in his *Historia*.[97] Henry's account deviates in places from Geoffrey's narrative, and Arthur's fate is one such instance. The Englishman writes: 'Mortuum tamen fuisse Britones parentes tui negant. Et eum uenturum sollempniter expectant.' (But the Bretons, your ancestors, refuse to believe that he died. And they solemnly await his return.)[98] In this passage, Henry is not faithfully summarizing Geoffrey's narrative. The addressee, Warinus Brito, has not been conclusively identified and might be an epistolary framing device.[99] Here, we do not find proof that the Brittonic peoples actually believed that Arthur would return. Instead, we find an example of an Anglo-Norman, namely Henry of Huntington, stating that, according to the Bretons, Arthur will return. Henry was not afraid to modify his summary of Geoffrey's *Historia* to align more closely with his understanding of Brittonic culture. Henry may well have 'corrected' Geoffrey's account of Arthur's fate using William of Malmesbury's *Gesta regum Anglorum*.

The twelfth-century Anglo-Norman *Description of England*, which may date from as early as the reign of King Stephen (1135–54), also deserves mention in this context.[100] In this anonymous text the figure of Arthur is referenced as somehow supportive of the Welsh struggle for independence and sovereignty over all of Britain. As mentioned at the outset of this chapter, Gillingham's selective use of lines 218–28 of the Anglo-Norman

[96] See Neil Wright, 'The Place of Henry of Huntingdon's *Epistola ad Warinum* in the text-history of Geoffrey of Monmouth's *Historia regum Britannie*: A Preliminary Investigation', in *France and the British Isles in the Middle Ages and Renaissance: Essays by Members of Girton College, Cambridge, in Memory of Ruth Morgan*, ed. Gillian Jondorf and D. N. Dumville (Woodbridge, UK: Boydell, 1991), 73–4.

[97] Henry, archdeacon of Huntingdon, 'Epistola ad Warinum', ed. and trans. Diana Greenway, in Henry, Archdeacon of Huntingdon, *Historia Anglorum*, ed. and trans. Diana Greenway (Oxford: Clarendon Press, 1996), 558–9.

[98] Henry of Huntingdon, 'Epistola ad Warinum', 580–1.

[99] Henry of Huntingdon, 'Epistola ad Warinum', 559 n. 2. Wright believes that Warinus was a historical person of Breton descent, (Place of Henry of Huntingdon's *Epistola*', 74).

[100] 'The Anglo-Norman *Description of England: An Edition*', ed. Alexander Bell, in *Anglo-Norman Anniversary Essays*, ed. Ian Short (London: Anglo-Norman Text Society, 1993), 43. Also see Lesley Johnson, 'The Anglo-Norman *Description of England*: An Introduction', in *Anglo-Norman Anniversary Essays*, ed. Ian Short (London: Anglo-Norman Text Society, 1993), 11–30. Johnson believes that this text was 'composed probably soon after 1139 and certainly before the end of the twelfth century' (11).

Description of England bears almost all the weight of his argument that the twelfth-century Arthur was generally understood as a Celtic champion and threat to the Anglo-Norman rulers of the British Isles. Without summarizing the context of the lines, Gillingham offers this translation:

> Well have the Welsh revenged themselves
> Many of our French they have slain
> Some of our castles they have taken
> Fiercely they threaten us
> Openly they go about saying
> That in the end they will have all,
> By means of Arthur, they will have it back
> They will call it Britain again.[101]

Now, if we read these lines in isolation, the division between 'our French' and the Welsh and 'their' Arthur is striking. The Anglo-Norman author evidently understands Arthur to be a Welsh national hero. Gillingham, however, does not take into account the author's formulation of his own cultural identity. In the Anglo-Norman *Description of England* we find three separate cultural groups: the French (Anglo-Normans), the English, and the Welsh. Before defining himself in opposition to the Welsh, the author prides himself on his own 'French' cultural heritage and differentiates himself from the English. For instance, when explaining how a king from Wessex eventually united the Anglo-Saxon kingdoms under his rule and divided the newly formed England into shires, the poet writes:

> A chascun sun nun donat,
> En engleis 'scire' l'apelat,
> Mes nus ki romanz savum
> D'autre maniere les numum:
> Ço que 'schire' ad nun en engleis
> 'Cunté' ad nun en franceis.[102]
>
> (He gives to each one its name. In English he called it 'scire', but we, who know *romanz*, refer to them in another way. That which has the name 'shire' in English has the name 'county' in French.)

Asserting his 'French' cultural identity is a point of pride for our anonymous poet. At line 179, he turns his attention to Wales and begins naming its principal regions and the number and location of its bishops and archbishops. The poet then comments on the condition of Wales, and here we find the Arthur reference:

---

[101] Gillingham, 'Cultivation of History', 37.
[102] 'Anglo-Norman Description of England', 39, lines 63–8.

Ore n'i ad cité remis,
Kar destruit est tut le païs,
Premierement par les Seisuns,
Puis par la guere des Bretuns;
De l'autre part puis que Franceis
Vencu orent les Engleis
E orent cunquis la terre
Par feu, par faim e par guerre.
L'eve passerent de Saverne,
As Waleis si murent guerre,
De la terre mult conquistrent
E mult grieves leis i mistrent,
Kar les Galeis enchacerent,
Des lur la terre herbergerent
E si i firent mult chastels
Qui mult part sunt e bons e bels.
Mais nepurquant suventesfeiz
Ben s'en vengerent les Waleis.
De noz Franceis mult unt ocis,
De noz chastels se sunt saisiz;
Apertement le vont disant,
Forment nus vont maneçant,
Qu'a la parfin tute l'avrunt,
Par Artur la recoverunt,
E cest païs tut ensement
Toldrunt a la romaine gent,
A la terre sun nun rendrunt,
Bretaine la repelerunt.[103]

(Now no city remains there, for the entire country was destroyed, first by the Saxons, then by the war of the Britons; on the other side, the French have since vanquished the English and conquered the land by fire, by famine, and by war. They passed over the waters of the Severn and moved war against the Welsh, conquered much of the land and put in place many harsh laws there. For they chased the Welsh away, and some of their men took up residence on the land and thus made many castles there, which are extremely good and attractive. But, nevertheless, the Welsh avenged themselves well many times for it. They have killed many of our French folk; they have seized our castles; they are saying it openly, threatening us that in the end they will have it all. Through Arthur they will recover it, and they will take this country altogether in the same way from the Romance-speaking people. They will give the land back its name. They will call it Britain again.)

---

[103] 'Anglo-Norman Description of England', 43, lines 201–28.

The poet presents the French as the latest in a line of occupiers of the British Isles, coming after the English, who displaced the Britons. He initially refers to the French in the third person. The French overcame the English. The French dispossessed the Welsh. But, when speaking of Welsh retaliations, the poet numbers himself among the French (*noz Franceis*), and he expresses concern about how the Welsh were taking his countrymen's castles (*noz chastels*).[104] These are local Marcher concerns, and there is no clear indication that the text was written for a royal audience. In fact, Marcher lords, as is well known, enjoyed a substantial degree of autonomy from the crown of England.[105] In short, the Anglo-Norman *Description of England* does not necessarily reflect the crown's perspective on the figure of King Arthur.

The Welsh threat, as reported by the author of the Anglo-Norman *Description of England*, coincides with Geoffrey's *Prophetiae Merlini*, but for one notable detail: the British savior is Arthur, not Cadwallader and Conan. What *par Artur* means is unclear. Even if we understood the author's meaning and knew for a fact that the *Description of England* had been composed in the Welsh Marches, we could not automatically assume that it was representative of Welsh beliefs or practices. We can, however, regard the text as an indicator of an Anglo-Norman understanding of Welsh belief between 1133 and the close of the twelfth century.

In his *Vita Merlini* of 1150, Geoffrey of Monmouth delivers his final word on Arthur's fate. Yet again, he avoids taking a firm stance on the matter but allows for the possibility of Arthur's eventual return. Whereas the *Prophetia Merlini* are delivered by a youthful Merlin during the reign of Vortigern, who rules before Uther and Arthur, the *Vita Merlini* is set during the reign of Conan, who usurps the throne from Arthur's chosen successor, Constantine. The aged Merlin explains Arthur's fate to Taliesin. Merlin says that the steersman Barinthus transported Arthur, who had been gravely wounded at the Battle of Camlann, to the 'Insula Pomorum' (Island of Apples), also known as the 'Insula Fortunata' (Fortunate Island),[106] and there Morgen, an expert in herbal medicine, receives

---

[104] There are examples from 1164–6 and 1175 of the Welsh referring to the Anglo-Normans as 'the French'; see *Brut y Tywysogion, or Chronicle of the Princes: Red Book of Hergest Version*, 2nd edn., ed. and trans. Thomas Jones (Cardiff: University of Wales Press, 1973), 146–7 and 162–3. The text will henceforth be cited as *Red Book of Hergest Brut*. Also see Seán Duffy, 'Henry II and England's Insular Neighbours', in *Henry II: New Interpretations*, ed. Christopher Harper-Bill and Nicholas Vincent (Woodbridge, UK: Boydell, 2007), 135.

[105] See John E. Morris, *The Welsh Wars of Edward I: A Contribution to Mediaeval Military History, Based on Original Documents* (Oxford: Clarendon Press, 1901), 11.

[106] Geoffrey of Monmouth, *Vita Merlini*, 100–1, lines 907–8; 102–3, lines 930–2.

Arthur honorably, inspects his wounds closely, and gives him a positive prognosis provided he stay with her and accept her treatment.[107] Thus it seems that Arthur is fated to live on in an Elysium. But Geoffrey, through the character of Merlin, dismisses the notion that Arthur will return to play an active role in British affairs – at least in the short term. As Merlin describes the Saxon depredation of British lands, Taliesin interjects:

> 'Ergo necesse foret populo transmittere quemdam
> et mandare duci festina nave redire,
> si jam convaluit, solitis ut viribus hostes
> arceat et cives antiqua pace reformet.'[108]

('Then the people must send someone to call on our leader to return in a fast ship. If he has recovered, he can exercise his old vigour to fend off the enemy and re-establish the nation in its old state of peace'.)

Here, Taliesin articulates *exspectare Arthurum*. Geoffrey, through Merlin, allowed for this eventuality but states that it would not occur for a very long time, not until after Conan and Cadwallader should restore Britain to its pristine glory.[109] This clarification is largely consistent with the *Prophetia Merlini*, which states that the Bellicose Boar will come forth from Conan. Geoffrey in the *Vita Merlini* appears to have been leaving room for the possibility that the former Boar of Cornwall and the future Bellicose Boar are one and the same.

After 1150, references to Arthur as the hope of the British race begin to appear with greater regularity. Whether the idea of *exspectare Arthurum* originated with the Brittonic Celts or the Anglo-Normans was now a moot question. The Anglo-Normans represented *exspectare Arthurum* as a Brittonic belief, and the court of Henry II was intent on deriding it and mocking the aptitude of the Welsh more broadly.

Arthur in 'Arthurian' literature from the reign of Henry II

Much like the Arthur of Geoffrey's *Historia*, Henry II ascended the throne of a kingdom rife with internal unrest and external threats. Whereas Arthur faces the Saxons, Henry found himself at odds with the Celtic descendants of Arthur, the Welsh. In the first decade of his reign, Henry also sought to attain suzerainty over the duchy of Brittany and confronted local opposition.[110] Arthur, by virtue of being a restorer of

---

[107] Geoffrey of Monmouth, *Vita Merlini*, 102–3, lines 935–8.
[108] Geoffrey of Monmouth, *Vita Merlini*, 102–3, lines 954–7.
[109] Geoffrey of Monmouth, *Vita Merlini*, 102–5, lines 958–75.
[110] See J. A. Everard, *Brittany and the Angevins: Province and Empire, 1158–1203* (Cambridge, UK: Cambridge University Press, 2000), 35.

peace to a troubled kingdom and a *rex imperator*, was the ideal aspirational paradigm for Henry II, but Arthur, as the personification of the Breton Hope (widely understood to mean the reestablishment of Brittonic rule over all the British Isles and the expulsion of all foreigners), was not an uncomplicated model for the Plantagenet king.[111] The literature on Arthur from the reign of Henry II reflects this tension.

The writers associated with the Angevin court endeavored to wrest the 'historical' Arthur from the 'fabulous' Breton Hope and to claim Arthur as an *English* royal forebear for Henry II. There are two overarching trends in this process. One is the recasting of Arthur into an idealized and nearly superhuman prefiguration of Henry II. This acculturation I term the 'Angevinization' of Arthur. It is particularly evident in the depiction of Arthur's style of kingship, social display, political influence, and territorial holdings. Here we are witnessing the development of a secular typology, Henry II as the new Arthur.

The other trend is the dismissal of the 'Brittonic' literal interpretation of the Breton Hope on intellectual and theological grounds. This tendency fits into the aforementioned colonial discourse, where the French-speaking colonizers of Britain emerge as dynamic, culturally advanced, and righteous Christians entitled to rule all of Britain while the native Celts are presented as barbarians and bad Christians. The Brittonic Other takes on many of the negative attributes that we have seen attached to the Jewish Other, especially the charges of stupidity and misplaced faith.[112] Here we see the advancement of the figural interpretation of *expectare Arthurum* and the debasement of the literal interpretation of it. My discussion of these patterns will proceed diachronically.

Less than a year after Henry II's elevation to the throne of England (19 December 1154), the Jersey-born cleric and poet Wace (d. after 1174) composed for the Angevin court the *Roman de Brut* (1155), a French-language reworking of Geoffrey's *Historia*.[113] The move to recast British

---

[111] Turner, 'England in 1215', 22.

[112] See Miriamne Ara Krummel, *Crafting Jewishness in Medieval England: Legally Absent, Virtually Present* (New York: Palgrave Macmillan, 2011), 133–5, 199 n. 78.

[113] Wace, *Roman de Brut*, ed. and trans. Judith Weiss as *A History of the British: Text and Translation*, rev. edn. (Exeter: University of Exeter Press, 2002). I have also consulted Wace, *Roman de Brut*, ed. Ivor Arnold, 2 vols. (Paris: Société des anciens textes français, 1938–40), but my subsequent citations are to Weiss' edition. We do not know for certain that Henry II or his queen, Eleanor of Aquitaine (c. 1122–1204), commissioned the *Brut*. In his *Roman de Rou* (1160–c. 1174), Wace speaks of the royal couple as his benefactors and he twice mentions that Henry made him a prebend of Bayeux as a reward for his services. See Karen M. Broadhurst, 'Henry II of England and Eleanor of Aquitaine: Patrons of Literature in French?', *Viator* 27 (1996): 56–9, 70–2.

history for the Angevin court is evident in the opening lines of the *Brut*, at least in the majority of the surviving manuscripts. Most copies introduce the history of the kings of Britain as part of the history of the kings of England.[114] This action suggests continuity in rule over the British Isles as opposed to the presentation of the kingdom of England as a distinct entity that supplanted the ancient kingdom of Britain. This move also accords with what Davies has classified as the first English response to the British problem: 'to hijack much, if not most, of the Matter of Britain and to convert it into a colourful backcloth for the history of England before the coming of the English'.[115]

Wace also transformed Arthur into a paragon of Angevin chivalric kingship and a figural type for Henry II. It has often been suggested that Wace modeled his representation of Arthur after Henry II as a flattering nod to the poet's probable sponsor.[116] As David Rollo has noted, '[t]he two monarchs become types for one another: Arthur is historically anterior and his exemplarity patterns the celebration of Henry; yet Henry is the new paradigm of monarchy on which the translated Arthur is subtly remodeled'.[117] Yet the figure of Arthur as depicted by Wace was not simply an idealized representation of Henry; he was a prescriptive model for the king. Wace supplied the Plantagenets with new incentives to continue to make Arthur their own. The poet transformed Geoffrey's Arthur, a conqueror in the Norman mold, into a courteous, just, and mighty *roi-chevalier*.[118] Why did Wace see fit to place so much emphasis on Arthur's knighthood? An answer lies in Henry's personal history.

Henry II was a self-made monarch, whose rise to power in England was a consequence more of his martial accomplishment than of his royal birth. Henry's parents, Count Geoffrey of Anjou (d. 1151) and Matilda, had long struggled to reconsolidate the landholdings of Henry I of England, including the duchy of Normandy (secured in 1144) and the kingdom of England, but it was Henry Plantagenet who, by force of arms, ultimately succeeded in winning his place as heir to England's throne from Stephen of Blois in 1153.[119] Henry, although he could and did boast of being the son of an empress, was lacking in royal descent on

---

[114] Wace, *Roman de Brut*, 2–3, lines 1–8. See David Rollo, *Historical Fabrication, Ethnic Fable and French Romance in Twelfth-century England* (Lexington, KY: French Forum Publishers, 1998), 136, n. 8.

[115] Davies, *First English Empire*, 48.

[116] See Noble, 'Patronage, Politics, and the Figure of Arthur', 164.

[117] Rollo, *Historical Fabrication*, 111.

[118] Wace, *Roman de Brut*, 226–7, lines 9017–32.

[119] See John D. Hosler, *Henry II: A Medieval Soldier at War, 1147–1189* (Leiden: Brill, 2007), 37–51.

his father's side. Henry II was the son of a count, not of a king. Yet Henry was an accomplished military leader. Conversely, Henry's Capetian rival, Louis VII of France (r. 1137–80), although possessing all the advantages of birth, lacked knightly accomplishment. Emphasizing nobility of character and deeds as the principal qualities of a good king seems to have been how Henry's writers compensated for his lack of royal paternity. [120] Thus, the glorification of the *roi-chevalier* model of kingship was very much in Henry's interest.[121] Wace's Arthur functioned as the ancient forerunner of Henry II, one that lent ideological support to Henry's style of kingship and undermined Louis VII's manner of rule. It must be noted that Henry did prohibit tournaments in England during his reign; knights desirous of *gloria armorum* were obliged to travel overseas to compete in such events.[122] Cultivating a chivalric persona was evidently less important to Henry than preserving public order and eliminating the opportunity that tournaments provided for his barons to come together and conspire against him. Nonetheless, Wace made Arthur into a legitimizing predecessor for Henry II as Geoffrey of Monmouth had done a generation earlier for the successors of Henry I.

Henry II seems to have been especially in need of this legitimization. As Turner points out, Henry had assembled his Angevin empire through a combination of inheritance, marriage, and conquest. This empire did not map onto any pre-existing political entity and, complicating matters further, Henry held Normandy, Anjou, and Aquitaine under the suzerainty of the king of France.[123] Through his representation of Arthur and Arthur's empire, Wace gave Henry the heroic forebear and imperial precedent he needed, particularly in cases of confrontation with the king of France. In the passage above, Wace also seems to be suggesting to Henry that by displaying courtesy and generosity he could become (like Arthur) the trendsetter and envy of Western Europe, far outshining his Capetian rival. And, for what it is worth, in the opinion of the thirteenth-century St. Albans chronicler Matthew Paris (d. 1259),

---

[120] See Amaury Chauou, '*Arturus redivivus*: Royauté arthurienne et monarchie politique à la cour Plantagenêt (1154–1199), in *Noblesses de l'espace Plantagenêt (1154–1224), Table ronde tenue à Poitiers, le 13 mai 2000*, ed. Martin Aurell (Poitiers: Centre d'études supérieures de civilisation médiévale, 2001), 76–7.

[121] See Amaury Chauou, *L'Idéologie Plantagenêt: Royauté arthurienne et monarchie politique dans l'espace Plantagenêt, XIIe–XIIIe siècles* (Rennes: Presses Universitaires de Rennes, 2001), 136.

[122] William of Newburgh, *Historia rerum Anglicarum* 5.4, in 'The Fifth Book of the "*Historia rerum Anglicarum*"', in *Chronicles of the Reigns of Stephen, Henry II, and Richard I*, vol. 2, ed. Richard Howlett. RS 82/2 (London: Longman & Co., 1884), 422.

[123] See Turner, 'England in 1215', 21–3.

Henry II had succeeded in matching his legendary forebear. In an entry in his *Historia Anglorum* (c. 1250), entitled *de auctoritate regis Henrici II*, Paris states that in 1176 the respective envoys of Manuel I Komnenos, emperor of Constantinople (r. 1143–80), the Holy Roman Emperor Frederick I (r. 1155–90), Heinrich der Löwe, duke of Saxony (r. 1142–80), Count Philip I of Flanders (r. 1168–91) and an assortment of other magnates spanning the breadth of Christendom flocked to Henry II's court at Westminster for the king's advice. Matthew Paris then adds:

> Et alii, aliis temporibus et locis, pro suis negotiis dirigendis, ad curiam regis magnifici Henrici, immo etiam Francorum electi primates, velut ad scolam prudentiæ et justitiæ, undique confluxerunt; ita ut viderentur Arthuri tempora renovari.[124]

> (And other men, in other times and places, so that they may obtain advice concerning their affairs, flocked from everywhere to the court of the magnificent King Henry, even the elect peers of France, as if to a school of prudence and justice; such that the age of Arthur seemed to be renovated.)

Paris wrote this entry about sixty years after Henry II's death, but the passage speaks to the rivalry that existed between the courts of England and France, going on to offer a flattering comparison of the historical Henry II with the legendary Arthur (a figure that somewhat ironically had been crafted in literature as an idealized version of Henry I and then of Henry II).

Despite the potential ideological benefits offered by the figure of Arthur, Henry II had still to contend with the 'British problem'. Wace's treatment of this issue did not diverge greatly from that of Geoffrey of Monmouth. Neither linked Arthur with the Welsh. In terms of geographical boundaries, Arthur's principal kingdom, Logres, was very much an antecedent to the post-Conquest kingdom of England. Additionally, in the Galfridian tradition (including Wace), Arthur subdued the giant Ritho of Mount Aravius (Mount Snowdon) and the giant of Mont-Saint-Michel. The two giants could be interpreted as representatives of North Wales and Brittany respectively, and Arthur's victory over them can likewise

---

[124] Matthew Paris, *Historia Anglorum sive ut vulgo dicitur, Historia Minor, item, ejusdem abbreviatio chronicorum Angliæ*, ed. Frederick Madden, 3 vols. RS 44 (London: Longmans, Green, Reader, and Dyer, 1866–9), I, 397–8. This entry is a reworking of an account on the same subject by Roger Wendover (*fl.* 1230–5). Roger does not include the Arthur comparison in his discussion. See *Rogeri de Wendover liber qui dicitur flores historiarum ab anno domini MCLIV, annoque Henrici Anglorum regis secundi primo*, ed. Henry G. Hewlett, 3 vols., RS 84 (London: Longman, 1886–9), I, 107.

be seen as subordination of both territories to Loegrian (English) rule.[125] Wace, following the vulgate version of Geoffrey's *Historia*, also states that the Welsh of his day had degenerated from the greatness of their British ancestors.[126] An implication of this assertion is that although the Welsh possessed stronger linguistic and racial ties to Arthur than did Henry II, a substantial negative change to their nature had occurred such that they were not capable of producing another Arthur. Unlike Geoffrey, Wace did attest that the *Bretun* (seemingly a collective category for all those of Brittonic ancestry) still await King Arthur's return.[127] In this he appears to have been following the examples of William of Malmesbury and Henry of Huntington mentioned above. Writers subsequent to Wace did more than sneeringly identify the myth of Arthur's return with the British Other; they pointed to it as evidence of Welsh, Cornish, and Breton primitivism.

One way in which *exspectare Arturum* was derided was through mock epistolary. Possibly the earliest specimen of this is '[L]ittere quas misit Arturus inuictus rex Britannie Hug. capellano de Branno super sequanam cum palefrido. Anno Domini .m.c.lvii.' ([A] Letter that Arthur, the unconquered king of Britain sent to Hugo, chaplain of *Brannum* on the Seine, with a palfrey in the year of the Lord 1157.)[128] This text survives as an interpolation in four manuscript copies of Geoffrey's *Historia*. The earliest extant codex containing the letter, Oxford, Bodleian Library, MS Bodley 233, dates from the first half of the fourteenth century. But the inclusion of the year 1157 in the heading of two manuscript copies of the letter suggests that the text is a twelfth-century composition. The date and provenance of this curious letter are an open question, but why would an author refer back to such a seemingly trivial event that happened many years earlier? The author of the letter seems to have used a Capetian

---

[125] See Faletra, *Wales and Medieval Colonial Imagination*, 44.

[126] Wace, *Roman de Brut*, 372–3, lines 14851–4.

[127] Wace, *Roman de Brut*, 332–3, lines 13279–80.

[128] This is Julia Crick's transcription of the rubric introducing 'Arthur's Letter' in the earliest surviving manuscript known to contain it: Oxford, Bodleian Library, MS Bodley 233 (*S. C.* 2188) (first half of the fourteenth century, medieval provenance: ?Britain). See Crick, *HRB Summary Catalogue*, 219–21 and *HRB Dissemination and Reception*, 92–3. For descriptions of the three other manuscripts known to contain Arthur's Letter, see Crick, *HRB Summary Catalogue*, 10–11, 244–5, 323–4. Also see Hans Thurn, *Die Handschriften der Universitätsbibliothek Würzburg / Handschriften aus benediktinischen Provenienzen: Amorbach. Kitzingen. Münsterschwarzach ...* (Wiesbaden: Harrassowitz & Co., 1973), 136 (b).

model for the royal styling.[129] The mention of a place on the Seine further supports a Continental provenance. The letter reads:

> Arturus Dei gratia utriusque Britannie rex desideratissimus .H. uenerabili capellano salutem et expectationis tante fructuosam retribucionem. Occulta cordis desideria .uii. nocte mensis septimi septem Dei famuli[130] nobis sepcies reuelauerunt. Quiescant ergo intima suspiria. Appropinquat enim manifestacionis nostre gloria. Affectus cotidiani maturos inuenient effectus. Si[nu]s uniuerse matris nequaquam tibi aperietur quo usque tetrathas [sic] occidentis et aquilonis regulos ante fortitudinem manus nostre corruisse uidebis. Adhuc modicum et ecce moriganis [sic] optatos expetens amplexus ignem frigescere stupebit. Recurret ad consuetum antique artis auxilium et societatis fastidium renouacione doloris euincere temptabit. Uerum tamen medulle nichil mouebuntur quoniam lapide celitus inmisso purpurei riuuli cessabit inundatio. Tunc duo mondi [sic] climata imperio nostro pariter munientur. Terraque a Ioue [sic] ad Isium [sic] libere tibi pro dignitate tue promocionis famulabitur.[131]

(Arthur by the grace of God the most desired king of both Britains gives greetings and a fruitful retribution of so much expectation to the venerable chaplain Hugh. On the seventh night of the seventh month, seven servants of God revealed seven times to us the hidden desires of the heart. Therefore, let inner sighs rest. For the glory of our manifestation grows near. Daily affects will come upon mature effects. The bosom of the universal mother will never be opened up to you until the time that you will see the four petty kings of the West

---

[129] By 1157 'Dei gratia rex' had long been in the superscription of French royal charters, but it only entered English royal usage in 1172–3. Our author was either aping the English royal usage after 1172 or utilizing the French royal formula. If the text was written around 1157, then 'Dei gratia rex' suggests Continental provenance. See Françoise Gasparri, *L'écriture des actes de Louis VI, Louis VII et Philippe Auguste* (Geneva: Librairie Droz, 1973), 20–1; Nicholas Vincent, 'The Charters of King Henry II: The Introduction of the Royal *Inspeximus* Revisited', in *Dating Undated Medieval Charters*, ed. Michael Gervers (Woodbridge, UK: Boydell, 2000), 98–9, 110–12. In France, from the reign of Louis VII (1137–80) onward, the king consistently referred to himself in the first person plural. See Georges Tessier, *Diplomatique royale Française* (Paris: Picard, 1962), 214–15. In England, Henry II's immediate successor Richard I was the first to use the plural of majesty in royal letters. See Nicholas Vincent, 'Why 1199? Bureaucracy and Enrolment under John and his Contemporaries', in *English Government in the Thirteenth Century*, ed. Adrian Jobson (Woodbridge, UK: Boydell, 2004), 41. If the letter dates from 1157, the author of the 'Arthur's Letter' was likely following the French royal style. If the model was English, then the author was probably writing after 1189 and referring back to events in 1157.

[130] Cf. Tobit 12:15. In angelology there are seven angels who serve as intercessors for mankind with God.

[131] Crick, *HRB Dissemination and Reception*, 93.

and North fall before the strength of our hand. Yet a little while and behold: Morgan seeking the desired embraces will stun the fire into freezing. She will return to the accustomed aid of her ancient art, and she will try to overcome her loathing of society by renewal of grief. But nevertheless hearts will not be moved since with a stone sent down from heaven the flood of the purple stream will cease. Then two climes of the world will be defended together by our rule. And the land from Jove to Isis will freely serve you on account of the dignity of your promotion.)

Arthur is writing to provide encouragement to Hugh the chaplain. Arthur foresees Hugh's advancement but knows it will only occur after Arthur's own triumphant return (which unfortunately will be preceded by a time of tribulation). The author of Arthur's Letter seems to be implying that Hugh does not have the slightest chance of obtaining promotion. Arthur's Letter has a mock-heroic quality. Its language is apocalyptic, but the principal purpose of the document – to convey that an ecclesiastical promotion will be long in coming – is trivial.

The apocalypticism in the text also serves to mock Arthur, the Brittonic peoples, and the very idea of Arthur's survival and expected return. Arthur assumes two roles in the letter. He is both a seer and the prophesied world emperor. It is humorous that Arthur the Seer directly foretells his own future glory as Arthur the World Emperor. Arthur introduces himself as 'rex desideratissimus' (most desired king). *Desideratissimus* and *desideratus* are not uncommon designations in Latin epistolary, but in religious literature they have a more specific connotation. In the post-exilic Book of Haggai, the eponymous prophet receives a vision in the second year of Darius (520 BCE) on the twenty-first day of the seventh month. The Lord of Hosts (*Dominus exercituum*)[132] encourages the remnants of His Chosen People to keep to their faith and to rebuild the Temple in Jerusalem. Arthur's Letter exhibits specificity

---

[132] See Haggai 2:1–10. The Books of Haggai and Zechariah both contain predictions of the triumphant coming of the Messiah and are probable sources of inspiration for Arthur's Letter. The heaven-sent stone mentioned in Arthur's Letter is analogous to the stone which the Lord of Hosts places before Joshua the High Priest and the stone with seven facets, which are the eyes of the Lord that range over the whole earth, that is imparted to Zerubbabel, both of which are mentioned in the Book of Zechariah. The author of Arthur's Letter, if not using the Books of Haggai and Zechariah as direct referents, was certainly mixing and matching apocalyptic elements, a common practice in apocalyptic writing. The repetition and prominence of seven, a number symbolizing totality or perfection, in Arthur's Letter also points to the Book of Zechariah and the Book of Revelation. Arthur's role in Arthur's Letter parallels Haggai, Zechariah, and John the Evangelist.

with respect to day, month, and year, much like the Book of Haggai. As rendered in the Latin Vulgate, Haggai reads:

> 'Adhuc unum modicum est, et ego commovebo caelum et terram et mare et aridam, et movebo omnes gentes, et veniet desideratus cunctis gentibus, et implebo domum istam gloria,' dicit Dominus exercituum.[133]

> ('Yet one little while, and I will move the heaven and the earth and the sea and the dry land, and I will move all nations, and the desired of all nations shall come, and I will fill this house with glory,' saith the Lord of hosts.)

The Church fathers understood *desideratus* to signify Jesus Christ, and 'rex desideratus' is a way of referring to Jesus. We see this usage of *desideratus* in one of the seven O Antiphons, which were sung in the medieval Western Church on the last seven days of Advent. The O Antiphon in question is 'O Rex Gentium', which was sung on 22 December. Arthur as the self-proclaimed 'utriusque Britannie rex desideratissimus' invites comparison to Jesus Christ as 'desideratus cunctis gentis'. Arthur seems to believe that his return will be even more eagerly anticipated than Christ's Second Coming – at least by his adherents. Derision of Arthur and the Breton Hope through comparison with Christ and *Heilsgeschichte* had a precedent in Herman of Tournai's vignette about the Cornishman with a withered hand who was seeking healing from Marian relics whilst also obstinately proclaiming that King Arthur was still alive.[134]

---

[133] Haggai 2:7–8.

[134] In support of my reading of Arthur's Letter as a satirical reworking of elements from the Book of Haggai, I wish to call the reader's attention to the coverage of the birth of Arthur Plantagenet of Brittany (29 March 1187) in the *Chronicon Britannicum*, a set of annals extending from 211 (the death of Septimus Severus at York) to 1356 (the siege of Rennes by Henry of Grosmont). Arthur of Brittany, the grandson of Henry II of England, was born at Easter and the entry in the *Chronicon* reads: 'MCLXXXVII: Natus est Arturus filius Gauffridi ducis Britanniae, desideratus gentibus, in Pascha Domini' (1187: Arthur, a son, who is desired by the peoples (of Brittany), is born to Geoffrey, duke of Brittany, at Easter). Here the writer is describing the Breton Hope for Arthur using the Judeo-Christian language for the expectation of the Messiah. Arthur of Brittany is perhaps mockingly introduced as the fulfillment of this hope. The fact that Arthur's birth occurred at Easter may have precipitated the use of 'desideratus gentibus', but it is equally possible that there was a pre-existing tradition for using 'desideratus gentibus' to modify *exspectare Arthurum*. See 'Chronicon Britannicum ex collectione veteri MS Ecclesiæ Nannetensis', ed. Gui Alexis Lobineau in Alexis Lobineau, *Histoire de Bretagne, composée sur les titres et les auteurs originaux*, vol. 2 (Paris: Louis Guerin, 1707), col. 34; 'Chronicon Brittanicum', ed. Pierre Hyacinthe Morice, in Pierre Hyacinthe Morice, *Mémoires pour servir de preuves à l'histoire ecclésiastique et civile de Bretagne*, vol. 1 (Paris: Charles Osmont, 1742), col. 6.

Who is the addressee of Arthur's Letter and what was its immediate relevance in 1157? No one to date has offered a convincing identification of *Brannum super Secanam* (Brannum-sur-Seine), and it might be a fictional place.[135] The ascription of the letter to 1157 and the mention of four petty kings of the North and West (*tetrathas occidentis et aquilonis reguli*) are, however, suggestive of a real-world parallel. If we allow the Arthurian portion of Geoffrey of Monmouth's *Historia regum Britannie* to inform our reading of Arthur's Letter, then the four petty kings are most likely those of Scotland, Cornwall, Demetia, and Venedotia, all of whom swear fealty to Arthur at his great Caerleon coronation feast. If Arthur's Letter had been written with Henry II in mind, the four petty kings may signify the reigning monarch of the kingdom of Scotland (north of England) and the rulers of the three leading principalities in Wales (west of England): Deheubarth in southern Wales, Powys in central Wales, and Gwynedd in northern Wales.

The year 1157 is also suggestive of a real-world parallel, for it was a critical year for Henry II in terms of Scottish and Welsh relations. In the first half of that year, King Máel Coluim (Malcolm) IV of Scotland (r. 1153–65), aged sixteen, came to the court of Henry II to perform homage for his English landholdings. Henry, knowing the Scots to be in a position of weakness with such a young king on the throne, took back Northumberland and its castle of Newcastle-upon-Tyne, Bamburgh, Westmoreland, and Carlisle in Cumberland, thereby re-establishing the northern border of England to its former state under Henry I of England. Later in 1157, Henry II mounted his first military campaign in the British Isles as king of England, an invasion of the kingdom of Gwynedd in northwest Wales.[136] In July 1157, the very same month that Arthur reportedly had his vision, Henry personally led his army into northern Wales. They were ambushed at Counsylth (near Flint), and an erroneous

---

[135] Elisabeth van Houts believes the addressee to be Hugh of Braine Castle (in the diocese of Soissons), which belonged to Agnes de Baudemont and her second husband (after 1152), Robert of Dreux, brother of Louis VII. See her 'Latin and French as Languages of the Past in Normandy during the Reign of Henry II: Robert of Torigni, Stephen of Rouen, and Wace', in *Writers of the Reign of Henry II: Twelve Essays*, ed. Ruth Kennedy and Simon Meecham-Jones (New York: Palgrave Macmillan, 2006), 58–9, 73 n. 44. I am not persuaded by this identification because this Braine is located on the Aisne, not on the Seine, and is usually called Brana, and not Brannum, in Latin. See *Le Chartrier de l'abbaye prémontrée de Saint-Yved de Braine, 1134–1250*, ed. Olivier Guyotjeannin (Paris: École des chartes, 2000), 161. For passing suggestions that the letter alludes to Henry II's military campaigns in Brittany or Wales, see Crick, *HRB Dissemination and Reception*, 92 n. 7 and Van Houts, 'Latin', 58–9.

[136] See Hosler, *Henry II*, 52–4; Duffy, 'Henry II', 132.

rumor circulated that the king had been killed in the attack.[137] Despite this inauspicious start to the campaign, Henry ultimately succeeded in forcing Prince Owain of Gwynedd to perform homage to him. Having obtained hostages from Owain, Henry also ensured that his presence in northern Wales would continue to be felt in the years to come by fortifying the castles of Rhuddlan and Basingwerk.

Slightly earlier, by about 1155, Henry had become involved in the politics of Brittany. In July 1156, the king had compelled his brother Geoffrey to recognize him as heir to the county of Nantes in the event that Geoffrey should die (which he did on 26 July 1158). Thus by 1157, Henry was well on his way to becoming *rex utriusque Britannie*, which was part of the royal styling adopted by Arthur in his letter. Did the author of Arthur's Letter intend for his audience to conclude that Henry's incursions on Arthur's former lands would bring about his 'long awaited' return or that in 1157 Henry was on his way to becoming Arthur's equal?

Judging by the stated date of the letter, 1157, which is included in two of the four manuscript witnesses of the text (the earliest copy and the most recent copy), it would appear that the four petty kings of the West and North are those of Wales and of Scotland, but the author of Arthur's Letter might also have be alluding to Henry's success against the petty kings of Ireland in 1171–2. Henry landed at Waterford in October of 1171 and received shortly thereafter recognition as *dominus et rex Hyberniæ* and oaths of perpetual fealty from Dermot MacCarthy, king of Cork; Donald O'Brien, king of Limerick; Donald, king of Ossory; Tieran O'Rourke, king of Meath; and from other magnates and bishops of Ireland.[138] Here we again see four petty kings fall before an invading king.

The language of praise for Henry II in Gerald of Wales' earliest major work, *Topographia Hibernica* (c.1186–8),[139] is strongly evocative of Arthur's

---

[137] William of Newburgh, *Historia rerum Anglicarum* 2.5, in *Chronicles of the Reigns of Stephen, Henry II, and Richard I*, vol. 1: Containing the First Four Books of the *Historia rerum Anglicarum of William of Newburgh*, ed. Richard Howlett, RS 82/1 (London: Longman & Co., 1884), 108.

[138] Roger of Howden, *Chronica Magistri Rogeri de Houedene*, ed. William Stubbs, 4 vols. RS 51/1–4 (London: Longmans, Green, Reader, and Dyer, 1868–71), II, 29–30. Also see Duffy, 'Henry II', 138–9.

[139] The first recension of the *Topographia Hibernica* was 'begun before Gerald left Ireland in May 1186, and completed before March 1188, when he presented a copy to Archbishop Baldwin'; Gerald returned to this work and added and modified its content multiple times over his lifetime. See Bartlett, *Gerald of Wales*, 213–14. For an edition of the first recension, see Gerald of Wales, *Giraldus Cambrensis in Topographia Hibernie: Text of the First Recension*, ed. John J. O'Meara, in *Proceedings of the Royal Irish Academy* 52, sec. C, n. 4. (1949): 113–78. For an amalgamated version, see Gerald of Wales, *Topographia Hiberniæ*, ed. James F. Dimock, in *Giraldi Cambrensis opera*, vol. 5, ed. James F. Dimock, RS 21/5 (London: Longmans, Green, Reader, and Dyer, 1867), 3–204.

Letter. In a section on the victories of Henry II, Gerald writes: 'Certant enim cum orbe terrarum uictorie uestre: cum a Pyreneis montibus usque in occiduos et extremos borealis occeani fines, Alexander noster occidentalis, brachium extendisti' (Indeed, your victories wrestle with the world: when you, our Alexander of the west, have extended your arm from the Pyrenees mountains right up to the westernmost and northernmost ends of the ocean).[140] Gerald's representation of Henry II as ruler of the North and West calls to mind Arthur's Letter. Also in his *Topographia Hibernie*, Gerald mentions Jove (who is named in Arthur's Letter) when describing Henry's successes in Ireland. He writes: 'In occiduis enim occeani finibus Ioue tonante, occidentales reguli, tonitruis eius attoniti, pacis adepte benefitio fulminis ictum preuenerunt.' (For in the western ends of the ocean with Jove thundering, the western petty kings, astonished by his thundering, prevented the strike of lightning by the aid of an acquired peace.)[141] Even more evocative of Arthur's Letter is Gerald's encomium for Henry II, which appears at the close of the *Topographia Hibernie*:

> Qualiter igitur titulis et triumphis uestris Hibernicus orbis accesserit; quanta et quam laudabili uirtute, occeani secreta, et occulta naturæ deposita transpenetraueris…qualiter fulguranti aduentus uestri lumine attoniti, occidentales reguli, tanquam ad lucubram auicule, ad uestrum statim imperium conuolauerint[?][142]

> (In what way, then, has the Irish world been added to your titles and triumphs? By how great and by how praiseworthy a virtue were you able to penetrate the secrets of the ocean and the hidden treasures of nature? … How by the light of your shining arrival the petty western kings, astonished, as much as small birds at a lamp, flew round at once to your rule?)

The classical and natural imagery in Gerald's *Topographia* is quite similar to that in Arthur's Letter. I would not hazard to say that Gerald's writing inspired the composition of Arthur's Letter or vice versa, but I do maintain that Arthur is being conspicuously fashioned after King Henry II in Arthur's Letter.

---

[140] Gerald of Wales, *Topographia Hibernie First Recension*: 176–7. This praise also appears in the later recensions of the *Topographia Hibernie* as well as in his other writings. See Gerald of Wales, *Topographia Hiberniæ* 3.9, p. 149; Gerald of Wales, *De principis instructione liber* 2.21, ed. George F. Warner, in *Giraldi Cambrensis opera*, vol. 8, ed. George F. Warner, RS 21/8 (London: Eyre and Spottiswoode, 1891), 199.

[141] Gerald of Wales, *Topographia Hibernie First Recension*, 162. Henry's involvement is emphasized in later recensions. See Gerald of Wales, *Topographia Hiberniæ* 3.9, p. 149.

[142] Gerald of Wales, *Topographia Hibernie First Recension*, 177.

There is one further detail about Gerald's *Topographia Hibernie* that warrants mention. The H-manuscript, which is grouped with the first recension, and the subsequent recensions of the text justify Henry's overlordship of Ireland using Arthur's Caerleon coronation feast as a precedent.[143] This passage appears in *Topographia Hibernie* 3.8, which, perhaps not coincidentally, is the section of the text that immediately precedes the references to Henry as 'Alexander noster' and ruler of the North and West quoted above.

Despite the similarities in language between Arthur's Letter and Gerald's *Topographia Hibernie*, it still seems that the author of Arthur's Letter was focusing on the military successes of Henry II in 1157 rather than on the king's later campaigns in Ireland. There were certainly more than four rulers at any given moment in twelfth-century Ireland who could have been dubbed *reguli*. Given that 1157 was such a successful year for Henry II, its inclusion in two of the manuscript copies of Arthur's Letter does not appear to have been coincidental. Regardless of the precise historical context of Arthur's Letter, Arthur's vision (or delusion) of martial grandeur coincided with what Henry II was on the brink of achieving. Comparison of Gerald's panegyric on Henry II and Arthur's Letter shows an alignment of the presentations and agendas of Arthur and Henry II. The author of Arthur's Letter was seeking to communicate two things. First, it is foolish to interpret the myth of Arthur's survival literally – to believe that the original King Arthur would return in the flesh as a latter-day Lazarus. Second, one should interpret the myth figuratively and recognize Henry II of England as the fulfillment of the myth – as a second King Arthur. Whom does Arthur's Letter serve? It serves Henry II and the Arthurian pretensions of the Plantagenet dynasty.

The similarities as well as the apparent conflicts of interest between Arthur and Henry are also explored in the *Draco Normannicus* (c. 1167–9),[144] a pro-Plantagenet metrical Latin work written by Étienne of Rouen (d. after March 1170), a monk of the abbey of Bec-Hellouin.[145] In *Draco Normannicus* 2.17–23 there is a mock letter exchange between a Breton magnate named Rolland, an immortal Arthur (personifying the Breton

---

[143] Gerald of Wales, *Topographia Hibernie First Recension*, 161, n. 430.

[144] Étienne de Rouen, *Draco Normannicus*, in *Chronicles of the Reigns of Stephen, Henry II, and Richard I*, vol. 2, ed. Richard Howlett, RS 82/2 (London: Longman & Co., 1884), 589–762. For analysis of the text, see J. S. P. Tatlock, 'Geoffrey and King Arthur in "Normannicus Draco"', *Modern Philology* 31, n. 1 (1933): 1–18; n. 2 (1933), 113–25; Siân Echard, *Arthurian Narrative in the Latin Tradition* (Cambridge, UK: Cambridge University Press, 1998), 85–93.

[145] The *Draco Normannicus* shows signs of familiarity with Henry's court. See Tatlock, 'Geoffrey and King Arthur', 123–4.

Hope), and Henry II of England. Étienne chose a real-life conflict, Henry II's punitive campaigns against his Breton opponents, as the occasion for this instance of mock epistolary. In 1166, Henry invaded Brittany and compelled Conan IV to surrender the duchy to him. The two men arrived at a peace agreement whereby Conan's daughter, Constance of Penthièvre (c.1161–1201), would marry Henry's fourth son Geoffrey (1158–86) and rule Brittany with him. According to Robert of Torigni, in 1166 King Henry received pledges of fealty from almost all the barons of Brittany.[146] The very next year, however, certain stalwart Bretons and other confederates, including Rolland of Dinan, refused to render him service. Henry responded by laying waste to their lands. This conflict had yet to be resolved when Étienne was writing *Draco Normannicus*.[147] Rolland of Dinan has been identified as the personage behind 'Arturi dapifer, Rollandus' (Rolland, steward of Arthur),[148] who in Étienne's work, while fleeing from Henry II, dispatches an urgent plea for aid 'ad Arturum olim Britanniæ regem ... qui tunc apud antipodes degebat' (to Arthur, formerly king of the Britons ... who was then residing among the Antipodes).[149]

Just as the conflict constituting the subject of the letter exchange was rooted in contemporary developments, so too did Rolland's resort to the Breton Hope have contemporary resonance. In a commentary on the *Prophetia Merlini* written by a certain Alanus between 1167 and 1174, we find Arthur's *dubius exitus* glossed as a divergence of opinion regarding Arthur's mortality. Alanus adds that if any man dared to preach in the streets of Brittany that Arthur was dead, he would be lucky to return to tell about it without having been inundated with curses and pummeled by stones.[150] Given that the hope of Arthur's return is the topic for satire in *Draco Normannicus* and that belief in Arthur's survival was said to be strong in Brittany (in the late 1160s and early 1170s), it is conceivable that the Breton opponents to Henry II rallied behind the figure of Arthur.

---

[146] Robert of Torigni, *Chronica Roberti de Torigneio*, in *Chronicles of the Reigns of Stephen, Henry II, and Richard I*, vol. 4, ed. Richard Howlett. RS 82/4 (London: Eyre and Spottiswoode, 1889), 228. Also see Everard, *Brittany and the Angevins*, 45.

[147] Robert of Torigni, *Chronica*, 228, 236–8.

[148] Étienne of Rouen, *Draco Normannicus*, 2.18.945, p. 696. See Tatlock, 'Geoffrey and King Arthur', 118–19.

[149] Étienne of Rouen, *Draco Normannicus*, 2.18, p. 696.

[150] *Prophetia Anglicana, Merlini Ambrosii Britanni ...* (Frankfurt: Typis Ioachimi Bratheringii, 1603), 17. Also see Clara Wille, 'Les prophéties de Merlin interprétées par un commentateur du XIIe siècle', *Cahiers de civilisation médiévale* 51, n. 203 (2008): 223–34. Wille contends that the commentator in question was Alan of Flanders, bishop of Auxerre (r. 1152–67), who retired to Clairvaux, where he wrote the second *Vita* of Saint Bernard.

Nevertheless, in the context of this Breton campaign, Arthur was not strictly an icon of the Breton resistance. John of Salisbury (d. 1180) and the then-exiled archbishop of Canterbury Thomas Becket (r. 1162–70) saw Henry's success in Brittany as an indication that he might be the prophesied Bellicose Boar, i.e. the Second Arthur. Evidence of this appears in a July 1166 letter from John of Salisbury to Becket in which John details how Henry II was faring in his siege of Fougères (lasting June to mid July 1166). John writes:

> Instat enim tempus, ut aiunt, quo aquila rupti federis, iuxta Merlini uaticinium, frenum deauratura est, quod apro eius datur, aut modo fabricatur in sinu Armorico..... Adiciunt quod potentissimis Britannie proceribus, excepto comite Eudone, confederatus est federe mutuo. Nonne sic ferus singularis aut singulari proximus aper, qui depascitur et conculcat uineam Domini, cohiberi poterit et infrenari? Ego quidem sic illam interpretor prophetiam, expectans ut aquila quacumque subornatione incommoditates istas inauret; nisi forte Alexander noster, Merlini cognatus et oraculorum eius interpres prudentior aliud sentiat. De his hactenus.[151]

> (It is said that the time is at hand when the eagle of the broken covenant, according to Merlin's prophecy, shall gild the bridle, which is being given to his boar or being forged now in the Breton peninsula … They say too that he [i.e. Ralph, lord and defender of Fougères] has made a treaty of alliance with all the most powerful Breton leaders, excepting Count Eudo.[152] Cannot the wild boar, a beast who is *singular* [perhaps *sanglier* (boar)][153] or very near it, who wastes and tramples on the Lord's vineyard, be tamed and harnessed in this way? So I interpret the prophecy, looking to the eagle to drive him on and so gild these disadvantages. But perhaps our Alexander,[154] Merlin's kin and a wiser interpreter of his oracles, thinks otherwise. Enough of this.)

John's sympathies were with the Breton resistance, and this letter was composed prior to Henry's taking of Fougères on 22 July 1166. What is particularly striking is that John, as I understand him, here represents Henry II as a conflation of the king girt with the teeth of the boar and the Bellicose Boar. John's interpretation of the *Prophetia* serves as evidence

---

[151] John of Salisbury, 'Thome Cantuariensi archiepiscopo Iohannes Saresberiensis' (Letter 99), in *The Correspondence of Thomas Becket, archbishop of Canterbury, 1162-1170*, vol. 1: Letters 1–175, ed. and trans. Anne J. Duggan (Oxford: Clarendon Press, 2000), 452–5.

[152] Eudo de Porhoët, son-in-law of Conan III, duke of Brittany, declared himself count of Brittany in 1148. Eudo was Henry II's chief opponent in the English king's 1166–7 campaign to win the duchy. See *Correspondence of Thomas Becket*, 455, n. 10.

[153] I thank Professor Dorothea Kullmann for suggesting this possibility.

[154] Duggan has identified this Alexander as Alexander Llywelyn (Cuelin), Becket's crossbearer. See *Correspondence of Thomas Becket*, 455, n. 12.

of Arthur's polyvalence in twelfth-century thought. For some, Arthur signified the ferocious Angevin invader; for others he was an awe-inspiring (Breton) resistance fighter. With this duality in mind, let us now consider Étienne's treatment of Arthur in *Draco Normannicus*.

Étienne of Rouen, like John of Salisbury, conflated the king girt with the teeth of the boar and the Bellicose Boar and applied these Arthurian labels to Henry II in his *Draco Normannicus*. Recounting the death of King Stephen of Blois and the transfer of power to Henry of Anjou, Étienne writes:

Ut jus divinum statuit, post tempore parvo
Rex obit, inde duces dant diadema duci.
Montibus instat aper, galeati transvolat umbram,
Merlinus merulæ vocibus ista canit.[155]

(As divine law ordained, after a short while the king died, and then the dukes gave the crown to the duke. The boar stood atop the mountains, and flew across the shadow of the helmeted man. Merlin sang these things by the voices of a blackbird.)

At least two commentators on the *Prophetia Merlini* interpreted the Boar-Toothed King as King Stephen. Étienne, in contrast, links the Boar-Toothed King with Henry II.[156] Furthermore, Étienne conflates the Arthur-like Boar-Toothed King with the Bellicose Boar, the later counterpart to the Boar of Cornwall. Thus, according to Étienne, Henry II, the Boar-Toothed King, and the Bellicose Boar (*Arthurus redivivus*) are all one and the same.

Étienne also constructs a situational parallel between Arthur and Henry II that reveals Henry II to be the new Arthur. In the *Historia regum Britannie*, Arthur receives a letter condemning his imperialist endeavors from Lucius Tiberius, the standard bearer of an empire long past its prime. In *Draco Normannicus*, Henry II receives an analogous letter from King Arthur, likewise the figurehead of a past empire. As Tatlock has noted, the Roman defiance begins: 'Lucius rei publicae procurator Arturo regi Britanniae quod meruit' (Lucius, procurator of the republic, wishes Arthur, king of Britain, his just deserts),[157] while Arthur's defiance begins, 'Arturus magnus, fatorum lege perennis, / Henrico juveni, quod meruisse putat' (Arthur the Great, eternal by the law of the fairies, settles what Young Henry deserved).[158] As Francesco Marzella has recently observed with respect to *Draco Normannicus*:

---

155 Étienne of Rouen, *Draco Normannicus* 1.9.357–60, p. 605.
156 See Hammer, 'Commentary on the *Prophetia* Merlini', 17 and *Prophetia Anglicana, Merlini Ambrosii Britanni*, 84.
157 Geoffrey of Monmouth, *Historia regum Britannie* 158.415, pp. 214–15.
158 Étienne of Rouen, *Draco Normannicus* 2.20.969–70, p. 697; see Tatlock, 'Geoffrey and King Arthur', 6.

Arthur represents the old and Henry is the new, the first the arrogant king who threatens war and the second is the one who with his deeds is scaring the lord of the old empire. Henry is not only a second Alexander, he is also the new Arthur whose accession was foreseen by Merlin the prophet, the new *aper* or *leo* who will substitute the *Cornubiae aper*.[159]

In *Draco Normannicus*, there are two Arthurs: the eternal Arthur, a ghost of his former self, who lives and reigns in an Otherworld, and Henry II, the up-and-coming Arthur who lives and reigns in the world of the living. With this in mind, let us now turn our attention to the representation of King Arthur in the *Draco Normannicus*.

It is widely held that Étienne crafts Arthur as the personification of the Breton Hope and as a parody of the Arthur of Geoffrey's *Historia*.[160] In this way Étienne lampoons the myth of Arthur's survival. The eternal Arthur of the *Draco Normannicus* exists outside the bounds of credibility and has definite pagan overtones from classical mythology. For example, Arthur, as we have seen, is styled 'Arthur the Great, eternal by the law of the fairies'. He enjoys the gift of clairvoyance. Instead of receiving his information from the seven servants of God as is the case in Arthur's *Letter*, Étienne's Arthur understands the workings of the Fates.[161] Étienne's account of Arthur's miraculous survival is similar to that of the *Vita Merlini* but more outlandish:

> Saucius Arturus petit herbas inde sororis,
> Avallonis eas insula sacra tenet.
> Suscipit hic fratrem Morganis nympha perennis,
> Curat, alit, refovet, perpetuumque facit.
> Traditur antipodum sibi jus; fatatus, inermis,
> Belliger assistit, prœlia nulla timet.
> Sic hemispherium regit inferius, nitet armis,
> Altera pars mundi dimidiata sibi.[162]

> (Wounded Arthur, from there, seeks the herbs of his sister. The sacred island of Avalon holds these. Morgan, the eternal nymph, thus

---

[159] Francesco Marzella, 'Letters from the Otherworld: Arthur and Henry II in Stephen of Rouen's *Draco Normannicus*', *Tabularia*. Autour de Serlon de Bayeux: la poésie normande aux XIe–XIIe siècles (2017), 10 (http://tabularia.revues.org/2858accessed 17 June, 2017).

[160] Michael Faletra, 'Narrating the Matter of Britain: Geoffrey of Monmouth and the Norman Colonization of Wales', *Chaucer Review* 35, n. 1 (2000): 77–82; Mildred Leake Day, 'The Letter from King Arthur to Henry II: Political Use of the Arthurian Legend in *Draco Normannicus*', in *The Spirit of the Court: Selected Proceedings of the Fourth Congress of the International Courtly Literature Society (Toronto 1983)*, ed. Glyn S. Burgess and Robert A. Taylor (Cambridge, UK: D. S. Brewer, 1985), 154.

[161] Étienne of Rouen, *Draco Normannicus* 2.19.958–62, pp. 696–7.

[162] Étienne of Rouen, *Draco Normannicus* 2.20.1161–8, p. 703.

takes her brother, cares for him, nourishes him, restores him and makes him everlasting. Jurisdiction over the Antipodes is bestowed upon him; thus fated, the warrior defends the unarmed and fears no conflicts. Thus he rules the lower hemisphere; he is resplendent in arms. The other half of the world is his.)

By removing Arthur from the mundane world, by making him subject to the rules of an enchanted world, Étienne trivializes his continued existence. Later in the work, the character of Arthur, speaking in the third person (and almost breaking the fourth wall) even acknowledges that his destiny defies belief: 'Quis fuit Arturus vel quis sit, cernis. At ista / Non jactando loquor, sed tibi pando sacra.' (Who Arthur was or who he might be, you decide. But I do not speak these things in boast, rather I impart unto you sacred truths.)[163] The use of the perfect indicative (the definite past) and present subjective (conveying uncertainty) of the verb *esse* (to be) hints at the existence of two Arthurs: the old Boar of Cornwall (Arthur Pendragon) and the new Bellicose Boar (almost certainly Henry II).

At the end of the string of correspondence, Étienne's Henry II has the final word. His remarks imply that Arthur's continued existence and revelations are theologically problematic. On account of his mother's death, Henry resolves to hold Brittany under Arthur's authority, and he sends a letter to Arthur declaring the following:

> Cedo sed ad tempus; nam tota Britannica tellus
> Tum mihi tum natis est referenda meis.
> Hanc sub jure tuo, sub pace tua teneamus;
> Jus tibi, pax nobis, totaque terra simul.
> Hæc quia concedis, valeat tua vita perennis,
> Nam mea sub Christi jure perennis erit.[164]

> (I concede but for a time; for all British soil must be returned to me and to my sons. Let us hold it under your law, under your peace. The law is yours, the peace is ours, and all the land as well. Because you concede these things, let your everlasting life prevail. For my life will be eternal under the law of Christ.)

In this concluding statement, Étienne's Henry stresses that eternal life may only be achieved *sub Christi iure*. Arthur's questionable version of eternal life is not part of the economy of salvation.

Étienne mocks the Breton Hope, and his Arthur functions as its personification, but Étienne's characterization of Arthur is more nuanced than that. The eternal Arthur is, it is true, a blowhard, but alongside the

---

[163] Étienne of Rouen, *Draco Normannicus* 2.20.1175–6, p. 704.
[164] Étienne of Rouen, *Draco Normannicus* 2.22.1277–82, p. 707.

caricature are traces of the noble Arthur of Galfridian history, the *bonus rex* and exemplar of imperial kingship. Étienne's Arthur endeavors to relate to Henry II, or to present himself in terms that Henry II would admire. Arthur, in his opening address to Henry II, serves as a model of kingly probity:

> Naturalis habet probitas animusque virilis,
> Ut prius indicat prœlia, deinde gerat.
> Dedignatur enim prosternere more latronum,
> Quorum stat sceleris fraude necare dolo.
> Provocat, ostentat pro viribus arma, cohortes,
> Quæ sibi bellica vis; palificare studet.
> Talis Alexandri virtus, et Cæsaris ardor,
> Usus et iste mihi semper ad arma fuit.[165]

> (Natural uprightness and manly courage hold that one announces conflicts first and then wages them. For he disdains to knock down [his foe] in the manner of those brigands whose crime it is to kill by trick and by fraud. He calls out his enemy, he displays as his strength his troops and his arms and he strives to show what force of war is his. Such was the virtue of Alexander and the ardor of Caesar, and this was always my custom at arms.)

In this instance we again see Arthur as a *speculum regis*. Arthur's remarks may function as an indictment of Hugh Capet, who, as Étienne discusses elsewhere, seized the throne of France by trick (*dolus*) from Charles of Lorraine, the last Carolingian claimant to the throne of France, in 987.[166]

The 'historical' Arthur also has a complex identity, one that is more imperialistic than nativistic. Rolland addresses Arthur as 'trino regi' (thrice king), but singles out the Bretons as Arthur's people.[167] Arthur, however, boasts in his letter to Henry:

> Substravi Britones armis, Anglosque subegi,
> Francorum domui turgida colla jugo.
> Sic triplicis regni diademata tunc tria gessi
> Solus, in his terris par mihi nemo fuit.[168]

> (I laid low the Britons [seemingly the Amorican Bretons] with arms, I subjugated the English. I subdued the stiff necks of the Franks by a

---

[165] Étienne of Rouen, *Draco Normannicus* 2.20.971–8, p. 697. A similar sentiment is expressed by the figure of Arthur in the *Gesta regum Britanniae*, a ten-book versified version of Geoffrey's *Historia*. See *Gesta regum Britanniae* 169.429–34, in *The Historia Regum Britannie of Geoffrey of Monmouth V: Gesta regum Britanniae*, ed. and trans. Neil Wright (Cambridge, UK: D. S. Brewer, 1991), 224–5.
[166] Étienne of Rouen, *Draco Normannicus* 3.3.246–54, p. 720.
[167] Étienne of Rouen, *Draco Normannicus* 2.18.947, p. 696.
[168] Étienne of Rouen, *Draco Normannicus* 2.20.981–4, p. 698.

yoke. Thus I alone wore the three crowns of the triple realm. In these lands no one was my equal.)

Here, the Bretons, the English, and the French are all conquered peoples. None receives preferential treatment. Furthermore, Arthur recollects how 'Anglia nostra potens' (our powerful England) brought forth Constantine and Helena, and adds, 'Hos imitans, armis Anglorum jura reposco, / Angligeni regni qui diadema gero.' (Imitating them, I claim the rights of the English with arms, I who wear the crown of the English realm.)[169] When speaking for himself, Étienne's Arthur is preoccupied with his own title and legacy. He neither shows preference for his British kinsmen nor identifies exclusively with this ethnic group. He even goes so far as to liken himself to Henry II's ancestors 'Rollo, domuit qui Francica colla' (Rollo, who subdued the necks of the Franks) and William the Conqueror, 'dux Angligenum qui diadema capit' (the duke, who seized the crown of the Englishmen), but greater than the two combined.[170] Arthur endorses conquest by battle, which underpins Henry II's rule as well. Thus, Étienne of Rouen communicates that the Breton Hope was an aberrant belief of degenerate Brittonic Celts but preserved the 'historical' Arthur as an aspirational model for Henry II.

Also critical to establishing Arthur's imperialistic identity and to linking him with Henry II is the number three. As noted above, Arthur is styled thrice king. Marzella has recently called attention to the fact that Arthur's emphasis on wearing the triple-crown likens him to that other great Christian emperor, Charlemagne.[171] In Book One, Étienne writes of the Frankish monarch: 'Francos, Romanos, Alamannos possidet unus; Unica vis unum sic tria regna facit.' (One is master of the Franks, the Romans, and the Germans; a single force thus makes three kingdoms one.)[172] The monk twice underscores Charlemagne's tripartite rule in Book Three.[173] To Marzella's valuable observation, I wish to add that Étienne, after chronicling Henry's ascendency to the throne of England, eulogizes the monarch in an imperial fashion involving the number three.

[169] Étienne of Rouen, *Draco Normannicus* 2.20.1134–6, p. 702.

[170] Étienne of Rouen, *Draco Normannicus* 2.20.999–1000, p. 698.

[171] Marzella, 'Letters', 11: 'And even if Stephen does not say it, his audience might remember that Alexander is traditionally considered a kind of *rex trinus*, ruling over the three parts of the world: Europe, Asia and Africa.'

[172] Étienne of Rouen, *Draco Normannicus* 1.14.565–8, p. 613.

[173] Étienne of Rouen, *Draco Normannicus* 3.10.715–20, p. 735; and 3.14.1164–74, p. 749. On the subject of tripartite rule by Arthur, Alexander, Charlemagne, and Henry, see Marzella, 'Letters', 11.

Immediately after recounting Henry's elevation to the throne of England, Étienne writes:

> Julius in terris Macedonis astat in armis,
> Exprimit iste duos sensibus, ense, manu.
> Nec minor eloquio, vi mentis, culmine morum,
> Ortu, divitiiis, nobilitate ducum.
> Mundi pars minor huic, fidei sed luce refulget:
> Hac superatur ab his, hac superavit eos.
> Terror Francigenis, galeatus murus in armis,
> Militiæ splendor, nobilitatis apex.
> Summus ubique leo vi nulla cedere novit,
> Fulguris instar habens hostibus ense fremit.
> Obtinet hic solus quod jam fuit ac genitoris
> Pictavisque ducis, nec minor ipse tribus.
> Unit tres unus, sic et tria perficit unum,
> Una trium virtus, imperium fit idem.
> Quidquid tres probitatis erant transivit in istum,
> Cernitur in tanto vivere quisque trium.[174]

(He stands as a Julius [Caesar] in lands, as the Macedonian [Alexander the Great] in arms, and he imitates both of them in senses, sword, and hand. Nor is he inferior to them in speech, force of mind, loftiness of character, origin, riches, and nobility of his dukes. A smaller part of the world belongs to him, but it shines brightly with the light of faith. In the former he is surpassed by them; in the latter he has surpassed them. Terror to the French, a wall helmeted with arms, splendor of knighthood, apex of nobility. The highest lion knows to yield to no force anywhere. Having the likeness of lightning, he roars at his enemies with his sword. He alone obtains what is his already, as well as his father's and the duke of Poitou's [his father-in-law's]. Nor is he less than three. One [person] combines into three, and thus one [realm] completes three. One strength of three, an empire becomes. Whatever probity the three had passed into him. Each of the three is seen to live in such a man.)

By Étienne's reckoning, Henry, like Arthur and Charlemagne, enjoyed a tripartite, 'imperial' rule. He held the kingdom of England and the duchy of Normandy from his mother Matilda (and maternal grandfather Henry I); he held Anjou, Maine, and Touraine from his father Geoffrey of Anjou; and he held Aquitaine, Gascony, and Poitou through his wife, Eleanor of Aquitaine (and her father, William X of Aquitaine).

---

[174] Étienne of Rouen, *Draco Normannicus* 1.10.363–78, pp. 605–6.

The tripartite empire analogy that Étienne sought to create between Arthur, Charlemagne, and Henry II in his three-book Latin epic is tenuous and contrived. What led him to this construct? A possible answer lies in the third chapter of the third book of *Draco Normannicus*. In 1167, the year that Henry II's mother Matilda died (a death that King Arthur reportedly foresaw thanks to his clairvoyant abilities and fairy connections), there were three portents in the sky: in March a comet was seen in the skies over Paris; in July a circle radiated around the sun; and in September the moon appeared red.[175] With respect to these portents Étienne remarks: "Hæc diversa quidem, non unum sed tria signant, / Quæ tamen hæc extent dicere nemo valet.' (What truly these diverse things, not one but three, signify, what indeed they stand for, no one is able to say.)[176] Nonetheless, he suggests that it has to do with the clash between Henry II and Louis VII, and acknowledges that the appearance of a comet is suggestive of 'jura novi regni' (the rights of a new realm).[177] In the very next chapter, Étienne reports how Heinrich der Löwe, duke of Saxony, Henry II's son-in-law, came to Henry's court on behalf of Emperor Frederick. Frederick sought to persuade Henry II not to admit vassalage to the king of France because, according to Frederick's reckoning, Henry was every bit Louis of France's equal – nay superior – with respect to strength, honor, and royal dignity.[178] The emperor then reportedly offered Henry II military assistance, and even promised to lead a division of his army personally, should the English king wish to depose Louis VII. The emperor justified this offer on the grounds that Louis was the heir of Hugh Capet, not of Charlemagne, and that Hugh Capet took France from the descendants of Charlemagne by guile. Arthur, as noted above, appears to have alluded to this act of fraud in his opening remarks to Henry II. Frederick claimed that he was the rightful heir to Charlemagne and that he sought to take the throne of France by the forces of the empire. Frederick attempted to entice Henry to ally with him against Louis by stating that the aforementioned comet foretold their victory and that he would grant France to Henry's heir.[179] Elsewhere in the *Draco Normannicus*, Étienne shows himself to be a staunch opponent of the Capetians and sympathetic to Frederick's cause.[180]

---

[175] Étienne of Rouen, *Draco Normannicus* 3.3.141–8, p. 716.

[176] Étienne of Rouen, *Draco Normannicus* 3.3.159–60, p. 717.

[177] Étienne of Rouen, *Draco Normannicus* 3.3.161, p. 717 and 3.3.170–90, pp. 717–18.

[178] Étienne of Rouen, *Draco Normannicus* 3.4.233–8, p. 720.

[179] Étienne of Rouen, *Draco Normannicus* 3.4.243–70, pp. 720–1.

[180] See, for example, Étienne's account of the rise of the House of Capet (987) and the death of Charles of Lorraine (992) in *Draco Normannicus* 1.27.1277–82, p. 641. For an illuminating discussion of how the *Draco Normannicus* favors a Hohenstaufen and Plantagenet alliance against Capetian France, see Irene Harris, 'Stephen of Rouen's *Draco Normannicus: A Norman Epic*', in *The Epic in History*, ed. Lola Sharon Davidson, S. N. Mukherjee, and Z. Zlatar (Sydney: Sydney Association for Studies in Society and Culture, 1994), 116–24.

Étienne's aim thus appears to have been to situate Henry II in a noble lineage of emperors and conquerors such as Alexander the Great, Julius Caesar, King Arthur, and Charlemagne, and to encourage the king to resist the Capetian Louis VII and perhaps even to depose him. Étienne dismisses Brittany's supposed ethnic connection to Arthur in favor of Henry II's titular connection to him. Likewise, Étienne dismisses the special French connection to Charlemagne in favor of Frederick I's imperial connection to him. Étienne seems to have wanted Henry II to follow in Arthur's footsteps by conquering France and becoming the Bellicose Boar prophesied to sharpen his tusks in the forests of France.

A comprehensive analysis of the reception and political exploitation of the figure of King Arthur in twelfth-century England and France cannot overlook the representation of the king in the Arthurian verse romances of Chrétien de Troyes (fl. 1160–90).[181] In Chrétien's two earliest surviving romances, Erec et Enide (c. 1170) and Cligés (c. 1170–6), there is evidence of Angevinization of Arthur.[182] Chrétien does not specify a patron or dedicatee for either work and, in all likelihood, he was searching for a benefactor at that time. It is probable that Chrétien had hoped to find patronage at Henry's court. Fashioning Arthur after Henry II seems to have been an element in Chrétien's bid for royal support, a strategy that Wace had employed years earlier.

Constance Bullock-Davies has noted that in Cligés, Chrétien exhibits knowledge of the topography, tides, and city names of southern England, and on this basis she concludes that the poet had spent time in England before relocating to Champagne and then Flanders.[183] However, all of the

[181] For an excellent overview of the characterization of Arthur in Chrétien's five Arthurian romances, see Peter S. Noble, 'Chrétien's Arthur', in Chrétien de Troyes and the Troubadours: Essays in Memory of the Late Leslie Topsfield, ed. Peter S. Noble and Linda M. Paterson (Cambridge, UK: St. Catharine's College, 1984), 220–37.

[182] The dating of Erec et Enide to 1170 is widely accepted. See Stefan Hofer, 'Alexanderroman–Erec und die späteren Werke Kristians', Zeitschrift für romanische Philologie 60 (1940): 245–61. For the dating of Cligés, see Anthime Fourrier, 'Encore la chronologie des œuvres de Chrétien de Troyes', Bulletin Bibliographique de la Société Internationale Arthurienne 2 (1950): 80–1. Citations for Erec et Enide are from Christian von Troyes: sämliche Werke, nach allen bekannten Handscriften, vol. 3, Erec und Enide, ed. Wendelin Foerster (Halle: Max Niemeyer, 1890); the translations provided are from Erec and Enide, trans. Carleton W. Carroll, in Chrétien de Troyes, Arthurian Romances, ed. William W. Kibler (London: Penguin Books 1991), 37–122. Citations for Cligés are from Christian von Troyes: sämliche Werke, nach allen bekannten Handscriften, vol. 1, Cliges ed. Wendelin Foerster (Halle: Max Niemeyer, 1884), and the translations provided are from Cligés, trans. William W. Kibler, in Chrétien de Troyes, Arthurian Romances, ed. William W. Kibler (London: Penguin Books, 1991), 123–205.

[183] Constance Bullock-Davies, 'Chrétien de Troyes and England', Arthurian Literature I (1981): 1–61. Her analysis has influenced Faletra, Wales and Medieval Colonial Imagination, 103–5.

particulars that Bullock-Davies cites as evidence of first-hand familiarity with England could just as easily have been acquired second-hand either through discussion with travelers to England or by consulting nautical maps and the like.[184] Indeed, one of the distinctive features of *Cligés* is the extent to which the romance is grounded in real-world geography. In the romance's geography, Chrétien mentions not only such English places as Windsor, Oxford, Wallingford (near Oxford), and Southampton but also Regensburg (noting how it lies on the Danube), the Black Forest, and Cologne (the site of a tournament and a festival).[185] In addition to King Arthur and the emperor of Constantinople, the German emperor and the duke of Saxony are characters in this work. Furthermore, passing references are made to Cæsarea (Palestine), Toledo (Spain) and Candia (Crete), as well as to the wealthy commercial centers of Pavia and Piacenza in Lombardy.[186] This smattering of place names and land features shows that Chrétien's knowledge was not England-specific and that he need not have resided in England. However, as shown above in the writings of the St. Albans chronicler Matthew Paris, the *nuntii* of the emperor of Constantinople, the Holy Roman emperor, and the duke of Saxony all flocked to Henry II's court at Westminster in mid November 1176, which fits with the putative date of composition of *Cligés*.[187] The dramatis personae of Henry II's life in 1176 are *mutatis mutandis* the dramatis personae of Arthur's world in *Cligés*. Regardless of whether Chrétien was at England's court, he no doubt was informed of the notable happenings there and drew upon this knowledge to flatter Henry II and to seek his patronage.

Near the conclusion of *Erec et Enide*, we find the strongest indications that Chrétien characterized Arthur as an idealized version of Henry II. After Erec's father, King Lac of Estre-Gales, dies, Erec asks Arthur to crown him king. Arthur happily agrees and declares that he will crown both Erec and his consort Enide on Christmas Day at Nantes, where the king would be holding a plenary court. Chrétien, declaring his enthusiasm about the occasion, writes that kings and counts from sundry lands were present: Arthur had summoned to Nantes all the highborn lords and ladies from Normandy, Brittany, Scotland, Ireland, England, Cornwall, Wales, Anjou, Maine and Poitou.[188] This guest list, as Anthime Fourrier long ago observed,

---

[184] I thank Professor Dorothea Kullmann for calling this fact to my attention.
[185] Chrétien de Troyes, *Cligés*, 107, lines 2664–8; 108–9, lines 2692–706; 137, lines 3395–3400.
[186] Chrétien de Troyes, *Cligés*, 193, lines 4746–7; 213, line 5200.
[187] See Matthew Paris, *Historia Anglorum*, I, 397–8.
[188] Chrétien de Troyes, *Erec et Enide*, 237, lines 6644–55; Chrétien de Troyes, *Erec and Enide*, 118.

corresponds to the territorial dimensions of Henry's Angevin Empire from 1169 to 1170, when the king held direct possession of Ireland.[189] Yet the barons of France are, as Schmolke-Hasselmann has noted, conspicuously absent,[190] and this might reflect the hostilities between Henry II and Louis VII, which had escalated into proxy skirmishes between April 1167 and January 1169.[191] Chrétien, like Wace before him, writes at length about how Arthur, the paragon of good kingship, was foremost with respect to power and largesse. Chrétien even writes that Arthur was more powerful, rich, and generous than Alexander the Great and Caesar.[192] In this description we again find a great compliment predicated on a great display of generosity. Chrétien seems to have been hinting at the possibility that Henry, after the fashion of Arthur, should fund his literary endeavors.

The correspondence between the world of Arthur and the world of Henry II in the Nantes Christmas court scene has inspired scholars to look for a historical precedent underpinning it. Henry II's Christmas court at Nantes in 1169 is a strong candidate.[193] On that occasion, Henry II as suzerain and Henry's son Geoffrey as duke of Brittany received pledges of fidelity from the bishops and barons of Brittany.[194] The union of Erec and Enide has been interpreted as a nod to the engagement of Geoffrey and Constance of Brittany.[195] Though these suggestions reside in the realm of conjecture, the parallels between life and art here have proven strong enough to win widespread agreement that *Erec et Enide* contains a compliment to Henry II of England.[196] If the figure of Arthur had been perceived as a threatening

---

[189] Fourrier, 'Encore la chronologie', 73.
[190] See Beate Schmolke-Hasselmann, 'Henry II Plantagenêt, roi d'Angleterre, et la genèse d' Erec et Enide', *Cahiers de civilisation médiévale*, n. 95–6, (1981): 243; Beate, Schmolke-Hasselmann, *Der arturische Versroman von Chrestien bis Froissart*, trans. Margaret and Roger Middleton as *The Evolution of Arthurian Romance: The Verse Tradition from Chrétien to Froissart* (Cambridge, UK: Cambridge University Press, 1998), 233–4.
[191] See Hosler, *Henry II*, 63–5.
[192] Chrétien de Troyes, *Erec et Enide*, 237–8, lines 6656–85.
[193] Fourrier, 'Encore la chronologie', 72–4; Bullock-Davies, 'Chrétien de Troyes and England', 52; Schmolke-Hasselmann, 'la genèse d' Erec et Enide', 243–4.
[194] Only in 1181 when he married Constance did Geoffrey officially succeed to the duchy of Brittany. See Everard, *Brittany*, 48. Also see W. H. Jackson, *Chivalry in Twelfth-Century Germany: The Works of Hartmann von Aue* (Cambridge, UK: D. S. Brewer, 1994), 15.
[195] See H. C. R. Laurie, 'The Arthurian World of *Erec et Enide*', *Bulletin Bibliographique de la Société International Arthurienne* 21 (1969): 117–18. The coronation of Erec by Arthur might allude to the coronation of Henry's eldest son, Young Henry, which was directly orchestrated by Henry II in June of 1170. See L. T. Topsfield, *Chrétien of Troyes: A Study of the Arthurian Romances* (Cambridge, UK: Cambridge University Press, 1981), 58–9; Noble, 'Chrétien's Arthur', 226.
[196] See Jackson, *Chivalry in Twelfth-Century Germany*, 14.

specter (rather than as a kingly predecessor) to Henry II, why would the figure of Arthur have been selected as a means of flattering Henry II?

In *Cligés* there is further suggestion that Chrétien was fashioning Arthur after Henry II. At the beginning of the romance, Chrétien equates contemporary England with Arthurian Britain when he writes that Alexander, the father of the eponymous protagonist 'ala de Grece an Angleterre, / Qui lors estoit Bretaigne dite' (went from Greece to England, which in those days was called Britain).[197] Although expressly aware that the use of the word England in the context of Arthurian Britain was anachronistic, Chrétien, like Wace before him, does not shy away from it. When Alexander and his retinue of Greeks arrive at the port 'desoz Hantone' (below Southampton), they ask if the king is in 'Angleterre' and are told that he is at 'Guincestre' (Winchester).[198] Winchester is, of course, the home and burial place of the Wessex kings and was the capital of England during the Anglo-Saxon and early post-Conquest periods.[199] Arthur is thus presented anachronistically as an English king in *Cligés*.[200]

Near the close of the romance, Cligés complains to his great-uncle King Arthur that his other uncle Alis, the tyrannical emperor of the East, perjured himself and unjustly disinherited him. Arthur then organizes an expedition to Constantinople. At this juncture Chrétien writes:

> Por ostoiier feit aparoil
> Li rois si grant, qu'ainc le paroil
> N'ot neis Cesar ne Alixandre.
> Tote Angleterre et tote Flandre,
> Normandie, France et Bretaingne,
> Et toz çaus jusqu'as porz d'Espaingne
> A feit semondre et amasser.[201]

> (The king's preparations were on such a grand scale that neither Caesar nor Alexander ever equalled them. All England and all Flanders, Normandy, France, and Brittany, and everyone as far as the Spanish passes [Pyrenees], were convened and assembled.)

Again Arthur's world reflects the geopolitical realities of twelfth-century Western Europe, and Arthur's wealth and resources correspond to those of

---

[197] Chrétien de Troyes, *Cligés*, 1, lines 16–17; Chrétien de Troyes, *Cligés*, 123.
[198] Chrétien de Troyes, *Cligés*, 12, lines 287–94.
[199] See Bullock-Davies, 'Chrétien de Troyes and England', 11.
[200] Further suggestion of a likening of Arthur to Henry in *Cligés* can be seen in King Arthur's unexplained desire to travel to Brittany, a trip that prompts Arthur to entrust Count Angrés of Windsor with the guardianship of the realm during his absence. See *Cligés*, 17, lines 422–3. As Bullock-Davies has noted, Henry from the 1160s onwards made frequent trips to Brittany ('Chrétien de Troyes and England', 13).
[201] Chrétien de Troyes, *Cligés*, 276–7, lines 6699–705; Chrétien de Troyes, *Cligés*, 204.

the Angevin kings. This is most apparent when we compare Arthur's muster in *Cligés* with that of Richard I of England (r. 1189–99), as described by the anonymous chronicler of Béthune (c.1220).[202] In *Cligés*, however, Chrétien lists France as falling under Arthur's muster, and Arthur's empire cannot be said to coincide precisely with Henry's Angevin Empire. A flattering embellishment of Henry's sphere may be at play here.[203] In the writings of Wace, Étienne of Rouen, and Chrétien of Troyes, we can trace a tendency to make explicit the associations between King Arthur and the post-Conquest kings of England that remained implicit in Geoffrey's *Historia*.

Before departing from Chrétien's Arthurian *oeuvre*, there is one further matter of consequence to our discussion, namely the poet's unflattering representation of the Welsh. Michael Faletra has written at length about how Chrétien in all of his Arthurian romances tends to portray the Welsh as racially inferior.[204] The most poignant and familiar example of this tendency occurs at the beginning of *Perceval*. Five of Arthur's knights outfitted from head to toe in shining and clinking armor ride into the Waste Forest in Wales. There they encounter a garrulous, ill-mannered, and poorly dressed Perceval. One of Arthur's knights seeks information from the youth but to no avail. Another of Arthur's knights, in frustration, then comments: 'Sire, sachiez bien entresait / Que Galois sont tot par nature / Plus fol que bestes en pasture' (Sir, you must be aware that all Welshman are by nature more stupid than beasts in the field).[205] This speaker, an Arthurian knight, defines himself in opposition to the Welsh. Based upon the manner in which he is speaking, he is presumably not of Welsh heritage. It is quite easy to read him as a colonizer, who is contemptuous of the rustic natives he encounters in his travels. The knight appears to voice French (and perhaps Anglo-Norman) prejudice against the Celts. Although quite a few of Arthur's men, including Erec of Estre-Gales, seem to have been of nominally Brittonic extraction, the Arthurian identity is represented, at least in *Perceval*, as something greater than and distinct from Welsh or Brittonic identity.

---

[202] 'Extrait d'une chronique française des rois de France par un anonyme de Béthune', ed. Léopold Delisle, in *Recueil des historiens des Gaules et de la France* 24, n. 2 (1904): 758.

[203] See Bullock-Davies, 'Chrétien de Troyes and England', 30. Also see Noble, 'Chrétien's Arthur', 226.

[204] See Faletra, *Wales and Medieval Colonial Imagination*, 125–33.

[205] Chrétien de Troyes, *Le Roman de Perceval ou Le Conte du Graal, Édition critique d'après tous les manuscrits*, ed. Keith Busby (Tübingen: De Gruyter, 1993), 12, lines 242–4. For this translation see Chrétien de Troyes, *The Story of the Grail (Perceval)*, trans. William W. Kibler, in Chrétien de Troyes, *Arthurian Romances*, ed. William W. Kibler (London: Penguin Books, 1991), 384.

Arthur in 'non-Arthurian' literature from the reign of Henry II

Looking beyond the prophecies, chronicles, and romances in which Arthur plays an integral role (either as principal actor or as figurehead), we now turn our attention to passing references to Arthur in 'non-Arthurian' works dating from the reign of Henry II.

We shall begin with the acclaimed poet Walter of Châtillon (*fl.* 1170–80). In his most celebrated work, the *Alexandreis* (c. 1176–84), Walter makes just one reference to Arthur:

> Pallanthea domus Roma crescente superbit,
> Gadibus Herculeis Hyspania, thure Sabei,
> Francia militibus, celebri Campania Bacho,
> Arthuro Britones, solito Normannia fastu.[206]

> (The Palatine house takes pride in Rome's growth, Spain in [its] Herculean Gades, Sabaea in [its] incense, France in [its] knights, Campania in its celebrated wine, the Britons in Arthur, and Normandy in customary arrogance.)

Walter states that the Britons take pride in *their* Arthur. It is unclear whether he means the Armorican Bretons specifically or the Brittonic Celts collectively. Either way, a twelfth-century French writer saw the Brittonic Celts as having a proprietary claim to Arthur. Walter also mentions Arthur in his *Tractatus sive Dialogus contra Judaeos*,[207] and here we find one of the earliest examples of an explicit likening of the Breton Hope to Jewish messianism. Walter structures his 'libellum in Judæos' (booklet against the Jews) as a dialogue that he had with Baldwin of Valenciennes, a canon of Braine (a Premonstratensian abbey in the diocese of Soissons not far from Châtillon-sur-Marne). The stated purpose of the work is to restrain the 'linguam falsiloquam' (lying tongue) of Jews who deny that Jesus is the saviour anticipated in the Hebrew Bible.[208] Walter places himself at Châtillon-sur-Marne in the work,[209] and for this reason the *Tractatus* is believed to have been one of Walter's earlier writings, which he wrote either before or during his teaching stint at Châtillon-sur-

---

[206] Walter of Châtillon, *Alexandreis* 7.409–12, ed. Martin L. Colker (Padua: Antenore, 1978), 191.
[207] Walter of Châtillon, *Tractatus sive Dialogus ... contra Judaeos*, in *PL* 209, ed. Migne, col. 424, prologue.
[208] Walter of Châtillon, *Tractatus sive Dialogus ... contra Judaeos*, col. 424–5. Also see Anna Sapir Abulafia, 'Walter of Châtillon: A Twelfth-century Poet's Engagement with Jews', *Journal of Medieval History* 31, n. 3 (2005): 270.
[209] Walter of Châtillon, *Tractatus sive Dialogus ... contra Judaeos*, col. 450.

Marne (c.1171–6).[210] The parallel between the Breton Hope and Jewish messianism appears in the prologue of the work: 'Cujus misericordiæ particeps Ecclesia, sponsum ad generales nuptias venturum expectat; Synagoga vero adhuc velamen ante oculos habens, ut Britones Arcturum, primum ipsius præstolatur adventum.' (The Church, a partaker of Christ's mercy, expects the bridegroom who will come to universal nuptials. The Synagogue, however, still having a veil over its eyes, awaits His first coming, as the Britons await Arthur.)[211] The basis for the analogy between the British and the Jewish Hope is clear: both groups are waiting for their own special saviour. What does the British / Jewish analogy tell us about Walter's opinion of the Breton Hope? Walter evidently selected the Breton Hope because he expected that his audience would regard it as a misplaced hope that would never be fulfilled.

Walter's British / Jewish analogy also contains within it a great insult against the Celts. It implies that the Breton Hope was not simply an empty hope but also a source of spiritual corruption. As David Berger has noted, it was a common practice for Christian writers to use Jews as a 'standard for evaluating all sorts of sinners, heretics and pagans'.[212] Walter of Châtillon even goes so far as to treat the continual refusal of the Jews to embrace Jesus as their savior as evidence that the Jews were under the influence of Satan and susceptible to the misdirection of the Antichrist. [213] Walter thus places *exspectare Arthurum*, which he ascribed to 'the Britons', in the same spectrum of false belief. This categorization alerts the reader to the ethnic-provincialist aspect of *exspectare Arthurum*. The analogy hints at the possibility that the Britons made Arthur into their special messiah, their false idol, and it suggests that this was a rustic belief that interfered with their appreciation of Jesus as messiah. This message is contained in Herman of Tournai's *Miracula*, Arthur's Letter, and Étienne of Rouen's *Draco Normannicus*. In the case of the *Draco Normannicus*, *exspectare Arturum* is presented as analogous to paganism and *rusticitas* rather than to Davidic messianism. The British / Jewish analogy might have already been an established cliché when Walter was writing his *Tractatus*.

---

[210] Walter of Châtillon, *The Shorter Poems: Christmas Hymns, Love Lyrics, and Moral-Satirical Verse*, ed. and trans. David A. Traill (Oxford: Clarendon Press, 2013), xvii–xviii.

[211] Walter of Châtillon, *Tractatus sive Dialogus … contra Judaeos*, col. 424, prologue.

[212] See Berger, 'Attitude of St. Bernard', 104–5.

[213] See Walter of Châtillon, 'Dum contemplor animo seculi tenorem', in *The Shorter Poems: Christmas Hymns, Love Lyrics, and Moral-Satirical Verse*, ed. and trans. David A. Traill (Oxford: Clarendon Press, 2013), 210–11. Also see Abulafia, 'Walter of Châtillon', 277–9.

We do not know precisely when Walter composed his *Tractatus*, but it was probably written in the first half of the 1170s, and in that very same window of time Peter of Blois (c. 1130–1212) used the British Hope / Jewish messianism analogy in two of his letters. Peter of Blois became associated with the court of Henry II around 1174 and is thought to have collected his letters at the behest of Henry II.[214] In *Epistola* 34 (c. 1172), Peter of Blois complains to his cousin Peter Mimet, bishop of Périgueux (r. 1169–82), about empty promises of a generous reception by a common acquaintance: 'Adhuc benignioris eventus vota concipio, et fortasse venturum cum Britonibus præstolor Arturum, et Messiam cum Judæis expecto' (Still I expect the promises of a more generous outcome and perhaps I stand ready with the Britons for Arthur to come and with the Jews I expect the Messiah to come). [215] In *Epistola* 51 (c. 1170?), Peter is similarly seeking gratuity for services rendered – this time from Joscelin de Bohun, bishop of Salisbury (r. 1142–84), for attending to the education of the bishop's nephews in Paris. Communicating exasperation, Peter writes: 'Adhuc etiam promissam expecto gratiam, fortasse sicut Arcturum Britannia, sicut Judæa Messiam' (To this very moment I expect the promised gratuity, perhaps just as Britain expects Arthur, just as Judea expects a Messiah).[216] In both cases, *exspectare Arthurum* is emblematic of a misplaced and unfulfilled hope. Peter uses the Arthurian reference in the context of a disappointed expectation of liberality and courtesy – virtues that Geoffrey of Monmouth, Henry Huntingdon, Wace, and countless other writers used to define Arthur.[217] The relative chronology is unclear, but it is possible that Peter of Blois read Walter's *Tractatus*.[218] Walter's writings were well known at Henry's court. Regardless, it seems quite likely that speaking of the Brittonic Celts waiting for Arthur and the Jews waiting for the Messiah was common in the English royal court and on the Continent.

---

[214] See Peter Dronke, 'Peter of Blois and Poetry at the Court of Henry II', *Mediaeval Studies* 38 (1976): 191.

[215] Peter of Blois, 'Epistola 34', in *Petri Blesensis Bathoniensis archidiaconi Opera Omnia*, vol. 1: *Epistolæ*, ed. John Allen Giles (Oxford: I. H. Parker, 1847), 113–14.

[216] Peter of Blois, 'Epistola 51', in *Petri Blesensis Bathoniensis archidiaconi Opera Omnia*, vol. 1: *Epistolæ*, ed. John Allen Giles (Oxford: I. H. Parker, 1847), 156.

[217] Arthur's generosity is also underscored in the Latin narrative satire *Architrenius*, which was completed by the Norman *Magister Iohannes de Hauvilla* in 1184. In that text Arthur leads an army of the generous against the forces of Avarice. See Johannes de Hauvilla, *Architrenius* 6.1, ed. and trans. Winthrop Wetherbee (Cambridge, UK: Cambridge University Press, 1994), 144–5.

[218] Peter of Blois, it should be noted, wrote his own polemic against the Jews. See Peter of Blois, *Contra perfidiam Judæorum*, in *PL* 207, ed. Migne, col. 823–70. It does not, however, contain the British–Jewish comparison.

Peter also pokes fun at the Breton Hope in a lyric poem he writes for the court of Henry II, which is entitled 'Quod amicus suggerit'. The poem is a debate between a courtier (*Curialis*) and a warner (*Dehortans*) over whether one should partake of all the worldly pleasures that the court has to offer or forsake them in hope of salvation. *Curialis* declares in the eighth strophe:

> sompniator animus
> respuens presencia
> gaudeat inanibus–
> quibus si credideris,
> expectare poteris
> Arturum cum Britonibus![219]

> (Let the dreamer reject the things of the present and rejoice in inane hopes – if you can believe in such things, you might as well wait for Arthur with the Britons!)

Peter, much as Walter had done, uses the British Hope as a rhetorical example of a senseless and hopeless belief. The speaker *Curialis* argues that there is no empirical evidence to support religion and therefore there is no more reason to believe in it than in the Breton Hope. For the reference to the Breton Hope to have any literary effect, there must have been a general consensus that the idea of Arthur's return was patently false.

The last significant reference to the Breton Hope that I have found in non-Arthurian literature from the reign of Henry II appears in the final lines of the third book of the *Ilias* (c. 1180–5) by Joseph of Exeter (*fl.* 1180–94). Scorning the Greek pantheon, Joseph asserts 'Non fabula celum, / Sed virtus non ficta, dabit' (heaven's won by real good life, not lying tales),[220] and he casts doubt on the survival of Castor and Pollux, adding:

> Sola tamen Fatis Ledeum Lesbos amorem
> Concessisse negat raptosque secuta Lacones,
> Quos nec apud Frigios, mediis nec repperit undis,
> Credidit esse deos sterilique reversa favore
> Diis urbes auxit, thure aras, marmore templa.
> Sic Britonum ridenda fides et credulus error
> Arturum exspectat exspectabitque perenne.[221]

---

[219] Peter of Blois, 'Quod amicus suggerit', ed. and trans. Peter Dronke, in Peter Dronke, 'Peter of Blois and Poetry at the Court of Henry II', *Medieval Studies* 38 (1976): 208. I have provided my own translation.

[220] Joseph of Exeter, *Frigii Daretis Yliados libri sex* 3.455–6, in *Werke und Briefe von Joseph Iscanus*, ed. Ludwig Gompf (Leiden and Cologne: Brill, 1970), 137; for the translation provided, see Joseph of Exeter, *Iliad*, trans. A. G. Rigg (Toronto: Centre for Medieval Studies, 2005), 61 (http://medieval.utoronto.ca/ylias, accessed 18 November 2013).

[221] Joseph of Exeter, *Frigii Daretis Yliados* 3.467–73, p. 137.

(Lesbos alone claimed Leda's loving sons were saved from death, and said the twins were seized and never found amid the wreck of Troy or in the ocean's waves; they held that they were gods; though spurned by fruitless faith, they swelled towns, altars, shrines, with gods and scent and stone – just like the foolish British hope and trusting faith that waits for Arthur to return – and always will!)

Just as Walter uses the example of the Breton Hope to undermine Jewish religious beliefs, here Joseph uses it to show that pagan religious practices are ineffectual. Joseph's remarks also connect with Étienne's *Draco Normannicus* in an interesting way: where Étienne emphasizes the pagan qualities of the Breton Hope to dismiss it, Joseph comments that pagan worship is about as efficacious as faith in Arthur's return.

The overwhelming message of all these references is that the Breton Hope is a ridiculous idea and one that is characteristic of and seemingly exclusive to the Brittonic Celts. But, as we have observed, such non-Brittonic paragons of Christian learning as John of Salisbury gave thought to the prophecies of Merlin. The English and French probably did not fear the actual return of Arthur, but it is plausible that they feared the potential of Arthur as a rallying figure for the Brittonic Celts. Did the English and French compensate for this putative anxiety through satirical writings? One could argue that this was the case in *Draco Normannicus* and in Arthur's Letter, where the Breton Hope is a major subject. Yet, in the writings of Walter of Châtillon, Peter of Blois, and Joseph of Exeter, Arthur and the Breton Hope are not the primary focus. References to Arthur and the Breton Hope were only included because they served the purposes of their respective authors, namely to discredit Judaism, to complain about a lack of generosity, and to point out the futility of pagan worship. The potency of the Breton Hope as a rhetorical device is predicated on recognition of the idea's absurdity.

As has been shown above, the poets of Henry II's court dismissed the Breton Hope as inane and un-Christian. The target of their criticism was not Arthur *per se*, but rather the 'Britons' who supposedly believed in Arthur's return. This attack fits into the wider prejudicial stereotype of the Celtic peoples, particularly of Wales, as intellectually and culturally inferior. Did the Welsh and Bretons truly believe that King Arthur would be their avenger, or was this idea an unfounded English prejudice? Did twelfth-century non-Celtic authors (specifically Henry's courtiers) truly think that the Celts believed in the Breton Hope? Was there a conscious misrepresentation of Celtic culture? These questions cannot be answered definitively. A variety of twelfth-century writers nonetheless defined Arthur's relationship with the Brittonic Celts as one-sided and one-dimensional: *exspectare Arthurum*. If the Celtic connection to Arthur could be said to consist solely in *exspectare Arthurum*, then the Brittonic claim to Arthur would likewise appear laughable. This brand of propaganda, which predates the discovery of Arthur's remains, constituted one means by which the Angevin kings of England alienated Arthur from the Brittonic Celts and expropriated him as their spiritual predecessor.

Conclusion

Remarks made on Geoffrey's *Historia* by a late twelfth-century scribe who identifies himself as 'Bernardus' epitomize the central argument of this chapter.[222] After copying Joseph's *Ilias* but prior to copying Geoffrey's *Historia*, Bernardus inserted two of his own Leonine verse poems into the codex that he was compiling. He titled these short poems: 'Versus contra Daretem' and 'Versus contra fidem Britonum' respectively. The 'Versus contra fidem Britonum' directly precedes the *Historia regum Britannie* in two late twelfth-century manuscripts – Douai, Bibliothèque Municipale, MS 880 and Douai, Bibliothèque Municipale, MS 882 – and it functions as a foreword to the text.[223] The title 'Versus contra fidem Britonum' appears to have been inspired by Joseph of Exeter's mention of the *fides Britonum* (3.472–3). It reads:

> Arturi gesta, Clyo, mihi scribere praesta,
> Quae non incesta nec falsa puto, sed honesta.
> Id tamen impurum reor errorem subiturum
> Quod putat Arturum Britto fatuus rediturum.
> Post vitae cursum prohibit mors cuique recursum:
> Si redit hic rursum, Britto vertetur in ursum.[224]

> (Clyo, give me the ability to write down the deeds of Arthur, which I do not believe to be corrupted or false, but honest. Nevertheless, I think it a foul error in so far as the foolish Briton thinks Arthur will return. Death prohibits anyone from returning after the course of his life has run out. If this one returns again, the Briton will be transformed into a bear.)

---

[222] See Jacob Hammer, 'Some Leonine Summaries of Geoffrey of Monmouth's *Historia regum Brittaniae* and Other Poems', *Speculum* 6, n. 1 (1931): 114–23.

[223] Julia Crick dates Douai, Bibliothèque Municipale, MS 880 to the second half / last quarter of the twelfth century and states that its medieval provenance is the Abbey of Anchin (Benedictine, diocese of Arras) (*HRB Summary Catalogue*, 93–4). She dates Douai, Bibliothèque Municipale, MS 882 to the last quarter of the twelfth century and states that its medieval provenance is Saint Rictrudis, Marchiennes (Benedictine, diocese of Cambrai-Arras) (94–7).

[224] Bernard, 'Versus contra fidem Britonum', ed. Jacob Hammer, in Jacob Hammer, 'Some Leonine Summaries of Geoffrey of Monmouth's *Historia regum Brittaniae* and Other Poems', *Speculum* 6, n. 1 (1931): 123.

These verses emphasize on one hand that the Breton Hope is absurd and on the other that the *Historia*, by virtue of the reference to the muse Clyo, is indeed a work of history. Here, we observe a distinction between the 'Arthur of history' and the 'Arthur of "Celtic" myth'. As I have argued with particular reference to Étienne of Rouen's *Draco Normannicus*, the late, great 'King Arthur of history' was an aspirational model for the Plantagenets. The Breton Hope was not an ominous threat to the Angevin court; it was a 'straw man' that facilitated the dismissal of the Brittonic ethnic and cultural connection with Arthur. The existence of the 'Breton Hope' was also useful in another way for the Plantagenets. If Arthur were not fated to return literally (physically healing and reawakening as if from death or a deep sleep) then perhaps he might return figuratively (a new king might possess his spirit and equal or surpass Arthur for his accomplishments). Henry II, as we have seen, was portrayed as Arthur-like. In the writings of Wace, Étienne, and Chrétien, Henry II is shown to be the new Arthur.

2
Arthurianism during the reign of Richard I, 1189–1199

Arthur of Brittany and the discovery of Arthur's bones

The competition for Arthur's legacy during Henry II's reign manifested as a contest of ideas involving rival interpretations of history and political prophecy. Was Arthur primarily a Brittonic resistance fighter or a conquering sovereign? Did Arthur die? Was he destined to return and, if so, how? As Henry's reign drew to its close, the political exploitation of the figure of Arthur in the Plantagenet world moved beyond hermeneutics in two notable ways. First, at Easter (29 March) 1187, the posthumous son of Geoffrey Plantagenet by Constance of Penthièvre, duchess of Brittany, was born at Nantes. He was christened Arthur and acclaimed the long-awaited *Arthurus redivivus*. Second, around the year 1191, Arthur's remains were 'discovered' and excavated at the Benedictine abbey of Glastonbury in Somerset. Both events had major implications for the Arthurian tradition. The birth of the new Arthur, who was of Plantagenet and Breton stock, was heralded as the fulfillment of the Breton Hope. The discovery of Arthur's bones, if genuine, stood as positive proof that King Arthur had truly died, was buried, and would not rise again in fulfillment of the prophecy – at least in his original body.

These two real-life developments in the Arthurian tradition are the focus of this chapter. The genesis of these events has considerable implications for our understanding of Arthurianism in Plantagenet England. For instance, if the Crown orchestrated the Glastonbury discovery, then it is reasonable to conclude that the Plantagenet kings perceived the Breton Hope as an enduring threat to their rule.[1] Henry II's stance in relation to the naming of his grandson Arthur is also consequential. If Henry approved of the name choice, then we are

---

[1] See Griffiths, *Early Vaticination in Welsh*, 37. Jean-Christophe Cassard has read the finding of Arthur's remains as part of the English royal strategy of capturing the ancient glory of Britain. This, in his opinion, constituted psychological warfare geared toward disarming the Welsh inhabitants of the island and establishing the Angevin kings as the legitimate heirs to Arthur ('Arthur est vivant!', 143). Also see Gillingham, 'Context and Purposes', 103; Aurell, 'Henry II and Arthurian Legend', 388.

observing a heightened appropriation of King Arthur for the hegemonic interests of the Plantagenets: Henry was making his grandson the new focalization of the Breton Hope.[2] On the basis of his lineage, Arthur of Brittany had unique potential in this regard. Not only was his maternal grandfather, Conan IV, a native duke of Brittany, his maternal grandmother, Margaret, was sister to two successive kings of Scotland: Malcolm IV (r. 1153–65) and William I (r. 1165–1214). Arthur boasted the princely blood of Brittany, England, and Scotland, which positioned him well to claim to be the rightful *rex totius Britannie*, as King Arthur had done according to Geoffrey's *Historia*.[3] If, however, Constance of Penthièvre named her son Arthur in defiance of Henry's wishes, then there is cause to infer that the figure of King Arthur had not been successfully coopted by Henry II and that he remained an emblem of native resistance.

Narratives of the Glastonbury discovery

The reported discovery of Arthur's remains at Glastonbury is in the opinion of some scholars the 'watershed moment' that allowed for the 'historicizing and Anglicizing of Arthur'.[4] It is undeniably an important event in the medieval Arthurian tradition, but whether it was *the* development that enabled Arthurianism by the post-Conquest kings of England is questionable. Arthurianism, at least as a textual activity, had been underway since the outset of Henry II's reign.

The earliest accounts of the discovery and excavation of Arthur's bones fall into two textual groups. One is the writing of Gerald of Wales (c. 1146–c. 1223), which does not specify an exact date for the find but credits Henry II (d. 6 July 1189) for providing the information that led to the discovery. The other group is typified by the *Chronicon Anglicanum* (covering the years 1066–1224) of the Cistercian abbey of Coggeshall in Essex. In the *Chronicon Anglicanum*, which is attributed to the house's fifth abbot, Ralph of Coggeshall, the discovery of Arthur's grave is described as a fortuitous accident. The chronicler reports that a certain monk expressed a great desire during his lifetime to be buried between the remnants of

---

[2] An inescapable analogy is found in Tudor England: Henry VII (r. 1485–1509) named his firstborn son and heir Arthur (1486–1503).

[3] See Ostmann, 'Die Bedeutung der Arthurtradition', 229–30, who calls attention to the potential benefit of Arthur of Brittany's Scottish ancestry to the high nobility of England.

[4] James P. Carley, 'Arthur in English History', in *The Arthur of the English: The Arthurian Legend in Medieval English Life and Literature*, rev. edn., ed. W. R. J. Barron (Cardiff: University of Wales Press, 2001), 48. Also see Gillingham, 'Context and Purposes', 103;

two ancient pyramids located in the grounds of Glastonbury Abbey. After his death, when the monks of the community were honoring his wishes, they unearthed a sarcophagus with a leaden cross. The cross identified the remains as Arthur's and the burial site as Avalon.[5] The *Chronicon Anglicanum*'s account of the discovery does not mention Henry II at all. The year it assigns to the event is 1191, two years after King Henry's death.

Gerald of Wales wrote about the Glastonbury discovery in two separate works. The earlier account occurs in the twentieth chapter of the first distinction of his *De principis instructione*.[6] Its date of composition is a complicated matter. In his catalogue of shorter works (c. 1217), Gerald comments that *De principis instructione* was one of the first works that he undertook but one of the last that he released; concern for personal safety was the cause for the delay.[7] In the first version of his *Itinerarium Kambrie* (1191), Gerald announces that he was at work on *De principis instructione*.[8] He released an initial version of the first distinction in the 1190s as a stand-alone piece, but this version is lost. Only a single copy of *De principis instructione* survives: London, British Library, MS Cotton, Julius B. xiii (fourteenth century). In this manuscript, the first distinction appears alongside the second and third distinctions. We know that the surviving version of the first distinction is a recension written between 1216 and 1217 because in it Gerald expresses support for Prince Louis Capet's claim to the throne of England and tells an anecdote about Prince Louis that dates from 1216.[9]

In *De principis instructione*, Gerald states that he visited Glastonbury during the abbacy (15 September 1189–93) of Henry of Sully (d. 1195) and that Abbot Henry personally showed him Arthur's skull and one of his massive shinbones.[10] Gerald seems to have consulted written accounts of Arthur's devotion to Glastonbury. This is apparent from Gerald's opening remarks about the discovery of Arthur's tomb in *De principis instructione* 1.20:

> Arthuri quoque Britonum regis inclyti memoria est non supprimenda,
> quem *monasterii Glastoniensis egregii*, cujus et ipse patronus suis

[5] Ralph of Coggeshall, *Chronicon Anglicum*, ed. Joseph Stevenson, RS 66 (London: Longman, 1875), 36.

[6] Gerald of Wales, *De principis instructione* 1.20, pp. 126–9.

[7] Gerald of Wales, 'Catalogus brevior librorum suorum', ed. J. S. Brewer, in *Giraldi Cambrensis opera*, vol. 1, ed. J. S. Brewer, RS 21/1 (London: Longman, Green, Longman, and Roberts, 1861), 423. For the dating of the 'Catalogus', see Bartlett, *Gerald of Wales*, 220.

[8] Gerald of Wales, *Itinerarium Kambriæ* 1.4, p. 53; Bartlett, *Gerald of Wales*, 69.

[9] See Warner's introduction to *De principis instructione liber*, xx; Bartlett, *Gerald of Wales*, 70.

[10] Gerald of Wales, *De principis instructione liber* 1.20, p. 126.

diebus fuerat præcipuus et largitor ac sublevator magnificus, *historiæ* multum extollunt.

(Also the memory of Arthur, the glorious king of the Britons, ought not be suppressed, whom the *histories of the famous monastery of Glastonbury* – of which he himself had been an extraordinary donor and supporter during his life – greatly extol.)

The monks of Glastonbury probably showed Gerald accounts of their institutional history during his visit.

Scholars, taking Gerald at his word, have traditionally regarded the entry in *De principis instructione* as the earliest description of the discovery.[11] If Gerald did visit Glastonbury, then the trip must have occurred before December 1193, for in that month Henry of Sully was consecrated bishop of Worcester.[12] Chronological incongruities in Gerald's account cast doubt on the reliability of his narrative, however, and there is reason to question whether the entry on the discovery of Arthur's grave was part of the original release of the first distinction. There are, it should be noted, extensive pro-Capetian additions, such as praise of Louis VII and Philippe II (some of which can be dated to 1214), appearing in the very same section in which the discovery of Arthur's remains is reported. Thus, we cannot rely on the completion of the first distinction of *De principis instructione* as a *terminus ante quem* to date the discovery of Arthur's remains.

Gerald's second account of the discovery appears in his final work, the *Speculum ecclesie*, which also survives in just one manuscript: London, British Library, MS Cotton, Tiberius B xiii. The section that details the discovery of Arthur's remains was damaged in the Cottonian Library Fire of 1731. In *Speculum Ecclesiæ* 2.8, Gerald speaks of the abbot as having been consecrated bishop of Worcester (r. 1193–5).[13] So, with respect to the *Speculum ecclesie* entry, there can be no doubt that Gerald was writing from hindsight on or after 4 December 1193. In *Speculum ecclesie*, moreover, Gerald refers to the Fourth Lateran Council of 1215, and R. W. Hunt holds that Gerald completed the preface after 1219.[14]

---

[11] See W. A. Nitze, 'The Exhumation of King Arthur at Glastonbury', *Speculum* 9, n. 4 (1934): 358; Antonia Gransden, 'The Growth of the Glastonbury Traditions and Legends in the Twelfth Century', in *Glastonbury Abbey and the Arthurian Tradition*, ed. James P. Carley (Cambridge, UK: D. S. Brewer, 2001), 44; Richard Barber, 'Was Mordred Buried at Glastonbury? Arthurian Tradition at Glastonbury in the Middle Ages', in *Glastonbury Abbey and the Arthurian Tradition*, ed. James P. Carley (Cambridge, UK: D. S. Brewer, 2001), 154.

[12] Gransden, 'Glastonbury Traditions and Legends', 45 n. 76.

[13] Gerald of Wales, *Speculum Ecclesiæ* 2.8, p. 47.

[14] See R. W. Hunt, 'The Preface to the "Speculum Ecclesiae" of Giraldus Cambrensis', *Viator* 8 (1977): 196–7.

Not long after Gerald would have visited Glastonbury, the Cistercian monk Ralph of Coggeshall wrote his entry on the discovery of Arthur's bones. Scholars have not given as much attention to the Coggeshall entry because it was assumed that the *Chronicon Anglicanum* as a whole was written shortly before its 1224 endpoint.[15] Yet David Carpenter, with an eye to Ralph's characterization of King Richard and King John, has made a study of the composition of the *Chronicon Anglicanum* and has concluded that the section containing the discovery of Arthur's tomb was written much earlier. Having considered internal evidence as well as the codicological features of an early working draft of the *Chronicon Anglicanum*, London, British Library, Cotton Vespasian D. x,[16] Carpenter holds that Ralph wrote the *Chronicon* in installments and that 'the first section of the chronicle was completed in or soon after 1195, while a second (that between 1195 and 1200) was written in or soon after 1201'.[17] The year 1195 marked the safe return of Richard I from captivity and is, in Carpenter's assessment, a stopping point for the chronicle.[18] If Carpenter's dating of Ralph's entries is accurate then Ralph presumably wrote his account of Glastonbury discovery within two years of Gerald's visit to the site. It is uncertain which version of the discovery was written first – the Giraldian version involving Henry II or the Coggeshall version in which Henry II is absent. However, I will offer evidence that the Coggeshall version came first.

There is another Cistercian account of the discovery of Arthur's remains that has received a fair amount of scholarly attention. It appears

---

[15] See, for example, Gransden, 'Glastonbury Traditions and Legends', 44.

[16] D. A. Carpenter, 'Abbot Ralph of Coggeshall's Account of the Last Years of King Richard and the First Years of King John', *English Historical Review* 113, n. 454 (1998): 1212, 1214. Also see F. M. Powicke, 'Roger of Wendover and the Coggeshall Chronicle', *English Historical Review* 21, n. 82 (1906): 286.

[17] Carpenter, 'Abbot Ralph of Coggeshall's Account', 1214.

[18] See Carpenter, 'Abbot Ralph of Coggeshall's Account', 1215. Carpenter notes a change in formatting beginning with the 1196 entries. He also observes that the St. Albans chronicler Roger of Wendover's own *Flores Historiarum* (to 1235) shows signs of being informed by the *Chronicon Anglicanum* up to 1195, which suggests that the version to which Roger had access terminated in 1195. See Roger of Wendover, *Flores Historiarum*, I, 203. Additionally, he calls attention to a tonal element that pertains to the dating of the sections of the *Chronicon*: Ralph's remarks about King Richard up to 1195 were almost entirely positive, and this suggests to Carpenter that Ralph was not writing from hindsight. Beginning in 1196, though, Richard placed substantial financial demands on his subjects that damaged the king's reputation at home in England, and the harm is palpable in the chronicles written after Richard's death.

in the *Annals of Margam* in Glamorgan.[19] Unlike Ralph's *Chronicon Anglicanum*, the date of composition of this text appears to be proximate to the conclusion of its entries, 1232.[20] Chronicles do, of course, tend to contain a patchwork of earlier historical writings, which means that the Margam account of the Glastonbury discovery might derive from an earlier account. The wording of the Margam and Coggeshall entries on Arthur's grave match almost verbatim, but the Margam account is slightly longer and contains two additional sequences of text. The first concerns the discovery of the remains of another woman and man at Arthur's gravesite; the second concerns the etymology of Avalon and the identification of the woman and man as Queen Guinevere and Mordred respectively.[21] Both sequences of additional lines appear to be interpolations from the writings of Gerald of Wales. The discovery of a woman's bones and her uncorrupted hair, which comes as a tangential and supplemental detail in the *Annals of Margam*, is mentioned in *De principis instructione*,[22] and is a focal point in the *Speculum ecclesie*. In fact, Gerald devotes an entire chapter of the second distinction of the *Speculum ecclesie* 2.8 to this episode. Here, Gerald faults a Glastonbury monk who was present at the excavation for his worldly desire and draws attention to the fact that all material things wither away. The second additional sequence in the *Annals of Margam*, which explains that Avalon contains within it the British word for apple, *aval*, is quite similar to remarks made by Gerald in *De principis instructione*. Although one could argue, as Gransden and Barber have done, that there was a common exemplar behind all of the surviving accounts,[23] it is curious that Roger of Wendover did not use this putative exemplar and instead relied on the briefer Coggeshall version. Barber has argued that the Margam version contains a more 'authentic' copy of a lost exemplar, but a simpler explanation – or at least one that requires less speculation – is that the *Annals of Margam* is a composite text that replicates the *Chronicon Anglicanum* account (c. 1195) with supplements from the writings (c. 1217–23) of Gerald of Wales. It should be remembered that the Margam text was finished in 1232, nine years

---

[19] *Annales de Margan (A.D. 1066–1232)*, in *Annales Monastici*, vol. 1, ed. Henry Richards Luard. RS 36/1 (London: Longman, Green, Longman, Roberts, and Green, 1864), 21–2.

[20] See Robert B. Patterson, 'The Author of the "Margam Annals": Early Thirteenth-Century Margam Abbey's Compleat Scribe', *Anglo-Norman Studies* XIV (1992): 197–210.

[21] *Annales de Margan*, 21–2.

[22] Gerald of Wales, *De principis instructione* 1.20, p. 127.

[23] See Gransden, 'Glastonbury Traditions and Legends', 44–5; Barber, 'Was Mordred Buried at Glastonbury', 153–4.

after Gerald is thought to have died. Thus, we need not postulate the existence of a lost exemplar to explain the textual history of the accounts of the discovery of Arthur's remains.

Before examining the Giraldian accounts, let us first consider the leaden cross that is mentioned in all of the reports of the event. According to the *Chronicon Anglicanum*, the cross bore the following inscription: 'Hic jacet inclitus rex Arturius, in insula Avallonis sepultus.' The accounts of the inscription vary only slightly in terms of orthography and syntax in the non-Giraldian descriptions of it. Gerald of Wales includes 'cum Wenneuereia vxore sua secunda' in his two accounts. The leaden cross, or a later reproduction of it, was still in existence when the antiquary John Leland visited Glastonbury in 1533, but the artifact has since disappeared.[24] A woodcut rendering of it, most likely derived from a sketch drawn by Leland, appears in William Camden's *Antiquitates Britanniae* (1607).[25] Except for the position of the word 'sepultus', Ralph's account of the inscription is the closest to Camden's woodcut.

With respect to the wording of the epitaph alone, there are two significant clues that the leaden cross was a forgery. First, a genuine burial marker would not carry its own location, for this would be self-evident both to the party responsible for the burial and to the onlookers. Whoever was responsible for the inscription wanted to make the point that Glastonbury was Avalon. And, so far as I am aware, prior to the twelfth century there was no suggestion that Glastonbury was Avalon. Second, the description of Arthur as 'inclitus rex' in the epithet is suggestive of forgery. The earliest historical accounts of Arthur do not refer to the figure as a king. The ninth-century *Historia Brittonum*, for example, famously refers to him as 'dux bellorum'.[26] To the contrary, the epithet on the cross seems to depend on Geoffrey of Monmouth's concluding

---

[24] See Oliver D. Harris, '"Which I have beholden with most curious eyes": The Lead Cross from Glastonbury Abbey', *Arthurian Literature* XXXIV (2018): 96–7. Harris has made a persuasive argument that John Leland is the last uncontestable first-hand witness to the physical survival of the leaden cross, and Harris adds, '[i]t seems increasingly likely that it was lost at or very shortly after the dissolution of Glastonbury abbey in 1539' (125). For earlier discussions of the cross, see Edward Donald Kennedy, 'Glastonbury', in *The Arthur of Medieval Latin Literature: The Development and Dissemination of Arthurian Legend in Medieval Latin*, ed. Siân Echard (Cardiff: University of Wales Press, 2005), 111 and David Carlson, 'Anglo-Latin Literature in the Later Middle Ages', in *The Cambridge Companion to Medieval English Culture*, ed. Andrew Galloway (Cambridge, UK: Cambridge University Press, 2011), 198–9.

[25] Harris, 'The Leaden Cross from Glastonbury Abbey', 106. Camden, according to Harris, first copied the image in the 1580s, but the 1607 version was adapted by the block-cutter shortly before publication.

[26] See Carlson, 'Anglo-Latin Literature', 199.

remarks about King Arthur in the *Historia regum Britannie*: 'Sed et *inclitus ille rex* Arturus letaliter uulneratus est; qui illinc ad sananda uulnera sua in insulam Avallonis euectus....'[27] As Stephen C. Morland has observed, it is extremely likely that 'whoever decided the wording on the cross had read Geoffrey of Monmouth'.[28] Indeed, the maker of the cross seems to have taken special care to match up the inscription with *Historia regum Britannie* as closely as possible, perhaps to lend credibility to the idea that the bones were indeed those of Arthur. The identification of Glastonbury with Avalon and the reference to Arthur as 'inclitus rex', both of which appear in the inscription, belong to the same ideological context.

The letterforms of the epitaph on the leaden cross are also a point of interest and debate. David Carlson maintains that the letters are characteristic neither of the Arthurian period (400–600 CE) nor of the twelfth century; he adds, 'if the cross is a forgery, it is a careful one. The letter-forms appear to mimic those of the earliest documents (tenth-century charters) held in Glastonbury at the time of the exhumation.'[29] Aelred Watkin has observed that the letterforms in Camden's reproduction of the leaden cross are 'almost identical' to those contained on a twelfth-century tympanum found on the north door of St. Mary's Church at Stoke-sub-Hamdon, a village in the South Somerset district of Somerset, not far from Glastonbury.[30] Oliver Harris, the most recent commentator on this matter, believes 'the closest comparisons to the letter-forms of the lead cross' are to be found on old coins, such as the silver penny of Cnut (r. 1016–35), but not exclusively on pre-Conquest coins.[31] The letterforms on the leaden cross are best described as twelfth-century archaicizing monumental characters modeled after the oldest specimens of monumental inscription on hand, be they coins or charters. Let us now consider Gerald of Wales and his accounts of the discovery.

As noted above, Abbot Henry of Sully is said to have given Gerald a guided tour of the discovery. It is unclear precisely why Gerald went to Glastonbury in the early 1190s. He may have visited Glastonbury to

---

[27] Geoffrey of Monmouth, *Historia regum Britannie* 178.81–2, pp. 252–3.

[28] See Stephen C. Morland, *Glastonbury, Domesday and Related Studies* (Glastonbury, UK: Glastonbury Antiquarian Society, 1991), 60.

[29] Carlson, 'Anglo-Latin Literature', 199.

[30] See James P. Carley, 'The Discovery of the Holy Cross of Waltham at Montacute, the Excavation of Arthur's Grave at Glastonbury Abbey, and Joseph of Arimathea's Burial', in *Glastonbury Abbey and the Arthurian Tradition*, ed. James P. Carley (Cambridge, UK: D. S. Brewer, 2001), 305, n. 10.

[31] Harris, 'The Leaden Cross from Glastonbury Abbey', 113. Harris adds, 'what does seem entirely possible is that the designer of the cross, in cutting the inscription, used the lettering of old coins as his model in order to lend it an appropriate aura of antiquity' (114).

sate his curiosity after hearing of the discovery. Gerald, in his *Topographia Hibernica* and in his *Expugnatio Hibernica* (1188–9), announces his intention to write a *Topographia Britannica*, where he planned to discuss the ethnography of Wales and Scotland and elaborate on the Irish invasion and settlement of Scotland.[32] In the first recension of the *Descriptio Kambriae* (c.1194), Gerald expresses his continued desire to write a *Topographia Britannica* in which he would elaborate further on certain issues not already covered in his works on Wales, including an analysis of the courage of the Britons, especially in the time of 'Arturi nostri famosi, nec dicam fabulosi' (of our famous, and I will not say fabled, Arthur).[33] Gerald seems, though, to have abandoned the *Topographia Britannica* by 1215. For in the 1215 recension of the *Descriptio Kambriæ*, Gerald addresses some of the issues he intended to take up in the *Topographia Britannica*, including a reference to Arthur. Gerald may have traveled to Glastonbury between 1193 and 1195 in order to conduct research for his projected *Topographia Britannica*. Robert Bartlett has recently argued that much of the material originally intended for the *Topographia Britannica* found its way not only into the 1215 recension of the *Descriptio Kambriæ* but also into the 1216–17 recension of *De principis instructione*. Gerald's account of the discovery of Arthur was quite possibly one of these recycled materials.[34] However, there are also other possibilities for why Gerald documented the discovery.

Gerald was in royal service from 1184 to 1194, and the English crown may have dispatched him to document the Arthurian find. The discovery of the grave of the king on 'English' soil certainly reinforced the understanding of Arthur as a precursor to the Plantagenet kings of England. The analysis of John Gillingham and Martin Aurell encourages us to assume that the English royal court was keen for the bones of Arthur to be found and that there was considerable royal involvement in the documentation of the discovery. Gerald, as a royal official and Welsh liaison, may have been a part of this process. The discovery was not a prerequisite for use of the figure of King Arthur by the English crown, but this does not mean that that royal court did not have a hand

---

[32] For a discussion of the window of composition (1197–1214) and probable character of the *Topographia Britannica*, see Bartlett, *Gerald of Wales*, 182 n. 17.

[33] Gerald of Wales, *Descriptio Kambriæ* 2.2, ed. James F. Dimock, in *Giraldi Cambrensis opera*, vol. 6, ed. James F. Dimock. RS 21/6 (London: Longmans, Green, Reader, and Dyer, 1868), p. 208.

[34] Professor Bartlett suggested this possibility to me following his plenary talk: '"The dullest thing that Giraldus ever wrote": Book One of "Instruction for a Ruler"' (plenary lecture for the conference entitled 'New Perspectives on Gerald of Wales: Texts and Contexts', Harvard University, Cambridge, MA, 11 April 2015).

in the discovery or that it did not dispatch Gerald to document the event. However, if the Crown had assigned him this task, we would expect him to say so.

Another possible explanation for Gerald's journey to Glastonbury is that Abbot Henry of Sully asked him to document the event. Gransden has tentatively suggested that the Glastonbury community commissioned Gerald to compose an account of the discovery. Around the year 1129, another abbot Henry of Glastonbury, Henry of Blois (r. 1126–71), had outsourced the monastery's first great historiographical project to William of Malmesbury. William produced a treatise maintaining that Glastonbury was the oldest Christian religious community in Britain. This work, *De Antiquitate Glastonie Ecclesie*, was completed around 1135.[35] Gerald was perhaps, as Gransden has suggested, a successor of sorts to William of Malmesbury.[36] He was the ideal candidate for the task of producing the definitive account of the discovery of Arthur's bones. He was half-Welsh and knew some Welsh; he was well educated, indeed Paris-trained; he was a man of high standing, indeed a royal official who had served as an advisor to Prince John in Ireland in 1185; and, most importantly, Gerald was an expert on the legendary history of Britain and the prophecies of Merlin.[37] Who would be better to document the discovery?

However, three aspects of Gerald's personal history do not support Gransden's hypothesis. First, as the *Speculum ecclesie* illustrates, Gerald did not hold monks in high regard. Second, Gerald was independently wealthy and did not require the patronage of the Glastonbury community. Third, and most importantly, nowhere does Gerald mention taking up a commission on behalf of the Glastonbury community. Regardless of whether he traveled to Glastonbury on his own initiative, on behalf of the Crown, or at the request of the monastic community, Gerald was the recipient of a Glastonbury-endorsed narrative. Gerald, at least in his surviving writings, embraces this narrative and seems to have lent his talents to upholding it.

---

[35] See J. Armitage Robinson, 'William of Malmesbury "On the Antiquity of Glastonbury"', in *Somerset Historical Essays* (London: Oxford University Press, 1921), 3–4. The copies of *De Antiquitate Glastonie Ecclesie* that survive are heavily interpolated. See John Scott, *The Early History of Glastonbury: Edition, Translation and Study of William of Malmesbury's* De Antiquitate Glastonie Ecclesie (Woodbridge, UK: Boydell, 1981), 4–5.

[36] Gransden, 'Glastonbury Traditions and Legends', 32–3.

[37] In the preface to the third book of his *Expugnatio Hibernica* (c. 1189), the 'Liber vaticiniorum', Gerald promised to deliver a Latin translation of the prophecies of Merlin Silvester of Celidon. See Gerald of Wales, *Expugnatio Hibernica*, ed. and trans. A. B. Scott and F. X. Martin (Dublin: Royal Irish Academy, 1978), 252–7.

In the 1215 recension of his *Descriptio Kambriæ*, Gerald takes on one of the most challenging objections against the historicity of Arthur, namely the question of why the sixth-century British writer Gildas did not mention Arthur in his *De exidio et conquestu Britanniæ*. Gerald came up with a rational explanation for Gildas' conspicuous omission using Caradoc of Llancarfan's *Vita Gildæ* (c. 1130–50).[38] According to Caradoc, Gildas had been a contemporary of Arthur, the king of all Great Britain, and Gildas was disposed to love and obey Arthur always.[39] But such was not the case with the holy man's twenty-three Scottish brothers. They refused to recognize Arthur as their lord. The eldest and most distinguished of Gildas' brothers, Hueil, launched a series of raids against Arthur from the north. Arthur eventually killed Hueil in battle on the island of Minau. Gerald seized upon this narrative to explain why Gildas failed to mention Arthur in his surviving historical works. Gerald writes that, according to the Britons, Gildas destroyed all the outstanding books that he had written about Arthur because he was upset that Arthur had killed his brother.[40] Gerald's defense of the historicity of Arthur from an existing 'Arthurian' source is a prime example of Gerald's ingenuity. As we will see, Gerald used this same intertextual apologetic technique to link the details of the Glastonbury discovery with the pre-existing Arthurian tradition.

If Gerald had included this Gildas material in the first recension of *Descriptio Kambriæ* 2.2, which was completed in the 1194 and dedicated to Hubert Walter, archbishop of Canterbury (r. 1193–1205), there would be good reason to believe that Gerald had in fact visited Glastonbury during the tenure of Henry of Sully. The abbot presumably would have shown Caradoc's *Vita Gildæ* to Gerald at that time. But, as stated above, the passage only appears in the 1215 version dedicated to Hubert's eventual successor, Stephen Langton, archbishop of Canterbury (r. 1207–28).[41] Thus, we do not have any independent verification but only Gerald's own remarks that this assignment came during Abbot Henry of Sully's tenure (1189–93). Gerald's familiarity with Glastonbury's history and legend is

---

[38] See Caradoc of Llangarfan, *Vita Gildæ*, in *Two Lives of Gildas by a Monk of Ruys and Caradoc of Llancarfan*, ed. and trans. Hugh William. Cymmrodorion Record Series (1899; repr., Felinfach: Llanerch Enterprises, 1990), 84–103.

[39] Caradoc of Llangarfan, *Vita Gildæ*, 90.

[40] See Gerald of Wales, *Descriptio Kambriæ* 2.2, p. 209. This explanation by Gerald does not entirely coincide with Caradoc's account of Gildas' reaction to the news that his beloved brother had been slain by Arthur. According to Caradoc, Gildas prayed for the soul of Arthur, his brother's murderer, fulfilling the apostolic commandment to love your persecutors (Luke 6:27). See Caradoc of Llangarfan, *Vita Gildæ*, 92.

[41] On the date of the recensions of *Descriptio Kambriæ*, see Dimock, *Giraldi Cambrensis opera*, vol. 6, xxii. On the difference between the first and second recension, see xxix–xxx and 208 n. 9.

only palpable in his later writings, namely from the second decade of the thirteenth century. Let us now consider Gerald's narrative of the discovery.

Gerald's account of the discovery of Arthur's tomb is far more elaborate than that of the *Chronicon Anglicanum*. The *Chronicon Anglicanum* account does not engage with the pre-existing Arthurian tradition. The serendipitous quality of its discovery narrative arguably made its veracity subject to doubt. Gerald, however, acted as an apologist of sorts for the discovery and offered a far more carefully crafted story. As is the case in the *Chronicon*, Gerald states that the body of Arthur was found at Glastonbury between two stone pyramids.[42] These pyramids are the topic of a chapter in William of Malmesbury's *De Antiquitate Glastonie Ecclesie*. The pyramids reportedly were located a few feet from the old church of Glastonbury and bordered the monk's cemetery. The accounts of Gerald and the *Chronicon Anglicanum* are in agreement about the location of the burial site, but Gerald adds that Arthur was buried no less than sixteen feet down and that Arthur's sarcophagus was not made of stone but rather from a hollowed-out oak.[43] The discovery of Arthur's body at such a depth does not fit well with the *Chronicon Anglicanum* narrative because it is improbable that the monks would dig so deep merely to bury one of their brethren. However, this depth was not arrived at from out of the blue. William of Malmesbury in his *Vita Sancti Dunstani* (c. 1125) – yet another work dedicated to the monks of Glastonbury – states that Dunstan, who was abbot of Glastonbury in the middle decades of the tenth century, had the base of the cemetery raised.[44] As James Carley has noted, if a discovery of an ancient grave were to be made, it would have to have been made at a great depth.[45] It is probable that either Gerald himself or the monks were aware of Dunstan's raising of the cemetery, and Gerald (perhaps in consultation with the monks) refashioned the narrative to coincide with this knowledge. It should also be noted that

---

[42] See William of Malmesbury, *De Antiquitate Glastonie Ecclesie* 32, ed. and trans. John Scott, in John Scott, *The Early History of Glastonbury: Edition, Translation and Study of William of Malmesbury's* De Antiquitate Glastonie Ecclesie (Woodbridge, UK: Boydell, 1981), 84–5.

[43] Gerald of Wales, *De principis instructione liber* 1.20, p. 128.

[44] See the prologue of William of Malmesbury, *Vita Sancti Dunstani*, in *Memorials of Saint Dunstan, Archbishop of Canterbury*, ed. William Stubbs, RS 63 (London: Longman, 1874), 250, which establishes that the *vita* was dedicated to the Glastonbury community. For Dunstan's order that the monks' cemetery be elevated, see 1.16, pp. 271–2.

[45] Carley, 'Discovery of the Holy Cross of Waltham', 304 n. 8. Carley has made a compelling case that *De inventione Sanctae Crucis nostrae in Monte Acuto et de ductione ejusdem apud Waltham* (c. 1177), which was written by a secular canon from Waltham, was known to the monks of Glastonbury and constituted 'some sort of vague model for the organisation of the excavation at Glastonbury in 1190/91' (305).

in *Speculum ecclesie* 2.8, Gerald states that the discovery occurred in the sacred cemetery dedicated by Saint Dunstan.[46]

The detail that Arthur's coffin was a hollowed-out oak is more perplexing. It may reflect knowledge of ancient burial practice or perhaps it was dreamed up by someone who knew that oaks were trees sacred to the Celts and Druids. It is also possible that the monks did actually unearth a hollowed-out oak containing human remains in or around 1191, which they decided were those of Arthur. We cannot say with confidence, though, that an actual dig occurred or that human remains were found in hollowed-out oaks at a depth of at least sixteen feet. This may have been a fabrication by someone who was steeped in the abbey's history or at least familiar with William of Malmesbury's *Vita Sancti Dunstani*.

Gerald was probably the one who reconciled the particulars of the Glastonbury dig with the established Arthurian tradition. Creativity was required in order to achieve this harmonization, for nowhere in the prophecies of Merlin do we find reference to a sixteen-foot-deep grave or a hollowed-out oak. Moreover, a wooden casket would seem a rather humble repository for such a paragon of regal magnificence. What had these details to do with the existing Arthurian tradition? Why, except for the inscription on the leaden cross, should anyone believe the bones were those of Arthur? The solution arrived at by 'Gerald' was to associate these details with the difficulty of finding Arthur's grave, which had been emphasized in the Welsh 'Stanzas of the Graves' (*Englynion y Beddau*) and in William of Malmesbury's *Gesta regum Anglorum*. As the reader will recall, the seeming impossibility of finding Arthur's grave provided the core of the argument *ex silencio* in favor of *exspectare Arthurum*. Indeed, Gerald, near the beginning of his account of the discovery, makes reference to the *fabulæ* that speak of Arthur's body as 'quasi phantasticum in fine, et tanquam per spiritus ad longinqua translatum, neque morti obnoxium' (almost fantastical in [its] end, spirited far away as it were and not susceptible to death).[47] Gerald brings this supposed marvel down to earth by asserting that the body was indeed found at Glastonbury in recent times, and he alludes to the 'historical' Arthur's ongoing war against the Saxons to explain the peculiar circumstances. He writes: 'Ideoque tam profunde situm corpus, et quasi absconditum fuerat, ne a Saxonibus post necem ipsius insulam occupantibus, quos tanto opere vivens debellaverat et fere ex toto deleverat, posset nullatenus inveniri' (The body was buried so deep and was, as it were, hidden so that it would not be able to be found by the Saxons occupying the

[46] Gerald of Wales, *Speculum Ecclesiæ*, 2.8, p. 47.
[47] Gerald of Wales, *De principis instructione* 1.20, p. 127.

island after his death – the Saxons whom, when he was alive, he had fought with so much exertion that he had almost entirely annihilated them).[48] This claim may have been inspired by a very similar narrative in William of Malmesbury's *De Antiquitate Glastonie Ecclesie*, which tells of how the remains of Dunstan were translated from Canterbury to Glastonbury in order to prevent the Danes from desecrating his tomb. A monk of Glastonbury, who was specially chosen for the task of hiding Dunstan's bones, placed them in a small wooden receptacle with special markings. He then buried the wooden container most secretly in Glastonbury's larger church beneath a stone cut out for this purpose.[49] At Glastonbury, the elaborate measures taken to conceal Dunstan's remains from Danish marauders parallel those 'anteriorly' taken to conceal Arthur's remains from Saxon marauders.

Gerald was able to connect the specific details of the Glastonbury discovery to Arthurian history (the struggle against the Saxons) and to the folk tradition regarding Arthur's unknown resting place. He managed to transform the great difficulty in finding Arthur's remains from being a liability that fueled the Breton Hope into being an asset that helped to corroborate the Glastonbury discovery – to explain why it took so many centuries for this discovery to be made. This is a point that has not been sufficiently emphasized in the existing scholarship on the topic. Gerald's integration of the Glastonbury discovery into the pre-existing Arthurian tradition is an element that is sorely lacking from the *Chronicon Anglicanum* account. Gerald possibly devised his more intricate narrative as an improvement on the *Chronicon* account, harmonizing the archeological history of Glastonbury abbey with the Arthurian tradition.

In his later work, the *Speculum ecclesie*, Gerald embeds the discovery of Arthur even more deeply in the established Arthurian tradition. Gerald acknowledges the existence of the myth of King Arthur's survival but derides it as a foolish Brittonic belief.[50] He harkens back to the pronouncements made by William of Malmesbury and Wace that the historical truth of Arthur had become the stuff of fiction.[51] By evoking this truism, Gerald obtains freedom to take liberties with the existing traditions surrounding Arthur's end. His approach is to preserve everything from tradition that is useful to him, to 'correct' what he cannot use, and to hold up the authority of the English crown and the religious community of Glastonbury to privilege his own version of events.

---

[48] Gerald of Wales, *De principis instructione* 1.20, p. 128.
[49] See William of Malmesbury, *De Antiquitate Glastonie Ecclesie* 24, pp. 74–7.
[50] See Gerald of Wales, *Speculum Ecclesiæ* 2.9, pp. 48–9.
[51] William of Malmesbury, *Gesta regum Anglorum* 1.8 (I, 26–7). Also see Wace, *Roman de Brut*, 246–7, lines 9785–99.

Gerald is able to affirm that Camlann was the site of Arthur's last battle, that the king's opponent there was Mordred,[52] and even that Arthur's kinswoman Morganis (whom we have seen mentioned in Geoffrey's *Vita Merlini* and in Étienne of Rouen's *Draco Normannicus*) transported Arthur to Avalon. Gerald is unwilling, however, to countenance that Morganis took a gravely-injured-but-still-living Arthur to Avalon to have his wounds healed. This detail leaves too much room open for belief in Arthur's continued existence. Gerald argues instead that Morganis took Arthur's corpse to Avalon for burial in its sacred cemetery and that the removal of Arthur's mortal remains from the scene of battle was the reason why the British and their bards were accustomed to make up stories insisting that Morgan brought Arthur to Avalon in order to be healed of his wounds and that once healed, the king, strong and powerful, will return to rule the Britons, so that they themselves may lead, just as they used to.[53] Gerald adds 'propter quod, ipsum expectant adhuc venturum sicut Judæi Messiam suum, majori etiam fatuitate et infelicitate, simul ac infidelitate decepti' (on account of this, they still expect him to come just as the Jews – who are even more misled by foolishness, misfortune, and also infidelity – expect their Messiah).[54] Gerald touts the Plantagenet position on Arthur, namely the almost wholesale acceptance of Geoffrey's account of Arthur's life as fact and the repudiation of all reports of the king's survival as bogus on the grounds that they are the product of Brittonic ignorance and folly. Gerald also includes the British–Jewish analogy, which, as we have seen, Walter of Châtillon and Peter of Blois employed in their works. Once again, by matching the Glastonbury discovery narrative up so closely with the existing Arthurian narrative Gerald may have been trying to reinforce the credibility of the find, but he also opened it up to challenge insofar as its believability became contingent on the Avalon–Glastonbury linkage.

Gerald also states that Henry II told the monks of Glastonbury where to look for the remains of Arthur and that the English king ordained that Arthur's remains be translated honorably. Superficially, there are good reasons for accepting that King Henry was the orchestrator of the discovery. Such a find was beneficial to Henry II ideologically speaking. The discovery of the bones on English soil encouraged the perception of Arthur as an English king whose royal legacy – potently encapsulated in his physical remains – were in the capable hands of the House of Plantagenet.[55] Just as it

---

[52] Gerald of Wales, *Speculum Ecclesiæ* 2.9, p. 50.
[53] Gerald of Wales, *Speculum Ecclesiæ* 2.9, p. 49.
[54] Gerald of Wales, *Speculum Ecclesiæ* 2.9, p. 49.
[55] See Carley, 'Arthur in English History', 48; Rouse and Rushton, 'Arthurian Geography', 228.

has been argued by scholars that the English (including Henry II) perceived the Breton Hope as a threat, so too has it been argued that the discovery of Arthur's remains was Henry II's response to this supposed threat.[56]

We have, however, valid cause to question whether the aged king was the driving force behind this *coup de grâce* against the Breton Hope. In the final two decades of his reign, Henry II did not have a pressing need – at least in terms of Anglo-Welsh relations – to demonstrate that Arthur was dead and buried. By 1172 Henry had arrived at a peace settlement with the native princes of Wales. They, including Prince Rhys ap Gruffydd of Deheubarth (r. 1155–97), accepted Henry as overlord of Wales. Emblematic of the settlement, Henry conferred the office of justiciar upon Rhys. By the settlement of 1171–2, King Henry's overlordship was confirmed. The English king even received military assistance from the Welsh in putting down the rebellion of 1173. The Welsh princes, in turn, received assurances from Henry that he would not allow his Anglo-Norman Marcher lords to encroach upon their lands. This peace proved enduring. As Davies has noted, '[t]he settlement of 1171–2 marks the end of an era. No English king would again invade Wales for almost forty years.'[57] The discovery of Arthur's remains would have been of greater utility to Henry when tensions with Wales were at their height, namely in the aftermath of Henry's lackluster expedition of 1165, when he failed to overcome the allied forces of Wales' princes. The Anglo-Welsh détente that characterized the later years of Henry II's reign casts doubt on the necessity of disproving the Breton Hope.

Gerald, however, declares that King Henry II had explained everything to the monks of Glastonbury just as he had heard it from a Welsh singer of ancient history.[58] In *De principis instructione*, Gerald does not provide a timetable for the three-part process of suggestion, discovery, and translation of Arthur's remains. Instead, he rather unhelpfully remarks that the remains of Arthur were found 'in nostris diebus'.[59] Timing matters greatly in this particular case because Henry II died on 6 July 1189 – well before the conventional dating of the discovery, 1191. If demonstrating that King Arthur was dead and buried had been crucially important to Henry, why did he not put greater pressure on the monks to dig in the place that he indicated? The delay on the part of the monks to fulfill the king's wishes is, to say the least, curious.

In *Speculum ecclesie*, Gerald is more precise about when the discovery

---

[56] See Cassard, 'Arthur est vivant!', 143.
[57] Davies, *Age of Conquest: Wales*, 54.
[58] Gerald of Wales, *De principis instructione*, 1.20, p. 128.
[59] Gerald of Wales, *De principis instructione*, 1.20, p. 126.

occurred. He claims that King Henry told the abbot where to dig 'pluries, sicut ex gestis Britonum et eorum cantoribus historiis rex audierat' (many times, just as the king had heard it from the deeds of the Britons and in the histories [sung] by their bards)[60] and then adds that

> [d]ictus autem abbas corpore reperto, monitus quoque dicti regis Henrici marmoreum ei sepulchrum fieri fecit egregium, tanquam patrono loci illius præcipuo, qui scilicet ecclesiam illam præ cæteris regni cunctis plus dilexerat, terrisque largis et amplis locupletaverat.[61]

> (The aforesaid abbot, with the body having been discovered, upon the advice of the aforesaid King Henry, had an outstanding sepulchre made for him [Arthur], just as for an outstanding patron of that place, who had loved specifically that church before all the rest in the realm and enriched it with large and ample lands.)

Gerald's remarks suggest that Henry envisioned the translation of Arthur's remains prior to their discovery. Yet the *dictus abbas* mentioned above was, according to Gerald, Henry of Sully,[62] and Gerald's narrative presents a glaring chronological inconsistency. The appointment of Abbot Henry of Sully (15 September 1189) occurred two months after Henry II's death (6 July 1189), but the abbacy of Glastonbury had been vacant since the death of Robert of Winchester in 1180. It is, however, possible that King Henry had made the suggestion to Henry of Sully before he became abbot of Glastonbury. Gerald is vague about when and where this exchange occurred, but he implied that it happened while Henry of Sully was abbot of Glastonbury.[63] Perhaps Gerald was deliberately vague about details he knew were inaccurate. Gerald was, admittedly, 'very vague in matters of dating, even in giving dates of events in his own career'.[64]

---

[60] Gerald of Wales, *Speculum Ecclesiæ*, 2.9, p. 49.

[61] Gerald of Wales, *Speculum Ecclesiæ*, 2.10, p. 51.

[62] Gerald of Wales, *Speculum Ecclesiæ*, 2.8, p. 47.

[63] This apparent discrepancy in Gerald's *Speculum Ecclesie* did not go unnoticed by medieval authors. John of Glastonbury called attention to this issue in his fourteenth-century chronicle but did not wrestle with it. See *Chronicle of Glastonbury Abbey: An Edition, Translation and Study of John of Glastonbury's Cronica sive Antiquitates*, ed. James Carley, trans. David Townsend (Woodbridge, UK: Boydell, 1985), 180–1. Another fourteenth-century chronicler, Ranulf Higden (d. 1364), dated the discovery to 1177. See Ranulf Higden, *Polychronicon Ranulphi Higden, Monachi Cestrensis*, vol. 8, ed. Joseph Rawson Lumby. RS 41/8 (London: Longman, 1882), 60. By Higden's dating, Henry II would have made his recommendation to Robert of Winchester, who was abbot from 1173 to 1180.

[64] Scott, *Expugnatio Hibernica*, xix. Given that Gerald is thought to have composed the *Speculum Ecclesie* near the end of his life, over two decades after the Glastonbury discovery, his memory might have been failing him. See Nitze, 'Exhumation of King Arthur', 358.

It is conceivable that Henry II suggested the dig to the monks and that the monks were slow to respond.[65] If so, we can extrapolate that finding Arthur's bones was not a pressing concern for Henry II. Yet another possibility is that Henry's involvement was a contrivance of the monks of Glastonbury geared towards enhancing the credibility of the find, putting the royal seal of approval on the discovery as it were.[66] In order to evaluate this possibility, we need to review the institutional history of Glastonbury Abbey around the time of the discovery, in particular the abbey's relationship with the English crown.

When Abbot Robert of Winchester died in 1180, Henry II assumed nominal control of Glastonbury Abbey and postponed the anticipated abbatial election indefinitely. This course of action was in Henry's interest, for, when the abbey was without an abbot, the king was entitled to its revenues. Henry II was in the habit of collecting ecclesiastical revenues in this fashion.[67] But on St. Urban's Day (25 May) 1184 his hold over Glastonbury ceased to be lucrative. A terrible fire decimated nearly all of the monastery's great buildings, including its main church as well as the old wooden church, *Vetusta Ecclesia*, which was widely held to have been the oldest Christian house of worship in Britain.[68] The magnitude of Henry's contribution to the Glastonbury reconstruction efforts is unclear. An institutional history of Glastonbury covering the years 1126–1291, the *Libellus de rebus gestis Glastoniensibus*, attributed to Adam of Damerham, states that Henry II had compassion for the monks of Glastonbury on account of their calamity; he made his chamberlain, Ralph FitzStephen, the overseer of the repairs, and FitzStephen was to spend the 'totum residuum de redditibus' (the entire remainder of the rents) on the repair and reconstruction of the abbey's old church and other buildings.[69] Sir

---

[65] See Gransden, 'Glastonbury Traditions and Legends', 49.

[66] Charles T. Wood favored this interpretation. See his 'Guenevere at Glastonbury: A Problem in Translation(s)', in *Glastonbury Abbey and the Arthurian Tradition*, ed. James P. Carley (Cambridge, UK: D. S. Brewer, 2001), 88–9.

[67] James P. Carley, *Glastonbury Abbey: The Holy House at the Head of the Moors Adventurous* (Woodbridge, UK: Boydell, 1988), 22. Gerald of Wales, in his *Expugnatio Hibernica*, reproached Henry II for this very practice. See his *Expugnatio Hibernica* 1.46, pp. 130–1.

[68] Carley, *Glastonbury Abbey*, 22.

[69] Adam of Damerham, *Libellus de rebus gestis Glastoniensibus*, ed. Thomas Hearne. 2 vols. (Oxford: E Theatro Sheldoniano, 1727), II, 334; John of Glastonbury, *Cronica* 94, 174–5. The meaning of this statement is unclear. Carley understands Adam to mean that Henry gave Ralph FitzStephen 'carte blanche to spend the full abbatial revenues on rebuilding the church' (*Glastonbury Abbey*, 22). Gransden holds that 'after the fire Henry II allowed what revenues remained after the monks had been provided with their necessities, to contribute to the rebuilding rather than go to the royal exchequer' ('Glastonbury Traditions and Legends', 48).

William Henry St. John Hope, upon inspection of 'all the Pipe Rolls of the reign of Henry II', was 'able to say positively that from 1184 onward they do not contain anything to show that the Abbey of Glastonbury received any help from the Royal Exchequer'.[70] Nonetheless, Ralph FitzStephen's sound management enabled great and rapid progress to be made in the Glastonbury rebuilding project.[71]

The situation changed when Richard I succeeded Henry II as king of England (6 July 1189). The *Libellus* states that Richard turned his attention to matters of war, to the great detriment of Glastonbury and its building work; the new king also installed his kinsman, Henry of Sully, 'virum de regia stirpe progenitum' (a man sprung from the royal stock), as abbot.[72] The author of the *Libellus* condemned this royal appointee as a greedy and mercenary figure whose primary concern was his own advancement.[73] The fourteenth-century chronicler John of Glastonbury gives insight into the climate at the abbey under Henry de Sully's rule. He writes that Abbot Henry did not devote himself to the rebuilding of the abbey but instead enfeoffed his men on the church's land and did much that upset the monks. The monks, out of concern for the continuance of the construction, took matters into their own hands and dispatched some of their confreres to fundraise for them with the aid of relics and indulgences of various bishops.[74] In the mid 1180s, as the foundations were being laid for the new church structures, the monks of Glastonbury 'rediscovered' the remains of St. Dunstan (d. 988).[75] They also put forth a 'charter of St. Patrick' that tells of how Patrick came to Glastonbury, brought together twelve hermits of the district into communal life, and became Glastonbury's first abbot.[76] The

---

[70] W. H. St. John Hope, 'Notes on the Abbey Church of Glastonbury', *Archaeological Journal* 61, n. 1 (1904): 187.

[71] Adam of Damerham, *Libellus*, II, 335; John of Glastonbury, *Cronica* 96, 178–9.

[72] See Adam of Damerham, *Libellus*, II, 341; John of Glastonbury, *Cronica* 98, 180–1. For further confirmation see *Gesta regis Henrici Secundi Benedicti abbatis / The Chronicle of the Reigns of Henry II and Richard I, A.D. 1169–92 Known Commonly under the Name of Benedict of Peterborough*, ed. William Stubbs, 2 vols. RS 49 (London: Longmans, Green, Reader, and Dyer, 1867), II, 85; Gervase of Canterbury, *Chronicle of the Reigns of Stephen, Henry II, and Richard I*, in *The Historical Works of Gervase of Canterbury*, vol. 1, ed. William Stubbs. RS 73/1 (London: Longman, 1879), 458.

[73] Adam of Damerham, *Libellus*, II, 341. John of Glastonbury, *Cronica* 99, 182–5.

[74] John of Glastonbury, *Cronica* 99, 184–5.

[75] See William of Malmesbury, *De Antiquitate Glastonie Ecclesie* 24–5, pp. 74–9.

[76] St Patrick's charter, which survives as an interpolation to William of Malmesbury's *De Antiquitate Glastonie Ecclesie*, tells of how Patrick hewed his way through dense woods to reach an ancient oratory atop Glastonbury Tor. Patrick reportedly granted an indulgence to all pious Christians who would follow in his footsteps. See William of Malmesbury, *De Antiquitate Glastonie Ecclesie* 9, pp. 55–9. Scott has suggested that the stories about St. Patrick were 'probably put together about 1220' (27).

purpose of these 'pious frauds' was to increase the prestige of Glastonbury, to encourage pilgrimage and bequests, and to give the monastic community leverage in its ongoing conflict with the bishop of Bath. The bones of Arthur were a secular attraction but analogous to the monks' pious frauds.

Financial and political matters became even worse for Glastonbury when King Richard elevated Henry of Sully to the see of Worcester on 4 December 1193 and permitted Savaric FitzGeldewin, bishop of Bath (1192–1205), to replace Henry as abbot. Bishop Savaric was intent on making Glastonbury fall under his ecclesiastical jurisdiction, which would enable him to draw upon the abbey's wealth. Savaric, it should be noted, had gone on crusade with Richard I and was Emperor Heinrich VI's cousin. While Richard was a prisoner of Heinrich VI (23 March 1193–4 February 1194), Savaric acted as a negotiator on the English king's behalf. In return for Savaric's services, Richard wrote to Pope Celestine renouncing his royal patronage of Glastonbury and requesting the creation of a dual episcopal see of Bath and Glastonbury that would oversee the affairs of the abbey.[77] Bishop Savaric sought to reduce the monks' sumptuary allowances and was therefore extremely unpopular at Glastonbury.

These desperate times moved the monks of Glastonbury to take desperate measures, and there is record of at least one instance in which they misrepresented Henry II's generosity to their community. The *Libellus* and John's *Cronica* preserve a 'Forma magni priuilegii Henrici regis secundi' in which Henry reportedly declared that he would lay a foundation for the church of Glastonbury and repair it more magnificently as a work to be finished by himself or his heirs. According to this charter, Henry also ordered a diligent search for the charters and privileges of his predecessors, including *inclitus Arthurus*, concerning Glastonbury. In addition to being a statement of commitment to the rebuilding of Glastonbury abbey by Henry II on his own behalf and that of his heirs, this undated document guarantees a great many rights and privileges to the religious community at Glastonbury, not the least of which is the sought-after declaration that the abbey was and should remain completely free of the jurisdiction of the bishop of Bath.[78]

---

[77] See Robin Sutherland-Harris, 'Authority, Text, and Genre in Accounts of Diocesan Struggle: The Bishops of Bath and Glastonbury and the Uses of Cartulary Evidence', in *Authorities in the Middle Ages: Influence, Legitimacy, and Power in Medieval Society*, ed. Sini Kangas, Mia Korpiola, and Tuija Ainonen (Berlin: Walter de Gruyter, 2013), 109, 109, n. 4.

[78] Adam of Damerham, *Libellus*, II, 337–40; John of Glastonbury, *Cronica* 95, pp. 175–7. Also see Charles T. Wood, 'Fraud and its Consequences: Savaric of Bath and the Reform of Glastonbury', in *The Archaeology and History of Glastonbury Abbey: Essays in Honour of the Ninetieth Birthday of C. A. Ralegh Radford*, ed. Lesley Abrams and James P. Carley (Woodbridge, UK: Boydell, 1991), 273–83.

As R. W. Eyton has demonstrated, however, the document is a forgery because the testators were not together on the day and place listed.[79] The actual date of composition of this forged charter is unclear. Its content, as stated above, is preserved in the thirteenth-century Glastonbury *Libellus* and in John of Glastonbury's fourteenth-century *Cronica*. The earliest extant manuscript of the *Libellus* is Cambridge, Trinity College, MS R.5.33, fols. 21–73v (thirteenth century). According to Gransden, the prologue and narrative up to 1230 of the Trinity College manuscript was written in 'a hand datable to c. 1247'.[80] Thus the charter was forged prior to 1247. It surely was drafted after the death of Henry II, and it is logical to assume that the appointment of Savaric as abbot in 1193 was its impetus. Savaric died in 1205, but conflict with the see of Bath did not entirely disappear until Jocelin of Wells (r. 1206–42), Savaric's successor as bishop of Bath, formally renounced his claim to Glastonbury Abbey in 1219.[81] The forgery would have been of the greatest utility between 1193 and 1219, and hence this is the most probable window for its composition.

Within this time frame are a few specific occasions for which the document may have been drafted. Prior Harold of Glastonbury, along with some of his fellow monks, went to the royal court at Winchester at Easter (2 April) 1195 in hopes that King Richard would hear their plea for independence from the see of Bath. The following year, two monks journeyed to Normandy to petition the king again on behalf of the convent of Glastonbury.[82] The Glastonbury-based reports of Henry's generosity to the abbey (encapsulated in the forged privilege) might have been designed to win royal support. If all of the kings of 'England' from Arthur through to Henry II had supported Glastonbury, was not Richard I also under a moral obligation to aid the community in its time of need?[83]

In 1198, King Richard reversed his earlier decision and threw his support behind the monks of Glastonbury. He wrote to the Roman Curia stating that only under duress had he given his assent to Bishop

---

[79] See R. W. Eyton, *Court, Household, and Itinerary of King Henry II Instancing also the Chief Agents and Adversaries of the King in his Government, Diplomacy and Strategy* (London: Taylor, 1878), 262, n. 3. Also see St. John Hope, 'Notes on the Abbey Church of Glastonbury', 186–7.

[80] Antonia Gransden, 'Damerham, Adam of (d. in or after 1291?)', *Oxford Dictionary of National Biography*, Oxford University Press, 2004; online edn., Sept. 2013 (http://www.oxforddnb.com/view/article/93, accessed 31 January 2015).

[81] See Sethina Watson, 'The Bishop and his Cathedral Cities', in *Jocelin of Wells: Bishop, Builder, Courtier*, ed. Robert Dunning (Woodbridge, UK: Boydell, 2010), 79–80.

[82] John of Glastonbury, *Cronica* 101, pp. 186–7; Adam of Damerham, *Libellus*, II, 359–60.

[83] Julia Crick has interpreted the discovery in this way. See her 'The British Past and the Welsh Future: Gerald of Wales, Geoffrey of Monmouth and Arthur of Britain', *Celtica* 23 (1999): 72.

Savaric and that he had since annulled the bishop of Bath's annexation of Glastonbury. Richard had the monks of Glastonbury choose a new abbot, and he confirmed William Le Pie for the position. Perhaps the forgery was drafted with the Curia as its intended audience. But Richard's early death and an adverse decision by Pope Innocent III in the summer of 1200 prevented abbot-elect William Le Pie from receiving papal confirmation.[84] After Savaric's death in 1205 the monks of Glastonbury again appealed to Pope Innocent III seeking the restoration of Glastonbury's former autonomy.[85] It is possible that the charter was forged in the lead-up to this plea, but given the emphasis placed on England's kings in the document, the charter was more probably intended for either Richard I or John.

Interestingly, Gerald begins his entry on Arthur in *De principis instructione liber* 1.19 by emphasizing Arthur's Marian devotion and generosity to Glastonbury as reasons why he was an exemplar of good Christian kingship worthy of imitation. He remarks: 'Præ cunctis enim ecclesiis regni sui sanctæ Dei genitricis Mariæ Glastoniensem ecclesiam plus dilexit et præ cæteris longe majori devotione promovit.' (Indeed, before all the other churches of his realm, he loved the Glastonbury Church of Mary the holy mother of God more and, before all the rest by far, he advanced it with greater devotion.)[86] Did the Glastonbury monks show Gerald the forged charter of Henry II? It is possible, but Caradoc, in his *Vita Gildæ*, states that Arthur was a generous donor to the Glastonbury community.[87] *De Antiquitate Glastonie Ecclesie* also details Arthur's grants of land to Glastonbury.[88] That being said, nowhere in the *Vita Gildæ* or in *De Antiquitate Glastonie Ecclesie* is Arthur's patronage of the Glastonbury Church of Mary (the Lady Chapel) rationalized as an expression of Arthur's well-known special devotion to the Virgin Mary. This linkage may well be another example of Gerald's ingenuity. Not only does Gerald align the discovery of Arthur's remains with pre-existing tradition, he is able to explain Arthur's generosity and devotion to Glastonbury in the same fashion.

To sum up, the account of the discovery of Arthur's remains contained in the *Chronicon Anglicanum* appears to be the earlier narrative. Gerald visited Glastonbury Abbey after hearing of the discovery – most likely as fieldwork for his planned *Topographia Britannica* – and the monks of Glastonbury likely informed Gerald that Henry II had been involved in the discovery.

---

[84] Also see Sutherland-Harris, 'Authority', 110.

[85] See John of Glastonbury, *Cronica* 107, pp. 198–9.

[86] Gerald of Wales, *De principis instructione liber* 1.20, p. 126.

[87] Caradoc of Llangarfan, *Vita Gildæ*, 92.

[88] See William of Malmesbury, *De Antiquitate Glastonie Ecclesie* 34, pp. 86–9 and 69, pp. 140–1.

Rival traditions concerning Arthur from Sicily and Wales

When it came to establishing the credibility of the discovery of Arthur's remains, the critical question was not Henry II's involvement, but rather whether Glastonbury had once been known as Avalon. Otherwise, as Gransden has observed, the identification of the bones as those of Arthur and Guinevere hinged on the authenticity of the inscription found on the leaden cross.[89] The idea that Glastonbury was Avalon found expression in English chronicles. One of the earliest known examples of this is the *Gesta regum* (extending from Brutus to the year 1210) of the Benedictine monk and chronicler Gervase of Canterbury (d. c.1210), which succinctly states that Arthur, having been wounded, died and was buried at Glastonbury.[90] Statements of this sort did not, however, put Arthur's fate to rest. Other ideas about Arthur's destiny were circulating at roughly the same time as the Glastonbury excavation.

From Sicily came an alternative tradition regarding Arthur's fate that seems to have been contemporary with the Glastonbury discovery. Gervase of Tilbury (c. 1152–c. 1222) states in his *Otia imperialia* (1214) that King Arthur was sighted in a remote area of Mount Etna (also known as Mongibello) during his lifetime.[91] The story of the Arthur-sighting goes as follows: a groom entrusted with the care of the bishop of Catania's palfrey lost his charge, which galloped off into the dark recesses of Mount Etna. The groom chased after the horse along a narrow path and advanced into a wide and beautiful plain full of delights of every kind. In this *locus amoenus*, comparable to the Fortunate Island described in Geoffrey's *Vita Merlini*, the groom arrived at a marvelously constructed palace, and there he found Arthur.[92] Arthur asked the groom the purpose of his visit and, upon learning of his visitor's troubles, the king returned the palfrey to

---

[89] Gransden, 'Glastonbury Traditions and Legends', 50.

[90] Gervase of Canterbury, *The Gesta Regum with its Continuation*, in *The Historical Works of Gervase of Canterbury*, vol. 2, ed. William Stubbs, 3–324. RS 73/2 (London: Longmans, 1880), 19.

[91] Gervase of Tilbury, *Otia Imperialia* 2.12, ed. and trans. S. E. Banks and J. W. Binns (Oxford: Clarendon Press, 2002), 334–5. Gervase had been in the service of Henry II and had begun to write what was to become the *Otia imperialia* for Henry II's son, Young King Henry (1155–83). After Young Henry's untimely death in 1183, Gervase entered into the service of Henry II's son-in-law, William II, king of Sicily (r. 1166–89). Gervase was at Salerno in June 1189 and remained in Italy until William's death (16 November 1189) at which time Tancred of Lecce (d. 20 February 1194), an illegitimate cousin of William II, usurped the throne and placed under house arrest William's widow Joan, the daughter of Henry II. It is possible that Gervase learned of the Arthur-sighting at Mount Etna while in the king of Sicily's employ. See H. G. Richardson, 'Gervase of Tilbury', *History* 46, n. 157 (1961): 107. Also see Roger Sherman Loomis, 'King Arthur and the Antipodes', *Modern Philology* 38, n. 3 (1941): 298.

[92] Gervase of Tilbury, *Otia Imperialia* 2.12, pp. 336–7.

him and explained the reason for his own extended stay there. Arthur said that he remained afflicted by 'antiquis in bello cum Modredo nepote suo et Cilderico duce Saxonum pridem commisso uulneribus quotannis recrudescentibus' (old wounds received when he had joined battle long ago with his nephew Mordred and Cheldric, duke of the Saxons; these wounds broke open afresh every year).[93] Gervase concludes his entry by reporting that he heard from the locals of Catania that Arthur sent marvelous gifts to their bishop.

As is the case in Étienne of Rouen's *Draco Normannicus*, Arthur in the *Otia imperialia* inhabits a liminal space between the living and the dead. The fires of Etna, the site of Arthur's resort, were popularly understood to be an entrance to the otherworld, which is sometimes represented as a pagan paradise but negatively regarded by Christians as the pits of hell.[94] Elsewhere in the *Otia Imperialia*, Gervase provides a brief account of Arthur's *res gesta* and journey to Avalon that is largely consistent with the Galfridian narrative. The one notable divergence is Gervase's claim that Arthur's wounds would break open anew each year and therefore required regular treatments by Morgan.[95] Gervase wove together what he learned (or invented) about the Sicilian Arthurian tradition into the Avalon convalescence as described in Geoffrey's *Historia* and *Vita Merlini*. The added element of Arthur's debilitating wound makes the prospect of his heroic return from Avalon seem all the more implausible.

The *Otia Imperialia* is the earliest known attestation of Arthur at Etna. There are, however, indications of interest in the 'materia brettone' in southern Italy from the middle of the eleventh century.[96] What has been regarded as the strongest evidence of Arthurian interest in southern Italy appears on a pavement mosaic in the central nave of the cathedral of Otranto (c. 1163–5).[97] There we find a depiction of a figure labeled 'REX

[93] Gervase of Tilbury, *Otia Imperialia* 2.12, pp. 336–7.
[94] See Gervase of Tilbury, *Otia Imperialia* 2.12, p. 336 n. 41 and Loomis, 'King Arthur and the Antipodes', 299 n. 41. Also see Henri Bresc, 'Excalibur en Sicile', *Medievalia* 7 (1987): 11.
[95] Gervase of Tilbury, *Otia Imperialia* 2.17, pp. 428–9.
[96] Edmund Garratt Gardner, *Arthurian Legend in Italian Literature* (London: J. M. Dent & Sons, 1930), 11.
[97] Inscriptions on the pavement state that Archbishop Ionathas of Otranto commissioned sections of the mosaic in the eleventh indiction (between January and August) 1163 and the fourteenth indiction (between September and December) 1165 respectively and that the work was accomplished through the hand of 'Presbyter Pantaleon'. See Walter Haug, *Das Mosaik von Otranto: Darstellung, Deutung und Bilddokumentation* (Wiesbaden: Reichert, 1977), 11–12. For a fuller description and analysis of the mosaic, see Manuel Castiñeiras, 'D'Alexandre à Arthur: L'imaginaire normand dans la mosaïque d'Otrante', *Cahiers de Saint-Michel de Cuxo* 37 (2006): 135.

ARTVRVS' astride a horned beast. Arturus is holding a club and doing battle with a four-legged, spotted cat-like creature generally thought to be the demon cat Chapalu. The mosaic is not in pristine condition; it has suffered the ravages of earthquakes and interventionist restoration work in the nineteenth century. Modifications to the figure of Arthur have been made, but this is still generally thought to have been part of the original composition.[98] If we take it for granted that the Arthurian scene is original, his appearance in the mosaic serves to document awareness of the Matter of Britain, and perhaps familiarity with the story of Arthur's combat with Chapalu. Given that Sicily was a Norman realm, knowledge of Arthur there is not surprising.

Another faint hint of the existence of the idea that Arthur is forever resting on an island in the Mediterranean Sea is contained in the 'vulgate version' of the *Bataille Loquifer*, an Old French epic of the Guillaume d'Orange Cycle, which appears to be of Sicilian provenance.[99] In this epic, three fays abduct the protagonist, Renoart au Tinel, as he is sleeping by the seashore and transport him to a remote place which they refer to as 'Avalon, noste cité vaillant'.[100] Much like the other Avalons that we have encountered, the Avalon of the *Bataille Loquifer* is a place of great abundance. There, Renoart finds Arthur in the chief hall of his castle. The king's companions include Gawain, Yvain, and Perceval of the Round Table, Roland, and an assortment of fairy folk. Arthur is a less courteous host in the *Bataille Loquifer* than in other narratives, for he forces Renoart to do battle with the monstrous Chapalu.[101] After allowing the cursed beast to drink the blood of his heel, thereby enabling the creature to revert to its true human form, a perturbed Renoart demands answers from this 'roi Artus apelé' (king called 'Arthur').[102] Arthur agrees to explain himself and begins by confirming that he is indeed the much-talked-about Arthur. The king then informs Renoart that Avalon is home to fairies and those who have passed away from the world of the living.[103] There is, however, no explicit identification of Avalon as Mount Etna in this text. Moreover, the date of composition of the *Bataille*

---

[98] In the early nineteenth century (prior to 1814), A. Millen made a set of sketches of the Modena pavement mosaic, which are now housed in the Cabinet des Estampes of the Bibliothèque National, Paris. Millen's sketch reveals that part of Arthur's forehead, his entire right arm and a large part of his ride's neck were lost.

[99] For a modern edition of this text, see *La Bataille Loquifer*, ed. Monica Barnett (Oxford: Blackwell, 1975).

[100] *La Bataille Loquifer*, 129, line 3634.

[101] *La Bataille Loquifer*, 131–3, lines 3735–90.

[102] *La Bataille Loquifer*, 136, lines 3896–7.

[103] *La Bataille Loquifer*, 136, lines 3898–908.

Loquifer is uncertain and debated.[104] None of the surviving manuscripts predates the thirteenth century.[105] Therefore we cannot safely treat the text as an earlier analogue to Gervase's Arthurian entry.

In contrast to the Glastonbury discovery of Arthur's remains, the Mount Etna narrative does not appear to have served any immediate political purposes. Later in this chapter we will consider in detail Richard I's stay in Sicily (1190–1), during which time Richard bestowed the supposed sword of King Arthur on William II's successor, Tancred. This gift, which was presented at Catania, may have increased interest in the figure of Arthur in Sicily, which possibly led, in turn, to the development of the tradition that Arthur was convalescing at Mount Etna. The arrival of the Plantagenet princess Joan in Sicily in 1177 could also account for this development. While we have no attestations of Arthur at Mount Etna prior to Gervase's *Otia Imperialia*, the idea resurfaces in the thirteenth century.[106] Was the idea of Arthur at Etna an extremely recent development when Gervase was writing – possibly a consequence of Richard I's visit? In the absence of more conclusive evidence this question must remained unresolved.

Another seemingly timely account of Arthur's fate, one that seems to have posed a graver challenge to the Glastonbury narrative, is the *Vera historia de morte Arthuri*, which survives in at least one instance as an interpolation in the First Variant Version of Geoffrey's *Historia* and elsewhere as a distinct text that circulated with the vulgate version of the *Historia regum Britannie*.[107] The *Vera historia* does not include Glastonbury at all in its account of where and how King Arthur met his end but allocates a central role to the kingdom of Gwynedd in northwest Wales, whose royal house of Aberffraw boasted such eminent native princes of Wales as Gruffydd ap Cynan (r. 1081–1137), Owain ap Gruffydd (r. 1137–70) and

---

[104] Some scholars have taken this to mean that the epic was first written anywhere from 1120 to 1150, which roughly corresponds to the reign of William I of Sicily (1154–66). Other scholars believe that it was written during the reign of William II of Sicily (1166–89). See *Bataille Loquifer*, 29–30.

[105] See *Bataille Loquifer*, 2–5.

[106] See Caesarius of Heisterbach, *Dialogus miraculorum* (c. 1221), vol. 5, ed. Horst Schneider (Turnhout: Brepols, 2009), 2204–5; 'Detto del Gatto Lupesco', in *Poeti del Duecento*, vol. 2, ed. Gianfranco Contini (Milan: Riccardo Ricciardi, 1960), 288–9, lines 25–34; *Esclarmonde*, ed. Max Schweigel, in *Esclarmonde, Clarisse et Florent, Yde et Olive, drei Fortsetzungen der Chanson von Huon de Bordeaux, nach der einzigen turiner Handschrift zum erstenmal veröffenlicht*, ed. Max Schweigel (Marburg: N. G. Elwertische Verlagsbuchhandlung, 1889), 126, lines 3457–72; *Floriant et Florete* (after 1268), ed. and trans. Annie Combes and Richard Trachsler (Paris: Honoré Champion, 2003), 496, lines 8242–50.

[107] See *Vera historia de morte Arthuri*, ed. and trans. Michael Lapidge, in *Glastonbury Abbey and the Arthurian Tradition*, ed. James P. Carley (Cambridge, UK: D. S. Brewer, 2001), 115–41.

Llywelyn ('the Great') ap Iorwerth (r. 1195–1240). The date of the text is uncertain. Given that the narrative directly responds to *Historia regum Britannie*, it postdates Geoffrey's work. The earliest surviving manuscript of the *Vera historia* (London, Gray's Inn 7, fols. 60r–61r) dates from the dawn of the fourteenth century; thus 1138–1300 is the window of dating for the *Vera historia*. The short text could have been written before or after the production of Arthur's remains at Glastonbury. Yet Gerald of Wales makes no direct mention of the *Vera historia* in any of his surviving writings. This offers a faint indication that it postdates Gerald (d. c. 1224).

The *Vera historia*, whenever it was composed, cannot be harmonized with the Glastonbury narratives of Arthur's end. According to it, Arthur did not meet his end as a consequence of his fateful battle with Mordred; rather, the badly injured king received a fatal wound shortly thereafter from a poisoned spear made of elm, the men of Gwynedd's weapon of choice.[108] Even then, the king did not die immediately. He had himself taken to *Venedocia* (Gwynedd), here identified as home to the Isle of Avalon, for its beauty and salubrious effects.[109] Once again, Avalon is depicted as a *locus amoenus*. Regardless of whether it was written before or after the Glastonbury discovery of Arthur, the *Vera historia* constituted a direct challenge to Gerald's association of Glastonbury with Avalon. Barring further evidence that Avalon was Glastonbury, it would seem that Gerald's story rested on the leaden cross.

The *Vera historia* then relates that while at Avalon (Gwynedd), Arthur took a turn for the worse and, knowing that death was near, confessed his sins to the archbishop of London and two additional bishops, namely Urien of Bangor and Urbegen of Glamorgan. The archbishop of Canterbury is conspicuously absent from this list of confessors, and the author does not explain the absence. Instead, the narrator mentions in an aside that the patron saint of Wales, David, archbishop of Menevia, would have been at Arthur's side had he not been seriously ill at the time.[110] At his terminal moment, Arthur, with hands outstretched to heaven, 'in

---

[108] See Gerald of Wales, *Itinerarium Kambriæ* 2.5, p. 123. Richard Barber makes this connection in 'The *Vera historia de morte Arthuri* and its place in Arthurian Tradition', in *Glastonbury Abbey and the Arthurian Tradition*, ed. James P. Carley (Cambridge, UK: D. S. Brewer, 2001), 110.

[109] *Vera historia de morte Arthuri*, 2, pp. 136–7.

[110] Michael Lapidge believes that the *Vera historia* was written in the context of one of the Welsh grass-roots movements to make St. David's an archbishopric independent of Canterbury. The first movement occurred during the episcopate of Bernard (r. 1115–48), and Gerald of Wales spearheaded a second movement c. 1200–3. Residual sympathies for Bishop Bernard's initiative in the later twelfth century prior to Gerald's activities cannot be entirely dismissed. See *Vera historia de morte Arthuri*, 124–8.

manus redemptoris suum commendabat spiritum' (commended his spirit into the hands of the Redeemer).[111] The narrator makes it abundantly clear that Arthur was a devout Christian. This Arthur placed his hope for salvation in Christ, not in the *fatorum lege* as Étienne of Rouen had insinuated. The narrator also makes it quite clear that Arthur died, which contradicts the Breton Hope as well as Gervase's account of Arthur's survival at Mount Etna. The *Vera historia* states unambiguously that Arthur's corpse was embalmed, that services were said for the king's immortal soul and that Arthur was set to be buried at a place of his own choosing, a certain small chapel which had been dedicated to his protectress, the Virgin Mary.[112] The author of the *Vera historia* then offers a rationalization for the Breton Hope. He explains that the apertures of the aforesaid chapel were too small to admit the corpse of Arthur, so it was decided that the king would be laid to rest outside, next to one of the chapel's walls. After exequies were said for the soul of the king within the tiny house of God, a torrential storm and an earthquake occurred outside. A mist then enveloped the bier containing Arthur's corpse, which lasted from nine o'clock in the morning until three in the afternoon. This mist reportedly absorbed the brightness of the lightning and blinded all onlookers. When the mist cleared, Arthur's remains were gone. This mysterious occurrence prompted debate and wild speculation as to the king's fate, even the possibililty of his miraculous survival.[113] The narrator,

---

[111] *Vera historia de morte Arthuri* 2, pp. 136–7.
[112] *Vera historia de morte Arthuri* 3, pp. 138–9.
[113] *Vera historia de morte Arthuri* 4, 138–41. In *La Mort le Roi Artu* (c. 1215–20), Arthur, following his final battle, repents for his sins at *la Noire Chapele*. See *La Mort le Roi Artu: roman du xiiie siècle*, ed. Jean Frappier (Geneva: Droz, 1954), 246. Arthur's knight Girflet, as soon as he leaves for a third time to throw Excalibur, sees a great and wondrous downpour near the king. See *The Death of Arthur*, trans. Norris J. Lacy. *Lancelot-Grail: The Old French Arthurian Vulgate and Post-Vulgate in Translation*, ed. Norris J. Lacy, vol. 7 (Cambridge, UK: D. S. Brewer, 2010), 129. This parallels the torrential storm in *Vera historia de morte Arthuri*. Next, in *Mort Artu*, Girflet sees Arthur sailing away with Morgan le Fay and other ladies. Three days later, Girflet returns to *la Noire Chapele* and sees a rich and marvelous tomb with an inscription stating that it contains Arthur's remains (251). The hermit who managed *la Noire Chapele* tells Girflet that some ladies had brought Arthur to the chapel and that he was buried there. We, like Girflet, must rely on the testimony of the hermit and on the inscription. Given that both the emphasis placed on a chapel as Arthur's final resting place and the ambiguity regarding Arthur's final resting place are common to these two texts, it is possible that there is a connection between them. Richard Trachsler believes that the *Vera historia de morte Arthuri* combines the narrative details of the French *Mort Artu* with those of Geoffrey's *Historia*. See Richard Trachsler, *Clôtures du cycle Arthurien: étude et textes* (Geneva: Droz, 1996), 9 n. 14, 133–4. Perhaps it is the *Mort Artu* that mixes and matches elements from Geoffrey's *Historia* and the *Vera historia*.

despite having already stated that Arthur died, uses this miraculous belief to rationalize and justify the belief that Arthur escaped death. The author also cautiously puts forth the idea that the king, far from leaving the building for some remote land of grace, actually became part of the fabric of the chapel dedicated to the Blessed Virgin in Avalon – Gwynedd – the seat of the royal house of Aberffraw. And, most conveniently for the House of Aberffraw, the *Vera historia* did not require the production of Arthur's remains.

Having considered Henry II's place in relation to King Arthur and the great discovery of Arthur's bones at Glastonbury, let us now turn our gaze to the positioning of Henry's offspring in relation to King Arthur prior to the close of the twelfth century.

Arthur of Brittany: Breton Hope or Plantagenet Hope?

Of Henry II's sons, Geoffrey of Brittany (1158–86) was most readily associated with Arthur. This pairing is evident in Gervase of Tilbury's *Otia Imperialia*, where Gervase provides profiles of Henry II's sons for their nephew, Holy Roman Emperor Otto IV (r. 1209–15).[114] Although Gervase extols his earlier patron, Young King Henry, as another Paris and another Hector, Geoffrey alone is flatteringly compared to Arthur:

> Successit proles tercia, comes aut pocius dux Brittonum, Arcturo fabuloso animali uirtute non inferior, strenuus, milicia pollens, liberalitate excelsus, probitate et magnanimitate incomparabilis, exactis paucis in uirtute immensa annis obiit.[115]

> (A third offspring follows, the count, or rather duke, of Brittany, not inferior in physical courage to the legendary Arthur, valiant, mighty in warfare, unsurpassed in generosity, beyond compare in uprightness and magnanimity; but after living for a few years with boundless virtue, he died.)

Geoffrey may have sought such a comparison during his lifetime, but he is not known to have done so. There were, however, multiple grounds for the association, the most immediate being Geoffrey's title as ruler of the Arthurian land of Brittany (r. 1181–6), which, as we have seen, Henry II obtained for him. Geoffrey was also an avid participant in tournaments. Gerald of Wales, who is generally critical of Geoffrey, acknowledges

---

[114] Otto IV was the third son of Henry's II's daughter, Matilda Plantagenet.

[115] Gervase of Tilbury, *Otia Imperialia* 2.21, pp. 488–9. I have modified Banks' and Binns' translation slightly. As the editors note, Gervase does not count in this list Henry II's firstborn son, who died as an infant.

that the duke was a 'miles egregius et eloquens, tam Ulixis heres quam Achillis' (an excellent and eloquent knight, as much an heir to Ulysses as to Achilles).[116] The Yorkshire cleric and chronicler Roger of Howden (d. 1201/2), who had served at the court of Henry II between 1174 and 1189, states that Geoffrey set out to rival his brothers Young King Henry and Richard of Aquitaine in knightly feats of arms as soon as Henry II knighted him at Woodstock in 1178.[117] Additionally, Geoffrey was a prince of cultural attainment. He was a patron of Occitan and Old French poets and may have produced a few compositions of his own.[118] Taking into account Geoffrey's ducal title, reputed athleticism, and courtliness, one can readily see why he prompted comparison to Arthur.

But contrary to Gervase's remarks, Geoffrey was not widely esteemed for *probitas*. Geoffrey engaged in political intrigue and shifted allegiances, although he was arguably no more duplicitous than his brothers.[119] Gerald of Wales characterizes Geoffrey as an ungrateful son to Henry, a malign force, an unctuous manipulator, and a hypocrite.[120] Roger of Howden reviles Geoffrey as a son of iniquity for the part he played in the 1183 rebellion against his father.[121] Yet, as Judith Everard has noted, it is difficult to assess Geoffrey's character and motivations. We do not have any Breton chronicles from the second half of the twelfth century, and, for English chroniclers, Geoffrey was a secondary figure only relevant insofar as he advanced or impeded the interests of Henry II, Richard I, or John. Because Geoffrey frequently found himself at odds with his father and brothers in his bid to carve out his own base of power in Brittany, he does not have a positive legacy in English historiography.[122] This bias, as we shall see, also came to apply to his son Arthur.

In 1186, Geoffrey had an extended stay at the French royal court where he plotted with Philippe II against King Henry and Richard. The Augustinian

---

[116] Gerald of Wales, *Expugnatio Hibernica* 2.23, pp. 196–7; Gerald of Wales, *De principis instructione* 2.8, p. 172; Everard, *Brittany and the Angevins*, 125.

[117] Roger of Howden, *Chronica*, II, 166.

[118] Everard, *Brittany and the Angevins*, 125.

[119] Geoffrey sided with his brothers Young Henry and Richard against their father in the Great Rebellion of 1173–4. A decade later he allied with his younger brother John against Richard (June 1184) and repeatedly colluded with Philippe II of France, to whom he did homage for the duchy of Brittany in 1175. Philippe II was, of course, Henry II's chief royal adversary.

[120] Gerald of Wales, *De principis instructione* 2.11, p. 178.

[121] Roger of Howden, *Chronica*, II, 277. Everard contends that Geoffrey's chief drive was to secure the lands and honors that he had been promised by his father, Henry II, namely the county of Nantes, the duchy of Brittany, and the honour of Richmond. Everard does, however, acknowledge that Geoffrey's sights grew larger after the death of Young Henry (*Brittany and the Angevins*, 127, 137).

[122] Everard, *Brittany and the Angevins*, 123.

canon William of Newburgh (c. 1135–c. 1198) suggests that Geoffrey had designs on Anjou.[123] According to Gerald of Wales, it was during this visit that Philippe made Geoffrey seneschal of France,[124] an office that belonged to the count of Anjou in 'Angevin mythology'.[125] More precisely, Geoffrey's *Historia* and a version of the *Liber de compositione castri Ambazie* (c. 1140–7), which is itself partly derived from Geoffrey's *Historia*, hold that Arthur had bestowed the county of Anjou on his seneschal Kay.[126] In his *Philippide* (c. 1214–24), Guillaume le Breton (d. 1225), who served as a chaplain and envoy for Philippe II, also references Arthur's bestowal of Anjou onto Kay and claims that the hamlet of Chinon obtained its name from Kay.[127] A *Chronicon Universale* for the years 1155–1219, written by an anonymous chronicler of Laon, also highlights this piece of legendary history in its description of how King Louis VII had his son, the future Philippe II, crowned at Reims (1 November 1179). In attendance were the three sons of Henry II of England: Young King Henry; Richard, count of Poitou; and Geoffrey, who was about to perform homage for Brittany. The chronicler reported that the three brothers argued amongst themselves about which among them was entitled by ancient custom to the honor of *dapifer*, and

> ait rex iunior Anglorum, sibi deberi racione ducatus Normannie, cuius dux Kaius, qui Camum hedificavit, fuisse non ambigitur. 'Dignitas etiam pincerne michi racione comitatus Andegavie, cuius comes Bedverus pincerna fuit.' Annuunt omnes in gratiam ipsius.[128]

> (the junior king of England said there is no doubt that it was owed to him by reason of the duchy of Normandy, whose duke [was] Kay, who founded Chinon: 'the dignity of cupbearer belongs to me by reason of the county of Anjou whose count was Bedivere the Cupbearer'. All nodded in thanks to him.)

If this reported speech is based in fact, the sons of Henry II and members of the French court were familiar with Galfridian history (possibly through Wace's *Roman de Brut*), brought it up in conversation, and perhaps even

---

[123] William of Newburgh, *Historia rerum Anglicarum* 3.7, p. 235.

[124] Gerald of Wales, *De principis instructione* 2.10, p. 176.

[125] Everard, *Brittany and the Angevins*, 141.

[126] See Geoffrey of Monmouth, *Historia regum Britannie* 155.301–3, pp. 208–9; 'Liber de compositione castri Ambazie', in *Chroniques des comtes d'Anjou et des seigneurs d'Amboise*, ed. Louis Halphen and René Poupardin (Paris: Auguste Picard, 1913), 10.

[127] Guillaume le Breton, *Philippide* 8, in *Oeuvres de Rigord et de Guillaume le Breton: Historiens de Philippe-Auguste*, vol. 2: *Philippide de Guillaume le Breton*, ed. H.-François Delaborde (Paris: Librairie Renouard, 1885), pp. 224–5, lines 381–6.

[128] *Chronicon Universale anonymi Laudunensis von 1154 bis zum Schluss (1219) für akademische Übungen*, ed. Alexander Cartellieri and Wolf Stechele (Leipzig: Dyksche Buchhandlung, 1909), 30–1.

cited it to resolve contemporary disputes. One wonders whether the Young King Henry referenced this Arthurian precedent in jest. Even if the vignette in the *Chronicon Universale* is fictitious, it and the passages quoted from *Liber de compositione castri Ambazie* and Guillaume le Breton's *Philippide* attest to knowledge of Angevin Arthurian mythology in France in the second decade of the thirteenth century. In investing Geoffrey with the office of seneschal, the king of France may have knowingly assumed the role of Arthur and aimed to suggest that history would soon repeat itself: Geoffrey, Philippe's new seneschal, would soon also become the duke of Anjou.

Before the king of France and his seneschal could put their planned invasion of Anjou into effect, Geoffrey died of an undetermined illness in Paris (19 August 1186).[129] The duke's early death moved the celebrated troubadour Bertran de Born (c. 1140–1215) to compose a chivalric eulogy for him, 'A totz dic qe ja mais'. Bertran knew the sons of Henry II personally and had repeatedly tried to exploit their fraternal strife to his own advantage. In the 1180s, Bertran favored Geoffrey, whom he nicknamed 'Rassa', over his more immediate overlord, Richard of Aquitaine.[130] Bertran arguably knew how the duke wished to be memorialized. In the second stanza of his lament, Bertran expresses his desire that Geoffrey join the ranks of the best warriors the world had ever known, including Alexander the Great, Ogier, Raoul de Cambrai, Roland, Oliver, Aton, Estout, Naimes, Oristain, and William of Orange. This list does not include Arthur, but Bertran begins his fifth stanza declaring:

> S'Artus, lo segner de Cardoil,
> Cui Breton atendon e mai,
> Agues poder qe tornes sai,
> Breton i aurian perdut
> E Nostre Segner gazagnat.[131]

---

[129] Reports vary as to the cause of Geoffrey's death. See Everard, *Brittany and the Angevins*, 142–5. Roger of Howden states that Geoffrey died after being trampled by horse hooves *in conflictu militari* (*Chronica*, II, 309). Also see Albricus monachus Trium Fontium, *Chronica*, ed. Paulus Scheffer-Boichorst, in *MGH Scriptores* 23, ed. Georg Heinrich Pertz (Hanover: Hahn 1874), 859, which states that Philippe II held Geoffrey in great affection, had the late duke buried honorably at Notre Dame in Paris, and at his own expense arranged for prayers to be said in perpetuity for Geoffrey's soul.

[130] See Caroline Jewers, 'Another Arthur among the Troubadours', *Tenso* 24, n. 1–2 (2009): 27–8.

[131] Bertran de Born, 'A totz dic qe ja mais non voil', in *L'amour et la guerre: L'oeuvre de Bertran de Born*, ed. and trans. Gérard Gouiran (Aix-en-Provence: Université de Provence, 1985), 434, lines 33–7. For the translation provided, see Simon Gaunt and Ruth Harvey, 'The Arthurian Tradition in Occitan Literature', in *The Arthur of the French: The Arthurian Legend in Medieval French and Occitan Literature*, ed. Glyn Sheridan Burgess and Karen Pratt (Cardiff: University of Wales Press, 2006), 531.

(If Arthur, the lord of Cardeuil [Carlisle], whom the Bretons wait for henceforth, had the power to return to this world, the Bretons would have lost in exchange, and Our Lord would have won.)

The idea here is that Geoffrey of Brittany was more worthy than King Arthur. Bertran draws on the *exspectare Arthurum* motif to pay the highest compliment to the late lord of Brittany. It would seem that in 1186 the Bretons were still thought to have been awaiting Arthur's return, but the Breton Hope was by then a universal cliché. The events surrounding the birth of Geoffrey's posthumous son Arthur do, however, lend credence to the idea that the Bretons were rallying behind the figure of Arthur in the mid 1180s.

On Easter Day (29 March) 1187, a little over seven months after Geoffrey died, Constance of Penthièvre gave birth to his son at Nantes. The naming of the boy Arthur and his reception as Arthur reborn demonstrate an understanding of the Breton Hope that did not involve the physical return of the original Arthur. As a consequence of his parentage, place of birth, and given name, Arthur Plantagenet of Brittany was a son of two worlds. On the one hand he was a son of Celtic Brittany[132] and on the other a scion of the House of Plantagenet. By rule of primogeniture, Prince Arthur, assuming his uncle Richard I had no sons, was first in line to succeed Richard I as the ruler of the entire Angevin Empire. Given that the figure of King Arthur was of interest to the Plantagenets and to the Bretons, it is not immediately apparent whose idea it was to name the infant Arthur. So long as harmony existed between dynasty and duchy, Arthur of Brittany could be the Plantagenet Hope and the Breton Hope. Sadly for Prince Arthur, however, this was not to be. His place in the Plantagenet dynasty was always an open question. The impediment, actual or theoretical, that Arthur of Brittany posed to John's chances of succeeding Richard as lawful king led to a reintensification of the debate over whether the figure of King Arthur belonged to the Brittonic peoples or to the Plantagenets.

Because he died aged fifteen and because English chronicles tended to be biased against him, Arthur of Brittany is not a very accessible figure. The most fruitful way of analyzing him is to be cognizant of his allies and adversaries at each period of his short life, which can be divided into four distinct segments. The first stretches from his birth (29 March 1187) to

---

[132] The monk Albericus of the Cistercian abbey of Trois-Fontaines (which is on the border of Champagne and Lorraine) draws a direct genealogical connection between Arthur of Brittany and King Arthur in his *Chronica*, which was written between 1227 and 1241. See Albricus monachus Trium Fontium, *Chronica*, 859. The genealogical link offered by Albericus is probably his own invention, but this does not mean that individuals from the late twelfth century did not reach a similar conclusion regarding Arthur Plantagenet's maternal heritage.

Richard I's formal announcement of Arthur as heir apparent (6 October 1190). These first years were the least turbulent period of his existence. The second segment extends from October 1190 until about 1195. During this time, Arthur and his mother Constance enjoyed good relations with King Richard, but Arthur had John as an adversary. John was endeavoring to build local support in England as well as assistance from the French royal court in order to supplant Arthur as Richard's heir. The third segment extends from 1195 until roughly the time of Richard I's sudden death (6 April 1199). Constance was at odds with Richard I regarding how much local autonomy the duchy of Brittany – and she as its de facto ruler – would be permitted to enjoy within the Angevin Empire. From 1196 until around 1199, Arthur was in the care of Philippe II of France and was estranged from Richard I. During this third segment of time, more precisely between 1196 and 1198, William of Newburgh wrote his *Historia rerum Anglicarum* where he makes a series of negative comments about the Bretons, Arthur of Brittany, and the figure of King Arthur. The fourth and final segment of Prince Arthur's life extends from the death of Richard (6 April 1199) to Arthur's own premature death around 3 April 1203.[133] Arthur's murder almost certainly occurred on King John's orders. The chroniclers who supported John were not sympathetic to Arthur, and William of Newburgh seems to have numbered among them. With these circumstances in mind, let us now consider the life and myth of Arthur Plantagenet.

Arthur of Brittany was named after the illustrious King Arthur and was presented as the fulfillment of the Breton Hope. Confirmation comes in songs written by the Provencal troubadour Peire Vidal (d. c. 1205) and also in two continuations of the Angevin annals of the abbey of Saint-Aubin of Angers. In 'Pus tornatz sui en Proensa', Peire expresses happiness about returning to Provence after a lengthy trip to the Holy Land with Richard the Lionheart (1186–7) and also about the fact that he was forgiven for stealing a kiss from Lady Adelaide of Roquemartine, the wife of his patron Raimon Jaufre Barral, viscount of Marseilles (r. 1178–92). In the second stanza of the song, Peire declares:

> E sel que long' atendensa
> Blasma, fai gran falhizo;
> Qu'er an Artus li Breto
> On avion lur plevensa.
> Et ieu per lonc esperar

---

[133] For discussion of the precise date and circumstances of Arthur's death, see J. C. Holt, 'King John and Arthur of Brittany', *Nottingham Medieval Studies* 44 (2000): 90, 90 n. 36.

Ai conqist ab gran doussor
Lo bais que forsa d' amor
Me fetz a ma domn' emblar,
Qu'eras lo·m denh' autreiar.[134]

(Anyone who criticizes patient waiting makes a great mistake; for now the Bretons have their Arthur in whom they had their promise guaranteed. And I, too, through patience have gained with great sweetness the kiss which the force of love had made me steal from my lady and which now she grants me willingly.)

This is a new spin on the *exspectare Arthurum* motif: the Breton Wait is finally over, and the Bretons' extraordinary patience has turned out to be a virtue.[135] Peire treats Arthur of Brittany as Arthur's second coming, as the fulfillment of the Breton Hope. His passing allusion to the birth of Arthur Plantagenet suggests that he expects his audience to understand the reference.

Two closely related continuations (covering 1180–1212) of the *Annals of Saint-Aubin of Angers* further affirm that the birth of Arthur Plantagenet was presented as the return of King Arthur.[136] The B-version (Vatican, BAV, Reg. lat. 711, t. II, fols. 1–10) contains the following entry for the year 1187: 'Nascitur Arturus, Mars alter marte futurus, / Qui regnaturus civibus erit undique murus' (Arthur is born, who will be a second Mars in battle; he will reign and he will be a wall on every side for his countrymen).[137] The E-version (Paris, BnF, Lat. 4955, fols. 96–103) begins with a short prose entry stating that Arthur, son of Geoffrey of Brittany, son of King Henry of England, is born and then offers these verses: 'Nascitur Arturus, regali stirpe creatus. / Ut sit causa pacis nobis est ille legatus' (Arthur is born, sprung from royal stock. He has been bequeathed to us so that he may

---

[134] Peire Vidal, 'Pus tornatz sui en Proensa', ed. and trans. Veronica M. Fraser, in Veronica M. Fraser, *The Songs of Peire Vidal: Translation and Commentary* (New York: Peter Lang, 2006), 62, 64 (2, lines 10–18). I have modified this translation slightly, changing 'Arthur in whom they had such hope' to 'Arthur in whom they had their promise guaranteed' for greater accuracy.

[135] Peire uses this example again in another song about faithful love service and long, unrequited love: 'Ges pel temps fer e brau', which also dates from about 1187. See Peire Vidal, 'Ges pel temps fer e brau', ed. and trans. Veronica M. Fraser, in Veronica M. Fraser, *The Songs of Peire Vidal: Translation and Commentary* (New York: Peter Lang, 2006), 230, 232 (4, lines 31–40). The two critical lines are 39–40: 'Despos Artus en cobrat en Bretanha, / Non es razos que mais jois mi sofranha' (since the Bretons have rediscovered Arthur, it is not right that I should ever be lacking joy).

[136] For a discussion of the manuscript tradition of the *Annals of Saint-Aubin*, see Stéphane Lecouteux, 'L'archétype et le stemmata des annales angevines et vendômoises', *Revue d'Histoire des Textes*, n. s. 3 (2008), 253–6 and 261.

[137] *Annales de Sancti Albini Andegavensis*, in *Recueil d'Annales Angevines et Vendômoises*, ed. Louis Halphen (Paris: Alphonse Picard et Fils, 1903), 19.

be a cause of peace for us).[138] The E-text and B-text each preserve leonine couplets of dactylic hexameter. Their likeness suggests that they were excerpted from a larger poem celebrating Arthur's birth. It is unsurprising that this praise poetry was preserved at the Abbey of Saint-Aubin because Arthur of Brittany went on to assume the title of count of Anjou in April 1199; the nobility and high clergy of Anjou (and of Angers in particular) favored his authority over that of Prince John. The verses appearing in the Angevin annals bear comparison to court poetry that was written three centuries later for a similar occasion: Henry VII of England (r. 1485–1509) had the birth of his firstborn son and heir Arthur (1486–1503) celebrated by means of metrical poetry.[139] Quite similar to the *Annals of Saint-Aubin* on Arthur of Brittany are Pietro Carmeliano's verses in his *Suasoria Laeticiae* (1486) on the nativity of Prince Arthur Tudor.[140] Both blend Classical and Arthurian mythology. The repetition of 'Arthurus nascitur' in the Angevin annals and 'Nascitur ecce puer' in Carmeliano's *Suasoria* are evocative of messianic poetry, specifically Isaiah 9:6, which announces the birth of a small child (*parvulus*) who will bear the burden of government on his shoulders and be a prince of everlasting peace, justice, and righteousness. These lines also call to mind Virgil's Fourth Eclogue, which similarly anticipates the coming of a small child (*parvus puer*) who will inaugurate an age of heavenly peace and prosperity. It is widely agreed that Henry Tudor selected the name of Arthur for his firstborn son in an effort to popularize his new dynasty. The originator of the name choice for Arthur of Brittany and his or her motivations are however opaque.

Late twelfth-century histories state that the Bretons (in a few cases, Constance specifically) favored the name.[141] What appears to be the earliest chronicle treating the subject is the *Gesta regis Henrici Secundi et Gesta regis Ricardi* (completed c. 1192–3; henceforth *Gesta regis*), which is held by Gillingham and David Corner to be the work of Roger of Howden.[142] Of Arthur's birth, 'Roger' writes that in 1187 the countess of Brittany, who was also daughter of the sister of King William of Scotland, gave birth

---

[138] *Annales de Sancti Albini Andegavensis*, 25.

[139] See David Carlson, 'King Arthur and Court Poems for the Birth of Arthur Tudor in 1486', *Humanistica Lovaniensia* 36 (1987): 147–83.

[140] Pietro Carmeliano, *Suasoria Laeticiae* (London, British Library, MS Addit. 33776, fols. 2r–11v), ed. David Carlson, in 'King Arthur and Court Poems', 182–3, lines 255–82.

[141] Ostmann, 'Die Bedeutung der Arthurtradition', 228.

[142] For arguments that Roger of Howden authored 'Benedict's *Gesta Regis*', see John Gillingham, 'Roger of Howden on Crusade', in John Gillingham, *Richard Coeur de Lion: Kingship, Chivalry and War in the Twelfth Century* (London: Hambledon, 1994), 141–53; David Corner, 'The *Gesta Regis Henrici Secundi* and *Chronica* of Roger, Parson of Howden', *Bulletin of the Institute of Historical Research* 56, n. 134 (1983): 126–44.

on the night of the resurrection of the Lord at Nantes in Brittany to her firstborn son, 'quem Britones Arturum vocaverunt' (whom the Bretons called Arthur).[143]Another account comes from William of Newburgh:

> Natus est ei, ex Britannici comitis filia unica, filius posthumus; cui cum rex avus nomen suum imponi jussisset, contradictum est a Britonibus, et sollemni acclamatione in sacro baptismate Arturus est dictus. Sicque Britones, qui diu fabulosum dicuntur expectasse Arturum, nunc sibi cum multa spe nutriunt verum, juxta opinionem quorundam, grandibus illis et famosis de Arturo fabulis prophetatum.[144]

> (A posthumous son was born to Geoffrey by the only daughter of the count of Brittany; [and] when the king, the child's grandfather, had commanded that his name be given to the boy, his order was contradicted by the Bretons, and by solemn acclamation the child was called Arthur in holy baptism. And thus the Bretons, who are said to have awaited the celebrated Arthur for a long time, now full of hope, nourish a truth for themselves, at least according to the opinion of some, one prophesied in the grand, celebrated tales of Arthur.)

Historians of our own time have tended to trust William of Newburgh's account even though it is the only text claiming that Henry wanted his grandson to have his name.[145] W. L. Warren believes the ducal court

---

[143] See *Gesta regis*, I, 361. 'Roger' privileged Constance's Scottish heritage over her Breton blood and title when identifying her. See also Ralph de Diceto, *Ymagines historiarum* (A. D. 1148–1202), in *The Historical Works of Master Ralph de Diceto, Dean of London*, vol. 2, ed. William Stubbs, RS 68 (London: Eyre and Spotiswoode, 1876), 48.

[144] William of Newburgh, *Historia rerum Anglicarum* 3.7, p. 235. There is another noteworthy discussion of Arthur's birth, but it was written three centuries after the fact, and for this reason we cannot attach the same level of importance to it. The account is by the chanter and canon of l'Eglise Collegiale de Nostre Dame de Laval, Pierre Le Baud (c. 1450–1505). Le Baud is recognized as the foremost medieval authority on the history of Brittany, and he had access to Breton sources now lost to us. See Pierre Le Baud, *Histoire de Bretagne avec les chroniques des maisons de Vitré et de Laval*, ed. Ch. D'Hozier (Paris: Gervais Alliot, 1638). Le Baud writes that it was the Bretons who were responsible for selecting 'le nom d'Artur', and he adds that they chose this name 'en memoire du tres preux & renommé Artur Roy de la grand Bretagne' (199). Le Baud, in contrast to William of Newburgh, does not say that Henry II wanted his grandson to be named after him. Le Baud writes that King Henry II, when he heard of his grandson's birth, came to Brittany to see him and assembled all the aforementioned prelates and barons in Nantes, from whom he took and received the oath that they would be faithful to said Arthur and would guard his life and his land on his behalf (199). Everard has been unable to find this assembly attested elsewhere, but, as she notes, Henry did visit Brittany in September 1187 (*Brittany and the Angevins*, 157).

[145] Ostmann, 'Die Bedeutung der Arthurtradition', 227.

christened the boy after Brittany's own great cultural hero in hopes that the native Bretons would receive the 'half-Angevin' child as their own.[146] According to this reading, the ducal court in Brittany stood as the prime beneficiary of the name choice. Michael Jones interprets the name selection as on the one hand a 'bold assertion by Constance and her advisers of their desire to be free from Plantagenet domination' and on the other an acknowledgement that 'since Arthur was Henry II's only legitimate male grandson to date in the direct line, whatever hopes they may have entertained for independence, his life inevitably had wider horizons than Brittany alone'.[147] Jones thus offers two non-mutually exclusive readings of the decision. His initial suggestion is predicated on William of Newburgh's account. The latter statement is more open-ended and suggests that the choice of this name of great expectation spoke to Arthur's opportunities for elevation within the House of Plantagenet.

I hold that what precipitated the decision was the desire to win local Breton support (as Warren has suggested) as well as the aim to communicate that the boy, as heir to the Plantagenet Empire, was destined for greatness (as Jones has suggested).[148] William of Newburgh's story implies that Arthur, from the very moment of his birth, was under a foreign, subversive Breton influence; he was, for that reason, somehow less of a Plantagenet and not to be trusted with the throne of England. These sentiments were useful to John Lackland in his bid to supplant Arthur as Richard's successor. William of Newburgh's account of Arthur's naming possibly originated with John's partisans.

There are strong indications in the *Historia rerum Anglicarum* that William preferred John to Arthur. The author does not overlook John's failings but acts as an apologist for him. This kindness most likely reflects John's good standing in England in the latter half of the 1190s, especially in 1197. William, in his account of how John conspired with Philippe II to

---

[146] See W. L. Warren, *King John*, rev. edn. (Berkeley: University of California Press, 1978), 82.

[147] Michael Jones, 'Arthur, duke of Brittany (1187–1203)', *ODNB* (Oxford University Press, 2004) (http://www.oxforddnb.com.myaccess.library.utoronto.ca/view/article/704, accessed 1 Aug 2013).

[148] Judith Everard and Michael Jones call attention to the fact that following Arthur's birth in 1187 Constance began expressly associating Arthur with her authority in charters and this led them to conclude that '[n]ot only was she concerned with Arthur's future as duke of Brittany, but with his succession to the Angevin empire'. See *The Charters of Duchess Constance of Brittany and Her Family, 1171–1221*, ed. Judith Everard and Michael Jones (Woodbridge, UK: Boydell, 1999), xvi. See, for example, Constance's 'Confirmation of grants to the abbey of Beaulieu by Roland and Alain de Dinan and Duke Geoffrey, adding a grant of her rights on a hermitage and field etc. in the forest of Lanmeur (Rouen, soon after Easter 1187) [C 15]', 51–2.

block Richard's release from captivity in January 1194, did indeed refer to Prince John as a *hostis naturæ* (enemy of nature).[149] This is a damning epithet, but William goes on to explain why John betrayed his brother during the years 1189–94: Richard was, according to William of Newburgh, excessively generous to John in land grants prior to leaving on crusade in 1189, and this liberality had the unintended effect of making John even more covetous.[150] In this instance, William clearly writes with hindsight and is perhaps trying to mitigate John's treachery.

In the unfinished fifth and final book of the *Historia rerum Anglicarum*, William presents John as a reformed man. This retrospective vantage point is, I argue, how William saw John when writing his *Historia*. In a short chapter on the reconciliation that occurred between Richard and John in 1193, William writes that John redeemed himself for his prior excesses by assuming new duties and by going to battle faithfully and forcefully against the king of France.[151]

William of Newburgh's favoritism for John over Arthur is further detectable in his account of how John found out that Richard had selected Arthur as his successor. According to William, John learned of this through the stealthy actions of William Longchamp, bishop of Ely (r. 1189–1197), justiciar of England and Richard's chancellor. On 6 June 1190, Richard designated Bishop William guardian of England in his absence. The bishop had already become papal legate to England. William of Newburgh does not conceal his antipathy for this man; he characterizes him as a power-hungry tyrant who saw Prince John as the only force that stood in his way.[152] The bishop, according to William of Newburgh, sent two of his brothers to the court of William I of Scotland with the aim of convincing the king to agree to help set up his grandnephew – referred to in the text as *Arthurus Brito* (Arthur the Breton) – as the next ruler of England.[153] The bishop communicated to the Scottish king not

---

[149] William of Newburgh, *Historia rerum Anglicarum* 4.40, p. 402.

[150] William of Newburgh, *Historia rerum Anglicarum* 4.3, pp. 301–2. The same opinion is also expressed by the Benedictine monk and chronicler Richard of Devizes (c. 1250–c. 1200). See Richard of Devizes, *Chronicon Ricardi Divisiensis de rebus gestis Ricardi Primi regis Angliæ* 8, ed. Joseph Stevenson (London: Sumptibus Societatis, 1838), 7.

[151] William of Newburgh, *Historia rerum Anglicarum* 5.5, p. 424. When asserting that John fought bravely on Richard's behalf, William may have been referencing John's involvement in the capture of two leaders of Philippe II's forces, Philippe of Dreux, bishop of Beauvais, and William of Merlou on 19 May 1197. See John Gillingham, 'Historians Without Hindsight: Coggeshall, Diceto and Howden on the Early Years of John's Reign', in *King John: New Interpretations*, ed. S. D. Church (Woodbridge, UK: Boydell, 1999), 11; Roger of Howden, *Chronica*, IV, 16.

[152] William of Newburgh, *Historia rerum Anglicarum* 4.14, p. 335.

[153] William of Newburgh, *Historia rerum Anglicarum* 4.14, p. 335.

only that Arthur had a stronger claim to England than John by right of primogeniture but also that King Richard had dispatched letters from either Marseilles or Sicily declaring that he had designated his five-year-old nephew as his successor in the event that he should fail to return from crusade. The kingdom was to be held in safekeeping for Arthur until he should come of age.[154] William of Newburgh is skeptical of Bishop William's motives for setting up Arthur as Richard's successor:

> [d]enique, ne forte rege peregre moriente et Johanne rite succedente, propria exspiraret potestas, arte, ut dicitur, agendum putavit ut Johannes jam adultus non succederet, sed per successorem tenerum longi sibi temporis potestatem pararet.[155]

> (and then, so that in the event that the king should die while abroad John would be blocked from rightly succeeding and so that his [Bishop William's] own power would not run out, the bishop thought to bring it about by artifice, as it is said, that John, who was now an adult, not succeed, but by means of a successor of tender age the bishop might retain power for himself for a long time.)

Even if the chronicler's mistrust was founded, William Longchamp was telling the truth to the Scottish king and complying with Richard I's wishes. Richard had designated Arthur as his heir. Nevertheless, William of Newburgh regards John as the more legitimate and appropriate successor and chooses to refer to Arthur not as a prince of the royal blood but as an outsider.

William of Newburgh, after outlining the bishop's message for the Scottish king, states that the plot did not escape John's notice and that John 'conceptum rancorem subtili pro tempore cautela dissimulans, suæ parti quoscunque [sic] poterat prudenter allicere, artemque arte eludere studuit' (concealed for a time the rancor he had engendered through subtle caution, and he prudently strove to win over whomever he was able to his side and to cheat artifice through artifice).[156] John fashioned himself as a local hero standing up for English customs and liberties against the haughty outsider William Longchamp. John's 'chief propagandist', Hugh of Nonant, bishop of Coventry, circulated a letter in October 1191 that reviled William Longchamps as a lowborn and supercilious Frenchman who had nothing but contempt for the English. Roger of Howden

---

[154] William of Newburgh, *Historia rerum Anglicarum* 4.14, pp. 335–6.
[155] William of Newburgh, *Historia rerum Anglicarum* 4.14, p. 335.
[156] William of Newburgh, *Historia rerum Anglicarum* 4.14, p. 336.

included a transcript of this letter in his historical writings,[157] and William of Newburgh endorsed this negative characterization of the chancellor by characterizing him as a foreigner of obscure name, unproven both in fidelity or industry.[158] John brought many English lords over to his side through his 'populist campaign'.[159] And he, after a show of force at Nottingham and Tykehill in late July 1191, compelled William Longchamp to cease supporting Arthur's interests and to agree to hand over royal fortifications to John as the rightful heir in the event that Richard failed to return.[160] On 8 October 1191, John confirmed the privileges of the city of London and in return secured from its citizens oaths of support for his claim to the throne of England.[161] John then ousted the chancellor from power. The nativist sentiment that John stirred to unseat William Longchamp he also marshaled against his nephew Arthur.

Upon learning that Leopold V, duke of Austria, had captured Richard I near Vienna (late December 1192), John sought an alliance with Philippe II. The coverage of this development in the Annals of Dunstable Priory is of interest to us. It states that John, enticed by a desire to reign, crossed the sea and made a treaty with the king of France 'ut Arturum nepotem suum ab ea spe, quam Britones super ejus promotione conceperant, prorsus excluderet' (to the effect that his nephew Arthur would be utterly excluded from that hope, which the Bretons had conceived with respect to his promotion).[162] This entry implies that the Bretons hoped that their Arthur would preside over the entire Angevin Empire. The Dunstable annalist offers us an indication that John was at odds not only with the person of Arthur of Brittany but also with the understanding of Arthur of Brittany as the fulfillment of the Breton Hope.

Concomitant with the othering of Arthur of Brittany in England was a move to disassociate the figure of King Arthur from the Plantagenet dynasty.

---

[157] *Gesta regis*, II, 215–20; Roger of Howden, *Chronica*, III, 141–7, especially 142–3. See John Gillingham, *Richard I* (New Haven: Yale University Press, 1999), 228.

[158] William of Newburgh, *Historia rerum Anglicarum* 4.5, pp. 306–7.

[159] See John Gillingham, 'John (1167–1216)', *ODNB* (Oxford University Press, 2004) online edn, Sept. 2010 (http://www.oxforddnb.com/view/article/14841, accessed 21 Sept. 2013).

[160] William of Newburgh, *Historia rerum Anglicarum* 4.16, p. 339.

[161] *Gesta regis*, II, 214. Roger of Howden, *Chronica*, III, 141.

[162] *Annales Prioratus de Dunstaplia (A.D. 1–1297)*, in *Annales Monastici*, vol. 3, ed. Henry Richards Luard. RS 36/3 (London: Longmans, Green, Reader, and Dyer, 1866), 26. Roger of Howden reports that John traveled to Normandy in January 1193, did homage to Philippe for all of Richard's overseas lands – reportedly for England too – and promised to marry Philippe's sister Alys. Philippe, in return, promised John his full support in his bid to take possession of Richard's lands. See Roger of Howden, *Chronica*, III, 204.

As discussed at length in Chapter One, King Arthur had been remade as an idealized Plantagenet monarch. But as long as Arthur of Brittany was alive and well, John could not convincingly make the figure of King Arthur his own. Not only did the prince from Brittany bear the legendary king's name, he had Breton heritage and a stronger claim to the throne of England by strict primogeniture. What chance did John have of convincing the baronage of the English realm to support him over this promising son of prophecy? John resolved to discredit both Arthurs, the old and the new.

William of Newburgh's treatment of King Arthur in the *Historia rerum Anglicarum* attended to John's concerns. William depicts King Arthur as the cultural property of the Britons and denied the veracity of Geoffrey of Monmouth's account of King Arthur. At the very outset of his *Historia*, William denigrates the Britons and their history. With regard to Gildas' negative portrayal of the Britons in his *De excidio et conquestu Brittaniae*, William calls attention to the fact that Gildas writes that the Britons were neither strong in battle nor faithful in peace.[163] William then declares that Geoffrey of Monmouth, surnamed Arthur, in an effort to redeem the tainted legacy of the Britons, passed off fables about Arthur that were taken from the ancient yarns of the Britons and also his own embellishments as honest history written in Latin.[164] Further on in his proemium William again expresses his disbelief in Geoffrey's account of Arthur as well as his own disdain for the Britons as a people:

> cuncta, quæ homo ille de Arturo, et ejus vel successoribus vel, post Vortigirnum, prædecessoribus scribere curavit, partim ab ipso, partim et ab aliis constat esse conficta; sive effrenata mentiendi libidine, sive etiam gratia placendi Britonibus, quorum plurimi tam bruti esse feruntur, ut adhuc Arturum tanquam venturum exspectare dicantur, eumque mortuum nec audire patiantur.[165]

> (Everyone knows that everything this man cared to write about Arthur and about both his successors and his predecessors that came after Vortigern is a fabrication partly by him and partly by others; either on account of an unbridled passion for lying or even for the sake of satisfying the Britons, the majority of whom are held to be so irrational that they are said to expect that Arthur will still come and they do not suffer to hear that he is dead.)

What is particularly striking about this attack is the emphasis placed on how Arthur belonged to the Britons, not to the English. At the absolute

---

[163] William of Newburgh, *Historia rerum Anglicarum*, Prœmium, p. 11.
[164] William of Newburgh, *Historia rerum Anglicarum*, Prœmium, pp. 11–12.
[165] William of Newburgh, *Historia rerum Anglicarum*, Prœmium, p. 14.

latest, the Glastonbury discovery happened in 1193, and yet William makes no mention of it. William points out historical inconsistencies in Geoffrey's narrative, including the fact that, despite Geoffrey's and Gerald's claims to the contrary, there were no archbishops in post-Roman Britain prior to the advent of St. Augustine of Canterbury.[166] Then William calls King Arthur's illustrious legacy into question. As we have seen, the polite way of saying that Arthur's *res gesta* should not be taken too literally was to declare that Arthur deserves to be the subject of reliable history rather than false and dreaming fable. William of Newburgh dispenses with this pleasantry and delivers the most biting attack against Arthur's historicity of the medieval period. He asks how it could be that ancient history writers, who meticuluously fulfilled their charge of committing all details of note, great and small, to written record could pass over in silence such an incomparable man as Arthur whose acts were reportedly outstanding beyond measure. Repeating his rhetorical question, William asks: 'Quomodo, inquam, vel nobiliorem Alexandro Magno Britonum monarcham Arturum, ejusque acta, vel parem nostro Esaiæ Britonum prophetam Merlinum, ejusque dicta, silentio suppresserunt? (How could it be, I say, that they suppressed to silence either Arthur the monarch of the Britons and his acts, Arthur who was more noble than Alexander the Great, or Merlin the prophet of the Britons and his sayings, Merlin who was equal to our Isaiah?) [167] For William of Newburgh, Arthur was not *rex Angliæ* but *monarcha Britonum. Brito*, in this case, undeniably refers to the realm and inhabitants of the ancient kingdom of Britain. Yet, as we have seen elsewhere in his text, the Bretons reportedly regarded Arthur as theirs. William contempuously groups Arthur, king of the Britons (*Arturus, monarcha Britonum*), Arthur of Brittany (*Arturus Brito*), the false history of the Britons, and the contemporary Bretons into one category: the proximate, non-English other.

William may have felt compelled to point out the inconsistencies in Geoffrey of Monmouth's *Historia* purely because of concern for historical truth,[168] but politics likely were a contributing factor in William's decision

---

[166] William of Newburgh, *Historia rerum Anglicarum*, Prœmium, p. 16.

[167] William of Newburgh, *Historia rerum Anglicarum*, Prœmium, p. 17.

[168] See Anne Lawrence-Mathers, 'William of Newburgh and the Northumbrian Construction of English History', *Journal of Medieval History* 33 (2007): 339–57. Lawrence-Mathers contends that William of Newburgh was an adherent to the Northumbrian 'school' of thought that offered a 'self-consciously English vision of the past', exalted Bede's narrative of English history, and left no room for the heroics of King Arthur and the Galfridian narrative of history (341).

to dismiss Galfridian history.[169] Let us now take a step back in time and consider how Richard regarded his nephew Arthur of Brittany and the prince's illustrious ancient namesake.

Henry II's plans for his grandson are unknown. If, as William of Newburgh claims, the king wanted his grandson to have his name, then perhaps he thought the child might eventually succeed him. Richard I's plans for Arthur are less obscure. Richard in 1190 named Arthur as his successor. This was a logical choice because, as W. L. Warren has noted, Arthur, a mere toddler at the time of Richard's accession and a total stranger in England, posed no threat to him.[170] Richard formalized this decision during his stay in Sicily while en route to the Holy Land. The context of Richard's stay in Sicily offers us a glimpse of how King Richard was toying with the notion of his nephew and heir apparent as *Arthurus redivivus*.

Ostensibly, Richard went to Messina in order to rendezvous with Philippe II at this Sicilian port, but, as Gillingham has suggested, the English king seems to have been secretly waiting there for Berengaria of Navarre (c. 1165–1230), the eldest daughter of Sancho VI of Navarre (r. 1150–94).[171] Richard intended to marry her. The arrangement was clandestine because Richard was still betrothed to Philippe's sister Alys. Richard had been unwilling to repudiate the betrothal out of fear of upsetting Philippe and thereby jeopardizing their joint crusade.[172]

Upon arrival in Sicily, Richard had another piece of unresolved family business that demanded his attention. When Richard's brother-in-law William II died on 16 November 1189, Tancred of Lecce usurped the throne of Sicily and placed Joan (William's widow and Richard's sister) under house arrest.[173] The usurper king was loath to give Joan her dower

---

[169] Gransden has suggested that William's prologue may initially have been an independent 'political tract' commissioned by 'someone connected with the royal court'. See Antonia Gransden, 'Bede's Reputation as an Historian in Medieval England', *Journal of Ecclesiastical History* 32, n. 4 (1981): 416–18. Also see Crick, 'British Past and Welsh Future', 72.

[170] Warren, *King John*, 39.

[171] Gillingham, *Richard I*, 126–7. Philippe had arrived at Messina on 16 September 1190. See Roger of Howden, *Chronica*, III, 54.

[172] See John Gillingham, 'Richard I and Berengaria of Navarre', *Bulletin of the Institute of Historical Research* 53 (1980): 162–3; Gillingham, *Richard I*, 126–7.

[173] William had designated his aunt, Constance, the wife of Heinrich of Hohenstaufen, as his successor. Heinrich of Hohenstaufen (d. 1197), not long after the death of his father Frederick Barbarossa (10 June 1190), was to become Emperor Heinrich VI (r. 1191–7). Pope Clement III and the Sicilian nobility were both averse to the prospect of rule by a German king and therefore supported Tancred. See Jean Flori, *Richard Cœur de Lion*, trans. Jean Birrell as *Richard the Lionheart: King and Knight* (Westport, CT: Praeger, 2006), 96.

because it involved granting her the county of Monte Sant'Angelo, which was under threat of invasion from the rival claimant to the Sicilian throne, Heinrich of Hohenstaufen, the king of the Romans and son of Frederick Barbarossa.[174]

Richard arrived in Messina on 23 September 1190 with much pomp. This calculated display of magnificence was designed to intimidate Tancred, and it worked. Tancred agreed to release Joan at once.[175] Richard was still not appeased. William II had bequested a handsome legacy to Henry II in the event that the English king made good his planned crusade. Richard had now come to collect this legacy, which included valuable objects of gold and silver, 100 war galleys stocked with two years' worth of provisions, and vast quantities of grain and wine.[176] Tancred held that, since Henry II had predeceased William II, the legacy was null and void. Richard thought otherwise. Two days after Joan's arrival in Messina (30 September), Richard captured the fortified monastery of Bagnara in Messina and set up Joan and her household there. On 2 October, he occupied the Greek monastery of St. Saviour. Threatened by Richard's actions, the inhabitants of Messina took up arms against the Crusaders, and Richard found himself unable to stop the violence. Following a failed conference with Tancred's officials in Messina, Richard, on 4 October, had the entire city taken by force.[177] Two days later, Tancred, fearing the permanent loss of Messina, reached a settlement with Richard, which included a great marriage alliance. The text of the charter survives.[178] As part of the treaty Tancred agreed to pay 20,000 ounces of gold to settle Joan's dower and a further 20,000 ounces both as a quitclaim to resolve William's bequest and to serve as an offering for a marriage between his daughter and Richard's nephew Arthur.[179] In return, Richard promised that so long as he was in Sicily, he would provide military assistance to Tancred against all invaders.[180] Richard then dispatched a letter (dated 11 November 1190) to Pope Clement III (r. 1187–91) seeking the pope's blessing for the agreement. By these two royal acts, Richard made it known that, if he were to die without issue, Arthur of Brittany should

---

[174] Gillingham, *Richard I*, 133, n. 32.

[175] Flori, *Richard Cœur de Lion*, 96, 98; Roger of Howden, *Chronica*, III, 55.

[176] Roger of Howden, *Chronica*, III, 61. For a discussion of how Sicilian support for the crusading movement was imperiled by the rise of Tancred, see William of Newburgh, *Historia rerum Anglicarum* 3.28, pp. 285–6.

[177] Roger of Howden, *Chronica*, III, 56–8; William of Newburgh, *Historia rerum Anglicarum* 4.12, pp. 324–5.

[178] *Gesta regis*, II, 133–5.

[179] Roger of Howden, *Chronica*, III, 61.

[180] *Gesta regis*, II, 136; Roger of Howden, *Chronica*, III, 64.

succeed him.[181] In order see how Richard exploited the Arthurian aura surrounding his Breton-born nephew, we must delve ever more deeply into Richard's diplomatic relations with Tancred.

After making peace with Tancred, Richard was still awaiting Berengaria, who was late in leaving Navarre.[182] Joining her were Eleanor of Aquitaine and Count Philip of Flanders, the dedicatee of Chrétien's *Perceval*. By February 1191 the trio had reached Naples and were waiting for Richard's galleys to transport them to Messina. News of their imminent arrival was a source of anxiety for Philippe II and for Tancred. For Philippe, the arrival was blatant proof that Richard was determined to break off his betrothal with Alys, a turn of events that had the potential to embarrass the House of Capet. Tancred had much graver concerns than family honor; his political survival was at stake. He had learned that Eleanor had met Heinrich in Lodi near Milan on 20 January 1191 as they were both making their way to Sicily, she to oversee her son's marriage and he to move against Tancred.[183] The Sicilian usurper-king feared that Richard would betray him. Philippe played on Tancred's fears in order to block Berengaria's arrival.

After receiving warning of Richard's perfidy from Philippe II, Tancred interfered with Richard's wedding plans. He allowed Philip of Flanders to come to Messina but did not extend the same permission to Eleanor and Berengaria on the grounds that the port city could not accommodate their large retinue. Richard knew this to be a false pretense and arranged to meet with the king of Sicily in person at the foot of Mount Etna, Arthur's resting place according to Gervase of Tilbury. The pair met on 3 March 1191 and spent five days together. Tancred must have been attempting to discern Richard's intentions. Two contemporary chronicles, the *Gesta regis* (attributed to Roger of Howden) and Roger of Howden's *Chronica* (written in two stages between 1192–3 and 1201–2), state that, on 6 March 1191,

> rex Siciliæ dona multa et magna, in vasis aureis et argenteis, in equis et pannis sericis obtulit regi Angliæ: at hujusmodi non indigens, nihil eorum capere voluit præter annulum parvulum quendam, quem in signum mutuæ dilectionis accepit. Rex autem Angliæ dedit ei gladium optimum Arcturi, nobilis quondam regis Britonum, quem Britones vocaverunt Caliburnum. Præterea Tancredus dedit

[181] *Gesta regis*, II, 135; *Chronica*, III, 63. Also see King Richard's letter to Pope Clement concerning the Anglo-Sicilian peace treaty. A transcript of this text appears in *Gesta regis*, II, 136–8 and Roger of Howden, *Chronica*, III, 65.
[182] Gillingham, *Richard I*, 125.
[183] Gillingham, *Richard I*, 141; 'Richard I and Berengaria of Navarre', 164.

regi Angliæ quatuor magnas naves quas vocant Ufsers, et quindecim galeas.[184]

(the king of Sicily bestowed upon the king of England gifts, that were both numerous and great, in [the form of] golden and silver vessels, in horses and in silken garments, but Richard, who was not lacking in things of this sort, did not wish to take any of these items except a certain small ring, which he received as a token of their mutual affection. The king of England, however, gave to Tancred the finest sword of Arthur, who was once noble king of the Britons. The Britons called this sword 'Caliburn'. In addition, Tancred gave to the king of England four great ships, which they call 'Ufsers' [Huissiers], and fifteen galleys.)

This gift exchange seems to have led to a breakthrough, for on the following day the king of Sicily, according to the *Gesta regis,* declared to the king of England:

Nunc scio vere et certis indiciis comprobavi, quod ea quæ rex Franciæ mandavit mihi de vobis per ducem Burgundiæ, et per litteras suas, potius ex invidia processerunt quam ex amore quem erga me haberet. Ipse enim mandavit mihi quod nec pacem nec fidem mihi servastis; et quod conventiones inter nos factas transgressi estis; et quod in regnum istud non venistis nisi ut auferretis a me; sed et si vellem cum exercitu meo super vos venire, ipse auxiliaretur mihi quantum posset, ad vos et exercitum vestrum confundendum.'[185]

('Now I know truly and I have confirmed by certain pieces of evidence that those things which the king of France conveyed to me about you through the duke of Burgundy and through his letter proceeded out of envy rather than out of the love he had for me. For he sent word to me that you neither kept peace nor faith with me; and that you had transgressed the pact made between us; and that you came into this realm for no reason but to take it away from me; and that if I should wish to overtake you with my army, he would assist me as much as he could to confound you and your army.)

Richard remained in disbelief until Tancred produced Philippe's letter. This document gave Richard the ammunition he needed to extricate himself from his betrothal to Alys. After showing the letter to Philippe and accusing the French king of treachery, Richard was released from the marriage agreement. As an added bonus, Richard secured lordship

---

[184] *Gesta regis,* II, 159. Compare with Roger of Howden, *Chronica,* III, 97. In his *Chronica,* Roger refers to Arthur not as *quondam nobilis rex Britonum,* but as *quondam nobilis rex Angliæ.* See Gillingham, 'Context and Purposes', 103, n. 23.

[185] *Gesta regis,* II, 159. This reported speech is absent from Roger of Howden's *Chronica.*

over the duchy of Brittany for the English crown in perpetuity, albeit with acknowledgment that the French crown retained suzerainty over it.[186] Arthur was to swear homage to Richard rather than to Philippe for Brittany.

Since Roger of Howden is the only contemporary writer known to have reported Richard and Tancred's gift exchange, we cannot exclude the possibility that Roger invented this episode.[187] Roger is, however, thought to have been in close proximity to King Richard from 7 August 1190 to 25 August 1191, where he was acting as a representative for Hugh du Puiset, bishop of Durham (r. 1154–95).[188] Tancred had indeed been blocking the arrival of Eleanor and Berengaria at Messina. The story, even if fabricated, is deserving of attention.[189]

The gift of Caliburn to Tancred is perennially mentioned in biographies of Richard I and in Arthurian scholarship. For Gillingham, the fact that Richard went on the Third Crusade with a sword that had allegedly belonged to Arthur is sufficient indication that the Lionheart desired to be associated with Arthur.[190] Emma Mason regards the sword, quite rightly, as a 'secular relic', more specifically as a physical object that had absorbed the powers, prestige, and charisma of its previous possessor, King Arthur, and could impart these qualities to its current bearer.[191] The remarks of these two scholars prompt us to ask why Richard gave away 'a sword so rich in the symbolism of royal dignity, and bearing such an ideological weight' to Tancred, who was a relatively minor player on the European stage and a

---

[186] *Gesta regis*, II, 161; Roger of Howden, *Chronica*, III, 99–100.

[187] Michelle R. Warren, 'Roger of Howden Strikes Back: Investing Arthur of Brittany with the Anglo-Norman Future', *Anglo-Norman Studies* XXI (1998): 261.

[188] Corner, 'Roger, Parson of Howden', 140.

[189] See Gillingham, *Richard I*, 141: 'This is a curious story: however well informed Roger of Howden was, he is unlikely to have overheard the private conversation of two kings. None the less the fact that Eleanor and Berengaria were kept away from Messina suggests that Howden is doing more than simply repeating anti-French gossip.'

[190] Gillingham, 'Context and Purposes', 103. Richard I brought the dragon-ensign to battle in Messina (1190) and Palestine (1191). Tatlock finds no evidence of its use since Hastings (1066) by Harold I. The example of Uther Pendragon from Geoffrey's *Historia regum Britannie* 135.393–400, pp. 180–1 may have inspired Richard I. See J. S. P. Tatlock, 'The Dragons of Wessex and Wales', *Speculum* 8, n. 2 (1933): 226, 234–5. Support for this opinion exists in the *Otia Imperialia*, where Gervase of Tilbury states that King Richard carried the English war banner, which originated with Uther Pendragon, into battle against the 'pagans of Outremer'. See Gervase of Tilbury, *Otia Imperialia* 2.17, pp. 420–1.

[191] Emma Mason, 'The Hero's Invincible Weapon: an Aspect of Angevin Propaganda', in *The Ideals and Practice of Medieval Knighthood III: Papers from the fourth Strawberry Hill conference, 1988*, ed. Christopher Harper-Bill and Ruth Harvey (Woodbridge, UK: Boydell, 1990), 121, 128.

politically insecure one at that.[192] Mason has suggested that Richard, who already had an established knightly reputation, 'could perhaps afford to dispense with an Arthurian relic'.[193] But why did he do it? Mason and others hold that Richard gave the sword away with the understanding that he would receive ships in return. They contend that Richard was doing everything in his power to ensure the success of the Third Crusade and that this mattered more to Richard than being seen as a successor to Arthur. This interpretation is logical, for if Richard succeeded in leading his crusaders to victory, then his own place in chivalric history would be assured, not to mention his spiritual salvation. He would not stand in the shadow of King Arthur; he would surpass the legendary monarch.

I, however, have three concerns about this line of thought. First, implicit in this interpretation is the assumption that the exchange was a quid pro quo, with Richard knowing in advance that he would receive ships from Tancred in return for Caliburn. This may have been the case, but it is not clearly stated in the accounts. Second, why would Tancred give away so many ships for Arthur's sword? Third – and this is my main objection – the interpretation does not speak to the history of diplomacy between Richard and Tancred. The two kings had, as we have seen, struck an alliance in October 1190 whereby Richard's nephew and designated heir, Arthur of Brittany, was to marry a daughter of Tancred when she reached marriageable age. To understand Richard's motivation for parting with Caliburn as well as Tancred's desire to possess the sword, we must bear in mind the details of the October 1190 peace agreement.[194]

Tancred, from October 1190 to March 1191, had, as we have seen, ever-increasing doubts as to Richard's reliability, particularly regarding whether Richard would furnish military assistance and bring about the promised union between Arthur and Tancred's daughter. Richard must have sensed that his honor was being called into question during his time with Tancred at Catania. Evidence of this can be seen in Roger of Howden's *Chronica*. The day after the gift exchange, Tancred reportedly handed Philippe's letter to Richard. This letter stated that the king of England was a traitor and that he had no intention of upholding the peace that he made with Tancred.[195] Roger of Howden then reports the English king's reaction. Richard asserts, in dare I say Nixonian fashion, 'Proditor

---

[192] Flori, *Richard Cœur de Lion*, 402–3.
[193] Mason, 'Hero's Invincible Weapon', 130.
[194] Warren calls for a contextual reading of this gift exchange in her 'Roger of Howden Strikes Back', 263.
[195] Roger of Howden, *Chronica,* III, 98.

non sum, nec fui, nec ero; et pacem, quam vobiscum feci, in nullo sum transgressus, nec transgrediar quamdiu vixero.' (I am not a traitor, I never was, and I never will be; and I have in no way broken the peace that I made with you, nor will I for as long as I live.)[196] Richard perceived that his good name was under attack. With this in mind, let us consider the symbolism of the gift exchange.

Richard reportedly refused all material riches that Tancred had lavished upon him except a small ring, a token of their mutual affection. Richard then gave Caliburn to Tancred. Might there have been an understanding that Tancred would knight his son-in-law Arthur using the sword of the boy's legendary namesake around the time of the wedding? Michelle Warren has speculated along these lines, remarking: '[s]hould Arthur accede to the English throne, we can imagine him inheriting Caliburn from Tancred and returning it to England from whence Richard had carried it'.[197] Perhaps Richard even planned for Tancred to confer the belt of knighthood on his son-in-law Arthur. Richard may have thought to forestall Philippe, the liegelord of Brittany, from knighting Arthur.[198] A possible analogue is Henry I of England's selection of the young Geoffrey, count of Anjou, as a husband for his widowed daughter Matilda. Geoffrey of Anjou had yet to be knighted when the marriage contract was arranged. Henry I, according to Jean de Marmoutier's *Historia Gaufridi ducis Normannorum et comitis Andegavorum* (c. 1180), sent to his royal treasury for an ancient sword that had allegedly been forged by the swordsmith Weland. Weland, according to certain *chansons de geste*, had made Charlemagne's sword 'Joyeuse', Roland's sword 'Durendal', Olivier's sword 'Hauteclaire', and Anthénor's sword 'Flamberge'. With a sword forged by Weland, Henry I knighted his future son-in-law.[199]

---

[196] Roger of Howden, *Chronica*, III, 98.

[197] Warren, 'Roger of Howden Strikes Back', 271.

[198] In England, the king typically reserved the right to knight a vassal of comital status. See D'A. J. D. Boulton, 'Classical Knighthood as Nobiliary Dignity: The Knighting of Counts and Kings' Sons in England, 1066-1272', in *Medieval Knighthood V: Papers from the Sixth Strawberry Hill Conference 1994*, ed. Stephen Church and Ruth Harvey (Woodbridge, UK: Boydell, 1995), 94. As a result of an Anglo-Castilian wedding alliance (contracted 31 March 1254), it was agreed that Alfonso X of Castile (r. 1252–84) would knight his future brother-in-law Edward Plantagenet (1239–1307), aged fourteen. A dual knighting / marriage ceremony took place at Burgos on All Soul's Day 1254. Alfonso made Edward a knight. See Matthew Paris, *Chronica Majora*, ed. Henry Richards Luard, 7 vols. RS 57 (London: Longman, 1872–83), V, 449–50.

[199] Jean de Marmoutier, *Historia Gaufredi ducis Normannorum et comitis Andegavorum*, in *Chroniques des comtes d'Anjou et des seigneurs d'Amboise*, ed. Louis Halphen and René Poupardin (Paris: Auguste Picard, 1913), 179–80.

Richard's actions, specifically his acceptance of Tancred's ring and his gift of Arthur's sword, apparently persuaded Tancred that Richard intended to honor their arrangement. There does seem to have been interest in things Arthurian in Sicily, but in Tancred's hands Caliburn was visible and material proof that Tancred and Richard were allies and future in-laws. King Arthur's alleged ownership of the sword in the remote past may have been of less symbolic importance to Tancred than the fact that Richard had been its most recent possessor. The Anglo-Sicilian alliance had already proven efficacious: it dissuaded Tancred's Muslim subjects from rebelling against him.[200] Perhaps the king hoped that it would likewise discourage Heinrich VI from invading Sicily.

The Arthurian valence of Caliburn may have been of secondary importance to Tancred, but this was not true for the Plantagenets. How and where Richard obtained the sword remains a mystery. As Gillingham and Mason have suggested, the mere fact that Richard was in possession of Arthur's sword indicates that he saw himself as a successor to the king. Richard did not, in my opinion, value the sword lightly. He did not simply trade it in for four great ships and fifteen galleys. On the contrary, he put a plan in place whereby the Arthur of the Plantagenet dynasty would – when he came of age to wed and wield a sword – receive the blade of his legendary namesake. This arrangement is a great example of life enacting literature. Richard evidently was not averse to exploiting the idea that his nephew was *Arthurus redivivus*.

The Arthurian plans, if any, that Richard I had for Arthur remain a mystery and subject for speculation. The fact that Richard obtained from King Philippe lordship over Brittany suggests, as Warren has noted, that the king of England was determined to exercise political control over his widowed sister-in-law and Arthur. By acquiring lordship over Brittany, Richard removed the need for direct contact between Arthur and Philippe.[201] As Warren has also quite rightly emphasized, Richard selected a partner for Arthur who was not enmeshed in the ongoing Anglo-French conflict.[202]

One group that may have had some inkling about what Richard had in mind for his nephew was the enterprising Glastonbury community.

---

[200] *Gesta regis*, II, 141.

[201] Warren, 'Roger of Howden Strikes Back', 269.

[202] Warren, 'Roger of Howden Strikes Back', 266: 'Richard in fact had good reason to marry his heir south. Arthur's mother, Constance of Brittany, was the niece of William king of Scotland, as well as closely tied to the French court. For Richard, the Sicilian marriage foreclosed one path to a stronger Scottish / French alliance.'

They seem to have hoped to profit from Richard's choice of successor. The timing of the excavation and translation of King Arthur's remains in 1191, after the Anglo-Sicilian marriage alliance of October–November 1190, suggests this possibility. It should also be recalled that Henry of Sully was elevated to the abbacy by Richard I and that he was of royal blood. Did Richard or his court officials suggest to Abbot Henry that unearthing the bones of King Arthur would be an effective means of reinforcing the understanding that Arthur of Brittany was *Arthurus redivivus* – 'King Arthur is dead, long live King Arthur'? By translating the remains of the original Arthur, were the monks showing their loyalty to Richard I and hoping that this gesture would inspire Arthur of Brittany to endow their religious community with benefits and privileges? It is quite possible.[203] Indeed, Catalina Girbea has raised the intriguing possibility that it was Richard who called for the exhumation of Arthur's bones. Richard, she contends, was acutely aware that he had just ignited a dynastic quarrel by designating Arthur of Brittany as his successor; he may have hoped that the timely discovery and recovery of King Arthur's bones would be interpreted by his subjects as a sign of supernatural approval, possibly even divine sanction, for his choice of heir.[204]

There is also the distinct possibility that Laȝamon tailored his presentation of King Arthur in his *Brut* to suggest that Arthur of Brittany was *Arthurus redivivus* in order to counter the othering of King Arthur and Arthur of Brittany and lend ideological support to Arthur of Brittany's claim to the throne of England. As noted at the outset of Chapter One, Laȝamon's *Brut* was written some time between 1185 and 1216. J. S. P. Tatlock dates Laȝamon's *Brut* to the reign of Richard I, 1189–99, and bases this dating largely on his reading of line 14297 of the poem, which contains Laȝamon's twist on *exspectare Arthurum*: 'þat an Arður sculde ȝete cum Anglen to fulste' (that an Arthur should come again to aid the people of England). Tatlock holds that '[i]t is impossible not to see an allusion to Arthur of Brittany', and he sees 'almost uncanny agreement' between Laȝamon's words and William of Newburgh's account of the

---

[203] Charles T. Wood has suggested that the announcement of Arthur as Richard's heir prompted the discovery of Arthur's remains at Glastonbury. See Wood, 'Guenevere at Glastonbury', 88–9.

[204] Catalina Girbea, 'Limites du contrôle des Plantagenêt sur la légende arthurienne: le problème de la mort d'Arthur', in *Culture politique des Plantagenêt (1154–1224): Actes du colloque tenu à Poitiers du 2 au 5 mai 2002*, ed. Martin Aurell (Poitiers: Centre d'Études Supérieures de Civilisation Médiévale, 2003), 292.

christening of Arthur in the *Historia rerum Anglicarum*.[205] Although there is no obvious verbal correspondence between the two authors, Tatlock's contextualization of Laȝamon's *Brut* merits further exploration.

Tatlock's linkage of Arthur of Brittany's cause to Laȝamon's *Brut* does not rest solely on his interpretation of one line of text; he also calls attention to a curious addition that Laȝamon made to the legend of King Arthur. In Geoffrey's *Historia*, after Uther Pendragon's death, the noblemen of Britain assembled in Silchester, selected Uther's son Arthur as their king, and asked archbishop Dubricius to consecrate him as king. After mentioning the intensified threat that the Saxons posed to the Britons, Geoffrey writes that Dubricius and his fellow bishops crowned the fifteen-year-old Arthur as their king.[206] It is unclear how much time passed between Arthur's election and his coronation. No statement is made as to Arthur's location at the time of Uther's death. In the *Roman de Brut*, Wace writes that the bishops and barons of Britain came together after Uther's death. Wace does not specify the location of this meeting but says that the magnates collectively summoned Arthur to Silchester where they made him their king.[207] Nor does Wace reveal the whereabouts of Arthur when he received the message. Laȝamon, true to his tendency of amplifying source material with concrete details,[208] revises this episode slightly and adds an all-important detail: the great warrior-prince Arthur had been residing in Brittany.[209] By placing Arthur in Brittany, Laȝamon makes Arthur the 'Breton Hope' of

---

[205] Tatlock, *Legendary History*, 504. Tatlock's reading of the line has been challenged. See E. G. Stanley, 'The Date of Laȝamon's *Brut*', *Notes and Queries* 213 (1968): 87: '… the authorities cited by Tatlock hardly allow us to see Arthur of Brittany as the hope of the English, so that Tatlock's theory seems unconvincing from the point of view of the history of the period. A further point may be made, which, if not decisive against Tatlock's interpretation of the passage, certainly lends no support to it. The use of the indefinite article *an* with the personal name *Arður* is not likely to have had the sense "another", i.e. "another Arthur", viz. Arthur of Brittany. It seems to mean rather "some Arthur", i.e. the use provides an example … of a proper name used with the indefinite article as a common noun with the generalizing meaning "comparable to the individual in question".' Stanley's syntactical objection is a moot point: Arthur of Brittany could still have been the anticipated Arthur figure. His historical objection is contestable as well. It is certainly true, as shown above, that William of Newburgh, the principal authority cited by Tatlock, was no admirer of Arthur of Brittany. We cannot, however, responsibly conclude that *every* Englishman disliked Arthur of Brittany. John, as history shows, was successful in obtaining the requisite English support to secure the Crown, but that is not equivalent to obtaining universal English support. Glastonbury, as I shall suggest, may have been a base of support for Arthur of Brittany prior to John's coronation.

[206] Geoffrey of Monmouth, *Historia regum Britannie* 143.1–11, pp. 192–3.

[207] Wace, *Roman de Brut*, 226–7, lines 9005–12.

[208] See Tatlock, *Legendary History*, 489.

[209] *Laȝamon's Brut*, 508–9, lines 9893–905. See also *Laȝamon's Brut*, 512–13, lines 9909–22.

sixth-century Britain's nobility, and he harmonizes the biographical details of King Arthur and Arthur of Brittany. One might also draw an analogy between Richard I's 1190 succession announcement and Uther's choice of Arthur to succeed him.

If Tatlock's analysis is correct, Arthur son of Uther as the Breton Hope of post-Roman Britain was intended to serve as a prefiguration of Arthur son of Geoffrey as the Breton Hope of post-Conquest England. Again I wish to call attention to Tatlock's analysis, which accords very closely with the general thrust of my assessment of the place of Arthur of Brittany in Plantagenet dynastic politics in the 1190s:

> Though after Richard's death (6 April 1199) there seemed no chance of Arthur becoming king of England, at any time earlier an Englishman might have anticipated this. John had certainly given no one reason to hope for good from him as king, and by his record of conduct in Ireland especially to no one who knew recent events there. To Lawman prince Arthur may well have seemed a 'Breton Hope'.[210]

I agree with Tatlock on this point and would add, further, that Laȝamon's anglicization of King Arthur and British history more broadly is a definite counterpoint to – and possible reaction against – the othering of King Arthur and Arthur of Brittany undertaken by John's supporters and on display in William of Newburgh's *Historia rerum Anglicarum*.

If King Richard hoped to transform his nephew Arthur into a 'Plantagenet Hope', these plans collapsed in 1196. Richard, after his release from captivity (4 February 1194), fought to regain control of his possessions on the Continent. Brittany had in his absence attained a degree of autonomy that Richard found unacceptable. The king's solution was twofold. First, he pressured Duchess Constance, Brittany's de facto ruler, to reconcile with her estranged husband Ranulf III, earl of Chester and Richmond, whom Henry II had forced her to marry on 3 February 1189. It was Richard's wish that Ranulf take charge of Brittany as duke *jure uxoris*. Second, Richard wanted to assume custody of the nine-year-old Arthur. With Arthur at his court, Richard would have greater leverage over Constance and the lords of Brittany as well as the opportunity to influence the boy as he saw fit. Early in 1196, Richard ordered Constance to come to his court in Normandy. Ranulf captured her while she was in transit.[211] The Bretons blamed Richard for the abduction. In April, Richard came to Rennes for Arthur, but the boy's guardians spirited him away to inner Brittany. The Bretons and Richard came to an agreement whereby

---

[210] Tatlock, *Legendary History*, 505.
[211] See Roger of Howden, *Chronica*, IV, 7.

Constance would be released in exchange for hostages. When Richard failed to honor his side of the agreement, the Bretons swore fealty to Arthur,[212] and the boy assumed the title 'dux Brittanie'.[213] Arthur, in an act dated 21 August 1196, promised his Breton supporters that he would not make peace with Richard without including them.[214] According to Roger of Howden, when Arthur failed to obtain the release of his mother (August 1196), he sought sanctuary at the French royal court and razed the lands of his uncle. Arthur began following the pattern of his late father. Richard, in retaliation, assembled a great army and laid waste to Brittany.[215] In summer 1197, Richard and the Bretons came to terms, and Constance was released. Arthur, however, remained at the French royal court and stayed there until the latter half of 1198 or early 1199.[216] Despite Richard's best efforts, Arthur fell under the influence of Philippe II.

At the core of the Breton conflict, epitomized by the custody battle over Arthur, was a relatively straightforward political issue: the extent to which Brittany would be permitted to exercise local autonomy within the Angevin Empire. William of Newburgh adds an element of romance to his retelling of events in 1196, much as he had done in his account of Arthur's christening. William's 1196 portrayal suggests that the Bretons viewed the contest as a struggle for Arthur's soul. The fulfillment of the Breton Hope was at stake. William writes that the Bretons 'puerulum sibi Arturum sub magno hujus nominis omine nutriebant' (were raising the little boy Arthur for themselves under the great omen of his name) and that the magnates of Brittany would not hand him over more on account of a certain suspicion than on account of due caution.[217] Again William scorns Arthur and the Britons.

John's was not a smooth succession to the throne following Richard's early death (6 April 1199), and his supporters undertook to discredit Arthur

---

[212] Everard and Jones, *Charters of Duchess Constance of Brittany*, 109.

[213] Roger of Howden, *Chronica*, IV, 8; Everard, *Brittany and the Angevins*, 161.

[214] 'Promise made by Arthur to his Breton supporters, following the capture of Duchess Constance, that he would not make peace with King Richard without including them (Saint-Malo de Beignon, 21 August 1196) [A2]' in *Charters of Duchess Constance of Brittany and Her Family*, 117.

[215] Roger of Howden, *Chronica*, IV, 7; *Philippide* 5, pp. 130–1, lines 147–67. Guillaume adds that Arthur was then educated in Paris for several years with his exact contemporary, Philippe's son, the future Louis VIII.

[216] According to Everard, 'Arthur returned from the Capetian court around the beginning of 1199 and began to be associated in Constance's government of Brittany' (*Brittany and the Angevins*, 167). According to Michael Jones, in August 1198 Arthur 'renounced his fealty to Philip and agreed to be guided in relations with him by Richard'. See Jones, 'Arthur, duke of Brittany (1187–1203)', *ODNB* online.

[217] William of Newburgh, *Historia rerum Anglicarum* 5.18, pp. 463–4.

with even greater vigor.[218] They attacked the duke of Brittany's character and judgment and questioned his 'Englishness'. They also worked to establish John's fittingness to succeed Richard. Roger of Howden writes that Richard I, sensing imminent death from a gangrenous wound, willed that John be his successor as king of England.[219] However, this purported dying wish did not settle the matter. Initially Anjou, Maine, and Touraine supported Arthur's cause, as did the archbishop of Canterbury Hubert Walter (r. 1193–1205).[220] In England the response was varied.[221] On behalf of John stood the celebrated knight and earl of Pembroke William Marshal (c. 1147–1219). In the *Histoire de Guillaume le Maréchal* (c. 1219–26), there is an exchange between the archbishop and the Marshal over who should be chosen to replace Richard I. The archbishop declared that Arthur had the stronger claim,[222] but the Marshal vehemently opposed elevating Arthur to the throne on that grounds that

> Artur est en felon conseil
> Si est eschis e orgeillos,
> E si nos l'atraiom sor nos,
> Mal e ennui nus voldra querre,
> Qu'il n'eimme pas cels de la terre.[223]

> (Arthur has treacherous advisors about him and he is unapproachable and overbearing. If we call him to be over us, he will seek to do us harm and damage, for he does not like those in our realm.)

The Marshal, who himself held a fiefdom in Longueville, Normandy, characterized Arthur of Brittany as a foreigner unsympathetic to English interests. This instance of reported speech was written roughly twenty years after the event described, but it may nonetheless reflect ideas circulating in 1199.[224]

---

[218] Roger of Howden reports that King Richard, on 31 March 1194, summoned his brother John and Hugh of Nonant, bishop of Coventry, to court on the charge of conspiring with King Philippe. See Roger of Howden, *Chronica*, III, 241–2. According to the *Annals of Margam Abbey*, this charge against John combined with Arthur's stronger claim by primogeniture should have disqualified John from succeeding Richard. See *Annales de Margan*, 24–5.

[219] Roger of Howden, *Chronica*, IV, 83.

[220] See Roger of Howden, *Chronica*, IV, 86–7.

[221] Holt, 'King John and Arthur of Brittany', 87.

[222] *Histoire de Guillaume le Maréchal*, ed. A. J. Holden, trans. S. Gregory, historical notes D. Crouch, 3 vols. (London: Anglo-Norman Text Society from Birkbeck College, 2002–6), II, 94–5, lines 11880–3.

[223] *Histoire de Guillaume le Maréchal*, II, 94–5, lines 11886–90.

[224] Arthur of Brittany is not compared to his namesake in the *Histoire*. This distinction goes instead to Young King Henry. See *Histoire de Guillaume le Maréchal*, II, 182–3, lines 3572–82.

Arthur is not, however, universally reviled in historical writing. A lay chronicler from Tournai, Philippe Mousquet (d.c. 1245), valorizes Arthur of Brittany in his *Chronique rimée* of the history of the French kings from the fall of Troy until 1243. He introduces the prince as a worthy successor to his legendary namesake:

> Artus ot non li damoisiaus.
> Rouses estoit, mais moult fu biaus,
> Et moult estoit bien ensigniés,
> Simples, courtois et afaitiés,
> De grant amour s'iert obéis
> Al jovène signour Loéys.[225]

> (The young man had the name Arthur. He was red-haired but very handsome and very well brought-up. He was humble, courteous, and well bred. With great love he was obedient to the young lord Louis [the dauphin of France].)

Mousquet's description of Arthur's character stands in stark contrast to that of William Marshal. Arthur of Brittany provides an excellent example of how politics affects historical memory.

Arthur of Brittany did not become king of England upon Richard's death, but he took possession of Angers on Easter (18 April) 1199 and then paid homage to Philippe for possession of Anjou, Maine, Touraine, and Brittany.[226] The fight for control of the Angevin landholdings in France continued into September. In that month, Guillaume des Roches, seneschal of Anjou, betrayed his lord Arthur by capturing him and delivering him to King John, but Arthur and his mother soon escaped to Anjou.[227] They were reunited with the king of France, but the king temporarily betrayed their trust. In the treaty of Le Goulet (22 May 1200), Philippe recognized John as the rightful heir of Richard I, agreed that Arthur would not hold Anjou, Maine, and Touraine, and had Arthur perform homage to John for Brittany.[228] Arthur was, however, permitted

---

[225] Philippe Mousquet, *Chronique rimée de Philippe Mouskes*, ed. Baron de Reiffenberg (Brussels: M. Hayez, 1836–8), II, 313, lines 20579–84.

[226] Guillaume le Breton, *Gesta Philippi Augusti, Guillelmi Armorici Liber* 101, in *Oeuvres de Rigord et de Guillaume le Breton: Historiens de Philippe-Auguste*, vol. 1: *Chroniques de Rigord et de Guillaume le Breton*, ed. H.-François Delaborde (Paris: Librairie Renouard, 1882), 205.

[227] Roger of Howden, *Chronica*, IV, 96–7.

[228] See Walter Ullmann, 'Arthur's Homage to King John', *English Historical Review* 94, n. 371 (1979): 356–64 and Holt, 'King John and Arthur of Brittany', 88–9. For the text of the treaty, see Roger of Howden, *Chronica*, IV, 148–51.

to remain in Philippe's protective custody.[229] By April 1202, the concord between Philippe and John had collapsed, and Philippe released Arthur from his feudal obligations to John.

In 1202, Arthur again paid homage to the king of France and was betrothed to Philippe's six-year-old daughter Marie. According to the *Annals of Saint-Aubin*, this wedding engagement, which Philippe arranged without consulting King John, led to war between England and France.[230] The planned union elevated Arthur's political and social status. No longer could John restrict Arthur's consolidation of power and influence to the duchy of Brittany. Once again, a wedding alliance would play a determining role in his destiny.

At Gournai in July 1202, Philippe II conferred on Arthur the belt of knighthood, confirmed him as duke of Brittany, and promised him the counties of Anjou and Poitou if Arthur could take them by force.[231] It is tempting to speculate that the knighting ceremony involved Arthurian symbolism, but I have not found evidence confirming this. Guillaume le Breton states in his *Philippide* that Philippe presented Arthur with a new belt of knighthood in accordance with the ancient custom of the French.[232] The king of France then sent Arthur off with a detachment of about 200 men to launch an assault on John's landholdings in Aquitaine.[233] Arthur, with the aid of the nobles of Poitou, laid siege to the castle of Mirebeau where his grandmother, Eleanor of Aquitaine, was in residence. Eleanor sought assistance from John, who was then in Normandy. John hastened to Mirebeau with an outstanding force.[234] Arthur, according to all of the chroniclers, failed to wait for reinforcements and rashly attacked Mirebeau with too small a force. Guillaume le Breton attributes this

---

[229] See Roger of Howden, *Chronica*, IV, 115. Arthur's obligation to do homage to King John became a *casus* in juristic literature, namely *Quaestio* XIII of the *Collectio Azoniana*, namely whether a sovereign king may delegate his vassal to another vassal of lesser or equal standing. See the appendix to Ullmann, 'Arthur's Homage to King John', 363–4.

[230] *Annales de Sancti Albini Andegavensis*, 20.

[231] Rigord, *Gesta Philippi Augusti, Rigordi Liber* 138, in *Oeuvres de Rigord et de Guillaume le Breton: Historiens de Philippe-Auguste*, vol. 1: *Chroniques de Rigord et de Guillaume le Breton*, ed. H.-François Delaborde (Paris: Librairie Renouard, 1882), 152. See Guillaume le Breton, *Gesta Philippi Augusti* 113, p. 210. See also Mousquet, *Chronique rimée*, II, 313, lines 20593–6.

[232] Guillaume le Breton, *Philippide* 6, p. 162, lines 262–5.

[233] Rigord, 'Gesta Philippi Augusti, Rigordi Liber' 138, p. 152. Also see the account (c. 1220) of this event written by the Anonymous of Béthune in *Histoire des ducs de Normandie et des rois d'Angleterre publiée en entier, pour la première fois, d'après deux Manuscrits de la Bibliothéque du Roi*, ed. Francisque Michel (Paris: Jules Renouard, 1840), 92–3.

[234] See Ralph of Coggeshall, *Chronicon Anglicum*, 137.

tactical error to Arthur's eagerness to earn his spurs.[235] Might Arthur have felt pressure to match the exploits of his ancestor on this occasion?

Arthur surely was aware of the deeds of his namesake. He might even have known that, according to Geoffrey of Monmouth, Arthur was fifteen years of age when he became king and fought off the Saxons. Arthur of Brittany is not, however, known to have made any specific reference to his legendary namesake when he marched into Aquitaine. In his *Philippide*, Guillaume le Breton has Arthur deliver a moving speech to the Poitevins and his other supporters during this campaign. In his oration, Arthur seeks the counsel of the more seasoned warriors in his ranks but expresses a desire to postpone confrontation with King John until he has sufficient reinforcements from Philippe II. He also reasserts the justness of his cause and outlines the many wrongs that John has perpetrated against him and his men:

> Novi me quantum patruus meus oderit, et vos
> Quam sit crudelis, sitiens quam sanguis, et
> Seviat in cunctos quos casus subicit illi; [quam]
> Et modo nil curat quid ei rex auferat, ut qui
> Me solum querit, regna in mea sola protervit;
> Me, quoniam regi faveo, semperque favebo;
> Me, quia sceptra peto mihi debita jure paterno;
> Me, quia germanam repeto, quam carcere clausam
> Ipse tenet, metuens amittere regna per ipsam.[236]

> (I know how much my uncle hates me, and you know how cruel and how bloodthirsty he is, and how he rages against all whom fate puts under his sway. And now he does not care at all what the king [of France] takes away from him, such that he seeks me alone, [and] he attacks my realm alone; me, because I support the king [of France] and always will support him; me because I seek the scepters owed to me by paternal right; me, because I demand my sister back, whom he, fearing to lose kingdoms on her account, holds locked up in prison.)

Although, according to Guillaume le Breton, Arthur prefers to wait for reinforcements from the king, the Poitevins appeal to his vanity and convince him to lay siege to Mirebeau in order to capture his grandmother, Eleanor of Aquitaine. She, according to the Poitevins, was the mastermind of many of John's nefarious deeds. They advise him to take her hostage and use her as leverage in negotiations.[237] This section of

---

[235] Guillaume le Breton, *Gesta Philippi Augusti*, 113, p. 210.
[236] Guillaume le Breton, *Philippide* 6, p. 164, lines 326–34.
[237] Guillaume le Breton, *Philippide* 6, pp. 165–6, lines 358–83.

the *Philippide* does not provide evidence of specifically Arthurian heroics
on the part of the young duke of Brittany, but it does suggest that a desire
for glory and honor and a sense of youthful invincibility moved Arthur to
challenge King John's forces without sufficient manpower.[238]

According to the *Histoire des ducs de Normandie et des rois d'Angleterre*
(c. 1220) by the so-called Anonymous of Béthune, a verbal exchange
allegedly occurred at Mirebeau between Arthur and his grandmother,
Eleanor of Aquitaine, which perhaps reveals more about the duke's
character and the purpose of his campaign. The chronicle contains a
passage in which Arthur attempts to persuade Eleanor to exit the fortified
tower of Mirebeau:

> En cel point vint Artus, li cuens de Bretaigne, o les Poitevins devant
> .i. castel que on apiele Mirabiel, ù la roine Alienor, qui mere estoit
> au roi Jehan et ayoule Artu, estoit dedens. Quant Artus et li Poitevin
> vinrent devant le castiel, tantost lor fu la ville rendue; mais l[i]
> castiaus se tint. Artus fist tant que il parla à s'ayole, si li requist que
> ele s'en issist dou castiel et si emportast toutes ses choses, et s'en alast
> en boine pais quel part k'ele vorroit aler; car à son cors ne vaurroit-il
> faire s'onour non. La roine respondi qu'elle ne s'en istroit pas; mais,
> s'il faisoit que courtois, il se partiroit d'illuec; car assés troveroit
> castiaus que il poroit assaillir, autres que celui ù elle estoit dedens, et
> molt li venoit à grant mervelle que il asseoit castiel ù il savoit qu'ele
> estoit, ne il ne li Poitevin ki si home lige devoient estre. Artus ne li
> Poitevin ne s'en vaurrent partir, ains assaillirent le castiel; mais pas
> ne le prisent. Il se herbregierent en la ville, si i furent ne sai quans
> jors.[239]

(At that point Arthur, the count of Brittany, came with the Poitevins
before a castle that is called Mirebeau, where inside was Queen
Eleanor, who was the mother to King John and grandmother to
Arthur. When Arthur and the Poitevins came before the castle, the
town was handed over to them at once, but the castle held out.
Arthur was doing so much until he spoke to his grandmother, and
he asked that she get out of the castle and that she carry with her all
her things, and that she go from there in good peace anywhere she
would want to go, for to her person he only wanted to do honor. The
queen responded that she would not go forth from there, but if he
were to act as a courteous man, he would leave from there, for he
would find enough castles that he would be able to assail other than
that one that she was occupying, and it indeed came to her as a great
marvel that he was laying siege to the castle where he knew she was,

---

[238] See Ostmann, 'Die Bedeutung der Arthurtradition', 245.
[239] Anonymous of Béthune, *Histoire des ducs de Normandie et des rois d'Angleterre*, 93.

for neither he nor the Poitevins, who were his liege men, should be there. Neither Arthur nor the Poitevins wanted to leave from there. Rather, they attacked the castle, but they did not take it. They stayed in the town, and they were there for I do not know how many days.)

In this passage, Arthur claims to have only positive intentions with respect to his grandmother. Yet capturing her was, according to the *Philippide*, the purpose of his mission in Mirebeau. Eleanor, who knew his purpose, informed Arthur that courtesy dictated that he leave her in peace. It would appear that Arthur of Brittany did not actually intend to honor his word. Therefore, although he may have been lacking in mature wisdom, Arthur of Brittany should not be thought of as a naïve youth who blindly and idealistically trusted in his own greatness and the greatness of his name.

Victory was not in store for this young Arthur. John captured him on 1 August 1202 and imprisoned him at Falaise Castle until the end of January 1203. He then had him brought to Rouen. Arthur died there on the night of 3 April. The details and aftermath of Arthur's death will be explored in the next chapter. John also captured Arthur's elder sister, Eleanor of Brittany (b. 1182x4–1241), at Mirebeau. As daughter to Geoffrey of Brittany, Eleanor also posed a threat to John's legitimacy as king. For this reason, both John and his son and eventual successor, Henry III, kept her under house arrest for her entire life. The author of the first half of the *Chronicle of Lanercost* (1201–97) notes that she was first detained in private in the custody of William of Vieuxpont in Westmoreland at Burgh Castle, and after that at Bowes. From there she was put away at Corfe Castle, where she lived apart until her death.[240]

Arthur of Brittany failed in his quest to claim his birthright, and he fell far short of the martial and political success of his namesake. That being said, Arthur of Brittany's life did parallel King Arthur's in another way: both had an uncertain end. At least one anonymous medieval chronicler remarked upon this tragic coincidence. In a series of annals (covering 1202–25) that were written as a continuation of Roger of Howden's *Chronica* – possibly at Peterborough – there is the following entry under the year 1203:

---

[240] *Chronicon de Lanercost (1201–1346)*, ed. Joseph Stevenson (Edinburgh: Edinburgh Printing Company: 1839), 1, 12. For a discussion of the composition and authorship of the *Chronicon de Lanercost*, see A. G. Little, 'The Authorship of the Lanercost Chronicle', *English Historical Review* 31 (1916): 269–79. Little comments that the author had extensive first-hand knowledge of the Franciscan house of northern England and had also spent time at Oxford, and Little believes that the first half of the chronicle was composed between 1280 and 1297 (274–6).

Arthurus in prisona patrui sui Johannis regis Angliæ, dubium quo casu, de medio factus est, nec est inventum sepulcrum ejus usque ad diem hunc, ut dicitur, sed non absque vindicta Dei. Qui frangit omnem superbum. Britones quippe quasi de nomine augurium sumentes, Arthurum antiquum in isto resuscitatum imprudenter et imprudenter jactitabant, et Anglorum internecionem, regnique ad Britones per istum imminere translationem.[241]

(Arthur was in the prison of his uncle, King John of England. Doubt exists as to how he met his end, and his tomb has not been found up to this very day, as it is said, but not without the vengeance of God. He crushes all the proud. For the Britons, as it were, taking up the prophecy of his name, were boasting immodestly and imprudently that the Arthur of old had been brought back to life in this one, and that through him both the destruction of the English and the transfer of the realm to the Britons were imminent.)

The author of this passage takes familiar elements from the Arthurian tradition and applies them to Arthur of Brittany. The *exitus dubius* and Arthur's unknown grave now pertain to Arthur Plantagenet. The author's remarks about the vengeance of God suggest a bias in favor of King John's cause. The writer depicts Arthur as representing the hopes of the Bretons. No mention is made of Arthur's claim to the throne of England. In the passage above, we also see the prophecy of Merlin about the destruction of the English in its third iteration. Originally, the prophecy involved Cadwallader and Conan. Then it was transferred to King Arthur. And now, in this third case, Arthur of Brittany takes the place of his namesake. The author suggests that the Bretons saw their duke as the reincarnation of King Arthur. Arguably this is yet another example of an English writer mocking the Celtic Other for false belief. The author conveys that Arthur of Brittany was not truly a second King Arthur, but merely a pale imitation. The annalist ascribes the understanding of Arthur of Brittany as *Arthurus redivivus* to the Bretons, but, if my analysis is correct, Richard I was its chief architect and propagator.

---

[241] This collection of annals is commonly known as the 'Barnwell Chronicle' because one of the manuscripts that preserves it, British Library MS Add. 35, 168, has been located to the Augustinian priory at Barnwell in Cambridgeshire. See Walter of Coventry, *Memoriale fratris Walteri de Coventria*, ed. William Stubbs, 2 vols. RS 58 (London: Longman, 1872–3), II, 196. For an analysis of the manuscript tradition that postulates that the original version of the annals from 1202 was 'both composed and written at Peterborough', see Richard Kay, 'Walter of Coventry and the Barnwell Chronicle', *Traditio* 54 (1999): 141.

Conclusion

I have observed two contrasting English stances in relation to the figure of King Arthur during Richard I's reign. The first is the continued adoption of King Arthur as an English king and proto-Plantagenet monarch. Examples include the Glastonbury discovery of Arthur's remains on English soil, Richard's possession of Caliburn, and possibly the decision to name Geoffrey Plantagenet's posthumous son Arthur. The second stance is the rejection of King Arthur as a Brittonic Other. This sentiment is most palpable in William of Newburgh's *Historia rerum Anglicarum* and in the 'Peterborough' annals. Both stances had their origin in the discourse on King Arthur during the reign of Henry II. The two stances do not appear to reflect deeply entrenched ideological beliefs, but rather the more ephemeral politics of succession. In the next chapter we will consider the consequences of Arthur of Brittany's demise for the future of Plantagenet Arthurian self-fashioning.

3
Arthurianism during the reign of King John, 1199–1216

King John: the anti-Arthur

John Lackland is not known to have emulated King Arthur. The only exception – if it should be regarded as such – is an entry for December 1207 in the Rolls of Letters Patent preserved in the Tower of London, which states that King John received into his possession at Clarendon a 'magnam coronam que venit de Alemannia' (great sword that came from Germany), precious clothes and jewelry, and 'duos enses, scilicet ensem Tristami et alium ensem de eodem regali' (two swords, namely the sword of Tristam and another sword of the same royal).[1] When and whence Tristam's sword entered the royal treasury is unknown, but the aforesaid entry allows for the possibility that all the items named in it, including Tristam's sword, came from Germany.[2] The dean of Westminster, Arthur Penrhyn Stanley, believes that Emperor Otto IV (r.1209–15) gave Tristam's sword to his uncle, King John, in 1207.[3] E. M. R. Ditmas theorizes that the sword arrived in England in 1125 as part of the regalia that Matilda brought to England after the death of her husband Heinrich V.[4]

Aurell has suggested that King Henry II bestowed the sword on John when knighting him on *Laetare* Sunday (31 March) 1185 as a symbolic accompaniment to the appanage of Ireland and Cornwall – two lands where much of the Tristan narrative takes place.[5] Technically, Henry had already named John 'Lord of Ireland' at the Council of Oxford in

---

[1] See *Rotuli Litterarum Patentium in Turri Londinensi Asservati*, ed. Thomas Duffus Hardy, vol. I, part I (London: Commissioners of the Public Records of the Kingdom, 1835), 77b.

[2] Mason, 'Hero's Invincible Weapon', 131.

[3] See Arthur Penrhyn Stanley, *Historical Memorials of Westminster Abbey*, 2nd edn. (London: John Murray, 1868), 413; Joseph Loth, 'L'épée de Tristan', *Comptes rendus des séances de l'Académie des Inscriptions et Belles–Lettres* 67, n. 2 (1923): 119.

[4] See E. M. R. Ditmas, 'More Arthurian Relics', *Folklore* 77, n. 2 (1966): 93; E. M. R. Ditmas, 'The Curtana or Sword of Mercy', *Journal of the British Archaeological Association*, Third Series, 29 (1966): 122–33. For a discussion of what Matilda brought to England from the German imperial court, see K. Leyser, 'Frederick Barbarossa, Henry II and the Hands of St. James', *English Historical Review* 90, n. 356 (1975): 489–90.

[5] Aurell, 'Henry II and Arthurian Legend', 373.

May 1177.[6] But it was in 1185 that Henry sent his newly knighted son off on his first military campaign, the objective of which was to expand the Plantagenet foothold in Ireland. Tristan's first knightly adventure, according to tradition, had also been in Ireland: Tristan defeated the Irish giant Moholt, brother of the queen of Ireland, in single combat and freed Cornwall from a demand of tribute. A notch of Tristan's sword remained lodged in the dead giant's skull – a perpetual reminder of the knight's great victory.[7] If he bestowed the sword on John in 1185, Henry's intention might have been to suggest that the prince would achieve similar success in Ireland. Such an accomplishment so early in John's active life would indeed have been a notch in his belt of knighthood. Nonetheless, all of this would speak more to the Arthurian enthusiasm of Henry II than to that of John Lackland.

John's Irish expedition, although carefully outfitted by Henry II, ended in failure.[8] According to Gerald of Wales, John and his Norman entourage made an extremely poor first impression on the Irish. They reportedly pulled on the long beards of the Irishmen who came to greet them in peace. Worse yet, rather than honor commitments he made to his Irish supporters, John awarded grants of land to his latest knightly companions.[9]

The charges of poor leadership, lack of mature counsel, faithlessness, disrespect of the rights and customs of his subjects, and avarice – all quite antithetical to the qualities associated with King Arthur that we have seen thus far – were common critiques of John. In contrast to his elder brothers (Young King Henry, Richard I, and Geoffrey of Brittany), John was not interested in establishing a knightly reputation. According to Roger of Howden, when Richard I learned that John was conspiring against him with Philippe II in 1193, he remarked: 'Johannes frater meus non est homo qui sibi vi terram subjiciat, si fuerit qui vim ejus vi saltem tenui repellat' (my brother John is not the man to subjugate a land by force if someone will be there to put up even the slightest resistance against his force).[10]

---

[6] See Gerald of Wales, *Expugnatio Hibernica* 2.25, pp. 198–9; 2.32, pp. 226–7 and p. 350, n. 457. Also see Seán Duffy, 'John and Ireland: the Origins of England's Irish Problem', in *King John: New Interpretations*, ed. S. D. Church (Woodbridge, UK: Boydell, 1999), 225–6.

[7] See Chrétien de Troyes, *Erec et Enide*, 46–7, lines 1247–50, and the episode is recollected (but not narrated) in the surviving fragment of Béroul's *Tristan*. See Béroul, *Tristan*, ed. and trans. Norris J. Lacy, in *Early French Tristan Poems*, vol. 1, ed. and trans. Norris J. Lacy (Cambridge, UK: D. S. Brewer, 1998), 12–13, lines 27–8 and 16–17, lines 135–42.

[8] See Gerald of Wales, *Expugnatio Hibernica* 2.27, pp. 204–5.

[9] See Gerald of Wales, *Expugnatio Hibernica* 2.36, pp. 236–9; Roger of Howden, *Chronica*, II, 304–5.

[10] Roger of Howden, *Chronica*, III, 198.

Consistent with this reported speech is Gervase of Canterbury's statement that John's detractors mocked his smallness of stature and called him 'mollegladius' (softsword) because prudence more than bellicosity governed his thinking.[11] If reports of John's character do not sufficiently account for his apparent lack of interest in the figure of Arthur, then his conflict with Arthur of Brittany and suspected involvement in Arthur's untimely death more than suffices.

After Mirebeau, the perception of Arthur of Brittany as 'Arthurus redivivus' was no longer a major threat to John, but the figure of King Arthur posed a different sort of problem for him. In life and in death Arthur of Brittany had been, as J. C. Holt has so eloquently put it, 'John's albatross'.[12] Any evocation of King Arthur by John could not help but call unwanted attention to the disappearance of Prince Arthur. This chapter will focus on how the figure of King Arthur was used against King John. At no time during his seventeen-year reign was John free of the specter of Arthur of Brittany, and ultimately John came to be seen not as a new King Arthur, but as a new King Herod.

King John as Herodes redivivus

When John had Arthur imprisoned at Falaise Castle in Lower Normandy, the Bretons led a series of violent uprisings in an effort to secure their duke's release. John's advisors recommended that Arthur be blinded and castrated. John gave the order, but Arthur's custodian at Falaise, Hubert de Burgh, shielded the prince from harm. Hubert caused a rumor to be spread that Arthur had been released from confinement and died shortly thereafter on account of pain and heartache. According to the rumor, Arthur was buried at the Cistercian abbey of Saint-André-de-Gouffern. Hubert spread this fake news in an attempt to curb the king's ire as well as that of the Bretons. His plan backfired. The Bretons swore never to stop attacking John for the detestable injustice he had perpetrated against their lord. The Crown let it be known that Arthur was safe and sound. John had Arthur transferred to Rouen. The Bretons responded by collaborating with the king of France. Together they wrote to John calling for Arthur's release in exchange for hostages; they threatened military action should John fail to comply. Philippe was again using Arthur as a political pawn.[13]

---

[11] Gervase of Canterbury, *Gesta regum*, 92–3. Also see Jim Bradbury, 'Philip Augustus and King John: Personality and History', in *King John: New Interpretations*, ed. S. D. Church (Woodbridge, UK: Boydell, 1999), 348–9.

[12] Holt, 'King John and Arthur of Brittany', 103.

[13] Ralph of Coggeshall, *Chronicon Anglicum*, 140–1, 143.

Arthur would prove even more useful to Philippe dead than alive. Ralph of Coggeshall's *Chronicon Anglicanum* does not recount Arthur's death but states that in 1204 Philippe II was unwilling to make peace with John because he was confident that he would soon conquer all of the English king's French territorial possessions 'pro nece Arturi, quem in Sequana submersum fuisse audierat; unde et jurasse fertur quod nullo tempore totius vitæ suæ ab infestatione regis Johannis desisteret, donec eum toto regno suo privasset' (on account of the death of Arthur, whom he had heard was plunged into the Seine; and for this reason it is told that he had sworn that he would desist at no point in his life from attacking King John until he had deprived him of his entire kingdom).[14] Holt has questioned the chronological accuracy of this statement.[15] The entry was written retrospectively,[16] and we cannot be sure that Philippe had learned by 1204 that Arthur had drowned in the Seine.

The Margam annalist likewise reports that King Philippe knew of Arthur's death in 1204, but his chronological accuracy is also suspect. According to the Margam annalist, Philippe, upon receiving word of Arthur's death, summoned John to the court of France to account for Arthur's whereabouts. John reportedly did not dare to appear in court and fled from Normandy to England (5 December 1203). The annalist then states that the English king, after his retreat, never returned to France to answer for the death of Arthur. Philippe and the peers of France by judicial verdict deprived and disinherited John and his heirs from all the land and honors that the English king held from the crown of France.[17] The annalist does not specify when this trial took place, but the chronicler's remarks come directly before a description of the winter of 1204–5. The Margam annalist presents John's loss of Normandy in 1204 in tandem with the Capetian court's condemnation of John for the murder of Arthur. This linkage provides justification for Philippe's seizure of John's French territories.

Whether Philippe knew of Arthur's death as early as 1204 remains an open question that the Margam annalist cannot enable us to solve. His entries for 1204 were composed after John's death (9/10 October 1216).[18] Only from 1206 do we have evidence that the French king was confident

---

[14] Ralph of Coggeshall, *Chronicon Anglicum*, 145.
[15] Holt, 'King John and Arthur of Brittany', 100, n. 75.
[16] For a tentative dating of the 1202–5 segment of the *Chronicon Anglicanum* to 1205–7, see Carpenter, 'Abbot Ralph of Coggeshall's Account', 1228.
[17] *Annales de Margan*, 27–8.
[18] See *Annales de Margan*, 27, which mentions the end of John's days.

that Arthur was dead: in that year Philippe II arranged for his daughter Marie to marry the count of Namur as a replacement for Arthur.[19]

Details about Arthur's demise surfaced between 1206 and 1208. It was then that William de Briouze (c. 1153–1211), erstwhile companion of John, fell out of favor with the king. William seems to have been the source of incriminating rumors against John. As royal letters attest, William was often in the king's company around the time of Arthur's disappearance.[20] Money, according to King John, was at the root of their discord: William had incurred a substantial debt to the Crown and did not repay any part of the sum.[21] In March 1208, John began to apply pressure by demanding that William surrender one of his sons as collateral. William complied.[22] In that same year, John had demanded hostages from a great many of his barons as insurance lest Pope Innocent III (r. 1198–1216) declare John excommunicate and release them from their feudal obligations to him. When John's officials came to William's home seeking hostages, William's wife Matilda, according to Roger of Wendover (d. 1236), barred their entrance, exclaiming that she would not hand over her boys to King John 'quia Arthurum nepotem suum, quem honorifice custodisse debuerat, turpiter interfecit' (because he shamefully killed his nephew Arthur, whom he ought to have held in an honorable fashion).[23] The St. Albans chronicler then states that when the king's officials repeated Matilda's words, King John was gravely perturbed and had William's entire family seized. William, having been warned of this, fled to Ireland.[24]

Unsurprisingly, King John presents his break with William in a different way. According to the king, William attempted to retake by force three Welsh castles (Hay, Brecon, and Radnor), which he had pledged as a security for his outstanding debt to John. After his siege proved fruitless, William attacked Leominster, which was under the king's protection. He

---

[19] This was first noted by Charles Petit-Dutaillis, 'Le déshéritement de Jean sans Terre et le meurte d'Arthur de Bretagne: Étude critique sur la formation et la fortune d'une légende', *Revue Historique* 147, fasc. 2 (1924): 179. Also see M. Dominica Legge, 'William the Marshal and Arthur of Brittany', *Bulletin of the Institute of Historical Research* 55, n. 131 (1982): 23, and Kate Norgate, 'The Alleged Condemnation of King John by the Court of France in 1202', *Transactions of the Royal Historical Society*, New Series, 14 (1900): 67.

[20] See Holt, 'King John and Arthur of Brittany', 91; F. M. Powicke, 'King John and Arthur of Brittany', *English Historical Review* 24, n. 96 (1909): 671.

[21] 'The Complaint of King John against William de Briouze (c. September 1210), *The Black Book of the Exchequer Text*', ed. and trans. David Crouch, in *Magna Carta and the England of King John*, ed. Janet S. Loengard (Woodbridge, UK: Boydell, 2010), 168–79.

[22] See 'Complaint of King John', 173, n. 6.

[23] Roger of Wendover, *Flores historiarum*, II, 48–9.

[24] Roger of Wendover, *Flores historiarum*, II, 49.

then fled to Ireland, where he was sheltered by William Marshal, Walter de Lacy, and Hugh de Lacy.[25] The relationship between King John and William was in tatters by late 1208.

Around this time, a member of William de Briouze's household divulged the circumstances of Arthur's death to someone in communication with the Margam religious community.[26] William notably had been responsible for the administration of Glamorgan (the county in which Margam Abbey is located) from 1202 to 1207.[27] The *Annals of Margam* account of Arthur's murder, which was compiled after William de Briouze's death in 1211,[28] is quite detailed. It states that on the fifth feria before Easter (3 April 1202), John became drunk after dinner, killed Arthur with his own hand, attached a heavy stone weight to Arthur's corpse, and threw it into the Seine. The chronicler adds that the corpse became entangled in a fisherman's dragnet, was taken ashore and identified, and was secretly buried in the priory of Bec, which is called Saint-Marie-du-Pré, 'propter metum tyranni' (on account of fear of the tyrant).[29] This account coincides with the rumor that Philippe is said to have heard in 1204.

In 1210, after failing to compel William Marshal and Walter and Hugh de Lacy to hand over William de Briouze, King John went to Ireland to arrest him.[30] William once again evaded John. This time he escaped to France. Not so lucky were his wife Matilda and son William, who were captured at Galloway by Duncan of Carrick (d. 1250). A vengeful John let them starve to death at Windsor.[31]

In the safety of Philippe's court, William de Briouze gave a damning account of Arthur's death. Philippe II's chaplain, Guillaume le Breton, offered a Latin verse rendering of William's story in Book Six of the *Philippide*. The story goes as follows: King John tried to bribe his attendants to devise a clandestine means of killing Arthur, but no one wanted to be the perpetrator of such a sin.[32] The king then moved Arthur to the old tower of Rouen and placed him in William's custody. John revealed to William his heinous plans for Arthur. William protested his

---

[25] 'Complaint of King John', 175 and 175, n.19.
[26] Powicke, 'King John and Arthur of Brittany', 670–1.
[27] Powicke, 'King John and Arthur of Brittany', 670.
[28] Powicke, 'King John and Arthur of Brittany', 666, n. 19.
[29] *Annales de Margan*, 27.
[30] 'Complaint of King John', 176.
[31] See 'Complaint of King John', 177–8; Roger of Wendover, *Flores historiarum*, II, 49; Anonymous of Béthune, *Histoire des ducs de Normandie et des rois d'Angleterre*, 111–15.
[32] Guillaume le Breton, *Philippide* 6, p. 170, lines 475–6.

unwillingness to be a party to such an unspeakable treason; he then reportedly declared that he was no longer comfortable having Arthur in his care and returned Arthur – still healthy, unwounded and in good spirits – to King John.[33]

Guillaume's account of the parricide in the *Philippide* is largely consistent with that of the *Annals of Margam*. The one notable divergence concerns the question of premeditation. According to the *Annals of Margam*, John killed Arthur in a fit of drunken rage. According to the *Philippide*, John was guilty of cold-blooded murder. He purposefully absented himself from his court attendants for four days, obtained a small bark, and sailed to Rouen in the cover of darkness.[34] At midnight he had his nephew removed from the tower and placed on his bark.[35] Guillaume, no doubt for dramatic effect, writes that Arthur begged his uncle for mercy on the ground of their kinship,[36] but to no avail. Guillaume then in grisly detail writes that John seized Arthur by the hairs of his forehead and drove his sword up to its hilt into the gut of the screaming youth; after extracting it, he plunged the sword into Arthur's neck; after that, he cast Arthur's lifeless body into the waves of the Seine.[37] The *Annals of Margam* and the *Philippide* agree that John killed Arthur with his own hands and threw him into the Seine. William de Briouze, the originator of these narratives, died on 9 August 1211, but Philippe had the testimony he needed to justify his seizure of John's French landholdings and to sanction a Capetian invasion of England.

The cause of this invasion can be traced back to September 1215 when John ceased to feign compliance with the provisions of Magna Carta, which he had been compelled to sign on 15 June of that year. The rebels responded by inviting Prince Louis (1187–1226), the dauphin of France and childhood companion of Arthur of Brittany, to invade England and replace John as their king.[38] Louis agreed but did not begin sending troops until December 1215.

According to Roger of Wendover, Prince Louis and the barons of England cited John's alleged murder of Arthur as the grounds for regime change. The St. Albans chronicler provides a singular account of the objections of Louis and the barons of England against King John,

[33] Guillaume le Breton, *Philippide* 6, pp. 170–1, lines 478–90. Also see Legge, 'William the Marshal and Arthur of Brittany', 23.

[34] Guillaume le Breton, *Philippide* 6, p. 171, lines 493–507.

[35] Guillaume le Breton, *Philippide* 6, p. 173, lines 552–5.

[36] Guillaume le Breton, *Philippide* 6, pp. 173–4, lines 558–60.

[37] Guillaume le Breton, *Philippide* 6, p. 174, lines 561–6.

[38] Roger of Wendover, *Flores historiarum*, II, 172–4.

which were allegedly delivered in April 1216 to Gualo the papal legate in France and to the pope at Rome. The first *propositio* raised against the king of England is 'quod Arthurum nepotem suum propriis manibus per proditionem interfecit, pessimo mortis genere, quod Angli murdrum appellant' (that John killed his nephew Arthur with his own hands through treachery by the worst kind of death, which the English call 'murder').[39] The messengers of Prince Louis were evidently drawing on William de Briouze's account of Arthur's death. Next, they claimed that King John was condemned to death in the court of the king of France by the judgment of his peers.[40]

Pope Innocent III, who had received John as his vassal on 15 May 1213, did not support Prince Louis' planned invasion of England and refused to bless the campaign. The pope claimed that John's anointment as king of England made him superior in standing to the barons of France and precluded him from being condemned by them to death. Innocent III also deemed it unlawful for the French court to inflict a sentence of death on an absent man who had not been called to court, convicted, or condemned. Furthermore, in response to the matter of Arthur's death, the Pope is said to have replied:

> Multi imperatores et principes, et etiam Francorum reges, multos in annalibus occidisse leguntur innocentes, nec tamen quenquam illorum legimus morti addictum; et cum Arthurus apud Mirebellum castrum, non ut innocens, sed quasi nocens et proditor domini et avunculi sui, cui homagium et ligantiam fecerat, captus fuerit, potuit de jure morte etiam turpissima sine judicio condemnari.[41]

> (Many emperors and princes – and even kings of the Franks – are reported in annals to have slaughtered many innocents, and we do not read that any of them were sentenced to death; and since Arthur was captured at the castle of Mirebeau, not as an innocent man, but as one doing harm and acting as a traitor to his lord and uncle, to whom he had done homage and made allegiance, he could rightly be condemned to death, even to a most shameful death without a trial.)

Rebuffed by the Roman Curia, Louis still had recourse to the court of public opinion in order to justify his invasion of England. Guillaume le Breton, who authored the *Philippide* between 1214 and 1224, was happy to furnish the ideological support Louis needed. Guillaume in his *Philippide* encourages Prince Louis to continue in his father's work of growing the

---

[39] Roger of Wendover, *Flores historiarum*, II, 185.
[40] Roger of Wendover, *Flores historiarum*, II, 185.
[41] Roger of Wendover, *Flores historiarum*, II, 186.

Capetian Empire to the size of the Carolingian Empire at its height.[42] On account of his Capetian partisanship (and perhaps also his Breton ties), Guillaume le Breton damns King John.[43] After describing John's brutal murder of Arthur, Guillaume unleashes the following invective against John in the sixth book of his *Philippide*:

> Ecce Judas alter; Herodes ecce secundus,
> Qui pueros inter Messiam perdere querens,
> Ne regnum perdat, proprios occidere natos
> Postea non veritus, et regnum perdidit et se,
> Dum reliquos metuens natos sibi guttera rupit.
> Sic et Judeus statuit crucifigere Christum
> Consilio Cayphe, metuens amittere gentem
> Atque locum. Sed, eo crucifixo, perdidit omne
> Perdere quod metuit, translatus in extera regna,
> Servitioque datus, quem Vespasianus in omnes
> Dispersit ventos privatum regis honore
> Atque sacerdotis; quod vir desideriorum
> Et Moises olim fore sic cecinere prophete.
> Sic tibi continget Arturi morte, Johannes;
> Ejus per vitam metuisti perdere regnum,
> Ejus per mortem vita regnoque carebis.
> Antea quam fato fieres ludente monarcha,
> Patris ab ore tui *Sine-terra* nomen habebas;
> Ne pater ergo tuus sit in hoc tibi nomine mendax,
> Hec tibi mors addet rem nominis hujus et omen.
> Nam tibi fatalis venit hora, nec est procul a te,
> Qua, factus mortem cunctis odiosus ob istam,
> Fies et vives sine terra pluribus annis;
> Postea privatus regno, privabere vita.[44]

(Behold the other Judas; behold the second Herod, who, seeking to destroy the Messiah among boys so that he would not lose his kingdom, afterwards was not afraid to kill his own children and lost both his kingdom and himself. While fearing the surviving children, he broke his neck. And so the Jew decided to crucify Christ, by the advice of Caiaphas, fearing to lose his people and place, but, with Christ crucified, he lost all that he feared and was sent into foreign lands and given over to servitude. Vespasian cast him to all the winds, deprived

[42] Guillaume le Breton, *Philippide* 12, p. 380, lines 826–30.
[43] For a discussion of how Philippe II represented himself as *Carolus redivivus* and the patterning of the Capetians after their Carolingian predecessors, see Gabrielle M. Spiegel, 'The Reditus Regni ad Stirpem Karoli Magni: A New Look', *French Historical Studies* 7, n. 2 (1971): 162, 165–6, 170.
[44] Guillaume le Breton, *Philippide* 6, pp. 174–5, lines 575–98.

of the honor of a king and of a priest, just as the prophets, [Daniel] the man of desires and Moses, long ago prophesied would happen. John, the same thing will happen to you on account of the death of Arthur. Through his life you feared to lose your kingdom, through his death you will lose your life and your kingdom. Before you were made monarch by a trick of fate you bore the name 'Lackland' from the mouth of your father. Therefore, so that your father may not be a liar [in giving you this name], this death will add the fact and omen of this name. For the fated hour comes for you and it is not far off from you. Therefore, having been made loathsome to all on account of this death, you will become and you will live without land for many years. Later, deprived of your kingdom, you will be deprived of your life.)

This tour de force of typology stresses that John was destined to lose his realm on account of the murder he committed to secure it. Guillaume represents Arthur of Brittany as an innocent victim, arguably even a Christ-like martyr. We can push this analogy a bit further and see in Guillaume le Breton's choice of biblical imagery an allusion to Arthur as the messianic fulfillment of the Breton Hope. King John is, of course, fashioned as the new King Herod, the great slaughterer of the innocents. Herod, threatened by signs and prophecies that the Christ child would eventually rise to become the king of kings, attempted to bring about the infant Jesus' early death, but failed. Similarly, King John, threatened by his nephew's stronger dynastic claim to the throne of England and (as Guillaume would have us infer) by the great expectations surrounding Arthur's 'messianic' name, succeeded in bringing about his nephew's demise. In order to defame John, Guillaume thus makes Arthur of Brittany something of a messianic figure.[45]

The author of the first half of the *Chronicle of Lanercost*, a Franciscan writer from the north of England active in the last quarter of the thirteenth century, offers a similar typological reading, except that he uses imagery from both the Hebrew Bible and the Gospels:

Sed quia sæpe opes ac honores fidem dirimunt inter nobiles, advertens rex perfidus juvenem octodecim annos habentem, vultu decorum,

---

[45] In the 'Post-Vulgate' *Merlin* Continuation (c. 1230–40), King Arthur's actions bear resemblance to King John's treatment of Arthur of Brittany. King Arthur, much like Herod, is responsible for the endangerment of many innocent children in his realm. Merlin tells Arthur that a child born on a certain date is fated to destroy Arthur's kingdom. In an effort to circumvent this dire prophecy, Arthur has all the sons of Logres born in that month gathered up in a tower and then cast out to sea in a ship without a captain. See *La suite du roman de Merlin*, ed. Gilles Roussineau (Geneva: Droz, 2006), 56–65. For an English translation, see *The Post-Vulgate Cycle: The Merlin Continuation*, trans. Martha Asher. *The Old French Arthurian Vulgate and Post-Vulgate in Translation*, ed. Norris J. Lacy, vol. 8 (Cambridge, UK: D. S. Brewer, 2010), 35–40.

corpore procerum, populo gratiosum, ac sciens eum ex seniore fratre
majus jus in regnum habere, ac facile ad hoc posse induci propter
sui odium tam Brittos quam Anglicos, cepit insidias ponere juveni
puero ut eum eximeret de medio. Quemadmodum igitur Saul David
sancto insidiatus est ut eum lancea transfigeret cum pariete, sic
iste cœnanti sibi puerum jubet astare arcto inter ignem et mensam
spatio, ut in occulto penu-cultro perfoderet, et in ignem propelleret.
Sed spiritus innocentiæ signo sibi ostendit quid alius providit, et ab
irato tyranno semiustus hac vice secessit.[46] Igitur conceptum impius
complere proponens dolum ne detegeretur, et sic facere studens ne
promulgaretur, assumptis quodam vespere causa spatiandi dicto
juvene loco armigeri, et Willelmo de Vepount, barone, et domino
Westmeriæ, ac molendinario, ut dicitur, per aliquod spatium maris
in cymba ima se ab habitatione hominum separaverunt, et inter
eos, nescitur per cujus manum, conceptum facinus fini exitiali
deduxerunt. Sic a proprio solo, tanquam extra vineam,[47] verus heres
Angliæ ejectus est et dejectus.[48]

(But because wealth and honors often destroy faith between nobles,
the perfidious king [John], noticing that the youth was eighteen years
old, had a handsome face, a noble physique, and was agreeable to
the people, and knowing that Arthur had the greater right to the
kingdom from his elder brother and also that both the Bretons and
English could be easily led to that [i.e. making Arthur king] due to
their hatred of him [John], John began to lay traps for the young boy
in order to eliminate him from their midst. Therefore, just as Saul laid
a trap for holy David so that he might impale him to the wall with
a lance, so he [John] ordered the boy to stand by him, dining in a
narrow space between the fire and the table, so that he might secretly
pierce him through with a food knife and cast him into the fire. But
the spirit of innocence showed to Arthur by a sign what the other
[John] planned, and, half-burnt, he thus withdrew from the irate
tyrant. Therefore, the impious one planning to finish the treachery
he had started, lest it be revealed, and striving to make it such that
it was not publicized, on a certain evening took the said youth in
place of a squire out for a walk, along with William of Vieuxpont,
baron and lord of Westmoreland, and also a miller, as is said, and in a
very deep skiff they separated themselves by some space of sea from
where people live, and among them, it is not known by whose hand,
they led their planned crime to its deadly end. Thus from his own
soil – outside the vineyard, so to speak – the true heir of England was
thrown out and overthrown.)

[46] Compare with 1 Samuel 18:10–12; 1 Samuel 19:9–10.
[47] Compare with Matthew 21:39.
[48] *Chronicon de Lanercost*, 12.

This chronicler presents John not as another Herod, but rather as a second Saul: a king who, conscious of the fact that he had lost divine favor, became fiercely jealous of his position as king. Saul also became so envious of the popularity and accomplishments of a member of his royal household (the *Wunderkind* David) that he plotted to assassinate the young and innocent hero on multiple occasions. In this explicit biblical analogy, Arthur of Brittany emerges as the new David, who, in addition to enjoying the support of the lord and the divine right of kingship, became a messianic political and religious hero to the Israelites, a prefiguration of Jesus, and a key inspiration for both the myth of Arthur's return and Geoffrey of Monmouth's construction of the life of Arthur. The chronicler concludes his discussion of Arthur's demise by alluding to the Parable of the Tenants, which is recounted in the Gospel of Matthew. Jesus tells of how a landowner (God) plants a vineyard (the kingdom of God, the city of Jerusalem, and more specifically the Temple) and entrusts it to tenants (the chief priests of the Temple and the Pharisees). When the landowner's servants (God's prophets and faithful believers) come on behalf of the landowner in order to obtain the vineyard's produce, the tenants beat, kill, and stone them. Finally, the landowner sends his son and heir (Jesus) for the fruits of the vineyard, expecting the tenants to respect him. They instead seize him, eject him from the vineyard, and kill him in an effort to acquire his inheritance, the vineyard. Jesus then explains that the Lord expels the wicked tenants and replaces them with faithful ones. Through this allusion, the medieval chronicler quite clearly casts John as the faithless tenant / the Pharisees, and he explicitly makes Arthur the true heir, a Christ figure, who is cast off and slaughtered. Accordingly, the vineyard is not the kingdom of Israel, but rather the kingdom of England and the Continental possessions of the Angevin Empire. And the further significance of the allusion is that John is presented as warranting divine retribution in this life or the next.

Yet another example of a portrayal of Arthur as an innocent martyr occurs in a thirteenth-century commentary on Geoffrey of Monmouth's *Prophetia Merlini* (British Library, MS Cotton Claudius B vii, fols. 224r–233v). The commentary, which ends with events from the reign of Henry III (c. 1230), glosses *Historia regum Britannie* 114.101–2 as follows:

> *Principium eius* [i.e., Sextus Hiberniae = Johannes rex, filius regis Henrici] *etc.*: in principio regni sui valde dubitavit de Arturo nepote eius, ne superveniret et occuparet regnum super eum et valde affectavit ipsum Arturum apprehendere aliquo ingenio et tandem cepit eum in werra apud Mirabellum et de ipso affectum suum

implevit, cuius affectus *finis ad superos convolavit*, id est ad Deum et sanctos suos per martirium dicti Arturi.[49]

(*His beginning* [i. e. the Sixth of Ireland = King John, son of King Henry] *etc.*: in the beginning of his reign, King John thought about his nephew Arthur greatly, specifically about how he could prevent the boy from coming up and taking the kingdom from him, and John greatly aimed to apprehend Arthur himself by some trick. He finally captured him in war at Mirebeau and fulfilled his will with respect to him, whose inflicted *end flew to the heavens*, that is to God and his saints, through the martyrdom of the aforesaid Arthur.)

John again appears as an insecure monarch guilty of parricide and Arthur as a martyr who is among the saints in Heaven.

Arthur of Brittany was also remembered as a harbinger of John's destruction. This representation is detectable in Roger of Wendover's *Flores historiarum*. John reportedly went to Falaise in 1202 in order to convince Arthur to become his faithful man. Arthur responded with indignation, demanding that John return to him all the lands and possessions that Richard held at the time of his death. Arthur asserted that these things belonged to him by right of inheritance and that, if they were not returned at once, John would never enjoy a lasting peace. Arthur's imprudent words reportedly cost him his life. According to Roger, John killed Arthur in 1202 and shortly thereafter had himself crowned king of England by Hubert Walter.[50] King John then crossed the Channel to Normandy, and rumor simultaneously spread throughout Europe that he had killed Arthur by his own hand. For this reason, 'multi animos avertentes a rege semper deinceps, ut ausi sunt, nigerrimo ipsum odio perstrinxerunt' (many, turning their minds from John (as they dared) made unfavorable mention of him with the blackest hate).[51]

Roger of Wendover's description of events is not historically accurate: Archbishop Hubert crowned John not in 1202 but in 1199 when Arthur was very much alive. The liberties taken with history in Roger's *Flores historiarum* serve to indicate that John's reign was cursed from its very beginning. Not only did John usurp the throne from its rightful occupant (Arthur of Brittany), he ascended it in a state of mortal sin. The *Annals of Margam* conveys this message:

---

[49] 'MS Cotton Claudius B vii Commentary on the *Prophetia Merlini*', ed. Jacob Hammer, in Jacob Hammer, 'A Commentary on the Prophetia Merlini (Geoffrey of Monmouth's *Historia Regum Britanniae*, Book VII) (Continuation)', *Speculum* 15, n. 4 (1940): 412, lines 423–9.

[50] Roger of Wendover, *Flores historiarum*, I, 315–16.

[51] Roger of Wendover, *Flores historiarum*, I, 316.

In qua coronatione omnes graviter peccaverunt, tum quia idem
Johannes nullum jus in regno habuit, vivente Arthuro filio senioris
fratris sui Gaufridi comitis Britanniæ; tum quia licet aliquando hæres
regni fuisset, propter memoratam tamen proditionem abjudicatus
fuit et exhæredatus. Et quia omnes gravissime Deum offenderunt,
omnes postea per eum tanquam instrumento suæ offensionis puniti
sunt et afflicti.[52]

(In John's coronation all had sinned gravely not only because the
same John held no right to the realm, with Arthur the son of his
elder brother Geoffrey count of Brittany alive, but also because it
was recognized for some time that Arthur was heir to the realm.
On account of the aforementioned prodition John was deprived by
judicial verdict and disinherited. And because all had offended God
gravely, all were punished and afflicted afterward through him as
much as the instrument of their offense.)

Moreover, the author of the *Chronicle of Lanercost*, in the opening lines of
his work (which treat the events of 1201), remarks that 'Johannes destruxit
legitimum semen hereditarium successionis Anglicanæ.... Quod facinus
necdum, ut creditur a multis, æqua lance recompensatum, suspensa super
stabilitate regni corda reddit sapientium' (John destroyed the legitimate
seed of the hereditary succession of England.... That crime, which has not
yet been repaid in the scales of justice, as many believe, keeps the hearts
of the wise in suspense over the stability of the kingdom.)[53] It would thus
appear that the memory of Arthur of Brittany did far more harm to King
John than did Arthur himself. Indeed, remembrance of John's foul crime
lingered into the age of Shakespeare and his play *King John*.

The Arthurian pretensions of the Castilian royal court

As John was struggling to retain Normandy and Anjou, the ruling house
of Castile attempted to take Gascony. The Castilian claim to it had an
Arthurian dimension that provides unique insight into the relationship
between the Plantagenet dynasty, King John, and the figure of King
Arthur. In 1177, Henry II's daughter, Eleanor (or Leonor, 1162–1214) of
England, married Alfonso VIII of Castile (r. 1158–1214). Leonor is credited
as having been a transmitter of Arthurian literature to Iberia.[54] The first
known Castilian allusion to the Arthurian tradition (or more particularly,

---

[52] *Annales de Margan*, 24–5.
[53] *Chronicon de Lanercost*, 1.
[54] See William J. Entwistle, *The Arthurian Legend in the Literature of the Spanish Peninsula*
(London: J. M. Dent, 1925), 32–5, 47.

to King Arthur's death) occurs in the *Anales Toledanos Primeros* (to 1219). The critical passage appears to have been written during Leonor's reign or shortly thereafter.[55] Leonor, according to Alfonso VIII, brought Gascony to their union as her dowry. The Castilian position was that, upon the death of Eleanor of Aquitaine, Leonor and Alfonso were to come into joint possession of Gascony.[56] In 1205, a year after the old queen's death (1 April 1204), when Philippe II was seizing control of Poitou, Alfonso VIII tried to take Gascony. He failed, but the Castilian court did not abandon its claim.[57] Half a century later, Alfonso X, king of Leon and Castile (r. 1252–84), reasserted it.

Plantagenet heritage was the basis for the Castilian court's claim to Gascony. This fact is evident in a *planh* that was written in 1212 shortly after the death of Fernando of Castile (1189–1211), a son of Alfonso VIII and Leonor. The poem's author, the Gascon troubadour Guiraut de Calanson (*fl.* 1202–12), praised the late Castilian Infante by declaring not only that Fernando resembled three of his Plantagenet uncles, Young King Henry, Richard I, and Geoffrey of Brittany, but also that his person was the perfect amalgamation of their finer qualities.[58] King John is conspicuously absent from this list of Fernando's maternal uncles. The conflict between the English and Castilian courts coupled with John's infamy surely account for this omission. Also significant is how Guiraut opens his *planh*:

> Belh senher Dieus, quo pot esser sufritz
> Tan estranhs dols cum es del jov' enfan,
> Del filh del rei de Castella prezan,
> Don anc nulhs oms jorn no· s parti marritz
> Ni ses cosselh ni dezacosselhatz;
> Qu'en lui era tot lo pretz restauratz
> Del rei Artus, qu'om sol dir e retraire,
> On trobavan cosselh tug bezonhos.
> Ar es mortz selh que degr' esser guizaire,
> Lo mielhs del mon de totz los joves bos!

[55] See *Anales Toledanos Primeros*, ed. Henrique Florez, in *España Sagrada. Theatro Geographico-Historico de la Iglesia de España*, vol. 23: *Continuacion de las memorias de la Santa Iglesia de Tuy y Coleccion de los chronicones pequeños publicados, è ineditos, de la Historia de España*, 2nd edn. (Madrid: La Oficina de la Viuda é Hijo de Marin, 1799), 382.

[56] See Joseph F. O'Callaghan, *The Learned King: The Reign of Alfonso X of Castile* (Philadelphia: University of Pennsylvania Press, 1993), 151–2.

[57] See Eleanor C. Lodge, *Gascony under English Rule* (London: Methuen, 1926), 25–6.

[58] Guiraut de Calanson, 'Belh senher Dieus…(planh)', ed. Willy Ernst, in Willy Ernst, 'Die Lieder des provenzalischen Trobadors Guiraut von Calanso', *Romanische Forschungen* 44, n. 2 (1930): 331.

(Dear Lord God, how can such severe grief be borne as that for the young Infante, the esteemed son of the king of Castile, from whom no one ever departed sorrowful, without help or deprived of support, for in him was restored all the excellence of King Arthur, of whom men tell and narrate, in whom all the needy found help. Now he is dead, he who should be a guide, the best in the world of all good young men.)

This elegy is reminiscent of Bertran de Born's *planh* for Geoffrey of Brittany, 'A totz dic qe ja mais non voil', in which the poet declares that the return of Arthur would not be sufficient compensation for the loss of Geoffrey. Guiraut's 'Belh senher Dieus' is arguably even more evocative of a *planh* for Richard I written by Gaucelm Faidit (c. 1170–1202), a troubadour from Limousin, who had been in the service of both Geoffrey of Brittany and Richard the Lionheart. In his 'Fortz chausa es que tot lo major dan' (written shortly after Richard I's death in 1199), Gaulcelm asserts not only that the late Richard was more generous than Alexander and more worthy than Charlemagne and Arthur,[59] but also that it would take a truly noble-hearted and strong-minded prince to replace Richard and his brothers the Young King and Geoffrey of Brittany.[60] In asserting that Fernando was a fitting successor to the Young King Henry, Count Geoffrey, and Richard I, Guirant appears to have been directly responding to Gaucelm's *planh*. Fernando, according to Guirant, could have taken the place of these three brothers. Guirant, as an inhabitant of Plantagenet-ruled Gascony, was no doubt familiar with the use of King Arthur as exemplary comparison for the Plantagenet princes. His decision to compare Fernando to Arthur suggests that Guiraut saw Arthur as emblematic of the House of Plantagenet. By linking Fernando with Arthur, the adopted ancestor of the Plantagenets, Giraut emphasizes that the offspring of Alfonso and Leonor were rightful claimants to Plantagenet lands, specifically Gascony. In these Iberian writings, members of the Plantagenet dynasty are presented as successors to Arthur, but John is excluded from this honor.

A singular comparison of King Arthur and King John

John seems not to have cultivated a likeness to King Arthur, but this does not mean that the figure of Arthur was never used as a point of

---

[59] Gaucelm Faidit, 'Fortz chausa es que tot lo major dan', ed. Martín de Riquer, in Martín de Riquer, *Los Trovadores: Historia, literaria y textos*, 3 vols. (Barcelona: Editorial Planeta, 1975–92), II, 771 (n. 148), lines 10–18.
[60] Gaucelm Faidit, 'Fortz chausa es que tot lo major dan', II, 772, lines 46–54; Jewers, 'Another Arthur among the Troubadours', 30–2.

reference to judge John's rulership. However, only one direct comparison of King Arthur and King John has come to light, and it appears in the *Histoire des ducs de Normandie et des rois d'Angleterre*.[61] Its author, the Anonymous of Béthune, is thought to have come from Artois and to have been in the household of Robert of Béthune, who was one of the Flemish allies that came to John's aid in 1215.[62] The *Histoire* begins with the arrival of the Northmen in France and its last recorded event dates from 1220, and the bulk of it was written after John's death (19 October 1216).[63] The Anonymous of Béthune, it should be noted, offers many such critiques of John's character flaws, particularly his lechery, envy, and his many retreats from battle, which the author regards as demonstrations of cowardice.[64] Gillingham has made a study of the chronicle's coverage of the events from the accession of John (May 1199) to Prince Louis' departure from England (September 1217) and has observed a marked increase in thoroughness and specificity beginning in May 1213, which leads him to conclude that the author had access to 'diary-style written notes' beginning in 1213.[65]

The Arthurian comparison in the *Histoire* occurs in the context of John's return to and governance of England after he failed to retake Normandy and Anjou from Philippe II in 1206. Between 1207 and 1212, John sought to accumulate as much revenue as possible to finance another French campaign, imposing a heavy tax burden on his subjects and instituting brutal revenue-collection methods. The Anonymous of Béthune succinctly summarizes this, stating that John 'repassa en Engletierre, ù il fist puis molt de maus' (returned to England where he then did a great number of bad things)[66] and then specifying these evils:

> Or oiiés quel vie li rois Jehans mena, puis que il fu repairiés en Engletierre. Toute s'entente torna à deduire son cors: bois et rivieres antoit, et moult l'en plaisoit li deduis. Tant se fist douter par sa tierre ke toutes les gens tiesmoignoient que puis le tans le roi Artu n'avoit eu roi en Engletierre qui tant fust doutés en Engletierre, en Gales, en Eschoce ne en Yrlande, comme il estoit. Les bestes sauvages avoient tel pais k'eles passoient par les chans ausi priveement comme se che fussent brebis. Quant les gens erroient par les chemins, et

[61] See Ostmann, 'Die Bedeutung der Arthurtradition', 253.
[62] John Gillingham, 'The Anonymous of Béthune, King John and Magna Carta', in *Magna Carta and the England of King John*, ed. Janet S. Loengard (Woodbridge, UK: Boydell, 2010), 28–9.
[63] See Gillingham, 'Anonymous of Béthune', 33.
[64] Anonymous of Béthune, *Histoire des ducs de Normandie et des rois d'Angleterre*, 105.
[65] Gillingham, 'Anonymous of Béthune', 33.
[66] Anonymous of Béthune, *Histoire des ducs de Normandie et des rois d'Angleterre*, 109.

il les veoient paistre delés eus, et il poingnoient vers elles, ne s'en daignoient-elles fuir plus grant alure del trot u des petis galos; et quant chil qui les chaçoient arriestoient, elles arriestoient ausi.[67]

(Now hear what sort of life King John led after he had returned to England. He turned all his attention to amusing himself: he frequented the woods and rivers, and the amusement in it was very pleasing to him. He made himself so feared throughout his land that all the people testified that not since the time of King Arthur had there been a king in England who was so feared in England, in Wales, in Scotland and in Ireland as he was. The savage beasts had such peace that they would pass by the fields as unmolested as if they were sheep. When people would travel by the roads, and if they would see them pasture beside them, and when they would gallop towards them, the beasts would not bother to flee at a quicker pace than at a trot or a slow gallop, and, when those who would chase them stopped, they would stop also.)

As Holt has noted, the Anonymous of Béthune was referring to John's strict enforcement of Forest Law.[68] William the Conqueror began Forest Law when he designated select woodlands, tracts of arable land, and even towns and villages as the Royal Forest wherein beasts of the forest could roam free and be preserved for the king's hunting. In designated areas, the king's own legislation, Forest Law, prevailed, and violators did not have recourse to Common Law. If anyone was caught interfering with the land in any way, the said violator would have to appear either in local forest courts or (in more serious cases) in the next session of the nearest forest eyre, which was typically presided over by a chief justice of the Crown. King John, between 1207 and 1212, enforced Forest Law to an unprecedented extent, exploiting it for his optimal financial gain.[69] This was a major source of grievance against King John.

It is fitting that the Anonymous of Béthune evokes the name of King Arthur in the context of John's enforcement of Forest Law. Gervase of Tilbury, in his *Otia Imperialia*, which was completed only a few years earlier, states that the keepers of the royal forests in Great Britain or Brittany claimed that on some days at noon, and on other days shortly after nightfall when the moon was full, they often would see a band of

---

[67] Anonymous of Béthune, *Histoire des ducs de Normandie et des rois d'Angleterre*, 109.

[68] See James Clarke Holt, 'King John', in his *Magna Carta and Medieval Government* (London: Hambledon, 1985), 97–8.

[69] See Jane Winters, 'Forest Law', Early English Laws Project. University of London: Institute of Historical Research / King's College London (http://www. earlyenglishlaws.ac.uk/reference/essays/forest-law/#fn:19, accessed 13 December 2013); Warren, *King John*, 151–2.

knights on a hunt, who identified themselves as the *societas ou familia Arturi*.[70] Jean-Claude Schmitt has suggested that the foresters of the living king (for example, King John) used such stories of his preternatural counterpart, King Arthur, to scare subjects into obeying Forest Law.[71] The passage excerpted above does not confirm Schmitt's suspicion but is consistent with it.

The Anonymous of Béthune uses *puis le tans le roi Artu* to signify the remote past and to indicate that John's severity was without precedent in living memory. The chronicler also presents Arthur as an imperial monarch whose authority was felt not only in England, but also in Wales, Scotland, and Ireland. John achieved this distinction but for a short space of time. In 1211, he headed two expeditions into Gwynedd – the first royal campaigns into Wales since 1165. The latter of these campaigns was a stunning victory for the English king. For a short time thereafter, John held more land in Wales and was in a stronger position there than any of his post-Conquest predecessors.[72] John also assumed a leadership position in Scotland. In the summer of 1209 he was about to invade Scotland, but the ailing William I of Scotland bought him off. By the treaty of Norham (August 1209), William promised to pay fifteen thousand marks and handed over thirteen hostages and two of his daughters to the English king.[73] In 1211, before his political fortune took a turn for the worse, John appeared to be on his way to becoming a *rex totius Britannie* like the legendary King Arthur.[74]

Arthur as ideal king in the London Collection

Thus far, we have considered rival claims to Arthur that were divided along the lines of ethnicity and have also examined how two rival members of the same ruling family used Arthur in contrasting ways in their bid for power. A contest for dominance over the Arthurian narrative also developed along social lines. This tension became more conspicuous near the end of the reign of King John.

---

[70] Gervase of Tilbury, *Otia Imperialia* 2.12, pp. 336–7.

[71] See Jean-Claude Schmitt, *Les revenants: Les vivants et les morts dans la société*, trans. Teresa Lavender Fagan as *Ghosts in the Middle Ages: The Living and the Dead in Medieval Society* (Chicago: Chicago University Press, 1998), 120.

[72] See Ifor W. Rowlands, 'King John and Wales', in *King John: New Interpretations*, ed. S. D. Church (Woodbridge, UK: Boydell, 1999), 280, 284.

[73] See John Gillingham, 'John (1167–1216), King of England, and Lord of Ireland, Duke of Normandy and of Aquitaine, and Count of Anjou', *ODNB* (Oxford: Oxford University Press, 2004–13) (http://www.oxforddnb.com/view/article/14841?docPos=2, accessed 14 December 2013).

[74] See Walter of Coventry, *Memoriale*, II, 203.

When constructing the figure of Arthur in his *Historia regum Britannie*, Geoffrey of Monmouth provided an ideal king not only for the Plantagenet dynasty but also for the baronage of England. Geoffrey's Arthur, as we have seen, cherishes and richly rewards his knights for valor and faithful service. Even more importantly, he rules with the advice and consent of his nobles. The prime example of Arthur as a consensus decision-maker in Geoffrey's *Historia* is the king's response to the 'Roman threat'. After receiving a demand for tribute from Rome, Arthur requests the counsel of his greater magnates, including Duke Cador of Cornwall, King Hoel of the Brittany, and King Anguselus of Scotland, who are to help him decide whether he should declare war or sue for peace.[75] Arthur declares war on Rome only after he has the unanimous support of his barons.[76] Geoffrey of Monmouth's Arthur is thus a limited, feudal monarch.

In Chrétien de Troyes' *Erec et Enide* and *Cligés*, as in Geoffrey's *Historia* and Wace's *Brut*, Arthur is a just king who rewards his knights generously for their service; additionally, Arthur shines as an exemplary feudal king. He is an upholder of *costume* – customary law.[77] In *Erec et Enide*, Chrétien has Arthur enunciate his understanding of his duty as king. Arthur welcomes the advice and opinions of his vassals. He expressly avoids making new laws (whereby he could consolidate his authority at the expense of his vassals); instead, he upholds tradition, specifically the traditions of his father (*l'usage Pandragon*), and maintains the status quo.[78] This depiction of Arthur catered to the interests of the high nobility, who enjoyed the greatest number of feudal honors and privileges. Arthur's promise to be an impartial dispenser of justice could be interpreted as an expression of concern for the king's lesser knights.

Arthur, it is true, declines in competency in Chrétien's final three romances: *Lancelot*, *Yvain*, and *Perceval*,[79] but in one post-Chrétien verse romance, the *Roman d'Yder*, Arthur is not simply lethargic and inept, but downright sinister. In *Yder*, Arthur's much-celebrated magnanimity (*largesse*), courtesy, and justice give way to pettiness, covetousness, and

---

[75] Geoffrey of Monmouth, *Historia regum Britannie* 159.448–54, pp. 216–17.

[76] Geoffrey of Monmouth, *Historia regum Britannie* 162.531–4, pp. 220–1.

[77] See Erich Köhler, *Ideal und Wirklichkeit in der höfischen Epik. Studien zur Form der Frühen Artus- und Graldichtung,* trans. Éliane Kaufholz as *L'Aventure chevaleresque: Idéal et réalité dans le romans courtois* (Paris: Gallimard, 1974), 11–13; Schmolke-Hasselmann, *Evolution of Arthurian Romance*, 88–92.

[78] Chrétien de Troyes, *Erec et Enide*, 67–8, lines 1803–15.

[79] See Noble, *Chrétien's Arthur*, 233–4; Barbara N. Sargent-Baur, 'Dux Bellorum / Rex Militum / Roi Fainéant: The Transformations of Arthur in the Twelfth Century', in *King Arthur: A Casebook*, ed. Edward Donald Kennedy (New York: Routledge, 1996), 39–41.

tyranny. Arthur's imperialist drive knows no limit. He also becomes insanely jealous of his queen-consort Guinevere. Schmolke-Hasselmann believes that the *Roman d'Yder* dates from the reign of King John and its unusually negative portrayal of Arthur is a comment on the misrule of King John.[80] Her suggestion is intriguing but conjectural. Schmolke-Hasselmann does not provide any evidence to support her dating of *Yder* to between 1190 and 1220 despite the fact that this window of time is critical for her argument.[81] The precise date of composition of this text is unknown, and the only extant copy of *Yder*, Cambridge University Library, Ee. 4. 26, is an Anglo-Norman manuscript from the second half of the thirteenth century.[82] Schmolke-Hasselmann, however, employs circular logic when analyzing *Yder*: her interpretation of the work as political satire depends on her fairly narrow dating of the text, while her dating of the text, from all indications, rests on her construal of it. She observes the negative depiction of Arthur in *Yder* and is aware that John was extremely unpopular with his nobles. So, recognizing the possibility of a temporal and geographical overlap, she presumes a connection between the literary King Arthur and the historical King John. In framing *Yder* as an indirect commentary on John's rule, Schmolke-Hasselmann does not find it necessary to identify precise correspondences between the depiction of Arthur in *Yder* and that of John in contemporary writings. This reading is particularly problematic because John's successor, Henry III of England (r. 1216–72), also continually found himself in conflict with his barons, even from the earliest years of his reign. A case could be made, then, that the depiction of Arthur in *Yder* corresponds at least as closely to Henry III as to John. Yet we must be careful to recognize that the anonymous author of *Yder* need not have had one specific historical king in mind. The negative depiction of Arthur may even have been a remnant from the *Yder*-poet's source material. In any event, Arthur's negative characteristics in *Yder* suggest that its author was writing for an audience with an unfavorable view of its monarch or monarchy more broadly.

---

[80] See Schmolke-Hasselmann, *Evolution of Arthurian Romance*, 247. Also see Beate Schmolke-Hasselmann, 'King Arthur as Villain in the Thirteenth-century Romance *Yder*', *Reading Medieval Studies* 6 (1980): 31–2.

[81] Schmolke-Hasselmann's dating of *Yder* has not been challenged. See *The Romance of Yder*, ed. and trans. Alison Adams (Cambridge, UK: D. S. Brewer, 1983), 13–14.

[82] *Yder*'s first editor, Heinrich Gelzer, determines that the romance was written in the Western Norman dialect of Old French and believes that the work dates from 1223–5. See *Der altfranzösische Yderroman*, ed. Heinrich Gelzer (Dresden: Max Niemeyer, 1913), lxxix. On the basis of its rhymes, the text's most recent editor, Alison Adams, has concluded that '*Yder* originated in the Western part of mainland France and was written at the end of the twelfth or beginning of the thirteenth century' (*Yder*, 5).

Let us again step outside the domain of Arthurian literature proper to consider a cluster of Arthurian legal precedents that were more evidently fabricated in protest against King John's rule. These precedents are contained in a compilation of English customary law referred to as the 'London Collection' (Manchester, John Rylands University Library MS Lat. 155, fols. 4r–130v and London, British Library Additional MS 14252, fols. 6–124).[83] This collection contains juridical precedents and historical entries that range in purported date from the remote British past to recent obsequies for Richard the Lionheart.[84] The Collector consistently advances the interests of the citizens of London and is thought to have worked for the London Guildhall.[85] The precise date of the compilation is unknown, but it was, as evidenced by the obsequies, assembled after the death of Richard I (6 April 1199).[86] According to Derek Keene, the project was begun before the sealing of Magna Carta (15 June 1215). A list of the sheriffs who held office in London, which is contained in the Collection, reveals that material was still being added as late as 1217.[87] The London Collection, as has been noted by Walter Ullmann and others, expresses the principles of Magna Carta and employs some of the same language as the famous document.[88] But whereas Ullmann regards the

[83] Digital facsimiles of these manuscripts are viewable online. See 'Leges Anglorum Londoniis collectae (Leges Angl)', Early English Laws Project. University of London: Institute of Historical Research / King's College London (http://www.earlyenglishlaws.ac.uk/laws/texts/leges-angl/#manuscripts, accessed 11 October 2012). For dating and analysis of the manuscripts, see Derek Keene, 'Text, Visualisation and Politics: London, 1150–1250', *Transactions of the Royal Historical Society* 18 (2008): 80–1; Felix Liebermann, 'A Contemporary Manuscript of the "Leges Anglorum Londoniis collectae"', *English Historical Review* 28, n. 112 (1913): 732–45. Selections of the London Collection have been edited in Felix Liebermann, *Über die Leges Anglorum saeculo xiii ineunte Londoniis collectae* (Halle: Max Niemeyer, 1894) and in *Die Gesetze der Angelsachsen*, ed. Felix Liebermann, 3 vols. (Halle: Max Niemeyer 1903–16), I, *passim*. Also see Bruce R. O'Brien, 'Forgers of Law and their Readers: The Crafting of English Political Identities between the Norman Conquest and the Magna Carta', *Political Science and Politics* 43, n. 3 (2010): 467–73.

[84] See Liebermann, *Über die Leges Anglorum*, 80–2.

[85] O'Brien, 'Forgers of Law and Their Readers', 470.

[86] See John Gillingham, '*Stupor mundi*: 1204 et un obituaire de Richard Coeur de Lion depuis longtemps tombé dans l'oubli', in *Plantagenêts et Capétiens: Confrontations et héritages*, ed. Martin Aurell and Noël-Yves Tonnerre (Turnhout: Brepols, 2006), 401–6.

[87] Keene, 'Text, Visualisation and Politics', 80–1.

[88] See Walter Ullmann, 'On the Influence of Geoffrey of Monmouth in English History', in *Speculum Historiae: Geschichte im Spiegel von Geschichtsschreibung und Geschichtsdeutung*, ed. Clemens Bauer, Laetitia Boehm, and Max Müller (Freiburg: Karl Alber, 1965), 260–3; James Clarke Holt, 'Rights and Liberties in Magna Carta', in James Clarke Holt, *Magna Carta and Medieval Government* (London: Hambledon, 1985), 207–8.

text as a combination of justificatory document and political manifesto that was completed before the signing of Magna Carta and that perhaps influenced its drafting, the compilation could just as easily have been a consequence of Magna Carta, and its purpose may have been to provide precedents for the gains obtained in the great charter.[89]

Among the London Collector's interpolations are customs and liberties of the city of London as well as precedents from antiquity that served to legitimate the institutions and practices of the London Commune.[90] Ironically, it was Prince John who had formally recognized the London Commune and had sworn to protect its dignities and the dignities of the city of London. As noted in the previous chapter, John made this concession on 8 October 1191 in order to gain support for his bid to succeed Richard I.[91] In the two decades that followed John's rise to the throne, the relationship between the king and the leading citizens of the metropolis became strained. Beginning around 1212, St. Paul's became a center of opposition against him. In 1213, a great assembly of clergy and barons met there to voice complaints against the king's misrule.[92] The London Collection encapsulates the interests of these malcontents. Its author, in the words of Keene, 'outline[s] an ideal, but historically based structure of local government and political assembly, informed by common counsel, communes and an oath of brotherhood which united nobility, townsmen, and all people for the utility of the realm'.[93] Yet the Collector was also an English 'imperialist', who favored strong, but not autocratic, monarchy. Implicit in his utopian vision is a rejection of John's despotic rule.[94]

When the Collector found rhetorical manipulation of his sources insufficient for his ends, he interpolated additional laws, seemingly of his own design, some of which contain textual borrowings from Geoffrey's *Historia regum Britannie*.[95] King Arthur appears in three of these

---

[89] Ullmann, 'Geoffrey of Monmouth in English History', 261.

[90] See *Gesetze der Angelsachsen*, I, 656–7; Mary Bateson, 'A London Municipal Collection of the Reign of John', *English Historical Review*, 17, n. 67 (1902): 480–511; Mary Bateson, 'A London Municipal Collection of the Reign of John, Part II', *English Historical Review* 17, n. 68 (1902): 707–30.

[91] Derek Keene, 'From Conquest to Capital: St Paul's *c.* 1100–1300', in *St. Paul's: The Cathedral Church of London, 604–2004*, ed. Derek Keene, Arthur Burns, and Andrew Saint (New Haven: Yale University Press, 2004), 31.

[92] Keene, 'From Conquest to Capital', 31.

[93] Keene, 'Text, Visualisation and Politics', 87.

[94] See B. Wilkinson, *Constitutional History of Medieval England, 1216–1399*, 3 vols. (London: Longmans, Green, 1948–58), III, 84; Keene, 'Text, Visualisation and Politics', 83.

[95] See Ullmann, 'Geoffrey of Monmouth in English History', 258.

interpolations as a lawgiver, a conqueror, and a champion of local self-government. The figure serves as a 'historical' counterexample to acts of King John.

The first and briefest Arthur reference occurs at the conclusion of the laws of King Æthelstan (r. 924–39) as part of the aforementioned historical-biographical entry on that king. It states that King Æthelstan reigned for fourteen years from the southern to the northern boundaries of the kingdom of Britain, namely 'usque ad metas Arthuri quas corone regni Britannie constituit et imposuit' (right up to the boundaries of Arthur, which he established and imposed for the crown of the realm of Britain).[96] The London Collector thus evokes Geoffrey of Monmouth's depiction of Arthur as *rex totius Britannie*.[97] Æthelstan typifies this notion of *patria*, for he brought all of the kings of the island of Britain under his authority, including Hywel, king of the West Welsh, Constantine, king of the Scots, Owain, king of the people of Gwent, and Ealdred from Bamburgh.[98] Æthelstan, as noted by the London Collector, became the first Saxon ruler to have a border with the Scots and the first Saxon king of all England.[99] Subsequently, Æthelstan was styled *rex totius Britannie*.[100] Geoffrey of Monmouth was aware of Æthelstan's accomplishments, and at the close of the *Historia regum Britannie*, he notes that Æthelstan was the first Saxon to wear the crown of Britain.[101] The London Collector evidently observed similarities between the two kings, particularly the extent of their dominion, and he juxtaposed Arthur and Æthelstan.[102] In the London Collection, the two kings together set forth an imperial imperative – an Insular Manifest Destiny, as it were – to the contemporary kings of England, namely the attainment of full sovereignty over the British Isles.[103] To be a latter-day Arthur was to be in control of England, Scotland, and Wales.

For a brief time, between 1209 and 1212, John was praised as another *rex totius Britannie*, but after 1211 John scored very badly on this front. In mid August 1211, as John was planning a third expedition to Wales

---

[96] See Liebermann, *Über die Leges Anglorum*, 22.
[97] See Ernst H. Kantorowicz, *The King's Two Bodies: A Study in Mediaeval Political Theology* (Princeton: Princeton University Press, 1957), 346–7.
[98] *The Anglo-Saxon Chronicle D-text s.a.* 927, in *English Historical Documents, 500–1042*, 2nd edn., ed. Dorothy Whitelock (London: Routledge, 1979), 218.
[99] Sarah Foot, *Æthelstan: The First King of England* (New Haven: Yale University Press, 2011), 160–1.
[100] Foot, *Æthelstan*, 216.
[101] Geoffrey of Monmouth, *Historia regum Britannie* 207.594–8, pp. 280–1.
[102] See Keene, 'Text, Visualisation and Politics', 83–4.
[103] See Davies, *First English Empire*, 16–17.

in order to consolidate his authority there, he learned of a plot against his life. He called off the campaign and failed to fortify his holdings in Wales adequately.[104] The English threat inspired the Welsh to unite behind Llywelyn ap Iorwerth (the 'Great') of Gwynedd (d. 1240). Just as John had taken advantage of the discord among the three Welsh principalities, now Llywelyn was poised to exploit John's difficulties with his baronage. He did so to great effect. R. R. Davies notes that '[b]y 1213 the Welsh had more than recovered all the lands that they had lost to the king',[105] and Rowlands adds that '[b]y the time of John's death, the March had been severely battered and the Crown's territorial stake in Wales had been reduced to a rump in the south-east. Retreat on this scale eclipsed those losses incurred in Stephen's reign.'[106] The London Collector was writing after John's reversal of fortune and perhaps censuring John for his recent failures.

The Arthur of the London Collection is more than a passing model of imperial kingship; he is a lawgiver. His rather exceptional appearance in this capacity receives pride of place in the *Leges Edwardi Confessoris* section of the Collection. In the twelfth and thirteenth centuries, the Confessor was remembered as a gifted lawgiver, who actively encouraged the counsel of his nobles and promoted peace.[107] His reign was deemed a golden age and his laws exerted a 'talismanic force'.[108] The laws were of symbolic value to the monarchy, the clergy, and the nobility. Henry I and Stephen had confirmed the laws of Edward the Confessor at the time of their coronation in order to legitimize their contested claims to the throne, the clergy exploited the laws of the Confessor in order to claim privileges allegedly enjoyed prior to the Conquest, and the barons of the realm referenced Edward's laws on multiple occasions in order to remind the reigning monarch that his sovereignty was not absolute.[109] According to its prologue, the *Leges Edwardi Confessoris* was compiled at

---

[104] Rowlands, 'King John and Wales', 284.

[105] Davies, *Age of Conquest*, 297.

[106] Rowlands, 'King John and Wales', 286.

[107] D. A. Carpenter, 'King Henry III and Saint Edward the Confessor: The Origins of the Cult', *English Historical Review* 122, n. 498 (2007): 880–1.

[108] Patrick Wormald, *The Making of English Law: King Alfred to the Twelfth Century*, vol. 1: *Legislation and its Limits* (Oxford: John Wiley & Sons, 1999), 128–9.

[109] *Gesetze der Angelsachsen*, I, 522; Robert S. Hoyt, 'The Coronation Oath of 1308: The Background of "Les Leys et les Custumes"', *Traditio* 11 (1955): 241; 'The First Charter of Stephen', in *Select Charters and Other Illustrations of English Constitutional History, from the Earliest Times to the Reign of Edward the First*, ed. William Stubbs, 6th edn. (Oxford: Clarendon Press, 1888), 119. Also see Janelle Greenberg, '"St. Edward's Ghost": The Cult of St. Edward and His Laws in English History', in *English Law before Magna Carta: Felix Liebermann and* Die Gesetze der Angelsachsen, ed. Stefan Jurasinski, Lisi Oliver, and Andrew Rabin (Leiden: Brill, 2010), 275, 278.

the command of William the Conqueror in 1070.[110] In actuality, the *Leges* was 'likely produced sometime early in the reign of King Stephen by an episcopal steward at Lincoln Cathedral'.[111] Contrary to expectations arising from the preamble of the work, the treatise lists neither the laws in effect under Edward the Confessor nor those under William the Conqueror. Instead, it defines in thirty-three chapters the types of legally established peace and security that the Church and king had the power to create and administer. It concerns the separation of powers between Church and Crown in England.[112]

Although the *Leges Edwardi Confessoris* was subject to addition, revision, and then, in the case of the London Collection, interpolation, it remained a fixed point of reference in the ongoing power struggle between king, Church, and baronage. This fact is evident in King John's exchange with Stephen Langton, archbishop of Canterbury (r. 1207–28), on 20 July 1213 at Winchester Cathedral. As part of his reconciliation with Rome, John sought absolution from Langton for preventing him from taking up his metropolitan see. The archbishop absolved John but not before obliging him to swear to do away with unjust laws and to reinstitute the good laws of his ancestors, especially those of St. Edward.[113] A return to the laws of St Edward was a rallying cry of the discontented clergy and baronage, especially in the run up to Runnymede.[114] Just as the good King Arthur of Chrétien's *Erec et Enide* commits himself to upholding the laws and customs of his father, so it would appear that the high clergy and barons of early thirteenth-century England expected John to provide good justice, to respect the rights and privileges of his subjects, and to reinstitute the laws and customs of his more distant predecessor, St. Edward. What the *l'usage Pandragon* was for Chrétien's Arthur, the *leges regis Edwardi* was for King John. Yet the barons, under the pretext of seeking a return to the good laws of the past, were actually seeking new concessions from the king. The interpolation of later doctrines to the laws of Edward the Confessor 'under the guise of old and laudable custom' was part of this process.[115]

---

[110] *Gesetze der Angelsachsen*, I, 627.

[111] See Bruce R. O'Brien, '*Leges Edwardi Confessoris* (ECf1)' Early English Laws Project. University of London: Institute of Historical Research / King's College London (http://www.earlyenglishlaws.ac.uk/laws/texts/ecf1/, accessed 22 January 2013).

[112] O'Brien, '*Leges Edwardi Confessoris*, (ECf1)'; Greenberg, 'St. Edward's Ghost', 277–8.

[113] Roger of Wendover, *Flores historiarum*, II, 81, 84.

[114] See, for example, *Annales Monasterii de Waverleia (A.D. 1–1291)*, in *Annales Monastici*, vol. 2, ed. Henry Richards Luard. RS 36/2 (London: Longman, Green, Longman, Roberts, and Green, 1865), 282.

[115] James Clarke Holt, *Magna Carta*, 2nd edn. (Cambridge, UK: Cambridge University Press, 1992), 20, 115–16.

The Collector's practice of interpolation and the themes of his interpolations perpetuated this tendency. At those points where the *Leges Edwardi Confessoris* covered matters of contemporary relevance, the Collector wove in new material as seamlessly as possible. His aim was to create the illusion that his additions were part of the fabric of the original text.

With these patterns in mind, let us now consider the first appearance of Arthur in the London version of the *Leges Edwardi Confessoris*. Chapter Thirty-Two of the third recension of the *Leges Edwardi Confessoris* was of interest to the London Collector. It concerns the offices and administration of local self-government, and discusses how the English word 'aldermen' corresponds in meaning to the Latin 'seniores'.[116] The London Collector, replicating some of the wording of the third recension, equates the senators of Roman Britain with the aldermen of Anglo-Saxon England. This analogy affords him a segue for grafting a Galfridian interpolation onto the base text that served his purposes. After explaining how aldermen hold the same power and authority as their counterparts of Hundreds and Wapentakes, the Collector writes the aldermen should preserve the laws and liberties and rights and peace of the king and the just and ancient customs of the realm. He adds that whenever something truly unexpected or bad happens against the kingdom or its king, the aldermen should ring bells intemperately, which the Angles call 'motbele', and convoke all who live under the king's protection to meet at the 'folkesmoth', where they are to make provision for the expenses of the Crown 'per commune consilium' (through common counsel) and to see to it that the insolence of evildoers is reprimanded for the utility of the kingdom.[117] Next, the Collector writes:

> Statutum est enim, quod ibi debent populi omnes et gentes universe singulis annis, semel in anno scilicet, conuenire, scilicet in capite kalendarum Maii, et se fide et sacramento non fracto ibi in unum et insimul confederare et consolidare sicut coniurati fratres ad defendendum regnum contra alienigenas et contra inimicos, una cum domino suo rege, et terras et honores illius omni fidelitate cum eo seruare, et quod illi ut domino suo regi intra et extra regnum uniuersum Britannie fideles esse uolunt.

> Ita debent facere omnes principes et comites, et simul iurare coram episcopis regni in folkesmoth; et similiter omnes proceres regni et milites et liberi homines uniuersi totius regni Britannie facere debent in pleno folkesmot fidelitatem domino regi, ut predictum est, coram episcopis regni.

[116] *Gesetze der Angelsachsen*, I, 655.
[117] *Gesetze der Angelsachsen*, I, 655.

Hanc legem inuenit Arturus, qui quondam fuit inclitissimus rex
Britonum, et ita consolidauit et confederauit regnum Britannie
uniuersum semper in unum; huius legis auctoritate expulit Arturus
predictus Saracenos et inimicos a regno. Lex enim ista diu sopita
fuit et sepulta, donec Edgarus rex Anglorum, qui fuit auus Edwardi
regis, propinqui uestri, illam excitauit et in lucem erexit, et illam per
totum regnum firmiter obseruare fecit et precipit.[118]

(For it is established that all people of every race ought to convene
in that place once every year, namely on the first of May, to pledge
themselves collectively by an unbroken faith and sacrament to be
united as one as sworn brothers in order to defend the realm against
foreigners and against enemies, together with their lord the king,
and with him to protect all his lands and honors in all fidelity and
[to pledge] that they wish to be faithful to him as their lord king both
when inside and when outside the whole realm of Britain.

All princes and counts ought to do this, [namely] to swear
simultaneously in the presence of the bishops of the realm in folkmoot;
and similarly all the nobles of the realm and the knights and the
freemen of the whole and entire realm of Britain are to swear fealty to
the king in a plenary folkmoot, as has been said, in the presence of the
bishops of the realm.

Arthur, who once was the most famous king of the Britons, established
this law and in this way he bound together and united the entire realm
of Britain forever; the aforesaid Arthur, by the authority of his law,
expelled from the realm Saracens and [other] enemies. And this law
was put to rest and buried for a long time until Edgar, king of the
English, who was the ancestor of King Edward, your relative, revived
it and brought it back into the light [of day] and ordered that it be
observed steadfastly throughout the whole realm.)

The May Day fidelity pledge, which is introduced by the words 'Statutum
est', is the core of the *Lex Arthuri*. Arthur, it would seem, was also the
progenitor of the folkmoot and the ultimate guarantor of the laws and
liberties and rights and peace of the king and the just and ancient customs
of the realm.[119] The attribution of this legislation to him is consistent with
the representation of Arthur as an upholder of *costume*. The passage also
provides a precedent for Clause Thirteen of Magna Carta in which John
conceded to the city of London all its ancient liberties and free customs.[120]

---

[118] *Gesetze der Angelsachsen*, I, 655.

[119] Christopher N. L. Brooke and Gillian Keir, *London 800–1216: The Shaping of a City*
(Berkeley: University of California Press, 1975), 249. See also Gwyn A. Williams,
Medieval London: From Commune to Capital (London: Athlone Press, 1963), 254.

[120] 'Magna Carta, 1215', ed. and trans. James Clarke Holt, in James Clarke Holt, *Magna
Carta*, 2nd edn. (Cambridge, UK: Cambridge University Press, 1992), 454–5.

Under the guise of authentic customs sealed and approved by bygone kings of Britain and England, the author–compiler of the London Collection integrated legal fictions into the existing privileges of the London Commune. At Runnymede, King John agreed by Clause Thirteen to respect all the ancient liberties and free customs of the citizens of London. John may well have been expected to uphold the spurious material included in the London Collection. One could argue that when signing Magna Carta, John was 're-confirming' a law which had allegedly been instituted by King Arthur and which was first revived by King Edgar. When we consider the London Collection and Magna Carta in tandem, the borders between visionary legislation and actual legislation, legendary history and actual history, collapse.

A critical principle of Magna Carta that Arthur endorses in the London Collection is government *per commune consilium regni*. Clause Fourteen of Magna Carta defines how *commune consilium* is obtained. The king is to summon the high clergy and greater baronage through individual sealed royal letters, and he is to issue a general summons to all other royal tenants through his sheriffs and bailiffs. All recipients are to have at least forty days' notice of the assembly, and the summonses are to state clearly the date, place, and purpose of the gathering.[121] For Arthur, *commune consilium* was standard practice. The association of Arthur with the folkmoot, the oath of fidelity, and the concept of *commune consilium* were fittingly attributed to Arthur because of his appearance as a seeker of baronial consent in Geoffrey's *Historia*. The affirmation of the institutional integrity of the folkmoot provides legitimation for municipal laws made by the mayor and other barons of the city through common counsel, illustrates the merits of local government, and serves as a counter-example to King John's much-detested tendency to act without the counsel of his barons.[122]

The *Lex Arthuri* also reserved benefits for John and his successors were they to choose to respect it and the manner of kingship advocated by the London Collection as a whole. The most obvious advantage was, of course, the yearly pledge of fealty to the king. Also propitious, on the ideological level, was the assertion of direct royal continuity (beginning in the British period) that the law implies. The interpolation states that Edgar revived a dormant Arthurian law as opposed to establishing an analogous one of his own design.[123] The connection established in the London Collection between

---

[121] 'Magna Carta, 1215', 454–5.
[122] Keene, 'Text, Visualisation and Politics', 88.
[123] O'Brien has observed that the 'strange notion that laws can fall asleep and be reawakened years afterwards by later monarchs' originates from the 'third version of the *Leges Edwardi*'. See O'Brien, 'Forgers of Law and Their Readers', 469, 471.

Edgar and Arthur is an acknowledgment of the legendary British king's historicity and it also reveals a desire to retrofit Arthur into the English royal lineage. Edgar, following the example of Æthelstan, had asserted his 'pan-Britannic' pretensions at the outset of his reign. His coronation rite demanded that he be honored 'above all kings of Britain', and he was styled in one of his charters as 'king and emperor of ... the kings and peoples dwelling within the boundaries of Britain'.[124] The pairing of Arthur and Edgar reinforces the 'pan-British' imperial dimension of the figure of King Arthur.[125] It can be read as yet another exhortation for the ruling monarch to refocus attention on achieving rule over the whole of Britain.

The ethnic divide between the British ruling elite and their Saxon successors was also downplayed in the London Collection. Arthur reportedly expelled 'Saracens and enemies' from his realm. The Collector does not name the perfidious Saxons of Geoffrey's *Historia* in this entry. In a subsequent interpolation, 'De illis, qui possunt et debent de iure cohabitare et remanere in regno Britannie' (Concerning those who are able to and by right ought to live together and remain in the realm of Britain), he explains how King Ine of Wessex (r. 688–726), became the first English king to obtain the *monarchia tocius regni Anglorum* (monarchy of the entire kingdom of England) after the arrival of the Angles in Britain and how he took a Briton named Wallia as his wife and received the *benedicta corona Britannie* (blessed crown of Britain).[126] The Collector adds that, by the common consent of the realm and at the command of King Ine, the Anglo-Saxons and the Britons intermarried, and there was further fusion of the Angles, both of England and of Germany, and the Scots. In summary, he remarks:

> Et tali modo effecti fuerunt gens una et populus unus per uniuersum regnum Britannie miseratione diuina. Deinde uniuersi vocauerunt regnum Anglorum, quod ante uocatum fuit regnum Britannie. Uniuersi predicti semper postea pro communi utilitate corone regni insimul et in unum uiriliter contra Danos et Norwegienses semper steterunt; et atrocissime unanimi uoluntate in globum pro patria et pro communi utilitate contra inimicos pugnauerunt et bella atrocissime in regno gesserunt.[127]

> (And, in such a way, throughout the entire kingdom of Britain, they were made one clan and one people by divine compassion. Finally, what had previously been called the realm of Britain, everyone

---

[124] Davies, *First English Empire*, 37.
[125] Davies, *First English Empire*, 10.
[126] *Gesetze der Angelsachsen*, I, 658.
[127] *Gesetze der Angelsachsen*, I, 659.

called the realm of the Angles. All the aforesaid forever after for the common good of the crown of the realm together and as one always vigorously stood against the Danes and Norwegians; and unanimous in will they fought most savagely in a close-packed group for the *patria* and for the common good against enemies and they waged battles most savagely in the kingdom.)

This interpolation implies that all the native kings of England who succeeded Ine could rightly be considered heirs to Arthur's legacy by blood and by office.[128] Just as thirteenth-century Londoners could look back to the *Lex Arthuri* as the justificatory precedent for their folkmoot, so too could the reigning English monarch find a connection to King Arthur.

Why does the London Compiler underscore the unity of different peoples within England as one of the Collection's leading themes? Keene believes the cosmopolitan makeup of the city of London explains this choice.[129] Davies interprets this emphasis as the second of two English responses to the Brittonic claim to Arthur.[130] 'The first English response', according to Davies, was the representation of British History as a precursor to Post-Conquest English history, and the second solution was 'to cut the Gordian knot by denying that there was a problem'.[131] By asserting that full racial integration had been achieved in the British Isles and by treating all of England's inhabitants as a single racial and political entity, the London Collector attempts to make the debate over whether the English or the Welsh had a stronger claim to the legacy of Arthur a moot point. The interpretations of Keene and Davies are not mutually exclusive.

The second Arthurian interpolation in the *Leges Edwardi Confessoris* section advances the idea that Britain had undergone racial integration, suggesting that the Britons and the Norse were united in blood thanks to the agency of King Arthur himself. The Collector writes:

Arturus uero, qui fuit quondam inclitissimus rex Britonum, uir magnus fuit et animosus et miles illustris. Parum fuit ei regnum istud: non fuit contentus animus eius regno Britannie excessitque metas et fines regni huius, et subiugauit sibi uiriliter et strenue Scanciam totam, que modo Norweya uocatur, et omnes insulas

---

[128] Maurice Keen has also noted that the interpolation on Ine's marriage to Wallia gave justification for the English use of Arthurian history. See Maurice Keen, 'Arthurian Bones and English Kings, ca. 1180–ca. 1550', in *Magistra Doctissima: Essays in Honor of Bonnie Wheeler*, ed. Dorsey Armstrong, Ann W. Astell, and Howell Chickering (Kalamazoo: Medieval Institute Publications, 2013), 63–4.

[129] Keene, 'Text, Visualisation and Politics', 89–90.

[130] Davies, *First English Empire*, 48.

[131] Davies, *First English Empire*, 49.

ultra Scanciam … et omnes alias terras et insulas orientales occeani usque Russiam – in Lappam scilicet posuit orientalem metam regni Britannie – et multas alias insulas ultra Scanciam, usque dum sub septemtrione, que sunt de appendiciis Scanciae, que modo Norweia uocatur.[132]

(Arthur, who was once the most famous king of the Britons, was truly a great and courageous man and an illustrious knight. His realm seemed small to him; his mind was not content with the realm of Britain; for, it passed the limits and boundaries of this realm, and in an active and vigorous way he subjugated the whole of Scandinavia, which is now called Norway and all the islands beyond Scandinavia … and all other lands and eastern islands of the ocean right up to Russia – that is to say he placed the eastern limit of the realm of Britain in Lapland – and many other islands beyond Scandinavia right up to the North Pole, which pertain to the appendages of Scandinavia, which is now called Norway).

The Collector adds that Arthur, the greatest of Christians, had all of these northmen baptized, and that nobles of Norway then took their wives from the noble race of the Britons, and 'unde Norwegienses dicunt, se exisse de genere et sanguine regni huius' (for this reason, the Norwegians say that they arose from the race and blood of this realm).[133] Arthur even obtained confirmation from the pope that Norway would forever belong to the crown of Britain. He called it the *camera Britannie* (roof of Britain). On this account, according to the Collector, the Norwegians say that they are entitled to inhabit England and claim to be from the body of the British realm.[134]

In this interpolation, Arthur is presented as a *rex-imperator* in the Galfridian mould. The passage communicates that a king's faithful service to God brings him good luck in his military expeditions. This is a traditional teaching but particularly applicable to King John, who was deemed both a great sinner and a great military failure near the end of his reign. Arthur, unlike John, is described as a *miles illustris*. Arthur shares the same value system as his knights. Additionally, the London Compiler recasts the Norse, whom he previously brands pirates,[135] in a friendlier light.

In addition to underscoring the peace and concord among the peoples of England, two motivations for this refashioning suggest themselves.

---

[132] *Gesetze der Angelsachsen*, I, 659. For a source study of this curious entry, see Lynette Muir, 'King Arthur's Northern conquests in the "Leges Anglorum Londoniis Collectae"', *Medium Aevum* 37 (1968): 253–62.

[133] *Gesetze der Angelsachsen*, I, 660.

[134] *Gesetze der Angelsachsen*, I, 660.

[135] *Gesetze der Angelsachsen*, I, 634–5.

One, as noted by Keene, is economic. At the time of the composition of the London Collection, Norwegians and Gotlanders were key intermediaries for trade in eastern Baltic goods.[136] The second motivation is political. The Scandinavian interpolation seems to have been designed to affirm the Plantagenet claim to England and thereby increase the Collection's chances of receiving royal endorsement. This task entailed embracing the Scandinavian heritage of every king of England since Edward the Confessor, whose mother, Emma of Normandy, like William the Conqueror, was a direct descendent of Rollo the Viking.[137] The so-called *camera Britanniae* supported the idea that the Norse had shared ancestry with Britons and that they had the right to dwell in England. Consequently, William the Conqueror, as a Norman descended from Norsemen, was not to be regarded as an interloper in England. The Plantagenet kings now had at their disposal multiple grounds for claiming to be of Arthur's race. Empress Matilda (1102–67) passed on English and Norman heritage to her son Henry II and his successors. Geoffrey Plantagenet (1113–51) passed on to his son the county of Anjou, which according the *Historia regum Britannie*, Arthur had bestowed upon his seneschal Kay. Thanks to the London Collection, the Angevin, Norse (i.e. Norman), and English elements in the heritage of the Plantagenets could all be traced back to Arthur and his British kin.

The London Collection contains within it a carrot-and-stick approach to correcting King John's behavior. The stick was the threat of deposition; the carrot, the construction of a three-fold *stirps regia* traceable back to Arthur, which, in the event that the king improved his ways, promised military success and greater fidelity from his vassals.

Conclusion

The French royal court, the Castilian court, and the baronage of England all used King Arthur as an ideological weapon against King John. Capetian propaganda portrayed King John as a second Herod, who treacherously slaughtered his nephew, a youth of great expectation. This vilification of John provided justification for the Capetian seizure of King John's feudal possessions in France. In the poetry of the Castilian court, one obtains the sense that John was the 'black sheep' of the Plantagenet dynasty, who does not match his elder brothers in nobility of character

---

[136] Keene, 'Text, Visualisation and Politics', 96; Williams, *Medieval London*, 13.

[137] The London Collector was not, however, favorably disposed toward King Cnut and his sons. See *Gesetze der Angelsachsen*, I, 640.

or chivalric virtue. The troubadour Guiraut de Calanson communicates that Fernando of Castile was of finer Plantagenet stock than King John. Fernando, rather than his uncle King John, compared favorably to King Arthur. By this logic, Fernando (and by extension the Castilian branch of the Plantagenet royal family) deserved to rule a portion of the Angevin Empire. Additionally, during the reign of King John, the lords of England increasingly looked to King Arthur as a champion of their reformist cause. Geoffrey's *Historia* and Chrétien's *Erec et Enide* portray Arthur as an ideal feudal monarch, and the London Collection furnishes indisputable evidence of England's baronage applying this understanding of Arthur in real world affairs, specifically in the context of the First Barons' War of 1215–17. The London Collector cites the example of Arthur to check the Plantagenet king's authority and referenced him as a guarantor of the high nobility's ancient feudal rights and privileges. The usurpation of the Arthurian narrative for the high nobility's gain would, as we shall see, progress further during the reign of John's son, Henry III (r. 1216–72).

4
Arthurianism during the reign of Henry III, 1216–1272

Royal ambivalence to Arthur in an era of Arthurianism

Arthur of Brittany's death did not preclude Henry III from fashioning himself after King Arthur as it had King John. Henry III's lack of Arthurian distinction is more attributable to his dearth of charisma and chivalric aptitude. Henry lives on in historical memory as a monkish and dithering monarch. This 're de la semplice vita' (king of the simple life), as Dante refers to him,[1] was not manifestly opposed to Arthur but preferred the example of his canonized royal predecessors, particularly St. Edward the Confessor.[2] Henry's preferences are evident from the artistic and architectural works he commissioned. Henry III stands out not as a warrior king, nor as a great lawgiver, but as a castle-builder and patron of the arts who was personally involved in the interior design of the Palace Complex at Westminster, the processional gateway into the Tower of London, and the Great Hall of Winchester Castle.

With one possible exception that will be considered later in this chapter, Henry III is not known to have commissioned Arthurian art. This is a conspicuous absence and suggests that Henry III was not overly interested in Arthur. Most of Henry's commissions were images of traditional Christian scenes and iconography. Henry also commissioned many depictions of Edward the Confessor.[3] In terms of non-religious subjects, Henry favored the adventures of the Third Crusade and Richard I's duel with Saladin. Henry chose this theme for his royal chamber at Clarendon (2 July 1251)

---

[1] Dante Alighieri, *Purgatorio* 8.130–1, ed. and trans. Anthony Esolen (New York: Modern Library, 2003), 80–1. Also see Björn Weiler, 'Henry III Through Foreign Eyes – Communication and Historical Writing in Thirteenth-Century Europe', in *England and Europe in the Reign of Henry III (1216–1272)*, ed. Björn K. U. Weiler and Ifor W. Rowlands (Aldershot: Ashgate, 2002), 137–61.

[2] The St. Albans chronicler Matthew Paris (d. 1259), in a description of one of his encounters with the king (c. 1257), claims that Henry could name all the canonized kings of England from memory. See Matthew Paris, *Chronica Majora*, V, 617. Also see D. A. Carpenter, 'King Henry III and Saint Edward the Confessor: The Origins of the Cult', *English Historical Review* 122, n. 498 (2007): 865–91.

[3] See Tancred Borenius, 'The Cycle of Images in the Palaces and Castles of Henry III', *Journal of the Warburg and Courtauld Institutes* 6 (1943): 47–50.

and for a chamber in the Tower of London (1251).[4] The fondness for Richard I at the royal court is logical. Richard was the most distinguished king of England of recent memory and an internationally renowned crusader. Richard's example, together with that of Edward the Confessor, communicated the eminence and sacrality of the Plantagenet bloodline. Henry III also commissioned two pictorial projects involving Alexander the Great. At Clarendon, there was a Chamber of Alexander. It is first mentioned in a document from 1237. Henry also had the history of Alexander painted in the queen's chamber at Nottingham Castle (15 January 1252).[5] Given this imagery, it is curious that we do not have record of any Arthurian pictorial projects commissioned by Henry III.[6] Floor tiles (c. 1250–60) depicting key episodes from the romance of Tristan and Isolde do, however, survive. These were produced at Chertsey Abbey near Windsor and their superior quality suggests they were intended for a royal palace.[7]

It has been argued that 'Henry's taste for splendour was intended to reinforce an absolutist ideology of kingship.'[8] If this assessment is accurate, then the figure of King Arthur, who increasingly came to be understood as an exemplar of consensual monarchy and a proponent of chivalric kingship (according to which the monarch places himself, or is placed, under the same value system as his knights), was perhaps out of step with Henry's ideological agenda.[9] Henry held that it was

---

[4] See Borenius, 'Cycle of Images', 45; Charles Lock Eastlake, 'Scriptural and Historical Subjects Painted in England during the Reign of Henry III', in his *Materials for a History of Oil Painting* (London: Longman, Brown, Green, and Longmans, 1847), 555–6.

[5] See Borenius, 'Cycle of Images', 44.

[6] See Alison Stones, 'Arthurian Art since Loomis', in *Arturus Rex*, vol. 2: *Acta Conventus Lovaniensis 1987*, ed. Willy Van Hoecke, Gilbert Tournoy, and Werner Verbeke (Louvain: Leuven University Press, 1991), 27.

[7] Another set of tiles depicts Richard I's encounters with Saladin. See *Age of Chivalry: Art in Plantagenet England, 1200–1400*, ed. Jonathan Alexander and Paul Binski (London: Weidenfeld and Nicolson, 1987), 204.

[8] H. W. Ridgeway, 'Henry III (1207–1272)', *Oxford Dictionary of National Biography*, Oxford University Press, 2004; online edn., September 2010 (http://www.oxforddnb.com/view/article/12950, accessed 26 February 2015). For a discussion of Henry's high sense of royal authority, see M. T. Clanchy, 'Did Henry III Have a Policy?', *History* 53, n. 178 (1968): 203–19. David Carpenter, who has disputed (but not entirely disproven) the argument that Henry III saw himself as above the law of the realm, recognizes that Henry III was a stalwart upholder of what he understood to be the rights of the Crown; what Henry may have regarded as a defense of his rights, the baronage likely perceived as a violation of theirs. See D. A. Carpenter, 'Kings, Magnates, and Society: the Personal Rule of King Henry III, 1234–58', *Speculum* 60, n. 1 (1985): 39–70.

[9] See Dominique Boutet, *Charlemagne et Arthur: ou le roi imaginaire* (Paris: Librairie Honoré Champion, 1992), 42. Also see Beate Schmolke-Hasselmann, 'The Round Table: Ideal, Fiction, Reality', *Arthurian Literature* II (1981): 58.

his prerogative to choose who would be his servants and ministers; he preferred to act upon the advice of a small coterie of advisors. Henry's reliance upon 'foreign' favorites, in particular his wife's Savoyard uncles and his own Poitevin half-brothers, angered the barons of England, who felt that they were entitled to a place on the king's royal council. This was one of the formal grievances raised in the great baronial reform movement that began in 1258 and devolved into the Second Barons' War of 1264–7. Henry III's desire to augment – or at least maintain – his monarchical authority was at odds with the wishes of the great lords of his realm.

There is scant evidence that Henry III involved himself in the Arthurian tradition, but there is ample evidence that important political players around Henry III evoked the figure of Arthur. Moreover, Henry's fifty-six-year reign coincided with a critical period in the development of the medieval Arthurian tradition, namely the transmission, translation, and imitation of the earliest specimens of the *matière de Bretagne* across Europe, especially in the Holy Roman Empire, Iberia, and Scandinavia. Over the course of the thirteenth century, Arthur did not cease to be connected with the Brittonic peoples or with the Plantagenet dynasty, but we increasingly find Arthur abstracted from local ties. Monarchs across Europe began to be compared to Arthur, and writers across Europe participated in determining what it meant to be like King Arthur. The earliest attestation of knightly Arthurian role-playing dates from Henry III's reign. Such events undoubtedly impacted the contemporary reception of Arthur across Europe. In particular, the newly developed chivalric games known as 'round tables' also reinforced the understanding of Arthur as belonging to chivalric society.

As I shall illustrate, Henry III's subjects initially nursed Arthurian hopes for their boy king, who was placed on the throne at the tender age of nine, but Henry III's poor leadership of the French campaign of 1230 demonstrated that these hopes were misplaced. Henry III's younger brother Richard of Cornwall (1209–72) stepped in to fill this void. He cultivated an Arthurian identity through his refurbishment of Tintagel Castle, the supposed birthplace of King Arthur. Richard's investment in Tintagel occurred during the 1230s when it was unclear whether Henry would produce a royal heir and when it was still a distinct possibility that Richard would succeed his brother as king of England.

The Aberffraw House of Gwynedd also emerged as Arthurian imitators during Henry III's reign. Llywelyn ('the Great') ap Iorwerth (r. 1195–1240), and then his grandson Llywelyn ('the Last') ap Gruffudd (r. 1246–82), took advantage of Henry III's difficulties with his barons in order to increase Gwynedd hegemony in Wales. The princely self-representation of the two Llywelyns and the identification of Avalon with Gwynedd in the *Vera historia de Morte Arthuri* indicate that these Welsh princes were attempting to harness the memory of Arthur to their advantage. The Gwynedd dynasty seems to have claimed Arthur in tandem with its reconquest of land in the Welsh Marches. This example is the first strong indication of the Welsh adoption of Arthur for political gain that I have found, and it dates from the reign of Henry III.[10]

Henry III: The new Arthurian hope and its disappointment

On the night of 18–19 October 1216, King John died at Newark. He had been abandoned by most of the barons of England and even many of his household knights. England was in the midst of the First Barons' War (1215–17), and John's death did not bring an end to the conflict. Many barons remained faithful to the Capetian pretender to the throne. But the pope, most of the high clergy of England, and a powerful contingent of stalwart royalists, including William Marshal, threw their support behind John's eldest son, Henry of Winchester (b. 1 October 1207). A little over a week after John's death, the earl Marshal knighted the pre-adolescent prince, and, on 28 October 1216, the bishop of Winchester, Peter des Roches, assisted by the bishops Worcester and Exeter, crowned him 'Henry III' at Gloucester Abbey.[11] This event marked the beginning of Henry III's reign. Shortly thereafter William Marshal was made *rector* of the realm, and he entrusted Henry to the care of Peter des Roches, who went on to serve as the boy's official guardian until 1221.[12] On 12 November, the earl marshal and the papal legate Guala issued a modified version of Magna Carta with the aim of undercutting the dauphin's cause. Although support for Prince Louis dwindled, it took a military victory against the rebel faction at Lincoln on 20 May 1217, the capture of Louis' supply fleet at Sandwich (24 August), and a promise of lenient treatment for Louis' steadfast supporters to convince the dauphin to quit his invasion of England. The two sides came to terms on 12 September 1217.

Almost a decade later, on 8 January 1227, Henry, aged nineteen, held a council at Oxford and declared himself of full age. At this point Henry

---

[10] Ostmann observes that, during the reign of Henry III, more sources surface that represent Arthur as a hero of the Welsh. See Ostmann, 'Die Bedeutung der Arthurtradition', 258–9.

[11] Maurice Powicke, *The Thirteenth Century, 1216–1307*, 2nd edn. (Oxford: Clarendon Press, 1962), 1.

[12] See David Carpenter, *The Minority of Henry III* (Berkeley: University of California Press, 1990), 257.

began his 'personal rule', but the power behind the throne until July of 1232 was Henry's justiciar, Hubert de Burgh. There seems to have been a measure of optimism, even an Arthurian hope, surrounding the new king in the early years of his reign – at least until 1230. The *Histoire de Guillaume le Maréchal* (c. 1219–26) provides evidence of these great expectations. In the midst of extolling Young King Henry (1155–83) for retaining the services of worthy knights, the poet, in an aside, laments that the vices of sloth and covetousness have prevailed upon the hearts and minds of high-ranking men in England and that these men have placed the virtues of *chevalerie* and *largesse* in fetters. The biographer also complains that tourneying had given way to formal contests.[13] He then expresses hope that Henry will grow to cherish his knights, liberate *largesse*, and become a patron of old-fashioned tournaments. The poet adds:

> E Dex nos doint al tens venir
> Que nos veions ce avenir
> Que Merlins en profetiza,
> Quant des reis dist e devisa
> Ce que en est avenue puis,
> Esi comme el Brute le truis.
> Dex en tel point mete la terre
> A fei que li reis d'Engletere
> Recovre ce qu'il deit aveir,
> Qui par coveitise d'aveir
> E par traïson fu vendue!
> Mais, si Deu plaist, n'iert pas perdue.[14]

(And may God grant that in days to come we shall see come to pass what Merlin prophesied when he spoke of our kings and described what subsequently happened to them, as I find it written in the *Brut*. May God bring our land to its true allegiance so that the King of England regains what is rightfully his, which was sold off through acquisitiveness and treachery! If God please, it will not be forever lost.)

Becoming a champion of knighthood was, according to the poet, the way that Henry would obtain the support of his subjects and rebuild the Angevin Empire to its former glory.

Another statement of Arthurian hope for Henry III's rule appears in the illustrated and glossed copy of Geoffrey of Monmouth's *Prophetia*

---

[13] *Histoire de Guillaume le Maréchal*, I, 136–9, lines 2686–92.
[14] *Histoire de Guillaume le Maréchal*, I, 136–9, lines 2701–12.

Merlini, contained in British Library, Cotton MS Claudius B vii, 224r–233v. The manuscript is thought to date from the mid thirteenth century, and Alison Stones believes the *Prophetia Merlini* was 'commissioned in royal circles'.[15] The commentary concludes with a prediction that Henry III will equal King Arthur in greatness.[16] The textual occasion for this claim is the Cadwallader / Conan prophecy. The commentator behind Cotton Claudius B vii favors a figurative reading of the prophecy. He sees Cadwallader not as a Welsh political hero but as the personification of Great Britain; likewise, he reads Conanus as the personification of Brittany. The commentary explicitly names Henry III of England as its subject. It states that there will be a wedding alliance between England and Scotland. Henry will enjoy an alliance with Brittany and from there mount an invasion of France. He will conquer all the lands up to Andalusia in a manner analogous to that of Arthur, who came very close to conquering Rome. In this commentary, to be like Arthur is to be the ruler of Britain, of all the lands that the Plantagenets once held as part of the Angevin Empire, and of even more land.[17] The Arthurian hopes for Henry III expressed by William Marshal's biographer are also found in the Cotton Claudius B vii Merlin commentary. It is possible that royal propagandists, in an effort to build support for the Breton expedition, were suggesting that Henry III would emerge victorious.

Details of the commentary correspond with the political circumstances and rhetoric immediately preceding Henry III's 1230 expedition to Brittany. First comes the matter of the wedding alliances in Brittany and Scotland. Prior to the death of Louis VIII, Henry III and his advisors had hoped to form an alliance with Pierre de Dreux, duke of Brittany (r. 1213–37), and to draw him into conflict with the king of France. The English crown sought to regain Plantagenet lands lost to the Capetians, such as Normandy, Anjou, and Poitou. The lords of Gascony, throughout the 1220s, were seeking military aid from Henry III. According to the proposed Anglo-Breton alliance, Henry III was to marry Duke Pierre's daughter Yolande, and Henry would guarantee Pierre refuge in England from Louis VIII if needed.[18] Through the union, Pierre would also receive the honor of Richmond, which had been linked to the duchy of Brittany when it was under Plantagenet dominion. But after Louis VIII's death (8

---

[15] For the dating of this work, see Stones, 'Arthurian Art Since Loomis', 28. For a brief description of the manuscript, see Neil R. Ker, 'Membra Disiecta, Second Series', *British Museum Quarterly* 14, n. 4 (1940): 86.

[16] MS Cotton Claudius B vii; 'Merlin Commentary', 412–13, lines 470–7.

[17] MS Cotton Claudius B vii; 'Merlin Commentary', 412–13, lines 460–77.

[18] Powicke, *Thirteenth Century*, 93.

November 1226), Louis' widow, Blanche of Castile, acting as the regent and guardian of Louis IX (r. 1226–70), made Pierre a better offer. When the two concluded an agreement at Vendôme in March 1227, Pierre broke off his negotiations with the king of England. After the proposed Anglo-Breton alliance collapsed, Henry sought to marry Marjorie (1200–44), the youngest sister of Alexander II of Scotland (r. 1214–49), and he spent Christmas 1229 with the Scottish king at York. Henry's desire to wed Marjorie seems to have been the first condition, the Anglo-Scottish alliance, to which our Merlin Commentator alludes.

The second condition of the Merlin Commentary, the Anglo-Breton alliance whereby the duke of Brittany would counsel Henry in his campaign against France, dates from 1230. Early in 1229, Blanche of Castile and Pierre de Dreux came into conflict. A truce between England and France also expired in July 1229, and Henry began preparing for war. On 9 October 1229, Pierre traveled to England, and on 26 October he swore homage to Henry III for the duchy of Brittany. In January 1230, the duke of Brittany severed feudal ties with the crown of France. Henry then prepared for an invasion. In May, Henry landed in Nantes with great pomp but failed to inspire many of the Plantagenet dynasty's former French vassals to support his cause. At this point, matters were at a standstill. Hubert de Burgh dissuaded Henry from leading troops against the king of France's forces.[19]

On 8 June 1230 an English emissary, Ralph FitzNicolas, wrote a letter to the king's chancellor, Ralph, bishop of Chichester, and to the king's seneschal, Stephen of Segrave, describing how matters stood with Henry III at Nantes. FitzNicolas said that Henry was trying to win the support of the magnates of Poitou. The count of La Marche had defected to the king of France. FitzNicholas was, however, confident that Henry would enjoy the military service of most of the barons of Poitou, which would, according to Ralph, enable Henry to ride through Poitou to Gascony and, if need be, to return north to Brittany.[20]

Around this time, Namoros dau Luc wrote a *sirventés* (troubadour poem) that centers on the warlike hopes for Henry III. Assuming the name 'Sir Chantarel', the poet addresses the king of England directly and tells him that, if he were to cross the strait (*le détroit*; presumably the Loire) with arms, a crowd of barons would flock to his side. With the exception

[19] N. Denholm-Young, *Richard of Cornwall* (Oxford: Basil Blackwell, 1947), 17.

[20] 'Ralph FitzNicolas to Ralph, Bishop of Chichester, Chancellor, and Stephen de Segrave (Royal Letters, No. 914)', in *Royal and Other Historical Letters Illustrative of the Reign of Henry III*, vol. 1: 1216–35, ed. Walter Waddington Shirley. RS 27/1 (London : Longman, Green, Longman, and Roberts, 1862), 370–1.

of Roncevaux, all of the barons mentioned came from southwestern French territories that were either part of or proximate to the Angevin Empire. Sir Chantarel promises Henry III that if he were to undertake a military campaign in the south, he would have at his side the Angevins, Normans, and Bretons.[21] Alfred Jeanroy, the modern editor of this work, believes that the praise of Pierre de Dreux in the *sirventés* is a strong indication that Namoros dau Luc had the Breton duke as his patron and that it was Pierre who was encouraging Henry to take up arms.[22] It is also possible that the poem was commissioned by one of Henry's Gascon subjects.

After assuring Henry III of broad military support, Sir Chantarel explains to Henry how he should comport himself. He urges Henry to commit himself to the strenuous life of a knight rather than to give in to the easy life of princely pleasure. The reward for the former is the promise of military success.[23] This *sirventés* has much in common with the Cotton Claudius B vii Merlin Commentary. Both texts represent Pierre de Dreux as a powerful and wise ally to Henry III, invite Henry to lead an army through southern France and into Spain (or anticipate his doing so), recommend that Henry become a warrior king, and predict a great victory for Henry if he follows this course of action.

Contrary to the hopes of William Marshal's biographer, the prediction of the Merlin commentator, and the recommendations of Namoros dau Luc's *sirventés*, Henry III did not rise to the occasion. The king did not make any substantive moves against the French in his Breton expedition of 1230. As Powicke has observed,

> [t]he troubadours translated political and social relations in terms of splendid adventure. King Henry may have liked to picture himself in a world of this kind, but he was the last man to follow in the footsteps of Richard the Lion Heart. He preferred to buy rather than to fight his way, and so did many other princes.[24]

Henry's efforts, regardless of their form, were not successful. In fact, they were counterproductive. To quote Noël Denholm-Young, '[i]f any hopes had been cherished that Henry III would prove the warrior that he always imagined himself to be, they must have been shattered in the lamentable gaiety of his progress through France'.[25]

---

[21] 'Un sirventés politique de 1230', ed. Alfred Jeanroy, in *Mélanges d'histoire du moyen âge offerts à M. Ferdinand Lot* (Paris: Librairie Honoré Champion, 1925), 276.
[22] 'Un sirventés politique de 1230', 278–9.
[23] 'Un sirventés politique de 1230', 276–7.
[24] Powicke, *Thirteenth Century*, 96.
[25] Denholm-Young, *Richard of Cornwall*, 17.

In October 1230, Henry and his younger brother Richard (1209–72) fell ill and returned to England. The king left William (II) Marshal (1190–1231), second earl of Pembroke, in charge of his forces. The earl-marshal died in April 1231. The earl of Chester then took over the English forces. He had some success in Anjou, but the French army reached the border of Brittany in June 1231, and Pope Gregory IX (r. 1227–41) persuaded England and France to agree to a three-year truce. The French chronicler and monk of St.-Denis, Guillaume de Nangis (c. 1300), mocked Henry's poor showing in 1230, commenting that the king was afraid of Louis and that he returned to England with ignominy.[26]

Henry III and the round table game

William Marshal's biographer laments the disappearance of knight errantry and tourneying in England, and Henry III did not grow to become a supporter of these activities. As Denholm-Young has observed, '[t]he history of the tournament during the reign of Henry III illustrates as well as any isolated series of events can do the problem of a medieval king who was not a warrior'.[27] Pope Innocent II had officially prohibited tournaments in the ninth canon of the Council of Clermont in 1130. Henry often upheld the Church's policy.[28] Consequently, tournaments were organized by and for the baronage, and these events afforded the great lords of England opportunities to come together and conspire against the king.[29] The tournament as pretext for conspiracy against Henry is the opening justification Pope Gregory IX references when renewing the prohibition of tournaments in England.[30] Henry seems to have sought out this papal bull (27 February 1228).[31] On select occasions, however, Henry did permit tournaments to occur. In a writ dated 26 July 1228, Henry prorogued – rather than outright forbade – a tournament that his supporters had organized. He assured his men, including members of his own family, that he would seek papal permission for future

---

[26] See Weiler, 'Henry III Through Foreign Eyes', 138.

[27] N. Denholm-Young, 'The Tournament in the Thirteenth Century', in *Collected Papers of N. Denholm-Young* (Cardiff: University of Wales Press, 1969), 103.

[28] See Denholm-Young, 'Tournament in the Thirteenth Century', 98, 100.

[29] Denholm-Young, 'Tournament in the Thirteenth Century', 96.

[30] See *Foedera, Conventiones, Literæ, et cujuscunque generis acta publica inter Reges Angliæ...*, 2nd edn., ed. Thomas Rymer, 20 vols. (London: J. Tonson, 1704–35), I, 301.

[31] See Laura Keeler, *Geoffrey of Monmouth and the Late Latin Chronicles: 1300–1500* (Berkeley: University of California Press, 1946), 132.

tournaments in England.[32] In 1232, Henry allowed tournaments to take place at Dunstable, Stamford, Brackley, and Blyth, but this indulgence was rescinded on account of his imminent expedition in Wales.[33]

It is among the tournament prohibitions of 1232 that we find the first known documentary reference in England to a new type of hastilude, the 'round table'. In a royal writ entitled *De rotunda tabula prohibenda* (20 July 1232), Henry requests the services of his faithful subjects in Shropshire and threatens arrest and confiscation of chattels if, contrary to his prohibition, they should dare to tourney at the 'aforesaid table', and he forbids his vassals from partaking in any other tournaments in his realm until further notice.[34] The wording of the writ suggests that a 'round table' was a variety of tournament or close analogue. The round table ban was in part a consequence of Henry's need for manpower in Wales.

What, then, was the character of the round table game? Do we have sufficient evidence to conclude that it had a fixed character and set of rules, and if it did, was its character explicitly Arthurian? These are difficult questions to answer because the nature of the round table seems to have been common knowledge among the knightly class in the thirteenth century and did not require repeating.[35]

Scholars generally deem the round table a significant manifestation of Arthurianism,[36] but our thirteenth-century chronicle sources do not confirm this assumption. The earliest known attestation of chivalric Arthurianism occurred in Cyprus in 1223, but imitating 'les aventures de Bretaigne et de la Table ronde' is not necessarily synonymous with engaging in the round table game.[37] A systematic study of all available literary and documentary references to the round table game is required. Such a work is beyond the scope of the present study. I shall, however, provide a comparison of some of the earliest descriptions of round tables and integrate some additional primary sources into the conversation,

---

[32] See *Close Rolls of the Reign of Henry III Preserved in the Public Record Office*, 14 vols. (London: H. M. Stationery Office, 1902–38), I (A.D. 1227–31), 113.

[33] Denholm-Young, 'Tournament in the Thirteenth Century', 102–3.

[34] *Patent Rolls of the Reign of Henry III Preserved in the Public Record Office*, 6 vols. (London: Mackie and Co., 1901–13), II (A.D. 1225–32), 492.

[35] This point has been made by Martín de Riquer, *Caballeros medievales y sus armas* (Madrid: Universidad Nacional de Educación a Distancia, 1999), 158.

[36] See, for example, Michel Parisse, 'Le tournoi en France, des origines à la fin du XIIIe siècle', in *Das ritterliche Turnier im Mittelalter*, ed. Josef Fleckenstein (Göttingen: Vandenhoeck & Ruprecht, 1985), 205; Juliet Barker, *The Tournament in England 1100– 1400* (Woodbridge, UK: Boydell, 1986), 12–13, 66; Denholm-Young, 'Tournament in the Thirteenth Century', 107–9.

[37] Philippe de Novare, *Mémoires, 1218–1243*, ed. Charles Kohler (Paris: Librairie Ancienne Honoré Champion, 1913), 7.

namely a late medieval round table sermon and a late fourteenth-century Castilian description of a round table. As will be illustrated below, the round table game appears to have had a fairly consistent structure, but it, at least in its early days, was not explicitly Arthurian in character.

The closest to a contemporary definition of the round table, at least in historical writing, appears in Matthew Paris' *Chronica Majora* (c. 1259). Describing a round table that took place near Walden Abbey in Essex on 15 September 1252 – one that had been expressly forbidden in a royal writ issued nine days earlier – Matthew writes:

> …milites ut exercitio militari peritiam suam et strenuitatem experirentur, constituerunt non ut in hastiludio quod vulgariter torneamentum dicitur, sed potius in illo ludo militari qui mensa rotunda dicitur, vires suas attemptarent.[38]

> (…knights so that they might put their skill and hardiness to the test, saw fit not to try their prowess in the hastilude that is commonly called a tournament, but rather in that military game that is called a round table.)

As Joachim Bumke notes, '[w]hat exactly differentiated the two kinds of tournaments from each other is not made entirely clear by the historical sources'.[39] However, the difference may have had to do with the weapons employed. In his description of the Walden event, Matthew Paris remarks that Roger de Leybourne (c. 1215–71) used a sharp-pointed lance, contrary to the rules, and fatally wounded Arnulf de Munteny. The St. Albans chonicler's account of this 'accident' leads us to infer that the round table was a military game (*ludus militaris*) in which only lances with dull tips, *armes à plaisance*, were to be used.[40]

Although chroniclers and romancers alike tended to provide only vague, passing references to round tables, the anonymous Old French

---

[38] See Matthew Paris, *Chronica Majora*, V, 318. For the writ of prohibition, see *Close Rolls of the Reign of Henry III*, VII (*A.D. 1251–1253*), 251. David Crouch has suggested that Richard de Clare, earl of Gloucester and Hertford (1222–62), sponsored this round table. See David Crouch, *Tournament* (London: Hambledon and London, 2005), 42.

[39] Joachim Bumke, *Höfische Kultur: Literatur und Gesellschaft im hohen Mittelalter*, trans. Thomas Dunlap as *Courtly Culture: Literature and Society in the High Middle Ages* (New York: Overlook Duckworth, 1991), 262. The same ambiguity also applies to the more purely literary sources from the period. See Claude Lachet, *Sone de Nansay et le roman d'aventures en vers au Xiiie siècle* (Geneva: Editions Slatkine, 1992), 416.

[40] See Paris, *Chronica Majora*, V, 319. Also see Crouch, *Tournament*, 79. An excellent point of comparison to Matthew Paris' entry is a interpolation (c. 1390) to the Castilian crusader compilation *La gran conquista de Ultramar* (c. 1292–5). See also *Gran Conquista de Ultramar*, ed. Louis Cooper, 4 vols. (Bogotá: Publicaciones del Instituto Caro y Cuervo, 1979), I, 575–6.

verse romance *Sone de Nansay* (c. 1267–82) is an exception.[41] In this *Bildungsroman*, the eponymous hero, a son of the count of Brabant and ancestor to Godfrey de Boulogne, learns from his patron, the count of Saintois, about the nature of the round table game. Sone participates in four round tables over the course of the romance. They occur in Burgundy, Machault in the Ardennes, Montargis in the Gâtinais, and England.[42] According to *Sone de Nansay*, round tables were not simple, improvised affairs; rather, they involved extensive preparation, much heralding, and great expense.[43] The host would first select the date and place for the event. A large and attractive meadow surrounded on all sides by mountains was an ideal location because the common folk could sit on high and watch the proceedings.[44] Then, the host would determine the grand prize, which was to be presented to the eventual victor, the 'rois de la table'.[45] The presentation of trophies is not, however, a distinctive element of the round table. In *Sone de Nansay*, comparable awards, including a golden fleece, are presented to the champions of general tournaments as well.[46] In addition to paying for the grand prize, the countess who hosts the Machault round table also promises to cover the expenses for all knightly competitors and their ladies.[47] Such a display of *largesse* on the part of the patron seems to have been customary.

Hosting a round table entailed great construction costs too, for, according to *Sone de Nansay*, these events took place in an enclosed space. When explaining to his protégé Sone how the round table is established, the count of Saintois states that, once a place of combat is chosen, 'loges de fust' (wooden structures) are raised all around it.[48] David Crouch, who references Jacques Bretel's *Tournoi de Chauvency* (1285), glosses '*eschaufaus*' and '*loges*' as 'elevated stands ... laid out in a line immediately behind

---

[41] There are no firm indications as to the dating of this anonymous romance. It survives in a single manuscript: Turin, Biblioteca Nazionale, MS L. I. 13, which dates from the first half of the fourteenth century. For the dating provided, see Lachet, *Sone de Nansay*, 53–61.

[42] See Lachet, *Sone de Nansay*, 424.

[43] See Lachet, *Sone de Nansay*, 430.

[44] See *Sone von Nausay*, ed. Moritz Goldschmidt (Tübingen: Gedruckt für ded litterarischen Verein in Stuttgart, 1899), 35, lines 1327–30 and lines 1349–50. Also see Crouch, *Tournament*, 14, 118–20.

[45] *Sone von Nausay*, 35, line 1344.

[46] See Lachet, *Sone de Nansay*, 431; Crouch, *Tournament*, 36.

[47] *Sone von Nausay*, 250, lines 9661–3.

[48] In other texts, these are also referred to as 'beffrois' (bellfreys) or 'escafauts' (scaffolds). See Michel Parisse, 'Tournois et tables rondes dans "Sone de Nansay"', in *Études de langue et de littérature françaises offertes à André Lanly* (Nancy: Université Nancy II, 1980), 279.

the lists, for viewing the jousts'.[49] The *Sone*-poet adds that ladies and damsels, spectators and judges, and even the knightly participants themselves would sit in these stands and watch the competition.[50] In the case of the Machault round table, the knights that came to partake advised the patroness to have a pit made to enclose the jousters.[51] The enclosed jousting area was referred to as the 'table'.[52]

Sone de Nansay outlines the course of the round table game itself. Each jouster was expected to bring his *amie* to the event. At the outset of the round table, a certain number of competitors were designated defenders of the table, *chiaus dedens*. The rest constituted the challengers, *chiaus defors*. The number of insiders varied from event to event. Each insider was obliged to have his shield, containing his own unique heraldic insignia, hung on an available stake on the lists. The shields were all to be placed in a single row, presumably at the same height off the ground.[53] After hanging his shield, each insider returned to the *loges*. Each outsider wishing to joust was to advance to the table and then select an opponent from the ranks of the insiders by striking or overturning the man's shield.[54] Guards (*siergans*) stationed at the entrance gate ensured that no one except the jousters (and their ladies), called upon at a given time, entered the arena. Trespassers were subject to disqualification and forfeiture of person and possessions.[55] Once challenged, the defender had to enter the jousting arena through the aforementioned entrance gate. It was the duty of each *amie* to supply her knight with a lance.[56] She would also cheer on her champion with a kiss and words of encouragement.[57] Here we observe the incorporation of courtly love. The knights and ladies who watched the jousts were sometimes called upon to act as judges.[58] Although multiple matches could occur simultaneously, only single

---

[49] Crouch, *Tournament*, 124.
[50] *Sone von Nausay*, 31, 1175–80. For a similar description of Queen Guinevere, together with a company of noble ladies and maidens, sitting on *loges* and watching knights joust at one of Arthur's tournaments, see *Le roman de Tristan en prose (version de manuscrit fr. 757 de la Bibliothèque nationale de Paris)*, 5 vols. (vol. 1, ed. Joël Blanchard and Michel Quéreuil; vol. 2, ed. Noël Laborderie and Thierry Delcourt; vol. 3, ed. Jean-Paul Ponceau; vol. 4, ed. Monique Léonard and Francine Mora under the direction of Philippe Ménard; vol. 5, ed. Christine Ferlampin-Acher under the direction of Philippe Ménard) (Paris: Honoré Champion, 1997–2007), I, 222.
[51] *Sone von Nausay*, 250, lines 9667–82.
[52] See Parisse, 'Tournois dans *Sone de Nansay*', 279.
[53] See Parisse, 'Le tournoi', 196-7.
[54] *Sone von Nausay*, 253, lines 9781–6.
[55] *Sone von Nausay*, 255–6, lines 9875–84.
[56] *Sone von Nausay*, 31, lines 1181–3, and 254, lines 9825–7.
[57] *Sone von Nausay*, 37, lines 1407–10. Also see 282, lines 10920–8.
[58] *Sone von Nausay*, 35, lines 1330–4.

combat was permitted.[59] As soon as a competitor was knocked off his horse, he lost his mount, and both he and his lady were eliminated from the competition.[60] When describing the Machault round table, the *Sone*-poet writes: 'S'il toute jour pooit durer, / Il convient chialz dedens jouster' (If it is able to last the whole day, / it is necessary for those within to joust).[61] The insiders eventually had to compete against one another in order to determine who was to be the *rois de la table*.

Each day of jousting typically extended from dawn till dusk.[62] Feasting and festivities began immediately after the grand prize had been awarded.[63] The *Sone*-poet states that at the Machault Round Table there were two enclosures surrounded by ditches: one of the enclosures was for jousting and the other was for eating, dancing, and other festivities. The latter enclosure was covered with tents and very richly equipped.[64] Judging by this detail it does not appear that merrymaking occurred only at the terminus of the jousting period. The festive dimension of the round table event provided opportunity for Arthurian role-playing, but *Sone de Nansay* does not provide any examples of it. The assumption of Arthurian roles does not appear to have been an essential element of the round table game.

Thus far, my analysis of the character of the round table has depended almost exclusively on one work of literature, the *Sone de Nansay*. Its author offers a vivid picture of a round table game, but was his account true to life? Does it epitomize a standard type of round table engaged in by Europe's nobility during the thirteenth century?[65] The paucity of detailed descriptions makes comparative analysis difficult. However, the description of the knightly challenge appearing in *Sone de Nansay* coincides with the understanding of the customs of King Arthur's Round Table displayed in the notebook (Oxford, Magdalen College, MS 93, fol. 144) of the fifteenth-century English preacher John Dygoun (*fl.* 1406–45). Taking up the question of why the Son descended from Heaven more swiftly than the other two persons of the Trinity for the sake of man's salvation, the preaching guide begins by explaining:

> Legitur in gestis Arturi quod habuit milites nobiles de tabula rotunda
> et quando congregabantur simul, singuli super parietem castelli

---

[59] See Parisse, 'Tournois dans *Sone de Nansay*', 282; Parisse, 'Le tournoi', 197.

[60] *Sone von Nausay*, 31, lines 1185–90.

[61] *Sone von Nausay*, 253, lines 9787–8.

[62] See Lachet, *Sone de Nansay*, 168–9.

[63] *Sone von Nausay*, 35, lines 1352–4.

[64] *Sone von Nausay*, 253, lines 9793–8.

[65] Crouch has suggested that the *Sone*-poet wrote 'almost journalistically', drawing on his own experience of tournaments (*Tournament*, 14).

pendebant sua scuta. Et si quis scutum alicuius tangebant, possessor scuti cum tangente pugnabat. Ad propositum: Tres persone Trinitatis possunt vocari milites rotunde tabule, quia omnes sunt equales virtutis et potencie.[66]

(One reads in the exploits of Arthur that he had noble knights of the Round Table, and that when they were gathered together at the same time they hung up their shields on the wall of a castle. And if anyone touched someone else's shield, its owner fought with him who touched it. To our business: the three persons of the Trinity can be called knights of the Round Table, because all are equal in virtue and power.)

Although this copy dates from the fifteenth century, the *exemplum* appears to have been known in the mid fourteenth century, if not earlier.[67] In addition to validating *Sone de Nansay*'s account of how a knightly challenge was extended, the *exemplum* affirms that the round table contest involved single-combat encounters. It also leads us to infer that the ludic practice of hanging shields in a straight row along the lists approximated what was believed to have been a courtly practice of Arthur's knights of old. It is possible, however, that this defining element of the round table game was projected onto the confraternity of the Round Table and not vice-versa.

Also agreeing with the description of the round table offered in *Sone de Nansay* is the description of the 'tabla rodonda' provided in a late fourteenth-century interpolation to the Castilian crusader compilation known as *La Gran Conquista de Ultramar*.[68] The translator–compiler seems to have been writing for an audience less than familiar with the history and rules of the round table. The interpolation as a whole confirms that (1) the host bore the cost for the proceedings; (2) round tables involved circular spaces enclosed by tents and wooden structures; (3) the competitors were divided into two categories: insiders and outsiders; (4) the knightly challenge was ritualized; (5) the *amie* served as arms-bearer and morale booster for her champion; (6) the contest was limited to single-combat jousting; (7) falling off one's horse resulted in a loss; and (8) a great feast followed the jousting period. While the author of *Sone de Nansay* states that a round table held at the foot of a mountain was ideal, the author–compiler of the *Gran Conquista* sets the round table of his narrative in the middle of a mountain, where there are some very beautiful and large meadows.[69]

---

[66] The transcription and translation provided are by Lawrence Warner, 'Jesus the Jouster: The Christ-Knight and Medieval Theories of Atonement in *Piers Plowman* and the "Round Table" Sermons', *Yearbook of Langland Studies* 10 (1996): 136–7.

[67] See Warner, 'Jesus the Jouster', 139.

[68] *Gran Conquista de Ultramar*, I, 575–6.

[69] *Gran Conquista de Ultramar*, I, 575.

The most obvious divergence between *Sone de Nansay* and the *Gran Conquista* interpolation concerns whence the event obtained its name. According to the author–compiler of the *Gran Conquista*, the 'juego de la tabla redonda' (the game of the round table):

> ... ha este nombre porque, un día ante que se partan, ponen mesas de parte de dentro de aquellas tiendas, a la redonda, e comen allí todos aquel día lo major que pueden; e porque aquellas mesas son assí puestas en derredor, llámanle el juego de la tabla redonda, que no por la otra que fue en tiempo del rey Artus.[70]

> (...has this name because one day before they depart, they set up tables on the inside of those tents, in a circle, and there, on that day, all eat as well as they can; and since those tables are thus placed all around, they call it the game of the Round Table, and not on account of the other one that existed in the time of King Arthur.)

Either the 'table' refers to the jousting enclosure (as in *Sone de Nansay*) or to the circle of tables assembled at the culmination of the event (as in the *Gran Conquista* interpolation). The fact that the Castilian compiler feels compelled to add that the round table was not named after, or at least inspired by, Arthur's Round Table implies that his audience would have assumed that this was the case. Given that all known round table hastiludes postdate Wace's famous *Roman de Brut* (1155), which contains the earliest surviving textual mention of Arthur's Round Table, the association between the literary and the ludic round table was inescapable.

Putting aside the event's rather suggestive name and recognizing that Arthurian role-playing does not appear to have been an essential aspect of the round table game, let us consider whether the format of the game is particularly Arthurian. Michel Parisse believes that the knighthood of thirteenth-century Europe felt a yearning to match the likes of the Knights of the Round Table with respect to manner of combat and courteous behavior. A round table, in Parisse's assessment, was a means of wish fulfillment, an artificial setting where courage, skill, and *esprit du corps* across knightly society took precedence over hierarchy.[71] Indeed, Arthur, according to Wace, devised his Round Table for the very purpose of ending quarrels over precedence amongst his barons.[72] This dimension of the round table is treated in the preaching *exemplum*, for it states that those called *milites rotunde tabule* were regarded as *equales virtutis et potencie*. The hanging of shields all in a row or ring, a practice

---

[70] *Gran Conquista de Ultramar*, I, 576.
[71] Parisse, 'Le tournoi', 205.
[72] Wace, *Roman de Brut*, 244–5, lines 9747–60.

attributed to Arthur's knights and documented in the case of *chiaus dedens* at round tables, implies fraternity and equality in both contexts. Moreover, at round tables all participants congregated in the same tents, and the knightly contestants were invited to judge the military performance of their peers. The social exclusivity of these round tables to knightly society, with commoners only being permitted to watch from afar, also fostered a 'class ethics' and 'circle of solidarity' that extended from the highest barons to the lowliest squires.[73]

The round table is also thought by some scholars to have been a deliberate enactment of 'Arthurian' *courtoisie*. Parisse, as noted above, believes that thirteenth-century knights wanted to imitate the Arthurian approach to combat and courteous behavior.[74] Richard Barber has also interpreted the round table game as 'a kind of temporary association in which each member swore to obey set rules covering the combat. In effect, the ethos behind the regulations has become a desire to see "fair play".'[75] These readings reflect the influence of a seminal article by Ruth Huff Cline, who regards the round table as a series of 'strictly regulated' (single-combat) jousts and as a thirteenth-century innovation that drew upon the idealism of Arthurian literature to provide an alternative (or corrective) to the mêlée style tournament, which, from time to time, spiraled out of control and resulted in miniature wars.[76]

The descriptions of tournaments in Arthurian literature intersect with the rules of the round table game. The Prose *Tristan* (c. 1230–50), for example, contains multiple lengthy descriptions of Arthurian tournaments that may reflect the ideal tournament of the thirteenth century or perhaps even how the round table was conducted. One such tournament description, which Cline has identified as potentially shedding light on the thirteenth-century tournament ideal, states that all of the companions of the Round Table wore white coverings so that they could distinguish themselves from their opponents. The author of Prose *Tristan* proceeded to explain that 'la baniere de la Table Reonde' is 'cele baniere qu'il portoient as tornoiemens, non mie la baniere des mortex bactailles' (that banner which they carry to tournaments [and it is] not the banner of mortal battles).[77]

---

[73] See Erich Auerbach, *Mimesis: The Representation of Reality in Western Literature*, trans. Willard Trask (Garden City, NY: Doubleday Anchor Books, 1957), 119.

[74] Parisse, 'Le tournoi', 205.

[75] Richard Barber, *The Knight and Chivalry*, rev. edn. (Woodbridge, UK: Boydell, 2000), 210.

[76] Cline, 'Influence', 206. For further discussion of the round table as a military game created in response to the physical dangers posed by the traditional tournament, see Keeler, *Geoffrey of Monmouth and the Late Latin Chroniclers*, 133–4.

[77] *Tristan en prose*, I, 222. Also see Cline, 'Influence', 206.

More recently, David Crouch has called attention to an even more concrete example of how fatalities were avoided at Arthur's tournaments. According to the Prose *Lancelot*, one Christmas morning, King Arthur sanctions an improvised tournament in which 300 of his knights compete against 300 of Galehaut's knights with no more gear than lances and shields.[78] During this contest, the treacherous Meleagant, jousting on the side of Galehaut, targets Lancelot and

> ... demande une lance roide et grosse, si la fist molt bien aiguisier – et si ne le deust pas fere, se il fust loials chevaliers – et laisse corre a Lancelot et avise molt bien ou il ferroit. Et il fu voirs que Lancelos baoit a un autre chevalier que a lui ne de son agait ne se prenoit il garde.[79]

> (calls for a rigid and large lance, then he had it sharpened very well – and he would not have done this, if he were a loyal knight – and has a go at Lancelot and knows very well where to strike. And it was clear that Lancelot was going after another knight because he did not guard himself against him [Meleagant] nor against his surprise attack.)

In this vignette we observe an expectation of fair play as well as the expectation that *armes à plaisance*, also known as *armes courtoises*, be employed. The parallel between the real-life joust of Roger de Leybourne and Arnulf de Munteny, on the one hand, and the fictional one between Meleagant and Lancelot, on the other, is striking. By requiring that dulled lance tips be used and that a formal challenge be issued prior to each joust, by enforcing the rule of single combat, and by incorporating the performance of courtly love as a formal element of the game, the round table facilitated the practice of *courtoisie* along the lines of Arthurian literature. It enabled each competing knight to focus on besting his single opponent and permitted the lords and ladies in the *loges* above to focus on assessing his performance. The round table game is comparable to a chivalric romance in that both focus on the accomplishments of the individual as opposed to the collective.[80]

Additionally, because round tables were 'remarkable for their sumptuous settings, the extravagance of their largesse and their involvement of women in the pageantry which was carried over from the hastiludes into the peripheral celebration', it would indeed seem, as Juliet Barker has commented, that round tables were 'the ultimate celebration of Arthurian values'.[81] Nonetheless, this line of thinking should not be

---

[78] Crouch, *Tournament*, 114; *Lancelot, roman en prose du XIIe siècle*, ed. Alexandre Micha, 9 vols. (Geneva: Droz, 1978–83), I, 90.

[79] *Lancelot en prose*, I, 92 (my translation).

[80] See Parisse, 'Le tournoi', 211; Crouch, *Tournament*, 119.

[81] Barker, *Tournament in England*, 66.

pushed too far. Although we can safely regard the round table game as reflective of Arthurian values in broad terms, Arthurian role-playing, particularly through the bearing of Arthurian heraldic arms and the dramatic reenactment of episodes from Arthurian legend, seems not to have been a defining element of the game. The setting could, however, accommodate role-playing games in which the arms and personae of Arthur and his knights were assumed.[82] The association of the round table game with Arthur's renowned knightly order was, moreover, unavoidable. Hosting and participating in round tables games was undoubtedly a means of inviting a comparison to King Arthur. Returning now to Plantagenet England, Richard of Cornwall, brother of Henry III, found a unique way to court association with Arthur – not by competing in round tables but through property ownership.

Richard of Cornwall, an Arthurian pretender to the throne?

Henry III does not stand out as an Arthurian, but there are indications that his brother Richard (1209–72) cultivated an Arthurian likeness. Richard, the second son of King John and his queen, Isabella of Angoulême (c. 1188–1246), was named after his uncle, Richard the Lionheart. Until 17 June 1239, when Henry III had a son and heir by his queen, Eleanor of Provence (c.1223–91), Richard was the heir-presumptive to the throne of England.[83] On 30 May 1227, Henry made Richard the earl of Cornwall,[84] and in May 1233 Richard acquired the castle and grounds of Tintagel, King Arthur's reputed birthplace.[85] During the 1230s Richard oversaw the redevelopment of this Cornish castle. Oliver Padel holds that the earl's interest in the site stemmed from its 'literary renown',[86] and David Rollason has suggested that Richard's objective in purchasing and developing Tintagel was 'to associate himself with the fame and glory of King Arthur by becoming the lord of a castle on the site of his conception'.[87] Rollason also notes that Richard's interest in Tintagel seems

---

[82] The earliest example of an Arthurian-themed round table of which I am aware occurred in the small Picard village of Le Hem on the feast of Saint Denis (8–10 October), 1278, and it will be explored in the next chapter.

[83] See Denholm-Young, *Richard of Cornwall*, 22; Matthew Paris, *Chronica Majora*, III, 340.

[84] See Denholm-Young, *Richard of Cornwall*, 9.

[85] See David Rollason, 'From Tintagel to Aachen: Richard of Cornwall and the Power of Place', *Reading Medieval Studies* 38 (2012): 1.

[86] Padel, 'Some South-western Sites with Arthurian Associations', in *The Arthur of the Welsh*, ed. Rachel Bromwich, A. O. H. Jarman, and Brynley F. Roberts (Cardiff: University of Wales Press, 1991), 233.

[87] Rollason, 'From Tintagel to Aachen', 2.

to have been 'short-lived', however, for 'after a visit to Launceston in 1256 which may have taken in Tintagel, the castle was scarcely visited, if at all, by him or any of his successors'.[88] In January 1257, Richard was elected 'King of Germany', and he was crowned on 17 May 1257 at Aachen, the principal palace and burial place of Charlemagne. Richard's attention does indeed seem to have turned to Germany at this point, but can we say anything more about his earlier interest in Arthur?

In so far as I am aware, all existing scholarship has been content to recognize the Tintagel purchase and castle building as a prestige project for Richard without further comment. Tintagel, with its Arthurian connections, was surely the most prestigious seat of power in the earldom of Cornwall, but Richard's relationship with his brother in the 1230s should also be taken into consideration. Initially, Richard held the earldom of Cornwall only at Henry III's pleasure. The king reserved the right to overrule decisions made by Richard with respect to the earldom. This was a source of friction between the brothers. Following a disagreement on these grounds in July 1227, Richard entered into an alliance with William (II) Marshal and other barons of the realm. Richard, supported by seven other earls, objected to the policies of Henry's justiciar, Hubert de Burgh, and they made an armed protest at Stamford and threatened civil war in summer 1227. Henry assuaged Richard for the time being with further grants of land, including the honor of Wallingford (again at the king's pleasure), but the earl had now shown his readiness to collude with the barons of the realm.[89] It is also worthy of note that Richard, in August 1225, assumed the title of count of Poitou. He stood to gain greatly from Henry's Continental campaign of 1230, and he may have been disappointed that Henry III followed the advice of Hubert de Burgh and avoided direct engagement with the army of the French.[90] But what Nicholas Vincent terms 'the most significant breach' between the royal brothers was the marriage of Richard to Isabella Marshal, the sister of the earl of Pembroke and widow of Gilbert de Clare (late earl of Gloucester) on 30 March 1231, for '[b]y allying himself to the Marshal, Richard threatened to bring together two of the greatest baronial power blocs in opposition to the king and de Burgh.'[91]

---

[88] Rollason, 'From Tintagel to Aachen', 4.

[89] Denholm-Young, *Richard of Cornwall*, 10–15.

[90] This is the opinion expressed by Nicholas Vincent. See his 'Richard, First Earl of Cornwall and King of Germany (1209–1272)', *Oxford Dictionary of National Biography*, Oxford University Press, 2004; online edn., Jan. 2008 (http://www.oxforddnb.com/view/article/23501, accessed 28 Feb. 2015). For a different assessment, see Denholm-Young, *Richard of Cornwall*, 18.

[91] Vincent, 'Richard, First Earl of Cornwall'.

Richard of Cornwall's position in the 1230s was analogous to that of Arthur of Brittany in the 1190s. Both were first in line of succession to the throne of an unwed king. This fact grants us a new perspective on Richard's interest in Tintagel. Richard, by taking up residence at Tintagel, was arguably signaling that in him lay the fulfillment of the Arthurian hope for the Plantagenet dynasty. He was poised to be the new boar of Cornwall.

In 1231, two years before Richard purchased Tintagel, the relationship between Henry and Richard improved – at least for a time. On 10 August 1231, Henry granted Cornwall, Wallingford, Eye and Beckley to Richard as a hereditary fiefdom and Richard Marshal, Richard's brother-in-law, was granted the earldom of Pembroke. This development marked the beginning of the fall of the divisive Hubert de Burgh, which was brought to fruition the following summer. Initially, Richard favored Henry's new advisor, Bishop Peter des Roches, but he saw the decision of the Crown to hold a judicial eyre in Cornwall in January 1233 as further infringement upon his lordship. In March 1233, Richard Marshal and Richard of Cornwall joined forces in a campaign against the Welsh in Radnor. The two Richards conducted the expedition without royal sanction, and it prevented Henry from arriving at a truce with the Welsh. In June 1233, Henry again purchased his brother's loyalty, but this time it cost the earl his alliance with Richard Marshal.

Three political motives for why Richard of Cornwall would have been interested in cultivating an Arthurian likeness suggest themselves. First, he had a turbulent relationship with King Henry and may not have been averse to replacing his brother on the throne.[92] Second, Richard was the heir presumptive until 1239 and may have wished to communicate to the lords of the realm that he would make a good monarch. Third, Richard had possessions in Arthurian lands, namely Cornwall and the Welsh Marches. Communicating his likeness to Arthur might have had symbolic value within his seignorial domain. It should, however, be noted that Richard of Cornwall was not revered as a great warrior.[93] Matthew Paris preserves an account of French opposition (c. 1257) to Richard of Cornwall's election as 'King of Germany', and this *Francorum consolatio* declares him to be '[i]mbellis est et imbecillis, et in negotiis

---

[92] In support of this point, see the analysis of Denholm-Young, *Richard of Cornwall*, 22: 'By 1238 [the earl of] Chester was dead, and the baronial demonstration of that year depended upon Richard of Cornwall for leadership. He was still young and handsome and great hopes were entertained of him.'

[93] See Denholm-Young, 'Tournament', 103 and Vincent, 'Richard, First Earl of Cornwall'.

bellicis inexpertus' (unwarlike and weak and inexperienced in the ways of war).[94] The earl of Cornwall was by other accounts highly regarded for his prudence.[95]

The likelihood of Richard's inheriting the throne of England decreased when Henry married Eleanor of Provence (c. 1223–91) on 14 January 1236. In summer 1236, Henry made one of his few recorded visits to Glastonbury. David Carpenter believes the king took his new bride to see Arthur's alleged gravesite on that occasion.[96] Shortly thereafter, around the year 1238, King Henry III decided on a new decorative program for the great hall and an adjacent chamber (located in the south-east corner of the inner bailey) at Dover Castle.[97] It came to be believed that King Arthur himself, rather than Henry III, had constructed the great hall at Dover. A brevia from the fourteenth regnal year of Edward II (8 July 1320–7 July 1321) states:

> L'an de Grace quartre centz seissante neuisme, regna in Bretaigne Arthour le Glorious; cesti amenda le dit chastiel en plusieurs choses, et fist la sale, que ore est appelle Artoursale; et la chambre sa femme est appelle Guaonebour, id est, Thalamus Guanguare.[98]

> (the year of grace 469, Arthur the Glorious reigned in Britain; he fixed up the aforesaid castle and several other things, and made the hall that is now called 'Arthur's Hall'; and the chamber of his wife is called 'Guaonebour', that is the chamber of 'Guanguare'.)

It is unclear whether this piece of local history inspired (or was inspired by) Henry III's building project. Henry III may have decided on an Arthurian decorative theme for the great hall of Dover, which would account for the later belief that Arthur was responsible for the hall.[99] It

---

[94] Matthew Paris, *Chronica Majora*, V, 605.

[95] See Matthew Paris, *Chronica Majora*, III, 340.

[96] See Margaret Howell, *Eleanor of Provence: Queenship in Thirteenth-Century England* (Oxford: Blackwell Publishers, 1998), 7.

[97] For the dating of the project to *c.* 1238–40, see Allan Brodie, *Arthur's Hall, Dover Castle, Kent: Analysis of the Building. Historical Building Report* (Swindon: English Heritage, 2011), 3. R. Allen Brown, *Dover Castle, Kent (Ministry of Public Building and Works Official Guide-Book)* (London: Her Majesty's Stationery Office, 1966), 17.

[98] *Historia Fundationis Ecclesiæ S. Martini Dover*, in William Dugdale, *Monasticon Anglicanum: A History of the Abbies and Other Monasteries, Hospitals, Frieries, and Cathedral and Collegiate Churches, with their Dependencies in England and Wales*, vol. 4, ed. and rev. John Caley, Henry Ellis, and Bulkeley Bandinel (London: James Bohn, 1846), 533. Also see Stones, 'Arthurian Art Since Loomis', 27–8. Gawain's skull and Craddock's mantle are two other Arthurian relics associated with Dover. See E. M. R. Ditmas, 'The Cult of Arthurian Relics', *Folklore* 75, n. 1 (1964): 32–3.

[99] See Berard, 'King Arthur and the Canons of Laon', 108–9; Borenius, 'Cycle of Images', 46.

is possible that Henry commissioned an Arthurian decorative project to impress his new queen all the more with the romantic character of his realm.

It should also be noted that Henry was again at odds with his brother Richard until February 1238. Eleanor's Savoyard relatives were the new court favorites, and the secret marriage of Henry and Richard's sister Eleanor to Simon de Montfort greatly angered the earl of Cornwall. Perhaps the Dover Arthurian project was a riposte to Richard's work at Tintagel. Of course, it is also possible that Richard of Cornwall and Henry III were dabbling with Arthurianism without any definite political intention. However, the prospect of Richard of Cornwall's elevation to the throne of England seems to have been one motivating factor behind his building project at Tintagel.

'King Henry of England' in Arthurian prose romance

We do not have definite evidence that Henry III commissioned Arthurian art or architecture, but the king did possess a legendary sword called 'Curtana', which we could broadly categorize as Arthurian regalia. Additionally, during Henry III's reign, a 'King Henry of England' was credited for commissioning French prose translations of the exploits of King Arthur and his Knights of the Round Table. Let us first consider Henry III's sword.

We have already looked at King John's sword of Tristam. Interestingly, as Loomis has noted, '[a]fter King John's time we hear no more of Tristam's sword among the regalia, but instead there appears "Curtana," the short (French *court*) or blunt sword'.[100] Matthew Paris mentions *Curtana* in his *Chronica Majora* in the context of the coronation of Eleanor of Provence as queen consort (23 January 1236). The St. Albans monk states that during the ceremony, John of Scotland (d. 1237) exercised the honor of bearing the 'gladium Sancti Ædwardi, qui Curtein dicitur' (sword of St. Edward, which is called Curtein) in his capacity as earl of Chester.[101] Paris either did not know or downplayed the Arthurian pedigree of this sword. His attribution of it to Edward the Confessor is surely erroneous.[102] The author of the Prose *Tristan* dubs Tristan's sword 'Cortaine' towards the close of

---

[100] Roger Sherman Loomis, 'Tristam and the House of Anjou', *Modern Language Review* 17, n. 1 (1922): 29.
[101] Matthew Paris, *Chronica Majora*, III, 337–8. See also the 'Red Book of the Exchequer (Record Office), fol. 232', in *English Coronation Records*, ed. and trans. Leopold G. Wickham Legg (Westminster: Archibald Constable, 1901), 58.
[102] See Ditmas, 'More Arthurian Relics', 93.

the romance. He writes that, more than one hundred thirty years after the death of King Arthur, Charlemagne conquered all of England, and in a certain English abbey Charlemagne reportedly found the sword of Tristan and the sword of Palamedés. The author of the Prose *Tristan* goes on to state that Charlemagne kept the sword of Palamedés for himself

> et dona celle de Tristan a Ogier le Danoys, et c'estoit celle meesmes dont li Morholz avoit esté ocis. Et por l'oche qi i estoit la fist il Ogier acorcier, car elle li sembloit un pou trop longue et trop pesant, dont i la trova trop curte aprés cele ovraige, q'elle en fu puis Cortaine apellee.[103]

> (and gave that of Tristan to Ogier the Dane, and it was with this same sword that he (Tristan) had killed Morholt. And on account of the notch that was in it, Ogier had it shortened, for it seemed a little too long and too heavy for him. Then he found it too short after this work, and for this reason it was henceforth called 'Cortaine'.)

Did the Plantagenets come to refer to John's sword of Tristam as *Curtana* on account of this episode, or vice versa? The overlap in date between the composition of the Prose *Tristan* (1230–50) and the coronation of Eleanor (1236) makes the direction of influence difficult to discern.

Let us now consider the attribution of prose Arthurian romances, namely those of the Lancelot–Grail Cycle (c. 1215–35), to 'King Henry of England'.[104] The authors of the cycle do not state where it was written. Ferdinand Lot has noted that the works of the cycle showcase only a rudimentary knowledge of the geography of the British Isles and northwest France, and even then, the plain of Salisbury is mistakenly located close to the sea.[105] On the other hand, the *Estoire del Saint Graal* and *Mort le Roi Artu* display detailed knowledge of Meaux (Île-de-France, Dep. Seine-et-Marne). In the Prose *Lancelot* and the *Queste del Saint Graal* there are references to the *fête de la Madeleine*, which was very popular in Champagne and Brie. Lot is persuaded that the author was Champenois

---

[103] *Tristan en Prose* IV, 312.

[104] See Carol J. Chase, 'La fabrication du Cycle du *Lancelot-Graal*', *Bulletin Bibliographique de la Société International Arthurienne* 61 (2009): 262–3. Chase believes that *l'Estoire del Saint Graal, Le Lancelot, La Queste del Saint Graal* and *La Mort le roi Artu* were drafted before 1220 (270–1). The earliest manuscripts containing fragments of the Lancelot–Grail Cycle have been dated to c. 1220 (267–8) by Alison Stones based on her study of the manuscript decorations. This dating is upheld by Patrick Moran, *Lectures cycliques: Le réseau inter-romanesque dans les cycles du Graal du XIIIe siècle* (Paris: Honoré Champion, 2014), 328.

[105] See Ferdinand Lot, *Étude sur le Lancelot en prose* (Paris: Honoré Champion, 1918), 140–51 (esp. 140). Also see Jean Frappier, *Étude sur La Mort le roi Artu, roman du xiie siècle*, 3rd edn. (Geneva: Librairie Droz, 1972), 22.

and made use of Chrétien de Troyes' *Lancelot*, which was written at the request of Marie of Champagne.[106]

Although the authors of these prose works show no signs of familiarity with Normandy, Brittany, or the British Isles, the cycle recognizes a special connection between the Plantagenet kings of England and the figure of Arthur. The explicit Angevin connection to Arthur is present in the *Queste del Saint Graal* and the *Mort le Roi Artu*. At the conclusion of the *Queste*, King Arthur orders his clerks to record the adventures of the knights of his household and to have this narrative preserved for posterity at the fictional 'l'almiere de Salebiere' (the library of Salisbury).[107] Henry II of England's well-known clerk, jurist, and *raconteur*, 'Mestre Gautier Map' (Walter Map, c. 1130–1209/10), according to the romance, went to Salisbury and had the adventures of the Holy Grail translated from Latin into French 'por l'amor del roi Henri son seignor' (for the love of his lord, King Henry).[108] In the opening lines of *Le Mort le Roi Artu*, the author revisits this framing device and has 'King Henry' request that 'Walter Map' write about the demise of the heroes involved in the 'adventures of the Holy Grail'.[109] Henry II and Walter Map emerge as the latter-day counterparts to King Arthur and his clerks. There is also a visual dimension that further communicates this idea. As Alison Stones has noted,

> [t]he opening of *Mort Artu* is most often illustrated with a scene depicting a king ordering a scribe to write…. The 'historical context' in which King Henry II and Walter Map are invoked at the beginning of the text suggests, of course, that it is they who are represented in the pictures; but it is equally likely that another obvious overlay of meaning is be understood here – King Arthur and his scribe.[110]

Stones believes that the identity of the king depicted is left ambiguous to allow for a 'multi-valent reading' that empowers the viewer to decide.[111]

---

[106] The manuscript history of the Prose *Lancelot* supports Lot's theory. See his *Étude sur le Lancelot*, 130.

[107] Salisbury Plain was, according to *Mort Artu*, the location of Arthur's final battle against Mordred.

[108] *La Queste del Saint Graal: roman du xiiie siècle*, ed. Albert Pauphilet (Paris: Édouard Champion, 1923), 279–80. All translations from the *Queste* are from *The Quest for the Holy Grail*, trans. E. Jane Burns. *Lancelot-Grail: The Old French Arthurian Vulgate and Post-Vulgate in Translation*, ed. Norris J. Lacy, vol. 6 (Cambridge, UK: D. S. Brewer, 2010), 171.

[109] *Mort Artu*, 1. With respect to the manuscript illuminations of this passage, see Alison Stones, 'Illustrations and the Fortunes of Arthur', in *The Fortunes of King Arthur*, ed. Norris J. Lacy (Cambridge, UK: D. S. Brewer, 2005), 133–4.

[110] Stones, 'Illustrations and the Fortunes of Arthur', 134.

[111] Stones, 'Illustrations and the Fortunes of Arthur', 135.

The visual ambiguity itself communicates that Henry II was *Arthurus redivivus*. For those involved in the composition of the Lancelot-Grail Cycle, Arthur was part of the Plantagenets' cultural heritage. The authors of this cycle establish a direct literary genealogy between the two kings. Henry II and Walter Map are both part of the narrative framework of the Lancelot-Grail Cycle.[112] The evocation of King Henry, an indisputably historical English king who died three or four decades prior to the composition of the Lancelot-Grail Cycle, attests to the factuality of the Arthurian narratives contained in the prose romances. We are encouraged to assume that Arthur was every bit as historical as Henry II. The framework also adds temporal distance: the adventures of Arthur are ancient stories written down by the grandfathers of the present day. Henry III's grandfather, Henry II, had the narratives preserved. Gerald of Wales, as we have seen, analogously uses Henry II to authenticate the discovery of Arthur's bones at Glastonbury in his *De principis instructione* and his *Speculum ecclesie*. These two Latin works date, at least in their surviving versions, from roughly 1217 to 1223, and this window of years closely approximates the putative dating of the *Queste del Saint Graal* and *Mort Artu*. Might Gerald's actions have influenced the anonymous authors of these prose romances, or vice-versa? It is possible that there was a trend early in Henry III's reign of attributing things Arthurian to Henry II of England. It would appear that, in Henry III's time, Henry II was coming to be remembered as 'Arthur-like' and as a patron of Arthurian literature.

The narrative convention and framework of acknowledging a 'King Henry of England' as the great patron behind the translation of the adventures of Arthur and his Knights of the Round Table from Latin into French continued to be employed in prose Arthurian romances that postdate the Lancelot-Grail Cycle. For instance, the prologue attached to eight manuscripts of the *Guiron le Courtois* (also known as *Palamedes*)[113] and the epilogue to several manuscripts of the Prose *Tristan* recognize a 'King Henry of England' as patron of the respective works. Both romances are widely accepted as dating from the reign of Henry III. Is the 'King Henry of England' mentioned in these prose romances Henry II or Henry

---

[112] On this topic, see R. Howard Bloch, 'The Text as Inquest: Form and Function in the Pseudo-Map Cycle', *Mosaic* 8, n. 4 (1975): 108.

[113] The romance *Guiron le Courtois* (c. 1235) postdates the Lancelot-Grail Cycle and the Prose *Tristan* but was already known by 1240. See Roger Lathuillère, *Guiron le Courtois: Étude de la tradition manuscrite et analyse critique* (Geneva: Librairie Droz, 1966), 34.

III? Neither author specifies regnal numbers, and we know little about Henry III's literary taste.[114]

At the beginning of the prologue to *Guiron le Courtois*, the first-person speaker, Helis de Borron, gives thanks to God for granting him, a 'chevalier pecheour' (a sinful knight), the graces necessary to translate 'le livre du Bret'[115] and to conquer 'la bonne volenté du noble roy Henri d'Engleterre'.[116] The king was reportedly so pleased with the phrasing of 'le livre du Bret' that he entreated Helis to write another Arthurian work with content not covered elsewhere. Helis then provides a literary genealogy for this prose romance tradition, naming 'Luces de Gau', 'Gasses li blons', 'Gautiers Map', 'Robers de Borron', and himself.[117] In order to resolve whether 'Henri d'Engleterre' is Henry II or Henry III, we must take into account the other personages listed above, beginning with Luces de Gau.

In the most common prologue to the Prose *Tristan*, Luces introduces himself as an English-born knight, lord of the 'Chastel del Gat' near Salisbury, and as translator of the 'l'estoire de Tristan' from Latin into French as spoken in England.[118] As Emmanuèle Baumgartner has noted, the placement of Luce close to Salisbury, where 'Walter Map' professed to have found the Latin Arthurian source that became the basis of his *Queste del Saint Graal* suggests that the author of the Prose *Tristan* was situating himself within the same narrative framework.[119] That the author of *Guiron le Courtois* perpetuates the fiction that Walter Map was responsible for the Lancelot-Grail Cycle of Arthurian romances further supports this

---

[114] We have record of an illuminated psalter, which is listed in London, British Library, Harley MS 745, fol. 162b as 'in usum Henrici tercii Regis'. See Susan H. Cavanaugh, 'Royal Books: King John to Richard II', *The Library*, 6th ser., 10, n. 4 (1988): 305. Henry also owned romances. The Calendar of Liberate Rolls contains an entry dated 18 August 1237 in which the king orders sixteen *solidi* to be spent on clasps, hasps, and nails of silver for the king's great book of romances. See *Calendar of the Liberate Rolls Preserved in the Public Record Office: Henry III, vol. 1 A.D. 1226–1240* (London: Hereford Times Limited, 1916), 288.

[115] '*Guiron le Courtois*, le Prologue de Paris, Bibliothèque Nationale, f. fr. 338', ed. Roger Lathuillère, in Roger Lathuillère, *Guiron le Courtois: Étude de la tradition manuscrite et analyse critique* (Geneva: Librairie Droz, 1966), 175.

[116] '*Guiron le Courtois*: Le Prologue de Paris, Bibliothèque Nationale, f. fr. 338', 176.

[117] '*Guiron le Courtois*: Le Prologue de Paris, Bibliothèque Nationale, f. fr. 338', 176–7.

[118] *Le roman de Tristan en prose*, ed. Renée L. Curtis, 3 vols. (Cambridge, UK: D. S. Brewer, 1985), I, 39. The Prose *Tristan* exists in multiple versions. See Emmanuèle Baumgartner, 'Luce del Gat et Hélie de Boron, le chevalier et l'écriture', *Romania* 106 (1985): 326–40. Renée L. Curtis has made a systematic study of the appearances of Luce and Hélie and variations thereupon in the manuscript tradition of the Prose *Tristan*. See her 'Who Wrote the "Prose *Tristan*"? A New Look at an Old Problem', *Neophilologus* 67, n. 1 (1983): 35–41.

[119] Baumgartner, 'Luce del Gat', 338.

interpretation. Neither the English knight Luce nor the *Chastel del Gat* has been identified.

Likewise, Gasses li blons has not been conclusively identified. Hermann Suchier has suggested that he was a certain 'Acius Blundus', a member of a great family devoted to Henry II,[120] but Gaston Paris and Baumgartner hold that Gasses is Wace, who for a time enjoyed the patronage of Henry II.[121] This identification is plausible, but the curious reference to Wace as blond remains unexplained. All of the elements mentioned thus far point to Henry II of England as the king alluded to in the prologue to *Guiron le Courtois*.

The French knight or cleric Robert de Boron (*fl.* 1191–1212) is also an elusive figure. He wrote the French verse *Joseph d'Arimathie* (c. 1191) and also a verse *Merlin* of which only the first 504 lines survive. He identifies himself as Robert 'de Bouron' (thought to be Boron a village in Franche-Comté) in his *Joseph* and claims to have been in the services of a 'Gautier de Mont Belyal'.[122] This individual might have been Gautier de Montbéliard, lord of Montfaucon, who departed for the Fourth Crusade in 1202 and died that year.[123] Walter Map and Robert de Boron make for an interesting juxtaposition. Walter Map was certainly in the service of Henry II, but is not known to have actually written an Arthurian text; Robert de Boron, on the other hand, is not known to have been in the service of Henry II, but was in reality the author of at least one Arthurian text. The period of literary activity of the historical Robert de Boron (as opposed to Robert de Boron, the frame character) coincides not with the reign of Henry II but rather with those of Richard I and of King John.

The anonymous author of the 'Post-Vulgate' *Merlin* Continuation (also know as the Huth *Merlin*) repeatedly references 'mon signeur de Borron' as the authority for his narrative. The author implies that Robert

---

[120] See Hermann Suchier, *Geschichte der französischen Literatur, von den ältesten Zeiten bis zur Geganwart*, vol. 1 (Leipzig and Vienna: Bibliographisches Institut, 1900), 160; See Lathuillère, *Guiron le Courtois*, 23–4.

[121] See Gaston Paris, *La littérature française au moyen âge, xie–xive siècle*, 4th edn. (Paris: Librairie Hachette 1909), 110; Emmanuèle Baumgartner, 'Sur quelques constantes et variations de l'image de l'écrivain (xiie–xiiie siècle), in *Auctor & Auctoritas: Invention et conformisme dans l'écriture médiévale, Actes du colloque de Saint-Quentin-en-Yvelines (14–16 juin 1999)*, ed. Michel Zimmermann (Paris: École des Chartes, 2001): 398. Also see Anne Berthelot, *Figures et fonction de l'écrivain au XIIIe siècle* (Montreal: Université de Montréal, Institut d'Études Médiévales, 1991), 437–69.

[122] See Robert de Boron, *Joseph d'Arimathie: A Critical Edition of the Verse and Prose Versions*, ed. Robert O'Gorman (Toronto: Pontifical Institute of Mediaeval Studies, 1995), 334, line 3155–6.

[123] See Fanni Bogdanow, 'Robert de Boron's Vision of Arthurian History', *Arthurian Literature XIV* (1996): 19–52.

de Boron is overseeing his work.[124] At select moments in the 'Post-Vulgate' *Merlin* Continuation when the author does not wish to elaborate further regarding a given knight and his adventures, he asks his companion at arms, Hélie, to lighten his burden by treating some of his material in a short 'branke' (branch) of his book. [125] The prologue of *Guiron le Courtois* is in dialogue with this passage of the 'Post-Vulgate' *Merlin* Continuation, for it claims that Robert de Boron requested Hélie's involvement and that the two were companions in arms. Yet as Anne Berthelot has rightly noted, in the *Merlin* Continuation it is not Robert who claims that Hélie is his companion in arms; rather, it is the anonymous scribe who does so.[126] The later writer, 'Hélie de Boron', conflates Robert de Boron and his scribe.

In short, the great prose romances of the thirteenth century, namely those of the Lancelot-Grail / Vulgate Cycle, the 'Post-Vulgate' *Roman du Graal*, *Guiron le Courtois*, and the Prose *Tristan* have pseudo-historical narrative frameworks. In the Vulgate Cycle, it is clear that 'roi Henri', the patron of Walter Map, is Henry II. In the prologue to *Guiron le Courtois*, Henry II was certainly the patron of the Arthurian works of 'Gasses li blons' and Walter Map. It is not absolutely clear that Hélie's patron, the 'noble roy Henri d'Engleterre' is Henry II, but the author does not offer any indication to the contrary. The prologue does not address the passage of time in the sequence of literary production.

Let us, for the sake of argument, treat this narratological construct as factual. If the writers were working in fairly quick succession, if their work overlapped, and if this undertaking began early in the thirty-five-year reign of Henry II, then the king may well have patronized all the works from Luces de Gau to Helie de Boron. Alternatively, if we assume that the works were written over an extended period of time and were completed after the end of Henry II's reign in 1189, then it is possible that Henry III was Hélie's patron. We know that the Vulgate Cycle was, in reality, completed under Henry III as were the 'Post-Vulgate' *Merlin* Continuation, *Guiron le Courtois*, and the Prose *Tristan*. Are we to understand the narrative framework as contemporary to its date of composition, or did the authors of these prose romances backdate their works to the reign of Henry II? This question, which goes hand in hand with the question of the identity of the romance references to 'King Henry of England', has not received much critical attention. The same question

---

[124] References to Robert de Boron as the authority behind the text may be found in *La suite du roman de Merlin*, 16, 107, 115, 133, and 274.

[125] *La suite du roman de Merlin*, 194. Also see pages 310, 311, 524.

[126] Berthelot, *Figures et fonction de l'écrivain*, 447.

applies not only to the prologue of *Guiron le Courtois,* but also to the epilogue of the Prose *Tristan.*

The epilogue to the Prose *Tristan* also recognizes a 'King Henry of England' as the patron of the romance. Once again, which Henry is it? The epilogue begins with a declaration by the author that after much time and effort he has completed his work, and he thanks God for providing him with the strength and wisdom that he needed. Next, the author, who identifies himself as 'Helys de Bouron' (Hélie de Boron), makes reference to 'rois Henrri d'Engleterre', stating that the king has already read his work from beginning to end and is still reading it because he enjoys it so much. King Henry reportedly found more in the Latin book that had yet to be translated into French, and he asked 'Helys', both in person and through others, by letters and by his own mouth, to write another text that would contain the adventures that were absent from the present work and all others coming before it. Helys states that he will break for the winter. He then makes the promise that, in the spring, he will return the Latin book and write a new book that will include all that was omitted by 'Luces del Gait'; by Walter Map, who made the 'livre de Lancelot'; Robert de Boron; and by Helys himself in his previous work, and he concludes by saying: 'et je endroit moi merci mult le roi Henri monseignor de ce q'il loe le mien livre et de ce qe il li donne si grant pris'. (And I for my part thank my lord King Henry very much for praising my work and for attributing to it such great merit.)[127]

Two modern editors of the Prose *Tristan* have tentatively suggested that we read 'rois Henrri d'Engleterre' as Henry III of England. Christine Ferlampin-Acher writes that 'King Henry' *might* be Henry III, but acknowledges that the reference *could* be fictive.[128] Renée L. Curtis expresses slightly more confidence in her identification of King Henry as Henry III: 'if the claim for royal patronage is legitimate, the king referred to is Henry III'.[129]

Both Ferlampin-Acher and Curtis acknowledge that the claim of patronage might be fictional but do not explore the possibility that the dedication might be backdated. The *Queste* and *Mort Artu,* with their mention of Walter Map as translator–author, provide a precedent for backdating. If we allow the prologue to *Guiron le Cortois* to inform our reading of the epilogue to Prose *Tristan,* then we would assume that

[127] *Tristan en Prose,* V, 455–7 (fol. 263b of BN 757); for the English translation provided, see *The Romance of Tristan: The Thirteenth-century Old French 'Prose Tristan',* trans. Renée L. Curtis (Oxford: Oxford University Press, 1994), 326.
[128] *Tristan en Prose,* V, 30, 564 n. 174.
[129] *Romance of Tristan,* 338 n. 326.

Master Luce de Gat began his work during the reign of Henry II, for the prologue states that he is the first to translate the story of Tristan from Latin to French for the king. But, once again, it is unclear at what point and at what date 'Hélie de Boron' completed the project.

In contrast to Ferlampin-Acher and Curtis, Berthelot reads 'rois Henrri d'Engleterre' as Henry II of England. She interprets the prologue to *Guiron le Courtois* and the epilogue to the Prose *Tristan* as backdated in the fashion of the Lancelot-Grail Cycle.[130] If she is correct, one might ask why it was Henry II who was selected as the patron of the immense corpus of Arthurian prose romance. Why did the authors of these texts not make Richard the Lionheart its grand patron? Berthelot's response is that, for a mid thirteenth-century audience, Henry II's reign was sufficiently long, prestigious, and distant to encapsulate the corpus of prose Arthurian romance and to lend it legitimacy.[131]

To Berthelot's remarks, I wish to add two further observations of my own. First, the choice of Henry II as the prime mover of the Arthurian prose tradition is a strong indication that the king was remembered in the thirteenth century as having been, on some level, an Arthurian king, either in his self-representation or in his literary taste. Although I cannot rely upon this as evidence to support my argument in Chapter One that Henry actively cultivated an Arthurian likeness, the representation of Henry II in the prose Arthurian romances is certainly consistent with my stance. Second, it was rather convenient for the writers of Arthurian romance to refer to an undifferentiated 'Henry of England' as an active patron of Arthurian literature. It allowed for a confusion or conflation between the former king, Henry II, and his namesake, Henry III of England. The reference to 'Henry of England' as patron was possibly intended as both a compliment to Henry III and as a goad to inspire him to take after his 'grandfather' and become an active supporter of Arthurian literature and of the institution of knighthood. In any event, the great prose romances of the thirteenth century reinforce the existence of a special connection between King Arthur, who had his scribes record the deeds of the knights of the Round Table for posterity, and the Plantagenet King Henry, who desired that the Latin narratives of the Arthurian past be translated into French for the edification of his court. This conveys a *translatio imperii* and a *translatio studii* from the court of King Arthur to that of King Henry, the founder of the Plantagenet dynasty.

---

[130] Berthelot, *Figures et fonction de l'écrivain*, 453.
[131] Berthelot, *Figures et fonction de l'écrivain*, 452–3.

King Arthur and the House of Gwynedd

During the relatively un-Arthurian reigns of John and Henry, the House of Gwynedd developed Arthurian credentials. We last considered Wales in the context of the stunning reversal of 1213, when John lost all of his recent territorial gains. The English crown's direct territorial stake in Wales was reduced to a small section in the southeast. The Welsh rallied behind Llywelyn ap Iorwerth (r. 1195–1240), the self-styled 'prince of the whole of North Wales'.[132] Between 1212 and 1217, Llywelyn took advantage of the Welsh unification, the erosion of John's power, and the divided attention of the Welsh Marcher lords (largely a consequence of the First Barons' War). In 1212, Llywelyn, as spokesman for all the princes of Wales, struck a peace treaty with Philippe II of France, and, by 1218, Llywelyn ap Iorwerth had become the most powerful prince in Wales since the Norman Conquest.[133]

After King John's death, the regency government of Henry III was eager to make peace with the Welsh, and in 1218 it requested that Llywelyn persuade all the magnates of Wales to perform homage to Henry. This act, as Davies has emphasized, was a tacit acknowledgment by the English crown that Llywelyn ap Iorwerth had attained hegemony in native Wales.[134] At the signing of the Treaty of Worcester (1218), Llywelyn and all the other princes of Wales swore homage to Henry III. In return, they were allowed to retain most of the lands and castles they had won. A period of relative peace prevailed until Llywelyn's death in 1240.[135] During these years, Llywelyn set himself up as the high king of a Welsh federation over which he exercised *de facto* power.[136]

Although Llywelyn did not attempt to unify all of Wales into one principality, he did seek to construct a 'historical and legal mythology to justify Gwynedd's hegemony in Wales'.[137] He styled himself 'lord of Wales', used the plurality of majesty, and claimed that his liberty was equivalent to that of the king of Scotland.[138] Thirteenth-century advocates for the House of Gwynedd also developed narratives concerning the royal lineage of Gwynedd in order to support Welsh independence from England and to justify Venedotian hegemony in Wales. These narratives were interpolated

---

[132] Davies, *Age of Conquest: Wales*, 239.
[133] Davies, *Age of Conquest: Wales*, 244.
[134] Davies, *Age of Conquest: Wales*, 243.
[135] There were, however, three royal campaigns launched against Wales in this period. See Davies, *Age of Conquest: Wales*, 243–4, 298–9.
[136] Davies, *Age of Conquest: Wales*, 245.
[137] Davies, *Age of Conquest: Wales*, 246.
[138] Davies, *Age of Conquest: Wales*, 246.

into existing legal collections much as the Arthurian interpolations were in the London Collection. Particularly notable among these legal fictions is the story of Maelgwyn Gwynedd (d. c. 547).[139] Just as the House of Plantagenet used the sixth-century figure of Arthur to legitimate its claims to overlordship of the British Isles and Western Europe, the House of Gwynedd used the sixth-century figure of Maelgwyn to legitimate its claim to overlordship of Wales. But did the House of Gwynedd, and Llywelyn ap Iorwerth in particular, also use Arthur as propaganda?

One instance of Gwynedd Arthurian propaganda is the *Vera historia de morte Arthuri*, which was written at an undetermined moment before its inclusion in London, MS Gray's Inn 7 (c. 1300). As we have seen, *Vera historia* locates Avalon in Gwynedd and suggests that the remains of Arthur became part of the fabric of an Avalonian chapel dedicated to the Blessed Virgin. Just as the discovery of Arthur's remains in Glastonbury suggests that Arthur was a king of 'English' lands and a spiritual forebear of the contemporary kings of England, the claim that Arthur was buried in Gwynedd suggests that the House of Gwynedd enjoyed a special connection with Arthur. The *Vera historia*'s emphasis on the primacy of Gwynedd fits with the two Llywelyns' mission to justify their supremacy in Wales.

Llywelyn ap Iorwerth's political accomplishments enabled him to be portrayed as a latter-day Arthur. Like the Arthur of British history, Llywelyn stalled the seemingly inevitable march of foreign invasion. In Arthur's case the invaders were the Angles and Saxons; in Llywelyn's case, they were the Anglo-Norman Marcher lords and the Plantagenet kings of England. Also like Arthur, Llywelyn ap Iorwerth 'created a sense of national unity which had been previously wanting' and which would be developed further by his grandson Llywelyn ('the Last') ap Gruffudd.[140] Yet, in his obituary for Llywelyn ap Iorwerth, the annalist responsible for the *Annales Cambriae* continuation to 1288 does not recognize the Welsh prince as *Arthurus secundus*; rather he acclaims him as 'ille magnus Achilles secundus'.[141]

Upon Llywelyn's death (11 April 1240), the magnates of Wales broke faith with his son and chosen successor Dafydd. From the time of Dafydd's knighthood by Henry III (15 May 1240) to the time of his premature death on 25 February 1246, the House of Gwynedd suffered significant political

[139] Morfydd E. Owen, 'Royal Propaganda: Stories from the Law-texts', in *The Welsh King and His Court*, ed. T. M. Charles-Edwards, Morfydd E. Owen, and Paul Russell (Cardiff: University of Wales Press, 2000), 224–54, especially 'The Supremacy of Maelgwyn Gwynedd' (251–4).

[140] Morris, *Welsh Wars of Edward I*, 19–20.

[141] *Annales Cambriæ*, ed. John Williams ab Ithel, RS 20 (London: Longman, Green, Longman, and Roberts, 1860), 82.

setbacks. By 1247, the English royal position with respect to Wales was the strongest it had been since King John's victories in 1211.

The debasement of Wales, and of Gwynedd in particular, continued from the death of Dafydd ap Llywelyn (25 February 1246) until the ascendancy of his half-nephew Llywelyn ap Gruffudd. In early June 1255 at Bryn Derwin, Llywelyn ap Gruffudd defeated his brothers in battle and became the sole ruler of Gwynedd. From 1256 to 1258, Llywelyn had a string of victories against the English. He focused the ire of his Welsh compatriots against the English and presented himself as the liberator of Wales.[142] The image of Llywelyn ap Gruffudd as a Welsh freedom fighter shines through in the entry for 1256 in the Red Book of Hergest version of the *Brut*.[143] Like his grandfather and namesake, Llywelyn used his celebrity and military successes to establish his hegemony over native Wales.

We know that Llywelyn was able to unify the native Welsh behind him through their shared contempt for the English, but was Arthur part of his propaganda arsenal? A Cambro-Latin martial poem most commonly known as 'The Song of the Welsh' suggests that this was the case. The poem survives in two manuscripts. The earlier copy is Leiden, Bibliotheek der Rijksuniversiteit, MS Voss. Lat. F. 77, fol. 144r–v. This manuscript contains a letter of Pope Martin IV (10 January 1282), which furnishes a *terminus ante quem* for the compilation.[144] The Leiden manuscript contains, among other texts, a version of Robert of Torigni's *Gesta Normannorum ducum* and its two continuations, a copy of Geoffrey of Monmouth's *Historia regum Britannie*, a French regnal list (fol. 143v), and the terms of the pact of 1259 between Louis IX and Henry III. Owing to these contents, the manuscript is thought to be of Norman provenance.

---

[142] See Powicke, *Thirteenth Century*, 137–8.

[143] Davies, *Age of Conquest: Wales*, 310; See *Red Book of Hergest Brut*, 246–9.

[144] The second manuscript is Cambridge, Corpus Christi College, MS 181, which is from St. Mary's, York and was written in the first quarter of the fourteenth century. The Leiden manuscript is thought to date from the late thirteenth or early fourteenth century. See Crick, *HRB Summary Catalogue*, 126–8. For additional discussion, see Michael Lapidge and Richard Sharpe, *A Bibliography of Celtic-Latin Literature, 400–1200* (Dublin: Royal Irish Academy, 1985), 30–1. There are three modern editions of this poem. The first is 'The Song of the Welsh', in *Political Songs of England from the Reign of John to that of Edward II*, ed. and trans. Thomas Wright (London: Camden Society, 1839), 56–8. The second is 'Appel des Bretons aux armes', in *Poeseos popularis ante saeculum duodecimum latine decantatae reliquias*, ed. Edélstand du Méril (Paris: Brockhaus et Avenarius, 1843), 275–7. The third and most recent edition is 'Trucidare Saxones: A Cambro-Latin Martial Poem', ed. and trans. David Howlett, in David Howlett, 'A Triad of Texts about Saint David', in *St. David of Wales: Cult, Church and Nation*, ed. J. Wyn Evans and Jonathan M. Wooding (Woodbridge, UK: Boydell, 2007), 268–71. Also see Andrew Breeze, 'The Date and Politics of "The Song of the Welsh"', *Antiquaries Journal* 88 (2008): 190–7.

There is no consensus as to the date of 'The Song of the Welsh'. It references Richard I of England and therefore must have been written after he became king in 1189. Lapidge and Sharpe index the anonymous poem as having been composed c. 1200 but do not explain their reasoning.[145] David Howlett has performed a numerological analysis and believes that the poem was written for Saint David's Day (1 March) 1200.[146] His numerological argument is tenuous, and the dating he offers is consequently suspect. Thomas Wright suggested that the poem was written in the context of the Second Barons' War of the 1260s.[147] As will be illustrated below, this contextualization is far more compelling. The poem reads:

> Trucidare Saxones soliti Cambrenses
> Ad cognatos Britones et Cornubienses;
> Requirunt ut veniant per acutos enses,
> Ad debellandos inimicos Saxonienses.
> Venite jam strenue loricis armati;
> Sunt pars magna Saxonum mutuo necati,
> Erit pars residua per nos trucidati:
> Nunc documenta date qua sitis origine nati.
> Merlinus veredicus nunquam dixit vanum;
> Expellendum populum prædixit vexanum.
> Et vos hoc consilium non servatis sanum;
> Cernite fallaces quorum genus omne profanum.
> Prædecessor validus rex noster Arturus
> Si vixisset hodie, fuissem securus
> Nullus ei Saxonum restitisset murus;
> Esset ei[s] sicut meruerunt in prece durus.
> Procuret omnipotens sibi successorem
> Saltem sibi similem, nollem meliorem,
> Qui tollat Britonibus antiquum dolorem,
> Et sibi restituat patriam patriæque decorem.
> Hoc Arturi patruus velit impetrare,
> Sanctus [qui]dam maximus: Anglum ultra mare;
> Scimus festum Martis kalendis instare,–
> Ad natale solum Britones studeat revocare.
> Virtuosos filii patres imitantur;
> Sic Arturum Britones virtute sequantur:
> Quam probo, quam strenuo monstrant procreantur;
> Ut fuit Arturus sic victores habeantur![148]

---

[145] Lapidge and Sharpe, *Celtic-Latin Literature*, 30.
[146] Howlett, 'A Triad of Texts about St. David', 259–61.
[147] Wright, *Political Songs of England*, 56.
[148] 'Song of the Welsh', 56–8.

(The Cambrians, who are used to slay[ing] the Saxons, salute their relations the Britons and Cornish-men: they require them to come with their sharp swords in order to conquer their Saxon enemies. Come now, vigorously, armed with coats of mail; a great part of the Saxons are fallen in mutual slaughter, the remainder shall be slain by us: now is the time for you to show of what blood you are sprung. The soothsayer Merlin never said a thing that was vain; he foretold that the mad people should be expelled. And you do not keep this wise counsel; observe deceitful people of whom the whole race is accursed. If our valiant predecessor, King Arthur, had been now alive, I am sure not one of the Saxon walls would have resisted him; he would have been hard to them, spite of their prayers, as they have deserved. May the Omnipotent procure him a successor only similar to him, I would not desire a better, who may deliver the Britons from their old grievance, and restore to them their country and their country's glory. May it please the uncle of Arthur to obtain this for us, a certain very great saint, [to send] the Englishman over the sea; we know that his festival is approaching on the kalends of March (St. David's Day); may he make it his study to recall the Britons to their native land. Sons imitate their virtuous fathers, so let the Britons take Arthur for their example in valour; they show from what a good and brave man they are descended; as Arthur was, so let them be, conquerors!)

The hatred of the English is pronounced in this martial poem. Although the poet mentions 'Anglia' (England) and 'Anglus' (Englishman), he tends to refer to contemporary Englishmen as Saxons. The Saxons are presented as villainous others. The call to arms of the Bretons and the Cornishmen evokes Merlin's prophecy of a pan-Celtic alliance, but the Scots are not mentioned. We instead find a purely Brittonic alliance. The poet's mention of a Saxon internecine slaughter suggests an English civil conflict and is a clue as to the poem's time of composition. It is unclear whether the poet's comment that Merlin never uttered a falsehood should be read as an earnest or a sarcastic remark.

The Arthur of the 'Song of the Welsh' is a *dux bellorum* in the tradition of the *Historia Brittonum*. Galfridian tradition also informs the characterization of Arthur, for the poet references Arthur's single combat with Frollo and his conflict with Rome.[149] Arthur is also presented as the ancestor and special champion of the Brittonic peoples. The English could boast of Richard the Lionheart and the French of Charlemagne, but the Brittonic peoples are the sole inheritors of the legacy of Arthur

---

[149] 'Song of the Welsh', 58.

and the other legendary kings of Britain.[150] This poem interestingly does not allude to the myth of Arthur's survival or to the expectation of his return. Instead, Arthur features as one of four worthy ancient British heroes, whom the contemporary descendants of the Britons (the Welsh, the Bretons, and the Cornish) should imitate.[151]

If we assume that the 'Song of the Welsh' touches on contemporary political affairs, then it must predate the conquest of native Wales by Edward I of England in 1283. The reference to the internecine wars of the Saxons (the English) suggests either the First Barons' War of 1215–17 or the Second Barons' War of 1264–7. The latter was by all accounts the bloodier affair.[152] The Red Book of Hergest version of *Brut y Twysogyon* is especially pertinent to this discussion. In its entry for the year 1264, the *Brut* states that 10,000 of the royalist party died at Lewes (14 May).[153] This claim, although of doubtful veracity, is indeed staggering and constitutes a great English (or Saxon) mortality. The actual death toll at Lewes is uncertain.[154] Few members of the knightly class were slain. Powicke notes that the most common estimate for the death toll was between 2,000 and 3,000, but he favors the tally of 600 arrived at by the clerks who buried the dead Londoners and men-at-arms.[155] When recounting the subsequent royalist victory at the Battle of Evesham (4 August 1265), the Welsh writer again emphasizes the great loss of life on both sides.[156]

There are additional reasons that support the dating of 'The Song of the Welsh' to the Second Barons' War. The more prominent lords of the Welsh Marches, including Roger Clifford, John Fitzalan, John and Hamo Lestrange, and Roger Mortimer of Wigmore, were leading participants (on the royalist side) in this war. Much of the fighting that took place occurred either in the March or in the adjoining English counties. Men from the Marches and native Wales constituted a sizeable presence in the battles of Lewes and Evesham.[157] Llywelyn ap Gruffudd, moreover,

---

[150] 'Song of the Welsh', 58.

[151] 'Song of the Welsh', 56–9.

[152] See Sean McGlynn, 'Roger Wendover and the Wars of Henry III, 1216–1234', in *England and Europe in the Reign of Henry III (1216–1272)*, ed. Björn K. U. Weiler and Ifor W. Rowlands (Aldershot: Ashgate, 2002), 196.

[153] *Red Book of Hergest Brut*, 254–5.

[154] For an early fourteenth-century account of the mortality at the Battle of Lewes, see *Chronicle of Pierre de Langtoft*, ed. and trans. Thomas Wright, 2 vols. RS 47 (London: Longmans, Green, Reader, and Dyer, 1866–8), II, 142–3.

[155] See F. M. Powicke, *King Henry III and the Lord Edward: The Community of the Realm in the Thirteenth Century*, 2 vols. (Oxford: Clarendon Press, 1947), II, 466–7.

[156] *Brut y Tywysogyon – Hergest Version*, 256–7.

[157] Davies, *Age of Conquest: Wales*, 312–13; Llywelyn ap Gruffudd sent footsoldiers to Lewes in support of the barons and Londoners. See Morris, *Welsh Wars of Edward I*, 30.

took maximal advantage of the discord among the English. He formed an alliance with Simon de Montfort. In 1263 and the following year, he sent military aid to the Montfortians in the Marches. In return, de Montfort forced Prince Edward to surrender the county and honor of Chester to Llywelyn, who assumed direct control over it. On 19 June 1265, Llywelyn obtained from de Montfort

> recognition of his title as prince of Wales and his lordship over the magnates within his principality, confirmation of all lands which he and his allies had conquered, and the promise of castles and lands along the border with England, which would greatly enhance the security of Llywelyn's principality....[158]

The divisiveness and great mortality of the English in the Marches and the consequent military and political opportunity afforded to Llywelyn by the Second Barons' War lend support to Wright's dating of the poem. Morever, it is entirely possible that Llywelyn's supporters drafted 'The Song of the Welsh' in order to encourage Welshmen to take up arms against the royalists and to win back the Marches. Arthur provided a noble pedigree for the Brittonic peoples. 'The Song of the Welsh' reopens the question of whether post-Conquest England or the Celtic fringe had the worthier claim to the legacy of Arthur. The poem's answer is simple and straightforward: Arthur is part of the noble heritage of the Brittonic peoples, and the Plantagenets could only boast of Richard the Lionheart as their great chivalric prince. This contest over Arthur's legacy, as we shall see, would resurface during the reign of Edward I. The *Vera historia de Morte Arthuri* and 'The Song of the Welsh', however, are the two earliest examples I have found of the adoption of King Arthur by the Welsh for political gain.

Conclusion

The figure of Arthur typified Henry III's weaknesses as king. The Arthur of Galfridian history was an inspiring and victorious leader much loved by his subjects, and a promoter of knightly life. Further alienating Arthur from Henry III were the actions of the Gwynedd dynasty. As this Welsh house increased its hegemony in Wales at Henry III's expense, it also seems to have claimed Arthur as its ancestral champion. The figure of Arthur thus by contrast emphasized Henry's incompetence as king – his failure to win back the Angevin lands in France, his failure to halt the

---

[158] Davies, *Age of Conquest: Wales*, 314.

political and military resurgence of native Wales, and his acrimonious relationship with his own subjects. Henry III had neither the physical nor mental disposition to undertake the Arthurian brand of consensual, chivalric kingship, but Prince Edward, who paid careful attention to his father's failings, was a different case entirely. He sponsored and participated in tournaments and pursued his political agenda through Parliament. In the next chapter we shall observe the convergence of Edward the man and Arthur the mighty kingly model. Edward's reign stands in sharp relief with the reign of King Henry III.

5
Arthurianism during the reign of Edward I, 1272–1307

Arthurus redivivus: for business or for pleasure

The author of the *Chronicle of Lanercost* (to 1297) concludes his discussion of the murder of Arthur of Brittany, the 'verus heres Angliæ' (the true heir of England), with a vignette involving Henry III and Arthur's elder sister, Eleanor of Brittany. This encounter would have taken place within two years of her death (10 August 1241). The chronicler writes:

> Dicitur tamen quod rex Henricus, filius ejusdem Johannis, ante mortem suam, credens se non omnino juste regnare, obtulit dictæ dominæ Alienoræ, sorori Arthuri, coronam regni Angliæ, et resignavit ei totum jus quod habebat in regno, et illa recepit et tenuit per tres dies. Postea fecit dominum Henricum vocari et dixit ei, 'filius tuus Edwardus est valens juvenis et strenuus; ego concedo sibi totum jus meum.'[1]

> (It is said that King Henry, the son of the same John, before her death, believing that he was not reigning altogether justly, offered the crown of the realm of England to the said Lady Eleanor, sister of Arthur, and he resigned to her all the right that he held in the realm, and she received it and held it for three days. After that she had Lord Henry summoned and said to him: 'Your son Edward is a valiant and hardy youth. I concede to him all my right.')

The author of this segment is believed to have been active from 1280 to 1297 – well into the reign of Edward I (1272–1307) and for a good forty years after the recounted event. It should be noted, however, that the chronicler speaks of Eleanor's death as having happened 'in hac nostra ætate' (in this our age).[2] The factuality of the narrative is wholly undermined by the fact that Edward was only two years old at the time of Eleanor's death. He would not have been a *valens juvenis et strenuus*, but a mere *infans*. This vignette, however, is of the utmost relevance to our topic. It was surely devised during the reign of Edward I, almost certainly by one of the king's supporters. The narrative tells us that the disappearance

---

[1] *Chronicon de Lanercost*, 12–13. See Ostmann, 'Die Bedeutung der Arthurtradition', 271.
[2] *Chronicon de Lanercost*, 12.

of Arthur of Brittany cast a long shadow over the Plantagenet dynasty, one that lasted, so it would seem, for the entirety of Henry III's sixty-five-year reign and even into the reign of Edward I.

By giving Eleanor the crown of England, Henry III acknowledges that she is the *vera heres Angliæ*, and he atones for the heinous mortal sin of his father King John. Eleanor's voluntary concession of the crown on the third day – probably alluding to the Holy Triduum (the period between the death and resurrection of Jesus Christ) – functions to rehabilitate the tarnished House of Plantagenet. Most importantly, Eleanor of Brittany is said to have chosen Lord Edward as Arthur of Brittany's rightful heir and successor. Erased is the negative baggage of the lackluster reigns of John and Henry III. A new day has dawned in England, and Edward has Eleanor's blessing to be the 'new' Arthur of Brittany, and, by extension, the new King Arthur. This vignette offers a small taste of the royal campaign establishing Edward I as *Arthurus redivivus*.

The justification that Eleanor of Brittany offers for selecting Edward as Arthur of Brittany's successor is that Edward is a valiant and hardy youth. This rationale is also meaningful. For, after the death of Richard I, England had been without a chivalric monarch for over seventy years. Circumstances changed when Henry III's eldest son, Lord Edward, became king (r. 1272–1307). Edward, like his great-uncles the Young King Henry, Richard the Lionheart, and Geoffrey of Brittany, was an athletic prince who sought glory and honor in arms. A successor of Matthew Paris at St. Albans describes Edward as a man of great stature, bravery, and fortitude, who knew how to use arms and was battle-trained; the chronicler adds that word of Edward's military skill and probity spread to the four corners of the globe.[3] There was a basis for favorable comparison of Edward to his knightly great-uncles and also to King Arthur. Edward seized upon it. He evoked Arthur more systematically than any of his predecessors. Early in his reign, on 19 April 1278, he translated the bones of the most famous Arthur before the high altar of Glastonbury Abbey. He went on to preside over round-table games at Kenilworth in Warwickshire (1279), at Nefyn in North Wales (1284), and at Falkirk in the central lowlands of Scotland (1302). Edward also cited the historical precedent of King Arthur to uphold his claim to the kingdom of Scotland in a letter (1301) to Pope Boniface VIII (r. 1294–1303).[4]

---

[3] *Opus Chronicorum (MS Cotton Claudius D. vi., fols. 115a–134b)*, in *Chronica Monasterii S. Albani*, vol. 3, ed. Henry Thomas Riley. RS 28/3 (London: Longmans, Green, Reader, and Dyer, 1866), 26; Michael Prestwich, *Edward I*, rev. edn. (New Haven: Yale University Press, 1997), 108–22.

[4] 'Sanctissimo Patri Bonifacio', in *Anglo-Scottish Relations, 1174–1328: Some Selected Documents*, ed. and trans. E. L. G. Stones (Oxford: Clarendon Press, 1965), 192–219.

It is commonly held that Edward I was the first English monarch to fashion himself consistently after King Arthur.[5] In truth, this distinction belongs to Henry II. Edward I's Arthurian pretensions are, however, far more conspicuous in the surviving historical record. Whereas the scholarly conversation concerning Henry II and King Arthur has focused on whether the first Plantagenet king of England ever cultivated a likeness to Arthur at all, the discussion surrounding Edward I and King Arthur has consisted of enumerations of his notable Arthurian undertakings and a debate regarding the nature and degree of his interest in Arthur.

Two interrelated binaries have played a large role in the scholarship on Edward I's Arthurianism. First, there is the distinction between the 'Arthur of history' and the 'Arthur of romance'. Was Edward I more interested in the former or the latter? The 'Arthur of history' refers to the figure of Arthur as portrayed in the Latin and vernacular chronicle tradition deriving from Geoffrey's *Historia regum Britannie*. The accretions to Geoffrey's biography of Arthur, such as the accounts of the discovery of Arthur's remains and the Arthur interpolations in the London Collection of the *Leges Anglorum*, are included in this category. The 'Arthur of romance' refers to the characterizations of the king in vernacular Arthurian romances, both verse and prose. The historical phenomenon of Arthurian role-playing fits into the 'Arthur of romance' category because the names assumed in chivalric hastiludes and stories performed in festive interludes derive principally from the romance tradition.[6] The second binary pertaining to Edward I's Arthurian gestures is the business/pleasure dichotomy. Was Edward's Arthurian self-fashioning strictly a leisure-filled diversion for the king and his nobles, or was it a meaningful component in his statecraft? Clinging too tightly to these binaries is problematic. The business/pleasure dichotomy is, strictly speaking, a false dichotomy. But these poles (history versus romance, business versus pleasure) have functional value both for describing the course of the scholarly conversation and for assessing Edward's Arthurian gestures.

An influential early contributor to the discussion of Edward I's Arthurianism is Sir Frederick Maurice Powicke, who emphasizes King Edward's historical consciousness, remarking that the king knew 'how to appeal to history' and also 'tried to comprehend in his own rule the

---

[5] See Nigel Saul, *Chivalry in Medieval England* (Cambridge, MA: Harvard University Press, 2011), 75, 78. Also see Juliet Vale, 'Arthur in English Society', in *The Arthur of the English: The Arthurian Legend in Medieval English Life and Literature*, rev. edn., ed. W. R. J. Barron (Cardiff: University of Wales Press, 2001), 185.

[6] Artesian noblemen acted out episodes from Chrétien de Troyes' *Yvain* and *Perceval* at Le Hem in 1279. See below.

traditions of his land'.[7] Powicke makes this point with respect to Edward's handling of his Welsh adversaries. He comments that Edward 'would not allow Llywelyn and the Welsh to rely upon the memories of King Arthur and the belief in his return to save them'.[8] Edward is thought to have viewed Arthurian history as a potential threat to his territorial ambitions and consequently used it for his own ends. According to Powicke, the 'historical' dimension of the figure of Arthur vis-à-vis the Welsh mattered most to Edward I, and serious political considerations motivated his Arthurianism. The 'Arthur of romance' does not factor into Powicke's discussion.[9]

Powicke did not trivialize Edward's evocations of Arthur, but more recent commentators have done so. This trivialization is, in large part, a reaction against R. S. Loomis' classic article 'Edward I, Arthurian Enthusiast' (1953). In an earlier work, 'Chivalric and Dramatic Imitations of Arthurian Romance' (1939), Loomis provides a descriptive overview of Arthurian play and display during the Middle Ages and emphasizes that it was a long-lasting, pan-European vogue. In 'Edward I, Arthurian Enthusiast', Loomis moves beyond the where, when, and how of Arthurian spectacle to consider the more challenging question of why a medieval monarch would imitate King Arthur. Loomis concedes that the representation of Arthur as *rex-imperator* in Geoffrey of Monmouth's *Historia regum Britannie* was of ideological value to Edward I and that politics factored into Edward's Arthurianism. Nonetheless, his central argument is that quixotic sentiment was the leading motivation for Edward's sustained interest in Arthur.

Loomis introduces the business/pleasure dichotomy into the scholarly conversation on Edward I's Arthurianism. He makes the sweeping generalization that 'political calculations had little if anything to do with this extraordinary addiction to matters Arthurian in lands remote from Britain' and then argues that this international aristocratic vogue was the chief motivation behind Edward's own Arthurian undertakings.[10] His logic runs as follows: if the international vogue for Arthur in the thirteenth century was not inspired by political calculations, and if Edward's Arthurian undertakings were part of that vogue, then the said Arthurian gestures were not politically motivated. This logic is not compelling.

---

[7] Powicke, *King Henry III and the Lord Edward*, II, 724.

[8] Powicke, *King Henry III and the Lord Edward*, II, 724.

[9] See F. M. Powicke, 'King Edward I in Fact and Fiction', in *Fritz Saxl, 1890–1948, A Volume of Memorial Essays from his Friends in England*, ed. D. J. Gordon (London: Thomas Nelson and Sons, 1957), 132–3.

[10] Roger Sherman Loomis, 'Edward I, Arthurian Enthusiast', *Speculum* 28, n. 1 (1953): 114.

Arthurian spectacle performed within Arthur's former principal domain and by one of his titular successors surely would have had more immediate political resonance than its performance elsewhere by non-Insular nobles.

Loomis lists all of Edward's documented Arthurian activities of which he was aware, he mentions an Arthurian prose compilation that was dedicated to Edward and his queen, and he references the many Arthur/Edward comparisons in contemporary chronicles and other political writings. Loomis sets forth this array to convince his readers of the intensity of Edward's devotion to Arthur. Not addressed, however, is whether each Arthurian evocation has more to do with the chronicle tradition or the romance tradition. Loomis imposes false binaries on his subject matter. To his mind, Edward I was either the consummate Arthurian or an occasional dabbler, and either business (political expediency) or pleasure (quixotic sentiment) was the principal motivation for Arthurian gestures. Loomis' opinion that Edward was an Arthurian 'enthusiast' caught up in the international vogue for Arthurian (romance) literature has cast a long and heavy shadow and has led to a trivialization of Arthurianism as a purely recreational exercise.[11] Loomis' generalizations about the extent of Edward's Arthurian enthusiasm have also prompted equally sweeping generalizations to the contrary.[12]

For a fruitful consideration of Edward's Arthurian activities, we must contextualize each episode in terms of its immediate social and political context and also in terms of how it stands in relation to the Arthurian gestures of Edward's predecessors. What did Edward hope to accomplish through each act? Does the evocation reflect engagement with the 'Arthur of history', the 'Arthur of romance', or both? Do we have reliable indications of Edward's fondness for Arthur as entertainment? If so, what are they? To begin, I wish to call attention to some points of intersection between the living Arthurian tradition and Edward's personal history.

Arthur and the formative years of Lord Edward

There is no evidence of Arthurian indoctrination of the young Prince Edward within the royal household. This absence of evidence cannot, however, be construed as evidence of absence, for very little is known

[11] Loomis, 'Edward I, Arthurian Enthusiast', 125–6.
[12] See Constance Bullock-Davies, *Menestrellorum Multitudo: Minstrels at a Royal Feast* (Cardiff: University of Wales Press, 1978), xxxvii–iii; Prestwich, *Edward I*, 121–2; Thea Summerfield, 'The Testimony of Writing: Pierre de Langtoft and the Appeals to History, 1291–1306', in *The Scots and Medieval Arthurian Tradition*, ed. Rhiannon Purdie and Nicola Royan (Cambridge, UK: D. S. Brewer, 2005), 33.

about Edward's early education, including whether Edward learned to read and write.[13] Our picture of the English royal book collections before Tudor England is also far from complete.[14] For these reasons we do not know if Edward read, or was read, Arthurian texts as a youth. Michael Prestwich and Noël Denholm-Young speculate that Edward's mother, Eleanor of Provence (c. 1223–91), and his wife, Eleanor of Castile (1241–90), encouraged him to cultivate a courtly and chivalric character.[15] Judging by her bookholdings and household decorations, Eleanor of Provence was partial to romances, especially during the 1250s when Prince Edward was entering his adolescence. But her interests, at least based on what we know of palace decorations, seem to have centered on Richard the Lionheart and Alexander the Great. Henry III likewise does not seem to have promoted Arthur as a kingly model for his son. Indeed, Henry named his eldest son after Edward the Confessor.[16]

Edward's Spanish relations – his wife, Eleanor of Castile, and his brother-in-law, Alfonso X, king of Leon and Castile (r. 1252–84) – may have fostered a penchant for Arthurianism in Edward. They plausibly suggested that he regard himself as a successor of sorts to Arthur of Brittany. Prior to Edward's wedding, there had been friction between the English and Castilian courts. Alfonso VIII of Castile (r. 1158–1214), as we have seen, laid claim in 1205 to the duchy of Gascony, asserting that Leonor of England (1162–1214) brought it to their marriage as her dowry. Upon his elevation to the throne in 1252, Alfonso X revived this claim. This was more likely saber rattling than serious policy, but Alfonso, at least in his rhetoric, drew attention to the fact that he was a descendant of Henry II and Eleanor of Aquitaine through Leonor. He claimed to be the lawful successor in Gascony to none other than Arthur of Brittany, whom Philippe II had recognized as duke in 1202. Alfonso's threat was that, if the king of France succeeded in overturning Plantagenet rule in Gascony, Alfonso would press his claim. Henry III's court was concerned that the new Castilian king would devote all of his energies to taking Gascony.[17] In order to forestall a Castilian move on Gascony, the English court opted for an Anglo-Castilian alliance. As part of the treaty of Toledo (31 March 1254),

---

[13] Prestwich, *Edward I*, 6.

[14] See Jenny Stratford, 'The Early Royal Collections and the Royal Library to 1461', in *The Cambridge History of the Book in Britain*, vol. 3: 1400–1557, ed. Lotte Hellinga and J. B. Trapp (Cambridge, UK: Cambridge University Press, 1999), 256.

[15] Prestwich, *Edward I*, 6; N. Denholm-Young, *History and Heraldry, 1254–1310: A Study of the Historical Value of the Rolls of Arms* (Oxford: Clarendon Press, 1965), 47–8.

[16] Prestwich, *Edward I*, 4.

[17] See Powicke, *King Henry III and the Lord Edward*, II, 232.

which involved the marriage of Edward and Eleanor, Alfonso officially quit his claim to Gascony.[18] Prince Edward, aged fourteen, arrived at Burgos on 18 October 1254. Two weeks later, on All Soul's Day, Alfonso X knighted Edward and gave away the bride at the nearby Abbey of Santa María la Real de Las Huelgas, which Leonor of England had founded in 1187.[19] This union inaugurated Castile's 'long-standing friendship and alliance with England' and a good rapport between Edward and Alfonso.[20] Edward's knighting ceremony is not known to have had an Arthurian dimension, but from the Castilian perspective Lord Edward was the first legitimate duke of Gascony since Arthur of Brittany.

Very soon after his knighting and marriage to Eleanor, Lord Edward began training for the lists. On 4 June 1256, around the time of Pentecost, the prince participated in his first tournament, which was held at Blyth in Nottinghamshire. Matthew Paris (d. 1259) defines this event as a hastilude. He does not specify whether Edward first tested his mettle in a general tournament or in a round table but comments that many knights, including William Longspée III, were trampled. This detail is suggestive of a mêlée.[21] Blyth was by no means Edward's only experience of tournaments as a young man. The *Annals of Dunstable Priory* states that, in 1260, Lord Edward, with a great company of knights, crossed the Channel to overseas lands in order to gain experience in hastiludes.[22] The *Annals of Burton* adds that Edward won a great number of tournaments on the Continent.[23] In 1262, the prince was seriously wounded while competing in a tournament.[24] In 1267, Prince Edward, his brother Edmund Crouchback (1245–96) (earl of Lancaster), and his cousin Henry of Almain (a son of Richard of Cornwall) reversed the tournament policy of Henry III through a public edict. They allowed tournaments to be held in England on certain days and at select locations.[25] This action constituted

---

[18] Matthew Paris, *Chronica Majora*, V, 397.
[19] Matthew Paris, *Chronica Majora*,V, 449–50. See also *Tratado de la Iglesia de Burgos*, ed. Henrique Florez, in *España Sagrada: Theatro Geographico-Historico de la Iglesia de España*, vol. 26: *Contiene el estado antiguo de las Iglesias de Auca, de Valpuesta, y de Burgos justificado con instrumentos legitimos, y Memorias ineditas* (Madrid: La Oficina de Pedro Marin, 1771), 319–20.
[20] O'Callaghan, *Learned King*, 152.
[21] Matthew Paris, *Chronica Majora*, V, 557.
[22] *Annales Prioratus de Dunstaplia*, 216–17.
[23] *Annales de Burton (A.D. 1004–1263)*, in *Annales Monastici*, vol. 1, ed. Henry Richards Luard. RS 36/1 (London: Longman, Green, Longman, Roberts and Green, 1864), 499.
[24] *Annales Prioratus de Dunstaplia*, 218–19.
[25] *Chronicon vulgo dictum Chronicon Thomæ Wykes (A.D. 1066–1289)*, in *Annales Monastici*, vol. 4, ed. Henry Richard Luard. RS 36/4 (London: Longmans, Green, Reader, and Dyer, 1869), 212.

a return to the policy of Richard I, who had reintroduced the practice of holding tournaments in England after its prohibition under Henry II. In Loomis' opinion, '[t]here can be little doubt that Edward's love of tourneys was one reason for his interest in the romances of the Round Table'.[26] Round tables and other knightly festivities certainly provided occasion for the performance of Arthurian tales. Loomis' suggestion, although speculative, does hint at an interest on Edward's part in the 'Arthur of romance'.

Another consequence of Edward's knighthood and marriage was his endowment with land and acculturation into the baronial perspective on good kingship, which, more than anything else, seems to have informed Edward's understanding of King Arthur. At the urging of Alfonso X, on 14 February 1254 Henry III endowed Edward with ample possessions on the condition that these would not be alienated from the English crown.[27] Now, as a lord in his own right, Edward could and did identify with his fellow barons. In 1259 Edward entered into an alliance with Richard de Clare, earl of Gloucester, who was one of the leaders of the movement, and the prince joined the barons in calling for the ouster of Henry's 'bad counselors'.[28] Although by 1261 Edward had reconciled with his father and was henceforth a royalist, he understood the baronial call for fuller inclusion in the governance of the realm. This awareness factored into his rulership. Indeed, Bertie Wilkinson recognizes Edward I as 'the first English king to begin to take the nation into a real partnership in many major problems attending the working of the state'.[29] He adds that '[t]he problem of the king's inner council, which had distracted the land under Henry, was partly in abeyance under his son because Edward accepted and used freely the great council'.[30] The image of Arthur in fellowship with his Knights of the Round Table accorded with the baronage's vision of the ideal king. Michael Giancarlo holds that Edward exploited the 'Arthurian ideal of a strong king working in concert with a strong baronage, meeting in parliaments and assemblies that are both "noble" and communally representative'.[31] Edward appears to have done so to assuage baronial discontent and to enlist support for his military campaigns. Edward's

---

[26] Loomis, "Edward I, Arthurian Enthusiast', 115.

[27] Prestwich, *Edward I*, 11.

[28] *Opus Chronicorum*, 7; Prestwich, *Edward I*, 31–2.

[29] Wilkinson, *Constitutional History of Medieval England*, I, 56.

[30] Wilkinson, *Constitutional History of Medieval England*, I, 55; Powicke, *King Henry III and the Lord Edward*, II, 694–5.

[31] Michael Giancarlo, *Parliament and Literature in Late Medieval England* (Cambridge, UK: Cambridge University Press, 2007), 44; Wilkinson, *Constitutional History of Medieval England*, I, 9–10.

Arthurianism was not merely the stuff of idle affectation. It was part of his domestic policy.

Baronial acculturation informed Edward's practice of Arthurianism, and there is reason to believe that Edward was acquainted with a version of the *Leges Anglorum* that was similar to the London Collection. Edward's formal rhetoric resembled that of the London Collection, and his behavior bore comparison to that of the Arthur of the London Collection. One of the major precepts contained in the London Collection is that the property of the Crown should not be alienated and that, should it become alienated, it must be recovered.[32] This tenet of good kingship was not in the best interest of the baronage, but it offered Edward moral justification for the recovery of royal authority within England. The Barlings and Hagnaby chronicles (c. 1300) report that, as soon as he was formally anointed king by the archbishop of Canterbury on 19 August 1274, Edward immediately took off his crown, declaring that it would never rest on his head until he had retrieved the Crown lands that his father had alienated.[33] Edward also adopted the idea of *consilium commune*, which was embodied in the *lex Arthuri* of the London Collection. Evidence of this appears in a letter to Pope Gregory X, dated 19 June 1275, in which Edward declares that, by the oath he took during his coronation, he is obliged to preserve the rights of his realm unharmed and not to do anything concerning the Crown of the same realm without first seeking the required counsel of its magnates.[34] Edward also aspired to fulfill the Arthurian manifest destiny of a united kingdom of Britain, seeking to bring Wales and Scotland under his rule.

Edward's actions were consistent with those described in the London Collection but sometimes contrary to its purpose. Edward turned its language against the interests of the baronage and the local municipal authorities that the compilation had been designed to defend. The king launched a great inquiry into encroachments upon royal rights. Even the activities of local officials came under scrutiny. This investigation, which began in 1274, was the most rigorous and extensive since the compilation of the Domesday Book, and it uncovered rampant corruption. Edward addressed many of these issues legislatively through the issuance of the First Statute of Westminster in 1275. He also saw fit to institute the

---

[32] *Gesetze der Angelsachsen*, I, 635.

[33] 'Extracts from the Barling Chronicle', in *Chronicles of the Reigns of Edward I and Edward II*, vol. 2, ed. William Stubbs, RS 76/2 (London: Longman & Co., 1883), cxvii.

[34] 'Rot. Claus. 3 Ed. I. m. 9. in Ced.', in *The Parliamentary Writs and Writs of Military Summons...*, vol. 1, ed. Francis Palgrave (London: George Eyre and Andrew Strahan, 1827), 381–2.

quo warranto proceedings between 1278 and 1294: royal justices were instructed to issue prerogative writs to subjects of the Crown, and each recipient was in turn obliged to show by what warrant (*quo warranto*) he exercised his franchise(s).[35] As Michael Clanchy has noted, the *quo warranto* proceedings emphasized both the importance of history and the privileging of the written record as the basis for authority.[36] Edward's implementation of the *quo warranto* proceedings illustrates his historical consciousness, which extended to the 'Arthur of history'. In his later years, Edward cited the precedent of King Arthur's conquest of Scotland to establish by what warrant he was entitled to be suzerain of Scotland. Now that we have looked at how Edward's experiences as tournament participant and a feudal lord may have contributed to his understanding of Arthur, let us take into account his status as a Marcher lord.

As earl of Chester, Lord Edward witnessed the extent to which Llywelyn ap Gruffudd was a threat to the English crown and used Arthurianism for his purposes. The earls of Chester were charged with maintaining (and expanding) the western border of England against the princes of Gwynedd.[37] As Edward obtained his Welsh fiefdoms, Llywelyn ap Gruffudd was rising in power. In June 1255, Llywelyn became sole ruler of Gwynedd. The following year, Edward imposed harsh rule over the Four Cantrefs of Perfeddwlad and provoked the local population. Edward's Welsh subjects appealed to Llywelyn for succour. In autumn 1256, Llywelyn retook the Four Cantrefs, Meirionydd, northern Ceredigion, Builth, and Roger Mortimer's territory of Gwrtheyrnion. In 1257 he defeated the royal army near Carmarthen and took much of southern Powys. He also attacked Glamorgan, and in 1258 he obtained the allegiance of most of the magnates of Wales and thereafter assumed the title of 'prince of Wales'. [38] Llywelyn's success lay in the speed of his attacks, his use of guerilla warfare tactics, and his avoidance of pitched battles. In spring 1263, Edward returned to Britain from Gascony and, together with the Marcher lord Roger (III) Mortimer, went on a punitive mission through Gwynedd. The gains made on this mission evaporated by the time of the royalist defeat at Lewes (14 May 1264).[39] Simon de Montfort forced Prince Edward to hand over to Llywelyn Chester and all

---

[35] Michael Prestwich, *The Three Edwards: War and State in England, 1272–1377*, 2nd edn. (London: Routledge, 2003), 8–9.

[36] Clanchy, *From Memory to Written Record*, passim.

[37] Morris, *Welsh Wars of Edward I*, 3–4.

[38] David Walker, *Medieval Wales* (Cambridge, UK: Cambridge University Press, 1990), 113.

[39] *Red Book of Hergest Brut*, 246–7.

the lands in Wales that the Welsh prince had seized from him during the baronial uprising. If Llywelyn had been using King Arthur as a precedent for Welsh resistance against the English, then Edward most likely knew about it.

Another part of Prince Edward's life that has been associated with his later Arthurianism is his time on the Eighth Crusade (1270–4).[40] After Henry III had been restored to power and the rebellious barons punished, Edward followed in the footsteps of his crusading ancestor, Richard I. In August 1270, the prince and his wife departed for the southern French walled seaport of Aigues-Mortes, where they expected to meet up with Louis IX of France. The royal couple reached the main force in Tunis only to find that Louis had died and that a peace treaty had been concluded between the crusaders and the emir of Tunis. Edward was, nevertheless, determined to persevere in his sworn undertaking. The entire crusading party spent the winter of 1270–1 in Sicily and then arrived at Acre on 9 May 1271. Edward launched a series of raids against enemy strongholds. A peace treaty, which Edward opposed, was reached in 1272. While at Acre, Eleanor had one of her clerks, Maistre Richard, translate Vegetius' *De re militari* into Anglo-Norman.[41] In his translation of this late Roman compendium on war, Richard included a passing remark about Prince Edward's success at the pivotal skirmish of Kenilworth (1 August 1265).[42] The tailoring of the text to Edward's own life story strongly suggests that he was the work's intended audience. But what 'evidence' is there for the prince's 'strong concern with both the historic and the romantic traditions of Arthur'?[43]

A prose Arthurian compilation purportedly written while Edward I was on crusade recognizes him as a provider of source material and as the patron of the compilation itself. This composite text is known by several titles, including *Meliadus*, the *Roman du Roi Artus*, and the Arthurian Compilation of Rustichello of Pisa. It combines narrative material from the Prose *Tristan* and *Guiron le Courtois* with new episodes.[44] In the

[40] See Loomis, 'Edward I, Arthurian Enthusiast', 115.
[41] See Lewis Thorpe, 'Mastre Richard: A Thirteenth-century Translator of the "De re militari" of Vegetius', *Scriptorium* 6, n. 1 (1952): 40.
[42] See Lewis Thorpe, 'Mastre Richard at the Skirmish of Kenilworth?', *Scriptorium* 7, n. 1 (1953): 120.
[43] See Loomis, 'Edward I, Arthurian Enthusiast', 115.
[44] See Fabrizio Cigni, 'French Redactions in Italy: Rustichello da Pisa', in *The Arthur of the Italians: The Arthurian Legend in Medieval Italian Literature and Culture*, ed. Gloria Allaire and F. Regina Psaki (Cardiff: University of Wales Press, 2014), 21. For a complete facsimile of Rustichello's *Compilation* and for a transcription, see *Il romanzo arturiano di Rustichello da Pisa*, ed. and trans. (into Italian) Fabrizio Cigni (Pisa: Pacini Editore, 1994).

prologue to the work, Rustichello of Pisa (Rusticiaus / Rusticien) identifies himself as the author–compiler of the work and recognizes Edward as the provider of his source material:

> Et sachiez tot voirement que cestui romainz fu treslaités dou livre monseingneur Odoard, li roi d'Engleterre, a celui tenz qu'il passé houtre la mer en servise nostre Sire Damedeu pour conquister la saint Sepoucre. Et maistre Rusticiaus de Pise, li quelz est imaginés desovre, conpilé ceste romainz, car il en treslaité toutes les tresmervillieuse novelles qu'il truevé en celui livre et totes les greingneur aventures; et traitera tot sonmeemant de toutes les granz aventures dou monde. Mes si sachiez qu'il traitera plus de monseingneur Lanseloth dou Lac et de monseingneur Tristan, le fiz au roi Meliadus de Leonois, que de nul autre, por ce que san faille il furent li meillor chevaliers que fussent a lour tenz en terre. Et li maistre en dira de cist deus plusor chouses et plusor battailles que furent entr'aus que ne trueverés escrit en trestous les autres livres, pour ce que li maistre le truevé escrit eu livre dou roi d'Engleterre.[45]

(And know for certain that this book was translated from the book of my lord Edward, the king of England, in that time in which he passed overseas in the service of our Lord God in order to conquer the Holy Sepulchre, and Master Rusticiaus of Pisa, who is depicted above, compiled this romance, for he translated from it all the new marvels and adventures that he found in that book and he certainly dealt with all the adventures of the world, and know also that he will write more about Sir Lancelot du Lac and Sir Tristan, the son of King Meliadus of Loonis, than about others because they were undeniably the best knights who were alive in the world at that time, and the master will tell you about these two men several things and news that happened between them which one will not find written in all the other books because the master found them written in the book of the king of England.)

Another statement of the relationship between Rustichello and Edward occurs in an epilogue to the Compilation.[46] The epilogue affirms that Edward I also commissioned Rustichello's translation.[47] Are these claims

---

[45] *Il romanzo arturiano di Rustichello da Pisa*, 233. For an edition of the *Compilation* that features BnF, MS fr. 340 as its base text, see *Le roman en prose de Tristan; Le roman de Palamède et la compilation de Rusticien de Pise*, ed. Eilert Löseth (Paris: Emile Bouillon, 1890), 423–74.

[46] This epilogue is lacking from the earliest surviving copy of the Compilation, BnF, MS fr 1463, which concludes instead with the epilogue to the Prose *Tristan* by 'Hélie de Borron'. See *Il romanzo arturiano di Rustichello da Pisa*, 287. For the 'Rustichello epilogue' we must turn to the later fifteenth-century manuscript tradition, namely BnF MS fr. f. 355.

[47] *La compilation de Rusticien de Pise*, 472.

credible? Until fairly recently scholars have accepted the veracity of the Compilation's prologue and epilogue.[48] This attribution may, however, be analogous to those in the tradition of the *Queste del Saint Graal*, *La mort le roi Artu*, the Prose *Tristan*, and *Guiron le Courtois*, all of which recognize Henry II as patron despite the fact that the king had long been dead at the time of their actual composition.

Let us begin by taking into account what is known about Rustichello of Pisa. Rustichello has not been conclusively linked with 'any one of the Pisan Rustichellos, primarily notaries, who appear in archival documents of the time'.[49] What little we know of him comes from another literary work, the *Devisement du monde*, in which we are told that Marco Polo and Rustichello were in prison together in Genoa. Rustichello reportedly put Marco's observations into writing, completing this undertaking in 1298.[50] The *Devisement* became a great success, and Rustichello is principally remembered for his involvement in it.[51] We know nothing about Rustichello's movements other than that he is associated by name with Pisa and that he spent time in a Genoese prison. These two elements do situate him in the Mediterranean, and we can, of course, also place Edward in the Mediterranean between 1270 and 1274. As Richard Trachsler notes, since we do not know Rustichello's itinerary while Edward was going to or from the crusade, a meeting between Rustichello and Edward as described in the prologue could have taken place at any point during that four-year period.[52] Loomis has speculated that this exchange occurred during Edward's second stay in Sicily at the court of Charles of Anjou in 1273; at that time Edward learned of his father's recent death (16 November 1272).[53] The references to Edward in the prologue and epilogue as 'roi d'Engleterre' indicate that these sections were written after Henry III's death.

---

[48] Loomis embraces the statements as factual ('Edward I, Arthurian Enthusiast', 115), as do Parsons (*Eleanor of Castile*, 30) and Prestwich (*Edward I*, 118).

[49] Cigni, 'French Redactions in Italy', 23.

[50] Marco Polo, *Le Devisement du monde*, vol. 1, ed. Philippe Ménard (Geneva: Droz, 2001), 117.

[51] Cigni, 'French Redactions in Italy', 22; Richard Trachsler, 'Rustichello, Rusticien e Rusta Pisa. Chi ha scritto il romanzo arturiano?', in *'La traduzione è una forma': Trasmissione e sopravvivenza dei testi romanzi medievali*, ed. Giuseppina Brunetti and Gabriele Giannini (Bologna: Pàtron editore, 2007), 109–11.

[52] See Trachsler, 'Rustichello', 113; Loomis, 'Edward I, Arthurian Enthusiast', 115.

[53] Loomis, 'Edward I, Arthurian Enthusiast', 115; see Prestwich, *Edward I*, 82. It is also noteworthy that Edward underwent a lengthy convalescence owing to an infected dagger wound that he sustained while fending off an assassination attempt (June 1272). This seems to have been an appropriate time to listen to stories of Arthur and the like. Edward did not rush back to England to be formally anointed as king.

It is also possible that the dedication is a literary fiction. Consistent with the convention in the prose tradition of Arthurian romance, a 'roi d'Engleterre' features as the provider (and authenticator) of the Arthurian source material as well as the patron for the new translation. In the case of Rustichello's Compilation, the Plantagenet patron was not 'Henri d'Engleterre', but rather 'Edouart d'Engleterre'. The language of the alleged source text, 'livre monseingneur Odoard, li roi d'Engleterre', is not stated. Given that 'Rustichello' claims to have translated it, he seems to be implying that it was written in Latin.[54]

The second departure from the existing literary convention concerns the author's name. The author–compiler, although writing in French, does not select a name from the existing catalogue of prose Arthurian pseudonyms. Nor does he reference any of these pre-existing writers. 'Rustichello' does not arrange his Arthurian source material according to the internal chronology of the narrative. Rather, he presents the material as it came to him.[55] Additionally, he does not identify precisely where his narrative fits into the existing prose Arthurian canon. Dispensing with the historical frame of Henry II's court makes sense given these tendencies. It frees him from some of the impositions of the existing narrative framework. The author does, however, assure his reader that the material that he found in King Edward's book had not yet been translated. Rustichello seems to have been mimicking the existing prose Arthurian narrative framework without being bound to it.

Why does the author identify himself in the prologue as Rustichello of Pisa? The simplest answer is that Rustichello was indeed the author of the Compilation. In this scenario, Rustichello perhaps did not actually meet Edward, but the writer surely would have known that the prince had visited his part of the world. Rustichello might have used this knowledge to fabricate a meeting between himself and Edward in order to obtain authentication for his work. A second possibility is that an anonymous Franco-Italian author adopted 'Rustichello of Pisa' as a pseudonym. The author presumably would have selected the name owing to its recognizability. Trachsler believes this to have been the case. He calls attention to Rustichello's prominence in the prologue. Our earliest copy of the Compilation, BnF, MS fr. f. 1463 (late thirteenth century) has a miniature on the first folio of the prologue, and the text speaks of *Maistre Rusticiaus de Pise* as being depicted above. Trachsler notes that two later manuscript copies of the text also contain the textual

---

[54] See Trachsler, 'Rustichello', 121.
[55] Berthelot, *Figures et fonction de l'écrivain*, 467–8.

reference despite lacking the illumination, and upon consideration of the *stemma codicum*, Trachsler concludes that 'li quelz est imaginés desovre' was an original component of the text and not a later interpolation.[56] If he is correct, a depiction of *Maistre Rusticiaus de Pise* from the time of composition was intended to accompany the prologue. Trachsler contends that Rustichello's name and depicted image conferred *auctoritas* onto the text. Trachsler then poses a question: at what moment in time would Rustichello's name have had cachet? Would this have been so in the 1270s or only after the completion of the *Devisement du monde* (1298)? He concludes that the latter was the case and that the Compilation was probably written after 1298.[57] Additionally, Trachsler detects verbal echoes between the prologue of the *Devisement* and the prologue of the Compilation. This discovery leads him to suggest that the anonymous author of the Arthurian text used the prologue of the *Devisement* as a model.[58] This Arthurian writer used Edward's name as a guarantee of the text's veracity and Rustichello's name as a guarantee of its literary merit.

Trachsler's analysis is compelling but hinges on the assumption that Rustichello had not become famous until he completed the *Devisement*. I do not know of any evidence that contradicts Trachsler's assumption. The dating of the Compilation to after 1298 explains the reference to Edward as simply 'li roi d'Engleterre'. By then Edward had already translated the bones of King Arthur and had hosted multiple round tables. He had more than matched his great-grandfather, Henry II of England, as an Arthurian. The claim that Edward I provided Rustichello with an Arthurian text is most likely a consequence of Edward's known association with the figure of Arthur.[59] Let us now consider how Edward acquired this connection.

Edward I's Arthurianism between the Welsh Wars, 1277–82

A major focus of the first decade of Edward's reign was re-establishing English hegemony in Wales, and Edward's Arthurianism, at least initially, was directed towards one grand purpose: establishing his lordship over

---

[56] Trachsler, 'Rustichello', 114–16.
[57] Trachsler, 'Rustichello', 116–18.
[58] Trachsler, 'Rustichello', 117. Compare Marco Polo, *Devisement du monde*, I, 117 with *Il romanzo arturiano di Rustichello da Pisa*, 233.
[59] By the 1270s, Arthurian literature was something of a trademark of the English court. For example, the wedding of Edward I's brother Edmund to Blanche d'Artois in 1275 is thought to have occasioned the production of an English codex (Paris, Bibliothèque nationale, fr 123) containing the *Queste du Saint Graal* and *Mort Artu* of the Lancelot–Grail cycle. This codex was presented as a wedding gift to a member of the Artesian nobility. See Stones, 'Arthurian Art Since Loomis', 29.

Wales. Relations between Llywelyn and the English nobility had been strained since the close of Henry III's reign. By the Treaty of Montgomery (1267), Llywelyn obtained from Henry III formal recognition as 'prince of Wales' and hereditary right to the principality of Wales. These terms angered the Marcher lords who had lost landholdings in Wales. From amidst their ranks, Roger (III) Mortimer rose to become one of the three regents entrusted with the guardianship of England in the interim between Henry III's death and Edward's return from crusade. Llywelyn had performed fealty to Henry III in 1267, but refused to swear it to Edward *in absentia* for fear that Mortimer would plot against him.

When Edward returned to England (2 August 1274), he invited Llywelyn to his coronation (19 August 1274). The Welsh prince refused to attend. Later that year, the prince learned of a conspiracy against his life that had been hatched by his own brother, Dafydd ap Gruffudd, and Gruffudd ap Gwenwynwyn. Edward gave the conspirators sanctuary, and Llywelyn again refused to attend the English king at Chester and to do him homage by the set date of 22 August 1275.[60] In further defiance of Edward, Llywelyn arranged to marry Eleanor, the daughter of Simon de Montfort. Edward's forces captured her at sea as she was trying to reach Llywelyn's court, and they kept her in English custody. On 12 November 1276, the English king in council formally proclaimed Llywelyn a rebel.[61] Edward launched a massive invasion of Gwynedd in July 1277, and by September, in the face of Edward's vastly superior force, Llywelyn sued for peace.

The result was the Treaty of Aberconwy (9 November 1277). Llywelyn lost the right of homage from all but five minor lords.[62] He had to acknowledge that his brother Dafydd would inherit the patrimony of Gwynedd Uwch Conwy upon his death. Edward reinstated the crippling annual dues established under the Treaty of Montgomery along with additional annual dues for Anglesey. Llywelyn was, however, permitted to retain most of his landholdings, excluding the Four Cantrefs, and his princely title, which had now become an 'empty title' and 'a cruel memento of former days of glory'.[63] According to the treaty, Llywelyn was to restate his submission annually: twenty men from each of his cantrefs were to go before the English king's agents and swear that they would uphold the Treaty of Aberconwy and would compel the prince of Wales to uphold it. If Llywelyn failed to remain a faithful vassal to Edward,

---

[60] *Red Book of Hergest Brut*, 262–3.
[61] Davies, *Age of Conquest: Wales*, 333.
[62] Davies, *Age of Conquest: Wales*, 335.
[63] Davies, *Age of Conquest: Wales*, 335.

these men promised to withdraw from Llywelyn's fealty and homage.[64] On 11 November 1277, two days after the treaty was signed, Llywelyn swore fealty to Edward at Rhuddlan. Edward allowed Llywelyn to marry Eleanor de Montfort, and, on 13 October 1278, the Feast of St. Edward the Confessor, the king gave the bride away and provided the wedding feast.

The first cluster of Edward's known Arthurian activity occurred during the Anglo-Welsh interwar period from November 1277 to March 1282. It included Edward I's translation of King Arthur's bones, a change in coinage thought to have fulfilled one of the *Prophetia Merlini* prophecies, a round table at Kenilworth in Warwickshire, and Arthur / Edward I associations in heraldry and in the Arthurian verse romance *Escanor*. Edward seems to have sensed that the Welsh War of 1277 was not the final campaign he would wage against Llywelyn ap Gruffudd. In order to conduct another expedition into Wales, he needed to obtain his subjects' financial and military support. By representing himself as a second Arthur, he appealed to his subjects' romantic and chivalric sensibilities. Edward harnessed the Galfridian historical and prophetic tradition surrounding Arthur as well as the Arthurian romance tradition to accomplish his political objective in Wales.

Between Llywelyn's performance of homage at London in December 1277 and the wedding arrangements made at Rhuddlan in September 1278, Edward translated the bones of Arthur before the high altar of Glastonbury Abbey (19 April 1278).[65] The most detailed account of this event is contained in the *Libellus* attributed to Adam of Damerham (d. c. 1291). It reads:

> Die vero Martis proxima sequente fuit Dominus Rex, & tota Curia, ad sumptus monasterii in toto, quo die in crepusculo fecit Dominus Rex aperiri sepulcrum incliti Regis Arturi. Ubi in duabus cistis, imaginibus & armis eorum depictis, ossa dicti Regis miræ grossitudinis, & Gwunnaræ Reginæ miræ pulchritudinis, separatim invenit. Ymago quidem Reginæ plene coronata, ymaginis regis corona fuit prostrata, cum abscicione sinistræ auriculæ, & vestigiis plagæ unde moriebatur. Inventa eciam fuit scriptura super hiis singulis manifesta. In crastino vero, videlicet die Mercurii, Dominus Rex ossa Regis, Regina ossa Reginæ, in singulis paliis preciosis involuta, in suis cistis recludentes, & sigilla sua opponentes, præceperunt idem sepulcrum ante majus altare celeriter collocari, retentis exterius capitibus et genis utriusque propter populi

[64] Davies, *Age of Conquest: Wales*, 336–7.
[65] Edward I is attested at Glastonbury between Wednesday, 13 April 1278 (6 Edward I) and Thursday, 21 April 1278. Edward celebrated Easter Sunday at Glastonbury on 17 April 1278. See E. W. Safford, *Itinerary of Edward I*, 3 vols. (London: Swift (P&D) Ltd., 1974–7), I, 92–3.

devotionem, apposita interius scriptura hujusmodi: Hæc sunt ossa nobilissimi Regis Arturi, quæ anno incarnacionis dominicæ millesimo ducentesimo septuagesimo octavo, terciodecimo Kalend. Maii, per Dominum Edwardum, Regem Angliæ illustrem, hic fuerunt sic locata, præsentibus serenissima Alienora, eiusdem Domini Regis consorte, et filia Domini Ferandi Regis Hispaniæ, magistro Willelmo de Myddeltone, tunc Norwycensi electo, magistro Thoma de Bek, tunc Archidiacono Dorsetensi et prædicti Domini Regis Thesaurario, Domino Henrico de Lacy Comite Lyncolniæ, Domino Amadio Comite uel Salue me[66] Sabaudiæ, et multis aliis magnatibus Angliæ.[67]

(On the following Tuesday, the Lord King and the whole court were present, all at the expense of the monastery, on which day, at dusk, the Lord King had the sepulcher of the famous King Arthur opened. There he found separately in two chests, decorated with their portraits and arms, the bones of the said king, which were of an astonishing size, and those of Queen Guinevere, which were of astonishing beauty. Indeed the image of the queen was richly crowned; the crown on the image of the king was knocked off and there was a cut on his left ear, and there were traces of the wound on account of which he died. Noticeable writing was found over each of these. On the following day, namely Wednesday, the Lord King again enclosed the king's bones in their chest, wrapped in a precious pall, while the queen did the same for the queen's bones. They marked them with their seals and directed the tomb to be placed speedily before the high altar, while the heads and knees of both were kept out for the people's devotion. Writing of this sort was placed inside: 'These are the bones of the most noble King Arthur, which were placed here in such a way in the year of the Incarnation of the Lord 1278, on the thirteenth before the kalends of May by the Lord Edward, the illustrious king of England. Present was the most serene Eleanor, consort of the same lord king and daughter of Ferdinand the king of Spain, Master William de Middleton, then bishop-elect of Norwich, Master Thomas de Bek, then archdeacon of Dorset and treasurer of the said lord king, Lord Henry de Lacy, count of Lincoln, Lord Amadeus, count of Salveniæ, or Savoy, and many magnates of England.')

The *Annals of Waverley* and the *Annals of Worcester* also recount this event. The Worcester entry is the longer and more detailed of the two. It states that, on Easter Day, Edward and his queen were at Glastonbury with its abbot. Edward had the tomb of Arthur opened, but the cause of this action was, reportedly, unknown to many. Edward then collected the

---

[66] See Adam of Damerham, *Libellus*, 589 n. 4. John of Glastonbury's *Cronica* reads 'domino Amadio comite Saluenie, vel Sabandie' (count of Saluenie or Savoy) (246–7). Manuscript M. of Adam's *Libellus* reads: 'Comite Sabaudiæ'.

[67] Adam of Damerham, *Libellus*, 588–9.

bones of the king and had them placed decently in the treasury of the monastery until such time as he was able to relocate them to a more honorific spot.[68] Adam of Damerham states that Edward ordered that the bones be translated before the high altar and that the king assisted in their preparation for relocation. The actual placement of bones in that place of honor appears to have occurred later.[69]

In translating Arthur's remains, Edward was affirming that Arthur was dead and that the bones found at Glastonbury were in fact Arthur's. Juliet Vale holds that this 'tangible refutation of Arthur's legendary survival ... was highly pertinent in the context of his [Edward's] continuing conflict with Llywelyn, prince of Wales'.[70] This position assumes that the Welsh, by and large, believed that Arthur was undead. If, however, the *Vera historia de morte Arthuri* and 'The Song of the Welsh' reflect the perception of Arthur in Wales (or at least in Gwynedd), then it would appear that Llywelyn had no objection to the idea that the original Arthur was dead and would not return. The *Vera historia*, as we have seen, clearly states that Arthur died and that his bones were buried at Gwynedd. The 'Song of the Welsh' treats Arthur as a freedom-fighting example for all the Welsh to emulate. Nowhere does 'The Song of the Welsh' hint at Arthur's return or the birth of a second Arthur. Instead, it represents Arthur as just one member of a heroic Trojan line extending up to the present day and insists that Arthur's blood flows through the veins of all Brittonic Celts. Such a strong racial and political linkage between Llywelyn and Arthur did not necessitate a reincarnation narrative.

The translation of the remains of Arthur was not Edward's response to the Breton Hope; rather, it was more likely a refutation of *Vera historia*'s claim that Arthur was buried in Gwynedd. As stated previously, if Arthur died and was buried on what was to become English soil, then the kings of England had a stronger claim to his legacy. When King Edward and the leading magnates of England stood together and authenticated the Glastonbury discovery, they confirmed that Arthur belonged to them. Edward provided written confirmation of the bones' authenticity and put the skulls and knees of Arthur and Guinevere on public display. The wounds on the skull of the

---

[68] See *Annales Prioratus de Wigornia (A.D. 1–1377)*, in *Annales Monastici*, vol. 4, ed. Henry Richards Luard, RS 36/4 (London: Longmans, Green, Reader, and Dyer, 1869), 474. The Waverley entry neither mentions the attendance of the bishop nor contains the remark that Edward's purpose in translating the remains was unknown to many. See *Annales Monasterii de Waverleia*, 389.

[69] This point was made by Michelle P. Brown and James P. Carley, 'A Fifteenth-Century Revision of the Glastonbury Epitaph', in *Glastonbury Abbey and the Arthurian Tradition*, ed. James P. Carley (Cambridge, UK: D. S. Brewer, 2001), 194.

[70] Vale, 'Arthur in English Society', 187.

male skeleton coincided with Geoffrey's report that Arthur sustained a fatal head injury. Both Gerald of Wales and Adam of Damerham mentioned the trauma to the skull of the male skeleton as evidence that the bones were genuine. Thus by showcasing the skull of 'Arthur', Edward offered all visitors to Glastonbury material proof that the abbey housed the true remains of Arthur. The monks of Glastonbury were able to produce a physical corpse to support their claim of being Arthur's final resting place; the residents of Gwynedd, at least according to the *Vera historia*, could not provide the bones because they had vanished in a cloud of smoke.

The second exhumation of Arthur's remains did more than undermine the Gwynedd claim to Arthur's remains; it established Edward's special connection with Arthur. Edward achieved this by conducting what James Carley has termed 'the secular equivalent of the translation of saints' relics with the attendant identification of the king with the revivified saint'.[71] John Carmi Parsons has noted parallels between the second translation of Edward the Confessor's remains performed at Westminster by Henry III on 13 October 1269 and the second translation of Arthur's remains performed at Glastonbury by Edward on 19 April 1278. Parsons interprets Henry III's conspicuous devotion to the cult of the Confessor, and most importantly the 1269 translation, as the king's attempt to compensate for not being Edward the Confessor's direct lineal descendant. A similar dynamic existed between Edward I and Arthur.[72]

Edward was in attendance at his father's translation of the Confessor's remains in 1269, and Henry III's devotion to Edward the Confessor seems to have informed Edward's conduct of the Glastonbury translation. There are many points of analogy. In both 1269 and 1278, the reigning king made a public spectacle of moving his predecessor from an already honorable resting place to an even more prominent location. Ostensibly, Henry III was expressing his reverence for his sainted predecessor. He was also establishing himself in the eyes of the public as a spiritual successor to St. Edward. Indeed, as Parsons has noted, the presence of a king at the translation of a saint's relics associated the king with 'the saints' merits and (of greater significance in the present context) with the protection and continuation of their work on earth'.[73] The same held true for Edward I with respect to Arthur. Arthur was not a proven saint, but the figure of Arthur was regarded as a champion of the faith. The English royal couple's

---

[71] Carley, 'Arthur in English Society', 51.

[72] John Carmi Parsons, 'The Second Exhumation of King Arthur's Remains at Glastonbury, 19 April 1278', in *Glastonbury Abbey and the Arthurian Tradition*, ed. James P. Carley (Cambridge, UK: D. S. Brewer, 2001), 180, 182 n. 6.

[73] Parsons, 'Second Exhumation', 181.

hands-on involvement in the translation of Arthur and Guinevere conveys that they absorbed the qualities of their respective royal 'forebears' and counterparts. If Richard the Lionheart, Tancred of Sicily, and Arthur of Brittany stood to gain some of the energy of Arthur by wielding Caliburn, how much more of it did Edward obtain by touching the king's bones?

Although Edward reportedly left the skulls and knees of Arthur and Guinevere exposed on account of popular devotion, there is no evidence that Arthur was venerated as a local saint at Glastonbury. Edward does not appear to have regarded Arthur as a saint. Arthur's remains were only housed in a *cista* (chest). If they were being accorded the status of saintly relics, one would expect to find mention of the bones being placed in a *feretrum*, which is 'a bier (stretcher) used to carry the body of a saint; by extension, a chest-like container for a saint's body'.[74] The 1278 translation is best characterized as a royal funerary ceremonial with cult-like overtones suggestive of ancestor worship and hero worship. Yet if one were to regard the *ossa nobilissimi Regis Arturi* as having relic-like powers, one would conclude that Edward, who had contact with said relics, absorbed their energy. Perhaps this royal touch was seen as transforming Edward into *Arthurus redivivus*. Touching the bones alleged to be those of one of Britain's most celebrated kings surely must have been personally significant for Edward and Eleanor, but the act was also filled with serious political symbolism that pointed to the English king's very recent victory in Wales and to his imperial aspirations.

Edward undeniably accorded the bones of Arthur the honor and dignity due to a deceased monarch. Parsons has stated that Edward I's action can be read not only as a translation of saints' relics but also as a royal reburial. The episode can be understood as the use of 'royal funerary ceremonial in legitimizing succession'.[75] It is clear from Edward's involvement in the translation that he recognized Arthur as his titular predecessor and was aiming for a reciprocation of sorts – recognition of his own status as Arthur's successor.

Edward needed legitimation as Arthur's descendant in the same way that Henry III needed legitimation as St. Edward's descendant. The ties were not self-evident, and there was cause to communicate the relationships by means of conspicuous display. Both cases exemplify an observation made by Olivier de Laborderie regarding the Capetian and Plantagenet ideologies of kingship: the kings of France obtained their legitimation by emphasizing the sacralization of the *sang royal*, whereas the kings of England based their legitimation on the sacralization of the

---

[74] See John Crook, *English Medieval Shrines* (Woodbridge, UK: Boydell, 2011), 311.
[75] Parsons, 'Second Exhumation', 181–2.

office of kingship and of the land to which it was linked. He adds that, although the kings of England were not beyond manipulating genealogy – and we have seen this in the London Collection – they found 'adoptive ancestors' with whom they shared a spiritual affinity as opposed to an actual kinship by blood.[76] The idea of *Arthurus redivivus* was of far greater utility to the kings of England than to the princes of Wales because the latter already enjoyed indisputable ties of blood and language to Arthur. Edward I emphasized his titular kingly connection to Arthur and attempted to transform himself into the next Arthur by conducting a royal burial for Arthur and by touching Arthur's bones.

In 1279, Edward was involved in two events with Arthurian resonance: he oversaw a change in coinage that was chronicled as the fulfillment of a prophecy by Merlin, and he attended a round table hosted by Roger Mortimer at Kenilworth in Warwickshire. Arthurian considerations do not appear to have motivated Edward's issuance of the new coinage,[77] but a chronicler at St. Albans,[78] the author of the Red Book of Hergest version of the *Brut y Tywysogyon*,[79] and other contemporary writers interpreted the production of new round coins and the execution of those found guilty of coinage debasement as the fulfillment of one of Merlin's prophecies contained in Geoffrey of Monmouth's *Prophetiae Merlini*.[80]

---

[76] Olivier de Laborderie, 'Élaboration et diffusion de l'image de la monarchie anglaise (XIIIe–XIVe siècles)', in *Histoires Outre-Manche: Tendances récentes de l'historiographie britannique*, ed. Frédérique Lachaud, Isabelle Lescent-Giles, and François-Joseph Ruggiu (Paris: Presses de l'Université de Paris-Sorbonne, 2001), 45.

[77] England had not had a full recoinage since 1247, and the coins in circulation were in poor condition owing to wear and illicit clipping. Many coins were significantly underweight, which led to currency inflation and made the collection of taxes extremely difficult. In January 1279, Edward decided on total recoinage and established commissions for hearing the charges against coin dealers, clippers, and officials suspected of fraud at the exchanges and mints. In August 1280, Edward demonetized the previous 'long-cross' coinage and forbade its use. He introduced round half pennies and farthings into circulation as accompaniments to the traditional penny so that it would not need to be cut to make smaller change. See Prestwich, *Edward I*, 245–7.

[78] See *Willelmi Rishanger, Monachi S. Albani, Chronica (MS Cotton Faustina B. ix)*, in *Chronica Monasterii S. Albani*, vol. 2, ed. Henry Thomas Riley, 1–230. RS 28/2 (London: Longman, Green, Longman, Roberts, and Green, 1865), 94.

[79] *Red Book of Hergest Brut*, 268–9.

[80] Geoffrey of Monmouth, *Historia regum Britannie* 113.83–4, pp. 146–7. Alanus de Insula interpreted the prophecy within the context of the deeds of Henry I. See *Prophetia Anglicana*, 79. Geoffrey may have been alluding to Henry I, who in 1100 began imposing harsh penalties on counterfeiters. See 'Henry I's coinage regulations (Hn mon)', Early English Laws Project. University of London: Institute of Historical Research/King's College London (http://www.earlyenglishlaws.ac.uk/laws/texts/hn-mon/, accessed 20 August 2014). See Roger Ruding, *Annals of the Coinage of Great Britain and its Dependencies from the Earliest Period of Authentic History to the Reign of Victoria*, vol. 1 (London: John Hearne, 1840), 163.

The second notable Arthurian event of 1279, the Kenilworth Round Table, is briefly mentioned in multiple chronicles.[81] One of the more detailed entries is contained in the *Chronicon* (1066–1289) of Thomas Wykes, a canon regular of Oseney Abbey. Wykes writes that on the vigil of St. Michael (28 September) Roger Mortimer, with a great multitude of knights and ladies, gathered at Kenilworth for a 'famosissimus convivium', commonly called a 'rotunda tabula'; the ephemeral event reportedly marked Mortimer's farewell to arms.[82] The Dominican friar Nicholas Trevet's *Annales sex regum Angliæ* (1136–1307) adds that 100 knights and 100 ladies participated in this round table and that a great multitude of knights from a variety of realms came to that place for the exercise of arms.[83] The pro-royalist continuation of Matthew Paris' *Flores historiarum* from Merton College, Oxford (1265–1326), states that the round table occurred in Warwick, that many noble potentates from home and abroad convened at it, and that Mortimer was its captain.[84] Mortimer is a central figure in these accounts of the Kenilworth Round Table. Denholm-Young found documentary evidence indicating that Edward attended the Kenilworth Round Table of 1279.[85] Before exploring King Edward's role in the round table, let us consider that of the host of the event, Roger (III) Mortimer.

Mortimer was of both Welsh princely and English royal blood. His mother was Gwladys Ddu (d. 1251), the daughter of Llywelyn ap Iorwerth and Joan (the legitimized daughter of King John). Thus Roger's maternal grandfather was Llywelyn ap Iorwerth and his maternal great-grandfather was King John of England. Mortimer thus had a claim to Llywelyn ap Iorwerth's Welsh principality and 'Arthurian' ethnic descent.

[81] See *Annales Prioratus de Dunstaplia*, 281; *Annales Londoniensis*, in *Chronicles of the Reigns of Edward I and Edward II*, vol. 1, ed. William Stubbs, RS 76/1 (London: Longman, 1882), 88; *Chroniques de London depuis l'an 44 Hen. III* [1259] *jusqu'à l'an 17 Edw. III* [1343]', ed. George James Aungier (London: Camden Society, 1844), 16; *Annales Prioratus de Wigornia*, 477.

[82] *Chronicon Thomæ Wykes*, 281–2.

[83] Nicholas Trevet, *Annales sex regum Angliæ, qui a comitibus Andegavensibus originem traxerunt* (A.D. M.C.XXXVI.–M.CCC.VII.), ed. Thomas Hog (London: Sumptibus Societatis, 1845), 300.

[84] *Flores historiarum*, ed. Henry Richards Luard, 3 vols. RS 95 (London: Her Majesty's Stationery Office, 1890), III, 53.

[85] British Library, MS Cotton Domitian A. xii, fol. 111 places Edward in Kenilworth on 7 Kalends October (24 September) for four days, during which time Sir John Vesey and Reginald de Grey injured one another while jousting. See Denholm-Young, 'Tournament in the Thirteenth Century', 117, 117 n. 4. Safford placed Edward at Westminster or Middlesex from 19–25 September and at Eastwood or Essex from 28–9 September 1279 (*Itinerary of Edward I, 1272–1290*, 116). There is also a chronicle account that locates Edward at the Kenilworth Round Table, but it was composed in the late fourteenth century. This chronicle is contained in the so-called Wigmore Manuscript (University of Chicago Library 224).

Two of Roger's own descendants emphasized their Welsh and Arthurian background in their bids to rule England, namely Roger Mortimer, first earl of the March (1287–1330), who was co-regent (1327–30) with Queen Isabella for Edward III of England (r. 1327–77), and Roger Mortimer, fourth earl of the March (1374–98), who, for a time, was the heir presumptive of Richard II of England (r. 1377–99).[86]

Prior to the Kenilworth Round Table, Roger (III) Mortimer had been increasing in power and influence.[87] In 1247, he married Matilda de Briouze. Through this union he climbed to the first ranks of the baronage. Henry III had knighted Roger at the Whitsuntide court of 1253 in Winchester. Roger's chief adversary was his distant relative Llywelyn ap Gruffudd, who took Gwrtheyrnion from him in 1256 and then the cantref of Builth on 10 January 1260. Roger had been holding Builth on behalf of Prince Edward. Mortimer was a stalwart loyalist during the Second Barons' War, and he had helped organize Edward's escape from baronial captivity at Hereford Castle on 28 May 1265. He also provided sanctuary for Prince Edward at Wigmore and at Ludlow. At the Battle of Evesham, Roger Mortimer commanded one of the three royalist divisions, and an account in College of Arms MS 3/23B claims that Roger Mortimer struck the blow that killed Simon de Montfort. As mentioned above, Mortimer became one of three 'virtual regents' of the realm (1272–4). In the First Welsh War of 1277, Edward made Roger captain of Shropshire, Staffordshire, and Hertfordshire. Mortimer led one of the three divisions of the English forces. On 27 April 1279, just a few months before the Kenilworth Round Table, Edward appointed Roger Mortimer as 'principal keeper of the parts of Lampadervaur and all the lands of West Wales' during the king's pleasure.[88] Mortimer's choice of the round table as the form of his retirement celebration leads one to wonder if he was signaling aspirations for lordship over Wales. Mary Giffin has speculated that Mortimer 'used Arthurian legend to point out what might be done for England by a prince of the Welsh blood who was also loyal to the king'.[89]

The choice of Kenilworth as the site of the round table also appears to have been deliberate, but it had greater symbolic value for Edward than for Mortimer. Edward enjoyed military success at Kenilworth

---

[86] See Mary E. Giffin, 'Cadwalader, Arthur, and Brutus in the Wigmore Manuscript', *Speculum* 16, n. 1 (1941): 111.

[87] See J. J. Crump, 'Mortimer, Roger (III) de, lord of Wigmore (1231–1282)', *Oxford Dictionary of National Biography*, Oxford University Press, 2004 (http://www. oxforddnb.com/view/article/19352, accessed 22 August 2014).

[88] *Calendar of the Patent Rolls Preserved in the Public Record Office: Edward I.* 4 vols. (London: Her Majesty's Stationery Office, 1893–1901), I, 310.

[89] Giffin, 'Cadwalader, Arthur, and Brutus', 113.

on 1 August 1265. As noted above, the Anglo-Norman translation of Vegetius' *De re militari* mentions this achievement. After Simon de Montfort's death, a contingent of rebels occupied the nearly impenetrable Kenilworth Castle. In a letter dated 24 August 1264, Edward invited the rebel garrison to surrender or face the consequences of becoming recognized public enemies. Powicke has pointed out that this letter may have been Prince Edward's 'first recorded act of state, done by him as a responsible advisor of the crown'.[90] Kenilworth was the site of a rite of passage for Edward. Additionally, although Edward is thought to have had little to do with its terms, the Dictum of Kenilworth (31 October 1266) provided the basis for the resolution of the Second Barons' War.[91] Maurice Keen and Juliet Barker have noted that Edward was in the habit of memorializing his earlier victories by making them the setting for his round tables.[92] This trend seems to have begun with the Kenilworth Round Table of 1279.

Was the Kenilworth Round Table held in honor of Edward, Roger Mortimer, or both? It is worthy of note that since 1266 Kenilworth had been in the possession of Edmund of Lancaster, Edward I's younger brother.[93] Mortimer seems to have presided over a tournament near a castle that belonged to the king's brother.

Complicating further the details of the Kenilworth Round Table is the discussion of it in the late fourteenth-century *Wigmore Chronicle* (University of Chicago Library 224), which is thought to have been commissioned by the Mortimers, presumably when Roger Mortimer, fourth earl of March and sixth earl of Ulster (1374–98), was the presumptive heir to Richard II. Of interest to us is its genealogical roll-chronicle. On folios 51v–52r Brutus, Arthur, and Cadwallader are shown as ancestors to Gwladys Ddu. On folio 53v, under the arms of Roger Mortimer, there is an account of the 1279 Round Table. It states that Roger went to the hastilude of Kenilworth with his three sons (Roger, William, and Geoffrey), who were elevated first with military honors by King Edward I. Roger also brought with him 100 knights and as many ladies to the Kenilworth hastilude, which was arranged and held there for three days. The likes of these solemnities had reportedly never been seen in England before, and Mortimer began a round table there; on the fourth day the golden lion, the sign of triumph,

---

[90] Powicke, *King Henry III and the Lord Edward*, II, 504.

[91] See Prestwich, *Edward I*, 57.

[92] Maurice Keen and Juliet Barker, 'The Medieval English Kings and the Tournament', in Maurice Keen, *Nobles, Knights and Men-at-Arms in the Middle Ages* (London: Hambledon, 1996), 90.

[93] *Calendar of the Charter Rolls*, vol. 2 (London H. M. Stationery Office, 1906), 66.

was granted to him, and he led the aforementioned ones who were in attendance to Warwick.[94]

Many of the details contained in the Wigmore manuscript coincide with earlier chronicle accounts of the Kenilworth Round Table, but the statement that Edward raised Roger's three sons in military distinction is unique. Some support for this report is found in the *Annals of Worcester*, which, in the context of Llywelyn ap Gruffudd's decapitation (11 December 1283), refers to Roger's sons as knights.[95] The names of the brothers – Roger, William, and Geoffrey – occur in the same order as they do in the *Wigmore Chronicle*. Edward's role at the Kenilworth Round Table is not entirely clear, but reportedly he made new knights there.

Edward transformed what had previously been an occasion for the baronage to coalesce in opposition to the monarch into a corporate activity promoting unity between royalty and aristocracy. Henry III's failed policy with respect to hastiludes was to 'beat them' and Edward's successful policy was to 'join them' and to repurpose them for his own ends. At these events, King Edward played the part of King Arthur. In Chrétien's *Perceval*, King Arthur is introduced as 'li rois qui les chevaliers fait' (the king who makes knights).[96] Although the Kenilworth Round Table may have been held in honor of Roger Mortimer, it was King Edward I who had pride of place and who knighted the sons of Sir Roger. The ritual of knighthood enacts a special bond between the conferrer and the recipient. The recipient, to the fullest extent possible, is obliged to remain loyal to the lord who has knighted him. With the Second Barons' War still a fresh memory, such chivalric ties were of the utmost importance to King Edward. Dominique Boutet, with particular reference to the prose *Lancelot* (c. 1210), has observed that the figure of the king held sway over the nobility (in romances) by exercising his prerogative of hosting sumptuous plenary courts and dubbing new knights.[97] This is precisely the prerogative that Edward I exercised at round tables and other chivalric pastimes.

At the Kenilworth Round Table, Edward seems to have been drawing upon the 'Arthur of romance' for serious ends – to obtain greater loyalty and support from his subjects, particularly in preparation for his military

[94] 'Cartae ad Prioratum de Wigmore, in agro Herefordensi, spectantes, Num. II: *Fundationis et Fundatorum Historia'*, in *Monasticon Anglicanum: A History of the Abbies and Other Monasteries, Hospitals, Frieries, and Cathedral and Collegiate Churches, with their Dependencies in England and Wales*, vol. 6, part 1, ed. William Dugdale (London: T. G. March, 1849), 350.
[95] *Annales Prioratus de Wigornia*, 484–5.
[96] See Chrétien de Troyes, *Perceval*, 15, line 333.
[97] Boutet, *Charlemagne et Arthur*, 33–40.

ventures. When Edward came to the throne, he found England's feudal array inadequate for his expansionist agenda. He sought to increase the size and preparedness of England's host and aimed to bring into existence an 'effective knightly cavalry'.[98] The need for a stronger standing army of knights became palpable to Edward during the Welsh War of 1277. On 26 June 1278, Edward issued a distraint of knighthood, an ordinance obligating all gentlemen who were not yet knights but who possessed land valued at £20 or more or who received a knight's fee worth £20 or more to become knights and to perform the *servicium debitum* of the feudal host. Elevation to knighthood brought greater military and financial obligations to the king but few additional privileges. Edward was seeking to construct a stronger force from the ranks of his newly expanded knighthood and to raise sufficient revenue from scutage to maintain a standing army. Lists of twenty-pound landholders were compiled, and on 12 March 1279 Edward appointed commissioners to enforce the writ.[99]

The distraint of knighthood was not a thing of romance. It was not a distinction awarded to select noblemen who had proven their valor through daring deeds of arms or other valuable service; rather, it was a compulsory order imposed indiscriminately upon all noble subjects of the Crown who possessed the requisite means. The distraint had all the charm of an income tax. Edward seems to have compensated for this unappealing reality of knightly existence by harnessing the mystique and inspirational example of King Arthur and his Knights of the Round Table. In the thirteenth century, many barons of England celebrated their noble heritage by commissioning romances and chivalric biographies that immortalized their ancestors. Works of this variety exalted the lineage of the respective patron. Edward's response was to reignite the cult of heroic kingship. He allowed that knights of England's past were glorious but underscored that their renown came through faithful service to the Crown. Arthurian romances emphasize the greatness of Arthur's knights. But other parts of the Arthurian literary tradition, particularly Arthurian chronicles, emphasize the justice, piety, generosity, and military acumen of the king. Knights obtained their prestige through their attachment to King Arthur, the flower of chivalry.

Edward, by assuming the role of Arthur at round-table games, brought about a pro-monarchical recalibration of Arthurianism. Edward

[98] See Michael R. Powicke, 'The General Obligation to Cavalry Service under Edward I', *Speculum* 28, n. 4 (1953): 816; Morris, *Welsh Wars of Edward I*, 73; David Simpkin, *The English Aristocracy at War: From the Welsh Wars of Edward I to the Battle of Bannockburn* (Woodbridge, UK: Boydell, 2008), 186.

[99] Powicke, 'Obligation to Cavalry Service under Edward I', 818.

I was able to accomplish this because, unlike his father, he possessed the physical skills and courageous knightly persona that chivalric literature celebrated.[100] Edward was aware of the pretensions of England's nobility. By representing himself as a new Arthur, he challenged his barons to live up to the example of their celebrated ancestors. The king sensed that simulating the Arthurian realm would generate more knights (or at least more enthusiastic knights) than conscription through the distraint of knighthood and feudal obligation. Edward's Arthurianism thus can be seen as 'spin', designed to enhance Edward's own personal popularity and to accrue political, military, and financial support for his causes. This surely was a key consideration behind Edward's Arthurianism.

Another facet of the English chivalric experience during the reign of Edward I, which likewise had an Arthurian dimension, was heraldry, 'the systematic use of hereditary devices centred on the shield'.[101] And, as Gerald Brault has noted, 'the reign of Edward I with its eighteen armorials was the golden age of heraldry in Europe'.[102] Edward employed heralds at his court, and rolls of arms were useful to him when it came to mobilizing a host for war.[103] Rolls of arms became all the more necessary as a consequence of Edward's push to increase England's volume of knights. Lesser landholders and gentry, once compelled to become knights, wanted to be included with their social betters in armorials and other martial displays.[104] Edward seems to have encouraged such aspirations.

Of all the armorials dating from the late thirteenth century, the Heralds' Roll (c. 1279) is the one which, according to Denholm-Young, 'brings us closer than any other to the Arthurian interests of Edward I and his court, and is convincing testimony to the lasting influence of the Arthurian cult in the chivalrous society of the age'.[105] The Heralds' Roll is exceptional – at least in comparison to the other surviving rolls of the period – for its curious admixture of knights and kings of the present day with chivalric warriors and saint-kings of the past. Its creator assigned coats of arms to St. Edmund the Martyr (d. 869), St. Edward the Confessor, and Harold Godwinson (d. 1066), all of whom died before the advent of true heraldry. One also finds the supposed arms of Bevis of Hampton,

---

[100] See Simpkin, *English Aristocracy at War*, 186.
[101] Anthony R. Wagner, *Heralds and Heraldry in the Middle Ages: An Inquiry into the Growth of the Armorial Function of Heralds*, 2nd edn. (Oxford: Oxford University Press, 1956), 12.
[102] Brault, *The Rolls of Arms of Edward I*, I, 39; Wagner, *Heralds and Heraldry*, 50.
[103] Wagner, *Heralds and Heraldry*, 50.
[104] Simpkin, *English Aristocracy at War*, 20.
[105] Denholm-Young, *History and Heraldry*, 49. 'Heralds' Roll', in Gerard J. Brault, *The Rolls of Arms of Edward I*, vol. 1 (Woodbridge, UK: Boydell Press for the Society of Antiquaries of London, 1997), 79–137.

Fulk FitzWarin, Prester John (not present in the earliest fragment, but appearing in the later, longer copies), Gawain, Roland, and the four sons of Aymon. The Latin kingdom of Jerusalem, the Roman Empire, Constantinople, Armenia, Cyprus, and many of the leading kingdoms and duchies of Europe are also represented on the roll. The Heralds' Roll even boasts the arms of *la reyne* Eleanor of Castile and of *la weyle Reyne* (the old queen) Eleanor of Provence. The appearance of ladies on thirteenth- and fourteenth-century rolls of arms is quite unique.[106]

If the Heralds' Roll is, as Denholm-Young suggests, a testament to Edward I's Arthurianism, we would expect to find the arms of King Arthur on it. Are they there? This seemingly straightforward question defies a simple answer. First, it must be noted that in the medieval heraldic tradition there was no universal consensus as to the design of King Arthur's arms. According to Geoffrey of Monmouth and the Glastonbury chronicle tradition, Arthur had the image of the Virgin Mary on his shield.[107] From the second half of the thirteenth century onwards – particularly in manuscripts of Jacques de Longuyon's *Les Voeux du Paon* (1312), which provides the classic formulation of the *neuf preux* of chivalry – Arthur's arms were three crowns, frequently gold, on a blue field (*Azure, three crowns or*).[108] In the Heralds' Roll, St. Edmund bears these arms.[109] The arms of the 'Roy d'Engletere', namely those of Edward I, are '*Gules, three lions passant guardant or*'.[110] These are the Royal Arms of England that were formally established under King Richard I (c. 1198).[111] Interestingly, in Manuscript K of the Second Continuation of Chrétien's *Perceval*, Bern, Stadtbibliothek 113 (Lorraine, perhaps Metz, late thirteenth century),[112] King Arthur's shield is blazoned '*three leopards passant or*'.[113] Gerald Brault, who first called attention to this atypical coat of arms for King Arthur, has noted that '[t]he tincture of the field is missing; if it were red, identification with the Royal Arms of England would be certain'.[114] Nonetheless, the inventor of these

---

[106] Denholm-Young, *History and Heraldry*, 52.
[107] See Gerard J. Brault, *Early Blazon: Heraldic Terminology in the Twelfth and Thirteenth Centuries with Special Reference to Arthurian Literature* (Oxford: Clarendon Press, 1972), 23–5.
[108] See Cedric E. Pickford, 'The Three Crowns of King Arthur', *Yorkshire Archæological Journal* 38, n. 151 (1954): 373–82.
[109] 'Heralds' Roll', 85.
[110] 'Heralds' Roll', 85.
[111] Brault, *Early Blazon*, 21.
[112] See 'Second Continuation Mss *EKLMPQSTUV*', xix.
[113] Brault, *Early Blazon*, 22.
[114] Gerard J. Brault, 'Literary Uses of Heraldry in the Twelfth and Thirteenth Centuries', in *The Court Reconvenes: Courtly Literature Across the Disciplines*, ed. Barbara K. Altmann and Carleton W. Carroll (Cambridge, UK: D. S. Brewer, 2003), 18.

arms evidently was aiming to link the then reigning monarch, probably Edward I, to King Arthur.[115] Thus, if we take Manuscript K to inform our reading of the Heralds' Roll, the Royal Arms of England (the arms of Edward I) were synonymous with the arms of King Arthur.

There is, however, a complication. The arms of the 'Prince de Gales', namely Llywelyn ap Gruffudd, are contained on the Heralds' Roll, and in one manuscript copy the arms of Llywelyn are ascribed to 'Li Rey Arthur'. The manuscript in question is London, College of Arms MS. Everard Green Roll (c. 1526–30), which contains shields painted by Thomas Wriothesley.[116] It is unclear whether this is an unintentional error or an example of heraldic flattery directed toward Llywelyn. It is also unclear when the conflation first occurred. Perhaps it should simply be ascribed to the sixteenth-century herald Wriothesley.

'Heraldic flattery', Brault's term for the 'procedure by which an author, using an identical or a very similar coat, established a link between a character and the real-life individual who bore these arms', was not strictly limited to rolls of arms; it was employed in literature as well. We find it in Girart d'Amiens' *Escanor*, a long Arthurian verse romance dedicated to Queen Eleanor.[117] Girart's aim to honor King Edward and Queen Eleanor is apparent in the prologue of his romance. He declares that Eleanor was the most valiant queen who was born in Spain and that she was given in marriage to one of the greatest and wisest noblemen who ever lived, the king of England. Edward I, according to Girart, was feared in many lands on account of his good sense, nobility, and very strong prowess. Girart concludes his praise of Edward in the prologue by stating that his nature was thoroughly kingly.[118]

Brault has noted in *Escanor* that the arms of Aguises, 'rois d'Escoce' (king of Scotland), and of Escalos, 'rois de Gales' (king of Wales), approximate those of King Alexander III of Scotland (r. 1249–86) and of Prince Llywelyn of Wales as described in Walford's Roll (c. 1273).[119] He interprets these correspondences as heraldic flattery and believes that

---

[115] Brault, *Early Blazon*, 22; Brault, 'Literary Uses of Heraldry', 18.

[116] 'Heralds' Roll', 87.

[117] See Girart d'Amiens, *Escanor: Roman arthurien en vers de la fin du xiiie siècle*, ed. and intro. Richard Trachsler, 2 vols. (Geneva: Librairie Droz, 1994); Richard Trachsler, '*Escanor*', in *The Arthur of the French: The Arthurian Legend in Medieval French and Occitan Literature*, ed. Glyn Sheridan Burgess and Karen Pratt (Cardiff: University of Wales Press, 2006), 440–2.

[118] Girart d'Amiens, *Escanor*, I, 139–40, lines 22–40. At the conclusion of his romance, Girart prays for the wellbeing of Queen Eleanor and the rest of the English royal family. See II, 1002–3, lines 25915–25.

[119] See Gérard J. Brault, 'Arthurian Heraldry and the Date of *Escanor*', *Bulletin Bibliographique de la Société International Arthurienne* 11 (1959): 86.

Escalos (i.e. Llywelyn) is 'depicted in a favorable light'; this suggests to him that the romance was written when Edward and Llywelyn were at peace, namely between November 1277 and late March 1282.[120]

Girart likely drew inspiration from the contemporary arms of the king of Scotland and the prince of Wales. But arms aside, there is no reason to assume that Escalos is the literary incarnation of Llywelyn in *Escanor*. Brault did not call attention to the fact that Escalos is not the sole representative of Wales in the text. Standing beside Escalos are Torgas, 'li princes des Galois' (the prince of the Welsh), and an unnamed 'rois des Norgalois' (king of the North Welsh).[121] Llywelyn ap Gruffudd's title, as we have seen, was prince of Wales, not king of Wales, and his patrimony was in North Wales. Thus 'li rois des Norgalois' would have been a more accurate designation for Llywelyn, especially following his defeat in 1277. Complicating matters further, Trachsler, the most recent editor of *Escanor*, has suggested that the eponymous character 'Escanor le bel de la Blanche Montaigne' was based on, or at least loosely inspired by, Llywelyn, who held the lordship of Snowdonia.[122]

Trachsler has called attention to a particular element in the text that supports the reading of Edward as Arthur and Escanor as Llywelyn. One of the major plot elements in *Escanor* is a misunderstanding between Escanor le Bel and Arthur's nephew Gawain. As part of this unfolding conflict, Arthur leads a march against Traverses, the stronghold of Escanor le Bel's sister. This episode is evocative of Edward's victorious campaign of 1277.[123] The verse romance contains discussion of the logistics of Arthur's preparations for war, a realistic aspect of war in which Edward excelled.[124] When preparing his invasion of Snowdonia in 1276–7, Edward showed himself to be an excellent logistical planner. His ability to mobilize military forces on a massive scale, particularly in the context of the Anglo-Welsh wars, was a hallmark of his reign.[125] Arthur demonstrates this ability in *Escanor*, and this is almost certainly a compliment to Edward I. Traverses is not in North Wales, for Girart explicitly states that Arthur passed 'Norgales' en route there.[126] Moreover, Girart characterizes Traverses as a lush and cosmopolitan place, which

---

[120] Brault, 'Arthurian Heraldry and the Date of *Escanor*', 87.
[121] See Girart d'Amiens, *Escanor*, II, 708–9, lines 17128–36.
[122] See Girart d'Amiens, *Escanor*, I, 78.
[123] See Trachsler's introduction to Girart d'Amiens, *Escanor*, I, 78–9.
[124] Girart d'Amiens, *Escanor*, II, 697, lines 16788–802. Also see II, 699–700, lines 16849–61, which likewise shows Arthur provisioning and leading his troops.
[125] See Prestwich, *Edward I*, 564.
[126] Girart d'Amiens, *Escanor*, II, 702, lines 16930–5.

contrasts strongly with customary descriptions of Wales.[127] Nevertheless, the king of North Wales, King Escalos of Wales, Prince Torgas of Wales, Brianz des Illes, King Claudaz of Zeeland, and the king of Ireland come to Traverses as allies of Escanor the Great.[128] King Arthur must stand against all of his British neighbors. He wins the day thanks to the naval support he put in place for his cavalry and pedestrian forces.[129] Naval support was, of course, a key element in Edward's swift victory over Llywelyn. Edward had his troops launch a marine attack on the island of Anglesey off the northwest coast of Wales. Anglesey had been Llywelyn's breadbasket, and so, by taking Anglesey, Edward was able to starve out his Welsh opponents. Trachsler believes that the amphibious attack on Traverses in *Escanor* is a 'souvenir' of Edward's victorious campaign of 1277 against Llywelyn.[130]

By the close of *Escanor*, either through military conquest or marriage alliance, Arthur obtains a more complete lordship over the entire island of Britain.[131] This conclusion was perfectly consistent with Edward's political objectives. Although Rustichello's prose Arthurian Compilation has received more scholarly attention for its purported commissioning by Edward, *Escanor* speaks more directly to Edward's political objects and, as Schmolke-Hasselmann and Trachsler have suggested, was most likely designed, at least in part, as ideological support for Edward I.[132] Just as the Arthur in Wace's *Roman de Brut* was modeled after Henry II of England and reflects the Insular and Continental aims he had for his Angevin Empire, the Arthur in Girart d'Amiens' *Escanor* was modeled after Edward I of England and reflects the Insular aims he had for his English kingdom.

The favorable representation of Escalos, the king of Wales, is not sufficient grounds for concluding that *Escanor* was written in the period of peace between Edward and Llywelyn. Girart does, however, seem to have known about Edward's great attention to detail when provisioning his great campaigns, the earliest of which was the campaign of 1277. Girart dedicated the work to Queen Eleanor, who died on 28 November 1290. Thus the work seems to date from between 1277 and 1290, and the conventional dating of 1280 is quite plausible. Most importantly, according to the romance, King Arthur's kingly dignity and landholdings

---

[127] Girart d'Amiens, *Escanor*, II, 731–5, lines 17799–919.
[128] Girart d'Amiens, *Escanor*, II, 707–11, lines 17096–225.
[129] Girart d'Amiens, *Escanor*, II, 720, lines 17480–6.
[130] Girart d'Amiens, *Escanor*, I, 78 and II, 1017–18 n. 17483.
[131] Schmolke-Hasselmann, *Evolution of Arthurian Romance*, 271.
[132] Schmolke-Hasselmann, *Evolution of Arthurian Romance*, 268.

are far greater than those of any Welsh prince. *Escanor*, albeit a literary work, distinguishes the petty kings of Wales from the great imperial kingship of Arthur. *Escanor* can be seen as a literary complement to the 1278 translation of Arthur's remains at Glastonbury. Both promote the interpretation of Arthur as a proto-English king, a precursor to Edward I, and challenge the interpretation of Arthur as a proto-Welsh prince. Girart surely intended for his audience to derive pleasure from *Escanor*, but he also crafted it to reinforce Edward I's political ideology.

The Welsh War of 1282 and its aftermath

It was not Llywelyn but rather his brother Dafydd ap Gruffudd who ignited the next major Welsh uprising against English rule. On 22 March 1282, Dafydd captured Hawarden Castle and its lord Roger Clifford. Although Llywelyn had assumed leadership of the revolt by November, it is not clear at what point he joined Dafydd's cause. When the revolt began, Llywelyn's wife Eleanor was pregnant, and three months later she died giving birth to their daughter. It may have been the death of Eleanor (19 June 1282) and the decreased likelihood that Llywelyn would sire any legitimate male heirs that moved him to commit himself to his brother's rather desperate cause.[133] Llywelyn and Dafydd, despite their contentious history, were reconciled and stood together in defense of Welsh laws and customs.[134]

Edward responded by mounting a campaign that cost seven times more than the War of 1277. The English made steady progress, and by fall 1282 English troops had taken Anglesey and Perfeddwlad and were besieging Llywelyn in Snowdonia.[135] Between October and November 1282, Archbishop Peckham of Canterbury attempted to convince Llywelyn to surrender peacefully. Edward authorized the archbishop to offer Llywelyn a county somewhere in England valued at £1,000 and the possibility of a hereditary earldom in exchange for the quitclaim of Snowdonia and the total relinquishment of his princely authority to Edward.[136]

The 'Reply of the Welsh to Peckham' (11 November 1282) reveals that Llywelyn used the legendary history of the kings of Britain in his

---

[133] See J. Beverley Smith, *Llywelyn ap Gruffudd, Prince of Wales* (Cardiff: University of Wales Press, 1998), 506–10.

[134] *Annales Prioratus de Dunstaplia*, 291.

[135] *Annales Monasterii de Waverleia*, 398.

[136] See 'Articles proposed to Llywelyn', in *Registrum epistolarum fratris Johannis Peckham archiepiscopi Cantuariensis*, ed. Charles Trice Martin, 3 vols. RS 77 (London: Longman, 1882–6), II, 467; Davies, *Age of Conquest: Wales*, 351.

political discourse.[137] The document states that Llywelyn's counselors would not permit a peace to be brokered with the king of England involving the surrender of the four cantrefs and Anglesey because 'isti cantredi sunt de puro principis tenemento, in quibus merum jus habuerunt principes et prædecessores sui a temporibus Kambri filii Bruti' (these cantrefs are among the pure holdings of the prince, which the princes and their predecessors have held by unblemished right since the time of Kamber, the son of Brutus).[138] Llywelyn represents himself as a successor to Kamber rather than to Brutus or Locrinus. This choice, as J. Beverley Smith has observed, suggests that Llywelyn is conceding that Britain was in its ideal state when it was divided between Locrinus, Kamber, and Albanactus, that is between England, Wales, and Scotland. The reference to Kamber, although upholding the territorial integrity of Wales and Llywelyn's hereditary claim to it, is conciliatory. In fact, the Galfridian reference to the tripartite division of Britain contains a tacit acknowledgment that the ruler of Loegria (England) enjoyed primacy.[139]

The 'Reply of the Welsh to Peckham' also states that all of the landholders in Wales would not accede to the will of the English king because he was unfaithful to the pacts, oaths, and charters that he had already made with their prince. The prince of Wales, according to the 'Reply', was unwilling to accept the offer of English land valued at £1,000 because it would be procured through magnates who were striving to disinherit him so that they could have his lands in Wales. Moreover, the Welsh argued that it did not seem probable that Edward would allow Llywelyn to have land in England. For if the Welsh prince were not permitted to retain his sterile and uncultivated land in Wales, which was owed to him by ancient hereditary right, in no way would he be permitted to have land in England, which was cultivated, fertile, and abundant. Llywelyn responded to the king of England using Edward's own preferred idiom – an appeal to history. He clarified by what warrant he held his lands in Wales: it was his inheritance through his forebears in Wales from the time of Brutus, which was confirmed as his through the legate of the see of Rome. This was his final message to the king.[140]

The 'Reply of the Welsh to Peckham' was chiefly designed for internal consumption. Llywelyn emphasized that he prioritized his public and

---

[137] See Smith, *Llywelyn ap Gruffudd*, 543.
[138] 'Reply of the Welsh to Peckham', in *Registrum epistolarum fratris Johannis Peckham archiepiscopi Cantuariensis*, ed. Charles Trice Martin, 3 vols. RS 77 (London: Longman, 1882–6), II, 469.
[139] See Smith, *Llywelyn ap Gruffudd*, 543.
[140] 'Reply of the Welsh to Peckham', 469–71; Smith, *Llywelyn ap Gruffudd*, 543–4.

patriotic duty to Wales as a hereditary Cambrian prince over his private self-interest as a nobleman. By asserting that he would not accept a lordship in England because England's ways were foreign to him, he stressed the cultural difference between the two territories and reinforced that Edward was an interloper in Wales and not entitled to possess it. Llywelyn represented himself as a stalwart champion of Welsh history and culture who would not be dissuaded from upholding his noble cause. Llywelyn's grand response suggests a concern for his own posthumous legacy in Wales and a desire to obstruct Edward's consolidation of authority in Wales. Llywelyn made no mention of King Arthur in his exchange with Peckham.

Llywelyn's Trojan pretensions did not go unanswered. On 14 November 1282, Archbishop Peckham issued a response. The archbishop did not challenge the veracity of the legendary history of Britain. Nor did he deny that the Welsh had blood ties to the ancient Britons. He did, however, challenge the idea that the Brittonic Celts had a special claim to Britain as a whole or to Wales in particular. According to his reading of the legendary history of Britain, the Trojan Britons were not the first people to inhabit the island. They happened upon it, not directly through God's Providence but rather through consultation of augurs and the practice of idolatry. Hence the island did not belong to them by divine inspiration. These Trojans, according to Peckham, took the island by force from tall Germanic northerners. After the departure of the Romans, the Britons themselves suffered a similar reversal at the hands of another (seemingly related) group of tall Germanic northerners, the Saxons. Archbishop Peckham, in this way, deflates the idea that the Brittonic Celts had an aboriginal claim to Britain. He outlines a series of *translationes imperii*. Rather than glorify any single race of the rulers, he emphasizes that all who live by the sword die by the sword, implying that the Welsh under Llywelyn would soon suffer the same turn of fate.[141]

After an unsuccessful attempt by the English to cross the Menai Straits from Anglesey into Gwynedd and after Archbishop Peckham's negotiations with Llywelyn and Dafydd failed to divide the brothers, Edward became all the more determined to destroy the House of Gwynedd. He persuaded the community of the realm that Wales should be conquered once and for all or else it would pose a threat to future generations of Englishmen. The baronage supported the campaign, and Archbishop Peckham gave it his blessing.[142] Edward's Arthurian self-

---

[141] 'Peckham to Llewelyn', in *Registrum epistolarum fratris Johannis Peckham archiepiscopi Cantuariensis*, ed. Charles Trice Martin, 3 vols. RS 77 (London: Longman, 1882–6), II, 47–5.

[142] Smith, *Llywelyn ap Gruffudd*, 548–9.

fashioning played no small part in rallying the community of the realm in support of his Welsh mission.

Llywelyn then made a curious decision: he left Gwynedd, his ancestral land, in the care of his brother Dafydd and led his army into the Welsh Marches. According to a continuation to the *Flores historiarum*, the failure of the English to cross the Menai Straits, which resulted in the drowning of many English troops, encouraged Llywelyn to leave the security of Mount Snowdon, and the Welsh reportedly encouraged him in this undertaking because they held that according to a prophecy of Merlin he would soon be crowned with the 'crown of Brutus'.[143] The veracity of this claim is suspect because English chroniclers, with the benefit of hindsight, tended to characterize Llywelyn as a proud and foolish figure who placed faith in vaticination rather than in sound reason. The representation of Llywelyn as a man given to irrational and pagan belief seems to have been a false caricature crafted to detract from the prince's right to rule Wales. This attack also fits into the more generalized othering of the Welsh as brutish, foolish 'bad Christians'.

In contrast to the English accounts of Llywelyn's fateful decision to leave Gwynedd, the Peniarth MS 20 version of the Welsh vernacular *Brut y Tywysogyon* makes no mention of Llywelyn being spurred on by vaticination. Rather, it states that Llywelyn's purpose was to gain possession of Powys and Builth.[144] According to the *Annals of Dunstable Priory* and the *Hagnaby Chronicle*, one of the sons of the recently deceased Roger (III) Mortimer (d. 30 October 1282) convinced Llywelyn to leave for Builth in order to receive his homage.[145] Why would a Mortimer submit to Llywelyn? Shortly after Roger Mortimer's death Edward granted one of Roger's younger sons (also named Roger) a major part of Powys Fadog and made him lord of Chirk. The English king did not, however, rush to grant Edmund, the eldest surviving son of Roger III, his father's patrimony. There may have been some bad feeling between Edward and Edmund, or at least the semblance of ill will. As Smith notes, their apparent rancor, the restlessness of the local inhabitants, and Llywelyn's

---

[143] *Flores historiarum*, III, 57.

[144] *Brut y Tywysogyon or the Chronicle of the Princes, Peniarth MS 20 Version*, trans. Thomas Jones (Cardiff: University of Wales Press, 1952), 120. Also see *Brenhinedd y Saesson or The King of the Saxons, BM Cotton Claudius MS. Cleopatra B v and The Black Book of Basingwerk, NLW MS. 7006*, ed. and trans. Thomas Jones (Cardiff: University of Wales Press, 1971), 258–9; Smith, *Llywelyn ap Gruffudd*, 550.

[145] See *Annales Prioratus de Dunstaplia*, 292–3; *The Hagnaby Chronicle* (excerpt), trans. R. Geraint Gruffydd, in *1282 – Casgliad o Ddogfennau / A Collection of Documents*, ed. Rhidian Griffiths (Aberystwyth: Llyfrgell Genedlaethol Cymru, 1986), 17. Also see Smith, *Llywelyn ap Gruffudd*, 550–2.

own need to open a second front are all plausible explanations for why the Welsh prince saw fit to leave the security of Snowdonia for the Marches.[146] There were sensible reasons why Llywelyn exposed himself to great risk.

When Llywelyn arrived at Builth, a substantial English force, including Edmund Mortimer and Roger Mortimer (lord of Chirk), confronted him. The chronicles differ regarding the precise circumstances in which Llywelyn was struck down. Either through ruse or accident, he became separated from his main force. He was killed and then decapitated somewhere near Llanganten, above the River Irfon in Builth on 11 December 1282.[147] The Mortimers appear to have sown the seeds of his destruction by luring him away from Snowdonia.[148]

Edward's consolidation of power in Wales

Of greater concern to us than the tactical error that led to Llywelyn's death is the symbolism behind his decapitation. The *Annals of Dunstable Priory* state that the head of Llywelyn was delivered to King Edward at Rhuddlan in North Wales and was later taken to London and placed above the Tower of London for the public to see.[149] The Benedictine monk and chronicler Bartholomew Cotton (d. c. 1322) claims in his *Historia Anglicana* that, after Llywelyn's head was brought to the king in North Wales, Edward sent it first to Anglesey, where it was shown to his troops. Cotton adds that it was subsequently brought to London and that, on the day after the feast of St. Thomas the Apostle (21 December), Londoners went out to see the head with pipes and horns. The head was paraded through the boroughs of London with a great clangor. At dusk it was brought to the Tower of London and fixed to a rafter.[150] The *Chronicon* of Thomas Wykes elaborates slightly as to Edward's intentions regarding the head of his foe. It states that the king, reveling in his triumph, ordered that the head be brought to London and mounted atop the Tower of London as a sign of victory.[151] The head was a trophy of war and tangible proof that Llywelyn, Edward's chief opponent in Wales, was dead. In

---

[146] Smith, *Llywelyn ap Gruffudd*, 558–9.
[147] Smith, *Llywelyn ap Gruffudd*, 561–7 and Llinos Beverley Smith, 'The Death of Llywelyn ap Gruffydd: The Narratives Reconsidered', *Welsh History Review* 11, n. 2 (1982): 200–13.
[148] See Smith, *Llywelyn ap Gruffudd*, 551–2, 566.
[149] *Annales Prioratus de Dunstaplia*, 293.
[150] Bartholomew Cotton, *Historia Anglicana (A.D. 449–1298)*, ed. Henry Richards Luard, 2 vols. RS 16 (London: Longman, Green, Longman, and Roberts, 1859), 162–3.
[151] *Chronicon Thomæ Wykes*, 291.

decapitating the rebellious Welsh prince and delivering his head to the king of England, the English were also adhering to precedent. For, as Frederick Suppe has noted, in 1053 the head of Rhys ap Rhydderch had been presented to King Edward the Confessor, and in 1063 the head of Llywelyn's ancestor Gruffudd ap Llywelyn had been delivered first to Harold Godwinson and then to Edward the Confessor.[152]

The *Annals of Waverley* and the *Annals of London* indicate that the procession of Llywelyn's head through London and its placement atop the Tower of London had an Arthurian dimension too. The *Annals of Waverley* and the *Annals of London* state that Llywelyn was taken to London and crowned with ivy in order to fulfill a prophecy made by Merlin.[153] The Waverley Annalist conveys that the Welsh misinterpreted the *Prophetia Merlini* and mistakenly believed Llywelyn was their long prophesied liberator. By crowning Llywelyn's decapitated head with ivy in London, the English were fulfilling the letter of the supposedly 'Welsh' interpretation of the *Prophetia Merlini* – but for derisive effect. Llywelyn's being crowned with ivy calls to mind Jesus' being crowned with thorns. The symbolism in both instances was to ridicule the messianic expectations surrounding the wearer. The *Annals of Waverley* communicate that the contemporary Welsh had only an incomplete and imperfect understanding of their own prophetic tradition. Here again, I wish to call attention to the theological disputes between Jews and Christians as a fitting analogy. In Christian polemical writing, Jews are depicted as having an incomplete and imperfect understanding of the Bible and as rallying behind false political messiahs rather than embracing Jesus of Nazareth as the true savior. The *Annals of Waverley* and other such English chronicles present Llywelyn as a false political messiah. Furthermore, Jesus, according to Christian teaching, fulfilled existing prophecies but did so in an unexpected and seemingly unconventional manner. King Edward, politically and militarily speaking, was on his way to matching Arthur's greatness, but Edward's ethnic and cultural heritage made him an unconventional Arthur. Llywelyn proved not to be *Arthurus redivivus*. The possibility that King Edward was the true *Arthurus redivivus* remained alive.

The basis for the high prophetic hopes regarding Llywelyn, at least according to the *Annals of Waverley*, was the 1279 coinage reform. It is possible that the chronicler conflated the change in coinage, which was

---

[152] See Frederick Suppe, 'The Cultural Significance of Decapitation in High Medieval Wales and the Marches', *The Bulletin of the Board of Celtic Studies* 36 (1989): 159.
[153] *Annales Monasterii de Waverleia*, 398–9; compare with *Annales Londonienses*, 90 and *Flores historiarum*, III, 57.

seen as a fulfillment of the *Prophetia Merlini*, with another, unrelated Welsh prophecy, which involved the head of Brân the Blessed, who, according to Welsh legend, had been a *rex totius Britanniae*. In 'Branwen ferch Llŷr' (Branwen daughter of Llŷr), the first tale of the second branch of the Mabinogi (c. 1060–1200),[154] we are told that Brân was a crowned king of Britain who had been raised to the throne of London. Near the end of the prose tale, Brân, gravely wounded, instructs his companions-at-arms to cut off his head, carry it to the 'White Hill' in London (possibly Tower Hill), and bury it facing France.[155] Brân's men do not fulfill his request until eighty years after his decapitation, but all the while the head remains perfectly preserved. The text then states that, when his men at last follow his instructions, his 'burial was one of the Three Happy Concealments, and one of the Three Unhappy Disclosures when it was disclosed. For when the head was concealed no plague came across the sea to this island.'[156] Triad 37 of the *Trioedd Ynys Prydein* (The Triads of the Island of Britain) affirms that the head of Brân (Bendigeidfran) was indeed one of the Three Happy Concealments, that it was buried on White Hill in London, and that it protected the Isle of Britain from 'oppression' in broader terms.[157] The date of composition of the Welsh Triads is uncertain, but the oldest version that has come down to us is contained in a thirteenth-century composite manuscript: Aberystwyth, National Library of Wales, Peniarth MS 16. The relevant section of the manuscript copy has been dated to the third quarter of the thirteenth century and is therefore contemporary with the Anglo-Welsh conflict (1277–83).[158]

---

[154] The earliest surviving manuscript containing fragments from the Mabinogi (namely from the Second and Third Branches) is Aberystwyth, National Library of Wales, Peniarth MS 6, (c. 1225). The commonly accepted window of dating for the Four Branches is 1060–1200. Saunders Lewis believes that Henry II's invasion of Ireland in 1171 informed the composition of 'Branwen ferch Llŷr' and believes the works were composed in the 1170s or 1180s. Two of the leading discussions of this topic include Patrick Sims-Williams, 'The Submission of Irish Kings in Fact and Fiction: Henry II, Bendigeidfran, and the Dating of *The Four Branches of the Mabinogi*', *Cambridge Medieval Celtic Studies* 22 (1991): 31–61, and T. M. Charles-Edwards, 'The Date of the Four Branches of the Mabinogi', *Transactions of the Honourable Society of Cymmrodorion* (1970): 263–98.

[155] 'Branwen Daughter of Llŷr', in *The Mabinogion*, trans. Jeffrey Gantz (London: Penguin Books, 1976), 79.

[156] 'Branwen Daughter of Llŷr', 81.

[157] *Trioedd Ynys Prydein*, ed. and trans. Rachel Bromwich (Cardiff: University of Wales Press, 2006), 94.

[158] *Trioedd Ynys Prydein*, xvi. The linguistic features of the Peniarth MS 16 copy of *Trioedd Ynys Prydein* suggest to Rachel Bromwich that the text itself predates the manuscript and is perhaps from the early thirteenth century.

Of even greater interest is the version of *Trioedd Ynys Prydein* preserved in the Red Book of Hergest (Oxford, Jesus College MS 111), which dates from about 1400. In the discussion of the Fortunate Concealments it, in agreement with 'Branwen ferch Llŷr', states that Bendigeidfran's head was facing France, and it specifies that the oppression that the head would avert was Saxon oppression.[159] Most important is the Red Book of Hergest text's account of the Third Disclosure: 'Ac Arthur a datkudya6d Penn Bendigeituran o'r G6ynnvrynn. Kan nyt oed dec ganta6 kad6 yr Ynys honn o gedernit neb, namyn o'r eidaw ehun.' (And Arthur disclosed the Head of Bendigeidfran [Brân the Blessed] from the White Hill, because it did not seem right to him that this Island should be defended by the strength of anyone, but by his own.)[160] Edward, as will become apparent below, was familiar with another narrative contained in the *Mabinogion*, 'The Dream of Macsen Wledig', and it is conceivable that the English king, when he had Llywelyn's decapitated head hoisted up on a pike above the Tower of London, was referencing the fate of Brân the Blessed. According to the tale, Brân's head was concealed; it did not decay, and it protected Britain from invasion. In 1282, Llywelyn's head was prominently displayed, and it presumably did decay. The rotting head symbolized the fall of native Wales to English rule. It was a mockery of Welsh vaticination. This derisive gesture suggests awareness in the English court of Welsh traditions and the significance of decapitation.

The mythic symbolism of Llywelyn's end did not go unrecognized by Welsh writers, specifically Bleddyn Fardd, who in his 'Elegy for Llywelyn' (c. 1282), writes:

llas Bendigeidran gydvryd a chymrv
a chymro oedd hevyd
llas llywelyn llafn grevlyd,
Llas Arthvr benadvr byd[161]

(He of the same mind as Bendigeidfran has been killed, and it was a terror. It was affliction; Llywelyn of the blood-stained blade has been killed, Arthur has been killed, chieftain of the world!)

Here is an exemplary comparison between Llywelyn, Arthur, and Brân (Bendigeidfran), which illustrates that the fate of Llywelyn's head paralleled that of Brân's head. The poet Bleddyn does not dwell upon

---

[159] *Trioedd Ynys Prydein*, 94.
[160] *Trioedd Ynys Prydein*, 94–5.
[161] Bleddyn Fardd, 'Englynion marwnad' / 'Elegy in the "englyn" metre', ed. and trans. Tomos Roberts, in *1282 – Casgliad o Ddogfennau/ A Collection of Documents*, ed. Rhidian Griffiths (Aberystwyth: Llyfrgell Genedlaethol Cymru, 1986), 26–7.

the dishonor done to Llywelyn or his failure. Rather, he regards him as a martyr for Wales. J. Beverley Smith has suggested that Bleddyn's use of exemplary comparison in this instance came from his own poetic imagination. Edward's treatment of Llywelyn's head encouraged these associations.

The *Annals of Waverley*'s account of Llywelyn's death is not the only textual tradition indicating that Llywelyn and his Welsh brethren clung to the mistaken belief that he would be their savior. This idea is also communicated in the chronicle of a certain Walter (*fl.*1290–1305) writing at the Augustinian priory of Guisborough in north Yorkshire. Walter's source for this information might have been William le Latimer, a participant in the Welsh campaign of 1282, or Welsh troops who in the 1290s were passing through Yorkshire on their way to fight for Edward in Scotland.[162] Walter writes that King Edward sent the head to London, where it was placed in a silver garland as a sign of the prince, and a knight carried the head on a lance through the middle of Westcheap in London with a great entourage of citizens. It was at last placed with the lance on high above the royal tower as a public spectacle. And in this way a diabolical prophecy was fulfilled in which Llywelyn reportedly had placed his hope. For it was said, according to Walter, that when Llywelyn was proposing to move war against the king of England he asked a certain witch what would happen to him. And she, with diabolical advice, responded to him that he ought to continue audaciously in the endeavor, and he should know for certain that he, having been crowned, would ride on horseback through Westcheap in London. Walter adds that Llywelyn believed, on account of this prophecy, that he would become king of England, and that he persisted in this error to his death. Walter concludes his entry by remarking that what the devil does not fulfill in life he supplies in death.[163] Walter's entry conveys the same fundamental message as the *Annals of Waverley*, namely that Llywelyn's war against Edward was foolish and futile. The prince fell prey to his own hubris and trusted in vaticination. Interestingly, Walter does not identify the evil counsel as being the *Prophetia Merlini* or an interpretation of it. But both entries convey that the death of Llywelyn amounted to the death of a Welsh hope.

Although the English writers sought to show how Llywelyn was an *Arthur manqué*, Welsh poets eulogize him as a martyr for Welsh independence akin to Arthur with regard to his nobility of character and

[162] Smith, *Llywelyn ap Gruffudd*, 563.

[163] Walter of Guisborough, *The Chronicle of Walter of Guisborough, Previously Edited as the Chronicle of Walter of Hemingford or Hemingburgh*, ed. Harry Rothwell (London: Camden Society, 1957), 221.

his tragic end. We have already observed some of this valorization in Bleddyn Fardd's 'Elegy for Llywelyn', but we also find it in an elegy by Gruffudd ab yr Ynad Coch (son of the Red Judge; *fl.* 1282). Gruffudd introduces Llywelyn as his former benefactor and laments that a 'Saxon' ultimately robbed Llywelyn of his life.[164] The poet then describes Llywelyn as a lionlike, prosperous, and mighty king of Wales who was of the right lineage to rule Aberffraw. Like Arthur, Llywelyn was a great native Welsh hero who succeeded in keeping the Saxons at bay until his final tragic fall in battle. Gruffudd emphasizes Llywelyn's legitimacy as a Welsh monarch. Gruffudd writes that after Llywelyn's death, there was as much lamentation as there had been at Camlann, which, according to Geoffrey of Monmouth, was the site of Arthur's last battle.[165] Near the end of his elegy, Gruffudd uses the tragedy of the decapitation to ennoble Llywelyn: Llywelyn's head is a dragon's head, a Pendragon.[166]

The death of Llywelyn was a terrible blow to the Welsh cause, but the resistance movement continued, and its new head was Llywelyn's brother, Dafydd ap Gruffudd. In late December 1282, there appears to have been a gathering of Welsh magnates in which Dafydd was named 'prince of Wales and lord of Snowden'.[167] He and his Welsh allies faced overwhelming odds. By the end of April 1283, the English had secured the Marches, and Dafydd went into hiding. The English were able to recruit Welsh guides to track him. After great effort, Edward's soldiers finally captured Dafydd in the last week of June.[168] Edward, in a letter (dated 28 June 1283) to the magnates of England and to representatives of the shires and boroughs of London, rejoices in his victory and condemns the countless frauds and machinations perpetrated against the realm of England since time immemorial 'generibus lingua Walensium, ad instar vulpium' (by the peoples of the fox-like Welsh tongue).[169] Edward then speaks of the many massacres the Welsh committed against all manner

---

[164] Gruffudd ab yr Ynad Coch, 'Awdl farwnad' / 'Elegy in the "awdl" metres', ed. J. E. Caerwyn Williams, trans. Joseph P. Clancy, in *1282 – Casgliad o Ddogfennau / A Collection of Documents*, ed. Rhidian Griffiths (Aberystwyth: Llyfrgell Genedlaethol Cymru, 1986), 33.

[165] Gruffudd ab yr Ynad Coch, 'Awdl farwnad', 33.

[166] Gruffudd ab yr Ynad Coch, 'Awdl farwnad', 34.

[167] See *Littere Wallie, Preserved in Liber A in the Public Record Office*, ed. John Goronwy Edwards (Cardiff: University of Wales Press, 1940), 75, 77; *Chronicle of Pierre de Langtoft*, II, 180–1.

[168] Smith, *Llywelyn ap Gruffudd*, 576, 578.

[169] Edward I, 'A.D. 1283. Summons of Borough Members to a National Council', ed. William Stubbs, in *Select Charters and Other Illustrations of English Constitutional History, from the Earliest Times to the Reign of Edward the First*, 6th edn., ed. William Stubbs (Oxford: Clarendon Press, 1888), 467–8.

of men, women, and even little children, and of the depredations they made as much against English inhabitants as of those of Wales without fear of God or man.[170] Edward treats the Welsh-speaking people as an ignoble other. He then comes to the principal subjects of his letter, namely Llywelyn ap Gruffudd, formerly prince of Wales, and his brother Dafydd.[171] Edward repudiates the brothers for treachery and for spilling innocent blood. He states that God saw fit to bring an end to their atrocities, first through Llywelyn's early demise and then through the capture of Dafydd by his own countrymen.[172] This detail, commonly reported in the contemporaneous chronicles, supports Edward's negative characterization of the Welsh as a treacherous people, and it undermines the idea that Dafydd had the complete faith and devotion of his Welsh compatriots. The author of the *Annals of Waverley* likewise brands Dafydd as 'propriæ nationis impostor' (impostor of his own nation).[173]

On 30 September 1283, Dafydd was tried by all the baronage of England. The *Annals of Dunstable Priory* gives a detailed description of the justice he received. First, because Dafydd was convicted as a traitor to King Edward (who had made him a knight), Dafydd was dragged to the scaffold by a horse at a slow trot. Second, because Dafydd was convicted as a murderer of English noblemen, he was hanged alive. Third, because he committed his crimes during Easter time, an act of blasphemy, his viscera were cremated. Fourth, because he had plotted the death of the king in many places, his body was dismembered and parts were sent through the climes of England in order to frighten the wicked.[174] Lastly, and most importantly, the *Annals of Dunstable Priory* tells us that his head was affixed atop the highest stake on the Tower of London.[175] The Dunstable annalist does not explain the rationale behind this final humiliation. Dafydd's fate, of course, matches that of his brother Llywelyn, and other chronicle sources even state that Dafydd's head was placed beside Llywelyn's.[176] The Dunstable annalist adds the significant detail that Dafydd's head was turned towards the sea. The Dunstable annalist's addition provides further evidence that Edward, when having the brothers' heads affixed to a spike atop the Tower of London, was referencing the tale of 'Branwen ferch Llŷr'.

---

[170] Edward I, '1283 Summons', 467.
[171] Edward I, '1283 Summons', 468.
[172] Edward I, '1283 Summons', 468; Smith, *Llywelyn ap Gruffudd*, 578.
[173] *Annales Monasterii de Waverleia*, 400.
[174] *Annales Prioratus de Dunstaplia*, 294; Walter of Guisborough, *Chronicle*, 221; *Flores Historiarum*, III, 58–9.
[175] *Annales Prioratus de Dunstaplia*, 294.
[176] See Walter of Guisborough, *Chronicle*, 221; *Flores Historiarum*, III, 58–9.

In its discussion of the execution and dismemberment of Dafydd, the Lanercost chronicler compares the Welsh to the ancient Israelites, which is yet another attestation of the British/Jewish simile that we have observed so often in English historical writing. After detailing the dismemberment of Dafydd, the chronicler writes:

> Caput vero iniqui, ne putrefiendo deficeret, ferro est circumligatum, et in longo hastili eminenter Londoniæ ludibrio positum. Quemadmodum sanctus Jeremias Threnos metricos instituit pro destitutatione Judææ, sic gens Wallica planctum heroicum composuit pro sui principis morte, in desolatione suæ nationis, in cujus fine semper memoriam David adjiciunt cum maledictione, tanquam auctor fuit hujus miseriæ ...[177]

> (But the villain's head was bound with iron, lest it should fall to pieces from putrefaction, and set conspicuously upon a long spear-shaft for the mockery of London. Just as the holy Jeremiah composed metrical dirges for the desolation of Judaea, so the Welsh nation composed a heroic elegy upon the death of their Prince and the desolation of their nation, at the end whereof they always commemorate David with curses, forasmuch as he was the author of this misfortune ...)

Dafydd is presented here as a false prophet and false messiah. The imagery of iron appears both in the *Chronicle of Lanercost*, where it is used to bind and preserve Dafydd's decapitated head, and in Jeremiah 28:13, where Jeremiah, acting on behalf of the Lord, exposes Hananiah as a false prophet. Hananiah has prophesied that within two years he would be able to liberate exiles from Judah from King Nebuchadnezzar of Babylon's yoke of servitude. Jeremiah attacks Hananiah for giving the citizens of Judah false confidence and holds him culpable for creating a 'yoke of iron' for Judah, symbolizing even harsher servitude to Nebuchadnezzar. By this analogy, Dafydd is Hananiah. Both have appealed to the messianic hopes of their people, incited rebellion, and proved to be false saviors. For their own advancement, they have jeopardized the wellbeing of their people. Wales is Judea, England is Babylon, and Edward is the great conqueror, Nebuchadnezzar, the chosen instrument of God's wrath.

As Edward marched into the Welsh heartland, all but a few stalwarts surrendered. According to the *Annals of Dunstable Priory*, the Welsh came to believe that yet another of Merlin's prophecies was coming true. The chronicle states that, in accordance with the prophecy of Merlin, a great

---

[177] *Chronicon de Lanercost*, 113. Unless otherwise noted, English translations provided for this text are from *The Chronicle of Lanercost, 1272–1346*, trans. Herbert Maxwell (Glasgow: James Maclehose and Sons, 1913), 35.

desolation of the realm happened 'velut si flumina sanguine manarent' (just as if a river were flowing with blood).[178] These words allude to Merlin's prophecy of Cadwallader and Conan. But contrary to that prophecy, the Welsh were not rejoicing at the most recent turn of events, nor did Logres cease to be called 'England'.

The anonymous commentator behind the *Prophetia Merlini* appearing in Dublin, Trinity College MS 496 E. 6. 2 (first half of the fourteenth century) arrived at a Plantagenet-friendly solution to this thorny problem. He glosses *Nomine ... peribit* as 'Postquam Edwardus rex Walliam gladio adquisivit, vocatum est Bretland ab adiacentibus' (After King Edward acquired Wales by the sword, it was called 'Bretland' by those living nearby).[179] Jacob Hammer has noted that 'Bretland' is used to refer to Britain in the Norse *Tristams Saga ok Ísondar*.[180] If our anonymous commentator is indeed referring to the Norse term for the island of Britain, then he is casuistic. The Dublin Merlin commentary breaks off before offering an interpretation of the next line of the *Prophetia Merlini*, which concerns the Bellicose Boar from the line of Conan who will sink his tusks into the forests of Gaul. Might our commentator have been hoping that Edward would retake his ancestors' French possessions? It is impossible to say; King Edward is, however, the focus of the Trinity manuscript.[181] It conveys that Edward's conquest of Wales was the fulfillment the *Prophetia Merlini* and that Edward of England was paradoxically the unexpected yet expected hero of Welsh prophecy.

Translatio imperii after the conquest of native Wales

The death of Dafydd marked the end of native rule in Wales. King Edward made English law the law of the land.[182] This total transfer of power was expressed symbolically. The most important political and religious relics

---

[178] *Annales Prioratus de Dunstaplia*, 294.

[179] 'Dublin, Trinity College MS 496 Commentary on the *Prophetia Merlini*', in Jacob Hammer, 'An Unedited Commentary on the *Prophetia Merlini* in Dublin', Trinity College MS 496 E. 6. 2. (Geoffrey of Monmouth's *Historia regum Britanniae*, Book VII)', in *Charisteria Thaddaeo Sinko: Quinquaginta abhinc annos amplissimis in Philosophia honoribus ornato ab amicis collegis discipulis oblata* (Warsaw: Sumptibus Societatis Philologiae Polonorum, 1951), 88.

[180] Hammer, 'An Unedited Commentary on the *Prophetia Merlini* in Dublin', 88.

[181] See Marvin L. Colker, 'Two Previously Unprinted Chronicles of the Reign of Edward I', in *'A Miracle of Learning': Studies in Manuscripts and Irish Learning. Essays in Honour of William O'Sullivan*, ed. Toby Barnard, Dáibhí Ó Cróinín, and Katharine Sims (Aldershot: Ashgate, 1998), 101–21.

[182] *Willelmi Rishanger, Monachi S. Albani, Chronica*, in *Chronica Monasterii S. Albani, Chronica Monasterii S. Albani*, vol. 2, ed. Henry Thomas Riley. RS 28/2 (London, 1865), 106.

of Gwynedd were handed over to King Edward.[183] An English roll from 1284 listing royal *jocalia* (jewels) states that Edward obtained the matrices of the seals of Llywelyn, his wife Eleanor, and Dafydd.[184] Edward had the silver content of the matrices melted down in order to make a new chalice, which the king then entrusted to the new abbey of Vale Royal.[185] Through his appropriation and alteration of Gwynedd's treasured objects, Edward announced that the House of Gwynedd was extinct, and that he, Edward, was annexing the principality of Wales to the English crown.[186]

A series of English chronicles report that among the Welsh treasures that Edward received was King Arthur's crown. The *Annals of Waverley*, for instance, states:

> Item corona famosi regis Arthuri, qui apud Wallenses a longo tempore in maximo honore habebatur, cum aliis jocalibus pretiosis domino regi est oblata; et sic Wallensium gloria ad Anglicos, licet invite, est translata.[187]

> (Also, the crown of the famous king Arthur, who was held in the highest honor by the Welsh for a long time, with other precious jewels was presented to the Lord King, and thus the glory of the Welsh was passed on, although unwillingly, to the English.)

The entry clearly communicates that native Wales was no more. The English crown now, by means of *translatio imperii*, had the rights to the principality's past, present, and future.[188]

What exactly was the crown of Arthur? Could Edward embrace the idea that the crown of Arthur, the symbol of the kingly office that Edward claimed to possess already, had been in Welsh keeping until now?[189] Some scholars, in particular Juliet Vale and Robert Rouse, believe the *corona famosi regis Arthuri* and the *Talaith Llywelyn* (the coronet of Llywelyn) were

[183] See *Annales Monasterii de Waverleia*, 401.

[184] See Kew, National Archives, E. 101/351/14 discussed in Arnold Taylor, 'A Fragment of a Dona Account of 1284', in Arnold Taylor, *Studies in Castles and Castle-Building* (London: Hambledon, 1985), 199.

[185] See Taylor, 'Fragment of a Dona Account', 198–9.

[186] Davies, *Age of Conquest: Wales*, 356.

[187] *Annales Monasterii de Waverleia*, 401. Also see *Annales Prioratus de Wigornia*, 489; *Flores historiarum*, III, 59; *Chronica Willelmi Rishanger*, 107; *Annales Londoniensis*, 91; *Register and Chronicle of the Abbey of Aberconway; from the Harleian MS 3725*, ed. Henry Ellis (London: Camden Society, 1847), 12.

[188] Llinos Beverley Smith, 'Llywelyn ap Gruffudd and the Welsh Historical Consciousness', *Welsh History Review* 12, n. 1 (1984): 21.

[189] Arthur is described as wanting to wear a gold crown at his Caerleon feast in *The Chronicle of Pierre de Langtoft*, ed. and trans. Wright, I, 168–9. Pierre de Langtoft writes that William I obtained possession of Arthur's crown from Aldred of York, bishop and confessor. See I, 410–11.

one and the same.[190] A continuation of the *Flores historiarum* (London, British Library, MS Cotton Nero D ii), which was written in the priory of Rochester early in the fourteenth century, explicitly states that an 'Aureola' of Prince Llywelyn of Wales was one of the *jocalia* (jewels) that Alphonso, the eldest son and heir apparent of Edward I, obtained after Wales had been subjugated.[191] In 1284, Prince Alphonso, Edward I's eldest son, made an offering of Llywelyn's coronet at the shrine of St. Edward the Confessor at Westminster Abbey, and he died later that year.[192] The princes of Gwynedd had their own special coronet. This fact is confirmed by a passage appearing in the *Annals of Tewkesbury*, which states that, in 1240, on the day that Henry III knighted Dafydd ap Llywelyn and invested him with his father's lands, Dafydd bore the 'diadema minus, quod dicitur garlonde, insigne principatus Northwalliæ' (coronet, which is called 'garland', the emblem of the principality of North Wales).[193] Perhaps there indeed had been confusion or conflation of Garland and Arthur's crown. The implication of such a conflation is that there was some special connection between Arthur and the Welsh.

The appropriation of the Welsh insignia of power is the first notable example of a pattern of symbolic violence perpetrated by Edward I against his opponents. A second example, occuring shortly thereafter, was Edward's order to eliminate public access to the ancient site of the folkmoot in London. Edward had been seeking to bring the London Commune more tightly under his control.[194] On 10 June 1285, he took advantage of an outbreak of violence in the metropolis to issue a letter-patent declaring that the area around St. Paul's cemetery had become a haven for thieves and other evildoers and that it posed a threat to the peace and security of the canons and ministers of St. Paul's. The king empowered the deacon and chapter of the aforesaid cathedral to enclose the area with a wall and to incorporate it into the churchyard.[195] No longer could the site of the folkmoot serve as a rallying point for popular protest in London.

---

[190] See Vale, 'Arthur in English Society', 188; Robert Rouse and Cory Rushton, *The Medieval Quest for Arthur* (Stroud: Tempus, 2005), 91–5.

[191] See *Flores historiarum*, III, 61 n.1. For the description of the manuscript, see *Flores historiarum*, III, xxvi–ii.

[192] See *Flores historiarum*, III, 61.

[193] *Annales de Theokesberia (A.D. 1066–1263)*, in *Annales Monastici*, vol. 1, ed. Henry Richards Luard, RS 36/1 (London: Longman, Green, Longman, Roberts, and Green, 1864), 115; Vale, 'Arthur', 346 n. 25.

[194] See Williams, *Medieval London*, 250–1.

[195] See *Liber Custumarum Compiled in the Early Part of the Fourteenth Century with Extracts from the Cottonian MS. Claudius, D. ii*, in *Monumenta Gildhallæ Londoniensis: Liber Albus, Liber Custumarum et Liber Horn*, vol. 2, part 1, ed. Henry Thomas Riley, RS 12/2 (London: Longman, Green, Longman, and Roberts, 1860), 341.

The mayor at the time, Gregory de Rokesle, together with his aldermen challenged the constitutionality of this egregious act in front of the king's representative in the matter, John Kirkby.[196] This dispute afforded Edward an occasion to break up the autonomous commune and assume direct control of the city. The third great act of symbolic violence perpetrated by Edward I was his seizure in 1296 of the Stone of Scone, which was used in the coronation of Scottish kings. Bearing close analogy to the Welsh precedent of 1283, Edward, in 1296, confiscated this most prized Scottish 'national' symbol and delivered it to the shrine of St. Edward the Confessor at Westminster. He did so after his vassal, John Balliol, whom he had selected to be king of the Scots, rebelled against him.

Given Edward's pattern of behavior, it is hard to believe that the king would not have capitalized upon an alleged crown of Arthur if he seized one from Llywelyn's possessions. The consistency in wording of all of the chronicle accounts of the passing of the crown of Arthur to Edward and of the translation of the glory of Wales to England strongly suggests that the English chronicles shared a common source. Whatever the source of this entry and regardless of the veracity of the claim, there existed the idea that the House of Gwynedd had been in possession of a crown of Arthur, and the existence of this idea means that, despite Edward's best efforts, there lingered the perception that Arthur was a Welshman.

In his entry on how Edward obtained the crown of Arthur, the author of the early fourteenth-century *Annals of London* repeats the statement that the *gloria Wallensium* had been transferred to the English by the providence of God, and the chronicler adds: 'Et quicquid princeps Walliæ debuisset perfecisse, secundum prophetias, jam per dictum Edwardum completum est.' (And whatever the prince of Wales was supposed to have accomplished, according to prophecies, now has been completed through the aforementioned Edward.)[197] The *Annals of London*'s statement that Edward was the fulfillment of Welsh prophecy seems to have been expressing the image that the king was seeking to portray.

Edward aimed to supplant Llywelyn in multiple respects. The English king quite literally occupied Llywelyn's space by establishing his court at two of Llywelyn's prized residences, Abergwyngregyn and Caernarfon.[198] It was at Caernarfon, the ancient centre of Gwynedd, where Edward endeavored to replace Llywelyn as a hero of Brittonic prophecy.[199] Caernarfon was a place

[196] Williams, *Medieval London*, 254.

[197] *Annales Londoniensis*, 91

[198] See Davies, *Age of Conquest: Wales*, 355.

[199] See Arnold J. Taylor, 'The King's Works in Wales, 1277–1330', in *The History of the King's Works*, vol. 1: The Middle Ages, ed. H. M. Colvin (London: Her Majesty's Stationery Office, 1963), 369–95.

of historical imagination in the Middle Ages. Above the modern town of Caernarfon there existed a hilltop fort known as Segontium, which was the base of a Roman garrison from about 80 to 380. Constantius (c. 250–306) had a smaller fort built on a cliff above the River Seint in its immediate vicinity. Thereabouts a great number of coins featuring the images of Helena, the wife of Constantius, Constantine the Great (r. 272–337), and Constantine II (316–40) have been discovered.[200] In the twelfth century, Caernarfon was understood to have been the old city of the Emperor Constantine, son of Constans the Great.[201] Caernarfon was thus one of the seats of the ancient realm of Britain. In the *Vita Merlini*, Geoffrey of Monmouth has Merlin prophesy the Britons' internal conflict and struggle with the Scots, which would be the prelude to their downfall, and Merlin states: 'Urbs Sigeni et turres et magna palatia plangent / diruta donec eant ad prestina predia Cambri' (The towers and great palaces of Segontium will be torn down, and they will weep there until the Welsh go to their old domain).[202] The ruins of the towers of Segontium bear analogy to the 'wailing' Western Wall, the remanent of the Temple of Jerusalem. Both are reminders of past greatness and places of hope for future greatness. By occupying and building a great castle at Caernarfon, the English king showed that he was the one destined to reestablish the ancient kingdom of Britain.

Once again, the English court seems to have had knowledge of the Welsh prophetic tradition. This awareness is not surprising because English administrative records from 1285 onwards record an influx of Welshmen serving as minstrels at the royal court.[203] They almost certainly were the royal court's conduit to the prophecies and traditions of Wales. Edward was certainly aware of the legends surrounding Caernarfon. The same chronicles that inform us that Edward received Arthur's crown state that, in 1283 at Caernarfon, the body of Prince Maximus, the father of the noble Emperor Constantine, was found and was honorably placed in its church.[204] Once again, Edward oversaw a translation of the remains of

---

[200] See Roger Sherman Loomis, 'From Segontium to Sinadon – the Legends of a Cité Gaste', *Speculum* 22, n. 4 (1947): 521. Also see Tony Davenport, 'Wales and Welshness in Middle English Romances', in *Authority and Subjugation in Writing of Medieval Wales*, ed. Ruth Kennedy and Simon Meecham-Jones (New York: Palgrave Macmillan, 2008), 152.

[201] See *The History of Gruffydd ap Cynan: The Welsh Text*, ed. and trans. Arthur Jones (Manchester: Manchester University Press, 1910), 132–3.

[202] Geoffrey of Monmouth, *Vita Merlini*, 84–5, lines 616–17.

[203] See Constance Bullock-Davies, 'Welsh Minstrels at the Courts of Edward I and II', *Transactions of the Honourable Society of Cymmrodorion* (1972/1973): 108.

[204] *Flores historiarum*, III, 59. Also see *Annales Londoniensis*, 91. Also see *Chronica Willelmi Rishanger*, 107; *Annales Monasterii de Waverleia*, 401; *Annales Prioratus de Wigornia*, 489.

one of his ancient Brittonic 'forebears'. Magnus Maximus is thought have been the loose inspiration for the Maximianus who figures prominently in Book V of Geoffrey's *Historia* and for Macsen Wledig of Welsh legend.[205]

Edward built his castle of Caernarfon at the mouth of Aber Seint. Edward seems to have intended for Caernarfon to be understood as the realization of the 'Dream of Macsen Wledig' and to revive Caernarfon's legendary past during his own rule.[206] The castle's multicolored towers corresponded to the towers in 'The Dream of Macsen', and the combination of banded masonry with polygonal towers had but one 'celebrated precedent: the tile-laced Theodosian wall of Constantinople, the first Constantine's own city'.[207]

Edward's forces began the occupation of Caernarfon in May 1283, and the building works seem to have begun the very next month.[208] On 25 April 1284, Queen Eleanor gave birth there to the future Edward II of England (r. 1307–27). This Edward, as Taylor notes, 'was the first royal child to be born in Wales since the deaths of the two last princes of Gwynedd'.[209] Almost seventeen years later, on 7 February 1301, Edward I made Edward of Caernarfon 'prince of Wales' and earl of Chester at a Lincoln parliament. When he was constructing Caernarfon, the king quite likely intended for one of his surviving sons to have this title. The transference of the title of 'prince of Wales' to the heir-apparent of the English throne is another example of how Edward endeavored to have his royal house absorb the ancient dignities of the emperor-kings of Britain, distinctions that had been claimed by the House of Gwynedd.

In addition to Edward's grand displays that mocked Welsh interpretations of Merlin prophecies, his acquisition of the spoils of Wales, his physical habitation in the princely residences of the House of Gwynedd, and his castle-building on sites of great Welsh cultural significance, Edward saw to it that the ancient kings of Britain, the pre-Conquest Saxon and Danish kings of England, and his own post-Conquest forebears were shown to exist in one long line of regnal continuity. Such a line found expression

---

[205] See John J. Parry, 'Geoffrey of Monmouth and the Paternity of Arthur', *Speculum* 13, n. 3 (1938): 272–3.

[206] See Taylor, 'The King's Works in Wales', 370–1. Subsequent scholars have embraced this interpretation. See, for example, Prestwich, *Edward I*, 120, 214 and also Richard K. Morris, 'The Architecture of Arthurian Enthusiasm: Castle Symbolism in the Reigns of Edward I and His Successors', in *Armies, Chivalry and Warfare in Medieval Britain and France: Proceedings of the 1995 Harlaxton Symposium*, ed. Matthew Strickland (Stamford: Paul Watkins, 1998), 65.

[207] Taylor, 'The King's Works in Wales', 370.

[208] Taylor, 'The King's Works in Wales', 369, 371.

[209] Taylor, 'The King's Works in Wales', 371.

in a series of short chronicles and genealogical rolls that were written in Anglo-Norman in the last quarter of the thirteenth century and early years of the fourteenth century.[210] The oldest Anglo-Norman Prose *Brut*, which was produced at an undetermined moment in the reign of Edward I, is the supreme example of this production. The Prose *Brut* begins with Brutus' arrival in Britain and ends with the death of Henry III in 1272. As Julia Marvin has noted, the text 'forges a link between the Arthurian world and the world of its own time simply by representing the two in the pages of the same book as part of a single, continuous story'.[211]

The Anglo-Norman Prose *Brut* did, however, have a Welsh rival in the *Brut y Tywysogion* (*Chronicle of Princes*). Latin annals of various Welsh religious communities served as source material for a lost Latin work, the *Cronica principium Wallie*. The *Brut y Tywysogion* is a vernacular translation of this *Cronica*. The *Brut y Tywysogion* begins where Geoffrey's *Historia* left off, the death of Cadwallader in 682, and it terminates with the death of Llywelyn ap Gruffudd in 1282. Thus the oldest Anglo-Norman Prose *Brut* and the *Brut y Tywysogion* were contemporaneous works that stood as alternative continuations to Geoffrey's *Historia*. The *Brut y Tywysogion* communicates that the native princes of Wales were the true successors to the ancient British kings and that this line of direct continuity ended with Llywelyn, the last native princes of Wales. The Anglo-Norman *Brut*, on the other hand, features multiple *translationes imperii* from ancient Britain to Plantagenet England. It is unclear which *Brut* came first, the Welsh or the Anglo-Norman. Regardless, the defining attribute of all *Brut* chronicles – the use of the *Historia regum Britannie* as the starting point for Insular historiography – speaks to a recognition of the Galfridian history as an authoritative narrative of history. The marriage of Geoffrey's accounts of ancient history with familiar events from the more recent past involving such indisputably historical figures as Henry III and Llywelyn ap Gruffudd imparted a greater semblance of reality and immediacy to the content of Geoffrey's *Historia*.[212]

---

[210] See Olivier de Laborderie, 'A New Pattern for English History: The First Genealogical Rolls of the Kings of England', in *Broken Lines: Genealogical Literature in Medieval Britain and France*, ed. Raluca Radulescu and Edward Donald Kennedy (Turnhout: Brepols, 2008), 45–61.

[211] See *The Oldest Anglo-Norman Prose Brut Chronicle*, ed. and trans. Julia Marvin (Woodbridge, UK: Boydell, 2006); Julia Marvin, 'Arthur Authorized: The Prophecies of the Prose *Brut* Chronicle', *Arthurian Literature* XXII (2005): 89; Felicity Riddy, 'Reading for England: Arthurian Literature and National Consciousness', *Bulletin Bibliographique de la Société International Arthurienne* 43 (1991): 325.

[212] See Edward Donald Kennedy, 'Visions of History: Robert de Boron and English Arthurian Chroniclers', in *The Fortunes of King Arthur*, ed. Norris J. Lacy (Cambridge, UK: D. S. Brewer, 2005), 33.

The coda of the Anglo-Welsh struggle to claim Arthur and the legendary history of Britain, at least in so far as Edward I is concerned, is the round table that the English king hosted at Nefyn, a village on the northern shore of the Llŷn peninsula, during the last week of July 1284.[213] Nefyn was another one of the residences of the Gwynedd dynasty. Like Caernarfon, it was an ancient center and one of the very few places in northwest Wales that evinced both urban life and maritime activity.[214] The Nefyn Round Table receives brief mention in a handful of chronicles. The most informative entry appears in the *Annals of Waverley*, which state that counts, barons, and knights of the realm of England, as well as many magnates from overseas convened at Nefyn for a round table; the event was celebrated by those making sport in ring dances and in hastiludes against one another, and it was held as a mark of the triumph of the soldier who fought against the pride of the Welsh people.[215] Thus, the Waverley annalist explicitly refers to this round table as a celebration marking the defeat of the native Welsh. The chronicler also emphasizes that it was a well-attended, international event. This detail is underscored in other chronicle accounts, including the *Annals of Dunstable Priory*, which state that King Edward spared no expense in preparation for the round table so that it would be attended by a multitude of English and foreign knights.[216] Whereas the Kenilworth Round Table of 1279 had been dominated by Roger (III) Mortimer, King Edward was the undisputed patron of the Nefyn Round Table of 1284. By hosting the event, Edward did more than contribute to social cohesion in England; he obtained international recognition for the success of the campaign he helmed, and he rewarded his men for their service. This great Arthurian event illustrated that King Edward was *Arthurus redivivus*. He had dispensed with Llywelyn ap Gruffudd, who arguably had a stronger claim to Arthur's mantle. Edward was now celebrating his victory in his late adversary's domain. To Edward's Continental guests, Nefyn must have seemed a mysterious and alluring place straight out of an Arthurian romance. Edward was one step closer to becoming a *rex totius Brittaniae*,

---

[213] Edward is attested as being at Nefyn from Thursday, 27 July 1284, to Saturday, 29 July 1284. His whereabouts from 30 July until 2 August is unknown, but on 2 August 1284 Edward is attested at Bardsey and at Caernarfon. See Safford, *Itinerary of Edward I*, I, 193.

[214] See Davies, *First English Empire*, 31.

[215] *Annales Monsterii de Waverleia*, 402. Also see *Annales Prioratus de Wigornia*, 491; *Chronica Willelmi Rishanger*, 110; *Annales Cestrienses or Chronicle of the Abbey of S. Werburg at Chester*, ed. and trans. Richard Copley Christie (London: Lancashire and Cheshire Record Society, 1887), 114.

[216] *Annales Prioratus de Dunstaplia*, 314.

and he wanted his subjects and Europe's elite at large to recognize this development. Given the paucity of information about the Nefyn Round Table we cannot say how much it participates in the Arthurian romance tradition, but we can say that it was motived by 'business' and 'pleasure'.

The Gascon phase of King Edward's reign, 1286–9

From 13 May 1286 to 12 July 1289, Edward I was on the Continent. During this period, he devoted much of his energy to touring his duchy of Gascony and reforming its administration. He was also deeply immersed in Continental politics, brokering peace between the kingdoms of Aragon and France. This, then, is an appropriate juncture for us to consider the reactions to Edward's Arthurian activity by Europe's nobility more broadly speaking.

The Old French verse poem *Roman du Hem* (c. 1279), by the minstrel-poet Sarrasin, indicates that by the late 1270s Edward was already being recognized on the Continent as a successor to Arthur.[217] The *Roman du Hem* takes its names from its subject: a knightly *feste* that took place on the feast of Saint Denis (8–10 October) 1278 in the small Picard village of Le Hem on the Somme. The *feste* involved two days of single-combat jousting with *armes à plaisance*. Dramatic enactments of stock episodes found in Arthurian romance also took place. These Arthurian interludes, or 'aventures', as Sarrasin refers to them,[218] include the mockery of Sir Kay, the arrival of the Loathly Damsel at court, the physical abuse of a maiden by a dwarf, the heroics of the knight-errant, and Queen Guinevere as the presider at court.[219] The *feste*'s sponsors were two Artesian noblemen: Sir Aubert II de Longueval (d. 1286) and his neighbor Sir Huart de Bazentin. Two of Aubert's sisters played the parts of the 'Dame Courtoisie' and King Arthur's wife, 'la roine Genievre', respectively. Robert II, count of Artois (1250–1302), assumed the role of the great champion of the event, the *Chevalier au Lyon*, a knight of the Round Table. The Knight of the Lion, Yvain, was, of course, the subject of Chrétien de Troyes' fourth surviving romance. Sarrasin makes multiple direct references to Chrétien in the *Roman du Hem*. He even states that it was his intention to memorialize

---

[217] Sarrasin, *Le Roman du Hem*, ed. Albert Henry (Brussels: University of Brussels, 1939).

[218] Sarrasin, *Roman du Hem*, 126, lines 4600–7.

[219] See Nancy Freeman Regalado, 'Performing Romance: Arthurian Interludes in Sarrasin's *Le roman du Hem* (1278)', in *Performing Medieval Narrative*, ed. Evelyn Birge Vitz, Nancy Freeman Regalado, and Marilyn Lawrence (Cambridge: D. S. Brewer, 2005), 105.

the Le Hem *feste* in a manner comparable to the romances of Chrétien de Troyes.[220] Although one of the Longueval sisters played the part of Queen Guinevere, according to Sarrasin, no one assumed the role of Arthur. This conspicuous absence was, in the opinion of Juliet Vale, a compliment to Edward I, for it implied that only Edward was worthy to fill the role of Arthur.[221] 'Queen Guinevere' – who admittedly was not played by Queen Eleanor – presided over the festivities in Arthur's stead.[222] Early in the narrative, Dame Courtoisie advises Sir Huart and Sir Aubert to advertise their upcoming *feste* in England and in Upper Brittany (eastern Brittany) because in those places one would find valorous and hardy knights, good jousters, and worthy successors to Arthur's knights, and she adds:

> Cix qui en est sires et rois
> Est preus et largues et courtois,
> On le nomme roi Edouwart;
> Or prions Diu que il le wart,
> Qu'il vaut mix que je ne sai dire.[223]

(That one who is lord and king of it [Engletere] is worthy and generous and courteous, [and] is called Edward. Now we will pray to God that He watches over him because he is worth more than I know how to say.)

Edward did not attend the *feste* at Le Hem,[224] but was seen, at least by Sarrasin, as a worthy successor to the ancient British king. The Brittonic / Anglo-Norman divide does not appear to have been a major issue for Sarrasin. Indeed, he confuses the Trojans with the Anglo-Saxons.[225]

Sarrasin's praise for Edward I's knightly character comes immediately after an extended critique of Philippe III of France (r. 1270–85), whom the poet faults for the decline of knighthood in France. King Philippe III, contrary to the example of his illustrious predecessor, Louis IX, had a ban on tournaments proclaimed in his realm. According to Sarrasin, knightly skill and the values of honor, prowess, largesse, and courtesy then went into decline in France.[226] The knights of France, who were eager to prove

---

[220] Sarrasin, *Roman du Hem*, 14, lines 472–93.
[221] Juliet Vale, *Edward III and Chivalry: Chivalric Society and its Context, 1270–1350* (Woodbridge, UK: Boydell, 1982), 15.
[222] Regalado, 'Performing Romance', 107.
[223] Sarrasin, *Roman du Hem*, 9–10, lines 322–51.
[224] Edward is attested at Stafford on 8 October 1278, at Brewood and Stafford on 9 October, and at Brewood, Stourton, Torton, and Stafford on 10 October. See Safford, *Itinerary of Edward I*, I, 101.
[225] Sarrasin, *Roman du Hem*, 9–10, lines 322–51.
[226] Sarrasin, *Roman du Hem*, 2–6, lines 52–199.

their chivalric worth, flocked to England. In October 1279, shortly after the Kenilworth Round Table, Edward wrote to Philippe III, informing the French king that one of his knights, Jean de Prie, had heard of a tournament in England and had crossed the channel to attend it. Philippe III's successor, Philippe IV (r. 1285–1314), initially upheld the ban on tournaments in France. In 1290, another French knight, Jean de Nesle, journeyed to England in order to joust at a tournament.[227] Sarrasin's *Roman du Hem* shows us that Edward was recognized not only as a successor to Arthur but also as one of the finest champions of chivalry of his day. Edward's knightly image in relation to that of Philippe III and Philippe IV bears analogy to Henry II of England's vis-à-vis Louis VII and Philippe II. How did Edward I's chivalric one-upmanship affect his relationship with his French royal counterparts? This is a question that Malcolm Vale has raised. Vale believes that Edward was hoping to make Philippe III and Philippe IV envious of him and to inspire them to 'behave according to the chivalric code of kingly honour', in particular to respect Edward as a king in his own right rather than as a vassal of the French throne.[228]

Philippe IV was aware of Edward's Arthurian pretensions and on at least one occasion sought to deflate them. Although the relations between Edward and Philippe IV were initially cordial, by 1294 they had deteriorated to a state of open conflict, one that continued in earnest until 1299. Each king was vying for the favor of Count Guy of Flanders (r. 1251–1305). In 1297, Edward succeeded in winning Guy's support but failed to take complete advantage of this Anglo-Flemish alliance. Edward was unable to muster a large army for his Flanders campaign, and it proved a costly, embarrassing disaster. In 1299, a truce between the king of France and the count of Flanders collapsed, and Philippe IV sent a massive force to capture the county. The expedition was a success, and a harsh rule was imposed over Flanders. The Florentine chronicler Giovanni Villani (d. 1348) writes in his *Nuova Cronica* that a round table was held in Flanders in honor of the French king's visit.[229] Perhaps through his involvement in a round-table game at the site of the king of England's political and military debacle, Philippe was usurping, and thereby ridiculing, Edward's Arthurian idiom.

Hosting a round table and receiving favorable comparisons to King Arthur was not Edward's exclusive privilege. The Catalan soldier and historian Ramon Muntaner (d. 1336) writes in his *Crònica* that King Pere II

---

[227] See Malcolm Vale, 'Edward I and the French: Rivalry and Chivalry', *Thirteenth Century England* II (1987–8): 166.
[228] Vale, 'Edward I and the French', 166.
[229] See Giovanni Villani, *Nuova Cronica*, ed. Giovanni Porta, 3 vols. (Parma: Ugo Guanda Editore, 1991), II, 51.

of Aragon (r. 1276–85) brought together a greater assemblage of expert knights at his court than King Arthur ever did at his Round Table.[230] The chronicler also makes reference to round tables held by King Pere's successor, Alfonso III (r. 1285–91).[231] Muntaner states that Alfonso III and Edward I attended a round table together. In July 1287, Edward, acting on behalf of Philippe IV of France, sought to secure the release of Charles of Salerno, king of Naples (r. 1285–1309), from Aragonese captivity. If Edward managed to free King Charles from captivity, he would enhance his international reputation. Edward also wanted to marry off his daughter Eleanor to Alfonso. An Anglo-Aragonese marriage alliance promised to increase his political leverage with the king of France. Alfonso was aware of Edward's aims, and the English king was operating from a position of weakness in the negotiations.[232] At Oloron-Sainte-Marie, Edward made a great feast for the king of Aragon and his son, the lord Infante, which lasted for ten days. At its conclusion, Edward's daughter was betrothed to Alfonso, and in order to celebrate this engagement King Alfonso treated Edward and his queen to an even greater feast, which included jousts, martial exercises, and round tables.[233] Alfonso was no stranger to hosting round tables. The event had become a common knightly pastime in Europe,[234] but it was also exceptionally appropriate for celebrating a union with the House of Plantagenet. Edward seems to have been recognized on the Continent as having a special Arthurian identity. This did not, however, prevent European princes and lords from engaging in various modes of Arthurianism.

Edward I, King Arthur, and the Matter of Scotland

From 1291 until his death in 1307, Edward I sought to realize English rule over the kingdom of Scotland, and he enlisted the 'Arthur of history' in this cause. Over the course of this sixteen-year period Edward's officials began to use Geoffrey's legendary history of Britain as a justification for the English claim to Scotland. This *modus operandi* was not unprecedented.

---

[230] See Ramon Muntaner, *Crònica* 56, in *Les quatre grans cròniques*, ed. Ferran Soldevila (Barcelona: Editorial Selecta, 1971), 718.

[231] Muntaner, *Crònica* 162, p. 815.

[232] Prestwich, *Edward I*, 325.

[233] Muntaner, *Crònica* 166, p. 817.

[234] We have record of a round table hosted at Bar in 1294 by Jan I (r. 1288–94), duke of Brabant. During the round table Jan was struck down by a lance blow from a French knight and died the same day. See *Annales Prioratus de Dunstaplia*, 388–9. Jan I was the father of Jan II of Brabant (r. 1294–1312) and father-in-law of Margaret Plantagenet, another of Edward I's daughters.

Gerald of Wales, in his *Expugnatio Hibernica*, lists Arthur's conquest of Ireland as a precedent for Plantagenet hegemony over Ireland.[235] The London Collector cites Arthurian precedents to advance the interests of the baronage around the time of Magna Carta. And, during Edward's own reign, Llywelyn ap Gruffudd drew upon Galfridian history when refusing to surrender the principality of Wales. Edward, however, was the first English king known to have cited the 'historical' precedent of Arthur in official government documents, namely in a letter to Pope Boniface VIII. The figure of Arthur obtained a place in international diplomacy, and the 'business' aspect of Arthurianism took pride of place over the 'pleasure' element. Moreover, the concerned parties of Edward's efforts, Pope Boniface VIII and the 'rebellious' lords of Scotland, did not dismiss the historicity of Arthur out of hand. The Scots used Arthurian history to their own ends by claiming that Arthur was a tyrant of illegitimate birth and that Mordred, the son of Arthur's sister Anna and the 'Scottish' King Lot of Orkney, was the rightful king.[236]

Anglo-Scottish relations during Edward's reign were cordial until September 1290, when Margaret, 'the maid of Norway' (1282–90), died. She was the last direct descendant of Alexander III of Scotland (r. 1249–86) and had been recently engaged to Edward's eldest surviving son and heir, Edward of Caernarfon. At her death, the succession to the Scottish throne became open to dispute, and there were no fewer than thirteen competitors for it. Within a month of Margaret's death, tragedy also struck the English court. On 7 November 1290, Eleanor of Castile died. Edward entered a period of mourning, but in spring 1291, the English king returned to the business of government and took up the Scottish succession dispute. On 8 March 1291, the English king began issuing a string of letters under privy seal asking the religious communities in England to assemble all material in their chronicle holdings and confidential documents that concerned the status of and relations between the realms of England and Scotland. Edward sought assistance from the leading English monasteries in the fabrication of a precedent-based claim for English overlordship of Scotland. This action has been termed Edward's First Appeal to History. In essence, Edward was holding himself to the principle of the *Quo*

---

[235] See Gerald of Wales, *Expugnatio Hibernica* 2.6, pp. 148–9.
[236] On Scottish attitudes toward King Arthur, see Robert Huntington Fletcher, *The Arthurian Material in Chronicles, Especially Those of Great Britain and France* (Boston: Ginn & Company, 1906), 241; Karl Heinz Göller, 'König Arthur in den Schottischen Chroniken', trans. Edward Donald Kennedy as 'King Arthur in the Scottish Chronicles', in *King Arthur: A Casebook*, ed. Edward Donald Kennedy (New York: Routledge, 1996), 182–3; Flora Alexander, 'Late Medieval Scottish Attitudes to the Figure of King Arthur: A Reassessment', *Anglia* 93 (1975): 19.

warranto proceedings. He was seeking legal-historical examples in order to demonstrate by what warrant he was entitled to be overlord of Scotland. The idea of the appeal to history is, at least in the *Chronicle of Pierre de Langtoft*, credited to Edward's close advisor and frequent envoy, Anthony Bek, bishop of Durham (r. 1284–1311).[237]

The great majority of the extant responses start with Anglo-Scottish relations in the tenth century, beginning either with the reign of Edward the Elder (899–924) or Æthelstan (926–39). The responses of Glastonbury Abbey, Faversham Abbey (in Kent), and Waltham Abbey are exceptions. They include precedents drawn from the legendary history of Britain. The Glastonbury reply was recorded in a register. It uniquely references Caradoc of Llancarfan's *Vita Gildæ* (c. 1130–50). This saint's life, which Caradoc had written for the Glastonbury community, tells how King Arthur killed Gildas' brother Hueil, a Scottish rebel who had led raids on Arthur's kingdom of Britain. The entry suggests that Arthur, in eliminating Hueil, had effectively placed Scotland under British rule.[238] This material appears to have been Glastonbury's own original contribution to Edward's cause. The Faversham reply, which survives in a damaged copy, begins with a discussion of Brutus' rule over Britain. [239] It supplies excerpts and abbreviated summaries of the *Historia regum Britannie* beginning with Geoffrey's discussion of how Arthur was entitled by hereditary right to the monarchy of the entire island of Britain. It also mentions how Arthur achieved victory over the combined forces of Scots and the Irish but took pity on his adversaries when the clergy of Scotland begged him for mercy. The Faversham reply then includes Anglo-Saxon precedents. At this point the copy breaks off owing to damage. The Waltham reply, which also survives in a single damaged manuscript, cites the *Brut* as its source and tells of how Brutus rid Great Britain of giants and later divided the island between his three sons: Locrinus, Kamber, and Albanactus.[240] There is a lacuna caused by damage immediately after that. The reply terminates with a few entries on Anglo-Scottish relations in the time of Henry III of England.

It is a matter of conjecture why so few of the surviving responses include precedents drawn from the Galfridian chronicle tradition.

---

[237] *Chronicle of Pierre de Langtoft*, II, 190–1.

[238] See James P. Carley and Julia Crick, 'Constructing Albion's Past: An Annotated Edition of *De Origine Gigantum*', in *Glastonbury Abbey and the Arthurian Tradition*, ed. James P. Carley (Cambridge, UK, 2001), 368. See Caradoc of Llangarfan, *Vita Gildæ*, 84–103.

[239] See Francis Palgrave, *Documents and Records Illustrating the History of Scotland and the Transactions between the Crowns of England, Preserved in the Treasury of Her Majesty's Exchequer*, vol. 1 (London, 1837), 92–4.

[240] Palgrave, *Documents and Records*, 105–7.

Bernard Guenée believes that the monastic writers questioned its veracity. These respondents, in his opinion, had greater historical scruples than their king.[241] The omission may simply have been a consequence of the wording of the inquest. In all of the surviving versions of the request, Edward is seeking precedents concerning the realms of England (*Anglia*) and Scotland (*Scocia*).[242] Technically speaking, *Britannia* is not *Anglia*. The majority of the religious communities may have concluded that ancient British history was superfluous to their assignment.

At Norham on 6 May 1291, Edward's advisors sifted through the various returns and drafted a summary.[243] It does not contain examples drawn from the legendary history of Britain, but rather chronicle extracts from 901–1252. In short, the First Appeal to History, barring the replies from Glastonbury, Faversham, and Waltham, did not include Arthurian precedents. It was not until 1301 that Edward I included the figure of King Arthur among his list of historical precedents for lordship over Scotland.

Edward I and the 'ensaumple du noble rei sire Arthur'

For the years 1291 to 1300 I have not found record of Arthurian self-fashioning on the part of Edward I. However, these years coincided with the outbreak of the First War of Scottish Independence, and English chroniclers, most notably the author of the second redaction of the *Chronicle of Pierre de Langtoft*, assessed Edward's performance in this war against the example of King Arthur.[244]

When the competitors for the throne of Scotland met at Norham on 10 May 1291, Edward's advocate, Roger Brabazon, asserted that the king of England was the rightful overlord of Scotland and that the candidate of the English king's choosing should swear homage to Edward for the

---

[241] Bernard Guenée, 'L'enquête historique ordonnée par Édouard Ier, roi d'Angleterre en 1291', *Comptes-rendus des séances de l'Académie des Inscriptions et Belles-Lettres* 119, n. 4 (1975): 579.

[242] See E. L. G. Stones and Grant G. Simpson, *Edward I and the Throne of Scotland, 1290–1296: An Edition of the Record Sources for the Great Cause*, 2 vols. (Oxford: Oxford University Press, 1979), I, 222–4.

[243] Palgrave, *Documents and Records*, 134–7.

[244] On the authorship of Pierre de Langtoft's chronicle, see Jean-Claude Thiolier, 'Pierre de Langtoft: Historiographie d'Edouard Ier Plantagenet', in *Anglo-Norman Anniversary Essays*, ed. Ian Short (London: Anglo-Norman Text Society, 1993), 379–94; Thea Summerfield, *The Matter of Kings' Lives: The Design of Past and Present in the early fourteenth-century verse chronicles by Pierre de Langtoft and Robert Mannyng* (Amsterdam: Rodopi, 1998), 22–7. I am using Wright's edition throughout, but I have also consulted *Édition Critique et Commentée de Pierre de Langtoft, Le Règne d'Édouard Ier*, vol. 1, ed. Jean Claude Thiolier (Créteil: University of Paris XII, 1989). All modifications to the translation (aside from punctuation and capitalization) will be indicated.

northern realm. The competitors agreed to Edward's terms, and in July and August many of the Scots swore homage to Edward and recognized his suzerainty.[245] On 17 November 1292, Brabazon made known Edward's verdict in favor of John Balliol, who then did homage to King Edward at Newcastle upon Tyne (26 December 1292). Edward restored to him all his rights intact and unharmed, and all his castles. Thus the incumbent Scottish king acknowledged Edward's lordship over Scotland. On 30 November 1292, John Balliol was invested as king of Scotland at Scone.[246]

Shortly after Balliol became king, the magnates of Scotland began seeking release from English suzerainty. Whether Balliol initially supported these motions is a matter for debate. Notwithstanding, the Scots sought and received absolution from Pope Celestine V (r. 5 July–13 December 1294) for all oaths exacted from them under duress.[247] The chronicler Walter of Guisborough dates the rumblings of rebellion to 1295 and holds that the Scottish nobles had moved cautiously at first. They advised their king that his policy of accommodating English lords at his court was too costly and that he should send them away. In 1295, Edward wrote to Balliol seeking troops for his war against the king of France. Balliol tried to excuse himself from service by pleading his lack of power. As Edward continued to apply pressure, the nobles of Scotland reached a breaking point. The Scots held a Parliament at Scone, where they appointed twelve peers (four bishops, four counts, and four barons) as the rulers of Scotland. The peers then sought a Franco-Scottish alliance.[248]

In spring 1296, Edward led a successful campaign in Scotland, which resulted in John Balliol's surrender of the Scottish crown directly to Edward on 10 July. For a brief space of time, Edward had achieved the Arthurian manifest destiny of a united kingdom of Britain. Patriotic English chroniclers, such as the author of the *Chronicle of Bury St. Edmunds*, rushed to sing his praises as the new *rex totius Britannie*.[249] The chronicler behind the continuation of the second redaction of the *Chronicle of Pierre de Langtoft* is no exception. He states that in 1296 Edward fulfilled the prophecy of Merlin by bringing about the long-awaited union of Ireland, Scotland, England, Wales, and Cornwall, and he adds:

[245] See Matthew Strickland, 'A Law of Arms or a Law of Treason? Conduct in War in Edward I's Campaigns in Scotland, 1296–1307', in *Violence in Medieval Society*, ed. Richard W. Kaeuper (Woodbridge, UK: Boydell, 2000), 60.

[246] Walter of Guisborough, *Chronicle*, 238–9; *Chronicle of Pierre de Langtoft*, II, 192–5.

[247] G. W. S. Barrow, *Robert Bruce and the Community of the Realm of Scotland*, 4th edn. (Edinburgh: Edinburgh University Press, 2005), 83.

[248] Walter of Guisborough, *Chronicle*, 264.

[249] *Chronica Buriensis / The Chronicle of Bury St. Edmunds: 1212–1301*, ed. and trans. Antonia Gransden (London: Nelson, 1964), 133.

Reys n'y ad ne prince de tuz les countrez
Fors le ray Eduuard, ke ensi les ad joustez;
Arthur ne ayayt unkes si plainement les fez.
Desore n'y ad ke fere for purver ses alez
Sur li ray de Fraunce, conquere ses heritez,
Et pus porter la croyce où Jhesu Cryst fu nez.[250]

(There is neither king nor prince of all the countries except King
Edward, who has thus united them; Arthur had never the fiefs so
fully. Henceforth there is nothing to do but provide his expedition
against the king of France, to conquer his inheritances, and then bear
the cross where Jesus Christ was born.)

This comparison is yet another example of Arthur being understood
as the king who personifies the united kingdom of Britain. The 1296
victory, however, proved fleeting. Beginning in May 1297, William
Wallace (d. 1305) mounted an insurgency that showed King Edward
just how impermanent his conquest had been.[251] Wallace led his Scottish
countrymen to victory at Stirling Bridge (11 September 1297).

The continuator of the second redaction of the *Chronicle of Pierre de
Langtoft* (henceforth referred to as the Langtoft Continuator) responded
with an inversion of his use of Arthur. Instead of telling of how Edward
exceeded Arthur's accomplishments, the Langtoft Continuator now
explains how Edward fell short of Arthur's political and martial skill.[252]
The first time we encounter this 'ensaumple du noble rei sire Arthur'
(example of the noble king, Sir Arthur) is in the discussion of the renewal
of the Scottish conflict in 1297. The reason that Edward lost Scotland so
quickly was, according to the Continuator, his parsimony:

En gestes aunciens trouvoums-nous escrit
Quels rays et quels realmes ly rays Arthur conquist,
Et coment sun purchace largement partyst.
Roys suz ly n'avoit ke ly countredist,
Counte, duc, e baron, qe unqes li faillist,
En guere n'en bataille ke chescun ne suyst.
Ly rays sir Eduuard ad doné trop petyt;
Par quai à sun aler, quant en mer se myst
Vers ly roys de Fraunce, fet ly fu despit,

---

250 *Chronicle of Pierre de Langtoft*, II, 266–7.
251 See Prestwich, *Edward I*, 477.
252 For discussion of this use of the figure of Arthur, see Robert Stepsis, '*Pierre de
Langtoft's Chronicle*, an Essay in Medieval Historiography', *Medievalia et Humanistica*,
New Series 3 (1972): 56–7; Thea Summerfield, 'The Arthurian References in Pierre
de Langtoft's *Chronicle*', in *Text and Intertext in Medieval Arthurian Literature*, ed.
Norris J. Lacy (New York: Garland, 1996), 195–6.

Ke nes un de ses countes of ly le aler emprist.
La commune de Escoz la novele oyst,
Chescun la sue part sur çoe se joyst.
La route de raskaylle la guere renoue reprist.[253]

(In ancient histories we find written what kings and what kingdoms King Arthur conquered, and how he shared largely his gain. There was not a king under him who contradicted him, [nor any] earl, duke, or baron who ever failed him in war or in battle, but each followed him. The king, Sir Edward, has given too little; whereby at his departure, when he put to sea against the king of France, the affront was shown him that not one of his earls undertook the expedition. The commonalty of Scotland hears the news, each on his own part rejoices over it. The rabble of the lower people resumed war anew.)

The Continuator claims that Edward lost the support of his earls, dukes, and barons because he lacked Arthur's generosity. At this point in the text the continuator does not specify the type of generosity in which he finds Edward deficient, but later in the work he remarks that Edward should have granted the lands he had conquered in Scotland to his faithful vassals.

The Continuator, when stating that Edward lacked Arthur's generosity, could, of course, have been referencing Arthur's generosity in broad terms. For in numerous texts from the twelfth to the fourteenth century Arthur is presented as the embodiment of kingly *largesse* and magnanimity. But the reference is more specific; it points directly to the first book of the *Chronicle of Pierre de Langtoft*. The 'ensaumple du noble rei sire Arthur' in the continuation of Book Three echoes Book One's account of Arthur's generosity after conquering Ireland.[254] In Book One, Pierre repeats this idea, among other places, in his description of Arthur's Caerleon coronation feast.[255] The Continuator seems to have drawn upon these passages for his critique of Edward. The key to Arthur's success in Book One was his liberality. Arthur's men served him loyally because they knew that they would be well compensated. The argument of the Continuator is that Edward, in contrast to Arthur, was reluctant to redistribute Scottish land. His vassals complained about him, and they refused to go on Edward's Flanders expedition. Word of discord in England spread to Scotland and emboldened the Scots to rebel. Evidently, Edward's mercy for defeated

---

[253] *Chronicle of Pierre de Langtoft*, II, 296–7.
[254] *Chronicle of Pierre de Langtoft*, I, 160–1.
[255] *Chronicle of Pierre de Langtoft*, I, 176–7.

Scottish lords equated to a lack of generosity for the English lords who accompanied him on his Scottish campaign.[256]

The 'ensaumple du noble rei sire Arthur' is framed as a critique of Edward's lack of zeal for giving, but this perhaps should be read as a circumlocution for a more widespread critique of Edward's zeal for taking. The Langtoft Continuator's critique of Edward occurs amidst his coverage of the Crisis of 1297. Between 1294 and 1297, Edward was engaged in three major conflicts: the Anglo-French war in which he sought to retain possession of Gascony, the suppression of the Welsh rebellion of 1294–5, and the aforementioned Scottish campaign of 1296. These activities put a great strain on the Crown's financial and military resources. At the Salisbury Parliament of 24 February 1297, Edward sought baronial support for two expeditions that he was about to mount in Gascony and in Flanders against the forces of France. The earls, in particular Humphrey de Bohun (d. 1298), seventh earl of Hereford and hereditary constable of England, and Roger Bigod (d. 1306), fifth earl of Norfolk and hereditary marshal, refused to go on any expeditions across the Channel on the grounds that there were more imminent domestic threats to England's security.[257] Edward pleaded that the planned expedition to Flanders was for the honor and common profit of the realm and that he was bound by honor to send forces there on account of the terms of a treaty he had entered into with the king of the Germans. According to the Continuator, a precedent from the age of Arthur also justified his cause: King Philippe IV and his twelve peers had wrongfully taken possession of the land and the manors in Aquitaine that Arthur gave to Sir Bedivere, and which all the ancestors of King Edward and his father, King Henry, had held.[258] This Arthurian precedent is mentioned in Geoffrey's *Historia* and in the first book of the *Chronicle of Pierre de Langtoft*.[259] Edward may well have made this appeal to history, but it fell on deaf ears.

In February 1296, and then after the disappointing Salisbury Parliament, Edward attempted to conscript men who possessed the requisite financial means. In 1296, Edward ordered an inquest to determine who had land worth more than £40 per annum. These men were to be armed and ready

---

[256] Andrew Spencer, in response to this critique of Edward's Scottish policy, has observed that the king did not make major grants of land, at least not until 1306, because he was trying 'to reconcile the Scottish nobility to his rule'. See Andrew M. Spencer, 'Royal Patronage and the Earls in the Reign of Edward I', *History* 93, n. 309 (2008): 24. Also see Michael Prestwich, 'Royal Patronage under Edward I', *Thirteenth Century England* I (1986): 45.

[257] *Chronica Buriensis*, 138–9.

[258] *Chronicle of Pierre de Langtoft*, II, 278–81.

[259] *Chronicle of Pierre de Langtoft*, II, 166–9.

for active service at three weeks' notice. For this they would receive wages. In 1297, the summons was extended to men possessing land worth more than £20 per annum. These men were to muster at London on 7 May 1297. As Prestwich has noted, this summons supplanted the already unpopular distraint of knighthood. Edward, according to feudal custom, asked his constable, Humphrey de Bohun, to draw up registers of all who attended the muster. The earl refused. In the Articles of Grievance of 1297, the high clergy, earls, barons, and community of the realm complained that the king in his writ of summons did not specify the theater of battle. If, as rumor had it, Flanders was to be the place, then, according to the *Monstraunces*, they were not obliged to perform service there because 'neither they nor their predecessors or ancestors ever did service in this land', and they expressed concern that Scotland and other lands that were 'not yet properly settled' would rise up if they knew that a sizeable force had gone to Flanders.[260]

The grievance that Scotland had not been properly settled may have been a veiled way of suggesting that Edward should enfief his English lords with lands in rebellious Scotland before departing for Flanders. Edward did not do so; instead, he offered wages to all who would serve on his Flemish campaign. Few accepted his offer. Edward also came into conflict with the archbishop of Canterbury, Robert Winchelsey (r. 1294–1313), when the king attempted to impose clerical taxation for the defense of the realm. According to the Third Lateran Council of 1179, the clergy could pay taxes to a secular authority in a case of dire need, but it fell to the head of the clergy in that land to determine whether the secular authority's need was great enough.[261] Edward tried to compel the clergy to contribute by refusing to offer his protection to dioceses and religious communities that refused to provide the amount he sought from them.

Edward also upset the public at large by imposing a sixfold increase on the existing custom on wool. This *maltote* (evil toll), as it came to be known, was in effect from 29 July 1294 to 23 November 1297. Prises of corn, oats, wools, hides, oxen, cows, and salted fish accompanied it, and the purpose of these impositions was to provision Edward's army.[262] Many of the collectors of these items were corrupt, and the seizures were wildly unpopular.[263] In 1297, England was at the brink of rebellion;[264] both clergy

---

[260] 'Articles of Grievance (*Monstraunces*), 1297', in *English Historical Documents*, vol. 3: *1189–1327*, ed. Harry Rothwell (London: Routledge, 1975), 468–70.
[261] See Prestwich, *Edward I*, 415.
[262] 'The "Evil toll" (Maltote of 1294–7)', in *English Historical Documents*, vol. 3: *1189–1327*, ed. Harry Rothwell (London: Routledge, 1975), 468.
[263] Prestwich, *Edward I*, 419.
[264] Prestwich, *Edward I*, 401.

and laymen complained that the king was disrespecting the rights and privileges guaranteed to them under Magna Carta.[265] It is no coincidence that the Langtoft Continuator, in the midst of his coverage of the setbacks that Edward suffered in 1297, lists a series of political disasters drawn from history, including 'li rays Arthur surpris par tricherye' (King Arthur [who was] surprised through treachery).[266] The Continuator laments that no man corrected his ways by the example of another, and, addressing King Edward directly, he tells the king that he must do all in his power to aid his nobles in Gascony and be reconciled with the Church.[267]

In his coverage of the Edward's capture of Caerlaverock Castle (15 July 1300), the Langtoft Continuator again faults Edward for not matching King Arthur's example. He reproves Edward for not sharing his territorial gains with his English barons and for lacking Arthur's sternness and self-discipline, writing:

> Demore e traine feynte e lung matinez,
> Delit en luxure, e surfet en vesprez,
> Affiaunce en felon, des enemis pitez,
> Au fet e consail propre voluntez,
> Conqueste retenir sanz fere largetez,
> Eschurent les Bretons en antiquitez.
> Ensample puit home prendre de Arthur li senez,
> De touz jours fu primer en touz ses alez
> A matin e à vespre, de grant honestetez,
> Felons en companie, e gens des enemistez,
> Solunc lour desert, touz les ad jugez.
> Au fet e au consail estoit atemprés;
> Prince plus curteis de teres conquestez
> Entre Crestiens ne fut unqes neez.
> Par quei le vus di, la reson escotez,
> Si nostre rei eust fet les puralez
> Parmi Engletere, cum il avoit grantez
> Affermez par escrit, qe bien est testmoynez,
> E de la tere d'Escoce partiz e donez
> A ses barons Engleis, par droite quantitez,
> La tere depesca fust en ses poestez,
> E pardurablement les soens heritez.[268]

---

[265] 'Articles of Grievance (*Monstraunces*), 1297', 469.
[266] *Chronicle of Pierre de Langtoft*, II, 284–5.
[267] *Chronicle of Pierre de Langtoft*, II, 284–5.
[268] *Chronicle of Pierre de Langtoft*, II, 326–30. I have modified Wright's translation for greater precision and elected to follow the variant reading indicated above (depesca = de pieç'a), which is attested in two of the manuscripts consulted by Wright, C and D.

(Idleness and feigned delay, and long morning's sleep, delight in luxury, and surfeit in the evenings, trust in felons, compassion for enemies, self-will in act and counsel, to retain conquest without giving distributions of gain – [all these things] the Britons of old avoided. We may take the example of Arthur the wise; he was always the first in all his expeditions in morning and in evening, with great uprightness; felons in company, and hostile people, according to their desert, he judged them all. He was temperate in deed and in counsel; a prince more courteous in conquered lands was never born among Christians. Wherefore I tell you, listen to reason: if our king had performed the perambulations through England, as he had granted and strengthened by writing, as is well witnessed, and of the land of Scotland had distributed and given to his English barons, by just quantities, the land would, since long ago, be here in his power, and his possession forever.)

Yet again, there is a correspondence between the first book and the second redaction of the third book. Pierre de Langtoft, in his account of Arthur's campaigning in Book One, writes: 'Arthur ne demort, ne volt resposer' (Arthur does not rest, he is unwilling to repose).[269] How, then, does the example of Arthur pertain to Edward I? In the last two years of his reign, Edward suffered from poor health and had difficulty getting up for Mass in the mornings. It is possible that the Langtoft Continuator was mistaking Edward's infirmity for laziness.[270]

We come now to the Continuator's criticism of Edward for failing to perform perambulations. This criticism is an indictment of the king's word of honor and good faith.[271] Perambulation is a term used for the investigations into and the surveying of the forests of England. Its purpose is to determine the boundaries of the King's Forest. The Crown, as we have seen, readily prosecuted violators and imposed hefty financial penalties on those who used the land without permission. Edward's subjects had complained that the borders of the King's Forest were ill defined, and it was widely believed that the Crown had significantly overstated the extent of the royal landholdings. In 1297, Humphrey de Bohun, constable of England, and Roger Bigod, marshal of England, refused to serve King Edward on his next Scottish campaign unless perambulations of the King's Forest were performed. The king ordered perambulations that October, but the implementation of the order was

---

[269] *Chronicle of Pierre de Langtoft*, I, 160–1.
[270] See Michael Prestwich, 'The Piety of Edward I', in *England in the Thirteenth Century: Proceedings of the 1984 Harlaxton Symposium*, ed. W. M. Ormrod (Woodbridge, UK: Boydell, 1985), 122.
[271] Prestwich, *Edward I*, 518–19.

delayed. In April 1299, Edward attempted to extricate himself from the promise, and it was widely felt that he was breaking his word. Roger Bigod reportedly went to Edward in 1299 and entreated him to have the perambulations performed.[272] According to the Langtoft Continuator, Edward promised and swore that he would perform the perambulations after his upcoming wedding to Margaret of France (10 September 1299).[273] Yet Edward failed to honor his word and was forsworn. The Langtoft Continuator links Edward's moral failing in this regard to his military failure in Scotland during the winter of 1299 and summer of 1300.[274] The matter of the perambulations spoke to three faults in Edward: a breach of faith, a lack of justice, and avarice.

Let us now consider the comparison made between Edward's justice and Arthur's justice. The Langtoft Continuator critiques Edward I for having too much compassion for his enemies. When recounting the Parliament held at Bury St. Edmunds in November 1296, the Continuator writes:

> Des barouns de Escoce à cel parlement
> Ne fu resun renduz, ne doné jugement.
> Li rays est si curtays, de si pitouse talent,
> Et de si graunt mercy, jo cray certaynement
> Ke sa misericorde serra salvement
> A cels ke ount la mort deservy playnement,
> Et de fez [...][275] ataynt felonessement.
> La graunt pité de quer k'il ad eu sovent
> Des felouns de Gales, en parlent tote gent;
> Quant plus ad eu à fere pur sun avauncement,
> Meu li ount la guere, et fet destourbement,
> Dount ses alez aylliours lesser li covent.[276]

> (Of the barons of Scotland in this parliament was no account rendered, or judgment given. The king is so courteous, of such charitable feelings, and of so great compassion, I believe veritably that his mercy will be the salvation of those who have fully deserved death, and [...] attainted of acts of felony. Of the great generosity of heart which he has often shown to the felons of Wales, all people talk. When he had most work before him for his own advancement, they have raised war upon him, and given him trouble, through which he was obliged to abandon his expeditions elsewhere.)

---

[272] This issue was raised at a parliament called for 3 May 1299. See *Chronica Buriensis*, 152.

[273] *Chronicle of Pierre de Langtoft*, II, 318–19.

[274] *Chronicle of Pierre de Langtoft*, II, 320–1.

[275] There appears to be a lacuna here. The missing word might be 'esté'.

[276] *Chronicle of Pierre de Langtoft*, II, 274–7.

The Continuator is giving voice to the complaints of the English magnates in attendance at the Bury St. Edmunds Parliament of November 1296. The lords hoped that Edward would redistribute to them the lands he had conquered – with their help – from the barons of Scotland. On the contrary, Edward sought to win local support in Scotland through clemency. He allowed every Scottish castle garrison during the 1296 campaign to surrender on terms that guaranteed life and limb. He even allowed the garrison defending Berwick, the first castle he attacked, freedom of egress with horses and arms, the 'ultimate mark of respect for a defeated opponent'.[277] Edward must have hoped that granting extremely generous terms to the first garrison that he encountered would entice future opponents to surrender without resistance. The *Chronicle of Lanercost* states that after the seemingly conclusive English victory at Dunbar (27 April 1296) and the abdication of John Balliol, King Edward had it proclaimed that, throughout his entire progress, no one was to make seizures or fires, but rather was to purchase the necessary victuals at a just price.[278]

Lands in Scotland did indeed come into the king's peace. The sole surviving plea roll of Edward I's Army in Scotland 1296 is helpful on this front. It tells of how a certain Nigel de Greenlaw charged Robert de Bamburgh with seizing sheep maliciously *in terra pacis*, and this is said to have occurred on 9 May 1296.[279] Another entry in the plea roll confirms that Edward took parts of Scotland into his protection. It also, however, indicates that plundering was an acceptable course of action prior to the issuance of the king's peace.[280] Each land would enter the king's peace only after its defenders had surrendered. This strategy was, as Andrew Martinez has recently referred to it, a '"carrot and stick" situation'' whereby further towns and areas were more likely to swear obedience to the king as they knew that in doing so they would be spared the attention of his soldiers'.[281]

Edward's policy became even more conciliatory to the Scots after the surrender of John Balliol: the king's peace now extended both to Scotland's knighthood and its peasants. Edward had become direct sovereign lord of Scotland, and all lands that the king toured were under his peace.

---

[277] Strickland, 'A Law of Arms or a Law of Treason?', 68.

[278] *Chronicon de Lanercost*, 182; *Chronicle of Lanercost*, 149–50.

[279] 'A Plea Roll of Edward I's Army in Scotland, 1296', ed. Cynthia J. Neville, in *Miscellany of the Scottish Historical Society* 11, Fifth Series, iii (1990): 54–5 (n. 57).

[280] See 'Plea Roll, 1296', 90–1 (n. 126).

[281] Andrew Martinez, 'Disciplinary Ordinances for English Armies and Military Change, 1385–1513', *History* 102, n. 351 (2017): 373.

Edward's aim was to convey that he was the rightful and just ruler of the Scots. This 'policy of conciliation', as Richard A. Newhall has termed it in the context of Henry V's Agincourt campaign, aimed to minimize the likelihood of future insurrection.[282] The *Chronicle of Lanercost* recognizes Edward, after he had granted his peace to all the lands of Scotland, as a worthy successor to Arthur:

> Progressus est ulterius animositate regia in partes instabilium Moraviæ populorum, ubi post Arthurum nullum in antiquariis reperies permeasse, ut montes et silvas ac saxa prærupta, quæ indigeni solent reputare quasi castra, dispersis agminibus, perlustraret. Hæc omnia quanta pietate, quanta frugalitate prosecutus sit, testantur ejus remissiones, condescentiones, munera ac festa.[283]

> (With kingly courage, he [Edward] pressed forward into the region of the unstable inhabitants of Moray, whither you will not find in the ancient records that any one had penetrated since Arthur. His purpose was to explore with scattered troops the hills and woods and steep crags which the natives are accustomed to count on as strongholds. With what piety and frugality he performed all these things, let his pardons, condescensions, bounties, and festivals testify.)

Based on this passage, one might argue that Edward was like Arthur only with respect to the thoroughness of his conquest and exploration of Scotland, but emphasis is placed on Edward's probity immediately prior to and directly after the mention of Arthur's name. The reader is encouraged to infer that Edward conducted himself in a virtuous manner comparable to Arthur during his progress north.[284]

There is some ambiguity with respect to the Langtoft Continuator's understanding of courtesy. The writer faults Edward for being too courteous to his Scottish and Welsh adversaries but praises the example of Arthur, whom he recognizes as the prince most courteous with respect

[282] Richard A. Newhall, 'Henry V's Policy of Conciliation in Normandy, 1417–1422', in *Anniversary Essays in Mediaeval History by Students of Charles Homer Haskins Presented on his Completion of Forty Years of Teaching*, ed. Charles Holt Taylor and John L. La Monte (Boston: Houghton Mifflin, 1929), 205–29.

[283] *Chronicon de Lanercost*, 182; *Chronicle of Lanercost*, 150.

[284] Edward, after his progress through Scotland, returned to Berwick and on 28 August 1296 obtained another oath of fealty and homage, this time from 'two thousand Scottish freeholders, great and small, male and female – persons, that is, representative of Scottish landholding society as a whole', and Edward had these oaths recorded in an official royal instrument, the so-called Ragman Roll of 1296. See Neville, 'Widows of War', 115.

to conquered lands. The Continuator's meaning here is not entirely clear. He is probably not alluding to Arthur's clemency for defeated opponents, but rather to Arthur's generosity in redistributing captured lands to his faithful subjects. The Continuator seems to have been referencing Pierre de Langtoft's account of Arthur's merciful handling of the Scots once he marched into Moray, the very same land mentioned by the Lanercost chronicler.[285] The Langtoft Continuator was suggesting that Edward, during his campaign of 1296, was more lenient than Arthur had been during his Scottish campaign. Yet even Arthur eventually granted his peace once the bishop came to him in supplication. However, the 'excess' of courtesy and mercy for which the Continuator faults Edward is the 'virtue' that other medieval writers laud as courtesy.

The *Chronicle of Lanercost*, as noted above, states that King Edward had it proclaimed after the surrender of John Balliol that no one was to make seizures or fires, but rather was to purchase the necessary victuals at a just price. This type of proclamation is known as a disciplinary ordinance and we have record of its use by subsequent kings of England, notably Edward III on the Crécy campaign and Henry V on the Agincourt campaign. Interestingly, King Arthur, according to Wace's *Brut*, issued such an ordinance to his troops as they conquered Flanders and Bologne.[286] This passage in the *Brut* does not have its source in Geoffrey's *Historia*. It is an original addition by Wace. Pierre de Langtoft does not include these lines in Book One of his *Chronicle*, although, it was incorporated into the Middle English adaptation (c. 1338) of the *Chronicle of Pierre de Langtoft* by Robert Mannyng of Brunne.[287] Wace's addition was, however, influential. In *Escanor*, we find an even lengthier discussion of how Arthur instructs his men not to plunder enemy territory but rather to compensate the locals for items that they found themselves compelled to take.[288] The courteous manner of conquest exemplified by King Arthur in Wace's *Brut* and in *Escanor* was not an entirely idealized and impracticable abstraction. It was a policy that Edward implemented selectively when he was sure of victory and desirous of building goodwill with his new subjects. Edward's generosity, however, stopped short of adequate redistribution of lands to his English vassals and did not prevent the Scots from rebelling.

---

[285] *Chronicle of Pierre de Langtoft*, I, 154–7.
[286] Wace, *Roman de Brut*, 248–9, lines 9897–9904.
[287] Robert Mannyng of Brunne, *The Chronicle*, ed. Idelle Sullens (Binghamton, NY: Medieval and Renaissance Texts and Studies, Binghamton University, 1996), 344, lines 10530–5.
[288] Girart d'Amiens, *Escanor*, II, 720–1, lines 17484–501; II, 721–22, lines 17521–40.

The Langtoft Continuator initially recognizes Edward I as surpassing King Arthur in the swiftness with which the English king achieved victory in Wales and Scotland and reunited Britain. When Edward's successes proved ephemeral, the chronicler faults him for not living up to the virtues of Arthur, in particular Arthur's readiness to redistribute conquered lands to his faithful nobles. Given that the *Chronicle of Pierre de Langtoft* itself exists within the Arthurian chronicle tradition, it is not surprising that the Continuator links Edward I with the 'Arthur of history' rather than the 'Arthur of romance'. What is particularly fascinating about the continuation of the second recension of the *Chronicle of Pierre de Langtoft* is the extent to which the Continuator treats Arthur as directly relevant to the political situation in England, Scotland, Wales, and Gascony in the 1290s. This characteristic appears to be an event-effect of Edward's Arthurianism. Arthur was integral to the political discourse during Edward's reign.

Edward I's second appeal to history and King Arthur

In our exploration of Arthurianism during the Scottish phase of Edward's reign, the focus has been on the responses to the king's actions. Mention has not been made of round tables nor of any Arthurian evocations from the royal court. I have found no evidence of such activities until 1301, when Edward at last included the figure of King Arthur among his precedents for lordship over Scotland. Edward cited Arthur's successes against the Scots in response to Pope Boniface VIII's demand that the English king cease his campaigns north of the River Tweed. Why did Edward see fit to reference Arthurian precedents in 1301 given that he had not done so a decade earlier? As James Fergus Wilde has persuasively argued, Edward, when contending with the Roman Curia, whose antiquity and apostolic continuity with the past was beyond dispute, felt compelled to stress that the rights and privileges he exercised extended even further back, to pre-Christian times.[289]

On 27 June 1299, Pope Boniface VIII addressed *Scimus, fili* to Edward I, declaring that the realm of Scotland had belonged to the Holy Roman Church since ancient times and that it had never been a feudal possession of the kings of England.[290] The pope did not provide substantiation for

---

[289] James Fergus Wilde, 'History and Legend in the Chronicle of Peter of Langtoft' (Ph.D. diss., University of Manchester, 1997), 83.

[290] 'Bulla Pape Bonifacii', in *Anglo-Scottish Relations, 1174–1328: Some Selected Documents*, ed. and trans. E. L. G. Stones (Oxford: Clarendon Press, 1965), 162–5.

the Church's claim to Scotland.[291] He did, however, illustrate that Henry III had not been overlord of Scotland, and he reminded Edward that King Alexander III, when performing homage for his landholdings in England in October 1278, did not swear homage for Scotland. The pope, after rehearsing further developments in Anglo-Scottish relations, came to the matter of the Scottish request for Edward's adjudication of the Great Cause dispute. The pope censured Edward for abusing his special position when Scotland was without a head. He stated that Edward had acted without regard for what was right and proper and had used force and intimidation to achieve his ends. On these grounds, the changes that Edward brought about were determined not to have legal standing.[292] Pope Boniface invalidated the oaths of fealty given to Edward by King John Balliol and the citizenry of Scotland between 1292 and 1296. Furthermore, the pope charged Edward with committing grave injustices against the Church and the inhabitants of Scotland.[293] If Edward could not justify his claim to Scotland and if he failed to desist from his campaigning in Scotland, he ran the risk of excommunication and loss of domestic support for future military expeditions into Scotland. Boniface concluded *Scimus, fili* by declaring that he was claiming supreme jurisdiction over the matter of Scotland. He instructed Edward that, if he intended to persist in his claim to Scotland or any part of it, he should send a delegation with all pertinent documentation to the papal court within six months of receipt of the bull.[294]

Although *Scimus, fili* is dated 27 June 1299, Edward did not formally receive the bull until 27 August of 1300 when he was on campaign in Galloway.[295] The archbishop of Canterbury delivered it to the king at Sweetheart Abbey, Dumfries and then wrote back to Pope Boniface describing Edward's initial reaction. Archbishop Winchelsey reportedly approached Edward while he was at lunch with his army, and the king said he did not have time to hear his message that day. Later in the evening, two of the king's earls informed the archbishop that he could present the bull the following day. At that time, Edward had at his side his son Edward of Caernarfon as well as the earls, barons and knights who were part of his army. Edward is said to have listened respectfully to *Scimus, fili*, and to have had the document read publicly and explained in French to his men. The archbishop argued the pope's case. Edward sent the archbishop away

[291] 'Bulla Pape Bonifacii', 163 n. 2.
[292] 'Bulla Pape Bonifacii', 168–9.
[293] 'Bulla Pape Bonifacii', 172–3.
[294] 'Bulla Pape Bonifacii', 174–5.
[295] See Howard de Walden, *Some Feudal Lords and their Seals, 1301* (London: De Walden Library, 1903), ix.

and deliberated with his lords. Later, one of the king's officials went to the archbishop and explained that this business touched upon England and that the king was therefore required by the custom of the realm to obtain the counsel of all whom the affair concerned. Because some key lords were absent and had not been consulted, the king could not respond at that time.[296] In short, Edward simultaneously used the expectation of common counsel emphasized in Magna Carta as a stalling tactic and showed himself to be a good constitutional monarch. It was a brilliant move.

Edward then commissioned his Second Appeal to History. The wording of his second inquest did not differ in any substantial way from that of the first. The final product, however, included precedents for English rule over Scotland stretching back to ancient Britain. Edward commanded a search through the royal archives for material concerning Scotland on 13 November 1300, and the findings were brought to the Lincoln Parliament of 12 February 1301. As a consequence of the parliament, two letters were drafted. First came the aptly named Barons' Reply of 12 February 1301, which was written at Lincoln and boasts the seals of seven earls and sixty-four barons. In it, the barons declare that the kings of England have always held 'superior and direct dominion' over the realm of Scotland and that Scotland has never belonged to the Church.[297] On the grounds of ancient precedent and of the inalienability of the rights of the Crown, the barons state that they will not permit their king to bring his case before the papal court in the manner prescribed by *Scimus, fili.* Participation, they argue, would be tantamount to the surrender of the very rights that the community of England was seeking to uphold.[298]

The Barons' Reply appeals to ancient history and communicates that the kings of the Britons fell under the umbrella of the kings of England and stood as progenitors to Edward I. Edward's connection to British history came by virtue of his royal office (rather than through blood descent). The Barons' Reply may have been written strictly for domestic consumption. No record of payment for its dispatch to Rome survives, but copies of the letter and an Anglo-Norman translation of it did circulate in England.[299]

On 7 May 1301, Edward drafted his own letter to the pope, and a week and a day later he entrusted it to two country knights, Thomas Wale and

---

[296] Robert Winchelsey, 'Certificatorium super statu regni Scocie', in *Registrum Roberti Winchelsey Cantuariensis Archiepiscopi, A D. 1294–1313*, ed. Rose Graham, 2 vols. (Oxford: Oxford University Press, 1952–6), II, 572.

[297] 'The Barons' Reply to the Pope', ed. and trans. Howard de Walden, in de Walden, *Some Feudal Lords*, xviii–xix, at xviii.

[298] 'Barons' Reply', xviii.

[299] Prestwich, *Edward I*, 492.

Thomas Delisle, who delivered it to Boniface VIII at Anagni on 2 July.[300] Edward's letter states, in no uncertain terms, that his explanation of policy was not to be received as a legal plea.[301] Edward justifies his claim to Scotland without actually submitting to papal adjudication. The kingdom of England, as represented in Edward I's letter, is a political entity whose existence stretches back into the remote past rather than to the tenth-century formation of *Anglia*. The document discusses how the illustrious Trojan Brutus, after the fall of Troy, sailed with fellow countrymen to a certain island called Albion and how Brutus slew the giants that lived there, renamed the island Britain, and divided it between Locrinus, Albanactus, and Kamber. This material appears in Geoffrey's *Historia* and is also cited in the Faversham and Walden replies to the First Appeal to History.

After providing additional precedents from early British history that reinforced the primacy of Loegria (England), Edward evokes King Arthur.[302] He references two Arthurian episodes from Geoffrey's *Historia*. First comes the Loch Lomond episode, where Arthur besieges the rebellious Scots and Picts and lifts a blockade made by the Scots' Irish allies. According to Geoffrey, when Arthur overcame the Irish, he was free to wipe out the Scots and Picts. But when the local Scottish clergy came barefoot before Arthur with relics in tow begging for mercy, he granted them his peace.[303] This passage was extremely useful to Edward because it communicates that the Scots had a history of treachery against their overlords and establishes that Arthur (and Edward by extension) was not obligated to show them mercy.

By 1297, Edward did not see himself as engaging in an open war in Scotland (a war between two sovereign Christian princes) but as putting down an insurrection.[304] As has been underscored by Cynthia Neville and Matthew Strickland, the rebellion / open war distinction was all-important in the context of the First War of Scottish Independence: a rebellious vassal did not enjoy the same privileged status as an enemy combatant who was the subject of another sovereign prince. It was the prerogative of a king to decide how to punish treacherous vassals.[305] Although Edward

---

[300] E. L. G. Stones, 'The Mission of Thomas Wale and Thomas Delisle from Edward I to Pope Boniface VIII in 1301', *Nottingham Medieval Studies* 26 (1982): 13.

[301] 'Sanctissimo Patri Bonifacio', 192–5.

[302] 'Sanctissimo Patri Bonifacio', 196–7.

[303] Geoffrey of Monmouth, *Historia regum Britannie* 149.166–75, pp. 200–3.

[304] See *Chronicon de Lanercost*, 190; *Chronicle of Lanercost*, 163.

[305] See Cynthia J. Neville, 'Widows of War: Edward I and the Women of Scotland during the War of Independence', in *Wife and Widow in Medieval England*, ed. Sue Sheridan Walker (Ann Arbor: University of Michigan Press, 1993), 111–12. Also see Matthew Strickland, 'A Law of Arms or a Law of Treason? Conduct in War in Edward I's Campaigns in Scotland, 1296–1307', in *Violence in Medieval Society*, ed. Richard W. Kaeuper (Woodbridge, UK: Boydell Press, 2000), 40–1.

had secured these oaths of fealty and submission, Pope Boniface and the Scottish delegation held that they were nonbinding because they were obtained under duress. Thus an ancient precedent justifying Edward I's harsh treatment of the Scots was desirable. The religious community at Faversham recognized the potential utility of the Loch Lomond episode as early as 1291 and included it in their reply to Edward.

The second Arthurian and Galfridian passage that Edward alludes to in his letter is that describing Arthur's plenary court at Caerleon on Pentecost.[306] According to Geoffrey, Arthur summoned all the kings and vassals subject to him to attend this event. It was to be a supreme display of his temporal power and to serve as a confirmation of his vassals' total submission to him. After offering the precedent of Arthur, Edward's letter to the pope provides examples of English overlordship of Scotland beginning with Edward the Elder and ending with his version of recent Anglo-Scottish relations.

On 2 July 1301, Wale and Delisle arrived at the papal court. According to a later report by Wale, Pope Boniface received the king's letter favorably upon their arrival, but he did not make any sort of formal decision then and there.[307] Much as Edward put off answering Pope Boniface by asserting that he needed the common counsel of the community of his realm to act, Boniface maintained that he needed to hold a consistory.[308]

Prior to the arrival of Wale and Delisle, Boniface had received a delegation of three representatives from the Scottish opposition party. Their purpose was to convince the pope that Scotland had suffered unjustly at the hands of the English king.[309] After Boniface received Edward I's letter, he gave a copy to the Scottish delegation. One of its members, Baldred Bisset, prepared a point-by-point refutation of Edward's arguments, the *Processus Baldredi contra figmenta regis Anglie* (Baldred's pleading against the fictions of the king of England).[310]

Among its numerous rebuttals of Edward's claims, the *Processus Baldredi* argues that the post-Conquest kings of England had no right to claim precedents from the legendary history of Britain as their own. Baldred did not reject out of hand the veracity of the legendary history of Britain but

---

[306] Geoffrey of Monmouth, *Historia regum Britannie* 156.306–10, pp. 208–9.

[307] Stones, 'Mission of Thomas Wale and Thomas Delisle', 17–19.

[308] See Prestwich, *Edward I*, 495.

[309] R. James Goldstein, 'The Scottish Mission to Boniface VIII in 1301: A Reconsideration of the Context of the *Instructiones* and *Processus*', *Scottish Historical Review* 70, n. 188 (1991): 3.

[310] See Walter Bower, *Scotichronicon* vol. 6: Books XI and XII, ed. Norman F. Shead, Wendy B. Stevenson, and D. E. R. Watt, with Alan Borthwick, R. E. Latham, J. R. S. Phillips, and Martin S. Smith (Aberdeen: Aberdeen University Press, 1991), 168–89.

disputed the English interpretation of it on technical points, and he included some Scottish accretions to the Galfridian narrative.[311] After challenging the primacy of the kingdom of Loegria, Baldred argues that the contemporary kings of England did not have any hereditary connection with the ancient kings of Britain and that, therefore, the rights and privileges of the Britons did not apply to those of the reigning dynasty in England.[312] Bloodline and nation are emphasized to the detriment of Edward's more tenuous figural and geographical claims of affinity with the British kings. In effect, Baldred problematizes *translatio imperii*, contending that the transfer of rule from one ruling population to the next is not necessarily smooth and that there is not always continuity between one kingdom and its successor.[313] According to Baldred, Arthur was too far removed ethnically, temporally, and even in titular terms to be an applicable precedent for Edward I. Each new nation had its own set of customs and laws. England was not Loegria. Baldred concludes his *Processus* by entreating Pope Boniface to disregard Edward's case from antiquity on the grounds that it did not pertain to the present matter. Edward's letter and Baldred's response showcase rival perspectives on the applicability of the distant past to the circumstances of the present, especially in light of ethnic change.

Although Baldred's objection to *translatio imperii* obviated the need to address Edward's use of King Arthur as a precedent, address it he did and in multiple ways. Baldred tried to disqualify Arthur's legitimacy as a ruler. He claimed that Arthur was not the rightful heir to the throne of Britain, but rather a tyrant of illegitimate birth who blocked Mordred from ascending the throne and who conquered a variety of realms by force of arms. He added that these kingdoms returned to their former liberty when Mordred slew Arthur.[314] He classified Arthur as an aberration in history whose reign did not have lasting effects.

The *Scimus, fili* affair brought legendary British history and the figure of Arthur onto the international diplomatic stage in an official capacity that was unprecedented. Pope Boniface VIII did not, however, issue a definitive ruling as to the validity of Edward's Galfridian pretensions.[315] In this respect the *Scimus, fili* affair proved anti-climactic. In the summer of 1301, Pope Boniface permitted John Balliol to move from the custody of the Church into the protection of Philippe IV of France. This could be seen as a small victory for the Scots, but it was not the strength of the

---

[311] See Walter Bower, *Scotichronicon* 11.62, pp. 182–3.
[312] Walter Bower, *Scotichronicon* 11.61, pp. 180–3.
[313] Walter Bower, *Scotichronicon*, 9.62, pp. 184–5.
[314] Walter Bower, *Scotichronicon*, 9.62, pp. 184–5.
[315] Prestwich, *Edward I*, 495.

arguments of the opposing sides that determined Boniface's final stance. On the contrary, it was a consequence of changing political realities. After Boniface's relations with Philippe IV of France soured late in 1301, the pope looked upon Edward more favorably.[316] In August 1302, the pope commanded the bishops of Scotland to be reconciled with the king of England. He did not use his moral and spiritual authority to challenge the veracity of Galfridian history or to deny its relevance to Anglo-Scottish relations. The Crown was thus free to continue to use the legendary history of Britain in support of its cause.

The Falkirk Round Table

The *Annals of London* states that King Edward held a round table at Falkirk from 20 to 26 January in 1302.[317] Three and a half years earlier, on 22 July 1298, the king had won a victory there against William Wallace. It appears that as many as 2,000 English infantrymen died in the battle, though only a single English knight, Sir Brian de Jay, master of the Temple, fell. There were, however, a great many casualties on the Scottish side and the Scottish cavalry was forced to retreat. William Wallace survived the day but with a tarnished reputation.[318] Juliet Barker has suggested that Edward intended for the Falkirk Round Table to commemorate his victory there.[319] Falkirk was indeed, as Prestwich has noted, 'the only major battle fought by the king himself since Evesham'.[320] In 1279, as we have seen, Edward participated in a round table at Kenilworth, the site of a personal victory over the rebel barons; in 1284, he organized the round table at Nefyn to celebrate his victory over the Welsh. The Falkirk Round Table continued this pattern, but the Scottish resistance had not been permanently defeated.[321] Indeed, in January 1302 England and Scotland were in a truce set to expire that autumn. If Edward was not celebrating a total victory, what was he celebrating?

Perhaps Edward was celebrating the alliance that he had just concluded with Robert Bruce the Younger. Some time before 16 February 1302, Robert Bruce swore homage to Edward I for the earldom of Carrick.[322] The

---

316 See Prestwich, *Edward I*, 497; Stones, 'Mission of Thomas Wale and Thomas Delisle', 15.

317 See *Annales Londoniensis*, 104.

318 See Prestwich, *Edward I*, 480–2.

319 See Barker, *Tournament in England*, 91.

320 Michael Prestwich, 'Edward I (1239–1307)', *Oxford Dictionary of National Biography*, Oxford University Press, 2004 (http://www.oxforddnb.com/index/8/101008517, accessed 22 August 2014).

321 See T. F. Tout, *Edward the First* (London: Macmillan and Co., 1893), 214.

322 See E. L. G. Stones, 'The Submission of Robert Bruce to Edward I, c. 1301–2', *Scottish Historical Review* 34, n. 118, ii (1955): 124.

Bruce had been in rebellion against the king since 1297. Rumor that John Balliol had moved from papal protection into French protection and that the French were going to aid Balliol in reclaiming his crown of Scotland drove Robert Bruce into Edward's hands.[323] In return for Robert's faithful service, the king guaranteed that the Bruce would not be disinherited of his rightful lands in England and Scotland and that, if it should come about that Balliol regained effective rule of Scotland, Edward would allow the Bruce to pursue his claim.[324] Thus the round table may well have been held to celebrate the newly established concord between Edward and the Bruce. And, as Stones has noted, until 1306 the Bruce 'held a position of considerable trust in Edward's counsels'.[325] I have not, however, been able to place the Bruce at the Falkirk Round Table. The entry in the *Annals of London* does not mention the event's attendees, and this period in the Bruce's career is obscure.[326] We do not know if there were any Arthurian romance elements at the Falkirk Round Table, but once again practical politics – the celebration of an important alliance and the commemoration of a personal victory – appear to have been factors in its design.

The Feast of the Swans: Edward I's Arthurian swan song?

Edward's final act of Arthurianism was his orchestration of the Feast of the Swans, a grand knighting ceremony that took place at Westminster on Whitsunday (22 May) 1306. At the royal palace, the ailing king knighted his successor, Edward of Caernarfon, aged twenty-two, and invested him with the duchy of Aquitaine.[327] The prince, in turn, knighted approximately three hundred men at the abbey. Although the chroniclers have left a fair amount of information about the Feast of the Swans, we cannot say definitively that this feast was Arthurian. Edward did, however, draw upon the romantic flavor of knighthood to win the support of his subjects.

In 1306, Edward again found himself in need of a sizeable army. The English king had defeated many of the leaders of the Scottish independence movement in 1304. He had also captured, tried, and executed William Wallace in 1305. Success in Scotland, nonetheless,

---

[323] Stones, 'Submission of Robert Bruce', 129–31.
[324] See 'Sire Robert de Brus le Filz', in *Anglo-Scottish Relations, 1174–1328: Some Selected Documents*, ed. and trans. E. L. G. Stones (Oxford: Clarendon Press, 1965), 236–9; Prestwich, *Edward I*, 496.
[325] 'Sire Robert de Brus le Filz', 237, n. 1.
[326] See Stones, 'Submission of Robert Bruce', 131.
[327] Nicholas Trevet, *Annales sex regum Angliæ*, 408.

remained illusory. Edward was in the process of establishing a new system of rule in Scotland, and he chose Robert Bruce and John Comyn 'the Red' of Badenoch to act as counselors in this process. The Bruce had had the king's trust, for he was a kinsman to Edward through his marriage to Johanna, daughter of William de Valence, earl of Pembroke.[328] Yet the Bruce also had a legitimate claim to the throne of Scotland, and in 1305 he saw an opportunity to pursue it. In February 1306, the Bruce met Comyn at Dumfries. The former urged the latter to support his claim. Comyn refused.[329] The two men came to blows. According to Walter of Guisborough, the Bruce's men killed Comyn on the steps of the high altar at the church of the Friars Minor at Dumfries in such a manner that his blood touched the table of the altar.[330] The murder of Comyn and the Bruce's consolidation of power were the impetus for yet another English expedition to subdue Scotland. On 25 March, Robert the Bruce was crowned king of Scotland at Scone with the consent of four bishops, five earls, and the people of the land.[331]

On 1 March 1306, Edward was already beginning to make preparations for what was to be his eighth and final campaign in Scotland.[332] Five days later, Edward proclaimed throughout his realm his intention to knight Edward of Caernarfon, and he invited all noblemen who wished to become knights to come to London before Whitsunday in order to receive the necessary equipment so that they might receive a knighthood from him on the same day.[333] The Feast of Swans was a grand chivalric event designed to fill the ranks of the English host for the imminent campaign.[334] Edward's method of recruitment this time was a generous and honorable invitation to a grand royal event. Edward provided each applicant with rich ceremonial robes, the ritual bed, and knightly equipment, specifically a helmet, hauberk, lance, sword, and spurs.[335] On offer was a sumptuous feast in London and a knighthood alongside his son and heir. The event was different in character but similar in purpose to the distraints of knighthood.[336]

---

[328] Bullock-Davies, *Menestrellorum Multitudo*, x.

[329] Adam Murimuth, *Continuatio Chronicarum*, ed. Edward Maunde Thompson, RS 93 (London: Eyre and Spottiswoode, 1889), 8–9.

[330] Walter of Guisborough, *Chronicle*, 366–7.

[331] Walter of Guisborough, *Chronicle*, 367.

[332] Bullock-Davies, *Menestrellorum Multitudo*, xiii.

[333] *Flores historiarum*, III, 131; Bullock-Davies, *Menestrellorum Multitudo*, xv; Walter of Guisborough, *Chronica*, 367.

[334] *Flores historiarum*, III, 131.

[335] See Bullock-Davies, *Menestrellorum Multitudo*, xxii–xxiv.

[336] Bullock-Davies makes this point in *Menestrellorum Multitudo*, xv–xvi.

An author of one of the continuations of Matthew Paris' *Flores historiarum* offers a detailed account of the proceedings. It states that 300 young men (the sons of earls, barons, and knights) accepted King Edward's invitation.[337] Each youth received a robe befitting his social status and then sought out a place in tents and pavilions that had been specially constructed for the occasion in New Temple, for there was not enough room in the royal palace. Most of these candidates for knighthood made their vigil there, but the prince of Wales and a few other tyros of great name made their vigil at Westminster by the order of the king. The next morning, King Edward girded the belt of knighthood onto his son in the royal palace. Henry de Lacy, earl of Lincoln, and Humphrey de Bohun, earl of Hereford and constable of England, each attached a spur onto Prince Edward's feet.[338] The king formally bestowed upon his son the duchy of Aquitaine. The prince of Wales then knighted his companions at the altar of St. Peter in Westminster.[339] Great lords of the realm were knighted, including Roger Mortimer, son of Edmund Mortimer; Edmund, earl of Arundel; and John, earl of Warenne. The mayor of London, John le Blound, also received a knighthood.[340]

After the mass knighting, the Feast of the Swans began. The *Annals of London* state that the patriarch of Jerusalem, the bishop of Chester, the bishop of Rochester, and, according to the estimation of heralds, as many as 1,000 knights were in attendance at the feast.[341] Two chronicle sources, a continuation of the *Flores historiarum* and Nicholas Trevet's annals, provide especially detailed accounts. The *Flores* states that two swans adorned with gold nets were brought before the king. When he saw them, he swore an oath on the swans that he wished to be accomplished in Scotland, namely that he, dead or alive, would avenge the injury to the Holy Church, the death of John Comyn, and the injured faith of the Scots. Then the rest of the magnates reportedly swore the oath, declaring that they stood with him in good faith and were prepared to fulfill the royal wish in Scotland both during the life of the king and after his death with his son the prince.[342] Accounts of the Royal Wardrobe confirm that ornamented swans were involved in the festivities.[343] The *Continuatio Chronicarum* of Adam of Murimuth (c. 1274–1347) states that Edward swore an oath of vengeance against Robert the Bruce, but this

---

[337] *Flores historiarum*, III, 131.
[338] *Annales Londonienses*, 146.
[339] *Flores historiarum*, III, 132.
[340] *Annales Londonienses*, 146.
[341] *Annales Londonienses*, 146.
[342] *Flores historiarum*, III, 132.
[343] See Bullock-Davies, *Menestrellorum Multitudo*, xxxiii.

source does not provide much in the way of further detail.[344] For this we must turn to the entry by Nicholas Trevet. He sets the stage by seating 'rex in mensa, novis militibus circumdatus' (the king at table, surrounded by the new knights).[345] Then, Trevet says, in came a multitude of minstrels carrying a piece of fabric adorned with many elements so that they could invite the knights, especially the new ones, to swear to a certain deed of arms in the presence of a device (or swan?).[346] The king himself vowed that he would avenge the contempt brought against God and the Church by Robert the Bruce and that, once this was fulfilled, he would never again bear arms against Christians but would guide his path into the Holy Land and never return. The son of the king vowed that he would never spend two nights in one place. Intending to fulfill his father's vow as much as he was able, he went into Scotland. Trevet states that he does not recall the vow of the rest of the knights.[347] The continuation to the second redaction of Langtoft's Chronicle confirms that Edward, Prince of Wales, swore to obtain vengeance on Robert the Bruce.[348] All the chronicle accounts state that, directly after the Feast of the Swans, the prince and his men hastened into Scotland in order to fulfill their vows and that King Edward slowly followed after them.[349] The Feast of the Swans was the prelude to Edward's final Scottish campaign, which was framed as a great quest for vengeance against a traitor to the Crown and enemy of the Church.

We know the underlying purpose of the event, but was the Feast of the Swans Arthurian in character? Not a single chronicle source refers to the event as involving a round table or Arthurian role-playing. Only one historical source, the aforementioned continuation to Langtoft's Chronicle, makes reference to King Arthur in connection with the feast:

> Unkes en Bretayne puys qe Dieu fu nez
> N'estoyt tel nobleye en viles n'en citez,
> Forpris Karleoun en antiquitez,
> Quant sire Arthur luy reis i fust corounez.[350]

(Never in Britain, since God was born, was there such nobleness in towns or in cities, except Caerleon in ancient times, when Sir Arthur the king was crowned there.)

---

[344] See Adam Murimuth, *Continuatio Chronicarum*, 9. Also see Bullock-Davies, *Menestrellorum Multitudo*, xxxii–xxxiii.

[345] Nicholas Trevet, *Annales sex regum Angliæ*, 408.

[346] For this translation of *signum*, see Bullock-Davies, *Menestrellorum Multitudo*, xxxiv.

[347] Nicholas Trevet, *Annales sex regum Angliæ*, 409.

[348] *Chronicle of Pierre de Langtoft*, II, 380–1.

[349] See Nicholas Trevet, *Annales sex regum Angliæ*, 409.

[350] *Chronicle of Pierre de Langtoft*, II, 368–9.

As Bullock-Davies has noted, this exemplary comparison does not suggest that Edward assumed the role of Arthur during the Feast of the Swans.[351]

Although the surviving chronicles and documentary evidence do not provide any clear evidence that the Feast of the Swans was an instance of Arthurianism, the event does appear to have had an Arthurian ambience, broadly speaking.[352] Edward's offer of ceremonial robes and knightly equipment to all men of noble birth seeking knighthood is Arthurian, although not exclusively Arthurian. Chrétien famously describes Arthur in *Perceval* as the 'roi qui les chevaliers fait' (king who makes knights), and, in the Prose *Lancelot*, we learn that it was Arthur's custom to knight only those squires who were wearing his robes and bearing his arms.[353] This is a practice that befits and could pertain to any great king. Another somewhat vague hint that Edward assumed the role of Arthur at the Feast of the Swans was his positioning in relation to the newly dubbed knights. Trevet, in his account of the event, notes that Edward sat at table surrounded by the new knights. The image of a great king at table surrounded by his knights is certainly evocative of Arthur at the Round Table. Furthermore, Edward is the first to make an oath. This shows him to be a *roi-chevalier* and *primus inter pares*. It is suggestive, but does not constitute explicit evidence, of Arthurianism. The framing of a great punitive campaign as a quest is certainly romantic and arguably Arthurian in a general sense. However, as Loomis has noted, the taking of an avian oath had no known Arthurian precedent.[354] Prince Edward's oath not to spend two nights in a single place until he has obtained vengeance on the Bruce is also not exclusively Arthurian. Loomis notes the example of the eponymous hero of Chrétien's *Perceval*, who vows not to spend two nights under the same roof until he learns the location of the Grail and whom it served.[355] In the Prose *Lancelot*, Sir Gawain vows not to rest more than one night in any town until he has ascertained the identity of the anonymous white knight (Lancelot) that has been his savior.[356] Even so, Prince Edward's oath is still generically chivalric in its formulation. If the oath were said to be binding for a year and a day, the

---

[351] See the dismissal of the Arthurian comparison by Bullock-Davies, *Menestrellorum Multitudo*, xxix; Prestwich, *Edward I*, 121.

[352] See Loomis 'Edward I, Arthurian Enthusiast', 122–5.

[353] See Arthur's conversation with Niniène regarding the knighting of Lancelot in the Prose *Lancelot*, VII, 267.

[354] Loomis, 'Edward I, Arthurian Enthusiast', 124; Bullock-Davies, *Menstrellorum Multitudo*, xxxv.

[355] Chrétien de Troyes, *Perceval*, 201, lines 4727–36.

[356] See Sir Gawain's oath made before King Arthur in the Prose *Lancelot*, VII, 372.

standard length of an Arthurian quest in the prose Arthurian romance tradition, then the Arthurian resonance of the swan oath would be more definite. However, given the likening of Edward's Feast of the Swans to Arthur's Caerleon coronation feast and given Edward's long history of engaging in Arthurian self-fashioning, an Arthurian element in the 1306 Winchester feast is plausible.

In early summer 1307, Edward, despite being unfit to travel, was on the road again to Scotland, and he died on 7 July at Burgh by Sands. His body was transported to Waltham Abbey near London, where it lay embalmed on a bier.[357] It was not until 27 October that a grand funeral took place. The king was laid to rest at Westminster Abbey in a plain Purbeck marble sarcophagus that did not contain an effigy or image of the king. Edward's tomb was strikingly stark when compared to the gilt bronze effigy of Henry III or the canopied tomb of Edward I's brother, Edmund of Lancaster (d. 1296). Prestwich suggests that the plain marble sarcophagus was chosen for Edward either in direct imitation of the similarly unadorned marble sarcophagus of Louis IX of France or in imitation of the marble sepulchre that, according to Gerald of Wales, Henry II of England had ordered to be made for the supposed remains of Arthur and Guinevere.[358] Edward looked upon this unadorned marble tomb when he had the sepulchre of Arthur opened in late April 1278. It is therefore possible that the design of the tomb was an Arthurian allusion, though I have not found any historical sources that confirm this possibility.

Edward I was commemorated in at least two instances with reference to King Arthur. The continuation of the second redaction of Langtoft's Chronicle concludes with a eulogy stating that Edward was the most accomplished flower of Christian knighthood since Arthur, but still not as outstanding as Arthur.[359] In contrast, John of London, in his 'Commendatio lamentabilis in transitu magni regis Edwardi quarti', rates Edward even more highly than Arthur.[360] The introductory description of Edward in the 'Commendatio lamentabilis' is adapted from Peter of Blois' description of Henry II. It is followed by a series of lamentions for Edward, first by the pope, second by secular kings, third by his widow Queen Margaret, fourth by the bishops of his realm, fifth by the earls

---

[357] *Chronicle of Pierre de Langtoft*, II, 382–3.
[358] See Michael Prestwich, *Plantagenet England, 1225–1360* (Oxford: Clarendon Press, 2005), 44–5.
[359] *Chronicle of Pierre de Langtoft*, II, 378–81.
[360] John of London, 'Commendatio Lamentabilis in transitu magni regis Edwardi quarti secundum Johannem de Londonia', in *Chronicles of the Reigns of Edward I and Edward II*, vol. 2, ed. William Stubbs. RS 76/2 (London: Longman, 1883), 3–21.

and barons of his realm, sixth by the knights of his realm, seventh by the clergy, and lastly by the laity. The Arthur/Edward comparison occurs in the sixth (chivalric) section of the work. John of London, speaking for the knights, writes that, although Arthur conquered more lands than Edward (albeit lands with smaller populations), Edward did not suffer the indignities of foreign invasion or fatal betrayal by a kinsman.[361] As we have seen, the tributes to Llywelyn ap Gruffudd liken the Welsh prince to Arthur because both were native heroes who valiantly resisted foreign invasion until they fell in battle: Llywelyn at Llanganten in Builth and Arthur at Camlann. The tributes that compare Edward I to Arthur juxtapose the two kings' successes in conquering lands. Once again we observe the dualism between Arthur the resistance fighter and Arthur the champion of institutional authority and imperialist kingship.

Conclusion

Loomis, as we have seen, has argued that Edward was more interested in pretending to be King Arthur for his own amusement than for practical purposes. My study has pointed in the exact opposite direction. For each and every instance in which Edward is known to have participated in an Arthurian activity, I have been able to adduce a cogent political motivation. Arthurianism was not a trivial, passing conceit for Edward. It was a component of the king's statecraft, factoring into his domestic and foreign policy.

King Edward was a canny and grounded king who knew that impersonating King Arthur was a good public relations strategy. This was, I hold, Edward's leading motivation for evoking Arthur. Edward used the model of Arthur to show his barons that he was different from his unpopular, divisive, and ineffectual father, Henry III. Edward sought to heal the residual wounds of the Second Barons' War. He wanted to be seen as a monarch who, in contrast to his father, respected the laws and customs of his realm and ruled with the advice and consent of the community of the realm. Edward was aware that the image of Arthur sitting at table with his knights and consulting them as near equals potently captured the English baronage's collective vision of its ideal king.

Over the course of his reign, Edward reclaimed the figure of Arthur as a champion of the Plantagenet dynasty to the disadvantage of his baronage and the Welsh. He did this by *becoming* the baronial dream of Arthur and the 'Welsh' prophetic vision of Arthur. Edward did not

---

[361] John of London, 'Commendatio Lamentabilis', 15.

prohibit round tables; rather, he turned the tables into royal events. He assumed pride of place at them and thereby enhanced his Arthurian credentials. Edward I's readiness to preside over round tables, although it seems so natural in hindsight, was his innovation. Henry II, John, and Henry III had all prohibited the holding of tournaments in England; Richard I allowed tournaments to take place under certain conditions, but he is not known to have ever impersonated Arthur. By contrast, Edward was so successful at emulating Arthur that, at the 1279 round table held at Le Hem, which was well outside the English king's dominion, the place of the king was left vacant in deference to him.

Edward did not dismiss Welsh political prophecies out of hand. Instead he sought to capitalize on them, even going so far as to effect some of the prophecies in ways that bolstered his own legitimacy as ruler over the whole of Britain. The fact that expectations lingered that Arthur would return in some capacity no doubt further encouraged Edward to cultivate this likeness. By virtue of being an Insular monarch with an established – albeit dormant – Arthurian pedigree and by virtue of having knightly ability and experience, Edward had the prerequisites to suggest convincingly that he was Arthur reborn. Edward I revived a tradition of Arthurian imitation that had been begun by his great-grandfather, Henry II, was consciously rejected by his grandfather John, and allowed to lie fallow by his father Henry III. Edward's hands-on involvement in the second translation of Arthur's remains calls to mind the first translation of Arthur's remains, the plan for which Gerald of Wales, rightly or wrongly, credited to Henry II. Edward, by participating in the reinterment of Arthur, by fashioning himself after Arthur, and by explicitly citing Arthur as a precedent for his own Insular authority in his letter to Boniface VIII, achieved the anglicization of Arthur. He furthered Henry II's unfinished work.

Loomis is quite correct that Edward participated in a pan-European literary and ludic Arthurian vogue. The English monarch was not, however, passively playing along with a trend in aristocratic entertainment and self-expression. He was seeking to take control of it and channel it for his own personal gain – to enhance his own domestic and international standing. Edward was a keen observer (and partaker) of the tastes and interests of his contemporaries – the lords and citizens of England, Wales, and Europe at large. Edward also had a special gift for coopting the ideas and practices of his opponents to his own advantage. If he could persuade his subjects that he was the long-awaited second coming of the heroic and triumphant Arthur, then he could count on their loyalty, financial support, and military service. If he could likewise convince the inhabitants of Wales that he was Arthur reborn, then he stood to induce them to submit to his rule. If he could persuade nobles from other realms that he was *Arthurus redivivus*, then he might more easily obtain their respect, friendship, and support. The vogue for and entertainment value of things Arthurian is what made it a potent political tool.

Of course, Edward might also have taken quixotic pleasure in emulating Arthur, although the surviving historical evidence can neither affirm nor deny this motivation. What Loomis took to be the strongest indicator of Edward's personal fondness for Arthurian literature, Rustichello's reference to the king in his Compilation, appears to have been a *topos* characteristic of the thirteenth-century prose cycle of Arthurian romances. The Compilation's reference to Edward I does, however, speak to the ubiquity of the Arthur/Edward association during and immediately following the Plantagenet king's reign. Comparisons of Arthur and Edward I appeared in chronicles (both Arthurian and non-Arthurian), political prophecy, romances, heraldry, and public spectacle. Even coinage and a funerary monument arguably contributed to the *Arthuring* of Edward I.

With respect to the 'Arthur of history' versus 'Arthur of romance' binary, the surviving historical records favor the former. The international romance-based vogue for things Arthurian was undoubtedly part of the allure of the figure of King Arthur for Edward, but the explicit evocations of Arthur by Edward refer to Arthur's 'historical' accomplishments as king. Powicke is quite correct that the 'historical' dimension of Arthur, the figure's supposed historical status as the overlord of the whole of the British Isles and much of Europe, was what caught Edward's attention most of all. Edward's vision for a new and improved Plantagenet empire coincided with Arthur's empire as defined by Geoffrey of Monmouth. Given what we know of Edward's historical consciousness, it is logical that the 'historical' Arthur appealed most to him. Arthur became part of Edward's own *quo warranto* claim to the suzerainty of Scotland.

Edward I's 1301 letter to Boniface VIII wherein he cites the precedent of Arthur for rule over Scotland is the English king's most substantial contribution to the history and development of Arthurianism. Edward is the first king known to have cited the precedent of Arthur in a grand way on the European political stage. He had the audacity to do this in his letter to the highest moral and spiritual authority in Western Europe. Edward staked a measure of his own integrity on the veracity of Geoffrey of Monmouth's narrative of the deeds of King Arthur. To challenge this account of Arthur's life was to challenge the wisdom and authority of King Edward I. Edward's lasting contribution to Arthurianism was ensuring that Galfridian history obtained at least functional recognition as historical fact.

Conclusion

The Welsh chronicler and 'soldier of Calais', Elis Gruffydd (1490–1552), observes in his world history (Creation–1552) that the English criticize the Welsh for taking excessive pride in Arthur and, in defense of his countrymen, he delivers this riposte:

> Ac etto j mae yn vwy j son wyntt [sc. y Sayson] amdanno ef [sc. Arthur] no nnyni [sc. y Kymru]; kanis j maentt twy [sc y Sayson] yn dywedud ac yn koelio yn gadarn j kyuyd ef [sc. Arthur] dracheuyn j vod yn vrenin. Yr hrain yn i hoppiniwn a ddywaid j vod ef ynn kysgu mewn googoff dan vryn garllaw Glasynbri. Ac yn wir pe gellid hroddi koel j ai[r] ymrauaelion bobl o'r ardal hwnw, yvo ymddangoses ac a ymddiuannodd a llawer o bobyl mewn llawer modd hryuedd er ys trychant o vylnyddoedd.

> (And yet they [sc. the English] talk much more about him [sc. Arthur] than we [sc. the Welsh] do; for they [sc. the English] say and firmly believe that he [sc. Arthur] will rise again to be king. They in their opinion say that he is sleeping in a cave under a hill near Glastonbury. And indeed, if credence could be given to the word of various people of that region, he has for three hundred years been appearing to and conversing with many people in many a marvellous way.)[1]

Gruffydd's observation seems to have been as true for the twelfth century as it was for the sixteenth. We do not have any early Welsh, Cornish, or Breton statements of belief in King Arthur's survival, but, beginning with the *Gesta regum Anglorum* (c. 1125) of William of Malmesbury, we encounter a series of claims made by Anglo-Norman and Continental writers that the Welsh, Cornish, and Bretons believed Arthur had never died and would return.

---

[1] National Library of Wales, 5276D, 342r, transcribed and translated by Thomas Jones, 'A Sixteenth Century Version of the Arthurian Cave Legend', in *Studies in Language and Literature in Honour of Margaret Schlauch*, ed. Mieczysław Brahmer, Stanisław Helsztyński, and Julian Krzyżanowski (Warsaw: Polish Scientific Publishers, 1966), 179. Also see Ceridwen Lloyd-Morgan, 'From Ynys Wydrin to Glasynbri: Glastonbury in Welsh Vernacular Tradition', in *Glastonbury Abbey and the Arthurian Tradition*, ed. James P. Carley (Cambridge, UK: D. S. Brewer, 2001), 173; Ceridwen Lloyd-Morgan, 'Welsh Tradition in Calais: Elis Gruffydd and his Biography of King Arthur', in *The Fortunes of King Arthur*, ed. Norris J. Lacy (Cambridge, UK: D. S. Brewer, 2005), 91.

The English and Continental formulation of *exspectare Arthurum*, which was exploited by the court writers of Henry II, implies that Arthur escaped the way of all flesh and was a special messianic figure for his Brittonic kinsmen. This idea is at odds with the fundamental Christian teaching that Jesus Christ is the one true messiah and that salvation comes through him alone. The myth of Arthur's survival is a colonial construct, an ethnic fable, that demeans the Brittonic Celts, like the Jews, as a proximate other. It participates in a negative stereotype of the Celts as 'bad Christians' lacking in intelligence and moral rectitude. The narrative legitimizes the forcible invasion of Wales and Brittany. This political agenda speaks to the utility of the myth, but it does not account for why the English became particularly interested in the British Arthur and the idea of his return.

King Arthur, as presented by Geoffrey of Monmouth in the *Historia regum Britannie*, offered the Plantagenet kings of England and their Anglo-Norman vassals a near perfect past. The myth of King Arthur's return, only hinted at in Geoffrey's *Historia*, offered them the prospect of an equally pleasing future. This vision of the future was itself a return to or repetition of the idyllic past.[2] According to Geoffrey, Arthur succeeded in establishing a vast empire based in 'England' that had political and cultural hegemony over much of Western Christendom, especially France. This narrative was particularly attractive to the Plantagenets, as it epitomized their own political aspirations. Arthur, again according to Geoffrey, was a beneficent monarch who did not place himself above the law of the realm, respected the rights and privileges of his subjects, and sought and heeded his barons' counsel, sharing his prosperity with them and rewarding their good service. This *Pax Arthuriana* was wish fulfillment for the lords of the realm of England. Although we do not have any early Brittonic prophecies that speak of Arthur as a revenant savior, the Welsh did have myths involving other returning heroes. But their three most vaunted heroes of prophecy – Owain, Cadwallader, and Conan – were not known for having attained the imperial splendor Geoffrey ascribed to Arthur. For this reason, these authentic heroes of Welsh tradition failed to capture the imagination of the English. Exceptional political achievements in the putative past, coupled with the expectation that 'England' would see another *Pax Arthuriana*, made Arthur uniquely appealing. The idea of a return to an ideal Arthurian past offered a hopeful tone for Henry II's newly established Plantagenet dynasty.

---

[2] This interpretation of Arthur's appeal has been suggested by Caroline D. Eckhardt, 'Prophecy and Nostalgia: Arthurian Symbolism at the Close of the English Middle Ages', in *The Arthurian Tradition: Essays in Convergence*, ed. Mary Braswell and John Bugge (Tuscaloosa: University of Alabama Press), 119.

Adopting the persona of the post-Roman, Brittonic Arthur did, however, require some creative thinking on Henry's part. He had to coopt for himself all that was useful about Arthur whilst jettisoning the rest. This task posed two major obstacles. First, how might a Christian king make positive use of the myth of Arthur's return if the very proposition was contrary to Christian dogma? A solution lay in a figurative interpretation of *exspectare Arthurum*. The myth arguably anticipates the coming of a second Arthur as opposed to the second coming of the original Arthur. This is the idea of *Arthurus redivivus*. The second Arthur is not necessarily a reincarnation of the first Arthur. Rather, he could be understood as a typological successor to Arthur. A figurative and typological approach to *exspectare Arthurum* is not directly at odds with Christian dogma. This brings us to the second obstacle: would not this new Arthur have to be of Brittonic descent? Not necessarily, for Geoffrey of Monmouth had laid a foundation for believing that the crown and the land itself conferred a measure of spiritual connection and continuity that stretched across cultural and dynastic change. Henry II's primary domain was Loegria, and Loegria's borders were the same as those of England. Henry II was the crowned head of England/Loegria and the overlord of multiple petty kingdoms. Henry's circumstances paralleled those of Geoffrey's Arthur. Thus the return of Arthur could be interpreted figuratively, and the defining characteristic of Arthur itself was open to debate. Was Arthur first and foremost a cultural hero to the British race or was he first and foremost the king of Loegria/England? The supporters of Henry II, including Wace, Étienne of Rouen, and the anonymous author of 'Arthur's Letter', espoused the latter understanding, and it is a defensible position. We do not have any surviving record of Henry II's commissioning Arthurian literature or of this king's participating in any form of Arthurian pageantry, but such ludic events were not known to have existed prior to the early thirteenth century. The pairing of Arthur and Henry II in the literature of the period is unmistakable and does offer grounds for assuming the existence of an Arthurian conceit at Henry II's court.

In the final years of Henry II's reign and throughout the reign of Richard I, we can more readily trace Arthurian self-fashioning back to specific members of the Plantagenet dynasty. Henry II's son Geoffrey seems to have led the way in fashioning himself as a successor to Arthur, and he appears to have hoped that this self-representation would make his rule in the 'Arthurian' land of Brittany more palatable to his subjects. This policy reached new heights after Geoffrey's death when his son was named Arthur. Scholars have tended to accept William of Newburgh's account of the christening of Arthur – that Constance of Penthièvre and her Breton advisors selected the name against Henry II's expressed wishes. However, at the time of his birth in 1187, Arthur of Brittany had a very real prospect of someday inheriting the throne of England. Ten years later, when William of Newburgh was writing his *Historia regum Anglicarum* (*c*. 1196–8), John Lackland was actively trying to block Arthur from succeeding to the throne of England. William of Newburgh's account, which portrays the name choice as a Breton act of defiance against the king of England, is consistent with John's aims. The narrative communicates that Arthur of Brittany was not English, but rather a Breton Other. The choice of the name Arthur for Henry II's grandson reflects the Plantagenet hopes for the child's future greatness. Henry II may have even supported the choice. The production of King Arthur's bones at Glastonbury and Richard I's presentation of King Arthur's sword to Arthur of Brittany's anticipated father-in-law, Tancred of Sicily, support my reading of Plantagenet policy.

Geoffrey of Brittany's effort to appear as a native ruler of Brittany foreshadows Henry III's later attempts to make himself and his son (Edward I) seem more English. Henry III venerated St. Edward the Confessor and named his firstborn son and heir after the saint–king. The Arthurian pretension of the Plantagenets in Brittany is also a precursor to Edward I's later efforts to have his son (also named Edward) recognized as prince of Wales, replacing the recently extirpated House of Aberffraw. Edward saw to it that his child was born at Caernarfon, an ancient seat of power in North Wales, and he conferred on him the title of 'prince of Wales'. These are all instances of foreign invaders attempting to legitimize their rule by creating a place for themselves in what they understood to be the history of their conquered subjects.

The seventy-three years extending from the rise of John Lackland to the throne of England (1199) to the death of Henry III (1272) is a murky period in the history of Plantagenet Arthurianism and has not received much scholarly attention. During this time Arthurian interest was blossoming everywhere but at the English royal court. To make sense of this conspicuous absence, I have analyzed the personal histories and characteristics of King John and of Henry III respectively and juxtaposed my findings with the contemporary representations of King Arthur. John's role in the disappearance of Arthur of Brittany goes a long way in explaining his lack of use for King Arthur. John's military and political failings, his viciousness, and his despotic rule also account for why we do not find any evidence of Arthurian self-fashioning coming from this monarch. Henry III seems to have been more ambivalent about

Arthur. His sense of kingly exceptionalism, lack of knightly disposition, and resistence to parliamentary government help explain his lukewarm reception of Arthur. Henry III evidently did commission an Arthurian-themed Great Hall at Dover Castle. Perhaps this is an indication of some personal interest in things Arthurian on his part, but it could just as easily be interpreted as a gesture to please his queen, Eleanor of Provence, who was fond of chivalric romance.

Once again, it must be stressed that John and Henry III reigned when Arthurian literary interest and production was at a high point in Europe. The adaptation of French romances into other European vernaculars and the composition of the great prose Arthurian romances occurred during these years. The earliest records we have of round table events and Arthurian role-playing also date from the first half of the thirteenth century. What were the consequences of the absence of Arthurianism at the English royal court in a period of such interest in Arthur? To respond to this question I considered the situation in England, in Wales, and on the Continent.

The nobility of England looked to the Arthurian past as a golden age of prosperity and harmony between the king and his lords. A foundation for this, as we have seen, existed already in Geoffrey's *Historia*, but the idea of Arthur as the perfect feudal monarch continued to be developed in the London Collection of *Leges Anglorum*. Arthur appears to have been a hero of the baronial reform movement. Arthur's round table and institution of the folkmoot anticipated government by common counsel and parliamentary rule. In the early to mid thirteenth century, members of the nobility organized round table events against the wishes of Henry III. These events afforded the nobility opportunities to come together to bond and to complain about the policies of the king. It is not clear from the surviving records to what extent each round table was Arthurian in character. Although Arthur does not appear to have served the interests of the Plantagenets for three-quarters of the thirteenth century, the English nobility did continue to anglicize Arthur. They treated Arthur – much like St. Edward the Confessor – as a glorious ruler from the golden past whose example justified their resistance to the perceived tyranny of the present regime. From the perspective of the baronage, only after amicable relations between the Crown and the baronage were restored could political expansion begin again.

It was in the thirteenth century, during a lull of English royal Arthurian self-representation, that the first strong evidence I have found of Welsh employment of Arthur for political gain appears. This evidence comes in the form of two undated Latin texts, the *Vera historia de morte Arthuri* and the 'Song of the Welsh'. Neither work, it should be noted, disputes that Arthur died. Quite to the contrary, in the *Vera historia* Arthur's death is politically meaningful: a fatally wounded Arthur chooses to end his days in Gwynedd. This communicates that Arthur was a Welshman at heart. His burial in Gwynedd enabled the princely House of Aberffraw to claim a special connection with the ancient king. What the narratives of the discovery of King Arthur's remains at Glastonbury in the West Country of England did for the Plantagenets, the *Vera historia* did for the ambitious princes of North Wales, Llywelyn ap Iorwerth and Llywelyn ap Gruffudd. In the 'Song of the Welsh', Arthur is presented as a late, great warrior of the past. This political song also conveys that Arthur's blood flows through the veins of all the contemporary warriors of Wales; there was no need for one individual *Arthurus redivivus*. The Welsh Arthurian evocations mentioned above were produced when the House of Aberffraw was consolidating its authority in Wales and when there was civil strife in England. These factors were conducive to the Welsh adoption of Arthur.

Although King John and King Henry III were not Arthurians, the anonymous thirteenth-century Continental authors responsible for the *Queste del Saint Graal, la Mort le Roi Artu*, a prologue to *Guiron le Courtois*, and an epilogue to the Prose *Tristan* recognize a special connection between the House of Plantagenet and King Arthur. According to the narrative framework of these texts, King Arthur had the adventures of his Knights of the Round Table recorded in Latin, and Henry II of England had these Latin narratives translated into French at and for his court. Here we find a literary genealogy linking Arthur with the founder of the Plantagenet dynasty, Henry II. We know that this framework is a fiction because these texts were not written until the time of Henry III. Throughout the thirteenth century, despite the changing character and achievements of the Plantagenet monarchs, the kingdom of England was still widely and consistently acknowledged as the land of Arthur. Although Arthurian role-playing occurred all across Europe, the Continent did not produce any claimants to the mantle of King Arthur that rivaled the Plantagenet association with Arthur. Fernando of Castile, who had Plantagenet ancestry, is the one exception that proves the rule. Continental writers upheld the Plantagenet connection with Arthur.

Edward I reinitiated royal Arthurian self-fashioning, and his practice of it harkened back to the Arthurian gestures and chivalric kingship of Henry II and Richard I. Edward I, like Henry II, was the recipient of much Arthurian flattery during his reign. Wace models Arthur in the *Roman de Brut* after Henry II; Girart d'Amiens crafts Arthur in *Escanor* after Edward I. Wace alludes to the sophistication of Henry II's court through his description of Arthur's court; Girart compliments Edward I for his attentiveness to the logistics of war. In both instances, Arthur is portrayed as an imperial monarch superior in dignity to the petty kings of Wales, Scotland, and Ireland. This tendency preemptively dismisses the Arthurian pretensions of the native Welsh princes, and it favors the figurative interpretation of *Arthurus redivivus*. Gerald of Wales reports that Henry II had planned out the dig and translation of Arthur's remains at Glastonbury, and Edward I, perhaps taking direct inspiration from Gerald's narrative, participated in the second translation of Arthur's remains.

The idea of a post-Conquest king of England as a topological successor to Arthur was developed under Henry II, but Edward I was the king who executed this idea consistently and systematically. The first Anglo-Norman Prose *Brut* chronicles and an assortment of heraldic and genealogical rolls, all of which date from the reign of Edward I, draw a direct line from the British past to the Plantagenet present. All of these textualizations of Arthur affirm that he was a historical figure and that Geoffrey's account of Arthur's deeds was regarded as authoritative.

Like Richard I, Edward I went on crusade in the Holy Land and allowed tournaments to be held in England. Henry II, John, and Henry III viewed tournaments as opportunities for the baronage to conspire against their king. Edward I, in contrast, recognized tournaments and round tables as opportunities to inspire loyalty in his subjects. He presided over round tables and used them to celebrate his victories, reward his faithful servants, make new knights, and display his kingly magnificence. Edward I harnessed the international Arthurian vogue of his time for serious ends – to enhance his domestic and international standing, which in turn would enable him to obtain knightly service from his subjects and build alliances with lords on the Continent. At the dawn of the fourteenth century, Edward I evoked the Arthur of Galfridian history in support of his claim to suzerainty over Scotland. In doing so, he recognized Geoffrey of Monmouth's *Historia regum Britannie* as an authoritative text. He officially and unambiguously claimed the kings of Britain from Brutus to Arthur as his predecessors. Edward, in as much as he was able, completed the anglicization of Arthur and conferred a further measure of credibility and respectability onto the figure. Edward I's conquest of Wales and his success in eradicating the princely House of Aberffraw added substance to his Arthurian pretensions. After the deaths of Llywelyn ap Gruffudd and Dafydd ap Gruffudd, there was no one left to challenge Edward's claim to be *Arthurus redivivus*, and the English king made Welsh princely regalia and the Gwynedd seats of power his own. English royal Arthurianism did not, however, come to an end with the death of Edward I. It would reach new heights under Edward III, the Tudors, the Stuarts, and Queen Victoria. The legacy of Arthur remains to this day part of the fabric of British monarchy. In fact, Arthur appears in the full names of the two most immediate heirs to the throne: Charles Philip Arthur George, prince of Wales (b. 14 November 1948), and William Arthur Philip Louis, duke of Cambridge (b. 21 June 1982). Both are free to draw upon Arthur for their regnal name.

Bibliography

Primary sources

Adam of Damerham, *Libellus de rebus gestis Glastoniensibus*. Edited by Thomas Hearne. 2 vols. Oxford: E Theatro Sheldoniano, 1727.

Aelred of Rievaulx, *Liber de speculo caritatis*. In *Aelredi Rievallensis Opera omnia*, vol. 1: *Opera ascetica*. Edited by Anselm Hoste and Charles H. Talbot. Turnhout: Brepols, 1971.

—— *Liber de speculo caritatis*. Translated by Elizabeth Connor as *The Mirror of Charity*. Kalamazoo, MI: Cistercian Publications, 1990.

Albricus monachus Trium Fontium, *Chronica*. Edited by Paulus Scheffer-Boichorst. In *MGH Scriptores* 23. Edited by Georg Heinrich Pertz, 631–950. Hanover: Hahn, 1874.

Anales Toledanos Primeros, ed. Henrique Florez. In *España Sagrada: Theatro Geographico-Historico de la Iglesia de España*, vol. 23: *Continuacion de las memorias de la Santa Iglesia de Tuy Y Coleccion de los chronicones pequeños publicados, è ineditos, de la Historia de España*, 2nd edn., 382–401. Madrid: La Oficina de la Viuda é Hijo de Marin, 1799.

'The Anglo-Norman *Description of England*: An Edition'. Edited by Alexander Bell. In *Anglo-Norman Anniversary Essays*. Edited by Ian Short, 31–47. London: Anglo-Norman Text Society, 1993.

The Anglo-Saxon Chronicle D-text. In *English Historical Documents*, 500–1042, 2nd edn. Edited by Dorothy Whitelock, 218. London: Routledge, 1979.

Anglo-Scottish Relations, 1174–1328. Edited and translated by E. L. G. Stones. Oxford: Clarendon Press, 1965.

Annales Cambriæ. Edited by John Williams ab Ithel. Rolls Series 20. London: Longman, Green, Longman, and Roberts, 1860.

Annales Cestrienses; or, Chronicle of the Abbey of S. Werburg at Chester. Edited and translated by Richard Copley Christie. London: Lancashire and Cheshire Record Society, 1887.

Annales de Burton (A.D. 1004–1263). In *Annales Monastici*, vol. 1. Edited by Henry Richards Luard, 183–500. Rolls Series 36/1. London: Longman, Green, Longman, Roberts and Green, 1864.

Annales de Margan (A.D. 1066–1232). In *Annales Monastici*, vol. 1. Edited by Henry Richards Luard, 3–40. Rolls Series 36/1. London: Longman, Green, Longman, Roberts, and Green, 1864.

Annales de Sancti Albini Andegavensis. In *Recueil d'Annales Angevines et Vendômoises*. Edited by Louis Halphen, 1–47. Paris: Alphonse Picard et Fils, 1903.

Annales de Theokesberia (A.D. 1066–1263). In *Annales Monastici*, vol. 1. Edited by Henry Richards Luard, 43–180. Rolls Series 36/1. London: Longman, Green, Longman, Roberts, and Green, 1864.

Annales Londoniensis. In *Chronicles of the Reigns of Edward I and Edward II*, vol. 1. Edited by William Stubbs, 1–251. Rolls Series 76/1. London: Longman, 1882.

Annales Monasterii de Waverleia (A.D. 1–1291). In *Annales Monastici*, vol. 2. Edited by Henry Richards Luard, 129–411. Rolls Series 36/2. London: Longman, Green, Longman, Roberts, and Green, 1865.

Annales Prioratus de Dunstaplia (A.D. 1–1297). In *Annales Monastici*, vol. 3. Edited by Henry Richards Luard, 3–408. Rolls Series 36/3. London: Longmans, Green, Reader, and Dyer, 1866.

Annales Prioratus de Wigornia (A.D. 1–1377). In *Annales Monastici*, vol. 4. Edited by Henry Richards Luard, 355–562. Rolls Series 36/4 (London: Longmans, Green, Reader, and Dyer, 1869).

Anonymous of Béthune, 'Extrait d'une chronique française des rois de France par un anonyme de Béthune'. Edited by Léopold Delisle. In *Recueil des historiens des Gaules et de la France* 24, n. 2 (1904): 750–75.

—— *Histoire des ducs de Normandie et des rois d'Angleterre publiée en entier, pour la première fois, d'après deux Manuscrits de la Bibliothèque du Roi*. Edited by Francisque Michel, 1–209. Paris: Jules Renouard, 1840.

'Articles of Grievance (*Monstraunces*), 1297'. In *English Historical Documents*, vol. 3: *1189–1327*. Edited by Harry Rothwell, 469. London: Routledge, 1975.

La Bataille Loquifer. Edited by Monica Barnett. Oxford: Blackwell, 1975.

Bernard, 'Versus contra fidem Britonum'. Edited by Jacob Hammer, 123. In Jacob Hammer, 'Some Leonine Summaries of Geoffrey of Monmouth's *Historia regum Britanniae* and Other Poems'. *Speculum* 6, n. 1 (1931): 114–23.

Béroul, *Tristan*. Edited and translated by Norris J. Lacy. In *Early French Tristan Poems*, vol. 1. Edited by Norris J. Lacy, 12–199. Cambridge, UK: D. S. Brewer, 1998.

Bertran de Born, 'A totz dic qe ja mais non voil'. In *L'amour et la guerre: L'oeuvre de Bertran de Born*. Edited and translated by Gérard Gouiran, 431–44. Aix-en-Provence: Université de Provence, 1985.

Bower, Walter. *Scotichronicon*, vol. 6: Books XI and XII. Edited by Norman F. Shead, Wendy B. Stevenson, and D. E. R. Watt, with Alan Borthwick, R. E. Latham, J. R. S. Phillips, and Martin S. Smith. Aberdeen: Aberdeen University Press, 1991.

'Branwen Daughter of Llŷr'. In *The Mabinogion*, 66–82. Translated by Jeffrey Gantz. London: Penguin Books, 1976.

Brenhinedd y Saesson or The King of the Saxons, BM Cotton Claudius MS. Cleopatra B v and The Black Book of Basingwerk, NLW MS. 7006. Edited and translated by Thomas Jones. Cardiff: University of Wales Press, 1971.

Brut y Tywysogion or the Chronicle of the Princes, Peniarth MS 20 Version. Translated by Thomas Jones. Cardiff: University of Wales Press, 1952. *Red Book of Hergest Version*, 2nd edn. Edited and translated by Thomas Jones. Cardiff: University of Wales Press, 1973.

'Bulla Pape Bonifacii'. In *Anglo-Scottish Relations, 1174–1328: Some Selected Documents*. Edited and translated by E. L. G. Stones, 162–75. Oxford: Clarendon Press, 1965.

Caesarius of Heisterbach, *Dialogus miraculorum*, vol. 5. Edited by Horst Schneider. Turnhout: Brepols, 2009.

Calendar of Chancery Warrants: A.D. 1244–1326; Preserved in the Public Record Office. London: H. M. Stationery Office, 1927.

Calendar of the Charter Rolls, vol. 1: *Henry III, A.D. 1226–1257*; vol. 2: *Henry III–Edward I: A.D. 1257–1300*. London: H. M. Stationery Office, 1903–6.

Calendar of the Patent Rolls Preserved in the Public Record Office: Edward I. 4 vols. London: Her Majesty's Stationery Office, 1893–1901.

Caradoc of Llangarfan, *Vita Gildæ*. In *Two Lives of Gildas by a Monk of Ruys and Caradoc of Llancarfan*. Edited and translated by Hugh William, 84–103. Cymmrodorion Record Series. 1899. Reprint, Felinfach: Llanerch Enterprises, 1990.

Carmeliano, Pietro. *Suasoria Laeticiae* (London, British Library, MS Addit. 33776, fols. 2r–11v). Edited by David Carlson. In David Carlson, 'King Arthur and Court Poems for the Birth of Arthur Tudor in 1486'. *Humanistica Lovaniensia* 36 (1987): 174–83.

'Cartae ad Prioratum de Wigmore, in agro Herefordensi, spectantes, Num. II: *Fundationis et Fundatorum Historia*'. In *Monasticon Anglicanum: A History of the Abbies and Other Monasteries, Hospitals, Frieries, and Cathedral and Collegiate Churches, with their Dependencies in England and Wales*, vol. 6, part 1. Edited by William Dugdale, 348–55. London: T. G. March, 1849.

The Charters of Duchess Constance of Brittany and Her Family, 1171–1221. Edited by Judith Everard and Michael Jones. Woodbridge, UK: Boydell, 1999.

Le Chartrier de l'abbaye prémontrée de Saint-Yved de Braine, 1134–1250. Edited by Olivier Guyotjeannin. Paris: École des chartes, 2000.

Chrétien de Troyes, *Le Chevalier de la charrete (Lancelot)*. In *Christian von Troyes: sämliche Werke, nach allen bekannten Handscriften*, vol. 4: *Der Karrenritter (Lancelot)*. Edited by Wendelin Foerster. Halle: Max Niemeyer, 1899.

     Translated by William W. Kibler as *The Knight of the Cart (Lancelot)*. In Chrétien de Troyes, *Arthurian Romances*, ed. William W. Kibler, 207–94. London: Penguin Books 1991.

—— *Cligés*. In *Christian von Troyes: sämliche Werke, nach allen bekannten Handscriften*, vol. 1. Edited by Wendelin Foerster. Halle: Max Niemeyer, 1884.

     Translated by William W. Kibler. In Chrétien de Troyes, *Arthurian Romances*. Edited by William W. Kibler, 123–205. London: Penguin Books 1991.

—— *Erec et Enide*. In *Christian von Troyes: sämliche Werke, nach allen bekannten Handscriften*, vol. 3: *Erec und Enide*. Edited by Wendelin Foerster. Halle: Max Niemeyer, 1890.

     Translated by Carleton W. Carroll. In Chrétien de Troyes, *Arthurian Romances*. Edited by William W. Kibler, 37–122. London: Penguin Books 1991.

—— *Le Roman de Perceval ou Le Conte du Graal, Édition critique d'après tous les manuscrits*. Edited by Keith Busby. Tübingen: De Gruyter, 1993.

     Translated by William W. Kibler as *The Story of the Grail (Perceval)*. In Chrétien of Troyes, *Arthurian Romances*. Edited by William W. Kibler, 381–494. London: Penguin Books 1991.

Chronica Buriensis / The Chronicle of Bury St. Edmunds 1212–1301. Edited and translated by Antonia Gransden. London: Nelson, 1964.

Chronicle of Glastonbury Abbey: An Edition, Translation and Study of John of Glastonbury's Cronica sive Antiquitates. Edited by James Carley, translated by David Townsend. Woodbridge, UK: Boydell, 1985.

Chronicle of Pierre de Langtoft. Edited and translated by Thomas Wright, 2 vols. Rolls Series 47. London: Longmans, Green, Reader and Dyer, 1866–8.

—— *Édition critique et commentée de Pierre de Langtoft, Le Règne d'Édouard Ier*, vol. 1. Edited by Jean Claude Thiolier. Créteil: University of Paris XII, 1989.

The Chronicle of William de Rishanger of the Barons' Wars / The Miracles of Simon de Montfort. Edited by James Orchard Halliwell. London: Camden Society, 1840.

'Chronicon Britannicum ex collectione veteri MS Ecclesiæ Nannetensis'. Edited by Gui Alexis Lobineau, cols. 30–6. In Gui Alexis Lobineau,

Histoire de Bretagne, composée sur les titres et les auteurs originaux, vol. 2. Paris: Louis Guerin, 1707.

—— Edited by Hyacinthe Morice, cols. 1–8. In Hyacinthe Morice, *Memoires pour servir de preuves* à *l'histoire ecclésiastique et civile de Bretagne*, vol. 1. Paris: Charles Osmont, 1742.

Chronicon de Lanercost (1201–1346). Edited by Joseph Stevenson. Edinburgh: Edinburgh Printing Company, 1839.

Translated by Herbert Maxwell as *The Chronicle of Lanercost*. Glasgow: James Maclehose and Sons, 1913.

Chronicon Universale anonymi Laudunensis von 1154 bis zum Schluss (1219) für akademische Übungen. Edited by Alexander Cartellieri and Wolf Stechele. Leipzig: Dyksche Buchhandlung, 1909.

Chronicon vulgo dictum Chronicon Thomæ Wykes (A.D. 1066–1289). In *Annales Monastici*, vol. 4. Edited by Henry Richards Luard, 6–319. Rolls Series 36/4. London: Longmans, Green, Reader, and Dyer, 1869.

Chroniques de London depuis l'an 44 Hen. III [1259] jusqu'à l'an 17 Edw. III [1343]. Edited by George James Aungier. London: Camden Society, 1844.

Close Rolls of the Reign of Henry III Preserved in the Public Record Office, 14 vols. London: Her Majesty's Stationery Office, 1902–38.

'The Complaint of King John against William de Briouze (c. September 1210), *The Black Book of the Exchequer Text*'. Edited and translated by David Crouch. In *Magna Carta and the England of King John*. Edited by Janet S. Loengard, 168–79. Woodbridge, UK: Boydell, 2010.

Continuations of the Old French Perceval of Chrétien of Troyes, vol. 2: *The First Continuation, Redaction of MSS E, M, Q, U*. Edited by William Roach and Robert H. Ivy. Philadelphia: University of Pennsylvania Press, 1950.

Continuations of the Old French Perceval of Chrétien of Troyes, vol. 4: *The Second Continuation, Redaction of MSS EKLMPQSTUV*. Edited by William Roach. Philadelphia: American Philosophical Society, 1971.

Cotton, Bartholomew. *Historia Anglicana (A.D. 449–1298)*. Edited by Henry Richards Luard, Rolls Series 16. London: Longman, Green, Longman, and Roberts, 1859.

Dante Alighieri. *Purgatorio*. Edited and translated by Anthony Esolen. New York: Modern Library, 2003.

'Detto del Gatto Lupesco'. In *Poeti del Duecento*, vol. 2. Edited by Gianfranco Contini, 285–93. Milan: Riccardo Ricciardi, 1960.

Du Cange, Charles du Fresne, sieur, 'Arturum Exspectare', in Du Cange, et al., *Glossarium mediae et infimae latinitatis*, rev. edn. Niort, France: L. Favre, 1883–7.

Edward I of England, 'A.D. 1283. Summons of Borough Members to a National Council'. In *Select Charters and Other Illustrations of English Constitutional*

History, from the Earliest Times to the reign of Edward the First, 6th edn. Edited by William Stubbs, 467–9. Oxford: Clarendon Press, 1888.

Ekkehard of Aura, *Ekkehardi Chronicon Universale ad a. 1106*. Edited by Georg Heinrich Pertz. In *MGH Scriptores* 6. Edited by Georg Heinrich Pertz, 33–231. Hanover: Hahn, 1843.

Esclarmonde. Edited by Max Schweigel. In *Esclarmonde, Clarisse et Florent, Yde et Olive, drei Fortsetzungen der Chanson von Huon de Bordeaux nach der einzigen turiner Handschrift zum erstenmal veröffenlicht*. Edited by Max Schweigel, 93–126. Marburg: N. G. Elwertische Verlagsbuchhandlung, 1889.

Étienne de Rouen, *Draco Normannicus*. In *Chronicles of the Reigns of Stephen, Henry II, and Richard I*, vol. 2. Edited by Richard Howlett, 589–762. Rolls Series 82/2. London: Longman & Co., 1884.

'The "Evil toll" (Maltote) of 1294–7'. In *English Historical Documents*, vol. 3: *1189–1327*. Edited by Harry Rothwell, 468. London: Routledge, 1975.

'Extracts from the Barling Chronicle', in *Chronicles of the Reigns of Edward I and Edward II*, vol. 2. Edited by William Stubbs, cxiii–cxviii. Rolls Series 76/2. London: Longman & Co, 1883.

'Extrait d'une chronique française des rois de France par un anonyme de Béthune'. Edited by Léopold Delisle. In *Recueil des historiens des Gaules et de la France* 24, n. 2 (1904): 750–5.

Fardd, Bleddyn, 'Englynion marwnad' / 'Elegy in the "englyn" metre'. Edited and translated by Tomos Roberts. In *1282 — Casgliad o Ddogfennau/ A Collection of Documents*. Edited by Rhidian Griffiths, 26–7. Aberystwyth: Llyfrgell Genedlaethol Cymru, 1986.

'The First Charter of Stephen'. In *Select Charters and Other Illustrations of English Constitutional History, from the Earliest Times to the Reign of Edward the First*, 6th edn. Edited by William Stubbs, 119. Oxford: Clarendon Press, 1888.

FitzNicolas, Ralph. 'Ralph FitzNicolas to Ralph, bishop of Chichester, Chancellor, And Stephen de Segrave (Royal Letters, No. 914)'. In *Royal and Other Historical Letters illustrative of the Reign of Henry III*, vol. 1: 1216–35. Edited by Walter Waddington Shirley, 370–1. London: Longman, Green, Longman, and Roberts, 1862.

Flores historiarum. Edited by Henry Richards Luard, 3 vols. Rolls Series 95. London: Her Majesty's Stationery Office, 1890.

Floriant et Florete. Edited and translated (into French) by Annie Combes and Richard Trachsler. Paris: Honoré Champion, 2003.

Foedera, Conventiones, Literæ, et cujuscunque generis acta publica inter Reges Angliæ..., 2nd edn. Edited by Thomas Rymer, 20 vols. London: J. Tonson, 1704–35.

Geffrei Gaimar, *Estoire des Engleis*. Edited and translated by Ian Short. Oxford: Oxford University Press, 2009.

Geoffrey of Monmouth, *Historia regum Britannie*. Edited by Michael D. Reeve. Translated by Neil Wright as The *History of the Kings of England: An Edition and Translation of* De gestis Britonum. Woodbridge, UK: Boydell, 2007.

—— *The Historia regum Britannie of Geoffrey of Monmouth I, Bern, Burgerbibliothek, Ms. 568*. Edited by Neil Wright. Cambridge, UK: D. S. Brewer, 1985.

—— *The Historia regum Britannie of Geoffrey of Monmouth II, The First Variant Version: A Critical Edition*. Edited by Neil Wright. Cambridge, UK: D. S. Brewer, 1988.

—— *Vita Merlini*. Edited and translated by Basil Clarke. Cardiff: University of Wales Press, 1973.

Gerald of Wales, 'Catalogus brevior librorum suorum'. Edited by J. S. Brewer. In *Giraldi Cambrensis opera*, vol. 1. Edited by J. S. Brewer, 421–3. Rolls Series 21/1. London: Longman, Green, Longman, and Roberts, 1861.

—— *De principis instructione liber*. Edited by George F. Warner. In *Giraldi Cambrensis opera*, vol. 8. Edited by George F. Warner, 3–329. Rolls Series 21/8. London: Eyre and Spottiswoode, 1891.

—— *Descriptio Kambriæ*. Edited by James F. Dimock. In *Giraldi Cambrensis opera*, vol. 6. Edited by James F. Dimock, 155–227. Rolls Series 21/6. London: Longmans, Green, Reader, and Dyer, 1868.

—— *Expugnatio Hibernica*. Edited and translated by A. B. Scott and F. X. Martin. Dublin: Royal Irish Academy, 1978.

—— *Itinerarium Kambriæ*. Edited by James F. Dimock. In *Giraldi Cambrensis opera*, vol. 6. Edited by James F. Dimock, 3–152. Rolls Series 21/6. London: Longmans, Green, Reader, and Dyer, 1868.

—— *Speculum Ecclesiæ*. Edited by J. S. Brewer. In *Giraldi Cambrensis opera*, vol. 4. Edited by J. S. Brewer, 3–354. Rolls Series 21/4. London: Longman, 1873.

—— *Topographia Hiberniæ*. Edited by James F. Dimock, In *Giraldi Cambrensis opera*, vol. 5. Edited by James F. Dimock, 3–204. Rolls Series 21/5. London: Longmans, Green, Reader, and Dyer, 1867.

—— (*Giraldus Cambrensis in*) *Topographia Hibernie: Text of the First Recension*. Edited by John J. O'Meara. In *Proceedings of the Royal Irish Academy 52*, sec. C, n. 4 (1949): 113–78.

Gervase of Canterbury, *Chronicle of the Reigns of Stephen, Henry II, and Richard I*. In *The Historical Works of Gervase of Canterbury*, vol. 1. Edited by William Stubbs. Rolls Series 73/1. London: Longmans, 1879.

—— *The Gesta Regum with its Continuation*. In *The Historical Works of Gervase of Canterbury*, vol. 2. Edited by William Stubbs, 3–324. Rolls Series 73/2. London: Longmans, 1880.

Gervase of Tilbury, *Otia Imperialia*. Edited and Translated by S. E. Banks and J. W. Binns Oxford: Clarendon Press, 2002.

Die Gesetze der Angelsachsen. Edited by Felix Liebermann, 3 vols. Halle: Max Niemeyer 1903–16.

Gesta regis Henrici Secundi Benedicti abbatis / The Chronicle of the Reigns of Henry II and Richard I, A. D. 1169–92; Known Commonly under the Name of Benedict of Peterborough. Edited by illiam Stubbs, 2 vols. Rolls Series 49. London: Longmans, Green, Reader, and Dyer, 1867.

Gesta regum Britanniae. In *The Historia Regum Britannie of Geoffrey of Monmouth V: Gesta regum Britanniae*. Edited and translated by Neil Wright. Cambridge, UK: D. S. Brewer, 1991.

Gildas, *De excidio Britonum / The Ruin of the Britain and other Documents*. Edited and translated by Michael Winterbottom. London and Chichester: Phillimore, 1978.

Girart d'Amiens, *Escanor: roman arthurien en vers de la fin du xiiie siècle*. Edited by Richard Trachsler, 2 vols. Geneva: Librairie Droz, 1994.

Gran Conquista de Ultramar. Edited by Louis Cooper, 4 vols. Bogota: Publicaciones del Instituto Caro Y Cuervo, 1979.

Gruffudd ab yr Ynad Coch, 'Awdl farwnad' / 'Elegy in the "awdl" metres'. Edited by J. E. Caerwyn Williams. Translated by Joseph P. Clancy. In *1282–Casgliad o Ddogfennau/ A Collection of Documents*. Edited by Rhidian Griffiths, 30–4. Aberystwyth: Llyfrgell Genedlaethol Cymru, 1986.

Guillaume le Breton, *Gesta Philippi Augusti, Guillelmi Armorici Liber*. In *Oeuvres de Rigord et de Guillaume le Breton: Historiens de Philippe-Auguste*, vol. 1: *Chroniques de Rigord et de Guillaume le Breton*. Edited by H.-François Delaborde, 168–327. Paris: Librairie Renouard, 1882.

—— *Philippide*. In *Oeuvres de Rigord et de Guillaume le Breton: Historiens de Philippe-Auguste*, vol. 2: *Philippide de Guillaume le Breton*. Edited by H.-François Delaborde, 1–385. Paris: Librairie Renouard, 1885.

Guiraut de Calanson, 'Belh senher Dieus ... (planh)'. Edited by Willy Ernst. In Willy Ernst, 'Die Lieder des provenzalischen Trobadors Guiraut von Calanso', *Romanische Forschungen* 44, n. 2 (1930): 255–406.

'*Guiron le Courtois*: le Prologue de Paris, Bibliothèque Nationale, f. fr. 338'. Edited by Roger Lathuillère. In Roger Lathuillère, *Guiron le Courtois: Étude de la tradition manuscrite et analyse critique*, 175–80. Geneva: Librairie Droz, 1966.

Hagnaby Chronicle (excerpt). Translated by R. Geraint Gruffydd. In *1282 — Casgliad o Ddogfennau / A Collection of Documents*. Edited by Rhidian Griffiths, 17. Aberystwyth: Llyfrgell Genedlaethol Cymru, 1986.

Henry, archdeacon of Huntingdon, 'Epistola ad Warinum'. Edited and translated by Diana Greenway. In Henry, Archdeacon of Huntingdon, *Historia Anglorum*. Edited and translated by Diana Greenway, 552–83. Oxford: Clarendon Press, 1996.

—— *Historia Anglorum*. Edited and translated by Diana Greenway (Oxford: Clarendon Press, 1996.

Hériman de Tournai, *Miracula sancte Marie Laudunensis*. Edited and translated by Alain Saint-Denis as *Les Miracles de sainte Marie de Laon*. Paris: CNRS Editions, 2008.

Higden, Ranulf. *Polychronicon Ranulphi Higden, Monachi Cestrensis*, vol. 8. Edited by Joseph Rawson Lumby. Rolls Series 41/8. London: Longman, 1882.

Histoire de Guillaume le Maréchal. Edited by A. J. Holden. Translated by S. Gregory. Historical notes by D. Crouch, 3 vols. London: Anglo-Norman Text Society from Birkbeck College, 2002–6.

Historia Fundationis Ecclesiæ S. Martini Dover. In William Dugdale, *Monasticon Anglicanum: A History of the Abbies and Other Monasteries, Hospitals, Frieries, and Cathedral and Collegiate Churches, with their Dependencies in England and Wales*, vol. 4. Edited and revised by John Caley, Henry Ellis, and Bulkeley Bandinel, 533–4. London: James Bohn, 1846.

The History of Gruffydd ap Cynan: The Welsh Text. Edited and translated by Arthur Jones. Manchester: Manchester University Press, 1910.

Jean de Marmoutier, *Historia Gaufredi ducis Normannorum et comitis Andegavorum*. In *Chroniques des comtes d'Anjou et des seigneurs d'Amboise*. Edited by Louis Halphen and René Poupardin, 172–241. Paris: Auguste Picard, 1913.

Johannes de Hauvilla, *Architrenius*. Edited and translated by Winthrop Wetherbee. Cambridge, UK: Cambridge University Press, 1994.

John of London, *Commendatio Lamentabilis in transitu magni regis Edwardi quarti secundum Johannem de Londonia*. In *Chronicles of the Reigns of Edward I and Edward II*, vol. 2. Edited by William Stubbs, 3–21. Rolls Series 76/2. London: Longman, 1883.

John of Salisbury, 'Thome Cantuariensi archiepiscopo Iohannes Saresberiensis' (Letter 99). In *The Correspondence of Thomas Becket, Archbishop of Canterbury, 1162–1170*, vol. 1: Letters 1–175. Edited and translated by Anne J. Duggan, 452–5. Oxford: Clarendon Press, 2000.

Joseph of Exeter, *Frigii Daretis Yliados libri sex*. In *Werke und Briefe von Joseph Iscanus*. Edited by Ludwig Gompf, 77–210. Leiden: Brill, 1970.

Translated by A. G. Rigg as *Joseph of Exeter: Iliad*. Toronto: Centre for Medieval Studies, 2005.

Lancelot, roman en prose du XIIIᵉ siècle. Edited by Alexandre Micha, 9 vols. Geneva: Droz, 1978–83.

Translated by Samuel N. Rosenberg as *Lancelot, Part I*. In *Lancelot-Grail: The Old French Arthurian Vulgate and Post-Vulgate in Translation*, vol. 3. Edited by Norris J. Lacy. Cambridge, UK: D. S. Brewer, 2010.

The Latin Texts of the Welsh Laws. Edited by H. D. Emanuel. Board of Celtic Studies, University of Wales. Cardiff: University of Wales Press, 1967.

Layamon's Brut, or Hystoria Brutonum. Edited and translated by W. R. J. Barron and S. C. Weinberg. Harlow, UK: Longman Group, 1995.

Laȝamon, *Brut, Edited from British Museum MS. Cotton Caligula A.ix and British Museum MS. Cotton Otho C.xiii*. Edited by G. L. Brook and R. F. Leslie, 2 vols. London: Oxford University Press, 1963–78.

Liber de compositione castri Ambazie. In *Chroniques des comtes d'Anjou et des seigneurs d'Amboise*. Edited by Louis Halphen and René Poupardin, 1–24. Paris: Auguste Picard, 1913.

Liber Custumarum Compiled in the Early Part of the Fourteenth Century with Extracts from the Cottonian MS. Claudius, D. ii. In *Monumenta Gildhallæ Londoniensis: Liber Albus, Liber Custumarum et Liber Horn*, vol. 2, part 1. Edited by Henry Thomas Riley. Rolls Series 12/2. London: Longman, Green, Longman, and Roberts, 1860.

Littere Wallie, Preserved in Liber A in the Public Record Office. Edited by John Goronwy Edwards. Cardiff: University of Wales Press, 1940.

Magna Carta, 1215. Edited and translated by James Clarke Holt, 448–73. In James Clarke Holt, *Magna Carta*, 2nd edn. Cambridge, UK: Cambridge University Press, 1992.

Mannyng (of Brunne), Robert. *The Chronicle*. Edited by Idelle Sullens. Binghamton, NY: Medieval and Renaissance Texts and Studies, Binghamton University, 1996.

Map, Walter. *De nugis curialium*. Edited and translated by M. R. James. Revised by Christopher Nugent Lawrence and R. A. B. Mynors. Oxford: Clarendon Press, 1983.

Marcabru, 'Al prim comenz de l'invernailh'. In *Marcabru: A Critical Edition*. Edited and translated by Simon Gaunt, Ruth Harvey, and Linda Paterson. Cambridge: D. S. Brewer, 2000.

Marie de France, *Le Lai de Lanval*. Edited by Jean Rychner. Geneva: Librairie Droz, 1958.

La mort le roi Artu: Roman du xiiiᵉ siècle. Edited by Jean Frappier. Geneva: Droz, 1954.

Translated as *The Death of Arthur*. Translated by Norris J. Lacy. *Lancelot-Grail: The Old French Arthurian Vulgate and Post-Vulgate in Translation*, vol. 7. Edited by Norris J. Lacy. Cambridge, UK: D. S. Brewer, 2010.

Mousquet, Philippe. *Chronique rimée de Philippe Mouskes*. Edited by Baron de Reiffenberg, 2 vols. Brussels: M. Hayez, 1836–8.

Muntaner, Ramon. *Crònica*. Edited by Marina Gustà, 2 vols. Barcelona: Edicions 62, 1979.

The Chronicle of Muntaner. Translated by Anna Kinsky Goodenough. Hakluyt Society 50. London: Hakluyt Society, 1920–1.

In *Les quatre grans cròniques*. Edited by Ferran Soldevila, 665–944. Barcelona: Editorial Selecta, 1971.

Murimuth, Adam. *Continuatio Chronicarum*. Edited by Edward Maunde Thompson, 4–276. Rolls Series 93. London: Eyre and Spottiswoode, 1889.

The Oldest Anglo-Norman Prose Brut Chronicle. Edited and translated by Julia Marvin. Woodbridge, UK: Boydell, 2006.

Opus Chronicorum (MS. Cotton Claudius D. vi., fols. 115a–134b). In *Chronica Monasterii S. Albani*, vol. 3. Edited by Henry Thomas Riley, 3–59. Rolls Series 28/3. London: Longmans, Green, Reader, and Dyer, 1866.

Orderic Vitalis, *The Ecclesiastical History of Orderic Vitalis*, 6 vols. Edited and translated Marjorie Chibnall. Oxford: Clarendon Press, 1969–80.

Paris, Matthew. *Chronica Majora*. Edited by Henry Richards Luard, 7 vols. Roll Series 57. London: Longman, 1872–83.

—— *Historia Anglorum sive ut vulgo dicitur, Historia Minor, item, ejusdem abbreviatio chronicorum Angliæ*. Edited by Frederick Madden, 3 vols. Rolls Series 44. London: Longmans, Green, Reader, and Dyer, 1866–9.

The Parliamentary Writs and Writs of Military Summons…, vol. 1. Edited by Francis Palgrave. London: George Eyre and Andrew Strahan, 1827.

Patent Rolls of the Reign of Henry III Preserved in the Public Record Office, 6 vols. London: Mackie and Co., 1901–13.

Peter of Blois, *Contra perfidiam Judæorum*. In *Patrologia Latina*, vol. 207. Edited by J. P. Migne, cols. 823–70. Paris, 1855.

—— *Epistolæ*. In *Petri Blesensis Bathoniensis archidiaconi Opera Omnia*, vol. 1: *Epistolæ*. Edited by John Allen Giles. Oxford: I. H. Parker, 1847.

—— 'Quod amicus suggerit'. Edited and translated by Peter Dronke. In Peter Dronke, 'Peter of Blois and Poetry at the Court of Henry II', *Medieval Studies* 38 (1976): 206–9.

Peter the Venerable, *Adversus Iudeorum inveteratam duritiem*. Translated by Irven M. Resnick as *Against the Inveterate Obduracy of the Jews*. Washington: Catholic University of America Press, 2013.

Philippe de Novare, Mémoires, 1218–*1243*. Edited by Charles Kohler. Paris: Librairie Ancienne Honoré Champion, 1913.

'A Plea Roll of Edward I's Army in Scotland, 1296'. Edited by Cynthia J. Neville. In *Miscellany of the Scottish Historical Society* 11, 5th ser., iii (1990): 7–133.

Polo, Marco. *Le Devisement du Monde*, vol. 1. Edited by Philippe Ménard. Geneva: Droz, 2001.

Prophetia Anglicana, Merlini Ambrosii Britanni…. Frankfurt: Typis Ioachimi Bratheringii, 1603.

Pseudo-Methodius, *Apocalypse; An Alexandrian World Chronicle*. Edited and translated by Benjamin Garstad, 1–139. Cambridge, MA: Harvard University Press, 2012.

—— *Apocalypse* [R2]. Edited by Otto Prinz, 6–17. In Otto Prinz, 'Eine frühe abendländishe Aktualisierung der lateinischen Übersetzung des Pseudo-Methodios'. *Deutshes Archiv für Erforschung des Mittelalters* 41, n. 1 (1985): 1–23.

La Queste del Saint Graal: Roman du xiii siècle. Edited by Albert Pauphilet. Paris: Édouard Champion, 1923.

—— Translated by E. Jane Burns as *The Quest for the Holy Grail. Lancelot-Grail: The Old French Arthurian Vulgate and Post-Vulgate in Translation*, vol. 6. Edited by Norris J. Lacy. Cambridge, UK: D. S. Brewer, 2010.

Ralph of Caen, *Gesta Tancredi*. Translated by Bernard S. Bachrach and David S. Bachrach as *The Gesta Tancredi of Ralph of Caen: A History of the Normans on the First Crusade*. Aldershot, UK: Ashgate, 2005.

Ralph of Coggeshall, *Chronicon Anglicum*. Edited by Joseph Stevenson. Rolls Series 66. London: Longman, 1875.

Ralph de Diceto, *Ymagines historiarum* (A.D. 1148–1202). In *The Historical Works of Master Ralph de Diceto, Dean of London*, vol. 2. Edited by William Stubbs, 3–174. Rolls Series 68/2. London: Eyre and Spottiswoode, 1876.

'Red Book of the Exchequer (Record Office), fol. 232'. In *English Coronation Records*. Edited and translated by Leopold G. Wickham Legg, 57–65. Westminster: Archibald Constable, 1901.

Register and Chronicle of the Abbey of Aberconway; from the Harleian MS 3725. Edited by Henry Ellis. London: Camden Society, 1847.

Registrum epistolarum fratris Johannis Peckham archiepiscopi Cantuariensis. Edited by Charles Trice Martin, 3 vols. Rolls Series 77. London: Longman, 1882–6.

Richard of Devizes, *Chronicon Ricardi Divisiensis de rebus gestis Ricardi Primi regis Angliæ*. Edited by Joseph Stevenson. London: Sumptibus Societatis, 1838.

Rigord, *Gesta Philippi Augusti, Rigordi Liber*. In *Oeuvres de Rigord et de*

Guillaume le Breton: Historiens de Philippe-Auguste, vol. 1: *Chroniques de Rigord et de Guillaume le Breton*. Edited by H.-François Delaborde, 1–167. Paris: Librairie Renouard, 1882.

Robert de Boron, *Joseph d'Arimathie: A Critical Edition of the Verse and Prose Versions*. Edited by Robert O'Gorman. Toronto: Pontifical Institute of Mediaeval Studies, 1995.

Robert of Reims, *Historia Iherosolimitana*. Translated by Carol Sweetenham as *Robert the Monk's History of the First Crusade*. Crusade Texts in Translation 11. Aldershot, UK: Ashgate, 2005.

Robert of Torigni, 'Chronica Roberti de Torigneio'. In *Chronicles of the Reigns of Stephen, Henry II, and Richard I*, vol. 4. Edited by Richard Howlett, 81–315. Rolls Series 82/4. London: Longman & Co., 1890.

Roger of Howden, *Chronica Magistri Rogeri de Houedene*. Edited by William Stubbs, 4 vols. Rolls Series 51. London: Longmans, Green, Reader, and Dyer, 1868–71.

Roger of Wendover, *Rogeri de Wendover liber qui dicitur flores historiarum ab anno domini MCLIV, annoque Henrici Anglorum regis secundi primo*. Edited by Henry G. Hewlett, 3 vols. Rolls Series 84. London: Longman, 1886–9.

Rotuli Litterarum Patentium in Turri Londinensi Asservati. Edited by Thomas Duffus Hardy, vol. 1, part I. London: Commissioners of the Public Records of the Kingdom, 1835.

Rustichello da Pisa, *Compilation*. Edited as *Il romanzo arturiano di Rustichello da Pisa*. Edited and translated into Italian by Fabrizio Cigni. Pisa: Pacini Editore, 1994.

—— *Le roman en prose de Tristan; Le roman de Palamède et la compilation de Rusticien de Pise*. Edited by Eilert Löseth, 423–74. Paris: Emile Bouillon, 1890.

Sarrasin, *Le Roman du Hem*. Edited by Albert Henry. Brussels: University of Brussels, 1939.

'Un sirventés politique de 1230'. Edited by Alfred Jeanroy. In *Mélanges d'histoire du moyen âge offerts à M. Ferdinand Lot*, 275–83. Paris: Champion, 1925.

Sone von Nausay. Edited by Moritz Goldschmidt. Tübingen: Gedruckt für ded litterarischen Verein in Stuttgart, 1899.

'Song of the Welsh'. In *Political Songs of England from the Reign of John to that of Edward II*. Edited and translated by Thomas Wright, 56–8. London: Camden Society, 1839.

As 'Appel des Bretons aux armes'. In *Poeseos popularis ante saeculum duodecimum latine decantatae reliquias*. Edited by Edélstand du Méril, 275–7. Paris: Brockhaus et Avenarius, 1843.

As 'Trucidare Saxones: A Cambro-Latin martial poem'. Edited and translated by David Howlett. In David Howlett, 'A Triad of Texts about Saint David'. In *St. David of Wales: Cult, Church and Nation*. Edited by J. Wyn Evans and Jonathan M. Wooding, 268–9. Woodbridge, UK: Boydell, 2007.

La suite du roman de Merlin. Edited by Gilles Roussineau. Geneva: Droz, 2006. Translated by Martha Asher as *The Post-Vulgate Cycle: The Merlin Continuation*. In *Lancelot-Grail: The Old French Arthurian Vulgate and Post-Vulgate in Translation*, vol. 8. Edited by Norris J. Lacy. Cambridge, UK: D. S. Brewer, 2010.

Tratado de la Iglesia de Burgos. Edited by Henrique Florez. In *España Sagrada. Theatro Geographico-Historico de la Iglesia de España*, vol. 26: *Contiene el estado antiguo de las Iglesias de Auca, de Valpuesta, y de Burgos justificado con instrumentos legitimos, y Memorias ineditas*, 166–441. Madrid: La Oficina de Pedro Marin, 1771.

Le roman de Tristan en prose. Edited by Renée L. Curtis, 3 vols. Cambridge, UK: D. S. Brewer, 1985.

Le roman de Tristan en prose (version de manuscrit fr. 757 de la Bibliothèque nationale de Paris), 5 vols. Vol. 1 edited by Joël Blanchard and Michel Quéreuil. Vol. 2 edited by Noël Laborderie and Thierry Delcourt. Vol. 3 edited by Jean-Paul Ponceau. Vol. 4 edited by Monique Léonard and Francine Mora under the direction of Philippe Ménard. Vol. 5 edited by Christine Ferlampin-Acher under the direction of Philippe Ménard. Paris: Honoré Champion, 1997–2007. Translated by Renée L. Curtis as *The Romance of Tristan: The Thirteenth-century Old French 'Prose Tristan'*. Oxford: Oxford University Press, 1994.

Trevet, Nicholas. *Annales sex regum Angliæ, qui a comitibus Andegavensibus originem traxerunt (A.D. M.C.XXXVI.–M.CCC.VII.)*. Edited by Thomas Hog. London: Sumptibus Societatis, 1845.

Trioedd Ynys Prydein. Edited and translated by Rachel Bromwich. Cardiff: University of Wales Press, 2006.

Vera historia de morte Arthuri. Edited and translated by Michael Lapidge. In *Glastonbury Abbey and the Arthurian Tradition*. Edited by James P. Carley, 115–41. Cambridge, UK: D. S. Brewer, 2001.

Vidal, Peire. 'Ges pel temps fer e brau'. Edited and translated by Veronica M. Fraser. In Veronica M. Fraser, *The Songs of Peire Vidal: Translation and Commentary*, 229–33. New York: Peter Lang, 2006.

—— 'Pus tornatz sui en Proensa'. Edited and translated by Veronica M. Fraser. In Veronica M. Fraser, *The Songs of Peire Vidal: Translation and Commentary*, 62–5. New York: Peter Lang, 2006.

Villani, Giovanni. *Nuova Cronica*. Edited by Giovanni Porta, 3 vols. Parma: Ugo Guanda Editore, 1991.

Wace, *Roman de Brut*. Edited by Ivor Arnold, 2 vols. Paris: Société des anciens textes français, 1938–40.

—— Edited and translated by Judith Weiss as *A History of the British: Text and Translation*, rev. edn. Exeter: University of Exeter Press, 2002.

Walter of Châtillon, *Alexandreis*. Edited by Martin L. Colker. Padua: Antenore, 1978.

—— 'Dum contemplor animo seculi tenorem'. In *The Shorter Poems: Christmas Hymns, Love Lyrics, and Moral-Satirical Verse*. Edited and Translated by David A. Traill, 206–17. Oxford: Clarendon Press, 2013.

—— *Tractatus sive Dialogus ... contra Judaeos*. In *Patrologia Latina*, vol. 209. Edited by J. P. Migne, cols. 423–53. Paris, 1855.

Walter of Coventry, *Memoriale fratris Walteri de Coventria*. Edited by William Stubbs, 2 vols. Rolls Series 58. London: Longman, 1872–3.

Walter of Guisborough, Cronica *Walteri de Gyseburne: The Chronicle of Walter of Guisborough, Previously Edited as the Chronicle of Walter of Hemingford or Hemingburgh*. Edited by Harry Rothwell. London: Camden Society, 1957.

Walter Map, *De Nugis Curialium*. Edited and translated by M. R. James. Revised by C. N. L. Brooke and R. A. B. Mynors. Oxford: Clarendon Press, 1983.

William of Malmesbury, *De Antiquitate Glastonie Ecclesie*. Edited and translated by John Scott. In John Scott, *The Early History of Glastonbury: Edition, Translation and Study of William of Malmesbury's* De Antiquitate Glastonie Ecclesie, 40–167. Woodbridge, UK: Boydell, 1981.

—— *Gesta regum Anglorum*. Edited by Roger Aubrey Baskerville Mynors, completed Rodney Malcolm Thomson and Michael Winterbottom, 2 vols. Oxford: Clarendon Press, 1998–9.

—— *Vita Sancti Dunstani*. In *Memorials of Saint Dunstan, Archbishop of Canterbury*. Edited by William Stubbs, 250–324. Rolls Series 63. London: Longman, 1874.

Willelmi Rishanger, *Monachi S. Albani, Chronica (MS. Cotton Faustina B. ix)*. In *Chronica Monasterii S. Albani*, vol. 2. Edited by Henry Thomas Riley, 1–230. Rolls Series 28/2. London: Longman, Green, Longman, Roberts, and Green, 1865.

—— *Gesta Edwardi Primi, Regis Angliæ* (MS. Bibl. Regi. 14 C. i., and MS. Cotton Claudius D. vi.)'. In *Chronica Monasterii S. Albani*, vol. 2. Edited by Henry Thomas Riley, 411–21. Rolls Series 28/2. London: Longman, Green, Longman, Roberts, and Green, 1865.

William of Newburgh, *Historia rerum Anglicarum*. In *Chronicles of the Reigns of Stephen, Henry II, and Richard I*, vol. 1: *Containing the First Four Books of the* Historia rerum Anglicarum *of William of Newburgh.* Edited by Richard Howlett. Roll Series 82/1. London: Longman & Co., 1884.

—— 'The Fifth Book of the *"Historia rerum Anglicarum"'*. In *Chronicles of the Reigns of Stephen, Henry II, and Richard I*, vol. 2. Edited by Richard Howlett, 415–500. Rolls Series 82/2. London: Longman & Co., 1884.

Winchelsey, Robert. *Registrum Roberti Winchelsey Cantuariensis Archiepiscopi.* Edited by Rose Graham, 2 vols. Oxford: Oxford University Press, 1956.

Yder, The Romance of. Edited and translated by Alison Adams. Cambridge, UK: D. S. Brewer, 1983.

Der altfranzösische Yderroman. Edited by Heinrich Gelzer. Dresden: Max Niemeyer, 1913.

Secondary Sources

Abulafia, Anna Sapir. 'Jewish–Christian Disputations and the Twelfth-century Renaissance'. *Journal of Medieval History* 15, n. 2 (1989): 105–25.

—— 'Walter of Châtillon: A Twelfth-century Poet's Engagement with Jews'. *Journal of Medieval History* 31, n. 3 (2005): 265–86.

Age of Chivalry: Art in Plantagenet England, 1200–1400. Edited by Jonathan Alexander and Paul Binski. London: Weidenfeld and Nicolson, 1987.

Alexander, Flora. 'Late Medieval Scottish Attitudes to the Figure of King Arthur: A Reassessment'. *Anglia* 93 (1975): 17–34.

Alexander, Paul J. 'The Medieval Legend of the Last Roman Emperor and its Messianic Origin'. *Journal of the Warburg and Courtauld Institutes* 41 (1978):1–15.

Auerbach, Erich. *Mimesis: The Representation of Reality in Western Literature.* Translated by Willard Trask. Garden City, NY: Doubleday Anchor Books, 1957.

Aurell, Martin. 'Henry II and Arthurian Legend'. Translated by Nicholas Vincent, 362–94. In *Henry II: New Interpretations.* Edited by Christopher Harper-Bill and Nicholas Vincent. Woodbridge, UK: Boydell, 2007.

—— *La légende du Roi Arthur, 550–1250.* Paris: Perrin, 2007.

Barber, Richard. *The Knight and Chivalry,* rev. edn. Woodbridge, UK: Boydell, 2000.

—— 'The *Vera historia de morte Arthuri* and its Place in Arthurian Tradition'. In *Glastonbury Abbey and the Arthurian Tradition.* Edited by James P. Carley, 101–13. Cambridge, UK: D. S. Brewer, 2001.

—— 'Was Mordred Buried at Glastonbury? Arthurian Tradition at Glastonbury in the Middle Ages'. In *Glastonbury Abbey and the Arthurian Tradition.* Edited by James P. Carley, 145–59. Cambridge, UK: D. S. Brewer, 2001.

Barker, Juliet. *The Tournament in England 1100–1400*. Woodbridge, UK: Boydell, 1986.

Barnes, Geraldine. 'Arthurian Chivalry in Old Norse'. *Arthurian Literature* VII (1987): 50–102.

Barron, W. R. J. '*Bruttene Deorling*: An Arthur for Every Age'. In *The Fortunes of King Arthur*. Edited by Norris J. Lacy, 47–65. Cambridge, UK: D. S. Brewer, 2005.

—— 'The Idiom and the Audience of Laȝamon's *Brut*'. In *Laȝamon: Contexts, Language, and Interpretation*. Edited by Rosamund Allen, Lucy Perry, and Jane Roberts, 157–84. London: King's College London Centre for Late Antique and Medieval Studies, 2002.

Barrow, G. W. S. *Robert Bruce and the Community of the Realm of Scotland*, 4th edn. Edinburgh: Edinburgh University Press, 2005.

Bartlett, Robert. *Gerald of Wales, 1146–1223*. Oxford: Clarendon Press, 1982.

Bateson, Mary. 'A London Municipal Collection of the Reign of John'. *English Historical Review*, 17, n. 67 (1902): 480–511.

—— 'A London Municipal Collection of the Reign of John, Part II'. *English Historical Review*, 17, n. 68 (1902): 707–30.

Baumgartner, Emmanuèle. 'Luce del Gat et Hélie de Boron, le chevalier et l'écriture'. *Romania* 106 (1985): 326–40.

—— 'Sur quelques constantes et variations de l'image de l'écrivain (xii⁰–xiii⁰ siècle)'. In *Auctor et Auctoritas: Invention et conformisme dans l'écriture médiévale, Actes du colloque de Saint-Quentin-en-Yvelines (14–16 juin 1999)*. Edited by Michel Zimmermann, 391–400. Paris: École des Chartes, 2001.

Bennett, Matthew. 'Stereotype Normans in Old French Vernacular Literature'. *Anglo-Norman Studies* IX (1987): 25–42.

Berard, Christopher. 'King Arthur and the Canons of Laon'. *Arthuriana* 26, n. 3 (2016): 91–119.

Berger, David. 'The Attitude of St Bernard of Clairvaux toward the Jews'. *Proceedings of the American Academy for Jewish Research* 40 (1972): 89–108.

—— 'Mission to the Jews and Jewish-Christian Contacts in the Polemical Literature of the High Middle Ages'. *American Historical Review* 91, n. 3 (1986): 576–91.

Berthelot, Anne. *Figures et fonction de l'écrivain au XIIIe siècle*. Montreal and Paris: Université de Montréal, Institut d'Études Médiévales, 1991.

Blacker, Jean. *The Faces of Time: Portrayal of the Past in Old French and Latin Historical Narrative of the Anglo-Norman Regnum*. Austin: University of Texas Press, 1994.

Bloch, R. Howard. 'The Text as Inquest: Form and Function in the Pseudo-Map Cycle'. *Mosaic* 8, n. 4 (1975): 107–19.

Bogdanow, Fanni. 'Robert de Boron's Vision of Arthurian History'.

Arthurian Literature XIV (1996): 19–52.

Bonura, Christopher. 'When did the Legend of the Last Emperor Originate? A New Look at the Textual Relationship between *The Apocalypse of Pseudo-Methodius* and the *Tiburtine Sibyl*'. *Viator* 47, n. 3 (2016): 47–100.

Borenius, Tancred. 'The Cycles of Images in the Palaces and Castles of Henry III'. *Journal of the Warburg and Courtauld Institutes* 6 (1943): 40–50.

Boulton, D'A. J. D. 'Classical Knighthood as Nobiliary Dignity: The Knighting of Counts and Kings' Sons in England, 1066–1272'. In *Medieval Knighthood V: Papers from the Sixth Strawberry Hill Conference 1994*. Edited by Stephen Church and Ruth Harvey, 41–100. Woodbridge, UK: Boydell, 1995.

Boutet, Dominique. *Charlemagne et Arthur: ou le roi imaginaire*. Paris: Librairie Honoré Champion, 1992.

Bradbury, Jim. 'Philip Augustus and King John: Personality and History'. In *King John: New Interpretations*. Edited by S. D. Church, 347–61. Woodbridge, UK: Boydell, 1999.

Brault, Gerard J. 'Arthurian Heraldry and the Date of *Escanor*'. *Bulletin Bibliographique de la Société International Arthurienne* 11 (1959): 81–8.

—— *Early Blazon: Heraldic Terminology in the Twelfth and Thirteenth Centuries with Special Reference to Arthurian Literature*. Oxford: Clarendon Press, 1972.

—— 'Literary Uses of Heraldry in the Twelfth and Thirteenth Centuries'. In *The Court Reconvenes: Courtly Literature Across the Disciplines*. Edited by Barbara K. Altmann and Carleton W. Carroll, 15–26. Cambridge, UK: D.S. Brewer, 2003.

—— *The Rolls of Arms of Edward I*, 2 vols. Woodbridge, UK: Boydell Press for the Society of Antiquaries of London, 1997.

Bresc, Henri. 'Excalibur en Sicile'. *Medievalia* 7 (1987): 7–21.

Breeze, Andrew. 'The Date and Politics of "The Song of the Welsh"'. *Antiquaries Journal* 88 (2008): 190–7.

Broadhurst, Karen M. 'Henry II of England and Eleanor of Aquitaine: Patrons of Literature in French?' *Viator* 27 (1996): 53–84.

Brodie, Allan. *Arthur's Hall, Dover Castle, Kent: Analysis of the Building. Historical Building Report*. Swindon: English Heritage, 2011.

Brooke, Christopher N. L. and Gillian Keir, *London 800–1216: The Shaping of a City*. Berkeley: University of California Press, 1975.

Brown, Michelle P. and James P. Carley, 'A Fifteenth-Century Revision of the Glastonbury Epitaph'. In *Glastonbury Abbey and the Arthurian Tradition*. Edited by James P. Carley, 193–204. Cambridge, UK: D. S. Brewer, 2001.

Brown, R. Allen. *Dover Castle, Kent (Ministry of Public Building and Works Official Guide-Book)*. London: Her Majesty's Stationery Office, 1966.

Bullock-Davies, Constance. 'Chrétien de Troyes and England'. *Arthurian Literature* I (1981): 1–61.

—— '"Exspectare Arturum"': Arthur and the Messianic Hope'. *Bulletin of the Board of Celtic Studies* 29, n. 3 (1981): 432–40.

—— *Menestrellorum Multitudo: Minstrels at a Royal Feast*. Cardiff: University of Wales Press, 1978.

—— 'Welsh Minstrels at the Courts of Edward I and II'. *Transactions of the Honourable Society of Cymmrodorion* (1972/1973): 104–22.

Bumke, Joachim. *Höfische Kultur: Literatur und Gesellschaft im hohen Mittelalter*. Translated by Thomas Dunlap as *Courtly Culture: Literature and Society in the High Middle Ages*. New York: Overlook Duckworth, 1991.

Carley, James P. 'Arthur in English History'. In *The Arthur of the English: The Arthurian Legend in Medieval English Life and Literature*, rev. edn. Edited by W. R. J. Barron, 47–57. Cardiff: University of Wales Press, 2001.

—— 'The Discovery of the Holy Cross of Waltham at Montacute, the Excavation of Arthur's Grave at Glastonbury Abbey, and Joseph of Arimathea's Burial'. In *Glastonbury Abbey and the Arthurian Tradition*. Edited by James P. Carley, 303–8. Cambridge, UK: D. S. Brewer, 2001.

—— *Glastonbury Abbey: The Holy House at the Head of the Moors Adventurous*. Woodbridge, UK: Boydell, 1988.

Carlson, David. 'Anglo-Latin Literature in the Later Middle Ages'. In *The Cambridge Companion to Medieval English Culture*. Edited by Andrew Galloway, 195–216. Cambridge, UK: Cambridge University Press, 2011.

—— 'King Arthur and Court Poems for the Birth of Arthur Tudor in 1486'. *Humanistica Lovaniensia* 36 (1987): 147–83.

Carpenter, D[avid] A. 'Abbot Ralph of Coggeshall's Account of the Last Years of King Richard and the First Years of King John'. *English Historical Review* 113, n. 454 (1998): 1210–30.

—— 'King Henry III and Saint Edward the Confessor: The Origins of the Cult'. *English Historical Review* 122, n. 498 (2007): 865–91.

—— 'Kings, Magnates and Society: the Personal Rule of King Henry III, 1234–58'. *Speculum* 60, n. 1 (1985): 39–70.

—— *The Minority of Henry III*. Berkeley: University of California Press, 1990.

Cassard, Jean-Christophe. 'Arthur est vivant! Jalons pour une enquête sur le messianisme royal au moyen âge', *Cahiers de civilisation médiévale* 32, n. 126 (1989): 135–46.

Castiñeiras, Manuel. 'D'Alexandre à Arthur: L'imaginaire normand dans la mosaïque d'Otrante'. *Cahiers de Saint-Michel de Cuxo* 37 (2006): 135–53.

Cavanaugh, Susan H. 'Royal Books: King John to Richard II'. *The Library*, 6th ser., 10, n. 4 (1988): 304–16.

Chambers, E. K. *Arthur of Britain*, rev. edn. Cambridge, UK: Speculum Historiale, 1964.

Charles-Edwards, T. M. 'The Date of the Four Branches of the Mabinogi'. *Transactions of the Honourable Society of Cymmrodorion* (1970): 263–98.

Chase, Carol J. 'La fabrication du Cycle du *Lancelot-Graal*', *Bulletin Bibliographique de la Société International Arthurienne* 61 (2009): 261–80.

Chauou, Amaury. '*Arturus redivivus: Royauté* arthurienne et monarchie politique à la cour Plantagenêt (1154–1199)'. In *Noblesses de l'espace Plantagenêt (1154–1224), Table ronde tenue à Poitiers, le 13 mai 2000*. Edited by Martin Aurell, 67–78. Poitiers: Centre d'études supérieures de civilisation médiévale, 2001.

—— *L'Idéologie Plantagenêt: Royauté arthurienne et monarchie politique dans l'espace Plantagenêt (XIIᵉ–XIIIᵉ siècles)*. Rennes: Presses Universitaires de Rennes, 2001.

Cigni, Fabrizio. 'French Redactions in Italy: Rustichello da Pisa'. In *The Arthur of the Italians: The Arthurian Legend in Medieval Italian Literature and Culture*. Edited by Gloria Allaire and F. Regina Psaki, 21–40. Cardiff: University of Wales Press, 2014.

Clanchy, M[ichael]. T. 'Did Henry III Have a Policy?'. *History* 53, n. 178 (1968): 203–19.

—— *From Memory to Written Record: England 1066–1307*, 3rd edn. Oxford: Wiley-Blackwell, 2013.

Cline, Ruth Huff. 'The Influence of Romances on Tournaments of the Middle Ages'. *Speculum* 20, n. 2 (1945): 204–11.

Colker, Marvin L. 'Two Previously Unprinted Chronicles of the Reign of Edward I', in *'A Miracle of Learning': Studies in Manuscripts and Irish Learning. Essays in Honour of William O'Sullivan*, ed. Toby Barnard, Dáibhí Ó Cróinín, and Katharine Simms. Aldershot, UK: Ashgate, 1998, 101–21.

Collingwood, W. G. 'Arthur and Athelstan', *Saga-Book of the Viking Society for Northern Research* 10 (1928–9): 132–44.

Cook, John. *English Medieval Shrines*. Woodbridge, UK: Boydell, 2011.

Coote, Lesley A. *Prophecy and Public Affairs in Later Medieval England*. York: York Medieval Press, 2000.

Corner, David. 'The *Gesta Regis Henrici Secundi* and *Chronica* of Roger, Parson of Howden'. *Bulletin of the Institute of Historical Research* 56, n. 134 (1983): 126–44.

Crick, Julia. 'The British Past and the Welsh Future: Gerald of Wales, Geoffrey of Monmouth and Arthur of Britain'. *Celtica* 23 (1999): 60–75.

—— *The Historia regum Britannie of Geoffrey of Monmouth III: A Summary Catalogue of the Manuscripts*. Cambridge, UK: D. S. Brewer, 1989.

—— *The Historia regum Britannie of Geoffrey of Monmouth IV: Dissemination and Reception in the later Middle Ages*. Cambridge, UK: D. S. Brewer, 1991.

Crouch, David. *Tournament*. London: Hambledon and London, 2005.

Curley, Michael J. 'A New Edition of John of Cornwall's *Prophetia Merlini*'. *Speculum* 57, n. 2 (1982): 217–49.

Curtis, Renée L. 'Who Wrote the "Prose *Tristan*"? A New Look at an Old Problem', *Neophilologus* 67, n. 1 (1983): 35–41.

Davenport, Tony. 'Wales and Welshness in Middle English Romances'. In *Authority and Subjugation in Writing of Medieval Wales*. Edited by Ruth Kennedy and Simon Meecham-Jones, 137–58. New York: Palgrave Macmillan, 2008.

Davies, R. R. *The Age of Conquest: Wales, 1063–1415*. Oxford: Oxford University Press, 1987.

—— *The First English Empire: Power and Identities in the British Isles, 1093–1343*. Oxford: Oxford University Press, 2000.

Day, Mildred Leake. 'The Letter from King Arthur to Henry II: Political Use of the Arthurian Legend in *Draco Normannicus*'. In *The Spirit of the Court: Selected Proceedings of the Fourth Congress of the International Courtly Literature Society (Toronto 1983)*. Edited by Glyn S. Burgess and Robert A. Taylor, 153–7. Cambridge, UK: D. S. Brewer, 1985.

Dean, Christopher. *Arthur of England: English Attitudes to King Arthur and the Knights of the Round Table in the Middle Ages and the Renaissance*. Toronto: University of Toronto Press, 1987.

Dégh, Linda and Andrew Vázsonyi, 'Does the Word "Dog" Bite? Ostensive Action: A Means of Legend-Telling', *Journal of Folklore Research* 20, n. 1 (1983): 5–34.

Denholm-Young, N. *History and Heraldry, 1254–1310: A Study of the Historical Value of the Rolls of Arms*. Oxford: Clarendon Press, 1965.

—— *Richard of Cornwall*. Oxford: Basil Blackwell, 1947.

—— 'The Tournament in the Thirteenth Century'. In *Collected Papers of N. Denholm-Young*, 95–120. Cardiff: University of Wales Press, 1969.

DeVries, Kelly. 'The Use of Chronicles in Recreating Medieval Military History'. *Journal of Medieval Military History* 2 (2004): 1–16.

Ditmas, E. M. R. 'The Cult of Arthurian Relics'. *Folklore* 75, n. 1 (1964): 19–33.

—— 'The Curtana or Sword of Mercy'. *Journal of the British Archaeological Association*, Third Series, 29 (1966): 122–33.

—— 'More Arthurian Relics'. *Folklore* 77, n. 2 (1966): 91–104.

Dronke, Peter. 'Peter of Blois and Poetry at the Court of Henry II', *Medieval Studies* 38 (1976): 185–235.

Duffy, Seán. 'Henry II and England's Insular Neighbours'. In *Henry II: New Interpretations*. Edited by Christopher Harper-Bill and Nicholas Vincent, 129–53. Woodbridge, UK: Boydell, 2007.

—— 'John and Ireland: the Origins of England's Irish Problem'. In *King John: New Interpretations*. Edited by S. D. Church, 221–45. Woodbridge, UK: Boydell, 1999.

Eastlake, Charles Lock. 'Scriptural and Historical Subjects Painted in England during the Reign of Henry III'. In Charles Lock Eastlake, *Materials for a History of Oil Painting*, 552–61. London: Longman, Brown, Green, and Longmans, 1847.

Echard, Siân. *Arthurian Narrative in the Latin Tradition*. Cambridge, UK: Cambridge University Press, 1998.

Eckhardt, Caroline D. 'Prophecy and Nostalgia: Arthurian Symbolism at the Close of the English Middle Ages'. In *The Arthurian Tradition: Essays in Convergence*. Edited by Mary Braswell and John Bugge, 109–26. Tuscaloosa: University of Alabama Press, 1988.

Ellis, Bill. 'Death by Folklore: Ostension, Contemporary Legend, and Murder'. *Western Folklore* 48, n. 3 (1989): 201–20.

Entwistle, William J. *The Arthurian Legend in the Literature of the Spanish Peninsula*. London: J. M. Dent, 1925.

Everard, J. A. *Brittany and the Angevins: Province and Empire, 1158–1203*. Cambridge, UK: Cambridge University Press, 2000.

Eyton, R. W. *Court, Household, and Itinerary of King Henry II Instancing also the Chief Agents and Adversaries of the King in his Government, Diplomacy and Strategy*. London: Taylor, 1878.

Faletra, Michael A.'Merlin in Cornwall: The Source and Contexts of John of Cornwall's *Prophetia Merlini*'. *Journal of English and Germanic Philology* 111, n. 3 (July 2012): 304–38.

—— 'Narrating the Matter of Britain: Geoffrey of Monmouth and the Norman Colonization of Wales'. *Chaucer Review* 35, n. 1 (2000): 60–85.

—— *Wales and the Medieval Colonial Imagination: The Matters of Britain in the Twelfth Century*. New York: Palgrave Macmillan, 2014.

Faral, Edmond. *La Légende Arthurienne, études et documents*. 3 vols. Bibliothèque de l'École des Hautes-Études, fasc. 255–7. Paris: Librairie Honoré Champion, 1929.

Fletcher, Robert Huntington. *The Arthurian Material in Chronicles, especially those of Great Britain and France*. Boston: Ginn & Company, 1906.

Flood, Victoria. 'Arthur's Return from Avalon: Geoffrey of Monmouth and the Development of Legend'. *Arthuriana* 25, n. 2 (2015): 84–5.

Flori, Jean. *Aliénor d'Aquitaine: La reine insoumise*. Translated by Olive Classe as *Eleanor of Aquitaine: Queen and Rebel*. Edinburgh: Edinburgh University Press, 2007.

—— *Richard Cœur de Lion*. Translated by Jean Birrell as *Richard the Lionheart: King and Knight*. Translated by Jean Birrell. Westport, CT: Praeger, 2006.

Foot, Sarah. Æthelstan: The First King of England. New Haven: Yale University Press, 2011.

Fourrier, Anthime. 'Encore la chronologie des œuvres de Chrétien de Troyes'. *Bulletin Bibliographique de la Société International Arthurienne* 2 (1950): 69–88

Fowler, David C. 'Some Biblical Influences on Geoffrey of Monmouth's Historiography'. *Traditio* 14 (1958): 378–85.

Frappier, Jean. Étude sur La Mort le roi Artu, roman du xiie siècle, 3rd edn. Geneva: Librairie Droz, 1972.

Freeman, Edward Augustus. *The History of the Norman Conquest of England, its Causes and its Results*, vol. 5. Oxford: Clarendon Press, 1876.

Fries, Maureen. 'The Arthurian Moment: History and Geoffrey of Monmouth's *Historia regum Britannie*'. *Arthuriana* 8, n. 4 (1998): 88–99.

Gabriele, Matthew. *An Empire of Memory: The Legend of Charlemagne, the Franks, and Jerusalem before the First Crusade*. Oxford: Oxford University Press, 2011.

Galbraith, V. H. 'The St. Edmundsbury Chronicle, 1296–1301'. *English Historical Review* 58, n. 229 (1943): 51–78.

Gallais, Pierre. 'Bleheri, la cour de Poitiers et la diffusion des récits arthuriens sur le continent'. *Journal of the International Arthurian Society* 2 (2014): 84–113.

Gardner, Edmund Garratt. *Arthurian Legend in Italian Literature*. London: J. M. Dent & Sons, 1930.

Gasparri, Françoise. *L'écriture des actes de Louis VI, Louis VII et Philippe Auguste*. Geneva: Librairie Droz, 1973.

Gaunt, Simon and Ruth Harvey, 'The Arthurian Tradition in Occitan Literature'. In *The Arthur of the French: The Arthurian Legend in Medieval French and Occitan Literature*. Edited by Glyn Sheridan Burgess and Karen Pratt, 528–45. Cardiff: University of Wales Press, 2006.

Gerould, Gordon Hall. 'King Arthur and Politics', *Speculum* 2, n. 1 (1927): 33–51.

Giancarlo, Michael. *Parliament and Literature in Late Medieval England*. Cambridge, UK: Cambridge University Press, 2007.

Giffin, Mary E. 'Cadwalader, Arthur, and Brutus in the Wigmore Manuscript'. *Speculum* 16, n. 1 (1941): 109–20.

Gillingham, John. 'The Anonymous of Béthune, King John and Magna Carta'. In *Magna Carta and the England of King John*. Edited by Janet S. Loengard, 27–44. Woodbridge, UK: Boydell, 2010.

—— 'The Context and Purposes of Geoffrey of Monmouth's *History of the Kings of Britain*'. *Anglo-Norman Studies* XIII (1991): 99–118.

—— 'The Cultivation of History, Legend, and Courtesy at the Court of Henry II'. In *Writers of the Reign of Henry II: Twelve Essays*. Edited by Ruth Kennedy and Simon Meecham-Jones, 25–52. New York: Palgrave Macmillan, 2006.

—— 'Historians Without Hindsight: Coggeshall, Diceto and Howden on the Early Years of John's Reign'. In *King John: New Interpretations*. Edited by S. D. Church, 1–26. Woodbridge, UK: Boydell, 1999.

—— *Richard I*. New Haven: Yale University Press, 1999.

—— 'Richard I and Berengaria of Navarre', *Bulletin of The Institute of Historical Research* 53 (1980): 157–73.

—— 'Roger of Howden on Crusade'. In John Gillingham, *Richard Coeur de Lion: Kingship, Chivalry and War in the Twelfth Century*, 141–53. London: Hambledon, 1994.

—— '*Stupor mundi*: 1204 et un obituaire de Richard Coeur de Lion depuis longtemps tombé dans l'oubli'. In *Plantagenêts et Capétiens: confrontations et héritages*. Edited by Martin Aurell and Noël-Yves Tonnerre, 397–411. Turnhout: Brepols, 2006.

Girbea, Catalina. 'Limites du contrôle des Plantagenêt sur la légende arthurienne: le problème de la mort d'Arthur', in *Culture politique des Plantagenêt (1154–1224): Actes du colloque tenu à Poitiers du 2 au 5 mai 2002*. Edited by Martin Aurell, 287–301. Poitiers: Centre d'Études Supérieures de Civilisation Médiévale, 2003.

Goldstein, R. James. 'The Scottish Mission to Boniface VIII in 1301: A Reconsideration of the Context of the *Instructiones* and *Processus*'. *Scottish Historical Review* 70, n. 188 (1991): 1–15.

Göller, Karl Heinz. 'The Figure of King Arthur as a Mirror of Political and Religious Views'. In *Functions of Literature: Essays Presented to Erwin Wolff on his Sixtieth Birthday*. Edited by Ulrich Brioch, Theo Stemmler, and Gerd Stratmann, 55–79. Tübingen: M. Niemeyer, 1984.

—— 'König Arthur in den Schottischen Chroniken'. Translated by Edward Donald Kennedy as 'King Arthur in the Scottish Chronicles'. In *King Arthur: A Casebook*. Edited by Edward Donald Kennedy, 173–84. New York: Routledge, 1996.

—— 'The Legend of King Arthur's Survival and Its Political Impact'. In *The*

Legacy of History: English and American Studies and the Significance of the Past, vol. 1: *Literature*. Edited by Teresa Bela and Justyna Leśniewska, 74–93. Kraków: Jagiellonian University, 2003.

Gransden, Antonia. 'Bede's Reputation as an Historian in Medieval England'. *Journal of Ecclesiastical History* 32, n. 4 (1981): 397–425.

—— 'The Growth of the Glastonbury Traditions and Legends in the Twelfth Century'. In *Glastonbury Abbey and the Arthurian Tradition*. Edited by James P. Carley, 29–53. Cambridge, UK: D. S. Brewer, 2001.

—— *Historical Writing in England*, 2 vols. Ithaca, NY: Cornell University Press, 1974–82.

Greenberg, Janelle. '"St. Edward's Ghost": The Cult of St. Edward and His Laws in English History'. In *English Law Before Magna Carta: Felix Liebermann and Die Gesetze der Angelsachsen*. Edited by Stefan Jurasinski, Lisi Oliver, and Andrew Rabin, 273–300. Leiden: Brill, 2010.

Greene, Virginie. 'Qui croit au retour d'Arthur'. *Cahiers de civilization médiévale* 45, n. 180 (2002): 321–40.

Griffiths, Margaret Enid. *Early Vaticination in Welsh*. Edited by T. Gwynn Jones. Cardiff: University of Wales Press, 1937.

Guenée, Bernard, 'L'enquête historique ordonnée par Édouard Ier, roi d'Angleterre en 1291'. *Comptes-rendus des séances de l'Académie des Inscriptions et Belles-Lettres* 119, n. 4 (1975): 572–84.

Guerin, M. Victoria. 'The King's Sin: The Origins of the David-Arthur Parallel'. In *The Passing of Arthur: New Essays in Arthurian Tradition*, edited by Christopher Baswell and William Sharpe, 15–30. New York and London: Garland, 1988.

Hammer, Jacob.'A Commentary on the *Prophetia Merlini* (Geoffrey of Monmouth's *Historia regum Britanniae*, Book VII)'. *Speculum* 10, n. 1 (1935): 3–30.

—— 'A Commentary on the *Prophetia Merlini* (Geoffrey of Monmouth's *Historia regum Britanniae*, Book VII) (Continuation)'. *Speculum* 15, n. 4 (1940): 409–31.

—— 'An Unedited Commentary on the *Prophetia Merlini* in Dublin, Trinity College MS 496 E. 6. 2. (Geoffrey of Monmouth's *Historia regum Britanniae*, Book VII)'. In *Charisteria Thaddaeo Sinko: Quinquaginta abhinc annos amplissimis in Philosophia honoribus ornato ab amicis collegis discipulis oblata*, 81–9. Warsaw: Sumptibus Societatis Philogiae Polonorum, 1951.

—— 'Some Leonine Summaries of Geoffrey of Monmouth's *Historia regum Brittaniae* and Other Poems'. *Speculum* 6, n. 1 (1931): 114–23.

Harris, Irene. 'Stephen of Rouen's *Draco Normannicus: A Norman Epic*'. In *The Epic in History*. Edited by Lola Sharon Davidson, S. N. Mukherjee, and Z. Zlatar, 112–24. Sydney: Sydney Association for Studies in Society and Culture, 1994.

Harris, Oliver D. ' "Which I have beholden with most curiouse eyes": The Lead Cross from Glastonbury Abbey'. *Arthurian Literature* XXXIV (2018): 88–129.

Haug, Walter. *Das Mosaik von Otranto: Darstellung, Deutung und Bilddokumentation.* Wiesbaden: Reichert, 1977.

Helbert, Daniel. '"an Arður sculde ȝete cum": The Prophetic Hope in Twelfth-Century Britain', *Arthuriana* 26, n. 1 (2016): 77–107.

Hofer, Stefan. 'Alexanderroman – *Erec* und die späteren Werke Kristians'. *Zeitschrift für romanische Philologie* 60 (1940): 245–61.

Holt, James Clarke. 'King John and Arthur of Brittany'. *Nottingham Medieval Studies* 44 (2000): 82–103.

—— 'King John'. In James Clarke Holt, *Magna Carta and Medieval Government*, 85–109. London: Hambledon, 1985.

—— *Magna Carta*, 2nd edn. Cambridge, UK: Cambridge University Press, 1992.

—— 'Rights and Liberties in Magna Carta'. In James Clarke Holt, *Magna Carta and Medieval Government*, 203–15. London: Hambledon, 1985.

Hope, W. H. St. John. 'Notes on the Abbey Church of Glastonbury'. *Archaeological Journal* 61, n. 1 (1904): 185–96

Hosler, John D. *Henry II: A Medieval Soldier at War, 1147–1189.* Leiden: Brill, 2007.

Howell, Margaret. *Eleanor of Provence: Queenship in Thirteenth-Century England.* Oxford: Blackwell, 1998.

Howlett, David. 'A Triad of Texts about Saint David'. In *St David of Wales: Cult, Church and Nation.* Edited by J. Wyn Evans and Jonathan M. Wooding, 253–73. Woodbridge, UK: Boydell, 2007.

Hoyt, Robert S. 'The Coronation Oath of 1308: The Background of "Les Leys et les Custumes"'. *Traditio* 11 (1955): 235–57.

Hunt, R. W. 'The Preface to the *Speculum Ecclesiae* of Giraldus Cambrensis'. *Viator* 8 (1977): 189–213.

Jackson, W. H. *Chivalry in Twelfth-Century Germany: The Works of Hartmann von Aue.* Cambridge, UK: D. S. Brewer, 1994.

Jarman, A. O. H. 'The Arthurian Allusions in the Black Book of Carmarthen'. In *The Legend of Arthur in the Middle Ages presented to A. H. Diverres.* Edited by P. B. Grout, R. A. Lodge, C. E. Pickford, and E. K. C. Varty, 99–112. Cambridge, UK: D. S. Brewer, 1983.

Jewers, Caroline. 'Another Arthur among the Troubadours'. *Tenso* 24, n. 1–2 (2009): 20–46.

Johanek, Peter. 'König Arthur und die Plantagenets: Über den Zusammenhang von Historiographie und höfischer Epik in mittelalterlicher Propaganda'. *Frühmittelalterliche Studien* 21 (1987): 346–89.

Johnson, Lesley. 'The Anglo-Norman *Description of England*: An Introduction'. In *Anglo-Norman Anniversary Essays*. Edited by Ian Short, 11–30. London: Anglo-Norman Text Society, 1993.

Jones, Bedwyr L. 'Williams (Ifor) (ed.), Bromwich (Rachel) (trans.), "Armes Prydein"(Book Review)'. *Medium Aevum* 43 (1974): 181–5.

Jones, Thomas. 'A Sixteenth Century Version of the Arthurian Cave Legend'. In *Studies in Language and Literature in Honour of Margaret Schlauch*. Edited by Mieczysław Brahmer, Stanisław Helsztyński, and Julian Krzyżanowski, 175–85. Warsaw: Polish Scientific Publishers, 1966.

Kantorowicz, Ernst H. *The King's Two Bodies: A Study in Mediaeval Political Theology*. Princeton: Princeton University Press, 1957.

Kay, Richard. 'Walter of Coventry and the Barnwell Chronicle'. *Traditio* 54 (1999): 141–67.

Keeler, Laura. *Geoffrey of Monmouth and the Late Latin Chronicles: 1300–1500*. Berkeley: University of California Press, 1946.

Keen, Maurice. 'Arthurian Bones and English Kings, ca. 1180–ca. 1550'. In *Magistra Doctissima: Essays in Honor of Bonnie Wheeler*. Edited by Dorsey Armstrong, Ann W. Astell, and Howell Chickering, 61–70. Kalamazoo: Medieval Institute Publications, 2013.

Keen, Maurice and Juliet Barker, 'The Medieval English Kings and the Tournament'. In Maurice Keen, *Nobles, Knights and Men-at-Arms in the Middle Ages*, 83–99. London: Hambledon, 1996.

Keene, Derek. 'From Conquest to Capital: St Paul's *c.* 1100–1300'. In *St Paul's: The Cathedral Church of London, 604-2004*. Edited by Derek Keene, Arthur Burns, and Andrew Saint, 17–32. New Haven and London: Yale University Press, 2004.

—— 'Text, Visualisation and Politics: London, 1150–1250'. *Transactions of the Royal Historical Society* 18 (2008): 69–99.

Kennedy, Edward Donald. 'Glastonbury'. In *The Arthur of Medieval Latin Literature: The Development and Dissemination of Arthurian Legend in Medieval Latin*. Edited by Siân Echard, 109–31. Cardiff: University of Wales Press, 2011.

—— 'Visions of History: Robert de Boron and English Arthurian Chroniclers'. In *The Fortunes of King Arthur*. Edited by Norris J. Lacy, 29–46. Cambridge, UK: D. S. Brewer, 2005.

Ker, Neil R. 'Membra Disiecta, Second Series'. *British Museum Quarterly* 14, n. 4 (1940): 79–86.

Koch, John T. 'The Celtic Lands'. In *Medieval Arthurian Literature: A Guide to Recent Research*. Edited by Norris J. Lacy, 239–322. New York: Garland, 1996.

Köhler, Erich. *Ideal und Wirklichkeit in der höfischen Epik. Studien zur Form der Frühen Artus- und Graldichtung.* Translated by Éliane Kaufholz as *L'Aventure chevaleresque: Idéal et réalité dans le romans courtois.* Paris: Gallimard, 1974.

Krummel, Miriamne Ara. *Crafting Jewishness in Medieval England: Legally Absent, Virtually Present.* New York: Palgrave Macmillan, 2011.

de Laborderie, Olivier. 'Élaboration et diffusion de l'image de la monarchie anglaise (XIIIe–XIVe siècles)'. In *Histoires Outre-Manche: Tendances récentes de l'historiographie britannique.* Edited by Frédérique Lachaud, Isabelle Lescent-Giles, and François-Joseph Ruggiu, 37–51. Paris: Presses de l'Université de Paris-Sorbonne, 2001.

—— 'A New Pattern for English History: The First Genealogical Rolls of the Kings of England'. In *Broken Lines: Genealogical Literature in Medieval Britain and France.* Edited by Raluca Radulescu and Edward Donald Kennedy, 45–61. Turnhout: Brepols, 2008.

Lachet, Claude. *Sone de Nansay et le roman d'aventures en vers au Xiiie siècle.* Geneva: Editions Slatkine, 1992.

Lagorio, Valerie M. 'The Apocalyptic Mode in the Vulgate Cycle of Arthurian Romances'. *Philological Quarterly* 57 (1978): 1–22.

Lapidge, Michael and Richard Sharpe, *A Bibliography of Celtic-Latin Literature, 400–1200.* Dublin: Royal Irish Academy, 1985.

Lathuillère, Roger. *Guiron le Courtois: Étude de la tradition manuscrite et analyse critique.* Geneva: Librairie Droz, 1966.

Laurie, H. C. R. 'The Arthurian World of *Erec et Enide*'. *Bulletin Bibliographique de la Société International Arthurienne* 21 (1969): 111–19.

Lawrence-Mathers, Anne. 'William of Newburgh and the Northumbrian construction of English History'. *Journal of Medieval History* 33 (2007): 339–57.

Le Baud, Pierre. *Histoire de Bretagne avec les chroniques des maisons de Vitré et de Laval.* Edited by Ch. D'Hozier. Paris: Gervais Alliot, 1638.

Lecouteux, Stéphane. 'L'archétype et le stemmata des annales angevines et vendômoises'. *Revue d'Histoire des Textes,* n. s., 3 (2008): 229–62.

Legge, M. Dominica. 'William the Marshal and Arthur of Brittany'. *Bulletin of the Institute of Historical Research* 55, n. 131 (1982): 18–24

Le Saux, Françoise H. M. *Laʒamon's Brut: The Poem and its Sources.* Cambridge, UK: D.S. Brewer, 1989.

Leyser, K. 'Frederick Barbarossa, Henry II and the Hands of St James'. *English Historical Review* 90, n. 356 (1975): 481–506.

Liebermann, Felix. 'A Contemporary Manuscript of the "Leges Anglorum Londoniis collectae"'. *English Historical Review* 28, n. 112 (1913): 732–45.

—— *Über die Leges Anglorum saeculo xiii ineunte Londoniis collectae.* Halle: Max Niemeyer, 1894.

Lindahl, Carl. 'Three Ways of Coming Back: Folkloric Perspectives on Arthur's Return'. In *King Arthur's Modern Return*. Edited by Debra N. Mancoff, 13–29. New York: Garland Publishing, 1998.

Little, A. G. 'The Authorship of the Lanercost Chronicle'. *English Historical Review* 31 (1916): 269–79.

Lloyd-Morgan, Ceridwen. 'From Ynys Wydrin to Glasynbri: Glastonbury in Welsh Vernacular Tradition'. In *Glastonbury Abbey and the Arthurian Tradition*. Edited by James P. Carley, 161–77. Cambridge, UK: D. S. Brewer, 2001.

—— 'Welsh Tradition in Calais: Elis Gruffydd and his Biography of King Arthur'. In *The Fortunes of King Arthur*. Edited by Norris J. Lacy, 77–91. Cambridge, UK: D. S. Brewer, 2005.

Lodge, Eleanor C. *Gascony under English Rule*. London: Methuen, 1926.

Loomis, Roger Sherman. 'Arthurian Influence on Sport and Spectacle'. In *Arthurian Literature in the Middle Ages: A Collaborative History*. Edited by Roger Sherman Loomis, 553–9. Oxford: Clarendon Press, 1959.

—— 'Chivalric and Dramatic Imitations of Arthurian Romance'. In *Medieval Studies in Memory of A. Kingsley Porter*, vol 1. Edited by Wilhelm R. W. Koehler, 79–97. Cambridge, MA: Harvard University Press, 1939.

—— 'Edward I, Arthurian Enthusiast', *Speculum* 28, n. 1 (1953): 114–27.

—— 'From Segontium to Sinadon – the Legends of a Cité Gaste', *Speculum* 22, n. 4 (1947): 520–33.

—— 'King Arthur and the Antipodes'. *Modern Philology* 38, n. 3 (1941): 289–304.

—— 'The Legend of Arthur's Survival'. In *Arthurian Literature in the Middle Ages: A Collaborative History*. Edited by Roger Sherman Loomis, 64–71. Oxford: Clarendon Press, 1959.

—— 'Tristam and the House of Anjou'. *Modern Language Review* 17, n. 1 (1922): 24–30.

Lot, Ferdinand. Étude sur le Lancelot en prose. Paris: Librairie ancienne Honoré Champion, 1918.

Loth, Joseph. 'L'épée de Tristan'. *Comptes rendus des séances de l'Académie des Inscriptions et Belles–Lettres* 67, n. 2 (1923): 117–29.

Martinez, Andrew. 'Disciplinary Ordinances for English Armies and Military Change, 1385–1513'. *History* 102, n. 351 (2017): 361–85.

Marvin, Julia. 'Arthur Authorized: The Prophecies of the Prose *Brut* Chronicle'. *Arthurian Literature* XXII (2005): 84–99.

Marzella, Francesco. 'Letters from the Otherworld: Arthur and Henry II in Stephen of Rouen's *Draco Normannicus*'. *Tabularia*. Autour de Serlon de Bayeux: la poésie normande aux XIe–XIIe siècles (2017): 1–17, http://tabularia.revues.org/2858 (Accessed 17 June 2017).

Mason, Emma. 'The Hero's Invincible Weapon: an Aspect of Angevin Propaganda'. In *The Ideals and Practice of Medieval Knighthood III: Papers from the Fourth Strawberry Hill Conference, 1988*. Edited by Christopher Harper-Bill and Ruth Harvey, 121–37. Woodbridge, UK: Boydell, 1990.

McGinn, Bernard. 'Apocalypticism and Violence: Aspects of Their Relationship in Antiquity and the Middle Ages'. In *Scripture and Pluralism: Reading the Bible in the Religiously Plural Worlds of the Middle Ages and Renaissance*. Edited by Thomas J. Heffernan and Thomas E. Burman, 209–29. Leiden: Brill, 2005.

—— *Visions of the End: Apocalyptic Traditions in the Middle Ages*, rev. edn. New York: Columbia University Press, 1998.

McGlynn, Sean. 'Roger Wendover and the Wars of Henry III, 1216–1234'. In *England and Europe in the Reign of Henry III (1216–1272)*. Edited by Björn K. U. Weiler and Ifor W. Rowlands, 183–213. Aldershot, UK: Ashgate, 2002.

Meecham-Jones, Simon. '"Þe Tide of Þisse Londe"– Finding and Losing Wales in Laȝamon's *Brut'*. *Reading Laȝamon's* Brut: *Approaches and Explorations*. Edited by Rosamund Allen, Jane Roberts, and Carole Weinberg, 69–105. Amsterdam: Rodopi, 2013.

Mickel, Emanuel J. 'History as Pseudepigraphy'. *Romance Philology* 54, n. 1 (2000): 71–89.

Moll, Richard J. *Before Malory: Reading Arthur in Later Medieval England*. Toronto: University of Toronto Press, 2003.

Moran, Patrick. *Lectures cycliques: le réseau inter-romanesque dans les cycles du Graal du XIIIe siècle*. Paris: Honoré Champion, 2014.

Morland, Stephen C. *Glastonbury, Domesday and Related Studies*. Glastonbury, UK: Glastonbury Antiquarian Society, 1991.

Morris, John E. *The Welsh Wars of Edward I: A Contribution to Mediaeval Military History, Based on Original Documents*. Oxford: Clarendon Press, 1901.

Morris, Richard K. 'The Architecture of Arthurian Enthusiasm: Castle Symbolism in the Reigns of Edward I and His Successors'. In *Armies, Chivalry and Warfare in Medieval Britain and France: Proceedings of the 1995 Harlaxton Symposium*. Edited by Matthew Strickland, 63–81. Stamford: Paul Watkins, 1998.

Morris, Rosemary. 'King Arthur and the Growth of French Nationalism'. In *France and the British Isles in the Middle Ages and the Renaissance: Essays by Members of Girton College, Cambridge, in Memory of Ruth Morgan*. Edited by Gillian Jondorf and David N. Dumville, 115–29. Woodbridge, UK: Boydell, 1991.

Neville, Cynthia J. 'Widows of War: Edward I and the Women of Scotland during the War of Independence'. In *Wife and Widow in*

Medieval England. Edited by Sue Sheridan Walker, 109–40. Ann Arbor: University of Michigan Press, 1993.

Newhall, Richard A. 'Henry V's Policy of Conciliation in Normandy, 1417–1422'. In *Anniversary Essays in Mediaeval History by Students of Charles Homer Haskins Presented on his Completion of Forty Years of Teaching*. Edited by Charles Holt Taylor and John L. La Monte, 205–29. Boston: Houghton Mifflin, 1929.

Nitze, W. A. 'The Exhumation of King Arthur at Glastonbury'. *Speculum* 9, n. 4 (1934): 355–61.

Noble, James. 'Patronage, Politics, and the Figure of Arthur in Geoffrey of Monmouth, Wace, and Layamon'. *Arthurian Yearbook* 2 (1992): 159–78.

Noble, Peter S. 'Chrétien's Arthur'. In *Chrétien de Troyes and the Troubadours: Essays in Memory of the Late Leslie Topsfield*. Edited by Peter S. Noble and Linda M. Paterson, 220–37. Cambridge, UK: St. Catharine's College, 1984.

Norgate, Kate. 'The Alleged Condemnation of King John by the Court of France in 1202'. *Transactions of the Royal Historical Society*, new ser., 14 (1900): 53–67.

O'Brien, Bruce R. 'Forgers of Law and Their Readers: The Crafting of English Political Identities between the Norman Conquest and the Magna Carta'. *Political Science and Politics* 43, n. 3 (2010): 467–73.

—— 'Leges Edwardi Confessoris (ECf1)'. Early English Laws Project. University of London: Institute of Historical Research / King's College London (http://www.earlyenglishlaws.ac.uk/laws/texts/ecf1/, accessed 22 January 2013).

O'Callaghan, Joseph F. *The Learned King: The Reign of Alfonso X of Castile*. Philadelphia: University of Pennsylvania Press, 1993.

Ostmann, Alexander. 'Die Bedeutung der Arthurtradition für die englische Gesellschaft des 12. und 13. Jahrhunderts'. Ph.D. diss., Freie Universität Berlin, 1975.

Owen, Morfydd E. 'Royal Propaganda: Stories from the Law-texts'. In *The Welsh King and His Court*. Edited by T. M. Charles-Edwards, Morfydd E. Owen, and Paul Russell, 224–54. Cardiff: University of Wales Press, 2000.

Padel, Oliver J. 'The Nature of Arthur'. *Cambrian Medieval Celtic Studies* 27 (1994): 1–31.

—— 'Some South-western Sites with Arthurian Associations'. In *The Arthur of the Welsh*. Edited by Rachel Bromwich, A. O. H. Jarman, and Brynley F. Roberts, 229–48. Cardiff: University of Wales Press, 1991.

Paris, Gaston. *La littérature française au moyen âge, xie–xive siècle*, 4th edn. Paris: Librairie Hachette, 1909.

Parisse, Michel. 'Le tournoi en France, des origines à la fin du XIIIe siècle'.

In *Das ritterliche Turnier im Mittelalter*. Edited by Josef Fleckenstein, 175–211. Göttingen: Vandenhoeck & Ruprecht, 1985.

—— 'Tournois et tables rondes dans "Sone de Nansay"'. In *Études de langue et de littérature françaises offertes à André Lanly*, 275–86. Nancy: Université Nancy II, 1980.

Parry, John J. 'Geoffrey of Monmouth and the Paternity of Arthur'. *Speculum* 13, n. 3 (1938): 271–7.

Parsons, John Carmi. *Eleanor of Castile: Queen and Society in Thirteenth-Century England*. New York: St. Martin's Press, 1995.

—— 'The Second Exhumation of King Arthur's Remains at Glastonbury, 19 April 1278'. In *Glastonbury Abbey and the Arthurian Tradition*. Edited by James P. Carley, 179–83. Cambridge, UK: D. S. Brewer, 2001.

Pastoureau, Michel. 'Jouer aux chevaliers de la Table Ronde à la fin du Moyen Age'. In *Le goût du lecture* à la fin du *Moyen Âge*. Edited by Danielle Bohler, 65–81. Paris: Léopard d'Or, 2006.

Patterson, Robert B. 'The Author of the "Margam Annals": Early Thirteenth-Century Margam Abbey's Compleat Scribe'. *Anglo-Norman Studies* XIV (1992): 197–210.

Pelle, Stephen Anthony. 'Continuity and Renewal in English Homiletic Eschatology, *ca.* 1150–1200'. Ph.D. diss., University of Toronto, 2012.

—— 'The *Revelations* of Pseudo-Methodius and "Concerning the Coming of Antichrist" in British Library MS Cotton Vespasian D. xiv'. *Notes and Queries* 56, n. 3 (2009): 324–30.

Petit-Dutaillis, Charles. 'Le déshéritement de Jean sans Terre et le meurte d'Arthur de Bretagne: Étude critique sur la formation et la fortune d'une légende'. *Revue Historique* 147, fasc. 2 (1924): 161–203.

Peyton III, Henry H. 'The Myth of King Arthur's Immortality'. *Interpretations* 5, n. 1 (1973): 55–71.

Pickford, Cedric E. 'The Three Crowns of King Arthur'. *Yorkshire Archæological Journal* 38, n. 151 (1954): 373–82.

Powicke, F. M[aurice]. 'King Edward I in Fact and Fiction'. In *Fritz Saxl, 1890–1948, A Volume of Memorial Essays from his Friends in England*. Edited by D. J. Gordon, 120–35. London: Thomas Nelson and Sons, 1957.

—— *King Henry III and the Lord Edward: The Community of the Realm in the Thirteenth Century*, 2 vols. Oxford: Clarendon Press, 1947.

—— 'King John and Arthur of Brittany'. *English Historical Review* 24, n. 96 (1909): 659–74.

—— 'Roger of Wendover and the Coggeshall Chronicle'. *English Historical Review* 21, n. 82 (1906): 286–96.

—— *The Thirteenth Century, 1216–1307*, 2nd edn. Oxford: Clarendon Press, 1962.

Powicke, Michael R. 'The General Obligation to Cavalry Service under Edward I'. *Speculum* 28, n. 4 (1953): 814–33.

Prestwich, Michael. *Edward I*, rev. edn. New Haven: Yale University Press, 1997.

—— 'The Piety of Edward I'. In *England in the Thirteenth Century: Proceedings of the 1984 Harlaxton Symposium*. Edited by W. M. Ormrod, 120–8. Woodbridge, UK: Boydell, 1985.

—— *Plantagenet England, 1225–1360*. Oxford: Clarendon Press, 2005.

—— 'Royal Patronage under Edward I'. *Thirteenth Century England* I (1986): 41–52.

—— *The Three Edwards: War and State in England, 1272–1377*, 2nd edn. London: Routledge, 2003.

Regalado, Nancy Freeman. 'Performing Romance: Arthurian Interludes in Sarrasin's *Le roman du Hem* (1278)'. In *Performing Medieval Narrative*. Edited by Evelyn Birge Vitz, Nancy Freeman Regalado, and Marilyn Lawrence, 103–19. Cambridge: D. S. Brewer, 2005.

Richardson, H. G. 'Gervase of Tilbury'. *History* 46, n. 157 (1961): 102–14.

Riddy, Felicity. 'Reading for England: Arthurian Literature and National Consciousness'. *Bulletin Bibliographique de la Société International Arthurienne* 43 (1991): 314–32.

(de) Riquer, Martín. *Caballeros medievales y sus armas*. Madrid: Universidad Nacional de Educación a Distancia, 1999.

Roberts, Brynley F. 'Geoffrey of Monmouth and Welsh Historical Tradition'. *Nottingham Mediaeval Studies* 20 (1976): 29–40.

Robinson, J. Armitage. 'William of Malmesbury "On the Antiquity of Glastonbury"'. In Richard J. Armitage, *Somerset Historical Essays Somerset Historical Essays*, 1–25. London: Oxford University Press, 1921.

Rollason, David. 'From Tintagel to Aachen: Richard of Cornwall and the Power of Place'. *Reading Medieval Studies* 38 (2012): 1–23.

Rollo, David. *Historical Fabrication, Ethnic Fable and French Romance in Twelfth-Century England*. Lexington, KY: French Forum Publishers, 1998

Rouse, Robert Allen and Cory James Rushton, 'Arthurian Geography'. In *The Cambridge Companion to the Arthurian Legend*. Edited by Elizabeth Archibald and Ad Putter, 218–34. Cambridge: Cambridge University Press, 2009.

—— *The Medieval Quest for Arthur*. Stroud: Tempus, 2005.

Rowlands, Ifor W. 'King John and Wales'. In *King John: New Interpretations*. Edited by S. D. Church, 273–87. Woodbridge, UK: Boydell, 1999.

Rubenstein, Jay. 'Godfrey of Bouillon versus Raymond of Saint-Gilles:

How Carolingian Kingship Trumped Millenarianism at the End of the First Crusade'. In *The Legend of Charlemagne in the Middle Ages: Power, Faith and Crusade*. Edited by Matthew Gabriele and Jace Stuckey, 59–75. New York: Palgrave Macmillan, 2008.

Safford, E. W. *Itinerary of Edward I*, 3 vols. London: Swift, 1974–7.

Sargent-Baur, Barbara N. 'Dux Bellorum / Rex Militum / Roi Fainéant: The Transformations of Arthur in the Twelfth Century'. In *King Arthur: A Casebook*, ed. Edward Donald Kennedy, 29–43. New York: Routledge, 1996.

Saul, Nigel. *Chivalry in Medieval England*. Cambridge, MA: Harvard University Press, 2011.

Schmitt, Jean-Claude. *Les revenants: Les vivants et les morts dans la société*. Translated by Teresa Lavender Fagan as *Ghosts in the Middle Ages: The Living and the Dead in Medieval Society*. Chicago: Chicago University Press, 1998.

Schmolke-Hasselmann, Beate. *Der arturische Versroman von Chrestien bis Froissart*. Translated by Margaret and Roger Middleton as *The Evolution of Arthurian Romance: The Verse Tradition from Chrétien to Froissart*. Cambridge, UK: Cambridge University Press, 1998.

—— 'Henry II Plantagenêt, roi d'Angleterre, et la genèse d' Erec et Enide'. *Cahiers de civilisation médiévale* n. 95–6 (1981): 241–6.

—— 'King Arthur as Villain in the Thirteenth-century Romance *Yder*'. *Reading Medieval Studies* 6 (1980): 31–43.

—— 'The Round Table: Ideal, Fiction, Reality'. *Arthurian Literature* II (1981): 41–75.

Shwartz, Susan M. 'The Founding and Self-betrayal of Britain: An Augustian Approach to Geoffrey of Monmouth's *Historia Regum Britanniae*'. *Medievalia et Humanistica*, new ser. 10 (1981): 33–53.

Simpkin, David. *The English Aristocracy at War: From the Welsh Wars of Edward I to the Battle of Bannockburn*. Woodbridge, UK: Boydell, 2008.

Sims-William, Patrick. 'The Early Welsh Arthur Poems'. In *The Arthur of the Welsh: The Arthurian Legend in Medieval Welsh Literature*. Edited by Rachel Bromwich, A. O. H. Jarman and Brynley F. Roberts, 33-71. Cardiff: University of Wales Press, 1991.

—— 'The Submission of Irish Kings in Fact and Fiction: Henry II, Bendigeidfran, and the Dating of *The Four Branches of the Mabinogi*'. *Cambridge Medieval Celtic Studies* 22 (1991): 31–61.

Smith, J. Beverley. *Llywelyn ap Gruffudd, Prince of Wales*. Cardiff: University of Wales Press, 1998.

Smith, Llinos Beverley. 'The Death of Llywelyn ap Gruffydd: The Narratives Reconsidered'. *Welsh History Review* 11, n. 2 (1982), 200–13.

—— 'Llywelyn ap Gruffudd and the Welsh Historical Consciousness'. *Welsh History Review* 12, n. 1 (1984): 1–28.

Spencer, Andrew M. 'Royal Patronage and the Earls in the Reign of Edward I'. *History* 93, n. 309 (2008): 20–46.

Spiegel, Gabrielle M. 'The Reditus Regni ad Stirpem Karoli Magni: A New Look'. *French Historical Studies* 7, n. 2 (1971): 145–74.

Stanley, E. G. 'The Date of Laȝamon's *Brut*', *Notes and Queries* 213 (1968): 84–9.

Stepsis, Robert. *'Pierre de Langtoft's Chronicle*, an Essay in Medieval Historiography'. *Medievalia et Humanistica,* new ser., 3 (1972): 51–73.

Stock, Brian. *The Implications of Literacy: Written Language and Models of Interpretation in the Eleventh and Twelfth Centuries.* Princeton: Princeton University Press, 1983.

Stones, Alison. 'Arthurian Art since Loomis'. In *Arturus Rex,* vol. 2: *Acta Conventus Lovaniensis 1987.* Edited by Willy Van Hoecke, Gilbert Tournoy, Werner Verbeke, 21–78. Louvain: Leuven University Press, 1991.

—— 'Illustrations and the Fortunes of Arthur'. In *The Fortunes of King Arthur.* Edited by Norris J. Lacy, 116–65. Cambridge, UK: D. S. Brewer, 2005.

Stones, E. L. G. 'The Appeal to History in Anglo-Scottish Relations, Part I'. *Archives* 9, n. 41 (1969): 11–21.

—— 'The Mission of Thomas Wale and Thomas Delisle from Edward I to Pope Boniface VIII in 1301'. *Nottingham Medieval Studies* 26 (1982): 8–28.

—— 'The Submission of Robert Bruce to Edward I, c. 1301–2'. *Scottish Historical Review* 34, n. 118, ii (1955): 122–34.

Stones, E. L. G. and Grant G. Simpson, *Edward I and the Throne of Scotland, 1290–1296. An Edition of the Record Sources for the Great Cause.* 2 vols. Oxford: Oxford University Press, 1979.

Störmer, Wilhelm. 'König Artus als aristokratisches Leitbild während des späteren Mittelalters, gezeigt an Beispielen der Ministerialität und des Patriziats'. *Zeitschrift für bayerische Landesgeschichte* 35 (1972): 946–71.

Stow, Kenneth 'Conversion, Apostasy, and Apprehensiveness: Emicho of Floheim and the Fear of the Jews in the Twelfth Century'. *Speculum* 76, n. 4 (2001): 911–33.

Stratford, Jenny. 'The Early Royal Collections and the Royal Library to 1461'. In *The Cambridge History of the Book in Britain,* vol. 3: *1400–1557.* Edited by Lotte Hellinga and J. B. Trapp, 255–66. Cambridge, UK: Cambridge University Press, 1999.

Strickland, Matthew. 'A Law of Arms or a Law of Treason? Conduct in War in Edward I's Campaigns in Scotland, 1296–1307'. In *Violence in*

Medieval Society. Edited by Richard W. Kaeuper, 39–77. Woodbridge, UK: Boydell, 2000.

Summerfield, Thea. 'The Arthurian References in Pierre de Langtoft's *Chronicle*'. In *Text and Intertext in Medieval Arthurian Literature*. Edited by Norris J. Lacy, 187–208. New York: Garland, 1996.

—— *The Matter of Kings' Lives: The Design of Past and Present in the Early Fourteenth-century Verse Chronicles by Pierre de Langtoft and Robert Mannyng*. Amsterdam: Rodopi, 1998.

—— 'The Testimony of Writing: Pierre de Langtoft and the Appeals to History, 1291–1306'. In *The Scots and Medieval Arthurian Tradition*. Edited by Rhiannon Purdie and Nicola Royan, 25–42. Cambridge, UK: D. S. Brewer, 2005.

Summers, David A. *Spenser's Arthur: The British Arthurian Tradition and The Faerie Queene*. Lanham, MD: University Press of America, 1997.

Suppe, Frederick. 'The Cultural Significance of Decapitation in High Medieval Wales and the Marches'. *The Bulletin of the Board of Celtic Studies* 36 (1989): 147–60.

Sutherland-Harris, Robin. 'Authority, Text, and Genre in Accounts of Diocesan Struggle: The Bishops of Bath and Glastonbury and the Uses of Cartulary Evidence'. In *Authorities in the Middle Ages: Influence, Legitimacy, and Power in Medieval Society*. Edited by Sini Kangas, Mia Korpiola, and Tuija Ainonen, 107–22. Berlin: Walter de Gruyter, 2013.

Tatlock, J. S. P. 'The Dragons of Wessex and Wales', *Speculum* 8, n. 2 (1933): 223–35.

—— 'The English Journey of the Laon Canons', *Speculum* 8, n. 4 (1933): 454–65.

—— 'Geoffrey and King Arthur in "Normannicus Draco". *Modern Philology* 31, n. 1 (1933): 113–25.

—— 'Geoffrey and King Arthur in "Normannicus Draco". *Modern Philology* 31, n. 2 (1933): 1–18.

—— *The Legendary History of the Kings of Britain: Geoffrey of Monmouth's Historia Regum Britanniae and Its Early Vernacular Versions*. Berkeley: University of California Press, 1950.

Taylor, Arnold. 'A Fragment of a Dona Account of 1284'. In Arnold Taylor, *Studies in Castles and Castle-Building*, 195–204. London: Hambledon, 1985.

—— 'The King's Works in Wales 1277–1330'. In *The History of the King's Works*, vol. 1: *The Middle Ages*. Edited by H. M. Colvin, 293–408. London: Her Majesty's Stationery Office, 1963.

Tessier, Georges. *Diplomatique royale Française*. Paris: Picard, 1962.

Thiolier, Jean-Claude. 'Pierre de Langtoft: Historiographie d'Edouard

Ier Plantagenet'. In *Anglo-Norman Anniversary Essays*. Edited by Ian Short, 379–94. London: Anglo-Norman Text Society, 1993.

Thorpe, Lewis. 'Mastre Richard: A Thirteenth-century Translator of the "De re miltari" of Vegetius'. *Scriptorium* 6, n. 1 (1952): 39–50.

—— 'Mastre Richard at the Skirmish of Kenilworth?'. *Scriptorium* 7, n. 1 (1953): 120–1.

—— 'Merlin's Sardonic Laughter'. In *Studies in Medieval Literature and Languages in Memory of Frederick Whitehead*, ed. W. Rothwell, W. R. J. Barron, David Blamires and Lewis Thorpe, 323–40. Manchester, Manchester University Press, 1973.

Thurn, Hans. *Die Handschriften der Universitätsbibliothek Würzburg / Handschriften aus benediktinischen Provenienzen: Amorbach. Kitzingen. Münsterschwarzach...Wiesbaden*: Harrassowitz & Co., 1973.

Topsfield, L. T. *Chrétien of Troyes: A Study of the Arthurian Romances*. Cambridge, UK: Cambridge University Press, 1981.

Tout, T. F. *Edward the First*. London: Macmillan and Co, 1893.

Trachsler, Richard. *Clôtures du cycle Arthurien: Étude et textes*. Geneva: Droz, 1996.

—— 'Escanor'. In *The Arthur of the French: The Arthurian Legend in Medieval French and Occitan Literature*. Edited by Glyn Sheridan Burgess and Karen Pratt, 440–2. Cardiff: University of Wales Press, 2006.

—— 'Rustichello, Rusticien e Rusta Pisa. Chi ha scritto il romanzo arturiano?'. In *'La traduzione è una forma', Trasmissione e sopravvivenza dei testi romanzi medievali*. Edited by Giuseppina Brunetti and Gabriele Giannini, 107–23. Bologna: Pàtron editore, 2007.

Turner, Ralph V. 'England in 1215: An Authoritarian Angevin Dynasty Facing Multiple Threats'. In *Magna Carta and the England of King John*. Edited by Janet S. Loengard, 10–26. Woodbridge, UK: Boydell, 2010.

Twomey, Michael W. 'Pseudo-Methodius Revelations'. In *Sources of Anglo-Saxon Culture: The Apocrypha*. Edited by Frederick M. Biggs, 18–20. Kalamazoo: Medieval Institute Publications, 2007.

—— 'The *Revelations* of Pseudo-Methodius and Scriptural Study at Salisbury in the Eleventh Century'. In *Sources of Wisdom: Old English and Early Medieval Latin Studies in Honour of Thomas D. Hill*. Edited by Frederick M. Biggs, Thomas D. Hill, Charles D. Wright, and Thomas Hall, 370–86. Toronto: University of Toronto, 2007.

Ullmann, Walter. 'Arthur's Homage to King John'. *English Historical Review* 94, n. 371 (1979): 356–64.

—— 'On the Influence of Geoffrey of Monmouth in English History'. In *Speculum Historiae: Geschichte im Spiegel von Geschichtsshreibung und Geschichtsdeutung*. Edited by Clemens Bauer, Laetitia Boehm, and Max Müller, 257–76. Freiburg: Karl Alber, 1965.

Vale, Juliet. 'Arthur in English Society'. In *The Arthur of the English: The Arthurian Legend in Medieval English Life and Literature*, rev. edn. Edited by W. R. J. Barron, 185–96. Cardiff: University of Wales Press, 2001.

—— *Edward III and Chivalry: Chivalric Society and its Context, 1270–1350*. Woodbridge, UK: Boydell, 1982.

Vale, Malcolm. 'Edward I and the French: Rivalry and Chivalry'. *Thirteenth-Century England* II (1988): 165–76.

Van Houts, Elisabeth. 'Latin and French as Languages of the Past in Normandy during the Reign of Henry II: Robert of Torigni, Stephen of Rouen, and Wace'. In *Writers of the Reign of Henry II: Twelve Essays*. Edited by Ruth Kennedy and Simon Meecham-Jones, 53–77. New York: Palgrave Macmillan, 2006.

Vincent, Nicholas. 'The Charters of King Henry II: The Introduction of the Royal *Inspeximus* Revisited'. In *Dating Undated Medieval Charters*. Edited by Michael Gervers, 97–120. Woodbridge, UK: Boydell, 2000.

—— 'Why 1199? Bureaucracy and Enrolment under John and his Contemporaries'. In *English Government in the Thirteenth Century*. Edited by Adrian Jobson, 17–48. Woodbridge, UK: Boydell, 2004.

Wade, James. *Fairies in Medieval Romance*. New York: Palgrave Macmillan, 2011.

Wagner, Anthony R. *Heralds and Heraldry in the Middle Ages: An Inquiry into the Growth of the Armorial Function of Heralds*, 2nd edn. Oxford: Oxford University Press, 1956.

de Walden, Howard. *Some Feudal Lords and their Seals, 1301*. London: De Walden Library, 1903.

Walker, David. *Medieval Wales*. Cambridge, UK: Cambridge University Press, 1990.

Warner, Lawrence. 'Geoffrey of Monmouth and the De-Judaized Crusade'. *Parergon* 21, n. 1 (2004): 19–37.

—— 'Jesus the Jouster: The Christ-Knight and Medieval Theories of Atonement in *Piers Plowman* and the "Round Table" Sermons'. *Yearbook of Langland Studies* 10 (1996): 129–43.

Warren, Michelle R. 'Roger of Howden Strikes Back: Investing Arthur of Brittany with the Anglo-Norman Future'. *Anglo-Norman Studies* XXI (1998): 261–72.

Warren, W. L. *King John*, rev. edn. Berkeley: University of California Press, 1978.

Watson, Sethina. 'The Bishop and his Cathedral Cities'. In *Jocelin of Wells: Bishop, Builder, Courtier*. Edited by Robert Dunning, 67–98. Woodbridge, UK: Boydell, 2010.

Weiler, Björn. 'Henry III Through Foreign Eyes – Communication and

Historical Writing in Thirteenth-Century Europe'. In *England and Europe in the Reign of Henry III (1216–1272)*. Edited by Björn K. U. Weiler and Ifor W. Rowlands, 137–61. Aldershot, UK: Ashgate, 2002.

Weiss, Judith. 'Emperors and Antichrists: Reflections of Empire in Insular Narrative, 1130–1250'. In *The Matter of Identity in Medieval Romance*. Edited by Phillipa Hardman, 87–102. Cambridge, UK: D. S. Brewer, 2002.

Wilde, James Fergus. 'History and Legend in the Chronicle of Peter of Langtoft'. Ph.D. diss., University of Manchester, 1997.

Wilkinson, B. *Constitutional History of Medieval England, 1216–1399*, 3 vols. London: Longmans, Green, 1948–58.

Wille, Clara. 'Les prophéties de Merlin interprétées par un commentateur du XIIᵉ siècle'. *Cahiers de civilisation médiévale* 51, n. 203 (2008): 223–34.

Williams, Gwyn A. *Medieval London: From Commune to Capital*. University of London Historical Studies 11. London: Athlone Press, 1963.

Wood, Charles T. 'Fraud and its Consequences: Savaric of Bath and the Reform of Glastonbury'. In *The Archaeology and History of Glastonbury Abbey: Essays in Honour of the Ninetieth Birthday of C. A. Ralegh Radford*. Edited by Lesley Abrams and James P. Carley, 273–83. Woodbridge, UK: Boydell, 1991.

—— 'Guenevere at Glastonbury: A Problem in Translation(s)'. In *Glastonbury Abbey and the Arthurian Tradition*. Edited by James P. Carley, 83–99. Cambridge, UK: D. S. Brewer, 2001.

Wood, Juliet. 'Where Does Britain End? The Reception of Geoffrey of Monmouth in Scotland and Wales'. In *The Scots and Medieval Arthurian Legend*. Edited by Rhiannon Purdie and Nicola Royan, 9–24. Cambridge, UK: D. S. Brewer, 2005.

Wormald, Patrick. *The Making of English Law: King Alfred to the Twelfth Century*, vol. 1: *Legislation and its Limits*. Oxford: John Wiley & Sons, 1999.

Wright, Neil. 'The Place of Henry of Huntingdon's *Epistola ad Warinum* in the Text-history of Geoffrey of Monmouth's *Historia regum Britannie*: A Preliminary Investigation'. In *France and the British Isles in the Middle Ages and Renaissance: Essays by Members of Girton College, Cambridge, in Memory of Ruth Morgan*. Edited by Gillian Jondorf and David N. Dumville, 71–113. Woodbridge, UK: Boydell, 1991.

Acknowledgments

Upon publication of this book my first Arthurian quest is at an end. Far longer than the conventional year-and-a-day mission, mine has been a veritable Homeric *Odyssey*: Providence, Rhode Island, my Ithaca, and Toronto, my Troy. I have strayed into dense, dark woods and fallen into perilous rabbit holes. But, aided by a special few, I have arrived at the sought-after castle of completion.

It is my great pleasure to acknowledge those who helped me on this journey. First and foremost, I thank my mother, Jean Berard, and my father, Dr. Roger G. Berard, for encouraging me to pursue my bliss, both in work and in play, and for teaching me to be conscientious and determined. I love you both and miss you when I don't see you. I thank my high-school history teacher, Mrs. Joyce Conti, and undergraduate academic advisor, Dr. Constance M. Rousseau, for shepherding me into the Liberal Arts and the field of Medieval Studies respectively. Connie, thank you for championing me and showing me how to improve as an academic writer. Much along the same lines, I thank Dr. Dorothea Kullmann. It was in Professor Kullmann's course on Wace's *Roman de Brut* that Arthur took hold of me. Dorothea, it was you who taught me how to engage in close reading of primary sources in their original languages and how to trace patterns of influence. Your dedication to your students deserves the fullest possible recognition. I thank Dr. James P. Carley for sharing his professional wisdom and his singular knowledge of all things Arthurian, British, and esoteric. James has been my principal Arthurian mentor and the overlap of our scholarly interests is truly remarkable. I also thank Dr. Mark D. Meyerson, whose expertise in Jewish–Christian relations in medieval Europe enriched the breadth of my scholarship. In particular, my exploration of parallels between medieval Jewish–Christian and British–Anglo-Norman relations owes much to conversations had in Mark's office. I also wish to thank a few additional scholars who have been kind, generous, and supportive of my work. They include Dr. Alexander Andrée, Dr. D'Arcy Jonathan Dacre Boulton, Dr. Jonathan Good, and Dr. Richard Moll, who was the external examiner of my doctoral dissertation. I am grateful to my friends and classmates at the University of Toronto's Centre for Medieval Studies, including: Dr. Nicholas Sivulka Wheeler, Dr. Stephen Pelle, Dr. Andrew Reeves, Drs. Alice and Tristan Sharp, Drs. Rachel and Wayne Lott, Anthony J. Fredette, and Douglass W. Hamilton. I wish to single out two CMS friends for special thanks: Dr. Morris Belknap Tichenor and Dr. Ryan Buchanan Allen. Morris has proofread many of my Latin translations and, even more importantly, has welcomed me into his family as the godfather of his children. Ryan, accepting no remuneration other than gratitude, has read drafts of this book and has given me much constructive feedback. Ryan, model of magnanimity, you truly are the Prince Arthur to my Redcrosse Knight. You have saved me from infelicities and occasional bouts of despair, and the final product is stronger for your potent aid. Responsibility for all errors and omissions is, of course, my own.

Finally, I wish to thank a few institutions that have helped make this book and the process of writing it possible. I thank the friendly staff of Seven Grams Espresso Bar of Avenue Road, Toronto, and the Coffee Exchange of Wickenden Street, Providence. Your exquisite coffee and cheerful company helped me through the lonely parts of this work. I thank Caroline Palmer, my anonymous readers, and the team at Boydell & Brewer for publishing my work as part of its Arthurian Studies Series. Last, but not least, I thank my Alma Mater and current employer Providence College for making a financial contribution in support of the publication of this book.

Index

ARTHURIAN STUDIES